Introduction to
Politics

Robert Garner

Peter Ferdinand

Stephanie Lawson

OXFORD
UNIVERSITY PRESS

OXFORD
UNIVERSITY PRESS

Great Clarendon Street, Oxford OX2 6DP

Oxford University Press is a department of the University of Oxford.
It furthers the University's objective of excellence in research, scholarship,
and education by publishing worldwide in

Oxford New York

Auckland Cape Town Dar es Salaam Hong Kong Karachi
Kuala Lumpur Madrid Melbourne Mexico City Nairobi
New Delhi Shanghai Taipei Toronto

With offices in

Argentina Austria Brazil Chile Czech Republic France Greece
Guatemala Hungary Italy Japan Poland Portugal Singapore
South Korea Switzerland Thailand Turkey Ukraine Vietnam

Oxford is a registered trade mark of Oxford University Press
in the UK and in certain other countries

Published in the United States
by Oxford University Press Inc., New York

© Robert Garner, Peter Ferdinand,
Stephanie Lawson 2009

The moral rights of the authors have been asserted
Database right Oxford University Press (maker)

First published 2009

British Library Cataloguing in Publication Data
Data available

Library of Congress Cataloging in Publication Data
Data available

Typeset by SPI Publisher Services, Pondicherry, India
Printed in Italy by
L.E.G.O. S.p.A.

ISBN 978–0–19–923133–1

1 3 5 7 9 10 8 6 4 2

Introduction to Politics

Acknowledgements

Three members of the OUP editorial team deserve special thanks from the authors. Ruth Anderson, the Commissioning Editor, got us together in the first place and ensured the project ran smoothly from start to finish. Monika Faltejskova took on the difficult job of coordinating the writing schedule in the early stages and was succeeded by Emily Medina-Davis who whipped us into shape just as we were beginning to flag. We had a number of very convivial meetings at the OUP office in London where a lot of hard work was accompanied by several good meals. Finally, we also owe a debt of gratitude to a number of anonymous reviewers whose constructive criticisms of draft chapters have made the final product that much stronger.

Guided Tour of the Textbook Features

The text is enriched with a range of learning features to help you navigate the text material and reinforce your knowledge of politics. This guided tour shows you how to get the most out of your textbook.

Reader's Guide

Reader's Guides at the beginning of every chapter indicate the scope of coverage in the chapter, including the key concepts and debates that the chapter discusses.

> **Reader's Guide**
>
> This chapter explores the concept of power. It starts by defining power in the context of authority, before going on to discuss the classic threefold typology of authority put forward by the German sociologist, Max Weber. Some conceptual questions about power are then asked—is it the same as force, must it be exercised deliberately, is it a good thing, and can we ever eliminate it? The rest of the chapter is concerned with examining the methodological problems inherent in the measurement of power, particularly in relation to the theories of the state discussed in chapter one.

Boxes throughout the book provide you with extra information on and discussion of key concepts, key debates, and key thinkers, in a way that does not disrupt the flow of the main text.

> **Key Debate** Box 4.1
>
> Freedom and Cultural Pluralism
>
> Consider the following two cases:
>
> 1. In 2004 religious symbols in schools were banned by the French National Assembly. This included a ban on Muslim girls wearing a veil, and the wearing of Jewish skullcaps, Sikh turbans, and conspicuous Christian crosses.
> 2. It is estimated that well over 100 million women have been subject to circumcision. This practice (involving either the removal of some of, or the entire, clitoris) can lead to serious physical and psychological problems. Yet it is justified on

Case Study boxes demonstrate how political ideas, concepts, and issues manifest in the real world.

> **Case Study:** Box 11.5
>
> Venezuela and the Downfall of Liberal Democracy
>
> From the time when democracy was re-established in 1958, Venezuela had the reputation of the most stable and most liberal democracy in South America. Yet recent years have seen this system pushed aside by President Chavez in favour of a more populist democracy. It is a reminder that while liberal democracy may have been presented by Fukuyama as 'the end of history', this type of regime may be vulnerable too. How did it get into this situation?
>
> In 1958 former dictator Pérez Jiménez was overthrown in a military coup that led to the reintroduction of democracy. In October the leaders of the three main parties signed a pact at Punto Fijo that committed them to observing the same basic rules of the

Key Points

Each main chapter section ends with a set of key points that draw out the most important arguments developed within that chapter topic.

> **Key points**
>
> - Liberalism is the dominant political tradition in the West.
> - Liberalism has its classical and social reforming strands.
> - The core concept of liberalism is liberty, with the classical tradition emphasizing negative liberty and the social reforming tradition emphasizing positive liberty.
> - The prominence of the individual in liberal thought involves the downgrading of the community.
> - Liberals advocate equality of opportunity rather than equality of outcome.

Cross-references

Cross-references throughout the book help you to make connections between the chapters and to deepen your understanding of a particular topic. Page references and colour coding aid navigation.

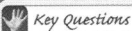

Key Questions

Carefully devised questions at the end of every chapter help you to assess your comprehension of core themes, and may also be used as the basis of seminar discussion and coursework.

Further Reading

An annotated further reading list is provided at the end of every chapter to help you to take your learning further and to locate the key academic literature relevant to the chapter topic.

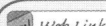

Web Links

Web links at the end of each chapter guide you to relevant learning material on the web.

Glossary Terms

Key terms appear in green in the text and are defined in a glossary at the end of the book to aid you in exam revision.

Guided Tour of the Online Resource Centre

www.oxfordtextbooks.co.uk/orc/garner/

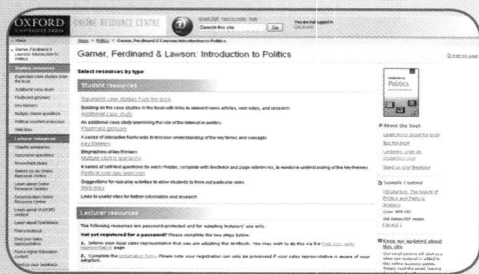

The Online Resource Centre that accompanies this book provides students and instructors with ready-to-use teaching and learning resources.

Expanded Case Studies from the Book

Ten key case studies from the book that deal with topical issues are developed further on the Online Resource Centre. The online case studies also include embedded links to relevant web reading, video, and audio to deepen your understanding of the case study and of its application in the real world.

Democracy, Rights, and Hunting

One interesting example of the potential conflict between the application of majoritarianism and the protection of rights is the debate about hunting. The hunting community in Britain has used a variety of arguments to support the continuation of hunting, but one recent strategy has been to employ the ideals of liberalism and the protection of individual rights. Here it has been argued that, despite the fact that hunting has been regularly opposed by a majority of British people in opinion polls and a majority of MPs in the House of Commons, it still does not justify a ban because it is illegitimate for a majority to impose its own moral views on the minority. To take such an action is a serious infringement of rights. This rights defence of hunting, however, fell on deaf ears despite the hunting community's attempt to undermine the legislative ban by appealing to the Human Rights Act.

Additional Case Study

An additional case study on the role of the Internet in politics will help you to gain an insight into the increasing role that the web plays in political life. Embedded links to relevant web reading, video, and audio bring this case study to life.

Flashcard Glossary

A series of interactive flashcards containing key terms and concepts has been provided to test your understanding of terminology from the book.

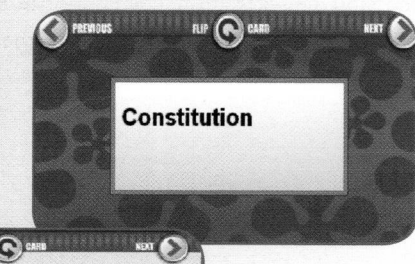

PREVIOUS   FLIP CARD   NEXT

Constitution

PREVIOUS   FLIP CARD   NEXT

The complex of relations between a state's governing institutions and the people, including the understandings that are involved. Most of these relations are usually codified in a single document.

Key Thinkers

Information on twenty key thinkers mentioned in the book is provided, including biographical details and information on their contribution to political science.

> **Woodrow Wilson**
>
> Woodrow Wilson (1856-1924) served as a Democratic US President from 1913 to 1921. He brought the US into the First World War in 1917 to help 'make the world safe for democracy', an idealist notion that has resonated in American foreign policy ever since. Wilsonian idealism was also reflected in attempts to establish a new international order at the end of the war along essentially liberal lines. A chief architect of the League of Nations, the centre piece of the new order, Wilson was unable to persuade a Republican- dominated Congress to join. But he was recognized for his efforts by the awarding of the Nobel Peace Prize in 1919. The first Chair in the emergent discipline of IR - the Woodrow Wilson Chair of International Politics at University College Wales, Aberystwyth - was established in the same year, also honouring his commitment to establishing a peaceful international order.

Multiple Choice Questions

A bank of self-marking multiple choice questions has been provided for each chapter of the text. It gives instant feedback on your answers to help strengthen your knowledge.

> **Question 1**
>
> Theories of political obligation are attempts to argue...
>
> ○ a) that we should all vote as often as possible
> ○ b) that we have no right to criticise the elected government.
> ○ c) whether or not we ought to obey the state.
> ○ d) that politicians ought to uphold the highest moral standards in their public and private activities.

Political Scenario Exercises

Role-play activities based on a particular political scenario have been created to help you deepen your appreciation of the real-life application of your textbook learning.

Web Links

The web links from the book are provided on the Online Resource Centre for easy access.

> www.political-theory.org
> On political theory in general, see the homepage of the 'Foundations of Political Theory' section of the American Political Science Association. Among other things, it will give you access to a wide range of key journals.
> www.politicaltheory.info
> The Political Theory Daily Review is a portal weblog that provides links to the latest news, publications, and reviews covering all fields of political theory and political philosophy.
> www.marxists.org
> For Marxist literature.
> www.ucl.ac.uk/bentham-project/

For Lecturers

Chapter Summaries

A detailed summary of each chapter is provided to help you quickly identify the topics, concepts, and debates that each chapter introduces the student to, for use during lecture, seminar, and tutorial preparation.

> **Chapter 15: Traditional Theories of International Relations**
>
> Theory is a way of organizing the basic elements of our thinking about the world around us, and we can neither explain nor understand that world without some kind of theoretical framework in which the 'facts' of international politics are arranged and made sense of. Two major bodies of theory - liberalism and realism - constitute the theoretical terrain of traditional IR. Each has offered competing explanations and solutions addressing the causes of war and the conditions of peace in the international sphere. IR's theoretical development also raised some important issues of methodology involving the search for objective knowledge on the one hand, and the place of norms and standards on the other. We also look at the 'English School' of IR which focuses on the idea of international society as well as maintaining an alternative methodological pathway to that of the 'scientism'. Finally, we consider theoretical developments in the form of neoliberalism and neorealism respectively. We should note that traditional theories of IR, while attempting to provide universally valid explanations of political behaviour, have been developed largely in 'the West' and therefore draw largely on European and North American experiences.

Discussion Questions

Discussion questions have been provided for use in seminars and tutorials. They are designed to draw out the themes and issues raised in each chapter.

> **Discussion questions**
>
> • What is a nation state? Does it matter whether the nation or the state came first?
> • Does the state require moral authority to enjoy domestic legitimacy?
> • Is state capacity simply a function of the level of economic development?
> • Or is it simply a function of longevity and habituation (viz Latin America as compared with sub-Saharan Africa)?
> • How far can theories of modern states in the West (see Hay et al.) be applied to states in the developing world?
> • After carrying out a democratic 'audit' of a particular country, what are your conclusions?

PowerPoint Slides

A suite of customizable PowerPoint slides has been included for use in lectures. Arranged by chapter, the slides may also be used as handouts in class.

> **Garner, Ferdinand & Lawson**
> **Introduction to Politics**
>
> Chapter 5: Traditional Ideologies

Brief Contents

Detailed Contents

Part 2   Comparative Politics   Peter Ferdinand

Part 3   International Relations   Stephanie Lawson

List of Boxes

List of Tables

About the Authors

Robert Garner

Robert Garner is Professor of Politics and Head of the Department of Politics and International Relations, at the University of Leicester. He was previously at the Universities of Buckingham and Exeter. He has published widely in the area of environmental politics in general and the politics and philosophy of animal rights in particular. His books include *Environmental Politics* (Macmillan, 2000), *Animals, Politics and Morality* (Manchester University Press, 2004), *The Political Theory of Animal Rights* (Manchester University Press, 2005), and *Animal Ethics* (Polity Press, 2005).

Peter Ferdinand

Peter Ferdinand is Reader in Politics and International Studies and Director of the Centre for Studies in Democratization at the University of Warwick. He is a former Head of the Asia-Pacific Programme at the Royal Institute of International Affairs (Chatham House). He is the author of *Communist Regimes in Comparative Perspective: The Evolution of the Soviet, Chinese and Yugoslav Models* (1992), and he has edited books on politics and political economy in Taiwan, Central Asia, Hong Kong, and on the Internet and democracy. His interests are in the politics of Pacific Asia, the former Soviet Union, democratization, and political economy.

Stephanie Lawson

Stephanie Lawson is Professor of Asia-Pacific Studies in the Department of Political Science and International Studies at the University of Birmingham. She has also held chairs in International Relations at the University of East Anglia and Macquarie University. Previous positions include Senior Lecturer in Politics at the University of New England and Fellow in International Relations at the Australian National University. Her main research interests focus on culture, ethnicity, nationalism and democracy, and combine comparative and normative approaches to the study of world politics. She is the author of many book chapters and articles dealing with these issues in the Asia-Pacific region as well as globally. Her recent books include *Culture and Context in World Politics* (2006), *Europe and the Asia-Pacific: Culture, Identity and Representations of Region* (2003), *International Relations* (2003), and *The New Agenda for International Relations: From Polarization to Globalization in World Politics?* (2002).

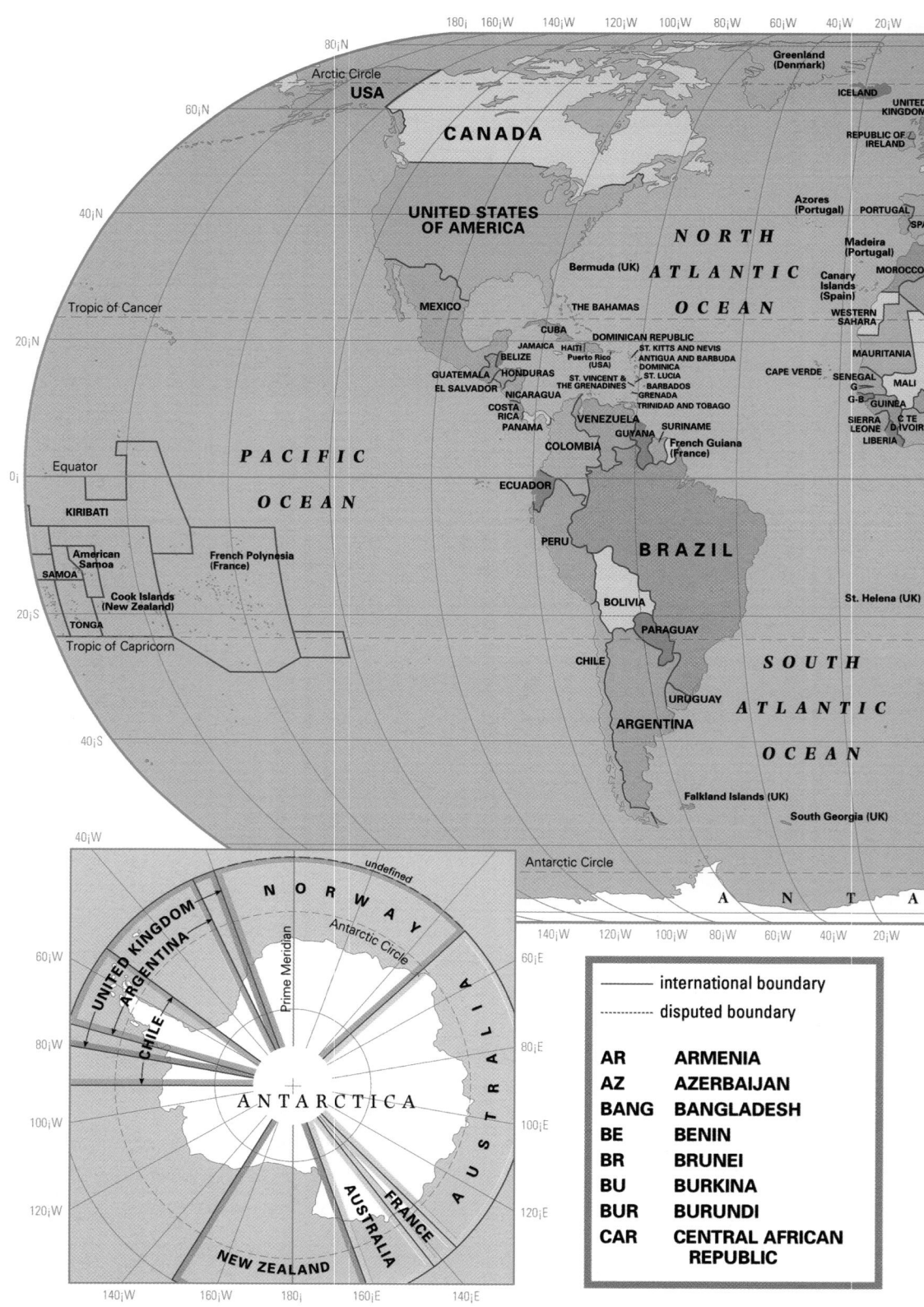

80¡N
80¡N   160¡W   140¡W   120¡W   100¡W   80¡W   60¡W   40¡W   20¡W

Arctic Circle
USA

Greenland
(Denmark)

ICELAND
UNITED
KINGDOM

60¡N

CANADA

REPUBLIC OF
IRELAND

40¡N

UNITED STATES
OF AMERICA

NORTH

Azores
(Portugal)   PORTUGAL
SPAIN

ATLANTIC

Madeira
(Portugal)

Bermuda (UK)

MOROCCO

Tropic of Cancer

MEXICO

OCEAN

Canary
Islands
(Spain)

20¡N

THE BAHAMAS

WESTERN
SAHARA

CUBA

MAURITANIA

DOMINICAN REPUBLIC

JAMAICA   HAITI
Puerto Rico
(USA)

ST. KITTS AND NEVIS
ANTIGUA AND BARBUDA
DOMINICA
ST. LUCIA

CAPE VERDE

SENEGAL
G-
MALI

BELIZE

GUATEMALA   HONDURAS

ST. VINCENT &
THE GRENADINES

BARBADOS

G-B   GUINEA

BU

EL SALVADOR

GRENADA

SIERRA
LEONE

C TE
D IVOIRE

GHANA

NICARAGUA

TRINIDAD AND TOBAGO

COSTA
RICA

VENEZUELA

LIBERIA

PACIFIC

PANAMA

SURINAME

COLOMBIA

GUYANA

French Guiana
(France)

0¡   Equator

OCEAN

ECUADOR

KIRIBATI

PERU

BRAZIL

American
Samoa

French Polynesia
(France)

SAMOA

St. Helena (UK)

Cook Islands
(New Zealand)

BOLIVIA

20¡S

TONGA

PARAGUAY

Tropic of Capricorn

CHILE

SOUTH

URUGUAY

ATLANTIC

ARGENTINA

40¡S

OCEAN

Falkland Islands (UK)

South Georgia (UK)

Antarctic Circle

40¡W

A   N   T   A

140¡W   120¡W   100¡W   80¡W   60¡W   40¡W   20¡W

undefined
NORWAY

60¡W
Antarctic Circle
60¡E

UNITED KINGDOM
ARGENTINA
Prime Meridian

AUSTRALIA

80¡W
CHILE
80¡E

100¡W
ANTARCTICA
100¡E

AUSTRALIA

120¡W
FRANCE
120¡E

AUSTRALIA

NEW ZEALAND

140¡W   160¡W   180¡   160¡E   140¡E

——— international boundary

- - - - - disputed boundary

AR	ARMENIA
AZ	AZERBAIJAN
BANG	BANGLADESH
BE	BENIN
BR	BRUNEI
BU	BURKINA
BUR	BURUNDI
CAR	CENTRAL AFRICAN REPUBLIC

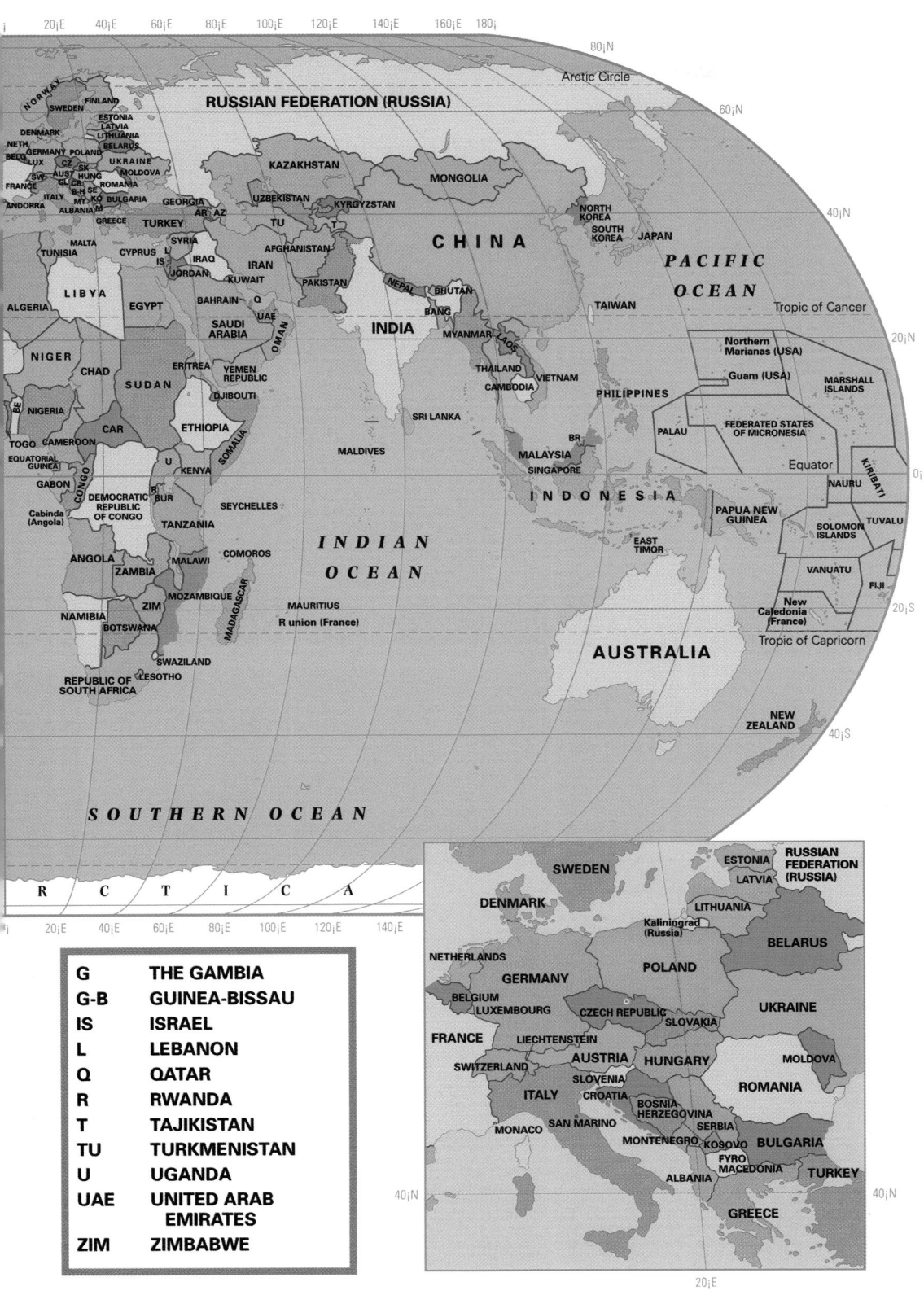

G	**THE GAMBIA**	
G-B	**GUINEA-BISSAU**	
IS	**ISRAEL**	
L	**LEBANON**	
Q	**QATAR**	
R	**RWANDA**	
T	**TAJIKISTAN**	
TU	**TURKMENISTAN**	
U	**UGANDA**	
UAE	**UNITED ARAB EMIRATES**	
ZIM	**ZIMBABWE**	

Introduction: The Nature of Politics and Political Analysis

by Robert Garner

Reader's Guide

This chapter will begin by seeking to define the nature of politics and the political, and asking whether politics is an inevitable feature of all human societies. Some time is spent examining the boundary problems inherent in an analysis of the nature of the political. Two are particularly notable. Should politics be defined narrowly, in the context of the state, or should it be broadly defined to encompass other social institutions? Secondly, is politics equivalent to consensus and cooperation, so that politics does not exist in the event of conflict and war? The chapter then goes on to distinguish between different forms of political analysis — the empirical, the normative, and the semantic — and outlines different approaches to the study of politics. Finally, it is asked whether politics can ever be a science to rival subjects in the natural sciences.

What is Politics?

Politics is a many-sided activity which is impervious to one simple definition. A crucial question is to ask what are the boundaries of the political? Should we draw them narrowly, at the risk of rejecting much of what might fairly be described as politics, or should we draw it widely, at the risk of diluting the term to the point of meaninglessness? Definitional rigour is not helped by the fact that politics is often popularly regarded in a pejorative sense, associated with corruption, intrigue, and conflict. By contrast, some political thinkers, such as Jean-Jacques Rousseau (1712–78) and J.S. Mill (1806–73) have regarded participation in political life as an extremely noble activity that should be encouraged.

➜ See chapter three, pages 75–6 for a discussion of the classical theory of democracy.

This pejorative critique actually provides a clue to what politics is about. For it might be argued that politics is associated with adversarial behaviour precisely because it reflects the conflictual nature of society, or, to use a less value-laden term, the fact that all societies of any complexity contain a range of different interests and values. Indeed, one popular definition of politics is that it is the process by which groups representing divergent interests and values make collective decisions. There are two assumptions here. The first is that all societies of any complexity must contain diversity, that humans will always have different interests and values, and therefore there will always be a need for a mechanism whereby these different interests and values are reconciled. The second assumption is that scarcity is also an inevitable characteristic of all societies. Since there is not enough to go around of the goods that people want, there needs to be some mechanism whereby these goods can be distributed.

Politics would seem, then, in the words of the American political scientist Harold Lasswell (1936), to be about 'Who Gets What, When, How?' Clearly, of great importance here is the way in which economic goods are distributed, as these are crucially important in determining the nature of society and the well-being of those who live within it. As we shall see in chapter four, competing theories of justice focus on a particular ordering of economic goods. However, there are other goods that humans value, status being of particular importance. It is no surprise, for instance, that the honours list in Britain has generated a great deal of controversy. The allegation that honours had been bought during Blair's era as Labour Prime Minister generated a good deal of publicity at least partly because it was widely perceived that status ought to be earned and not gained as a result of economic influence.

The study of politics prior to the nineteenth century was almost exclusively concerned with a study of values; that is, politics was equated with philosophy. Political philosophers asked, what is the good life? What, in other words, is the best kind of society for us to live in? Many different answers to this question have been provided over the centuries but, as Stoker (2006: 6) points out, a 'central divide for much of the last two centuries has been between those who prefer liberty over equality and those who prefer equality over liberty'.

In the twenty-first century, of growing importance is the conflict between liberty and security, a constant theme in this book, and particularly, in chapter four.

Is Politics Inevitable?

If we define politics in terms of differences, conflicts, and scarcity, then it might be, and has by many been, suggested that politics is an inevitable feature of all societies. Not all agree with this. For some, such a claim seriously underestimates the possibility of greater social cohesion based around agreement on core values. Marxists, in particular, suggest that, since differences of interests in society centre on the existence of competing social classes, the creation of a classless society offers the prospect of a society based on consensus and cooperation, one in which politics and the state is not necessary.

Politics, for Marx then, is seen in negative terms. It is about class conflict, and political power, as Marx and Engels famously insisted in the *Communist Manifesto* (1976: 105), and is 'merely the organised power of one class for oppressing another'. It logically follows from this that, once that conflict is ended through the overthrow of capitalism, there are no competing classes and therefore, by definition, no politics. For others, this Marxist vision is unrealistic—'ideal fancy' in Berlin's words (1969: 118) failing to take into account **human nature**'s tendency towards difference, striving, and competition. A modern version of this end of conflict thesis is associated with the 'end of history' or 'end of ideology' schools of thought (Bell, 1960; Fukuyama, 1992). Here, it is argued that in the post-1945 period liberal democratic values have gradually assumed a position of dominance across the world. It is true that the **Cold War** is now a thing of the past, that communism in Eastern Europe has been dismantled, and that growing affluence in the West has made it more difficult for left-of-centre parties to garner political support.

However, a cursory glance at world affairs seems to put this end of ideology thesis to the sword. As this book will reveal, in the world there are a number of alternatives to the liberal democratic model (Heywood, 2004: 71–2). Some of these alternatives have similarities with Western liberal democracy but also significant differences. The post-communist regimes of Eastern Europe, for instance, operate very differently because of their limited experience of democratic norms. Many East Asian regimes (such as China, Malaysia, Singapore, and so on) too, have put a greater focus on economic development sometimes at the expense of civil liberty and democratic procedures. The difficulty of establishing democracy in Iraq is also indicative of the limited application of the end of history approach. Finally, other alternatives are obviously completely different from the Western liberal democratic model. This applies to military regimes, often found in Africa, and Islamic regimes, particularly of the fundamentalist variety as in Iran, that put religious norms before liberty and democracy.

➜ See chapter one for a discussion of human nature.

Many fundamental conflicts remain in the world that require political resolution. Some are based on territory, others are based on political values, the most insoluble containing elements of both. Even in Western Europe, as witnessed, in particular, by debates over multiculturalism, conflict is rife. Further, as Gamble (2000: 108) points out, 'The notion that there are no longer any great ideological issues in the world . . . becomes bizarre in relation to the vast populations . . . in Africa, in Asia, in Latin America and in the former territories of the Soviet Union'.

→ See chapter six, pages 150–3 for a discussion of multiculturalism.

There is another sense in which politics is said to be superfluous, admirably identified and challenged by Gamble (2000). Gamble seeks to challenge what he sees as the pessimistic acceptance in the modern world that humans can no longer influence their destiny. According to this position, the forces of 'bureaucracy, technology and the global market' have led to the 'disenchantment of the world, in which the ability to change that world . . . has been lost, and lost irrevocably' (14). So-called **globalization**, in particular, signals the end of national autonomy (see chapters one and twenty). It no longer matters what allegedly sovereign governments do because we are controlled by global economic forces that no one can alter. As a result the 'space for politics is shrinking, and with it the possibility to imagine or to realise any serious alternative to our present condition. This it seems is our fate' (2–3).

Gamble seeks to argue that this is unduly pessimistic, a view shared by the authors of this volume. It would be wrong to suggest that there are no constraints, some of them severe, acting upon human will. We have to deal with the realities of the global market and dehumanizing technology; but it would be equally wrong to conclude that human agency can have no impact. Rather, there is a tension between impersonal forces and human will, a tension 'between politics and fate' that must be recognized and tackled.

Political Questions

Politics, then, is essentially a mechanism for making decisions about, in Lasswell's words, 'Who Gets What, When, How?' If we all had the same interests and values, and there was enough of everything to go around, there would be no need to make such decisions. We could have everything we wanted. Politics is predicated on the assumption that this is not the case. As a result, students of politics ask a number of questions about the decisions that are taken.

In the first place, they will ask what values do and should the decisions made serve? Do they serve, for instance, the values of justice or liberty and if so what do we mean by justice and liberty? Is a just decision one that is made in the interests of the few, the many, or all? Secondly, students of politics will ask who makes and should make the decisions taken? Is it one person who makes the decisions, or a few, many, or all? Is there anything special, it will be asked further, about democratic forms of government?

Key Debate   Box 0.1
Aristotle's Classificatory Schema

Aristotle (384–322 BC) argued that a symbol of good government was the degree to which the rulers ruled in the interests of all and not a sectional interest. As a result, he developed a sixfold classification containing three 'proper' forms of government and three 'deviant' forms of government. His preferred form of government was a monarchy. Democracy is regarded as a deviant form of government because it is regarded by Aristotle as the rule of the poor in their own interests, thereby equivalent to mob rule. However, he also thought (echoing Winston Churchill's comment many centuries later) that democracy is the least bad form of government (Cunningham, 2002: 7).

Number ruling	Rulers Rule in Interest of . . .	
	. . . All	. . . Themselves
One	Monarchy	Tyranny
Few	Aristocracy	Oligarchy
Many	Polity	Democracy

Table 0.1
Source: R. Dahl (1991), *Modern Political Analysis*, Englewood Cliffs, NJ: Prentice-Hall: 59

Are we more obliged to obey decisions taken in a democratic way than in other ways? These types of question formed the basis of Aristotle's famous sixfold classification of **political systems**. See **Box 0.1**.

The third main question that students of politics will ask is why are those taking decisions able to enforce them? Here, it is important to make a distinction between **power** and **authority**, concepts which are central to politics. We could say that rulers are able to enforce their decisions either because they have the power to do so or because they have the authority to do so. The former implies some form of coercion or sanction; that those with power are able to cause those without power to behave in a way they would not otherwise have done. Clearly, a regime that relies exclusively on the exercise of power, in the sense described above, is likely to be inefficient and unstable. Such a regime will only survive if it is able to impose coercion continually, a time-consuming and difficult exercise.

If a set of rulers has authority, on the other hand, force will not be necessary since authority is defined in terms of legitimacy. Authority, then, is defined here as legitimate power in the sense that rulers can produce acceptance by the ruled, not because they can

➔ See chapter two, for an exploration of the concepts of power and authority.

exercise coercion but because the ruled recognize the right of the rulers to exercise power. Converting power into authority, then, should be the goal of any set of rulers.

Key points

- Politics is usually predicated on the existence of competing interests and values in all societies of any complexity.
- For most commentators politics is inevitable precisely because all societies contain differences that have to be tackled in some way.
- The so-called 'end of ideology' thesis has also suggested that liberal democratic values have come to dominate throughout the world.
- This end of ideology thesis seriously exaggerates the lack of ideological conflicts existing in the world and the pre-eminence of liberal democratic values.
- Assuming differences of values and interests, politics becomes a study of which values and interests come to dominate, who is responsible for these decisions, and with what justification.

The Boundaries of the Political 1—State, Society, and the International Community

We have seen that politics is presaged on differences that human beings have, and how these differences, in interests and values, can be managed in a world where scarcity is inevitable. However, this only takes us so far in a definitional sense, because it does not touch upon boundary problems. Much of the definitional controversy surrounding politics relates to these boundary problems. Where does politics begin and end? For Leftwich (1984: 10), this is the 'single most important factor involved in influencing the way people implicitly or explicitly conceive of politics'.

For some, politics ought to be defined narrowly. According to this view, politics is associated with the activities of the state and the public realm, or with a particular type of decision-making based on building compromise and consensus. As a result, institutions other than the state, and dispute-resolving through violence or suppression, although important in their own right, are beyond the scope of politics. For others, as we shall see below, this narrow drawing of the boundary is to miss much of importance that might fairly be described as political.

Politics has traditionally been associated with the activities of the state. This narrow definition certainly helps to distinguish politics, however artificially, from other social sciences such as sociology and economics. As a result, subfields of politics such as political sociology and political economy, covered in this book, focus on the relationship between the state and society and the economy respectively. The state has traditionally been the centre of much political analysis because it has been regarded as the highest form of authority in a society. Put another way, in the words of the great German sociologist Max Weber (1864–1920), the state has a 'monopoly of the legitimate use of physical force in enforcing its order within a given territorial area' (Gerth and Mills, 1946: 77–8).

Such authority is tantamount to **sovereignty**. The state is sovereign in the sense that it is the supreme law-making body within a particular territory. Ultimately, it has the power of life and death over individuals. It can decide to put people to death for crimes they have committed and it can demand that individuals fight for their country in wars with other sovereign states. Defined in such a way, the state can be distinguished from the government in the sense that it is a much larger entity, containing not just political offices but also bureaucratic institutions, the judiciary, military and police and security services. The state can also be distinguished from civil society which consists of those non-governmental institutions—such as pressure groups, business organizations, and trade unions—to which individuals belong. It is these institutions that provide linkages between the individual and the state. See **Box 0.2**.

➡ See chapter twelve, page 276, for a discussion of civil society.

Without doubt, to include the activities of the state in a study of politics is necessary, albeit not necessarily sufficient. As we will see in Part 2 of this book, the study of government—its legislative, executive, and judicial functions—occupies a great deal of the political analyst's time. Chapters one and two reveal that the question of state power is central to the study of politics. As Barbara Goodwin (2007: 4) points out: 'Political theory may . . . be defined as the discipline which aims to explain, justify or criticize the disposition of power in society'. Political theory is therefore intrinsically linked to a study of **political obligation**. Why should we, it is asked, obey the state? Is there any particular form of the state that we can obey rather than others? Can we obey any state?

➡ See chapter three, page 82, for a discussion of political obligation.

Questions of political power more often than not focus on the state. However, some seek to draw the boundaries of the political much wider than the state. For these scholars, we can talk sensibly about politics existing in various types of group from the

Key Concept   Box 0.2
Civil Society

A term that is usually taken to refer to a range of private institutions existing between the individual and the state. This would include what are now referred to as interest groups representing things that people have in common, such as business, trade unions, religion, ethnicity, and so on. Hegel, the eighteenth and early nineteenth-century German philosopher, distinguished between the family, civil society, and the state, each offering increasing degrees of social integration. Others would want to include the family as an institution within civil society.

family to the international community. One fundamental question for students of politics, for instance, is the degree to which politics now exists beyond the state at a higher supranational level. There have always been those who have argued that the state is an oppressive institution and therefore ought not to exist (Hoffman, 1995). Arguably too, now, the focus of politics has begun to shift because in a practical sense we are living in a world which is becoming increasingly interdependent, where the forces of so-called **globalization** are placing increasing constraints on what individual so-called 'sovereign' states can do on their own.

It is certainly the case that the academic study of international relations has grown enormously in the past few years. The fact that a third of this book is devoted to the relationship between states is a reflection of the growing importance of this field. That said, it should also be recognized that the traditional so-called 'realist' approach to international relations still has the state as the key actor. In this model, the difficulty of securing agreement between states can act as a significant handicap on the successful resolution of supranational problems.

➜ See chapter fifteen, page 349, for a discussion of realism.

Another dent in the argument of those who draw the boundaries of the political in a narrow sense comes from those who argue that politics exists in the institutions of society below the state. Hay (2002: 3), for instance, makes this abundantly clear when he insists that 'the political should be defined in such a way as to encompass the entire sphere of the social'. Leftwich (1984) substantially agrees, arguing that 'politics is at the heart of *all* collective social activity, formal and informal, public and private, in *all* human groups, institutions and societies'. The term **governance**, often preferred now to government, reflects this by drawing the boundaries of the governmental process much wider to include not just the traditional institutions of government but also the other inputs into decisions affecting society such as the workings of the market and the role of interest groups. Indeed, this concurs with everyday discourse where it is common to hear about politics taking place in business organizations, universities, churches, sport, and the family.

Some ideological traditions concur with this wider view of politics. Radical feminists, for instance, see power deriving from the dominance of **patriarchy** in personal relationships and the family, and therefore the personal realm is acutely political. This is what is meant by the radical feminism slogan 'the personal is the political'. Classical Marxists, likewise, insist that political power derives from dominance in the economic realm. Similarly, whatever its internal divisions, and there are many, Islamic thought, deriving from religious scriptures, delves into all aspects of the social sphere down to the family and normative prescriptions that individuals are meant to follow. To deny the political nature of this thought further alienates politics from much of importance in the contemporary world.

➜ See chapter six, page 140, for a discussion on feminism.

Despite Leftwich's limitation above, it can also be questioned whether the boundaries of the political should stop at the human species. There would seem to be a strong case for incorporating at least some species of non-human animals as beings who are morally considerable and ought to have their interests considered in the political process (Garner, 2005). An even more radical position seeks to extend the boundaries of the political to encompass the whole of the natural world, a position designated as dark green ecology.

→ See chapter six, page 146, for a discussion on environmentalism.

There is an apparent danger in expanding the boundaries of the political in the ways suggested in the preceding discussion. If we do so, does not politics cease to be a distinctive discipline? How would we distinguish, say, between the work of the sociologist and that of the political analyst? Does not politics, in a very real sense, lose any separate identity?

Hay's response here is that this critique is confusing politics as an arena with politics as a process (2002: 72). For Hay, the distinctiveness of politics lies not in the arena within which it takes place but in 'the emphasis it places on the political aspect of social relations'. This 'political aspect' is then defined in terms of the 'distribution, exercise and consequences of power'. Politics, then, is about power, and occurs wherever the exercise of power takes place. Of course, Hay is not suggesting that politics explains everything there is to be known, or even the most important things to be known, about social relationships. Other disciplines—sociology, economics, psychology, cultural studies—have important explanatory roles too. 'Though politics may be everywhere', Hay (75) continues, 'nothing is exhaustively political'. As Dahl (1991: 4) explains, people 'experience many relationships other than power and authority: love, respect, dedication, shared beliefs and so on'.

The Boundaries of the Political 2—Politics as Consensus or Conflict?

There are those who suggest that politics is the art of finding peaceful resolutions to conflict, through compromise and the building of consensus. In so far as this fails to happen and military conflict or any kind of violence results as a consequence, then politics can be said to have been rejected or failed. Bernard Crick (1962) is perhaps the best-known advocate of this position. For him, politics is 'only one possible solution to the problem of order' (18). It is, for Crick, the preferable way in which conflicts can be resolved, a 'great and civilizing human activity' associated with admirable values of toleration and respect and fortitude (15).

In contrast to tyranny and oligarchy, both of which are concerned with coercing those who disagree with the ruling elite, political rule is concerned with incorporating competing groups in society. Crick argues that conciliation is most likely to occur when power is widely spread in society so that no one small group can impose its will on others. Unfortunately, as he recognizes, politics is a rare activity that is too often rejected in favour of violence and suppression. He therefore calls for its values to be promoted and persevered with.

A similar argument is put forward by Gerry Stoker. In a book widely regarded as a modern statement of Crick's position, Stoker (2006) argues that politics not only expresses the reality of disagreement and conflict in society but is also 'one of the ways we know of how to address and potentially patch up the disagreements that characterize our societies without resource to illegitimate coercion or violence' (7).

Stoker further argues that much of the present discontent about democratic politics is misplaced. Our expectations are too high. Rather than judging it by too exacting standards it should be recognized that politics, by its very nature, is messy, muddled and, in a very real sense, 'designed to disappoint' (10).

It might be best to describe the arguments put forward by Crick and Stoker as representing a particular kind of politics, rather than politics per se. It is true that conflicts and differences are at the heart of politics, but if we can only talk about politics when agreements are reached and compromises made then it would seem to be a very limited activity. In this sense, it is probably sensible to talk of the resort to force and violence and military conflict as politics by another means, as in the famous dictum by the nineteenth-century Prussian military strategist, Carl von Clausewitz.

A related point is that Crick has been criticized for linking politics closely with the practices of liberal democracies where power is commonly assumed to be widely dispersed. Like Crick, Stoker too comes close to equating politics with democracy. This is implied by the title of his book *Why Politics Matters* with a subtitle *Making Democracy Work*, as though the only politics worth talking about is democratic politics. It would seem strange if our definition forces us into a position which holds that those countries governed undemocratically by economic, religious, or military elites are not practising politics but should, as Crick and Stoker recommend, aspire to it. See **Box 0.3**.

Key Quotes Box 0.3
The Nature of Politics

A political system is 'any persistent pattern of human relationships that involves, to a significant extent, control, influence, power or authority'.   (Dahl, 1991: 4)

Politics is the 'the art of governing mankind by deceiving them'.   (Quoted in Crick (Issac D'Israeli, 1962: 16))

Politics 'can be simply defined as the activity by which differing interests within a given unit of rule are conciliated by giving them a share in power in proportion to their importance to the welfare and the survival of the whole community'.   (Crick, 1962: 21)

'Politics is a phenomenon found in and between all groups, institutions (formal and informal) and societies, cutting across public and private life. It is involved in all the relations, institutions and structures which are implicated in the activities of production and reproduction in the life of societies . . . Thus, politics is about power; about the forces which influence and reflect its distribution and use; and about the effect of this on resource use and distribution . . . it is not about Government or government alone'.   (Held and Leftwich, 1984: 144)

'Politics is designed to disappoint—that is the way that the process of compromise and reconciliation works. Its outcomes are often messy, ambiguous and never final'. (Stoker, 2006: 10).

Key Points

- Defining politics is beset by boundary problems.

- Some argue that the boundaries of the political ought to be drawn narrowly, recognizing the state as the key political institution. Others argue that politics ought to be drawn far more broadly to encompass power relations in social institutions such as the family or political institutions at the supranational level.

- The second boundary problem concerns the subject matter of politics, rather than its location. Here, there are those, such as Crick, who seek to define politics in terms of consensus-building and cooperation. For many, however, this definition is unduly limiting. Politics is not absent in undemocratic regimes or in periods of civil or international strife.

The Study of Politics

The study of politics dates back to at least the Greeks in the fifth century BC, the Greek philosophers Plato and Aristotle credited with being the founding fathers. Despite this, politics only became an independent discipline in higher education at the beginning of the twentieth century, previously being subsumed under other disciplines such as law, philosophy, and history. The American Political Science Association, the body of academics specializing in political studies, was formed in 1903 and its British equivalent, the Political Studies Association, in 1950 (Stoker and Marsh, 2002: 2).

The teaching of politics has traditionally distinguished between the study of political ideas (sometimes also referred to as theory or philosophy), the study of political institutions and processes within states, and the relations between states. This book is structured around these distinctions, yet, as we shall have cause to emphasize later in this introduction, they are far from being mutually exclusive. As Part 1 of this book shows, the study of political ideas contains a mix of conceptual analysis, coverage of the key figures in the history of political thought, and discussion of ideologies. The study of institutions and processes, too, covered in Part 2, can take a number of forms such as the examination of the institutions of a single state, comparisons of the institutions and processes of a number of states, political history, electoral politics, and public administration. Finally, students of international politics, examined in Part 3, focus, among other things, on the role of states or of a range of supranational actors and institutions, either historically or contemporaneously.

The Rise and Fall of Normative Analysis

In all three branches of the study of politics at least three major kinds of political analysis are utilized. First, students of politics engage in **normative analysis**. This type of political analysis asks questions of a valuational kind, and seeks to identify what is good or better with a view to recommending what we ought to want. It will ask, for instance, whether, when, and why we ought to value freedom, or democracy or equality and why should we obey the state. Many of the so-called 'greats' in the history of political thought, ranging from Plato's *Republic* through Thomas Hobbes' *Leviathan* to a more recent major work of political philosophy, John Rawls's *A Theory of Justice*, have all sought to set out what constitutes the 'good life', the kind of society and polity within which it would be desirable for us to live.

For much of the twentieth century, among the three forms of analysis identified above, normative analysis was the poor relation. In academia, a great deal of emphasis was placed upon empirical political science and also upon 'analytical' political philosophy, in which the meaning of concepts and the relation between them was considered. This was the so-called 'behavioural' revolution in which number crunching, particularly in relation to the study of electoral behaviour, was the gold standard. In this climate, pontificating on what kind of society and polity we ought to have—the basis of normative analysis—was regarded as, at best, unnecessary and, at worst, meaningless.

A variety of intellectual and practical political reasons have been put forward to explain what Peter Lasslett (1956: vii) described as the 'death of political philosophy', ranging from the growth of secularism (Dahl, 1991: 120), to the emergence, in the West at least, of consensus politics—whereby there was widespread agreement on the fundamental political principles. In the academic world, the decline of normative analysis was partly a product of the rise in status of **positivism**, an approach that seeks to apply the scientific methodology of the natural sciences to social phenomena. See **Box 0.4**. This approach was associated in particular with the French social scientist Auguste Comte (1798–1856), who argued that the scientific stage of history now upon us would dominate.

An extreme version of positivism was a school of thought known as logical positivism, centring around a group of philosophers known as the 'Vienna Circle' (see Ayer, 1971). For logical positivists, only statements which are empirically verifiable *and* those which sought to say something about the meaning of concepts and the relations between them are legitimate. Normative statements, seeking to make claims of a valuational kind, are regarded as meaningless.

 Key Concept Box 0.4
Positivism

An approach which holds that science must limit itself to those things that are observable, thereby insisting upon a clear separation between fact and value. At the extreme, positivism—in the form of the doctrine known as logical positivism—holds that only those statements that can be investigated by observation, and those that can be examined semantically, are worthwhile. Normative questions are regarded as more or less meaningless.

Normative political philosophy began to make a comeback in the 1960s and 1970s, partly as a result of the decline in consensus politics, and partly because of the emergence of new and innovative works of political philosophy, most notably Rawls's *A Theory of Justice*. Despite this, however, it should be recognized that a great deal of contemporary political philosophy is much more cautious and tentative than the grand narratives of the past. This is partly a recognition that normative questions present problems of a peculiar nature for the political philosopher. As we shall see below, empirical facts can play a part in the resolution of normative questions. However, for most scholars it still remains impossible to derive normative statements merely from empirical facts. This is the famous dictum that it is impossible to derive an ought from an is. Consider the premise that 'she is old and lonely and her health is frail' followed by the conclusion that 'you ought to help her' (Thomas, 1993: 14). Clearly, the conclusion does not follow from the premise unless we add another clause along the lines that 'we ought to help those who are old, lonely, and frail'. This, of course, is another normative statement not capable of empirical confirmation.

Given that we cannot resolve normative questions merely by invoking empirical facts, how then can we judge the validity of a normative statement? In other words, does this not mean that the logical positivists were right after all that normative statements are meaningless and attempts to adjudicate between competing values is a worthless exercise? As Dahl (1991: 118) asks, does this mean that asking the question whether democracy is better than dictatorship is equivalent to asking whether 'you like coffee better than tea'? In terms of ideologies, the problem is that different foundational values are adopted. Socialism and liberalism, for instance, adopt the foundational values of equality and freedom respectively. How can we evaluate between them?

There is 'no easy answer' (Wolff, 1996: 3) to this normative conundrum. One possible solution is offered by Dworkin (1987: 7–8), who cleverly argues that it is mistaken to regard modern political theories as offering different foundational values. Rather, he suggests, they all have a commitment to egalitarianism in the sense that they all hold that humans are worth the same and have an equal value.

Even if Dworkin is right, and it might be argued that he overestimates the compatibility between mainstream ideologies such as liberalism and socialism, it still remains the case that other political ideologies clearly do not hold that humans have an equal value; and yet, without any apparent means of assessing their worth, we are committed to saying that, say, slavery is as good as freedom, or racism is as good as racial tolerance. Intuitively, most of us would want to deny this relativism. How are we to judge between competing political and moral values?

In the first place, a relativist position does exaggerate the degree to which judgements on the validity of competing belief systems are not possible. Nagel (1987: 232), for instance, argues convincingly that it is possible to dismiss a particular belief 'in terms of errors in their evidence, or identifiable errors in drawing conclusions from it, or in argument, judgement and so forth'. Moreover, there are surely some conceptions of the good—health, bodily integrity, wealth, even liberty—to which everyone might aspire (Waldron, 1989: 74–5) as well as 'conceptions of the good which are manifestly unreasonable' (Arneson, 2000: 71). Of course, we may never be certain about the competing value of many conceptions of the good but, as Arneson (2000: 77) points out, 'if one sets the threshold of supporting reasons for public policy at the level of certainty, it is doubtful that any proposed policy can pass'.

Empirical and Semantic Analysis

The second type of analysis common to politics, as well as most other academic disciplines, is empirical. **Empirical analysis** seeks to identify observable phenomena in the real world with a view to establishing what is, rather than what ought to be. Empirical analysis, of course, is the basis of the natural sciences, and many so-called *positivist* political analysts seek to bring to bear what they see as the impartial and value free methods of the natural sciences to the study of political phenomena.

The third type of analysis commonly used in politics is analysis of a semantic kind. As its name suggests, this form of analysis is concerned with clarifying the meaning of the concepts we use. This is an important function in political studies. So many of the concepts used in politics have no commonly accepted definition, and, indeed, have been described as 'essentially contested concepts' (Gallie 1955–6). Defining what we mean by key terms such as democracy and freedom, then, is a crucial starting point.

In reality, the three forms of political analysis described above are not used independently of each other. As Wolff (1996: 3) succinctly points out, 'studying how things are helps to explain how things can be, and studying how they can be is indispensable for assessing how they ought to be'. Thus, in the first place, normative claims are, at least partly, based on empirical knowledge. In the case of Hobbes, to give one example, the normative claim that we ought to rely on an all-powerful sovereign to protect us derives from the largely empirical assumption that human nature is so brutally competitive that there is a great risk to our security without the protection of the so-called 'Leviathan'. Conversely, a great deal of empirical analysis presupposes some normative assumptions. This can be seen, in particular, in our choice of investigation. Thus, students of politics choose, say, to investigate the causes of war because it is assumed that war is undesirable and therefore we should try to eliminate it.

➡ See chapter one for a discussion on human nature.

It is instructive at this point to appreciate the differences between what might be called empirical and normative political theory. From a positivist perspective, the former refers to the generation of testable hypotheses of political phenomena. An example would be a hypothesis which postulated that democracy can only flourish in societies with a market economy and private ownership. Theory is usually taken to mean the normative goal of judging to which political goals we ought to aspire. In other words, it would ask whether a democratic political framework or a capitalist economic framework is desirable in the first place.

Two main responses should be made to the claim that we can separate political 'theory' from the study of political institutions and processes. First, those who study government without recognition of the key normative questions raised by political philosophers will only receive a partial picture of their discipline. Systems of government created by human beings are a reflection of normative beliefs. The American Constitution, to give one prime example, is a product of the 'Founding Fathers' vision of what a modern polity ought to be like, and developments in the constitution since its creation, allowing, for example, for universal suffrage for the election of the President, reflect modern normative thinking.

In addition to the importance of normative theorizing, it should also be noted that theorizing of an empirical kind is also a central part of the study of political institutions and processes. Theories are used in empirical work to try to order and make sense of the mass of information political researchers unearth, and to try and identify and explain relationships between observable phenomena. For example, much of the theoretical literature surrounding the study of relationships between states, considered in chapters fifteen and sixteen, relates to empirical, and not normative, phenomena.

A key element of the empirical approach to the study of political institutions and processes is the comparative method. Here, political analysts seek to develop testable generalizations by examining political phenomena across different political systems or historically within the same political system. To attempt an answer to the hypothesis posed above—that democracy requires the free market and private ownership—it is necessary to engage in a comparative examination of different regimes so that the relationship between political and economic variables can be better understood. It also, it might be added, requires semantic analysis of the concept of democracy, a term subject to many different definitions, as discussed in chapter three. To take another example, the proposition that electoral systems using a form of **proportional representation** tend to produce political and economic instability can be tested by comparing their use with regimes using alternatives such as the first-past-the-post system.

Deductive and Inductive Theories of Politics

Stoker and Marsh (2002: 3) point out that there are 'many distinct approaches and ways of undertaking political science'. However, it can be suggested, at the risk of simplification, that the most important approaches to the empirical study of politics can be divided into those using deductive reasoning, on the one hand, and those using inductive reasoning, on the other. The deductive method is associated with so-called rational choice theories of politics, and the inductive approach is most often associated with an approach known as

> **Key Concept** Box 0.5
> Behaviouralism
>
> An approach that developed, particularly in the United States, in the post-1945 period. It stresses the importation of the scientific method in the study of social phenomena. Objective measurement of the social world is the goal, values to be completely jettisoned from social enquiry. There is an assumption that human behaviour is capable of being measured in a precise way and generalizations derived from it. It reached its height of influence in political studies in the 1960s. Since then, it has been increasingly challenged by those who doubt the value-free nature of political studies and social enquiry in general.

behaviouralism. See **Box 0.5**. Both approaches had the effect of moving politics away from the formalistic and legalistic study of institutions and, particularly, constitutions.

Rational choice approaches to politics have become an increasingly important branch of the discipline. They focus on politics being a response to the problem of collective action, which, as this book will show, has applications both in the study of political institutions and processes, and in the study of international relations. In general, rational choice approaches start by making certain fundamental assumptions about human behaviour from which hypotheses or theories are deduced before being tested against the facts in the real world. The assumptions made are that human beings are essentially rational, utility maximizers who will follow the path of action most likely to benefit them. This approach has been used in so-called 'game theory' where individual behaviour is applied to particular situations. These 'games' reveal how difficult it can be for rational individuals to reach optimal outcomes, not least because of the existence of free-riders—actors who calculate that they can reap the benefits of collective action without paying any of the costs. In political science, the best-known applications can be found in the fields of voting and party competition and in interest group politics.

➜ See chapter three, pages 77–8, for a discussion of Downs's model of party competition.

One problem with the deductive method is precisely that its fundamental assumptions remain just that: assumptions which many regard as, at best, simplifications and, at worst, entirely inaccurate descriptions of human behaviour. Moreover, rational choice theory is awash with hypotheses about various aspects of the political process but is short on empirical tests of these hypotheses (Hay, 2002: 39–40). It is evident that rational choice theory is better able to predict outcomes deriving from certain stated premises than developing accurate empirical theories of the real world.

➜ See chapter ten, pages 246–7, for a discussion on interest groups.

Inductive approaches to politics, in contrast to deductive approaches, start with empirical observation from which explanatory generalizations are generated. For deductive approaches, then, theory is deduced from first principles before being tested, whereas for inductive approaches, theory follows observation and generalization. A classic version of inductivism is an approach known as behaviouralism which dominated Western, and particularly American, political studies in the 1950s and 1960s (see below). The behav-iouralists focused on political topics which, like voting behaviour, are quantifiable. Thus, to give one commonly cited example, empirical data on British voting behaviour during this period generated the generalization that voting is class-based, with the working class tending to vote Labour and the middle and upper classes tending to vote Conservative.

The weaknesses of the inductive method mirror those of the deductive method. While, as we saw, the latter approach is strong on theory but not so much on empirical testing, the reverse is true of the former. The inductive approach, in other words, tends to focus more on gathering empirical data than it does on the generation of theory. This traditional positivism was famously revised by the philosopher of science, Karl Popper (1902–94), who argued that rather than generating empirical data from which a hypothesis can be derived, the scientific method should be concerned with seeking to falsify a hypothesis. This had the effect, among other things, of making truth claims temporary; only as good as the next successful attempt to refute them. Verification can never be conclusive but falsification can be. More to the point, for our purposes here, it meant that positivists have tended, since Popper, to move away from using the inductive method and have shown more interest in the generation of hypotheses to be refuted.

Another weakness of the inductive method is that the type of hypotheses generated by inductivism tends not to be explanatory—in the sense of offering a casual link between generalizations. Rather, they tend to be merely patterns of statistical correlation (Hay, 2002: 79). Finding correlations between phenomena is not the same as the one explaining the other. To give an example, the identification of a statistical correlation between, say, social class and voting behaviour does not, by itself, explain why this correlation exists.

Key Points

- Political analysis involves three main approaches; empirical, normative, and semantic.

- Theorizing normatively about politics remains difficult and often contentious. While recognizing this, it should be noted that one can exaggerate these difficulties, and a moral relativism is not the inevitable consequence of political philosophy.

- In practice, these three forms of political analysis are not mutually exclusive. We need to know what is, before we can talk sensibly about what ought to be. Similarly, empirical analysis presupposes some normative assumptions.

- Empirical political analysis tends to use either inductive or deductive reasoning. The former can be illustrated by behaviouralism, the latter by rational choice theory.

Can Politics be a Science?

It is often asked whether social sciences, such as politics, can be, or ought to aim to be, scientific. This debate is a 'complex, voluminous and multi-faceted' one (Hay, 2002: 75), and we can only touch upon its major themes here. To a certain extent, the answer to the question depends upon whether we adopt a loose or rigid definition of science. Politics is quite clearly a science in the sense that it 'offers ordered knowledge based on systematic enquiry' (Stoker and Marsh, 2002: 11). Indeed, according to this definition, even normative analysis, when undertaken in a systematic way, can be described as scientific. A more rigid definition would involve applying the methodology of the natural sciences to the political realm, as is attempted in the behavioural approach discussed above. Here, an appropriate definition of science might be 'the ability to generate neutral, dispassionate and objective knowledge claims' (Hay, 2002: 87).

The attractions of developing a value-free and objective account of politics where we can identify the 'truth' about political phenomena, are obvious. However, the claims about a science of politics at this more rigid level can be challenged on two main grounds. In the first place, one can question whether the methods of natural science can be transferred to a social science such as politics. At a second, more fundamental, level, one can question whether the whole scientific enterprise, in both natural and social settings, is a valid and useful exercise.

At the first level, it is the social element of politics which is the key. Human beings, it is suggested, are unpredictable and are not amenable to unbending scientific laws in the way that, say, the workings of molecules are in the natural sciences. In other words, as Hay (2002: 50) points out, what makes the social sciences qualitatively different from the natural sciences is that the 'former must deal with conscious and reflective subjects, capable of acting differently under the same stimuli, whereas the units which comprise the latter can be assumed inanimate, unreflexive and hence entirely predictable in response to external stimuli'.

The unpredictability of human beings not only leads us to question the application of the 'scientific' method to the field of social studies, it also reminds us that social researchers often face ethical dilemmas in their work. We cannot treat human, or indeed animal, subjects with the same impunity that natural sciences treat inanimate objects. Humans, and animals, can feel emotional and physical distress that researchers have to take into account. Moreover, the prescriptions that might emanate from social research, or that might be derived from it by others, can have important ethical dimensions. An example here would be the implications of social research that led to claims being made about the importance of race, or gender, in determining intelligence and therefore political worth.

The only way of avoiding the conclusion that a science of society is difficult, if not impossible, because of the unpredictable nature of human beings, is to adopt an approach which claims that human behaviour can be determined. As we saw in the case of rational choice theory, however, it is doubtful if assumptions about human behaviour made in such accounts would stand the test of empirical observation. In addition, the study of politics is not value-free. As we saw earlier, we impose our own assumptions and norms on our work from the very start of a research project, the choice of which is imbued with our own sense of its importance. We might want to argue, too, that politics *should* be about values and norms. To attempt to exclude them is to miss much of what is valuable in a study of the political.

At a more fundamental level, the core of the scientific project has been challenged. Here, it might be argued that it is unfair to criticize politics for not being a science because there is no true value-free science in the first place. We should therefore question the claim that there can be a value-free exercise to which we can attach the label 'science', rather than solely questioning the scientific merits of politics. As Hay (2002: 87) remarks, the natural scientist, just like the social scientist, is 'socially and politically embedded within a complex and densely structured institutional and cultural landscape which they cannot simply escape by climbing the ivory tower of academe to look down with scientific dispassion and disinterest on all they survey'.

This idea that 'scientific' knowledge is, in part at least, socially constructed is the basis of the contemporary, so-called, 'interpretist' approach which has emerged to challenge positivism (see Bevir and Rhodes, 2002). To understand this critique a little better, it is important to understand the difference between the terms ontology and epistemology. Following Hay (2002: 61) we can say that **ontology** 'relates to *being*, to what *is*, to what *exists*'. In other words, an ontology asks what is there to know? For our purposes here, the key ontological question relates to whether there is a political world out there capable of being observed or whether this 'reality' is, at least to some degree, created by the meanings or ideas we impose upon it. **Epistemology** refers to the task of 'acquiring knowledge of that which exists' (63). In other words, it concerns itself with what can be known about what exists.

The definitional diversion is important because it enables us to make sense of the fundamental claims being made by those who insist that the study of politics can be a science. Thus, those adopting behavioural or rational choice approaches adopt a foundationalist ontology and a positivist epistemology, meaning, in short, an acceptance that a real world exists out there which can be discovered by empirical observations. Increasingly, though, this approach has been challenged by those writing from a so-called interpretivist standpoint. These scholars have ontologically challenged the very idea that there is an objective reality out there that is waiting for us to discover. As a result, rather than seeking to discover an objective reality that does not really exist, we should seek to examine the meanings that human beings themselves impose. From this perspective, then, a science of politics is impossible.

Key Points

- Behaviouralists, in particular, suggest that politics can have the scientific rigour of the natural sciences.

- Two challenges to this view were noted. In the first place, one can question whether the methods of natural science can be transferred to a social science such as politics.

- At a second, more fundamental, level, one can question whether the whole scientific enterprise, in both natural and social settings, is a valid and useful exercise.

Conclusion

This chapter has sought to introduce the reader to certain basic definitional features of politics, and some themes current within political analysis. The difficulty of studying politics, because of the lack of consensus on its meaning, has not been disguised. We suggest that having an open mind to what is 'political' prevents undue conservatism which would miss much that is important in the real world. The rest of this book operates in this vein.

Part 1, chapters one to six, continues the exploration of political ideas and ideologies, focusing on the state, power and democracy, freedom and justice, and traditional and new political ideologies. Part 2, chapters seven to thirteen, focuses on the study of political institutions and processes, with chapters on the main elements of the political system: constitutions, executives and legislatures, bureaucracies, parties and elections, the media and political culture. Part 3, chapters fourteen to twenty, deals with relationships between states. This section starts with a definition of key terms, and a historical account of the development of the states system, before going on to examine international relations theory, international security, diplomacy and foreign policy, international organizations and, finally, international political economy.

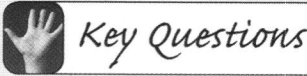 Key Questions

- What is politics?
- Is politics synonymous with the state?
- Is politics an inevitable feature of all societies?
- Distinguish between normative and empirical analysis in the study of political theory
- Can politics be a science?
- Should politics be seen in a positive light?
- What is the case for defining politics narrowly?
- How can we evaluate between competing normative claims?
- Evaluate the claims made by inductive and deductive approaches to political studies.
- 'Politics is generally disparaged as an activity which is shrinking in importance and relevance' (Andrew Gamble). Discuss.

 *Further Reading*

Crick, B. (1962), *In Defence of Politics*, London: Weidenfeld & Nicolson.
   This is a classic case for a particular interpretation of politics.

Dahl, R. (1991), *Modern Political Analysis*, Englewood Cliffs, NJ: Prentice-Hall.
   This is a classic account of the study of politics by a legendary American academic.

Gamble, A. (2000), *Politics and Fate*, Cambridge: Polity Press.
   Like Crick, this seeks to defend politics, but from the perspective of those who would decry the ability of humans to control their destiny.

Hay C. (2002), *Political Analysis*, Basingstoke: Palgrave.
   This cannot be bettered as a comprehensive and accessible account of different approaches to political science.

Marsh, D. and G. Stoker (eds) (2002), *Theory and Methods in Political Science*, Basingstoke: Palgrave.
   This is an extremely useful collection of articles setting out the field.

Stoker, G. (2006), *Why Politics Matter*, Basingstoke: Palgrave.
   This is a modern version of Crick's work, which defines politics in terms of consensus and democracy.

 *Web Links*

www.apsanet.org/
The American Political Science Association is the major American professional society for individuals engaged in the study of politics and government.

www.psa.ac.uk/
The Political Studies Association (PSA) of the United Kingdom, founded in 1950, is the British equivalent of the APSA. Its aim is to develop and promote the study of politics. The site gives details of its activities including publications and conferences, and contact details for about forty specialist groups within the association.

www.hyperpolitics.net/
Hyperpolitics is an innovative politics dictionary. It consists of an analytical tool created by Mauro Calise and Theodore J. Lowi that aids students and researchers in building up definitions of political science terms and concepts using conventional and online reference sources.

www.keele.ac.uk/depts/por/ptbase.htm
This site provides access to a useful directory of resources maintained by the School of Politics, International Relations and the Environment at Keele University. It includes a listing of web links relating to all aspects of political theory and political philosophy.

 Visit the **Online Resource Centre** that accompanies this book to access more learning resources. www.oxfordtextbooks.co.uk/orc/garner/

po·lit·i·co (p...

político, both

pol·i·tics (pə...

science of go...

litical entity,

of its interna...

with a sing...

government...

Part 1

Concepts and Ideologies

by Robert Garner

The six chapters in this section examine key political concepts and ideas. This is commonly described as political theory. By political theory is usually meant political philosophy which asks normative and semantic questions about political phenomena. Attempting to answer normative questions, as we pointed out in the introduction, can be aided by empirical analysis, although normative questions can never be answered decisively merely by the use of empirical facts. Moreover, political theory is a wider term which incorporates empirical analysis. Thus, chapters one and two spend a great deal of time discussing empirical theories which try to determine the location of power in the state.

Since the sixteenth century, political theory has been associated with—and has helped shape the character of—the nation-state, the varying types of which are described in chapter one. The key question for political theorists has been what legitimizes a state or, in other words, why should we obey it? This question of political obligation is discussed in chapter three. Moreover, concepts such as freedom and justice, examined in chapter four, were largely concerned with, in the former case, what limits ought to be placed on the state and, in the latter, what distribution of goods ought the state to pursue. Most of the ideologies covered in chapters five and six, are equally concerned with principles by which the state ought to be organized.

Political philosophy as an academic discipline has had a chequered recent history.

Some see the nineteenth century as the last great age of political philosophy, and put its decline down to the growth of secularism. As Dahl (1991: 120) points out, 'values could no longer be successfully justified by basing them on divinely revealed religious truths'. In addition, the status of philosophy in general had taken a hammering by virtue of the fact that the senseless destruction of human life in the Holocaust had occurred in what was regarded as the most philosophically sophisticated country in Europe (Horton, 1984: 115).

Coupled with this was the influence of a school of thought known as logical positivism, which challenged the worth of normative analysis of any kind (see Introduction), and the period of consensus politics in much of the West in the 1950s and 1960s was accompanied by economic prosperity. There was little purchase in justifying alternative political arrangements when the present ones—based on the mixed economy, the welfare state, and the nuclear deterrent—were working so well.

This cosy consensus was to change radically with challenges to American foreign policy in Vietnam in the 1960s and mounting economic problems in the 1970s and the polarization of political ideologies on offer. Suddenly, different world views were being promoted again and ideological politics made a comeback. At the same time, the influence of logical positivism began to wane. An important factor here was the emergence of significant new works of political philosophy in the 1970s, most notably John Rawls's *A Theory of Justice*, discussed in detail in chapter four.

Political theory is now facing another challenge: for it follows that the challenge to the modern state from the forces of globalization, discussed in various places in this book, question not only the sovereign state, but also political theory itself which grew up to theorize it. At the extremes, we could defend to the hilt the state-specific nature of much political thought by denying the claims made by advocates of globalization. Conversely, we could accept these claims and render the dominant state-specific school of political theory as redundant.

The truth probably lies somewhere in the middle. What is certain is that political theorists will increasingly have to grapple with the impact of globalization. Indeed, this is already beginning to happen. The case for cosmopolitan theories of democracy and justice, for instance, are considered in chapters three and four respectively. Moreover, those ideologies—such as environmentalism and multiculturalism—which are predicated on the reality of increasing interconnectedness of the peoples and nations of the world, form part of the subject matter of chapter six.

1

Politics and the State

Reader's Guide

This chapter begins by stressing the importance of the state and sovereignty to the study of politics. An attempt is made to provide an empirical typology of the state, before going on to outline various theories about the distribution of power in the state—namely pluralism, elitism, Marxism, and New Right theories. The chapter then proceeds to examine different views about what the role of the state ought to be, from the minimalist state recommended by classical liberal theory, to the pursuit of distinctive social objectives as recommended, in particular, by communitarian thinkers. Finally, the empirical and normative challenges to the state are reviewed.

1

The Political Importance of the State

The state is a notoriously difficult concept to define, and is a classic example of an essentially contested concept (Gallie, 1955–6). Some argue that 'the state is not a suitable concept for political theory, since it is impossible to define it' (Hoffman and Graham, 2006: 22). The fact that the state is difficult to define does not seem to be reason enough to refuse to try and define it, unless it is thought that the state does not actually exist, which virtually no one is claiming.

A classic definition of the state is provided by Weber who regards it as an institution claiming a 'monopoly of the legitimate use of physical force in enforcing its order within a given territorial area'. The state is therefore inextricably linked with **sovereignty**. Above all, this concept was developed by the French political philosopher Jean Bodin (1529–96) and the English jurist, William Blackstone (1723–80). The idea of the sovereign state denotes its superiority as the highest form of **authority** in a particular territory. There is, therefore, no higher authority within that territory, and, equally importantly, no external challenge to this authority. As chapters seven and fourteen will describe in detail, sovereign states emerged in the fifteenth and sixteenth centuries in Europe, replacing feudal societies which shared authority between the aristocracy and the Catholic Church (Tilly, 1975). Subsequent to this, most countries in the world have adopted, often through colonial rule, the sovereign state model, although stateless societies still exist in small communities of people, such as nomadic tribes.

The usefulness of the concept of sovereignty as a description of political reality, however, is debatable. In constitutional theory, states are sovereign but, in reality, states have always faced challenges from within and outside their borders, thereby, in practice, limiting their autonomy. In this sense, sovereignty has always been something of a myth. Here, there is a crucial distinction between *de jure* sovereignty, which refers to a legal right to rule supremely, and de facto sovereignty, which refers to the actual distribution of political power. As Held (1989: 216) points out: 'Sovereignty has been an important and useful concept for legal analysis, but it can be a misleading notion if applied uncritically as a political idea.' For example, the concept of sovereignty is of little use when discussing the phenomena of so-called 'failed states', where—as in Somalia—the state is unable to perform the functions of sovereignty.

➜ See chapter seven, page 164, for a discussion of the rise of the European state system

➜ See chapter fourteen, page 334, for more on the rise and spread of the state system

➜ See chapter seven, page 173, for a discussion of weak states

A Typology of the State

A classification of the state is usually organized around the degree to which it intervenes in society and the economy. At one end of this continuum is the so-called **night-watchman state** in which the state concentrates on ensuring external and internal security, playing little role in civil society and the economy where the economic market is allowed to operate relatively unhindered. The idea of a night-watchman state was a central characteristic of classical liberal thought and played a large part in shaping nineteenth-century British politics. It sees the state as having a protective role, seeking to uphold the rights—to life, liberty, and property—of individuals against external and internal threats.

The notion of a minimal state is an ideal type which has probably existed nowhere in reality. The degree, and character, of state intervention in the world today, however, differs enormously. In the so-called **developmental state**, for instance, there is a strong relationship between state and private economic **institutions** with the goal of securing rapid economic development. This model has been particularly prevalent in East Asia, where states have developed rapidly since 1945. Japan is the prime example of a developmental state (Johnson, 1995), but the model is also relevant to South Korea and even Malaysia, a so-called **illiberal democracy** (see below).

➡ See chapter twenty for an exploration of the relationship between the state and economic institutions.

Developmental states should not be confused with **social democratic** states which have a broader social and political objective. They are associated with attempts to secure greater social and economic equality, rather than just economic development per se. One of the criticisms of post-1945 British political and economic development is that Britain adopted a social democrat approach but neglected the developmental aspect (Marquand, 1988). This failure, it is argued, has hindered the social democratic project because greater social and economic equality is greatly assisted by general economic prosperity which provides a great deal more resources to redistribute.

States can also be defined in terms of their relationship to democracy or popular control of political leaders. Here, a useful distinction is to be made between **liberal democracies**, illiberal democracies, and **authoritarian** regimes (Hague and Harrop, 2007: 7–9). Liberal democracies—such as the United States, the United Kingdom, and India—are characterized by free and fair elections involving universal suffrage, together with a liberal political framework consisting of a relatively high degree of personal liberty and the protection of individual rights. Illiberal democracies—such as Russia and Malaysia—are characterized by elections but relatively little protection of rights and liberties, and state control over the means of communication. This creates a situation where opposition leaders and parties are disadvantaged and, as a result, there are relatively few transfers of power through elections.

Authoritarian regimes can be characterized in terms of the absence of fair elections and therefore the accountability of political rulers. About a third of people in the world live under regimes that can be described as authoritarian, most notably China—which contains just under 20 per cent of the world's population—and many states in the Middle East. The political elites in such regimes can derive from the military, royalty, ruling parties, or merely be individual dictators.

The degree of intervention in the economy and society can vary enormously in authoritarian regimes. At the extreme end is the totalitarian state, so-called because the

Photo 1.1 Hitler Shaking Hands

Adolf Hitler walks along the edge of a crowd and shakes hands with well-wishers.
Source: © CORBIS

state intervenes—often through a brutal and oppressive state police—in all aspects of social and economic life, under the guise of a transformative ideology. While liberal state theory postulates the existence of a civil society in which the state intervenes relatively rarely, in totalitarian states civil society is eclipsed. **Totalitarianism** is very much a twentieth-century phenomenon—associated, in particular, with Nazi Germany, Stalin's Soviet Union, and East Germany—although Iran, since the Islamic revolution in the late 1970s, has a number of totalitarian features.

Key Points

- However difficult it is to define, the state is undoubtedly a crucial institution for the political analyst.
- Sovereignty is a key defining feature of the state, although it is a concept that, arguably, has greater legal than political importance.
- It is possible to develop an empirical typology of the state from the minimalist night-watchman state, approximated to by nineteenth-century capitalist regimes at one end of the spectrum, to the totalitarian state of the twentieth century at the other.

The State and Power

Another dimension of the state relates to the relationship with **power**. Theories of the state more often than not provide different accounts of power distribution. These theories are primarily empirical accounts, seeking to describe the reality of power distribution rather than a normative aspiration. Clearly, it is essential to have an understanding of the concept of power itself, a task which is undertaken in chapter two. For now, it is necessary to note that an evaluation of the validity of the empirical theories of the state discussed in this chapter depends, to a large extent, upon the way in which the concept of power is defined and operationalized.

The need for an overarching theory of the state emerges from the need to be selective, to have some guide to the choosing of relevant information from the mass of factual evidence that can be unearthed. Choosing a theory of the state constitutes the analyst's criteria for selection and enables him or her to avoid drowning in a sea of information. In this chapter, we will look at three major theories of the state: pluralism, elitism, and Marxism, as well as considering the slightly more peripheral New Right theory of the state. There is another approach to the state put forward by feminists and this is deserving of an extended treatment provided in chapter six.

➔ See chapter six, page 140, for an exploration of feminism.

Pluralism

By the end of the 1960s, the pluralist approach, associated above all with the work of the American political scientist Robert Dahl (1963, 1971), dominated Western political science. It is possible to distinguish between different varieties of **pluralism**, some more accurate than others. In the classical pluralist position, society is seen as being composed of thousands of activities that have the effect of creating many different groups of all shapes and sizes. For pluralists, the existence of, often competing, groups is a natural feature of all societies of any complexity. The only way in which these groups can be prevented is through suppression, as they had been, for instance, in the old Soviet system.

For pluralists, the role of the state can also be defined in terms of the activities of groups. In this *political* pluralism, the state's role is to regulate and mediate between these groups. Some pluralists see the state as a neutral arbiter in this system, whereas some see it as a group in itself competing against others in society. The outputs of government are the result of group pressure. What governments do will be a mirror image of the **balance of power** of groups within society. It is important to note that pluralists are not saying here that all groups or interests are equal. Rather, pluralists are claiming that there are no predominant classes or interests within society, that all groups are able to make their voices heard in the political process, and that all groups get at least something of what they want.

As chapter twelve will explain in more detail, an interest group is an organization set up to promote or defend a particular interest or cause. It is common to distinguish between sectional groups, concerned to protect the—usually economic—interests of their members (such as trade unions or business organizations), and cause, or promotional, groups, designed to promote a particular group of people (for example, the homeless or the old) or an ideal (such as environmental protection or opposition to pornography).

➜ See chapter twelve, page 283, for a detailed discussion of interest groups.

Power in society for pluralists is diffuse or fragmented. In other words, in a pluralist state, most **interest groups** will be able to influence public policy outcomes to at least some extent. Dahl defines modern liberal democratic politics in terms of 'minorities rule' rather than majority rule, or **polyarchy** rather than democracy, to illustrate that politics is based upon the permanent interplay of numerous groups each constituting a minority. Successful political parties, then, are those that are able to forge a majority coalition of minority groups.

The pluralist conclusion that power is fragmented is based upon a number of related arguments. The first is that the bases upon which power rests are variable; that is, political influence is not dependent upon one particular resource. Rather, there are a variety of important resources—wealth, organization, public support, a group's position in the economy, the ability to exercise, or threaten to exercise, sanctions—which are not the preserve of a small number of groups. For example, a group of key workers such as miners or doctors may not be particularly wealthy or even have public support but can garner influence through the crucial functions they perform.

Secondly, even though it may seem that in a particular issue area one group or small set of groups is influential, the same groups are not influential in other issue areas. To give a classic example, it has traditionally been argued that the National Farmers' Union (NFU) in Britain is extremely influential within agricultural policy (Smith, 1990: 124–31). There is evidence to suggest that this is no longer the case (Smith, 1990: 212), but even when it was, the pluralist position is still upheld, the argument goes, because the NFU is not influential within other areas of policy, relating, say, to the economy, education, and health, where other groups are important. Thirdly, more often than not, it is the case that an influential group in a policy arena is challenged by a 'countervailing influence'. In the economic sphere, for instance, the influence of business groups is checked by the role of trade unions.

Pluralism to Elitism Continuum

The position we have just described can be classified as classical pluralism. It is possible to envisage a number of other approaches or theories of the state on a continuum between classical pluralism and classical elitism. The first of these is elite pluralism, sometimes described as **democratic elitism**. This revision of classical pluralism came about in the late 1950s and early 1960s following a sustained criticism of it. One of the major challengers was the American sociologist, C. Wright Mills (1956), who argued that power in American society is concentrated in the hands of a powerful elite, dominating the economic, military, and governmental spheres.

→ See chapter three, page 75, for discussion of the elitist theory of democracy.

The pluralist response to this led by Dahl (1958) was to accept that the classical pluralist assumption, that there is widespread participation in decision-making and that groups are themselves internally egalitarian, was misplaced. The existence of political elites, a small group of people playing a disproportionate role in groups, was accepted. Far from undermining the pluralist position, however, scholars such as Dahl suggested that it still existed because these political elites have divided interests and compete with each other to achieve their aims. Politics may be hierarchical, then, but rather than one homogeneous elite group, there are a multiplicity of competing elites. Pluralists, for instance, would see business as divided between, say, a financial and a manufacturing sector. Political power for pluralists can be represented diagrammatically, then, by a succession of pyramids and not just one.

Yet further down the continuum between pluralism and elitism is **corporatism**. See **Box 1.1**. Traditionally, corporatism referred to the top-down model where the state, as in the fascist model, incorporates economic interests in order to control them and civil society in general. This is also the corporatist model that can be applied to authoritarian states particularly in Asia.

→ See chapter five, page 129, for a discussion of fascism.

1

Modern societal or neo-corporatism, on the other hand, reflects a genuine attempt by governments to incorporate economic interests into the decision-making process (Held, 1989: 65). This modern version of societal corporatism shares with pluralism the belief that groups are a crucial part of the **political system**. Corporatism denies, however, that the competition between groups was as widespread, equitable, and fragmented as pluralists had suggested. Instead, corporatism points to the critical role played by economic elites. Government outputs are a product of a tripartite relationship between elites in government, business, and the trade unions. The insider role of economic elites was sanctioned by the state in return for the cooperation of these key interests in securing the support of their members for government policy.

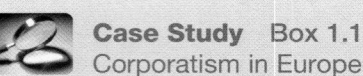

Case Study   Box 1.1
Corporatism in Europe

Corporatism, or neo-corporatism to be precise, has been particularly prevalent in certain European states. A survey of eighteen Western industrialized countries and Japan ranked Austria, Norway, Sweden, and the Netherlands as the top four most corporatist political systems, whereas New Zealand, Canada, the UK, and the USA were ranked as the least corporatist, and thereby closer to the pluralist model. The same study examined the factors explaining the existence of corporatism, arguing that the influence of social democracy in government is the most important variable, followed closely by the degree of consensus in the political system.   (Lijphart and Crepaz, 1991)

The Austrian system of 'social partnership' remains the most corporatist structure. The so-called *Sozialpartnerschaft* involves the organization of trade unions and employers in the 'big four' institutions, the trade union organization (OGB), and the three Chambers established by law with compulsory membership and the power to consider government bills before they are put before parliament. These are the Chamber of Labour (BAK), and the two employer chambers, the Economic Chamber (WKO), and the Chamber of Agriculture (PKLWK). This structure has traditionally been marked by the informality of relationships between the actors (Talos and Kittel, 2002). The key feature is the centralization and hierarchical character of the peak associations of labour and business.

Until the 1970s corporatism was largely applauded for its economic success. Since then, corporatism has decayed to some extent. A survey of Scandinavian corporatism, for instance, reveals that since the mid-1970s there has been a decline in the number of corporatist actors in public bodies, and the degree to which governments base decisions on corporatist-style agreements (Blom-Hansen, 2000). Even in Austria, corporatism has begun to weaken. While the structure remains intact, it has less public support, there is greater opposition from some rank-and-file organizations, and a more adversarial relationship between the chambers. As a result, government has become more autonomous, relying less on the peak associations of economic interests.   (Talos and Kittel, 2002: 44–8)

The form of corporatism we have been describing is shorn of much of the negative connotations associated with the top-down variety, associated with fascist regimes and authoritarian regimes such as China, which involve the state incorporating key interests in order to control them. Neo-corporatism, by contrast, is seen as a way of incorporating, and modifying, the key interests within civil society. It is argued that it has served a vital aggregation function.

Neo-corporatism has not, however, escaped criticism. In the first place, it is argued that governments tend, in practice, to be unduly influenced by business interests in corporatist arrangements. Even if trade unions are successfully integrated, neo-corporatism is still regarded as less open and democratic than a pluralist system because it is hierarchically organized, with power residing in the hands of economic elites. From the perspective of the New Right (see below), corporatism is condemned for failing to allow the market free reign, and thereby acceding to the, it is argued, unrealistic demands of sectional interests.

Elitism

At the other end of the spectrum from classical pluralism is the ruling elite theory of the state. While classical pluralists hold that Western liberal democracies have diffuse power structures, with a **plurality** of groups competing to influence the government, ruling elite theory holds that all society, whatever democratic rhetoric proclaims, is ruled by a single, unified, and self-conscious elite. Whereas the diagrammatical representation of elite pluralism is a series of pyramids, **elitism** can be represented by one pyramid containing an elite and the masses.

Elitism is particularly associated with a group of Italian scholars writing at the turn of the twentieth century (in particular, Robert Michels, Gaetano Mosca, and Vilfredo Pareto), although their work was built upon by later, mainly American, writers. The original elitists were concerned primarily with refuting Marx's vision of a future egalitarian society. For them, a ruling elite was an inevitable feature of all complex societies. The elitists claim to have discovered, in the words of Robert Michels, an 'iron law of oligarchy'; that is, in organizations of any complexity, whether they be political parties or interests groups, there will always be a dominant group controlling them. Elites come to dominate because of the resources they can muster, their psychological characteristics, or their position within society. Unlike Marxism, or ruling-class theory (see below), no one resource is necessarily crucial, so that it is possible to conceive of elites based upon military, administrative, and religious factors as much as economic ones.

Later scholarship on elitism came from the United States. Unlike the earlier Italian version, modern elitism has ceased to be anti-Marxist and has, instead, become a critique of pluralism. In other words, elitist thinkers such as C. Wright Mills (1956) and James Burnham (1941) have identified empirically the rule of elites but, rather than regarding this as inevitable or desirable, have argued that it is illegitimate and ought to be challenged.

Marxism and the State

An alternative to elitism is Marxism or ruling-class theory. Marxism has been a remarkably influential political ideology with, at one time, a large proportion of the world's population living under regimes proclaiming to be inspired by Marx's ideas. Marxism, of course, derives its inspiration from the work of the nineteenth-century German thinker, Karl Marx (1818–83). Marxism shares with elitism an acceptance of the fact that modern capitalist societies are dominated by a united, self-interested ruling group. Democracy in such societies, therefore, is a sham. Despite elections, the influence of the masses is minimal.

There are, however, two crucial differences between elitism and Marxism. In the first place, unlike elitists, Marxists are very specific about the character of the ruling group in capitalist societies. As we saw, elitists envisage ruling groups with a variety of resources. For Marx, the ruling group in pre-communist societies is always that social group or class that controls the means of production, and therefore has economic power. In capitalist society, then, the dominant class is the **bourgeoisie** and the dominated class is the proletariat (or working class), the latter defined in terms of its non-ownership of the means of production.

Marx produced a voluminous and disorganized body of literature, and it has been interpreted in a number of ways. The dominant interpretation of Marx attaches to him the view that that it is pointless for the working class to seek **emancipation** through gaining the vote and winning power through elections. This is not where real power lies. Rather, power lies within the economic sphere of society. In other words, those who have economic power also have political power. The working class, therefore, needs to win power by attacking its source in the economic sphere. Having said that there is some evidence that Marx was prepared to accept a greater autonomy for the state and that it was not perceived as simply the vehicle of the dominant class. This idea of the 'relative autonomy' of the state was taken up by later Marxists.

The second key difference between elitism and Marxism is that for the latter a communist revolution will bring about a truly egalitarian society, one in which a hierarchical society is abolished. By contrast, elitists argued, in response to Marx, that a hierarchical system of power relations is an inevitable feature of all societies of any complexity, and it is a utopian dream to think otherwise. Marx spent very little time describing in detail what this egalitarian society would look like, mainly because of his insistence that the downfall of capitalism would produce such a society, whatever he thought ought to happen.

➜ See chapter two, page 64, for a discussion of Marxist ideas on state power.

The New Right Theory of the State

A slightly different theory of the state was provided by a number of commentators, writing from the 1970s onwards, who can be classified as the New Right, a position whose antecedents were liberal free-market advocates such as Hobbes, Locke, and Adam Smith (see below). According to this position, the state has a tendency to expand its activities far beyond what is healthy for society. There are two main forces at work here. The first is external. Here, in a process that is coined as the 'economic consequences of democracy' (Britten, 1977), competitive electoral politics encourages politicians to offer ever-increasing benefits in order to attract votes, and once elected, governments then find it very difficult to meet the promises made to individuals and groups, sometimes sailing perilously close to bankruptcy.

The second force at work here for New Right thinkers is internal. Here, it is argued, in what has been called the 'over-supply thesis' (Dunleavy and O'Leary, 1987: 117–19), the state bureaucracy has a tendency to expand because it is in its self-interest to do so (Niskanen, 1971). To increase intervention and 'big' government, bureaucrats will forge relationships with interest groups. Both the bureaucrats and the groups have a vested interest in governments offering more, mainly financial, benefits.

For the New Right, then, the pluralist theory of the state is wrong on two main counts. First, the state is not neutral but serves its own interests. Secondly, the liberal democratic polity does not encourage stability and equilibrium as pluralists suggest. Rather, it has a tendency to lead to governing failure. The end result is 'a hyperpluralism of powerful groups confronting weak governments' (Dearlove and Saunders, 2000: 220).

The Empirical Dimension of the State

We have focused so far in this chapter on the empirical reality of the state, what the state does. When the role of the state is discussed, it is necessary to distinguish between the functions that the state does play, as a matter of fact, and the functions that it ought to play, as a matter of value. The theories of the state discussed above have both empirical and normative dimensions to them. An **empirical analysis** of a theory of the state would examine the degree to which it reflects the reality of any particular political system. As we shall see in chapter two, assessing the empirical adequacy of a theory of the state has a great deal to do with how political power is measured.

Here, we should just briefly note that an empirical critique of pluralism would be to say that it exaggerates the extent to which power is fragmented in liberal democratic societies. Indeed, pluralism has been criticized on the grounds that it too readily assumes that groups have a reasonable chance of influencing policy-making, whereas there is strong evidence to suggest that certain interests are much more powerful than others. We could engage, too, in an empirical critique of the elitist and Marxist theories of the state. Is it really credible to argue, for instance, that a ruling elite or a ruling class remains entirely untroubled by representative machinery in liberal democracies? Certainly, in addition, one can challenge many, if not all, of the claims made by Marx about the future direction of capitalism. Indeed, as we shall see in chapter five, post-Marxian Marxists did adapt classical Marxism to very different circumstances.

→ See chapter two, page 55, for a more developed critique of pluralism.

→ See chapter five, page 119, for a discussion of the development of socialist ideas.

Key Points

- There are a number of empirical theories of the state arranged on a continuum from classical pluralism at one end to ruling elite and Marxist theory at the other.

- Whereas pluralism sees the power structure as diffuse and fragmented, ruling elite and Marxist theories sees it as concentrated.

- The two key differences between ruling elite and Marxism are, first, that for the latter the dominant group is always that class that owns the means of production, distribution, and exchange, whereas for the latter the source of power can be varied. Secondly, Marxism postulates the existence of a future egalitarian society whereas ruling elite theory sees elites as an inevitable feature of all societies.

- It is possible to distinguish between an empirical and a normative examination of the state. In empirical terms, we can criticize pluralism, elitism, or Marxism for their failure adequately to describe the reality of the world as it is.

The Role of the State: What Ought the State to do?

Theories of the state can also be assessed on normative grounds; in other words, we can explore the degree to which they constitute adequate representations of how the state *ought* to be organized. The work produced in this area represents the core of political philosophy, which has as its fundamental aim the identification of the ideal polity and the good society. This question will occupy us also in chapters three and four, particularly in the context of the crucial question of **political obligation**. Here, however, we will merely sketch out some of the major answers to this normative question.

Pluralism and Elitism: A Normative Critique

There are two main normative critiques that can be made of pluralism. In the first place, it can be argued that the pluralist theory of the state devalues the idea of the general or public interest. Indeed, pluralism almost glories in the differences between people. It therefore accepts as given, the rather pessimistic view that society consists of a diverse range of competing, and sometimes hostile, interests. Secondly, the revised elite version of pluralism might also be criticized from a normative perspective on the grounds that it dismisses the importance of political participation. Thus, instead of accepting the competition between political elites as the best that can be achieved, political philosophers have argued that this is unacceptable from a democratic perspective and we ought to look at ways in which opportunities to participate can be enhanced.

➜ See chapter three, page 75, for a discussion of the elitist theory of democracy.

Ruling-elite theory as a description of the state makes no value judgement about the validity of elite rule. From this perspective, classical elitists at least are saying that, whether we like it or not, modern societies are dominated by a ruling elite. Students often confuse this empirical claim for a normative one. Of course, it is possible to justify elite rule on the grounds that the best should rule, uncluttered by the less able masses. The Greek philosopher Plato offers just such a scenario, justifying the rule of the so-called 'philosopher kings'. The modern theory of democratic elitism, examined in chapter three, is also based partly on a normative claim that elites ought to be left alone to govern because the masses tend to have authoritarian values. According to this position, mass participation in politics tends to result in instability and a climate of crisis (Dye, 2000). In these circumstances, apathy is to be encouraged.

The Liberal Social Contract Tradition

A classic means of determining what the role of the state ought to be is provided by the liberal **social contract** tradition. This is particularly associated with the work of the seventeenth-century liberal political thinkers Thomas Hobbes (1588–1679) and John Locke (1632–1704). Rousseau also employed the social contract, although, for reasons that will be explored in chapter four, it is questionable whether he can be described as a liberal. The social contract tradition is based around the idea of an imaginary **state of nature**, where individuals exist without government. In other words, it is argued that in order to find out what form of government is justified and why, we should try to consider what life would be like without the state. Social contract theorists envisage individuals coming together to decide the nature of the political system under which they will live. This approach was also adopted by a twentieth-century liberal political philosopher, John Rawls, whose ideas we will consider in chapter four.

Despite using the same social contract **methodology**, Hobbes and Locke provide very different versions of an ideal state. Much of the difference revolves around the issue of **human nature**, a key variable in political thought (see Plant, 1991, chapter one). Hobbes famously paints a picture of human nature as egotistical and competitive. Without government, life is very insecure. Indeed, in a well-known phrase, life in the state of nature, for Hobbes, is described as 'solitary, poor, nasty, brutish and short' (1651/1992: 186). As a result, a political system is necessary in order to impose order and ensure security, both from the risk of external threat and internal conflict. The ideal political system for Hobbes, then, is an all-powerful sovereign which Hobbes describes as the *Leviathan*.

John Locke, writing a little later, appears to be much less pessimistic about human nature and the ability of human beings to rub along without undue conflict. Because there are no immediate security considerations for Locke, individuals should choose to live under political rule only when it protects what individuals have in the state of nature (1690/1998). For Locke, individuals have **natural rights**, given by God, and these natural rights ought to be protected by the state. See Box 1.2. Locke promotes what became known as negative rights. These rights—to life, liberty, and property— are rights against societal and state interference.

➜ See chapter four, page 105, for an exploration of Rawls's Theory of Justice.

➜ For Hobbes' influence on international theory, see chapter fifteen, page 351.

Key Concept   Box 1.2
Natural Rights

It is common to make a distinction between natural rights and legal rights. Legal rights are those which exist within a particular society at a particular time. They are simply statements, then, of what the existing law is. Natural rights, on the other hand, are rights which humans are said to possess irrespective of the particular legal and political system under which they live. These are said to derive from **natural law**, a higher law, handed down from nature or God.

Modern liberal thinkers, writing particularly after 1945, have argued for the existence of positive rights. These are rights to things, such as free education and health care, that are enshrined in the United Nations Convention on Human Rights established in 1948. These positive rights have the potential to conflict with the negative rights promoted by Locke. In particular, the right to own property can conflict with other, more positive rights, and some political thinkers writing particularly from a Marxist perspective have criticized Locke for seeking to defend a possessive individualism which justifies selfishness, greed, and vast inequalities.   (Macpherson, 1962)

The Night-watchman State

➡ See chapter five, page 116, for a discussion of liberalism.

Both Locke and Hobbes were apologists for a free market economy and limited state interference, a tradition current in liberal thought up to the end of the nineteenth century. Classical liberals advocate a minimal state in order to maximize freedom. A modern version of this justification is provided by a group of thinkers and political actors known as the New Right, whose theory of the state we encountered above. The political popularizers of the New Right were political leaders such as Thatcher and Reagan, but the academic ballast was provided by political economists such as Friedrich von Hayek and Milton Friedman as well as political philosophers such as Robert Nozick.

➡ See chapter four, page 107, for a discussion of Nozick and the minimal state.

The New Right challenged the state interventionism that had become standard in post-1945 liberal democracies, centring on the welfare state, the mixed economy, and the use of demand management economic theory developed by John Maynard Keynes (1883–1946). Here, the state would seek to increase demand in the economy through public spending on various schemes, and these would be reined in when the increased demand threatened to create inflationary pressures. For the New Right school of thought, state intervention is counter-productive. It encourages individuals to overly rely on the state to provide welfare support, thereby stifling individual initiative and self-help. It is also inefficient, propping up unprofitable economic concerns and stifling the emergence of new lean and relevant ones. Finally, it is also unjust, failing to reward individual effort appropriately.

Utilitarianism

Another strand of liberal thought is the philosophy known as **utilitarianism**. The utilitarian theory of the state is associated with the work of the British political thinker, Jeremy Bentham (1748–1832). Bentham argues that the key to judging the effectiveness of a government is the degree to which it promotes the greatest happiness, or, as he sometimes put it, the greatest happiness of the greatest number (1948). Happiness, for Bentham, is associated with pleasure. In so far as governments do maximize happiness then they are valid, if they fall short of this goal then they are not. Bentham came to think that only if they are accountable to the electorate will rulers seek to maximize the happiness of all, rather than their own happiness. This forms the basis of the utilitarian theory of democracy.

The chief advantage of utilitarianism as a general ethical theory as well as a guide to political action, is that it is flexible enough to justify the attainment of what most would regard as important social goals. By focusing on the happiness of the community, rather than the protection of individual rights, it is able to sanction the kind of collective goals associated with the welfare state. On the downside, utilitarianism, or at least the classical version associated with Bentham, has been criticized for its aggregative character. See **Box 1.3**.

➡ See chapter three, page 73, for a description of the utilitarian theory of democracy.

Key Debate Box 1.3
Rights versus Utilitarianism

Traditionally, the two dominant approaches to ethics have been rights and utilitarianism. Until relatively recently, it was utilitarianism that held sway, but since the Second World War, rights theory has made a significant comeback. The following points should be borne in mind when considering the merits of the two approaches:

- Utilitarianism is a secular theory. It therefore 'does not depend on the existence of God, or a soul, or any other dubious metaphysical entity' (Kymlicka, 2002: 11). Earlier versions of rights tended to have such a religious overtone.

- By focusing on the consequences of an action, and not the motives of those responsible, utilitarians ask us to consider those who are affected by it, a laudable goal. On the other hand, utilitarianism is intuitively mistaken in assuming that there is nothing amiss in an action taken for malicious motives that inadvertently produces a desirable outcome. Conversely, it seems odd to condemn an action taken for the best of motives that produces undesirable consequences.

- Utilitarianism 'provides a clear and definite procedure for determining which acts are right or wrong' (Brandt, 1992: 113). By contrast, rights theory struggles with what to do in situations where rights conflict. For example, should the right to free health care or education be more important than the right to the fruits of one's own property?

- Utilitarianism is flexible enough to justify the attainment of what most would regard as important social goals. It is therefore more flexible and less individualistic than rights. On the other hand, as a **deontological** theory erights theory, unlike utilitarianism, seeks to protect individuals whose fundamental interests cannot, under normal circumstances, be sacrificed in order to promote the general welfare (Dworkin, 1978). It therefore avoids the aggregative consequences of utilitarianism, thereby ensuring that individual interests cannot be sacrificed for some greater good. As a result, 'it avoids the very counter-intuitive solutions to questions of distributive justice' that utilitarianism offers (Carruthers, 1992: 27). In Jones's words (1994: 62): 'There is no end to the horror stories that can be concocted to illustrate the awful possibilities that utilitarianism might endorse.' The persecution of a racial minority in the interests of a racist majority is one such example among many other possibilities.

Liberalism and Communitarianism

The classical liberal theory of the state, which is closely associated with pluralism, holds that the state should remain neutral as between different conceptions of the good. A liberal society's function, Arblaster (1984: 45) suggests, 'is to serve individuals, and one of the ways in which it should do this is by respecting their autonomy, and not trespassing on their rights to do as they please as long as they can do so without harm to others'. This **harm principle**, associated with J.S. Mill, is central to the liberal emphasis on freedom and toleration. It is also the central theme of John Rawls's later work as laid out in his *Political Liberalism* (1993).

➔ See chapter four, page 99, for a further discussion of the harm principle.

For much of its history, the major ideological opponent of liberalism came from the left, from Marxism in particular. In more recent years, however, the liberal theory of the neutral state has been challenged by a body of thought known as **communitarianism**. The label communitarian embraces a wide variety of views. In general, communitarian thinkers seek to re-establish the state as an institution with a role to play in uniting society around a set of values. This contrasts greatly with the liberal insistence that the state should allow a plurality of belief systems to exist. See **Box 1.4**.

Key Concept Box 1.4
Communitarianism

Since the 1970s, communitarianism has provided a more potent ideological challenge to liberalism than conservatism and socialism. Defining the basic thrust of communitarianism is difficult because of the disparate nature of its adherents, coming from the right and left of the political spectrum. The essence of the communitarian approach is an attack on what is perceived to be the asocial individualism of liberalism. This attack is both methodological and normative.   (Avineri and de-Shalt, 1992: 2)

- Methodologically, communitarians argue that human behaviour is best understood in the context of the social, historical, and cultural environments of individuals. Thus, 'it is the kind of society in which people live that affects their understanding both of themselves and of how they should lead their lives'. (Mulhall and Swift, 1996: 13)

- Some communitarian writing suggests that the basis of the communitarian critique of liberalism is the normative assertion that liberal theory accurately reflects liberal society and therefore ought to be transformed. Others suggest, methodologically, that liberal theory misrepresents the reality of modern societies where social ties are more important in determining the belief-systems of individuals than liberal theory has realized.   (Walzer: 1990)

Normatively, communitarians emphasize the value of communal existence, and the importance of being bound together by a shared vision of the good promoted by a perfectionist state—part of a tradition that can be traced back to Aristotle—on which particular emphasis is placed by MacIntyre (1985).

The State and the General Will

In many ways, the antecedents of communitarianism are those political philosophers, such as Jean-Jacques Rousseau (1712–78) and Georg Friedrich Hegel (1770–1831), who suggested that the state and morality are inextricably linked. Thus, for Rousseau, the state should be judged by the degree to which it upholds the **general will**. This is the will that binds people together and can be contrasted with the selfish or partial will existing within everyone.

Rousseau thinks that the general will can only emerge in small-scale communities. The German philosopher Hegel, on the other hand, seeks to apply a very similar objective for the state to modern nineteenth-century Prussia. Hegel distinguished between the state, **civil society,** and the family, seeing the state as the embodiment of the general interest, in which the partiality and self-interest of civil society and the family would be superseded. This elevated view of the state is in sharp contrast to Marx's wholly negative view of the

→ See chapter three, page 83, and chapter four, page 93, for more on the general will.

Short Biography   Box 1.5
Georg Wilhelm Friedrich Hegel (1770–1831)

The German philosopher Hegel was born in Stuggart in 1770. After a varied career as a personal tutor and a head teacher in a school, Hegel took the post of Professor of Philosophy at the University of Heidelberg in 1816. Two years later he was invited to take the prestigious chair of philosophy at the University of Berlin, where he stayed until his death in 1831.

His main work of political theory was the *Philosophy of Right*, published in 1821 (1942). His starting point is to deal with the political and social dissatisfaction existing in the Prussia of his day, social fragmentation being the major difficulty. He moves from an attempt to suggest reforms to create a more homogeneous society to, in the *Philosophy of Right*, a philosophical understanding of the modern world. Very basically, he argues that if we appreciate the unifying role played by the state, transcending the partial unity provided by the family and civil society, then we can be happy with our world.

Hegel has often been seen as an apologist for what was, in reality, a repressive and far from inclusive regime existing in Prussia during his day. His most eminent critic was Karl Marx who, despite being an advocate of Hegel's philosophy in his younger days, came to criticize him. He turns Hegel's philosophy on its head by arguing, first, that human history can be explained by the developing of material forces rather than, as Hegel had argued, by the development of the mind or the realm of ideas. Secondly, Marx argued that the point of philosophy was to change the world rather than merely explaining it. In other words, Marx argued that in order to achieve the goal Hegel had set—a unified and inclusive polity—it was necessary to change it so that, in particular, the existing divisive class system was abolished.

state as an instrument of exploitation. In fact, Marx was originally a follower of Hegel but came to see that the reality of the state in Prussia was very different from the glorified version of it provided by Hegel. As a result, Marx came to see that the point of political philosophy was not, as Hegel had thought, to interpret the world, but to change it. See **Box 1.5**.

The Anarchist Theory of the State

The normative theories we have identified do not challenge the need for some form of state to organize political affairs. Anarchists, however, question the very need for a state. Although anarchist thought dates back to the nineteenth century, and has preoccupied the minds of some great political theorists, its impact on modern politics is limited.

Anarchists' abhorrence of the state is based on its corrupting influence, which undermines a human being's tendency to be morally upstanding. This basic principle, however, raises more questions than it answers; for instance, who is to perform the functions of the state? How are the egalitarian aspirations of the dominant socialist strand of **anarchism** to be achieved without authority structures to enforce it? If there is a need for some authority structure—as some anarchists recognize—can this be consistent with the claim that this will inevitably lead to a loss of freedom? These themes will be considered further in chapter five.

➡ See chapter five, page 132, for an exploration of anarchism.

Key Points

- A normative critique of pluralism focuses on its downgrading of the public or general interest, while a normative critique of elitism focuses on the degree to which elites ought to rule.

- The liberal social contract tradition, represented most notably by Hobbes and Locke, provide different reasons to justify the state, the former focusing on security, the latter on the protection of natural rights.

- Other normative theories of the state seek to justify a limited role (the New Right), the state's pursuit of happiness or preference satisfaction (utilitarianism), the upholding of moral pluralism (liberalism), and a critique of the state in general (anarchism).

- One of the key debates in modern political theory is that between the liberal and the communitarian theory of the state. The former upholds a version of moral pluralism, whereas the latter seeks moral uniformity. The antecedents of the communitarian position reside in the attempts, by political philosophers such as Rousseau and Hegel, to justify obedience to a state promoting the general will.

Wither the State?

The state is now under sustained attack as a variety of scholars seek to challenge its utility and very existence. There are empirical and normative dimensions to this debate. From the former perspective, it is suggested that certain modern developments have made the state increasingly redundant. From the latter perspective is the long-standing view that the state is an exploitative institution that ought to be done away with. This derives its major impetus from the ideas of Marx.

Is the State 'Hollowing Out?'

The 'hollowing out' thesis (Jessop, 1990) suggests that in a variety of ways, the state no longer plays the significant role that it used to. The major slant here is the **globalization** thesis. This is the view that the world has become so economically and politically interdependent that there is little room for manoeuvre for nation-states. To the extent that this is true, there is clearly a gap between the political theory of the sovereign state, articulated at the beginning of this chapter, and the reality of politics in the modern world. Globalization undoubtedly, then, has a significant impact on political studies as an academic discipline. The focus of politics, and particularly political theory, has been on

Photo 1.2
Activists demand illegal whale meat aboard the Panamanian-flagged *Oriental Bluebird* be refused by customs. Greenpeace provided Japanese officials with documentary evidence of meat being transferred at sea from the whaling fleet in the Southern Ocean—a violation of the Convention on International Trade in Endangered Species (CITES).
Source: © Greenpeace/Naomi Toyoda

➔ See chapter twenty for a discussion of the relationship between the state and international economic institutions.

the nation-state. In addition, the dominant tradition in international relations has been the realist tradition, which postulates a state system consisting of individual autonomous and competing sovereign states. Globalization challenges both assumptions.

The issue of globalization will be considered in more detail later in this book. For now, it should be noted that we can adopt empirical and normative approaches to it. From an empirical perspective, the major impetus behind globalization is the internationalization of the economy. With the growth of multinational corporations—which have emerged to rival the power of states—and the liberalization of world trade, it is argued, the economic policies of individual states are now determined elsewhere (Ohmae, 1995). Partly as a result of greater economic **interdependence**—together with improved communication technology and the emergence of global environmental problems— supranational institutions (whether they be intergovernmental organizations, such as the World Trade Organization, or non-governmental organizations, such as Green- peace) have emerged to challenge further the power of states.

As a result, critics argue, the realist school postulating the key role of sovereign states, is time-bound, dating from the Peace of Westphalia in 1648. We are now, it is suggested, in a period of 'new Medievalism' where 'as in medieval Europe, sovereignty is shared among societies that interact in an ongoing way' (Cunningham, 2002: 203; see also Slaughter, 2003: 190). Others argue that the globalization thesis exaggerates the reality, that sovereign states still have a great deal of autonomy and were never, anyway, as self-contained as is often made out (Robertson, 1992).

From the latter perspective, it can be argued that the liberation of world markets is a positive development, facilitating greater prosperity. In addition, global environmental problems require global solutions that are beyond the reach of sovereign states. Finally, it is argued that globalization also facilitates **cosmopolitanism**, the goal of achieving peace, toleration, and justice in a world where we owe our allegiances to humanity—a form of global **citizenship**—rather than to partial entities such as the state (Heater, 1999). Others do not see the nation-state as an obstacle to cosmopolitanism, and suggest that a system of markets unencumbered by the state is a negative phenomenon, exacerbating inequality in the world and increasing exploitation, particularly in developing countries.

One final point here is that it is not just globalization that represents a threat to the autonomy of the nation-state. In addition, as we saw in the introduction to this book, the reality of decision-making is that the state is in partnership with a range of social and economic institutions. Government has now been replaced by **governance**. Included in those now sharing power with the state are substate institutions such as, in Britain, the Scottish and Welsh authorities established by devolution proposals in recent years, as well as the supranational institutions that are the subject of the globalization debate. This overlapping system of governance has been described as **neo-medievalism** as a result of its similarity to the system of authority in the Europe of the Middle Ages before the emergence of the state.

A Critique of the Marxist Theory of the State

The state has always been criticized by anarchist thinkers and is regarded by Marxists as an exploitative institution that ought to be transcended. The dominant interpretation of classical Marxism (the Marxism associated with the writings of Karl Marx himself) operates with a very simplistic definition of politics and the state. For classical Marxists, the state is merely a vehicle for the exercise of power by the dominant class, so that once classes are abolished, the state itself is abolished, or, in the words of Marx's collaborator, Fredrich Engels, 'withers away'. A communist society requires no enforcing state because the end of capitalism transforms human nature fundamentally. In other words, once classes are abolished, then conflict between individuals that is significant is a thing of the past.

Many scholars have argued that this is all too simplistic (see Plamenatz, 1963: 351–408). In the first place, it is argued that complex societies contain many different sources of division or conflict. Getting rid of classes therefore only ends one source of conflict. Others, based on aspects of life such as religion, culture, or types of work, will still exist and have to be dealt with presumably by an institution such as the state. The experience of the communist states of Eastern Europe backs up this critique of Marxism, for once the constraints of communist control were released, numerous interests, previously suppressed, emerged. As a result, it might be argued too that politics resumed, after it had been artificially suppressed.

Moreover, the transformation of human nature envisaged by Marx, it is argued, is also overly simplistic. There is something in the claim that to reduce the level of economic inequality will have an impact on the behaviour of individuals, reducing crime based on acquisitiveness. Marx is justly famous for having pointed this out. However, it is a large step from this to the claim that society can exist effectively without the need for differential rewards as incentives for contributing to it. One of the problems here is Marx's assumption that communism would end material scarcity, which, from the perspective of the twenty-first century, seems remarkably misplaced. As a result of all of these factors, it seems likely that a state would be necessary in a communist regime in order to achieve the desired egalitarian goals. Some would argue that this involves the illegitimate suppressing of the natural urge that individuals have to be different and better than others. Others would argue that this is a necessary price to pay in order to create a fairer and more equal society.

Conclusion

In this chapter we attempted to define the state, before going on to provide empirical typologies of it, and a consideration of various interpretations of how the state ought to be organized. We saw that one of the most important typologies of the state centres on the distribution of power. Here, we identified empirical theories of the state on a continuum from the open and diffuse picture painted by classical pluralism to the closed and hierarchical picture painted by elitists and Marxists. These theories can be criticized on empirical grounds—they do not provide an accurate description of how the state is organized—and on normative grounds—they do not provide polities to which we ought to aspire.

Certainly, theories of the state, with the possible exception of Marxism, do not emphasize enough the external constraints operating on the state in the modern world, and these globalizing tendencies will be a constant theme of this book. Chapters three and four will continue an exploration of how the state ought to be organized, and what it ought to do. In the next chapter, however, we will look closely at the concept of power, not least because this will help us to understand how difficult it is to investigate which of our theories of the state is the most accurate description of a particular political system.

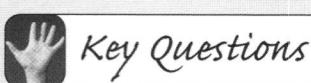 *Key Questions*

- What is the state?
- What functions should the state perform?
- Can we do without the state?

- Compare and contrast the pluralist, elitist, and Marxist theories of the state.
- How adequate is the pluralist theory of the state?
- Critically examine the Marxist theory of the state.
- Provide a normative critique of pluralism and elitism.
- Do you prefer Locke's or Hobbes' theory of the social contract?
- How effective is the communitarian critique of liberalism?
- Are the state's days numbered?

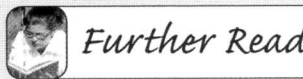

Further Reading

Held, D. et. al. (2005), *Debating Globalization*, Cambridge: Polity.

This provides a very useful collection of articles on globalization taking all sides of the debate.

Hoffman, J. (1995), *Beyond the State*, Cambridge: Polity.

This provides a normative critique of the state, while also outlining the different approaches considered in this chapter.

James, A. (1986), *Sovereign Statehood*, London: Allen & Unwin.

This is a detailed conceptual account of sovereignty. Argues that the concept remains useful in understanding modern politics.

Parry, G. (1969), *Political Elites*, London: Allen & Unwin.

This is a relatively old book but still cannot be bettered for the way in which it expertly surveys the literature on both classical elitism and pluralist versions of elitism.

Web Links

www.political-theory.org
On political theory in general, see the homepage of the 'Foundations of Political Theory' section of the American Political Science Association. Among other things, it will give you access to a wide range of key journals.

www.politicaltheory.info/
The Political Theory Daily Review is a portal weblog that provides links to the latest news, publications, and reviews covering all fields of political theory and political philosophy.

www.Marxists.org
For Marxist literature.

www.ucl.ac.uk/ Bentham-Project/.
The best source on Bentham, this is the website of the Bentham Project at University College London.

 Visit the **Online Resource Centre** that accompanies this book to access more learning resources. www.oxfordtextbooks.co.uk/orc/garner/

2

Political Power, Authority, and the State

Reader's Guide

This chapter explores the concept of power. It starts by defining power in the context of authority, before going on to discuss the classic threefold typology of authority put forward by the German sociologist, Max Weber. Some conceptual questions about power are then asked—is it the same as force, must it be exercised deliberately, is it a good thing, and can we ever eliminate it? The rest of the chapter is concerned with examining the methodological problems inherent in the measurement of power, particularly in relation to the theories of the state discussed in chapter one.

Power and Authority

We saw in the introduction to this book that **power** and **authority** are central concepts in politics. As Hay (2002: 168) states, in only slightly exaggerated terms, 'power is to political analysis what the economy is to economics'. Politics is about competing interests and values, and a key question is what interests and values come out on top in practice. To discover this, we need to know something about power, since those who have power over others can determine which interests and values will be adopted by political decision-makers.

We also saw that a common way of distinguishing between power and authority is to equate the former with coercion and the latter with consent. Authority, then, is defined here as legitimate power in the sense that rulers can produce acceptance by the ruled, not because they can exercise coercion but because the ruled recognize the right of the rulers to exercise power. Converting power into authority, then, is highly desirable. See **Box 2.1**. As Goodwin (2007: 328) points out: 'Where coercion creates obedience at a high cost in

Case Study   Box 2.1
The United States Supreme Court—Authority, Power, and Legitimacy

One useful example of the distinction between power and authority is the role of the Supreme Court in the USA. The Supreme Court is often said to be the most powerful arm of the American political system because of its established right (of judicial review) to declare actions of the executive and legislative branches as unconstitutional. This means that the decisions of elected bodies can be overridden by an unelected body. Members of the Supreme Court are chosen by the President and confirmed by the Senate but once appointed remain as justices for life unless removed for wrongdoing.

It is often asked whether the Supreme Court's apparent power is worrying in a democratic polity. The court has made many important political decisions relating to such controversial issues as race, abortion, and capital punishment, and yet its members are not elected and made accountable to the people.

One retort to the claim that the Supreme Court is exercising illegitimate power is to invoke the distinction between power and authority. Thus, it is important to note that the Supreme Court has no army or police force with which to enforce its decisions. In other words, it is unable to exercise power or, at the very least, it has to share power with the executive and legislative branches of the federal government. As a result, in order for its decisions to be accepted without the threat of coercion, the court relies on its authority. In other words, it has authority but not power. The Supreme Court would almost certainly lose its authority, and therefore its legitimacy, if it made decisions that are too divorced from public opinion. Supreme Court justices are therefore constrained by the need to remain an authoritative institution in the American polity.

manpower and equipment, authority can control both the minds and the behaviour of individuals at a very low cost'.

In terms of the exercise of power, there would seem to be two possible answers to the difficulty of applying coercion. One is to rule through so-called ideological control. In this scenario, rulers are able to maintain control through manipulating the preferences of the ruled so that these preferences reflect the interests of the rulers. Such control—associated with elitist thinkers and Marxist critiques of capitalist society (see below)—is much more effective in that it obviates the need for permanent scrutiny and coercion of the ruled. Nevertheless, as we shall see, its validity does depend upon the debatable assumption that individual preferences can be manipulated in such a way.

Some political theorists seek to link authority with philosophy and power with socio-logical analysis (Barry, 2000: 83). Here, authority is linked with right, with what ought to be, while power is conceived of as an empirical concept, with what is. This distinction, though, is problematic. As we noted above, authority can be a product of manipulation. Or, if one is suspicious of claims that people can be easily brainwashed, it might be argued that people are simply wrong, that they recognize as legitimate the wrong set of leaders.

There is no doubt, for instance, that Hitler had a great deal of authority within German society and yet few would want to claim that we therefore ought to regard the Nazi regime as legitimate. At the very least, we can agree with Goodwin's (2007: 331) assertion that 'a state's authority in the eyes of the people is not necessarily an indicator of its justice'. A linked argument is the case for saying that power is preferable to authority precisely on the grounds that, whereas the latter can be based upon manipu-lation, the former is based on coercion. And in the case of coercion, it is possible to recognize and act upon it (Goodwin, 2007: 331).

The second answer to the problem of coercion makes no such assumptions about the 'real' interests of the ruled. Rather, it simply asks how can any set of rulers make themselves legitimate in the eyes of the ruled? In other words, how can rulers convert power into authority? No set of rulers can survive very long without at least some authority. This then raises another question: on what is authority based? The question of when and why political systems are legitimate is a crucial one for political theorists. It is a topic we touched upon in chapter one when looking at what role, if any, the state ought to have, and it is a question to which we shall return in chapter three when we examine the claims of democracy.

The best-known attempt to come up with an analysis of the basis of authority was provided by Max Weber (Gerth and Mills, 1946). Weber regarded so-called 'legal–rational' authority as the predominant basis for authority in the modern world. To give an example of this, the American President is obeyed, not because he is charismatic or because he claims to have a divine right to rule, but because he holds the office of the President. We can go further than this. In the modern Western world, and indeed in many other parts of the world now, political institutions are accepted because they are subject to democratic principles. In other words, nowadays, the holder of the office of the American President

Key Concept Box 2.2
Weber and Authority

Max Weber (1864–1920), the German sociologist and social theorist, delivered a three-fold classification of authority. He recognized that these were ideal types, and all societies were likely to contain elements of the three types. Weber argued that the modern world exhibits a greater tendency towards legal–rational authority.

- **Traditional authority**—authority derived from traditional customs and values. A major example would be the principle of the divine right of kings, prevalent in European monarchies, whereby monarchies were said to be ordained by God to rule.
- **Charismatic authority**—authority derived from the personality traits of an individual. This is often associated with the leaders of authoritarian or totalitarian regimes, not least because such charismatic leaders tend to emerge at a time of crisis. This form of authority may be less important in modern liberal democracies where authority tends to be based upon status and not personal qualities. However, charisma still plays some part, being part of a political leader's armoury, particularly now that the media image of leaders is important, even in parliamentary systems such as Britain. Weber regarded charismatic authority as inherently unstable. This is because, since authority rests with an individual and not a set of rules, the death of this individual, or her loss of authority, will immediately lead to instability.
- **Legal–rational authority**—authority derived from the status of an office as part of a system of constitutional rules, in a democratic country, or a religious document such as the Koran in Islamic regimes.

has authority because he is elected. Indeed, the President remains the only part of the American polity whose **constituency** is the entire American electorate. See **Box 2.2**.

As Hoffman and Graham (2006: 5–11) rightly point out, although we can define power and authority separately, in practice all governments use both. Even in a **democracy** some exercise of power is necessary. This is not least because decisions taken by a majority (the classic way decisions are taken in a democracy) leave a minority who may be resentful that their view did not prevail. Thus, even though democratic states exercise much more authority than **authoritarian** states who exercise more power, the former have to exercise power at least some of the time and the latter always have some authority.

→ See chapter three, page 85, for a discussion of the problem of majority rule.

To put another spanner in the works, the distinction between authority and power is further clouded by the (likely) possibility that authority is granted to an institution, or an individual, precisely because it has power. It is true that not only do democratic regimes have to exercise power, but **totalitarian** regimes usually have some degree of authority, even if it is the charismatic authority associated with political leaders such as Stalin and Hitler.

As Heywood (2004: 136–41) points out, the concept of authority is now particularly contentious. Many bemoan the decline of authority, reflecting what they see as the decline of social deference. Conservative thinkers therefore seek to justify its importance, emphasizing the need for people to be led and protected (Scruton, 2001). Those from a liberal perspective, by contrast, while recognizing the importance of authority for social stability, also promote liberty which can challenge authority.

Conceptual Questions About Power

The meaning of power can be teased out a little further if we consider a number of questions about it.

Is Power the Same as Force?

It is often argued that there is a conceptual difference between power and force or coercion (Barry, 2000: 89–90). Power can be, and usually is, exercised by the threat of force. However, it might be argued that the actual use of force means that power has failed. For example, the USA clearly used a great deal of force in Vietnam, as well as, more recently, in Iraq. However, it palpably failed to gain obedience in the former and it is heading the same way in the latter. As Lukes (2005: 70) points out, 'having the means of power is not the same as being powerful'.

Must Power be Exercised Deliberately?

There are some who argue that power must be exercised deliberately. As Bertrand Russell (1872–1970), the great twentieth-century British philosopher, insisted, power is 'the production of *intended* results: the unforeseen effects of our influence on others cannot be called power' (1938: 25). The argument here is that it sounds intuitively odd to accord power to someone who has benefited from a situation which that person has not created. Nelson Polsby (1980: 208), the American political scientist, sums this up nicely by using the example of taxi drivers and the weather. Thus, taxi drivers surely benefit when it rains but they do not cause it to rain. It is merely an unplanned effect of the rain. As he points out, it is mistaken to regard this as an exercise of power by taxi drivers since showing that taxi drivers benefit from the rain 'falls short of showing that these beneficiaries created the status quo, act in a meaningful way to maintain it, or could, in the future, act effectively to deter changes in it'. As a result, 'Who benefits? . . . is a different question from who governs?' (209).

This debate is important because it relates to the argument (outlined below) put forward by some Marxists and elitists that the ruling class or elite exercises power, not because of its own **agency**, but because economic structures automatically benefit it and disadvantage others. It is to outcomes that we ought to look then if we want to see the true location of power. Of course, this sits uneasily with the claim that power is about intended effects; about, in other words, agency over structure. Maybe this is merely a matter of semantics. We can dispute that certain structures—the capitalist system for instance—do inevitably benefit some and disadvantage others. What we cannot do is to dispute the effect of structures that do actually benefit some and disadvantage others. This may not be an exercise of power, if we define power in terms of intended effects, but it is clearly politically significant. Maybe domination is a better word to use in this situation than power.

Is Power a Good Thing?

Some political thinkers would argue that whether or not power is good depends upon the uses to which it is put. From this perspective, using power to achieve certain desired outcomes is positive. As Lukes (2005: 109) points out, there are 'manifold ways in which power over others can be productive, transformative, authoritative and compatible with dignity'. By contrast, using power to harm others is negative. From a liberal perspective, however, power is always undesirable because 'every exercise of power involves the imposition of someone's values upon another' (Barry, 2000: 99). This is why liberals recommend limitations on power in the form, for instance, of a separation of powers to prevent one branch of government from exercising too much power.

It is not clear, however, that the exercise of power is necessarily undesirable, whatever the consequences. It is logically possible, for instance, to think of a situation where A might know B's real interests better than B does herself, so that A exercising power over B would be to act in B's interests. An example here would be the relationship between a parent and a child. Liberals could still contend, however, that such a power relationship is illegitimate because, whatever the motive, the exercise of power still infringes the individual's freedom. There are two responses to this. The first is to say that we are faced with a choice between two incommensurable concepts (freedom and intervention for good) and there is no sure-fire way of arbitrating between them. The second is to say that it is logically possible, however unlikely, for A to use her power to insist that B is free. Using the law to abolish human slavery would be a good example of this. It is possible to conceive of someone who wishes to remain in slavery and, in this case, power would be used to make them free.

Can We Eliminate Power?

A related question is whether it is ever possible for power to be dispensed with. Can a society in which no one exercises power over anyone else exist? Here, the work of the French philosopher Michel Foucault (1926–84) is instructive. Foucault is usually taken as offering a challenge to the work of those, such as Habermas (1929–), Marcuse (1898–1979) and Lukes, who, as we shall see below, imply that power is illegitimately exercised and ought therefore to be curtailed. For Foucault, power is ubiquitous, it is everywhere, and power relations between individuals are inevitable.

In his work *Discipline and Punish* (1977), for instance, Foucault argues that the history of legal punishment in France is superficially progressive because extremely violent punishment gave way to regimented incarceration. In reality, however, these are only two ways of achieving the same objective. Both involve power relations and both involve domination. History, for Foucault, then, is 'an endlessly repeated play of domination' (quoted in Hay, 2002: 191). Because power is ubiquitous, there is no possibility of liberation from it, although we can, as Foucault shows, change its focus and implementation. Lukes (2005: 107), who disputes this conclusion (and also denies that Foucault should be interpreted in this way) asks the question raised by Foucault, should we give up thinking 'of the very possibility of people being more or less free from others' power to live as their own nature and judgment dictate?' Foucault answers this in the affirmative. Lukes is less pessimistic.

Key Points

- The concepts of power and authority are usually taken to differ over the issue of legitimacy, the former implying the use or threat of sanctions, the latter reflecting a set of rulers' right to rule.

- A key question for students of politics is the degree to which power is converted into authority. Weber's threefold classification remains the best-known attempt. He argues that modern political authority is legal–rational in nature rather than being based on tradition or charisma.

- Typical questions asked about power, upon which different answers are provided, include whether power is the same as force, whether power can be said to be exercised without the intention of doing so, whether the exercise of power can ever be good, and, a related question, whether we can ever eliminate power relationships.

Power and Theories of the State

We saw in the last chapter that theories of the state centre on the distribution of power. These theories might be used to describe the power structures in different societies. We might be justified, for instance, in claiming that various clearly undemocratic regimes in the world exhibit characteristics equivalent to ruling elite theory, or even Marxist theory, whereas the liberal democratic regimes in the West are more clearly pluralist oriented. What we cannot claim, however, is that all of these theories of the state correctly analyse the power structure existing in any one polity. In other words, we cannot claim that a country such as the United Kingdom is at one and the same time capable of being explained in Marxist and **pluralist** terms. A pluralist account of UK politics would look very different from a Marxist account (see the discussion in Dearlove and Saunders, 2000, chapter nine). Having said this, it is possible to argue that, at a micro level, different policy networks within a particular polity exhibit different power structures some being more open than others (see Smith, 1993 and the discussion in chapter seven).

How, then, do we go about determining which of these theories of the state provides a more accurate description of reality in, say, Britain or the USA? Such a task is enormously difficult and one of the main reasons for this difficulty is the problems involved in measuring the exercise of power. These problems stem largely from the fact that, as we shall see, power has been conceptualized in a number of different ways. These different conceptualizations of power were articulated in a classic account of the concept provided by Stephen Lukes (2005) in a book originally published in 1974.

This became known as the 'faces of power' debate, because Lukes distinguishes between three dimensions or faces of power, himself preferring the third dimension as the most comprehensive. He starts, however, by offering us a definition of power which, he holds, is universally acceptable. This definition is as follows: 'A exercises power over B when A affects B in a manner contrary to B's interests' (Lukes, 2005: 30). This only takes us so far because there is disagreement over the way in which A can act contrary to B's interests.

Pluralism and Lukes's Three Dimensions of Power

The way in which power is conceptualized has a significant bearing on the empirical validity of theories of the state. To see how this is so, let us return to the pluralist theory of the state. Pluralists adopt a decision-making approach to measuring power, which is equivalent to the first dimension of power. The first face of power is where, in Robert Dahl's words, 'A has power over B to the extent that he can get B to do something that B would not otherwise do' (quoted in Lukes, 2005: 16).

This is otherwise known as the decision-making approach, in that the method used by pluralist researchers is to look at the decisions made and the preferences of those groups involved in decision making in a particular set of policy domains. It is then suggested that if a group's aims are met or partly met then they have power (see Hewitt, 1974). If no one group gets its way on all occasions, then the pluralist model is affirmed. The advantage of the decision-making approach utilizing the first face of power is that it is eminently researchable. Indeed, numerous so-called 'community power' studies in the late 1950s and 1960s were undertaken in the USA, most of which confirmed the pluralist theory of the state (Dahl, 1963; Polsby, 1980).

Clearly the decision-making approach could lead to non-pluralist conclusions; that is, it is possible that one group or a small number of groups get their way in the decisions made and the decision-making approach will pick this up. However, critics of pluralism suggest that the pluralist **methodology** is more than likely to generate pluralist conclusions

Photo 2.1

An aerial view of Iridimi Camp in Chad, that is housing refugees from Sudan.
Source: UN photo by Eskinder Debebe

(Moriss, 1975). In the first place, the pluralist methodology makes no attempt to rank issues in order of importance. Clearly, some issues are more important than others, and it may be the case that an elite group allows other groups to prevail in the lesser issues while ensuring that it gets its way in the more important ones. See **Box 2.3**.

Secondly, it is assumed that the barriers to entry for groups in the political system are low, that is, pluralists assume that if a group of people have a case to put or a grievance to express, then it is easy for them to enter the decision-making arena to express it. Clearly, however, this is a dubious assumption. Some groups—such as the unemployed or the homeless—may not have the resources or the expertise to organize effectively even if they wanted to.

Other groups may not bother to organize because they anticipate little success. By focusing on the active groups in the decision-making arena, therefore, pluralists may well miss a range of interests which, for whatever reason, never appear within it.

Key Debate Box 2.3
The First Face of Power and its Critics

Pluralists typically adopt a decision-making methodology, what Lukes (2005) describes as the first face of power. The decision-making approach is illustrated in Table 2.1. This table shows the outcome of four issues on which three groups took positions.

	Issue 1	Issue 2	Issue 3	Issue 4	Total
Group A	WON	WON	LOST	LOST	2
Group B	WON	WON	WON	LOST	3
Group C	LOST	LOST	LOST	WON	1

Table 2.1 The Pluralist Decision-making Approach
Adapted from Hay (2002: 174)

This table shows that all the groups to a range of decisions got their way at least some of the time. For example, the decisions taken on 1 and 2 met with the approval of Groups A and B while Group C achieved its goal on Issue 4. Pluralists would conclude from this that no one group was able to get its way on all issues, and that power is therefore widely dispersed.

It is possible that the decision-making approach can generate non-pluralist conclusions. In the example in Table 2.1, for instance, it might have been found that Group A got its way on all four issues and groups B and C lost out. However, the critics of pluralism suggest that the decision-making approach as set out in Table 2.1 is likely to generate pluralist conclusions.

One of the reasons for this, the critics argue, is that pluralists tend to assume that all issues are of the same political importance as all others. As Table 2.2 illustrates, this can distort the political reality. What it misses is the possibility that an elite group gets its way on the most important issue or issues, leaving other groups to get their way on the less important ones. Therefore, in the example below, Group C gets its way on fewer issues but yet gets its way on the issue weighted most highly (Issue 4).

Imagine, for instance, that groups A and B are trade unions and Group C is a business organization. Further imagine that Issues 1–3 establish for workers an extra 15 minutes' break at various parts of the working day, and Issue 4 grants to employers a right to prohibit strike action. Clearly, Issue 4 is much more important for business interests and is a serious restriction on trade unions; yet a pluralist methodology would fail to take this into account as an exercise of power by one group.

	Issue 1	Issue 2	Issue 3	Issue 4	Total
Weighting	1	1	1	5	
Group A	WON	WON	LOST	LOST	2
Group B	WON	WON	WON	LOST	3
Group C	LOST	LOST	LOST	WON	5

Table 2.2 Pluralism and Issue Preferences
Adapted from Hay (2002: 177)

Moreover, thirdly, is the related assumption that those issues discussed in the decision-making arena are the most important ones. In other words, it ignores the possibility that an elite group, or indeed a ruling class, can determine what will and will not be discussed. It is here that the second and third faces of power identified by Lukes can be invoked. The second face of power involves what Bachrach and Baratz (1963)—two American political scientists working in the 1960s—described as 'non-decision-making'. Here, an elite group operating behind the scenes can prevent certain issues from ever entering the decision-making arena.

For Bachrach and Baratz, then, power has two faces, the readily observable type as defined by the first dimension and a not so readily observable realm of non-decision-making. Power, for them, 'is also exercised when A devotes his energies to creating or reinforcing social and political values and institutional practices that limit the scope of the political process to public consideration of only those issues which are comparatively innocuous to A' (Bachrach and Baratz, 1970: 7). Non-decision-making, it is being suggested, usually operates in the interests of the most powerful who stand to gain most from inaction. Bachrach and Baratz advocate using both faces of power to gain a more rounded picture of the power structure.

Although undoubtedly difficult, it is possible to identify cases of non-decision making, where issues of importance to some groups have not appeared on the political agenda. A number of empirical studies (Crenson, 1971; Blowers, 1984) have attempted to show how this has occurred. A starting point is to identify covert grievances, grievances that clearly exist but which are never openly discussed. The next step is to identify reasons for non-decision-making. A number of possibilities present themselves. Issues may be excluded because of the use of force. Equally, they may be excluded because there is consensus among politicians on an issue therefore denying the electorate a choice. Similarly, issues can be excluded by the use of rules or procedures. In the latter category can be included the common tactic of taking the heat out of an issue by referring it to a legislative committee or, in the British context, a Royal Commission, thereby postponing the need to make a decision.

Another cause of non-decision-making is the so-called 'law of anticipated reactions'. We have already seen how this can impact on a group's decision not to enter the decision-making arena. It can also, however, influence the attitude of decision-makers themselves. A study by the American political scientist Charles Lindblom (1977), for instance, argued that business interests hold a privileged position in the decision-making arena because of their position in the economy; that is, governments recognize that businesses can help to deliver desirable economic scenarios—low unemployment and inflation—and as a result will always be likely to concede to business demands. This power of business is enhanced even further when governments have to deal with multinational companies who have the option to take their businesses to another country.

The crucial point here is that business interests do not have to lobby decision-makers or demonstrate on the street to be heard. Pluralist researchers adopting the decision-making approach, will not, therefore, identify business interests as one of a number of interests with a stated position. Rather, governments will automatically consider business interests because they anticipate their influence.

The first and second faces of power assume that political actors are aware of their own interests. The second, and much more insidious, way in which an elite group or ruling class can set the political agenda, it is suggested, is their ability to shape the demands which groups articulate in the decision-making arena. This is the third dimension of power. See **Box 2.4**. For Lukes (2005: 27), 'A may exercise power over B by getting him to do what he does not want to do, but he also exercises power over him by influencing, shaping or determining his very wants'. See **Box 2.5**.

The critique of pluralists here is that they take it for granted that the preferences expressed by individuals and groups are in their interests. No attempt is made by

Key Debate Box 2.4
Crenson, Lukes, and Air Pollution

Stephen Lukes, in his now classic study of power, argues that it is possible to determine empirically cases where individuals can be manipulated so that the wants they express are different from their actual interests. He cites the well-known study by the American political scientist Matthew Crenson that looked at air pollution policy in two American cities (Lukes, 2005: 44–8), as an example of how this can be done.

Crenson (1971) asks why the issue of air pollution was raised in some American cities but not in others. He looks in detail at two cities in the state of Indiana. One, East Chicago, introduced air pollution controls in 1949 and the other, Gary, waited until 1962. Crenson's explanation for this is that the latter city was dominated by one powerful steel company whose reputation for power prevented the issue from being raised, and when it was impossible to ignore, influenced the content of the legislation that emerged. It was not just that the industry prevented supporters of pollution control from getting a hearing (an example of non-decision-making), although that was part of the story. In addition, support for pollution controls was weak because, Crenson (1971: 27) claims, there was an element of ideological control too in which 'local political institutions and political leaders' exercised 'considerable control over what people choose to care about and how forcefully they articulate their cares'.

Lukes argues that Crenson's study reveals a genuine case where the real interests of people are different from the wants they express. As he remarks, 'there is good reason to expect that, other things being equal, people would rather not be poisoned', and yet it appears they were prepared to be (Lukes, 2005: 48).

Using this study in support of the third face of power is, as a number of commentators have noted, enormously problematic. The assumption both Crenson and Lukes make is that it was in the interests of people in East Chicago and Gary to have pollution control legislation. Therefore, in Gary, the people articulated their 'real' interests and achieved pollution control legislation whereas in East Chicago they did not. However, this assumption is dubious, to say the least. It could equally be argued that residents of Gary were well aware of the benefits that air pollution legislation might bring but were equally aware of the economic drawbacks. They were well aware, in other words, that paying the costs of such legislation would make the company less profitable and might lead to redundancies and reduced pay.

It may or may not be the case that pollution control legislation has economic consequences. Arguably, at the level of the individual industrial unit, unemployment and reduced pay would be the result of pollution control, although the benefits to society as a whole (including economic ones) may outweigh these costs. That, however, is little consolation to those whose livelihoods depend upon continued employment at the unit being threatened. This would be the case particularly where, as in Gary, one company dominates the economy.

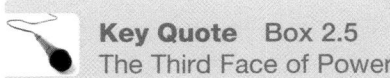

Key Quote Box 2.5
The Third Face of Power

'Is it not the most insidious exercise of power to prevent people, to whatever degree, from having grievances by shaping their perceptions, cognitions, and preferences in such a way that they accept their role in the existing order of things, either because they can see or imagine no alternative to it, or because they see it as natural or unchangeable, or because they value it as divinely ordained and beneficial?' (Stephen Lukes, 2005: 28)

pluralists to ascertain how individuals and groups come to hold the preferences they do. For elitists and Marxists this is a serious omission, since the ability of dominant groups to exercise ideological control is a key aspect of the exercise of power. By shaping individual preferences—through control over the means of communication and socialization—a ruling elite or class can prevent demands which challenge its interests from ever reaching the political agenda (for example, see the discussion of the power of the media in chapter twelve). In this way, an apparently pluralistic polity—with freedom of association, free elections, and so on—is, in reality, nothing of the sort.

➡ See chapter twelve, page 287, for a discussion of the power of the media.

Key Points

- Determining the empirical validity of the theories of the state discussed in chapter one depends upon an analysis of power.

- Pluralists use what Lukes calls the first face of power, focusing on the decision-making arena.

- This approach, while capable of producing non-pluralist conclusions, does not, it is argued, provide the complete picture. It misses, first, the possibility that a political elite or ruling class can avoid making decisions on certain key issues (the second face of power) and can, secondly, ensure that the wants expressed by political actors are not those that will damage the interests of the ruling group.

Interests and Power

Despite the force of their arguments, the critics of pluralism are faced with well-rehearsed methodological difficulties of their own; for if power is exercised in more subtle ways, how do we go about measuring it? We saw that it is possible, albeit difficult, to identify non-decision-making but how do we go about determining if individual preferences have been shaped by dominant forces in society?

The assumption of the third face of power is that one can distinguish between what individuals or groups perceive to be in their interests, and what is, in fact, actually in their interests. It is not impossible to conclude accurately that someone is acting against their best interests. Imagine, for instance, that the dominant ideology of a university, accepted by all of the students, is that it is necessary go out drinking the night before an exam on the spurious grounds that this will enhance your performance the following day. Imagine further that the university has shares in a local brewery and that it is likely to further benefit when students fail their exams and have to pay additional fees to resit them. Here, it is possible to conclude that an ideology benefits those in power and is not in the interests of the students.

Unfortunately, however, the identification of cases where individuals are clearly acting against their best interests are rarely as simple as that. Take the issue of smoking (Dearlove and Saunders, 2000: 368). Are we to say that those who continue to smoke, despite being aware of the health problems caused by it, are acting against their best interests? In some cases, undoubtedly, people would have given up smoking if they had been aware of the damage it was going to cause to their health; but others, well aware of the potential health costs, may insist that they want to continue smoking because of other perceived benefits— that it relaxes them, prevents them putting on weight, provides an ice breaker in social situations—or because they value other things over a long life. In these situations, are we still to say that these people are acting against their best interests?

There is an ever-present danger here of being extremely and unjustifiably patronizing towards individuals, a 'we know best' mentality. In reality, the researcher has to be careful to avoid his or her own subjective preferences from intervening. See **Box 2.6**. For example, imagine that one finds that there is widespread support for the existence of nuclear weapons and the argument that this acts as a deterrent against hostile powers also holding nuclear weapons. For the political analyst to argue that this belief is not in the interests of those holding it requires the imposition of an extremely contentious— and therefore political—judgement that, for instance, nuclear weapons are expensive and only encourage other countries to have them too. Others, of course, argue that the nuclear deterrent is in the interests of the people because it helps to maintain peace. Many political questions are similarly subjective and it is difficult to sustain the view that support for one value over another constitutes a failure to act in one's own interests. If a poor person, for instance, prefers freedom over equality are we to say that person is being manipulated? Such a position risks illegitimately denying the importance of one particular view of how society is organized over another.

Key Quote Box 2.6
A Critique of the Third Face of Power

'The problem (with the third face of power) . . . is the deeply condescending conception of the social subject as an ideological dupe that it conjures up. Not only is this wretched individual incapable of perceiving her/his true interests . . . But rising above the ideological mists is the enlightened academic who from his/her perch in the ivory tower may look down to discern the genuine interests of those not similarly blessed'. (Colin Hay, 1997: 47–8)

One innovative critique of the third face of power is provided by Scott (1990). He argues that researchers tend to confuse willing compliance, suggesting ideological manipulation, with a political strategy exercised by dominated groups. Such groups may superficially absorb and articulate the dominant world-view of the rulers, but underneath a counter-culture exists which challenges these dominant norms. This kind of strategy, Scott argues, is apparent in cases of slavery, serfdom, caste domination and, at a micro level, in relations between prisoners and warders and teachers and students. Lukes (2005: 127–8) does not challenge the ingenuity of Scott's research, but raises doubts about the correctness of its interpretation. Scott ignores the public evidence, suggesting the willing compliance of dominant groups, in favour of focusing on private transcripts which, he claims, reveal a deliberate strategy of quiescence. But why should we regard this evidence as more important than other information suggesting ideological conformity? At the very least, it 'does not show there is also not widespread consent and resignation' (Lukes, 2005: 131).

Political Elites

Given the difficulty of establishing that real interests are being thwarted, many critics of pluralism fall back on the existence of political elites. Here, it is argued, if it can be shown that those occupying the top positions in a variety of institutions have similar social and educational backgrounds, then this provides evidence of the possibility that a ruling elite or class does exist. This approach is, superficially at least, a fruitful one. In almost every elite group in a society such as Britain, those occupying the top positions are drawn disproportionately from the middle and upper classes and from those with public school and Oxbridge educations. Similarly, C. Wright Mills (1956), in his study of American centres of power, found overlapping social and educational backgrounds.

The problem with the political elite approach is that it arguably does not tell us very much at all about the exercise of power. Common sense tells us that political elites exist, but their existence is not necessarily incompatible with the pluralist position. As we saw in chapter one, pluralists accept the existence of elites but argue that providing these elites compete with each other then the basis of the pluralist position is maintained. To demonstrate the existence of a ruling elite or class, we have to establish that there is a coherent, conscious, and conspiratorial group which dominates decision-making.

→ See chapter one, page 30, for an exploration of pluralism.

In other words, establishing the existence of a ruling elite or class requires us to ask how far do elite groups share a common set of values and beliefs which is distinct from the rest of society? Secondly, how far do the aims of elite groups prevail? It is by no means clear that either of these conditions exist in a **liberal democracy** such as Britain, although the extent to which they do should, in principle, be capable of being researched. The problem is that it requires the type of empirical research of observable phenomena that critics of pluralism have already rejected.

2

Key Points

- It is extremely difficult to show conclusively that a political demand is not in the real interests of those who express it.

- Elite background studies do tend to reveal similar patterns of recruitment. However, the existence of a shared social and educational background does not prove the existence of a ruling elite or class.

Marxism and Power

The methodological problems we have identified above are as applicable to Marxist accounts as they are to elitist ones. Marxists, for instance, have emphasized the ability of the ruling class to exercise ideological control over the proletariat. They are therefore subject to the same critique that it is difficult to distinguish 'real' interests from perceived interests.

Marx famously pointed out that, 'the ideas of the ruling class are in every epoch the ruling ideas' (McLellan, 1980: 184). As a result of ideological control, the proletariat, for Marxists, are subject to 'false consciousness', and this explains their lack of revolutionary fervour. Marx tended to assume that a revolutionary class consciousness would arise spontaneously as a result of objective economic developments. As we shall see in chapter five, subsequent Marxists such as Lenin have argued for the need for a revolutionary party to articulate and promote the proletariat's 'real' interests.

➡ See chapter five, page 119, for an exploration of the development of socialism.

The concept of false consciousness is a theme developed by many post-Marxian Marxists. The Italian Marxist Antonio Gramsci (1891–1937), for instance (from whom Lukes borrows extensively) emphasized the ability of the ruling class ideologically to manipulate the proletariat through their 'hegemony', and regarded the role of intellectuals as crucial in challenging this domination (1971). Similarly, the neo-Marxist thinker Herbert Marcuse (1898–1979) stressed that the capitalist state creates a situation where a large part of the population are led to believe that the state is benign, if not beneficial, whereas the reality is that the state is exerting power. The evidence for this is provided by those occasions when the state is forced to react violently to public protest (1964).

Marxists, like elitists, have struggled to explain how it is that the ruling class rules despite the existence of universal suffrage and competitive elections. Marx himself, of course, had not faced this problem as he was writing at a time when the suffrage was limited to a small number of wealthy men. Marxists, such as Ralph Miliband (1924–94), have tended to fall back on three arguments here (1978). In the first place, they note the similar social and educational backgrounds of state and economic elites. Again, however, this falls prey to the critique outlined above, that such backgrounds do not show conclusively the existence of a cohesive, conspiratorial ruling class.

Secondly, Marxists, such as Miliband, argue that business interests represent a particularly powerful interest group. Again, the power of business can be challenged, on pluralist grounds, by noting the countervailing power of non-business interests and also by the state which Marxists have arguably failed to show always acts in the interests of business. Thirdly, Marxists (as well as elitists) argue that we ought to focus, not on the way decisions are made and who is involved in the decision-making arena, but on the outcomes of decision-making. Who wins and who loses from the decisions taken? According to the who wins and who loses position, we only have to look, it is argued, at the inequalities in most societies, including liberal democracies, to see that a particular group benefits. As Westergaard and Resler (1975: 141) state in their classic, Marxist, account of the class structure:

> Power is visible only through its consequences: they are the first and the final proof of the existence of power. The continuing inequalities of wealth, income and welfare that divide the population are . . . the most visible manifestations of the division of power in a society such as Britain.

From this, it is assumed that the group that benefits exercises power, and therefore that an elitist or Marxist approach is a more accurate description of modern political systems.

We saw earlier in this chapter that it is questionable whether outcomes such as these can be equated with power without the intended actions of a human agent. More specifically, although it is true that a great deal of inequality does still exist in most capitalist societies, it would be wrong to claim that universal suffrage and the coming to power of left-of-centre governments has had no impact on the distribution of resources. The creation of the welfare state and the introduction of free education in modern liberal democracies has undoubtedly improved the lives of many people. Indeed, arguably, the consequences of affluence, not least relating to the environment, have become as big a problem in the developed world as poverty.

Marxists counter the argument that the welfare state and other social reforms 'disprove' their central thesis. In the first place, they would argue that the creation of the welfare state was instrumental for the owners of capital because good healthcare and educational provision is essential for a productive workforce. Secondly, there is the argument that reforms benefiting the working class are made only when social unrest would have been the result had concessions not been made.

Both of these arguments have their problems. In the first place, not all social benefits can be shown to be in the direct interests of the dominant economic class. Some, such as, say, measures to improve productivity might be, but it is difficult to see free higher education in subjects in the humanities and social sciences in the same way. Secondly, the argument that reforms have averted social unrest and even revolution is weak, partly because it is impossible to disprove. We cannot possibly know for sure what the consequences of not granting concessions would have been. Moreover, if the ruling class are continually making concessions, then the question must be asked: how far do they remain a ruling class?

A more sophisticated Marxist account, which takes account of some of the weaknesses outlined above, is the structural Marxism associated mainly with the Greek

➡ See chapter six, page 146, for a discussion of the relationship between economic growth and environmental protection.

Marxist Nicos Poulantzas (1936–79), who in the late 1960s and 1970s engaged in a sustained debate with Miliband, the exponent of a more traditional Marxism (Poulantzas, 1973, 1976). Poulantzas, a disciple of the French structuralist Marxist Louis Althusser (1918–90), moves us from an account based on agency to one based on structure; that is, he argues that benefits in society may be distributed in a particular way not because of the intentional actions of individuals but because of the structure of the situation. In the economic sphere, capitalists, however kind and philanthropic they appear to be, are forced to act in particular ways—increasing profit primarily by bringing down wages—if they want to remain in business.

State personnel, too, are forced to act in ways that support the logic of the capitalist system. For Poulantzas, the state is able to act autonomously from the **bourgeoisie**, but this enables it to act in the long-term interests of the dominant class, even if, in some instances, the short-term interests of this class are set aside. Offering concessions to prevent social unrest is one such strategy. Offering free healthcare and education is not in the short-term interests of the bourgeoisie because paying for it eats into their profits. In the long-term, however, the ruling class benefits because of the creation of a healthier, more productive workforce, and a climate less likely to result in social unrest.

By emphasizing structure over agency Poulantzas, it might be argued, still falls foul of the claim that power can only be exercised deliberately. More specifically, he has been criticized for failing to explain why it is that the state behaves in the way he says it does (Hay, 1999). In other words, if the state is not directly controlled by the ruling class, why is it that it still acts in its long-term interests? Even more peculiar, why is it that it has autonomy which is only relative? There is an air of mysticism here which, perhaps, is the result of not paying enough attention to the attitudes and actions of individuals.

Key Points

- Marxists also emphasize the role of both ideological control and elite background studies, and therefore face similar problems to those seeking to justify a ruling elite position.

- Marxists also face difficulty in trying to explain how a ruling class can still be said to rule in a liberal democracy where universal suffrage has long been the norm and in which a welfare state now exists.

- Marxists tend to argue that universal suffrage does not dent the power of business interests, and that, in any case, much social welfare reform is in the interests of the dominant class.

- The structural Marxism associated with Poulantzas attempts, not always successfully, to deal with these problems. Political actors are forced to act in ways that promote the capitalist system because of the structure of the situation. Moreover, the state acts in the long-term interests of capitalism, even though in the short term it may seem to damage the interests of the class that is said to rule.

Conclusion

It is to be hoped that this chapter has been able to demonstrate how crucial the concept of power is to a study of politics. We have seen that semantic, normative, and empirical questions about power abound: what is it? Is it a good thing? How is it distributed? The answers to all of these questions are contested. Answers to the empirical question remain, perhaps, most disputed. Indeed, here, we reached something of an impasse.

On the one hand, we suspect that the conceptualization of power adopted by pluralists, although eminently quantifiable and researchable, is, at the very least, incomplete. On the other hand, the conceptualization of power most favoured by elitists and Marxists, although persuasive, is problematic because it appears unresearchable. This explains why the debate between exponents of competing theories of the state continues. This debate is, perhaps, less intensive than it was thirty years ago and this is partly, at least, to do with the question marks being raised against the efficacy of the state in an increasingly globalized world.

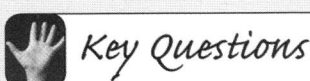 **Key Questions**

- What is the difference between power and authority?
- Is the exercise of power inevitable?
- Must power always be exercised deliberately?
- Is power the same as force?
- Is it desirable to eliminate the exercise of power?
- What are the methodological difficulties of determining the empirical validity of theories of the state?
- What are the implications for the pluralist theory of the state of Steven Lukes's second and third faces of power?
- Is power as thought control a viable concept?
- What does the character of political elites tell us about the distribution of power?
- Is there anything of value in the Marxist theory of the state?

Further Reading

Bachrach, P. and M. Baratz (1963), 'Decisions and Non-Decisions', *American Political Science Review*, 57, 632–42.
> This is a much-cited critique of the pluralist theory of the state which emphasizes the importance of non-decision-making.

Blowers, A. (1984), *Something in the Air: Corporate Power and the Environment*, London: Harper & Row.

Crenson, M. (1971), *The Un-Politics of Air Pollution*, Baltimore, MD: Johns Hopkins University Press.
> This is a study which attempts to put into operation Lukes's critique of the pluralist decision-making methodology.

Dahl, R. (1963), *Who Governs?*, New Haven, CT: Yale University Press.
> This is the classic example of the decision-making methodology associated with pluralism.

Lukes, S. (2005), *Power: A Radical View*, Basingstoke: Palgrave Macmillan, 2nd edn.
> This is a celebrated account of power. This second edition repeats the original account published in 1974 but also includes an essay defending it against critics.

Miliband, R. (1978), *The State in Capitalist Society*, New York: Basic Books.
> This is the best-known modern defence of the Marxist theory of the state.

Web Links

http://en.wikipedia.org/wiki/Power_(philosophy)
This is a useful summary of the power literature.

 Visit the **Online Resource Centre** that accompanies this book to access more learning resources at **www.oxfordtextbooks.co.uk/orc/garner/**

3

Democracy and Political Obligation

Reader's Guide

This chapter has two major aims: first, to explore key aspects of democratic theory, and secondly to examine the case for democracy being the major grounding for political obligation. The first objective will be fulfilled by examining the historical evolution of the term, as well as the debate between advocates of the protective theory and the participatory theory of democracy, and the cases, respectively, for deliberative democracy and cosmopolitan democracy. The second will be fulfilled by outlining why it is that democracy is seen as the major grounding for political obligation, examining alternatives to democracy, and considering the majoritarian implications of democracy.

3

What is Democracy?

Like many other political concepts, democracy is an essentially contested concept. It is a term with no precise and agreed meaning. Finding a definitional consensus for democracy is not helped by its emotive connotations. Democracy is a 'good' word. It is almost universally regarded in a favourable light. There are few countries in the world that would want to be labelled as undemocratic. Indeed, partly because of the collapse of the old Soviet Union and its satellites: 'Around two-thirds of all the countries in the world have a basic set of democratic institutions built around competitive elections that enable all adult citizens to choose and remove their government leaders' (Stoker, 2006: 7).

This expansion of competitive elections has led to the growing importance of so-called **illiberal democracies** or, as they are sometimes called, competitive authoritarian regimes or semi-democracies (Zakaria, 2003; Levitsky and Way, 2002). As we saw in chapter one, these are regimes in which, while elections are not blatantly rigged, elected rulers pay little heed to the protection of individual rights (such as free speech) once in power, and therefore opposition to rulers, who are able to manipulate electoral outcomes through control of the media and the use of the state apparatus, is difficult. As a result, the turnover of political leaders through competitive elections is small. In 2005, around thirty countries were described as only partly free (Hague and Harrop, 2007: 52). See **Box 3.1**.

➡ See chapter one, page 27, for a description of illiberal democracy.

The existence of illiberal democracies, however, raises a conundrum for students of democracy. For, while it is surely stretching the concept to breaking point if we insist that the label 'democratic' can be applied to, say, one-party states—in China (which describes itself as a 'democratic dictatorship') or in the old Soviet bloc countries—it is not so clear-cut that we should deny the democracy label to competitive authoritarian states.

 Case Study   Box 3.1
Singapore as an Illiberal Democracy

Singapore declared independence from Britain in 1963. Since then, its political institutions have been impeccably democratic, with **plurality**-based elections and a Westminster system of Parliament, Cabinet, and Prime Minister.

However, one party, the People's Action Party (PAP), has won control of Parliament in every election, and one individual, Lee Kuan Yew, was Prime Minister from 1959 to 1990. As a result, opposition parties have argued that it is essentially a one-party state. Of course, the dominance of one party is not necessarily inconsistent with a liberal democratic style of government. However, elements of Singapore's politics would point to it being an extreme example of an illiberal democracy, containing elements of both democracy and authoritarianism.

Thus, although elections are not rigged, the PAP has been accused of manipulating the political system. This has been achieved through censorship (the broadcasting media is state owned, newspapers are heavily controlled, and the use of satellite receivers is illegal), gerrymandering (where constituency boundaries are altered to benefit the ruling party), and the use of the legal system against opposition politicians. Moreover, liberal democratic values are rejected in general, with freedom of speech heavily curtailed and a draconian system of punishment involving the regular use of capital punishment. In general, economic development (where there has been a huge progress) is given a higher priority than democratic development.

Sources: Mauzy and Milne (2002); Worthington (2002)

It is probably the case that democracy does, justifiably, mean different things to different people; the question is, whether there is a core of meaning on which we can all agree. Very basically, democracy refers to a regime whereby political power is widely spread, where power in some way rests with the people. Democracy, then, has something to do with political equality. As Arblaster (2002: 7) points out, this definition is sufficiently vague to allow for a number of interpretations. Lively (1975: 30) suggests seven possibilities:

1. That all should govern, in the sense that all should be involved in legislating, in deciding on general policy, in applying laws and in governmental administration.
2. That all should be personally involved in crucial decision making, that is to say in deciding general laws and matters of general policy.
3. That rulers should be accountable to the ruled; they should, in other words, be obliged to justify their actions to the ruled and be removable by the ruled.
4. That rulers should be accountable to the representatives of the ruled.
5. That rulers should be chosen by the ruled.
6. That rulers should be chosen by the representatives of the ruled.
7. That rulers should act in the interests of the ruled.

Lively argues that numbers 1 to 4 are justified in being described as democratic whereas 5 to 7 are not (33–42). The crucial defining characteristic is accountability. The latter three definitions provide no means whereby the rulers can be removed by the ruled and therefore cannot be defined as versions of democracy. Number 7 allows for the inclusion of regimes, such as those subscribing to communism, who claim, despite the lack of competitive elections, to be democratic because the real interests of the many are promoted by rulers who are aiming for social and economic equality (Macpherson, 1966: 12–22).

This claim, however, is a logical mistake. The outcomes of a **political system** are separate from the means by which its rulers are chosen. It may be the case, as we will see below, that democracy (in the sense of a political system requiring regular competitive elections) is the most effective way of ensuring that rulers do act in the interests of the ruled. It may also be the case that the achievement of political equality requires a degree of economic equality; but ultimately, a benign dictatorship with the interests of her people at heart is not impossible. Many one-party communist states, of course, were far from being benign, arguably precisely because their leaders were not accountable. It is also questionable whether illiberal democracies, where rulers are able to manipulate elections and transfers of power are rare, uphold the accountability rule and can therefore be described as truly democratic. To add an extra layer of complexity, we will see later in the chapter that **liberal democracies** do not escape criticism from a democratic perspective because of the potential conflict between majoritarian decision making and the protection of individual rights.

Focusing on the first four of Lively's typology, we are still left with considerable variation. The first two are forms of **direct democracy**, whereas the latter two are forms of **representative democracy**. Direct democracy refers to a system whereby the people rule directly. The first definition on Lively's list seems impossible to be realized in anything but a very small-scale society. Even the second raises huge difficulties. Representative democracy is a more realistic proposition. This is where the people choose others to represent their interests. There can also be stronger and weaker versions of representative democracy. British MPs, invoking the great eighteenth-century parliamentarian Edmund Burke (1729–97), for instance, have for long insisted upon their independence from their constituents, so that on at least some issues (mainly moral ones such as capital punishment and abortion) they vote according to their conscience. Of course, it is debatable how far MPs can remain aloof from their constituent's views without negative consequences befalling them at a future election.

➡ See chapter nine, pages 209–10, for a quotation from Burke on the relationship between an MP and constituents.

Key Points

- The concept of democracy has a core meaning. It is about popular rule or the rule of the people. This can be interpreted in a wide variety of ways, although some regimes clearly do not exhibit any characteristics of the people having power, and others limit it extensively.

- Lively suggests that democracy requires the people to make decisions directly, or to choose, and be able to remove, those who make decisions on the people's behalf.

History

Democracy is a Greek term containing two words: *demos*, meaning the citizens within a city-state, and *kratos*, meaning power or rule (Arblaster, 2002: 15). The term was used to describe the practice of the Greek city-states. Many contemporary democratic theorists and activists look back to the Greek city-states with great affection, regarding them as providing a participatory model of democracy of which modern liberal democracies fall far short. In actual fact, direct democracy was possible precisely because a considerable number of people—most notably women, slaves, and foreigners—were excluded and did a great deal of the work that enabled citizens to engage in politics.

The Greek city-states practised direct democracy. More specialized and time-consuming tasks were allocated to a smaller number of office holders but office holders themselves were subject to regular rotation, chosen by lot by the rest of the community. Jury service was also a feature of Greek city-states so that all members of the community took it in turns to exercise justice.

For much of its history, democracy has been regarded in a negative light. The Greek philosophers—Plato and Aristotle, for instance—argued that democracy was synonymous with mob rule and was a perverted form of government, although the latter regarded democracy as the least bad of the three 'deviant' forms of rule: democracy, tyranny, and oligarchy (Cunningham, 2002: 7). Much the same picture applied to successive political thinkers. Neither of the key English political theorists of the seventeenth century, John Locke and Thomas Hobbes, were, for instance, democrats.

The French and American Revolutions

The tide began to turn with the French and American revolutions of the eighteenth century. Both revolutions proclaimed democracy as one of their goals, and both were influenced by the writings of the French political philosopher, Jean-Jacques Rousseau. The Americans endorsed democracy but were still wary of it. The Founding Fathers of the US Constitution, and most notably James Madison (1751–1836), were very keen to rid themselves of the absolute monarchy of George III. However, they were equally concerned about the effects of introducing majoritarianism. Majority tyranny was the ever-present danger of democracy. As a result, the Founding Fathers created a Constitution that set up a directly elected legislature, the House of Representatives, but at the same time checked it by separating power between it and the Senate (the other part of the legislature), the Executive branch headed by the President, and the Judiciary, headed by the Supreme Court.

The Nineteenth-century Move Towards Democracy

By the nineteenth century, democracy was beginning to take on more popular connotations in theory and in practice. Many countries began the long and slow road towards universal suffrage. In theoretical terms, the so-called utilitarian theory of democracy associated with Jeremy Bentham and James Mill was extremely influential. See **Box 3.2**.

Key Concept Box 3.2
The Utilitarian Theory of Democracy

The utilitarian theory of democracy is associated with the nineteenth-century British political thinker, Jeremy Bentham, who developed the theory in association with his chief disciple, James Mill. Bentham had initially not been concerned about democracy, feeling that an enlightened despot was just as likely to pursue the utilitarian aim of the greatest happiness. He came to change his mind after the failure of the British Government to implement any of his schemes of reform.

The utilitarian theory of democracy is based on the premise that democracy is necessary to ensure that those in government will remain accountable to those they govern. Bentham and Mill argued that, left to their own devices, members of government will maximize their own pleasure. They will only pursue the greatest happiness of all if their positions in power are dependent upon it. The function of elections is, therefore, a protective device to ensure that the preferences of the people are taken into account by decision-makers.

As the Marxist political theorist C.B. Macpherson (1911–87) (1977: 23–43) pointed out, the utilitarian theory was the first attempt to seek to apply democracy to a class-divided capitalist industrial society. This gave rise to liberal democracy, which denotes the linking of democracy with the kind of liberal principles originally associated with the industrial middle class. The linking together of democracy and capitalism raised the crucial question of how to reconcile political equality— to which democracy in its purest sense amounts — with economic inequality. The fear of many property owners at the time was that the arrival of universal suffrage would result in a political programme designed to create greater economic equality, thereby putting their privileged position at considerable risk.

Despite the rise of the Labour Party in Britain and similar socialist parties elsewhere, there was no great move towards a socialist political programme. Macpherson (1977: 62), and other left-wing academics such as Miliband (1972), argued that this was the product of trade union and Labour Party leaders betraying the revolutionary potential of the working class. We have seen in the past two chapters that there are a variety of reasons why the introduction of universal suffrage might not have brought about political equality. A classical Marxist account, for instance, would emphasize that power lies in the economic base, and the political realm is a mere reflection of this power. Without attacking the source of this power, then, the introduction of universal suffrage is going to have little impact. It is clearly true that, as many have noted, it is difficult to establish greater political equality in an economically unequal society. Without being a Marxist, it is clearly the case that economic clout often translates into political clout. From a non-Marxist perspective, political equality is not merely achieved by universal suffrage but also, even more importantly, by ensuring free and fair competition between organized groups in society. A fragmented pressure group universe results in greater democratic claims or, as Dahl (1971) points out, a **polyarchy** in which 'minorities rule'.

In the last thirty years or so, the democratic landscape has been transformed again with a doubling of the number of states having competitive elections. This is partly a product of the collapse of the Soviet bloc and the emergence of independent states in Eastern Europe, but it has also occurred in Southern Europe (Greece, Portugal, and Spain), Latin America (for example, Venezuela) and parts of Africa (for example, Botswana) and Asia (for example, Malaysia). From a democratic perspective, this has undoubtedly been an advance, even though, as we saw, the democratic credentials of the many illiberal states that have accompanied this wave of democratization can be questioned.

Key Points

- For much of its history, democracy has been regarded in a negative light.
- The turning point was the French and American Revolutions in the eighteenth centuries, after which democracy became a more desirable concept.
- The nineteenth century saw a sustained attempt to achieve universal suffrage in practice and to justify it in theory. The utilitarian theory of democracy, associated with James Mill and Bentham was really the first attempt to try to justify incorporating democracy into a class-divided society. This raises the question, why did not the advent of democracy bring about a more economically equal society?
- In the final quarter of the twentieth century there was an enormous expansion of regimes introducing competitive elections and proclaiming themselves democratic.

The Classical Versus the Elitist Theory of Democracy

By the twentieth century, democracy was largely shorn of its negative connotations. In academic political theory, the major dispute has been over two competing theories of democracy. On the one hand is the **elitist theory of democracy** (also sometimes called the 'revisionist' or 'protective' theory). This theory became prominent in the post-1945 period and is particularly associated with the Austrian economist and sociologist Joseph Schumpeter (1883–1950), who articulated his theory in the much-cited book *Capitalism, Socialism and Democracy*, originally published in 1942. Against this is the classical theory of democracy, sometimes also referred to as the 'participatory' or 'developmental' theory.

Schumpeter was reacting to what he saw as the inevitable role played by elites in modern polities. He therefore recognized the importance of the Italian elitists whom we encountered in chapter one. However, far from agreeing with their conclusion that democracy is a sham, Schumpeter argues that democracy can be reconciled with **elitism**. Schumpeter identifies what he describes as the prevailing classical theory of democracy, which he takes to be a model emphasizing the active participation of citizens in the making of political decisions. This model is associated with the practice of the Greek city-states, and the theories of Rousseau and the nineteenth-century British political theorist, John Stuart Mill. For Schumpeter, however, this model is both unrealistic and undesirable. See **Box 3.3**.

The classical model is unrealistic, Schumpeter argues, because mass participation is not a characteristic of modern democratic societies. Empirically, most people appear happy to leave

→ See chapter one, page 33, for an exploration of elitism.

Key Debate Box 3.3
Advocates of the Protective and Participatory Theories of Democracy

Protective theory	Developmental theory
Bentham	Greek city-states
James Mill	Rousseau
Schumpeter	J.S. Mill
Downs	G.D.H. Cole
	Bachrach
	Pateman

politics to a class of political elites. The classical model is also undesirable, Schumpeter argues, because the masses tend to be irrational and are liable to have authoritarian values and be seduced by charismatic and dictatorial leaders, a view echoed by Kornhauser (1960). It is no accident that Schumpeter was writing at a time when the rise of fascism in Germany and Italy had brought to power such leaders with the apparent consent, some of it enthusiastic, of a large proportion of the masses. Far from being a threat to democracy, then, elites become the protectors of democracy against the authoritarian values of the masses.

Schumpeter seeks to replace this classical theory of democracy with what he perceives to be a more desirable alternative. In a well-known passage, Schumpeter (1961: 269) redefines democracy as 'that institutional arrangement for arriving at political decisions in which individuals acquire the power to decide by means of a competitive struggle for the people's vote'. What is notable about this definition is that there is no emphasis on participation. Decisions are to be left to a political elite. What makes the system democratic, for Schumpeter, is the competition between elites. The voters in this model do not even choose between different sets of policies. They simply choose between different teams of leaders who then decide what policies to carry out.

Schumpeter's account has been built upon by other political scientists. In particular, account has been taken of intermediary groups such as trade unions and business organizations with elites of their own who compete with each other in trying to persuade the political leadership to adopt their policies. Kornhauser (1960) argued that this system of elites safeguards liberal democracies from either **totalitarian** or 'mass society'. Without the various intermediary groups, atomized individuals provide an opportunity for an elite to mobilize them and this may lead to the overthrow of the existing regime and its replacement by a new elite who may have totalitarian intentions.

This elitist theory of democracy held sway in political science circles for twenty or so years after the end of the Second World War. It was reinforced by the so-called 'economic

Key Debate Box 3.4
The Economic Theory of Democracy and its Critics

One version of the protective theory of democracy is the so-called economic theory of democracy. This is associated with the American political scientist, Anthony Downs (1930–), who wrote a hugely influential book on this issue in the late 1950s (1957). It is a good example of the use of the rational choice approach to political science (see Introduction).

Downs develops a sophisticated explanatory 'economic theory' of democracy, in which he tries to explain the nature of voter choice and party competition. Downs's theory is labelled economic because it shares certain fundamental principles with economics. In particular, advocates of the economic theory of democracy assume certain characteristics of human behaviour from which the theory is deduced. Humans are regarded as individualistic utility maximizers whose aim is to achieve benefits for themselves at the least possible cost.

For Downs, the behaviour of politicians and voters is analogous to the behaviour of producers and consumers in the economy.

- Political parties and politicians are equivalent to producers. Just as producers seek to maximize profit, politicians seek to maximize votes. Their only goal is to win power.

- Likewise, just as consumers seek the best buy for their money, voters seek to 'buy' at the cheapest possible price the set of policies that will serve their interests the most. As a result, parties must offer the voters what they want or they will not win enough votes to gain power.

Based on these simple principles, Downs constructs a whole model of competitive party politics. He suggests that voters can be located on an ideological continuum from left to right, and that political parties will seek to place themselves at the point where the majority of voters are situated, the vote maximization position.

There have been a number of pertinent criticisms of this model.

- It is overly simplistic. For example, it is inadequate to focus on just one ideological continuum, since that does not take into account the complexities of voter preferences. Moreover, voter choice is not simply about competing ideologies. A crucial dimension of voter choice is voter perceptions of the competence of politicians. This is not easily located on the kind of spectrum Downs uses (Stokes, 1963).

- It is by no means certain that voters and politicians behave in the way that Downs tells us they do.

  —Evidence suggests that at least some voters use their vote in an altruistic way on the grounds of principle rather than merely in their own self-interest.

3

— Similarly, to describe politicians as merely vote maximizers is surely too simplistic. Parties may recognize that they have to win votes in order to gain power, but this is different from saying that they have no principles they want to promote.

— Even more devastating for the economic theory of democracy is the evidence which suggests that many voters do not have the level of sophistication that the economic theory demands (Robertson, 1976: 177–81). According to the alternative party identification model, voters choose between parties, not on the basis of their perceptions of a party's particular policies, but because they have a long-standing psychological identification with a party. As a result, their support for a party does not change when the party's policies change.

— The economic theory of democracy also finds it difficult to explain why most people bother to vote at all (Barry, 1970: 13–22). For the economic theory, voting is a cost which is only worth paying if the benefits of voting outweigh these costs. Given this, it is only worthwhile voting if the vote makes a difference to the result. The chances of one vote making this amount of difference is minimal.

- The economic theory of democracy takes voter preferences as given. It therefore neglects to consider the possibility that these preferences are shaped by powerful forces in society, and not least by the political parties themselves, particularly when they have governmental power (Dunleavy and Ward, 1981).

theory of democracy' which built upon the earlier utilitarian model. See **Box 3.4**. These types of theory can be classified as 'protective' models of democracy, in the sense that they are concerned with ensuring that political leaders are accountable to the wishes of the voters. They are concerned, therefore, with democracy as a means to an end of voter utility maximization.

An alternative model can be described as a 'participatory' or 'developmental' model of democracy. This is enshrined in the classical theory of democracy, although this label contains as many differences as similarities. The developmental model is more concerned with democracy as an end in itself; that is, participation is itself enriching. It is not, as for the protective theory, a burden to be undertaken in order to ensure that politicians are accountable. Rather, participation is to be valued for the positive effect it has on individual characteristics. Individuals who participate, it is argued, become more virtuous and intelligent, they understand the need for cooperation, and their own self-worth increases as does their status in the eyes of others.

The antecedents of the developmental model are in the practice of the Greek city-states and the political philosophy of Rousseau, J.S. Mill, and the unjustly neglected British socialist thinker, G.D.H. Cole (1889–1959) (Wright, 1979). Support for it began to re-emerge in the 1960s. A new breed of radical democratic theorists began to challenge the elite theory (Bachrach, 1967; Duncan and Lukes, 1964; Pateman, 1970).

Photo 3.1

Aldermaston to London CND March—12 April 1968.
Source: Topfoto/PA

They argued that, by abandoning the participatory element, the elitist theory of democracy had lost sight of the true meaning of democracy. Any notion of rule by the people had been abandoned. What was needed, then, was the rediscovery of participation in the political process. These theoretical insights were accompanied by the rise of mass movements in the 1960s such as CND, protesting against nuclear weapons, the student protests particularly in France, and, a decade later, the grass-roots environmental movement.

Assessing the validity of these competing theories of democracy is a difficult task, not least because the meaning of the concept is disputed. Lively (1975: 40–1) argues that Schumpeter's theory is not democratic primarily because it does not fulfil the accountability criteria. This is because Schumpeter makes no recommendation on the frequency of elections, and his position would seem to justify, say, the election for life of a monarch. It is not clear, however, that this is Schumpeter's intention and most commentators have assumed the model includes a system of more or less regular competitive elections.

Two observations about these competing models of democracy are pertinent here. One is that if democracy can be defined first and foremost as political equality, then the elite

3

theory of democracy stretches the label to its absolute limits. Schumpeter was, arguably, trying to say that the rule of political elites, albeit in a competitive environment, is for a variety of reasons preferable to mass participation in politics. As a result, democracy ought to be limited in the interests of other goals such as stability and efficiency. In other words, Schumpeter is really espousing a mixed form of government combining democracy with other values. The problem is that, by the time Schumpeter was writing, democracy had such positive connotations that it was difficult for him to admit to wanting to limit it.

On the other hand, we can say that advocates of the developmental model must be able to show that their version of democracy is not undesirable and unrealistic, and this, indeed, is what much of the developmental literature seeks to do. For example, advocates of this model would say that political apathy is not inevitable, that people can be encouraged to participate more and, once they start, they will improve at it. Some may, perhaps, be less likely as a result to exhibit authoritarian values. Political apathy, they would continue, is partly a product of the lack of participation in decision making in the working environment. Of great importance to the developmentalists, therefore, is industrial democracy (Pateman, 1970). As Lively (1975: 38) astutely remarks, 'it does not follow from the fact that "classical" democracy does not exist that it cannot ever exist; nor does it force us to redefine democracy, for it might just as well lead us to the conclusion that Western systems are not democracies or are only imperfect democracies'.

Finally, advocates of the developmental model have to show that participation is possible (Arblaster, 2002: 84–5). Here, technological developments would seem to be on their side, offering the possibility of greater involvement in politics through, for instance, the use of the Internet and interactive television technology. In a large complex society, the use of referendums, whereby all electors vote on a particular issue, is a direct democratic way of increasing involvement. They are used in many countries, particularly Switzerland and the USA.

Deliberative Democracy

An off-shoot of the idea of democratic participation is a school of **deliberative democracy** (Bessete, 1994; Dryzek, 2000). This model of democracy, heavily influenced by the ideas of the German philosopher Jurgen Habermas, has been developed in the last twenty years or so. It builds upon the emphasis on participation by arguing that the process of public debate and argument leads to rational and more legitimate decision-making. It is not enough, then, for the existence of an opportunity to exercise a political choice. Rather, 'true' democracy allows for these choices to be developed after due discussion and reflection. It therefore does not assume that political choices are set in stone and unalterable. As Cunningham (2002: 165) points out, 'democracy on the deliberative conception should be more than voting, and it should serve some purpose other than simply registering preferences'.

Deliberative democracy cannot be accurately portrayed as another version of direct participatory democracy. This is partly because advocates of deliberative democracy are sceptical about the possibilities of direct democracy in large-scale modern societies, but also because it is doubted whether direct democracy can necessarily produce the kind of reflective deliberation required. The quality of participation is regarded as more important than its quantity (Held, 2006: 236–7). Recommendations for putting deliberative democracy into place include deliberative polling where a small section of the population engage in debates about some issues and are polled before and after the deliberation in order to see if their views have altered. The results would then be disseminated to a wider audience (Held, 2006: 247–8).

The advantages claimed for deliberative democracy include the point that it allows for toleration of other people's views in divided societies, and, in turn, might lead to greater consensus. It is regarded as a means by which altruism will triumph over the excessive dominance of private interests in liberal democracies. Moreover, decisions made as a result of deliberation are, it is suggested, more likely to have legitimacy and are more likely to be rational decisions, precisely because they were not taken in haste. The downside, it might be argued, is that anything other than superficial deliberation does take time (even if it does not follow the direct democracy model) and may, if widely adopted, lead to delays, or even paralysis, in decision making. In addition, the theory has been criticized for exaggerating the degree of consensus that can be reached in decision-making as a result of deliberation (Cunningham, 2002: 166).

Key Points

- The modern debate has been between exponents of the elite theory of democracy, on the one hand, and the participatory theory of democracy on the other.

- In the post-1945 period, the elitist theory, associated above all with Schumpeter, held sway. The classical theory, associated with participation and citizen involvement in decision making was regarded as undesirable and unrealistic.

- The elitist theory began to be challenged from the 1960s by a new breed of participationists, eager to show the developmental possibilities of greater citizen involvement. The success of their enterprise depends upon showing that greater participation is both desirable and realistic.

- The developmental theory has been built upon by exponents of deliberative democracy who suggest that political discussion is likely to produce more effective and legitimate decisions.

Why is Democracy Regarded as Special?

Politics in the West, and, indeed, much of the world, has become synonymous with democracy. Democracy is regarded as indispensable. But why is this? What is it about democracy that is so special? The usual answer to this question is that democracy is regarded as special because it is put forward as the main reason why we should obey the rules and laws of a political system. In other words, if one was to ask why it is that we are obliged to accept and obey the laws of our society, then the answer would be because they are democratically made.

This question of **political obligation**—on what grounds should we obey the laws of the state?—has been one of the central preoccupations of political theory. It is a crucial question, primarily because of the compulsory nature of the state. If we join a voluntary organization, such as a pressure group or a church, we have to accept the rules of that organization but if we do not like them we have the option of leaving. For most of us, we do not have the same option when it comes to the state. Some people may be able to go and live somewhere more to their liking, but for most people, that is not an option. Most of us do not have a choice when it comes to accepting the laws of the state, or at least if we choose not to obey the state, then we can expect sanctions to be applied against us.

Democracy seems to offer us the ideal grounding for political obligation because if we make the laws under which we live, then they are likely to be in our interests and therefore we get what we want. In other words, we do not lose anything as a result of being in a political community. Democracy, then, has a strong claim to be the political system that would be chosen by people in the **state-of-nature** scenario that we saw in chapter one has been a device used by **social contract** theorists. In other words, if a group of people came together to form a political system, the advantages of choosing democratic principles would be that they would all get a say in the laws under which they have to live. As a result, it can be argued, the freedom existing in the state of nature would be maintained in a democratic political system.

➡ See chapter one, page 37, for a discussion of the liberal social contract tradition.

Alternative Sources of Political Obligation

Before we go on to examine further the case of democracy as the ideal grounding for political obligation, it should be recognized that democracy is not the only one. In fact, democracy has only relatively recently been regarded as important. Three alternative approaches are particularly worth mentioning here, two of which you will be familiar with from chapter one.

We Ought to Obey the State because it Provides us with Security

This idea, as we saw, is associated with the seventeenth-century British political theorist, Thomas Hobbes. To reiterate, Hobbes argues that a sovereign who is strong enough to enforce stability is worth obeying. As soon as the sovereign's power weakens, however, we have no obligation to obey.

We Ought to Obey the State because it Protects our Natural Rights

This idea is associated with another British political thinker, John Locke. He argues that humans possess **natural rights**, given by God, before they enter into a political community. As a result, for such a political community to be legitimate, it must uphold and protect these rights. If it fails to do so, then we are entitled to revolt against it. Two brief observations at this point can be made about this approach to political obligation. The first is that, although Locke was not a democrat, his theory is not necessarily incompatible with democracy. Most democrats would argue that rights should be protected and would say that this is more likely to happen if the people have an influence on what the state does. There are some problems with this, which we will come back to later.

The second observation to note is that the key problem with rights as a grounding for political obligation is that it leaves open the question of *what* rights exist. Locke himself argued that the crucial rights to protect are the rights to liberty, life, and property. The problem with these rights is that they might be used to defend the status quo, to defend inequality and privilege. As we pointed out in chapter one, however, it is equally plausible to claim that we have other rights too—the right not to starve, for instance, or the right to a home, or education, or healthcare. Of course, these latter, social and economic rights, may conflict with the negative ones. It may be necessary, for example, to constrain, or even eliminate, property rights in order to generate enough resources to provide free healthcare or education.

More pertinently, from the perspective of the subject matter of this chapter, a democratic decision taken with the will of the majority may lead to the sacrifice of negative rights in favour of the achievement of more positive ones. Alternatively, the achievement of positive rights may be used as a reason, or as an excuse, for a failure to introduce democracy. For example, in China, the political leadership published a White Paper on democracy in 2005 in which the postponement of democratic reforms was justified partly on the grounds that economic development, and the achievement of better standards of living, were a priority (see web links). The upholding of (at least some) rights, then, is not necessarily compatible with democracy. Again, the consequences of this will be explored a little later in the chapter.

We Ought to Obey the State when it Pursues the General Will

The idea of the **general will** has been a popular theme in political theory but it is particularly associated with the eighteenth-century philosopher, Jean-Jacques Rousseau. For Rousseau, the general will can be contrasted with the selfish, particular, wills of individuals. It is tantamount, then, to the common good, something that is in the general interest of the community, that is, in the collective interests of society. This general will, then, amounts to more than the sum of particular wills. Rather, it is a genuine collective will, irrespective of the particular wills of members of the community. This approach to political obligation holds that if the state pursues this common, general interest—and not particular interests—then we have an obligation to obey it. Hegel adopts a very similar theory, whereby the state pursues the common interest, thereby transcending the particular interests pursued by families and by **civil society**.

Rousseau's arguments are more complex than has been suggested so far. We can coax them out by looking at what might be regarded as a key problem with his theory. We might respond to Rousseau and other advocates of the general will by asking what is so good about it? Why are we obliged to accept it? Why should I not be selfish and encourage the state to pursue a programme that is in my own selfish interests? We might answer by saying that we ought to obey the general will because it is the right and moral thing to do. The problem with this is that some people may deny the importance of this moral edict and still say 'I'm still not going to obey the general will because, on this occasion at least, it is not in my interests to do it'.

It is at this point that Rousseau's argument becomes a little more complex and contentious, for he wants to claim that not only should we promote the general will, but that this is what we *really* want to do. He even goes as far as to say that if we are forced to accept the general will, then we are being *forced to be free* (Rousseau, 1913). We are being forced to be free because we are being forced to accept what we really want to do.

It is not the place here to engage in a sustained critical analysis of Rousseau's political theory. We can say that it is heavily dependent upon the very existence of a community's collective will. Some political theorists suggest that that idea is a fiction. Of course, if this is the case, it becomes a potentially dangerous doctrine, open to abuse by a dictator who justifies tyrannical measures on the spurious grounds that they are in the public or collective interest (Talmon, 1952). Here, critics have been particularly scathing about the implications of Rousseau's claim that it is legitimate to force someone to be free. This aspect of Rousseau's theory relies on a particular conception of freedom and we will return to it in more detail in chapter four.

➜ See chapter four, page 93, for a discussion of Rousseau's idea of the general will and its implication for freedom.

For now, if we accept that Rousseau is right and that we all do really want to pursue the general will, it is important to recognize that he has solved the problem of political obligation. Remember that the study of political obligation is concerned with finding a political system which we can all obey because we want to. If we can do this, then we do not lose any freedom by joining together with others to create a political community. Rousseau (1913: 191) sets out his task as follows:

The problem is to find a form of association which will defend and protect with the whole common force the person and goods of each associate, and in which each, while uniting himself with all, may still obey himself alone, and remain as free as before. This is the fundamental problem of which the social contract provides the solution.

Rousseau's answer is that we can all obey a political system that pursues the general will and remain as free as we were before, because the general will is what we all want.

In other words, what the state wants to do, if it pursues the general will, can be unanimously accepted as representing the will of all. As we will see below, democracy finds it difficult, if not impossible, to achieve unanimity, and this raises question marks against its claim to provide an ideal form of political obligation.

Key Points

- Democracy is often regarded as the most important source of political obligation. This is because it is a political system that allows people to make decisions under which they can live. The freedom that individuals have in an imaginery state of nature is therefore maintained.

- There are, of course, others reasons we might invoke to explain our political obligation. We might, for instance, want to obey the state because it provides us with security (Hobbes) or because it protects our rights (Locke) or because it promotes the general will (Rousseau).

- If Rousseau is right that we always really want the state to promote the general will, he has solved the problem of political obligation. This is because even if we oppose the general will, we can be forced to be free. Our allegiance to the state, therefore, makes us as free as we were before a political community was created.

Is Democracy Special? The Problem of Majority Rule

After that detour, we will go back now and, armed with knowledge of alternative approaches to political obligation, further consider democracy's claim to be the ideal form of political obligation. Democracy, as we saw, is regarded as the primary modern ground for political obligation because if we participate in the making of the laws under which we live, these laws are likely to be in our interests and therefore we get what we want. The principal problem with democracy, however, is that we are very rarely going to arrive at unanimous decisions. As a result, democratic government means, in practice, following the view of the majority.

There are a number of problems with the majoritarian principle. In the first place, it is well documented that where there are more than two alternatives on which voters can have preferences, then it is difficult to reach a majority decision (Lively, 1975: 14–15). Of course, in practice too, many governments in the UK and Presidents in the USA are not elected with the majority of votes. This is explained by the use of first-past-the-post electoral systems, where the winning candidate merely has to gain more votes than any other candidate. Thus, in the 2005 British General Election, the Labour Party won only 35.2 per cent of the popular vote but 55 per cent of the seats.

Even if majority rule can be established, it is far from clear that it is the most appropriate political mechanism. For one thing, pure majority rule leaves open the possibility that a government can be elected with majority support but which then intends to deny the principle of majoritarianism in the future. The best example of this was in Algeria in 1991 when the Islamic Salvation Front won a majority of the seats (although not the votes) in the country's first multiparty elections. With a doubtful commitment to multiparty democracy, the military intervened, cancelling the second round, and banning all political parties based on religion. This was then followed by a violent civil war. This raises the question whether it is ever justified on democratic grounds to prevent a government with a majority of votes and/or seats from taking power.

Even if the principle of majoritarianism is maintained, however, there is the problem that arises from the fact that some people in every decision made are going to find themselves in a minority. Rousseau's solution to this problem is to say: provided that the laws carried are in accord with the general will, everyone unanimously will want to accept them because it is the right or moral thing to do. For Rousseau, then, there is no problem with the minority, but Rousseau's assertion that everyone would and should willingly accept the general will is contentious, to say the least. Therefore, if we assume that Rousseau's solution to the minority problem is flawed, then we are still left with the problem of the lack of unanimity; that is, if we accept that democratic decisions are those taken by majority votes, then what happens to those who find themselves in a minority? Do we still expect them to obey the law even though they did not support it?

There are some political philosophers who want to suggest that we cannot expect such people to obey a law which they did not support. One such political theorist, Robert Paul Wolff, in his book *In Defense of Anarchism* (1970), argues that those who find themselves in a minority are not obliged to accept the law; and because there is no solution to the majority rule problem, no government can ever be legitimate, requiring everyone to be obligated to it. For Wolff, the only legitimate kind of society is one that preserves individual autonomy. This, for Wolff, is an anarchist society, a society without government.

In practice, of course, we may just have to accept that democracy is not perfect, and console ourselves with the thought that at least a majority rule decision ensures that more people than not are on the winning side. What we can say is that the position of minorities is made much worse if the same people find themselves permanently in a minority. Usually, this does not happen because there are shifting or fluid minorities; that is, everyone can expect to be in a minority from time to time. As a result, the majority in any particular instance is less likely to harm the minority's interests fundamentally, because those in the majority know that at some future point they may find themselves in the minority.

The persecution of a minority is much more likely to take place where there is a permanent majority and a permanent minority. The classic case of this is in Northern Ireland, where traditionally most issues have been decided on ethno-nationalist lines with Protestants in the majority and Catholics in the minority on key issues. Clearly, such a situation is likely to cause problems and it was the persistent discrimination faced by the minority Catholic community that led to the resurgence of the troubles in the late 1960s. A form of rule known as **consociational democracy**, involving the sharing of power in divided societies, is one possible solution to this problem of entrenched minorities.

Cosmopolitan Democracy

We have focused exclusively in this chapter on democracy in connection with the city-state and, in more recent times, the nation-state. Given the forces of globalization, discussed elsewhere in this book, we should also mention the idea of **cosmopolitan democracy**. Here it is suggested (by, for example, Held, 2006: 304–9), that given that citizens of nation-states are increasingly affected, if not dominated, by forces happening beyond the boundaries of the particular nation state within which they live, then what matters now is ensuring that global forces are controlled by democratic means.

→ See chapter eight, page 196, for a further discussion of consociationalism.

Democratic theorists should therefore be focusing on ensuring that international institutions are both effective controllers of global developments and that they themselves are under democratic control. Held (2006: 306), for one, suggests the creation of regional parliaments with the power to make decisions binding in international law, and the introduction of referendums across national boundaries. The European Union would be a good model of this. Where the existing sovereign state fits into this model is not clear and as Hoffman and Graham (2006: 119) point out, rather undermines the radical force of Held's argument. For them (123), the 'concept of a "cosmopolitan democracy" can only be coherently sustained if the international community ceases to be composed of states'.

An alternative approach to the undemocratic implications of globalization is to 'urge *strengthening* the sovereignty of (democratic) states by defending their internal political structures against external constraint and interference' (Cunningham, 2002: 201). Of course, the cosmopolitan model is based on the assumption that globalization is a reality, a position challenged by those holding a realist view of international relations that still puts the nation state at the centre of political analysis.

Key Points

- The problem with democracy as a source of a political obligation is that few, if any, decisions are going to be made unanimously. As a result, the minority are going to have to accept decisions with which they disagree, thereby reducing their freedom.

- Some political philosophers, most notably Wolff, argue that because of the minority rule problem, no state can ever be legitimate.

- Fluid minorities are less of a problem than permanent minorities. The latter are more likely to lead to the oppression of a minority.

- More recently, in the light of the impact of globalization, political theorists have discussed the possibilities of cosmopolitan democracy, whereby supranational institutions and processes are democratized.

Conclusion

We have seen in this chapter that, however democracy is defined, it is almost universally feted. When we come to examine its claims to be the most important grounding for political obligation, however, we come up against the problem of what to do with the minority consequences of majoritarianism. We could reject democracy in favour of some version of the general will, whereby it is claimed that unanimity can be achieved, or we can recognize and deal with the minorities question.

The obvious solution to the problem of minorities is to introduce some device protecting their interests. Many political systems, including the USA, do just this by including a bill of rights protecting individuals against the majority. In the USA, this was included precisely because the Founding Fathers were concerned about the potential dangers of majority rule or majority tyranny as they called it. The problem here is that it must be questioned how democratic is such a bill of rights. Again, using the Supreme Court in the USA as an example, its members are not elected and not removable accept under the most extraordinary circumstances.

The protection of some rights—such as the right to free speech, the right to form political associations and, of course, the right to life—is essential for democracy to function. As we pointed out earlier, however, it is not clear that all rights, such as the right to property, are consistent with democracy. Maybe our conclusion should be that democracy is not as special as we previously thought. Perhaps it does not provide us with an adequate theory of political obligation, because of the problem of minorities, and maybe we should regard other principles, such as the protection of individual rights, as more important. See **Box 3.5**.

 **Case Study** Box 3.5
Democracy, Rights, and Hunting

One interesting example of the potential conflict between the application of majoritarianism and the protection of rights is the debate about hunting. The hunting community in Britain has used a variety of arguments to support the continuation of hunting, but one recent strategy has been to employ the ideals of liberalism and the protection of individual rights. Here it has been argued that, despite the fact that hunting has been regularly opposed by a majority of British people in opinion polls and a majority of MPs in

3

the House of Commons, it still does not justify a ban because it is illegitimate for a majority to impose its own moral views on the minority. To take such an action is a serious infringement of rights. This rights defence of hunting, however, fell on deaf ears despite the hunting community's attempt to undermine the legislative ban by appealing to the Human Rights Act.

What the hunting community fail to take into account in their argument, of course, is the interests of the animals being hunted. If we add that to the equation, then the moral legitimacy of the 'right' to hunting becomes less clear-cut. The abolition of pursuits such as bear-baiting and dog-fighting in an earlier era, and the existence of a general cruelty statute making it an offence to inflict unnecessary suffering on animals, is testament to this concern for animals which has been used to override an alleged human right.

A final point here is that it might be argued that this debate is, in any case, rather old-fashioned now, as it is has been transcended by a whole new, and much more pressing concern. This is the threat to democracy from the rise of globalization. Equally, it should be asked too whether democracy, particularly of the participationist and deliberative variety, is the most appropriate way to deal with some of the world's most intractable problems, and not least that of climate change. Arguably, here, the role of experts should be allowed full reign in order that the interests of the whole planet are put before the self-interested utility maximizing that passes for electoral choice in much of the world.

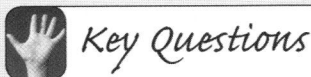

Key Questions

- What is democracy?
- Is it possible to reconcile elitism with democracy?
- Distinguish between direct democracy, democratic elitism, and representative democracy. Which is to be preferred?
- Is democracy special?
- Are we obliged to obey decisions taken democratically?
- Why should we obey the state?
- Critically examine the economic theory of democracy.
- Is democracy consistent with a class-divided society?
- Discuss the relationship between democracy and majority rule.
- Is cosmopolitan democracy possible and desirable?

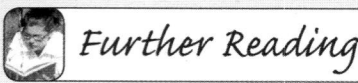 *Further Reading*

Held, D. (2006), *Models of Democracy*, Cambridge: Polity, 3rd edn.
> This is probably the best general text on democracy, coupling comprehensive descriptions with astute evaluation.

Macpherson, C.B. (1977), *The Life and Times of Liberal Democracy*, Oxford: Oxford University Press.
> This is a contentious account of the development of democratic thought and practice. Compelling reading.

Shapiro, I. (2003), *The Moral Foundations of Politics*, New Haven, CT: Yale University Press.
> This is an admirably concise account of the answers given by political theorists to the question of political obligation.

Wolff, R.P. (1970), *In Defence of Anarchism*, New York: Harper & Row.
> This is short and controversial but essential reading on the problem of political obligation.

 *Web Links*

www.chinadaily.com.cn/english/doc/2005-10/19/content_486206.htm.
The full text of the Chinese White Paper on Democracy.

www.freedomhouse.org.
A useful site that rates countries according to their degree of freedom and democracy.

 Visit the **Online Resource Centre** that accompanies this book to access more learning resources at **www.oxfordtextbooks.co.uk/orc/garner/**

Freedom and Justice

Reader's Guide

This chapter explores two related, but distinct, political concepts, justice and freedom. The difficulty of defining freedom is revealed by virtue of an examination of various competing constraints on our freedom. Berlin's argument that there are only two types of freedom is challenged by those who perceive there to be numerous conceptions of the concept. The chapter then explores the degree to which freedom is desirable. Various alternative values—equality, paternalism, happiness—that might conflict with freedom are considered, mainly in the context of the political thought of John Stuart Mill. In the second part of the chapter, the concept of justice is explored. Various criteria for determining the meaning of justice are identified, and discussed mainly in the context of the major competing theories of justice provided by Rawls and Nozick. Finally, the chapter considers alternative theories of justice which challenge the conventional liberal view that theories of justice should focus only on the nation-state and are applicable only to human beings.

Constraints on our Freedom

Like most other political concepts, freedom—or liberty (the terms are used interchangeably here)—is a difficult concept to define. Like democracy, part of the problem is that freedom is regarded as a 'good' concept, one which all governments should pursue. The reality, however, is that there may be good grounds for limiting freedom to pursue other goods that are valued. A starting point is to say that freedom is the opposite of constraint. Therefore, a commonsense definition of freedom is the absence of constraints or the absence of impediments. The problem is this only takes us so far, because most of the definitional controversy over freedom concerns the content of these constraints. In other words, political theorists disagree about what counts as a constraint. We might profitably begin, then, with an attempt to outline various possible constraints on our freedom.

Freedom and Democracy

The first possible constraint is *non-democratic forms of government*. In other words, how far is our freedom restricted by living in a non-democratic society? The answer would seem to be that there is no necessary relationship between freedom and the absence of democracy. It is possible to conceive of a benign dictatorship which grants a considerable degree of freedom to its people. Conversely, a democracy polity could conceivably limit freedom in a variety of ways. As Berlin (1969: 130) correctly points out: 'The answer to the question "Who governs me?" is logically distinct from the question "How far does government interfere with me?".'

Freedom and Physical Coercion

Perhaps the most obvious constraint on our freedom is when we are *physically coerced* by others. Here, we are unfree when others physically constrain us from doing what we want to do. The most obvious, and extreme, examples are imprisonment and slavery. It has been argued too that, in this category, an obvious restriction on freedom is the existence of law backed by sanctions. However, this is not as clear-cut as it first appears since we are, of course, free to break the law and either try to avoid detection or accept the punishment that comes with it. It seems odd, however, thereby to exclude the law as a constraint on our freedom. A response to this suggested by Barry (2000: 196) is to say that in many cases the costs of breaking the law—such as a long prison sentence or even the death penalty—are so high that, to all intents and purposes, they are equivalent to physical constraints.

Freedom and Physical Incapacity

We might want to add *physical incapacity* to this list, in the sense that we are unfree because we cannot do something that physical impairment prevents us from doing.

This might refer to a situation where an individual does not have an ability that other humans do, such as the ability to walk, or conditions which affect all humans, such as our inability to fly. These constraints, although clearly impediments, might not be worthwhile pursuing in so far as the situation is unalterable or beyond the control of human action. It is a different matter, however, if someone's disability is alterable and lack of resources prevents that person from living a normal life. In this case, the case for utilizing the language of freedom is compelling. In other words, human **agency** is necessary for an impediment to count as a constraint on our freedom.

Freedom, Rationality, and Morality

Some political theorists would also want to say that our freedom can be limited by a lack of *rationality* or *morality*. Only rational or moral behaviour, then, can be truly free. There is clearly something in the rationality argument. For example, we would not regard the supervision and direction of a person with senile dementia as a constraint on their freedom in the same way we would in the case of a normal healthy adult. In the same way, we do not regard the supervision and direction of children in the same way as we would with adults.

There are also weaknesses with the attempt to link freedom and rationality. We might want to say that supervizing and directing the behaviour of children or adults with senile dementia is a genuine restriction on their freedom (after all, we are preventing them from doing what they want to do) but that this restriction is justified in the pursuit of other goals, in this case protecting their safety. In addition, there are dangers in claiming that only rational behaviour is free, because it is by no means clear what the content of rational behaviour is. At the very least, this can encourage political leaders to impose their own version of rationality on to others, and justify paternalistic action on the grounds that it makes those subject to it freer.

Some of the arguments about equating freedom with rationality can also be applied to morality. Morality in this context is usually taken to mean behaviour that is selfless rather than selfish. In other words, we are free in so far as we behave morally or altruistically, acting in accordance with the common interest, or what Rousseau describes as the **general will**. Conversely, we are unfree in so far as we behave immorally or selfishly. This view, that freedom is linked to morality, is a central feature of one version of the so-called 'positive' theory of liberty. The main advocate is Jean-Jacques Rousseau. The credibility of this approach to freedom depends upon the validity of the assertion that what we really want to do is to behave morally, and in so far as we do not behave morally we are not doing what we really want to do. We become unfree, therefore, if we behave selfishly because ultimately we do not want to be selfish. It is in this sense that Rousseau, as we saw in chapter three, can argue that we can be 'forced to be free'.

➜ See chapter three, page 83, for more on the idea of the general will and its implications for freedom.

4

In response to the attempt to link freedom with morality, we might want to say that it seems to confuse two very different values. There may be a case when it makes sense to say that we can be freed from our desires—as in the case of, say, a paedophile who genuinely wants to behave in a different way. However, this requires a recognition from the individual himself that his behaviour is unacceptable, coupled with a desire to change it. The notion of forcing someone to be free goes further than this by arguing that someone can be coerced into behaving differently. There may be a case for saying that this is justifiable, and the state does intervene (as in the case of paedophiles) to try to change behaviour. However, it seems more appropriate to say in such cases that the state is imposing society's moral standards on individuals, not in order to make people freer but on the grounds that the moral principle is important enough to justify sacrificing freedom for.

Freedom and Psychology

The penultimate constraint to be identified refers to *psychological* influences on our behaviour. We saw above that we can be constrained by physical coercion. It might also be argued that we can be equally constrained psychologically; that is, we can be forced to behave in ways we really do not want to because of outside influences that affect the way we think. A very powerful example of this is advertising. It is often claimed that advertising creates wants that would otherwise not be there. This can apply to general commercial advertising as well as political advertising by parties and the state. A classic example here is the banning, in the UK and elsewhere, of tobacco advertising, on the ground that it encourages the dangerous habit of smoking that then creates an addiction difficult to shake off. The ability of a ruling group to influence, if not determine, the way that the masses think is an example of the 'third dimension' of power that we encountered in chapter two.

➔ See chapter two, page 55, for an exploration of the three dimensions of power.

Freedom and Economic Impediments

The final constraint that we can identify relates to *economic impediments*. If we regard freedom as merely the absence of externally imposed physical coercion, we would seem to be saying that freedom is best achieved if the state and society leave people largely to their own devices. Some political thinkers argue, however, that the state can, by intervening in the lives of individuals, do a great deal to increase freedom. In other words, an individual is not really free to develop as a human being and enjoy freedom if

Photo 4.1

A Marlboro billboard is on display near a road, 30 April 1997 in Los Angeles, Ca.
Source: Getty Images

she does not have enough to eat, or a roof over her head. This links freedom with power. As Gray (1991: 42) points out, 'for liberty to exist in any real sense, the agent must have the power to exercise it'. By intervening to provide, at least, a basic standard of living below which individuals cannot fall, then, the state can play a positive role in increasing the freedom of individuals to make something of their lives.

As with grounding freedom on notions of rationality and morality, however, it might be argued that advocates of this version of **positive liberty** are confusing liberty with other values; that is, preventing poverty, homelessness, and unemployment might be justified for a whole host of reasons, but these reasons are not the same as freedom. Clarity demands, it might be argued, that we should say that state intervention limits freedom in order to secure greater economic equality.

Key Points

- Since freedom is defined as the absence of constraints, the identification of constraints on our freedom is a useful starting point.

- Possible constraints can be divided into those that are external to us, and those that are internal to us, the latter including such characteristics as rationality and morality.

Determining the Nature of Freedom

The discussion above might lead us to suggest that we cannot resolve the question about the meaning of freedom. One way out of this impasse is to take on board a formulation suggested by MacCallum (1967). He argues that all genuine statements about freedom must contain three elements involving X (the agent), Y (the constraint), and Z (the objective). In this triadic relationship, X is free from Y to do or be Z. Political theorists, he argued, have disagreed over what ought to be included as X, Y, and Z but all have operated with the same conception. Thus, those who emphasize the importance of physical constraints (the Y factor) interpret the agent (the X factor) as an actual self and the objective (the Z factor) as an action. Those, on the other hand, who emphasize the importance of lack of rationality and morality as constraints, interpret the agent as a real (rational or moral) self and the objective as a state of mind.

The problem with MacCullum's formulation is that it only takes us so far. This is because, as we saw in the first section above, political theorists disagree on the content of the X, Y, and Z elements. As Gray (1991: 14) points out, MacCullum's formulation does not 'eliminate conceptual issues in relation to liberty, but simply displaces or conceals them as conceptual issues about what constitutes an X or Y or Z factor'. Better then to adopt the position that while 'there is only one *concept* of freedom . . . there are many *conceptions* of that concept' (6).

Negative and Positive Freedom

The view that there are many conceptions of freedom has been disputed by those who argue that essentially freedom can be divided into negative and positive varieties. The distinction between negative and positive freedom dates back to the Ancient Greeks (Gray, 1991: 7) but it is particularly associated with the Oxford political theorist, Isaiah Berlin (1909–97). Berlin famously argued, in an article first published in 1958, that these represent the two main, and distinct, conceptions of freedom. The negative conception is concerned with the question: 'What is the area within which the subject . . . is or should be left to do or be what he is able to do or be, without interference by other persons?' The positive conception, on the other hand, is concerned with the question: 'What, or who, is the source of control or interference that can determine someone to do, or be, this rather than that?' (Berlin, 1969: 121–2). Therefore, Berlin seeks to distinguish between the *area* of control, emphasized by **negative liberty**, and the *source* of control, emphasized by positive freedom. The ability of individuals to be self-governing, then, is crucial for advocates of the latter.

Berlin's purpose in making this distinction was primarily to defend negative liberty against advocates of the positive version. Indeed, he was violently opposed to the latter version, seeing it as an enemy of real freedom. This was because he argued that self-government usually involved the argument that genuine freedom requires that the 'real' (rational or moral) self be established over the 'actual' self. Berlin emphasized the illiberal implications of this move, discussed earlier in the chapter.

Berlin's approach has been heavily criticized (Gray, 1991: 8–11). In terms of the debate about the meaning of freedom, it is argued that Berlin has not demonstrated the existence of only two diametrically opposed conceptions of freedom. Positive freedom can be interpreted in a way that makes it close to the negative variety. As Barry (2000: 204) points out, the emphasis on self-mastery in the former may be interpreted as merely another means whereby constraints on individuals can be removed, with the difference being that these constraints are internal as opposed to the external variety emphasized by the latter. What we are then left with is still a number of different conceptions of freedom—based on the nature of the constraints—and not two different conceptions, as Berlin maintains.

Key Points

- MacCullum argues that a single conception of freedom can be identified, including statements about the agent, the constraint, and the objective.
- Berlin argues, by contrast, that there are only two types of freedom, negative and positive varieties.
- Other political theorists dispute both interpretations, arguing that there are many conceptions of freedom, each having a different interpretation of the nature of the agent, the constraint, and the nature of the objective to which freedom is directed.

Is Freedom Special?

Justifying freedom is a very different exercise from defining its character. The two, of course, are linked in the sense that our assessment of the value of freedom will be dependent upon what we think it is. It might be argued, for instance, that we can justifiably limit freedom in favour of greater equality. If, however, we have defined freedom in such a way that it requires state intervention in order to equalize resources so that freedom can be realized effectively by many people, then the two concepts are not as diametrically opposed as first thought.

Bearing this in mind, we can outline a number of justifications for freedom. Some political theorists argue that there ought to be a presumption in favour of freedom (Benn, 1971); that is, the burden of proof ought to rest with those who would limit freedom. However, this begs the question of why freedom ought to have such an exalted status. In other words, it presupposes some pre-existing argument in favour of freedom.

One such argument is that freedom is a basic human right (Hart, 1967). However, this argument also depends upon a prior argument in favour of rights, in general, and a right to freedom in particular. Dworkin (1978) does seek to provide such a justification by arguing that those freedoms that are necessary to ensure that individuals are treated with equal concern and respect (so-called 'strong' liberties) should be inviolable. Again, however, Dworkin tends to take as given the importance of his equality principle. Moreover, Dworkin's argument for upholding strong liberties has been criticized for its subjectivity. Is it not a matter of opinion, which liberties are to count as strong ones that uphold the right to equal concern and respect? (Gray, 1991: 106). This is particularly problematic if we accept that **cultural pluralism**—where competing norms of behaviour are regarded as acceptable—is deemed to be desirable. See **Box 4.1**.

Key Debate Box 4.1
Freedom and Cultural Pluralism

Consider the following two cases:

1. In 2004 religious symbols in schools were banned by the French National Assembly. This included a ban on Muslim girls wearing a veil, and the wearing of Jewish skullcaps, Sikh turbans, and conspicuous Christian crosses.

2. It is estimated that well over 100 million women have been subject to circumcision. This practice (involving either the removal of some of or the entire clitoris) can lead to serious physical and psychological problems. Yet it is justified on cultural and religious grounds and is still widely practised in Western and Southern Asia, the Middle East, and large parts of Africa. It has also been estimated that several thousand girls are circumcized every year in Britain.

These examples raise the important complication added by cultural pluralism to issues of freedom. Cultural pluralism describes a situation where different cultures adopt different norms of behaviour. On the one hand, should we seek, as in the first example, to limit cultural pluralism in the interest of national unity, thereby reducing freedom? On the other, as in the second example, should we allow cultural diversity even when this practice itself harms and denies freedom to others. The problem for those who would impose a universal standard of right and wrong, whereby it is not justified in restricting freedom for some things but is for others, is that they risk being accused of cultural imperialism.

Mill, Utilitarianism, and Freedom

One of the best-known defences of freedom was put forward by the British political philosopher, John Stuart Mill. Mill does not seek to justify a right to liberty. Rather, his arguments are coloured by his **utilitarianism**. In other words, Mill is arguing that freedom is conducive to the greatest happiness. There is another aspect to his thought that is important to note here too. Bentham had not sought to provide any content to happiness or pleasure. For him, it is the quantity of pleasure gained in any particular act that is crucial. Mill, on the other hand, famously revises the Benthamite principle by arguing that certain types of pleasure—the higher pleasures—are more valuable and ought to be pursued by individuals and the state. These are the pleasures associated with cerebral activities—literature, music, art, and so forth—as opposed to the bodily and more base pleasures (Mill, 1972).

Having established the basics of Mill's position, we can examine his theory of liberty. His essay *On Liberty*, originally published in 1859, is divided into two parts. In the first, he seeks to argue the case for the maximum possible freedom of thought and discussion. Even if an opinion being expressed is palpably false or hurtful to the sensibilities of others, Mill argues that it still should not be censored. True beliefs, he argues, will gain in vigour when they have to be upheld against objections, and false beliefs are more likely to be seen as such if they are open to public challenge. Mill strongly believes, too, that freedom of thought and expression is a means to social progress. Society, in other words, will be stronger if a wider variety of opinions and lifestyles are tried and tested.

In the second part of the essay, Mill seeks to argue the case for freedom of action. Here, Mill makes the well-known distinction between self and other regarding actions. This is the so-called **harm principle**. Only those actions that harm others (affecting them adversely) should be prevented by public opinion or the state. Self-regarding actions are not to be interfered with. We are entitled to warn of the dangers of pursuing a particular self-regarding path but we cannot, according to Mill, physically restrain someone. Mill is very clear, here, that actions which others find offensive, but which do not cause them physical or financial harm, are not to be seen as other regarding.

Freedom, Happiness, and Paternalism

Mill's thoughts on liberty have been very influential in determining the nature of state intervention in modern liberal societies. Laws legalizing homosexuality between consenting adults in many liberal democratic states, for instance, owe much to Mill's distinction between self and other regarding actions.

Case Study Box 4.2
Smoking and Liberty

The contemporary debate about smoking illustrates the difficulty of delineating the boundaries of freedom of action. The British Government's proposal for a total ban on smoking in pubs and clubs, came into force in July 2007. The main philosophical justification for the ban is that smoking harms those who are forced passively to inhale the smoke of others. This is a principle associated with J.S. Mill, who would argue that smoking in private where no one else will be harmed is legitimate.

If it can be established that passive smoking is harmful, which it seems it can, then the application of Mill's other regarding principle would seem to be clear-cut. Of course, it might be argued that non-smokers choose to frequent places, such as pubs and clubs, where others smoke; but if smoking is allowed in all pubs and clubs, as it was in Britain, then the choice of those who do not smoke is severely constrained. Moreover, the health risks of those who work in places where people smoke are even greater because of the amount of time they are exposed to smoke.

There are two criticisms of Mill's harm principle that do not challenge the smoking ban but rather suggest that it does not go far enough. The first is the argument that even smoking in private can, in most circumstances, harm others. This relates to the oft-stated criticism of Mill's harm principle that it is difficult to distinguish between self and other regarding actions. Thus, is it not the case that smoking, even in private, potentially harms others? If I become ill through smoking, as is likely, then this will impact upon family members who will be harmed—financially and emotionally—by my death or incapacity. Similarly, my ill health will have wider financial consequences, for the health service that has to treat me and the social benefit system that has to keep me if I am unable to work.

The second criticism is the point that, even if we can denote an action as being self-regarding, there are good grounds for suggesting that the state ought to intervene to stop individuals from harming themselves. This is the paternalistic critique of liberal-inspired freedom. Here, society and the state might step in to prevent me from engaging in an activity that they have good reason to believe will harm me. My health and well-being may, then, not be served by liberty, and indeed my happiness might be enhanced by restricting my freedom. In terms of smoking, it might be argued that the state should intervene on paternalistic grounds to ban it on the grounds that to do so will, in the long-run at least, improve the health of those who choose to smoke and thereby increase levels of happiness.

In formulating a critique of Mill, it is crucial, first, to note how his arguments for freedom are strongly influenced by the utilitarian framework of his thought. Thus, he argues for maximizing freedom of thought and discussion on the grounds that it will lead to social progress, through the development of greater knowledge. Knowledge was important for Mill because it facilitated the development of the higher pleasures. Likewise, Mill advocates freedom of action partly on the grounds that he thought humans were the best judges of what they want to do, and partly because he thought that making people free to choose what to do with their lives would be character-forming. In both cases, Mill is making the claim, then, that freedom makes humans happier.

It is by no means clear, however, that social progress will result from maximizing freedom of thought and discussion. Mill was arguably much too optimistic that in the marketplace of ideas, rationality and truth will prevail. It seems equally possible that the truth will need to be protected against its enemies. On utilitarian grounds too, it is not clear that freedom of thought and discussion will always promote happiness. One can readily think of cases where withholding the truth from someone may be in their best interests. Is it always in the best interests of someone to be told they have an incurable disease, particularly, in the case, say, of a disease such as multiple sclerosis, where the symptoms may be abeyance for some years? Clearly, there may be cases where it is not in a person's interests to be told such news; and yet, Mill is committed to freedom of thought and discussion as a universal principle.

Much of the debate about Mill has focused on his arguments for freedom of action. In the first place, it is regularly argued that the distinction between self and other regarding actions is unsustainable. Surely, it is suggested, there are few, if any, actions that affect the actor alone? Others have challenged Mill's view that actions which others find offensive, but which do not cause them physical harm, should be regarded as self-regarding. For instance, the British jurist Lord Devlin (1905–92)—echoing the sentiments of the eminent nineteenth-century judge James Fitzjames Stephen (1829–94)—argued that there is no such thing as private immorality, in the sense that even our private behaviour will have public consequences. Widespread drug-taking, for instance, will have effects on economic performance and on health-service resources. For Devlin (1965), then, society is held together by shared moral values, and excessive moral pluralism will be catastrophic for social stability.

We can also challenge Mill's assumption that freedom of action is conducive to happiness or well-being, as seen in the case study of smoking. See **Box 4.2**. Similarly, a utilitarian, committed to maximizing happiness in society, would have to take into account behaviour which others find offensive (whether written, said, or acted upon) but which do not directly harm them physically or financially. Such actions would have to be weighed against the benefits of allowing them to continue. See **Box 4.3**. This is highly relevant in an era when there have been many cases where religious sensibilities have been injured by, for example, the publication of blasphemous caricatures of religious beliefs. The publication, in 2005, of cartoons depicting the prophet Muhammad in a negative light in a Danish magazine is the classic recent case of this trend.

Key Debate   Box 4.3
Liberalism, Morality, and Freedom

It is a central part of the liberal canon that, however offensive, behaviour should not be prohibited by society or the state merely because it causes offence. Consider the following legal case reported in the *Guardian*.

Court of Appeal (Criminal Division)
Regina v Brown et al.
Before Lord Lane, Mr Justice Rose and Mr Justice Potts
19 February 1992
The defendants belonged to a group of sado-masochist homosexuals who had, over 10 years, willingly and enthusiastically participated in acts of violence against each other for the sexual pleasure engendered in the giving and receiving of pain. The acts took place in private at different locations including a room equipped as a torture chamber. The acts of genital torture involved the use of pain inflicting instruments—whipping with a cat-o'nine tails, caning, burning with a blow torch, branding with hot metal, hitting with a spiked glove, applying stinging nettles to the genital area . . . All the activities were carried out with the consent of the passive partner or victim. There was . . . no permanent injury . . . and no complaints to police.

Unfortunately for the participants, their activities were filmed on video and it was this evidence that resulted in the case being brought. In an original trial they were found guilty (under the Offences Against the Person Act 1861) and prison sentences were imposed.
   A number of questions can be asked about this case.

1.   Are there paternalistic grounds for prohibiting these activities?
2.   Are these activities self or other-regarding?
3.   Is your reaction determined by the nature of the activities or a general principle?
4.   Does such behaviour threaten the moral fabric of society?

To be fair to Mill here, however, remember that racially motivated writing or speeches could be prohibited on the grounds that they are other-regarding. This is the principle behind the prosecution in Britain of those—such as the British National Party leader Nick Griffen and the radical cleric Abu Hamza—deemed to be inciting racial hatred. Action was taken against them not because their comments were deemed to be offensive, although some of the things they said undoubtedly were, but because they were construed as an incitement for others to take racially motivated action to harm others.

Mill, Marx, and Socialism

Mill, of course, is putting forward a liberal theory of freedom, justifying limited state intervention and maximizing personal autonomy. This has been very influential in shaping the modern liberal theory of the state with its emphasis on neutrality and moral pluralism It should be noted, however, that Mill was equally aware of the poverty and squalor evident in nineteenth-century England, and the consequences of this for the enjoyment of freedom. Indeed, he recognized the challenge and, to some extent the value, of the socialist critique of liberalism that was emerging towards the end of the century. Mill can therefore be located on the cusp between the old **classical liberalism** and the **new liberalism** emphasizing social reform that came to dominate British politics.

➡ See chapter one, page 40, for more on the liberal theory of the state.

The socialist and, more specifically the Marxist, critique of the liberal theory of freedom centres on the impact of the inequality seen as the natural consequence of a capitalist economy. In the best-known Marxist account, Cohen (1979) points to the freedom to own property, and the resulting unequal ownership of property, as providing severe limitations on freedom for those who do not own property. In liberal capitalist regimes, the right to deprive others of the use of one's own property is a central feature. According to this approach, then, the freedom of the proletariat is necessarily constrained, and only when property is collectively owned can freedom be enhanced.

➡ See chapter five, page 117, for a discussion of the difference between classical and new liberalism.

Key Points

- Various reasons for valuing freedom have been put forward. These include freedom as a basic human right, freedom as a means to the end of happiness, and freedom as a means to self-development.

- J.S. Mill argues for maximizing freedom, only actions which are other regarding being suitable for state or societal intervention.

- A number of problems with Mill's formulation are evident. In particular, there is a case—on the grounds of maximizing happiness, or **paternalism**, or the pursuit of know-ledge—for limiting areas of freedom that Mill would regard as sacrosanct.

- The relationship between freedom and equality is a complex one, with those on the left arguing that equality is not necessarily a constraint on freedom.

The Meaning of Justice

Justice is yet another one of those political concepts that is difficult to define. Very basically, justice requires us to give to others what they are due or entitled to. This contrasts with charity. It may be morally good for us to contribute to a charity but we are under no obligation to do so. In the modern world, justice is a distributional concept, that is, it is concerned with how different resources—wealth, income, educational opportunities, and so on—ought to be distributed. It is a concept, then, that implies that resources are scarce, for if we had more than enough resources to go around, there would be no need to agonize over who should have them.

Photo 4.2   Aerial View of Haiti

Aerial view of Cap Haitien. Cap Haitien is Haiti's second largest city with an estimated population of 500,000 people. Date: 30 November 2005.
Source: UN photo by Sophia Paris

A distinction can be made between **procedural justice** and **social justice**. In the former case, justice involves the following of rules, irrespective of the outcomes, whereas the latter is more concerned about outcomes. Modern theories of social or distributive justice have identified a number of criteria that we might consider as guides to distribution (Miller, 1976: 24–31). We could say that resources ought to be distributed according to *need*, or *desert* (or *merit*) or a principle of pure equality. All theories of justice must involve equality, not in the sense that resources ought to be distributed equally, but that there ought to be consistency of treatment. This involves equality before the law and the principle that equals ought to be treated equally. Having accepted this, we may then decide that some humans are not equal with others in various respects and therefore differential treatment can then be justified. For instance, we might decide that since some people work harder than others, or are more talented than others, they ought to have more of the resources available for distribution.

A theory of justice based on need is particularly associated with socialism, as in the slogan 'from each according to his ability, to each according to his needs'. Even in modern liberal democracies, however, the existence of a welfare state amounts to a recognition that meeting needs is just, although such societies also adopt desert as a criteria for the distribution of resources once basic needs are met.

A **meritocratic theory of justice** advocates distributing resources to those who display some merit and therefore deserve to be rewarded. It is associated with liberalism. Merit can include a natural talent or it can refer to someone's propensity for hard work or a general contribution to society. A desert-based theory of justice regards it as just to differentially reward talent and hard work. In addition, it recognizes the social advantages of encouraging the development and employment of talent through the deployment of incentives. It is linked to the principle of equal opportunity, as to allow talents or hard work to be rewarded, it would seem unjust for an individual to start out with a structural disadvantage. It therefore would seem to demand educational and welfare opportunities for all to allow for the creation of a level playing field.

Key Points

- Justice is a distributional concept. What political theorists have mainly disagreed about is the criteria for distributing resources.

- Distributing resources based on need is problematic because it is not always clear what need consists of. In addition, it denies the importance of desert.

- Distributing resources based on desert takes account of incentives, but considerable state intervention would seem to be necessary in order to facilitate the equality of opportunity that the principle demands.

Rawls's Theory of Justice

The meaning of justice becomes clearer if we look at a particular account. The best-known is John Rawls's *A Theory of Justice*, published to much acclaim in 1971. See **Box 4.4**. Indeed, his lengthy book is regarded as the most important work of political philosophy published since the end of the Second World War. Rawls's account can be divided into two. First, there is the *method* he uses to arrive at his principles of justice and, secondly, the *principles* themselves.

Rawls (1921–2002) draws from the long-neglected **social contract** tradition associated with Hobbes and Locke. He seeks to devise a method for arriving at principles of justice to which everyone can consent. The problem with competing theories of justice is that they rest on judgements about values that are objectively irresolvable. Thus, how do we choose between a theory of justice emphasizing merit from one emphasizing needs? Does it not depend upon pre-existing normative arguments about, for example, whether one favours a more equal society or a freer one, or one which places greater store on individual efforts and achievements?

Rawls's answer to this is to devise a hypothetical situation in which, he argues, there will be unanimous support for particular principles of justice. Imagine, he asks, a so-called **original position** in which individuals are asked to meet and decide how they want their society to be organized. In this original position, the members will be under a 'veil of ignorance'; that is, they will have no idea what their own position in society will turn out

➜ See chapter one, page 37, for more on the social contract tradition.

Short Biography Box 4.4
John Rawls (1921–2002)

John Rawls was an American academic who spent most of his career in the Philosophy Department at Harvard University. Despite his retiring disposition, and his unwillingness to be involved in political debate, Rawls's major work, *A Theory of Justice* (1971) is widely regarded as one of the most influential works of political theory in the twentieth century, selling more than 300,000 copies in the USA alone. His rights-based theory of justice not only rejuvenated a discipline in apparent decline but also provided a major challenge to the, at the time, dominant utilitarian tradition.

Rawls's second book, *Political Liberalism* (1993) is concerned to demonstrate that his theory of justice only seeks to explore the basic political structure and not the wider area of ethics. In this wider sphere Rawls advocates the widest possible freedom for people to pursue different conceptions of the good life. This moral pluralism has become a central feature of the liberal creed.

to be. They do not know if they will be rich or poor, black or white, male or female, disabled or able bodied. Rawls also assumes that individuals in the original position will be self-interested, wanting the best for themselves. Finally, he also suggests that they will desire what he calls primary goods such as wealth, good health, education, and so on.

In the second part of the theory, Rawls outlines the principles he thinks will derive from individuals in the original position. There are two (Rawls, 1971: 302).

1. Each person is to have an equal right to the most extensive total system of equal basic liberties compatible with a similar system of liberty for all.
2. Social and economic inequalities are to be arranged so that they are both:
    (a) to the greatest benefit of the least advantaged . . . and
    (b) attached to offices and positions open to all under conditions of fair equality of opportunity.

Rawls adds that 1 (the liberty principle) has priority over 2, and 2(b) (the fair opportunity principle) has priority over 2(a) (the difference principle). This means, for example, that one cannot sacrifice liberty in order to achieve economic improvement, thereby ruling out slavery, where it is conceivable that individuals could have a relatively high degree of welfare but no liberty.

A Critique of Rawls

Rawls's work has generated a huge literature (see, for instance, Daniels, 1975; Wolff, 1977; Kukathas and Pettit, 1990). It is useful to distinguish between criticisms of his method, on the one hand, and his principles, on the other. In the former case, it has been questioned whether people in the original position would have produced the principles of justice at which Rawls arrives. His central claim is that, because they do not know where they will end up in the social strata, individuals behind the veil of ignorance will be conservative, in the sense of being unwilling to take risks.

It is not clear, however, that people in the original position would choose the kind of risk-averse strategy he suggests (Wolff, 1996: 177–86). Rawls calls it the 'maximin' strategy (maximizing the minimum) where we try to ensure that the worst possible scenario is as good as possible. It would clearly be extremely risky to adopt the other extreme (the 'maximax' strategy) whereby we seek to create a society where the rich are very rich and the poor are very poor; but, against Rawls, it can be argued that there is a middle way between these two extremes. We could, for example, opt for a society that has a great deal of inequality but which also protects the worst-off so they have basic protection. In this scenario, the average position in society would be considerably improved, but at the same time, if you did end up at the bottom of the social pile, it would not be totally catastrophic.

Rawls's reluctance to sanction the 'middle way' option leads some to suggest that he has merely created a method that will produce the outcomes he desires. There is some evidence for this. Rawls admits that he is not totally reliant on the heuristic device of the contract to derive his principles of justice. Rather, he adopts a procedure described as 'reflective equilibrium', whereby the principles derived from the original position are checked for consistency with our moral intuitions (Rawls, 1971: 20). Inevitably, then, the principles of justice arrived at will be, at the very least, influenced by already existing moral conventions.

This leads us to examine Rawls's principles of justice, irrespective of the method he uses to arrive at them. These principles have been criticized, from the left and the right. From the left, it has been argued that Rawls's difference principle is not as egalitarian as it seems (Wolff, 1977). Suspicions are aroused, in particular, by the priority given to liberty. Is it really the case that liberty should always be protected against any alternative? Here, Rawls's presumption of a general level of affluence is marked. The same cannot be said for many parts of the world where poverty is such a problem that liberty ought, and in many cases is, sacrificed in order to achieve a sustainable standard of living (see below).

From the right, Rawls's major critic has been the American philosopher, Robert Nozick (1938–2002). Nozick, writing from a libertarian perspective—heavily influenced by John Locke—in which the minimal state protecting property rights is the ideal, puts forward a procedural theory of justice; that is, he regards the way in which property is acquired as the key principle of justice and not the outcome of this acquisition. It is therefore a historical and not an end-state theory in which 'past circumstances or actions of people can create differential entitlements or differential deserts to things' (Nozick, 1974: 155). Provided that an individual's acquisition of property is fair, then she has a just entitlement to it. Nozick regards any attempt to redistribute property (defined in a wide sense to refer to anything possessed by an individual), even through taxation, as unjust.

Nozick therefore regards Rawls's end-state theory—that inequality is justified only when it benefits everyone, and in particular the worst off—as illegitimate. He notes that Rawls's principles are inconsistent. How can one hold that liberty should be prioritized and, at the same time, advocate a considerable redistribution of resources? Achieving the one precludes the other. For Nozick, any attempt to enforce patterns of justice, such as an end-state principle seeking to meet need, requires enforcing, which will involve restricting liberty. Left to their own devices, people's actions will always disrupt a particular pattern.

Nozick provides two provisos to his entitlement theory. In the first place, the original acquisition to property has to have been fair, in the sense that it was gained not by force or fraud. If it was acquired in such a way, then compensation is due. As critics have pointed out, it is clearly the case that much property has, in the past, been unfairly acquired. The levels of compensation that might be required to provide redress, and the difficulty of establishing how much is due, create huge difficulties for Nozick's theory (Barry, 2000: 151). The second proviso is that acquisition must not be inimical to the essential well-being of others. This, reasonably enough, rules out someone acquiring all the water or food supplies in a community and then denying it to others.

Intuitively, one might doubt that the consequences of Nozick's principles are just. It could, for instance, result in such inequalities that the poorest members of society are at risk of starvation. His attack on taxation as a form of forced labour can be regarded as an exaggeration. Moreover, it can be argued, as we saw earlier in the chapter, that redistributing resources actually increases liberty because it increases choices for the poor (Wolff, 1996: 194–5).

Key Points

- Rawls's theory of justice has been criticized for the method he uses to arrive at his principles of justice and the principles themselves.

- It has been argued that it is not necessarily the case that individuals in the original position will choose the principles Rawls says they will. There is a suspicion that he has manipulated the method in order to produce the outcome he desires.

- Rawls's principle of justice have been criticized from the left and the right. From the left, he is not regarded as egalitarian enough; from the right he is too egalitarian.

- Robert Nozick has provided the best-known critique of Rawls from the right. He argues that the kind of redistribution that Rawls calls for is illegitimate. Individuals should be entitled to hold the property they own without intervention from the state, provided that they have acquired it fairly.

Alternative Theories of Justice

Rawls and Nozick, although different in many ways, both put forward a theory of justice based on liberal ideas and limited their terms of reference to relationships between human beings within sovereign states. It is important to note that there are alternative theories of justice that are not similarly constrained.

Cosmopolitan Theories of Justice

The growing interconnectedness in the world of peoples and sovereign states has provided a fillip for extending justice beyond national boundaries. Limiting a discussion of justice to the internal affairs of wealthy Western states seems trivial, given the staggering inequalities between different parts of the world, particularly given the oft-made claim that the rich Northern states are at least partly responsible for the poverty in the South. This has led political theorists to develop theories of justice that are global in scope. See **Box 4.5**.

This so-called **cosmopolitan** approach to justice is based on the principle that our loyalties ought to be with human beings as a whole, rather than only those who happen to live within the boundaries of the state within which we reside. This idea, that human beings are equal members of a global citizenry, has a long history in political thought but the growing inequality between the North and the South in recent decades, and the greater recognition of this inequality, has made questions surrounding **global justice** 'one of the great moral challenges of the age' (Linklater, 2008: 555).

There is little agreement on what our moral obligations should be to those outsiders who do not belong to our community. At the extreme end, Singer (2002) puts forward the principle of unlimited obligation whereby we (in the rich North) are obliged to help others (in the poor South) even to the point of seriously eroding our own standards of living. A less extreme position is to apply Rawls's principles on a global scale, thereby justifying a greater degree of redistribution between the rich and the poor parts of the world (Beitz, 1979; Pogge, 1989).

➔ See chapter fourteen, page 325, for a further discussion of cosmopolitanism.

Case Study Box 4.5
Climate Change and Justice

Cosmopolitan theories of justice seek to impose a duty on individuals and states either to act positively to end injustices in the world or, at the very least, to refrain from acting so as to cause harm. Both practices feature in the politics of climate change. Cosmopolitans insist that rich industrialized countries should desist from continuing to burn fossil fuels at the rate they currently are. Equally, since these countries are held responsible for climate change, they are also obliged, it is argued, to assist those states in the developing world which have not been responsible for causing climate change but which are least able to deal with its consequences. Despite intensive international negotiations over the past two decades or so, neither outcome has materialized to the degree that many cosmopolitan theories of justice would advocate.

Communitarianism and Justice

An alternative to cosmopolitan theories of justice, and to liberal theories of justice in general is provided by **communitarianism**. Communitarians adopt a perfectionist theory of justice whereby the state articulates and aims to bring about a particular conception of the good, or a particular way of living. They also reject the universal nature of Rawls and Nozick's theory of justice, that is, liberal theories are designed to apply in all social settings, whatever the particular historical or cultural features of that particular society. Communitarians reject this universalism in favour of culturally specific justice claims. In other words, principles of justice should take into account the particular social and cultural character of the society for which they are designed. They will differ from society to society (Walzer, 1985).

The communitarian position provides an important critique of the cosmopolitan theory of justice. Communitarians regard the cosmopolitan notion of a global **citizenship** as naive—since our loyalties develop, and our identities are forged, within our own particular communities (Walzer, 1994). They also see it as undesirable as it is illegitimate to impose our own, liberal, conception of distributive justice on to other cultures. Somewhat ironically, support for this position is provided by Rawls himself who, in a later work (1999), does not think that we have a duty to apply a liberal conception of justice globally. Instead, all that should be expected of us is to live in peaceful coexistence with others, including a recognition of each other's **sovereignty** and the principle that states do not intervene in the affairs of others unless threatened.

Green Political Thought and Justice

➜ See chapter six, page 146, for more on the philosophy of environmentalism.

In recent years there has been the development of a body of Green political thought which challenges the view that justice can only be applied to currently living humans. There are a number of positions in this debate which can be put on a continuum. At the more moderate end, many philosophers have now raised the question whether justice ought to be applied to future generations of humans (see Barry, 1999). Of course, this **intergenerational justice** might clash with **intragenerational justice**. Put starkly, can we really justify cutting back on economic development for generations to come when there are so many people in the world who currently have a very low standard of living?

Some Green political theorists and moral philosophers want to go further than recognizing the justice claims of only human beings. There has been a sustained attempt, for instance, to apply justice to at least some non-human animals (Garner, 2005). Some Green political theorists want to go beyond humans and animals and include the whole of nature as recipients of justice. Some draw the line at living things (Taylor, 1986) whereas others want to include inanimate objects too, arguing that we can talk sensibly about applying justice to ecosystems, or biodiversity (Fox, 1984).

Key Points

- There have been challenges to the conventional liberal view that theories of justice should apply only within states and not between states and should be applicable only to human beings.

- Cosmopolitan theories of justice argue that we have obligations towards all humans and not just those residing within our own national boundaries.

- Communitarian theories of justice insist that principles of justice depend upon particular social, cultural, and historical experience and should not be regarded as universal, thereby challenging the cosmopolitan emphasis of universal global citizenship.

- Green theories of justice challenge the assumption that justice only applies to humans.

Conclusion

This chapter has employed the three major forms of analysis of the political theorist. We have spent time examining the meaning of liberty and justice (semantic analysis), and have tried to assess the values central to competing theories of liberty and justice (normative analysis). In undertaking the second task, empirical arguments come into play, although never decisively. An examination of freedom and justice has revealed how interconnected political concepts are. We cannot properly evaluate freedom, for instance, without considering how it relates to conceptions of justice. Such an exercise also involves considering the respective merits of freedom and equality, which for most, if not all, are seen as conflicting objectives. What we have seen too is that the essentially contested nature of political concepts makes it difficult to go beyond an exercise in semantics. For example, freedom has been regarded as a source of inequality, on the one hand, and as necessary for equality, on the other.

There is no doubt that theorists of freedom and justice now have to engage with the impact of **globalization**. Our greater knowledge of different cultures—enabled by technological developments which now give us a clearer picture of how different societies operate, and by increasing mobility leading to the emergence of multicultural communities—makes us more circumspect about the value of freedom and what practices should be regarded as legitimate restrictions on freedom. Likewise, there are increasing calls for the principle of justice to be applied globally to address the shocking inequalities between different parts of the world. These developments provide important challenges to political theorists, challenges which they will have to grapple with for some time to come.

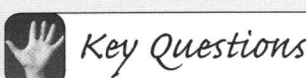 *Key Questions*

- What constraints exist on our freedom?
- Are there only two types of liberty, negative and positive?
- Is Mill's distinction between self and other regarding actions a viable principle?

- Should we maximize freedom of thought and expression?
- For what values, if any, would you want to limit freedom?
- Can justice exist without freedom?
- How valid is a needs-based theory of justice?
- Critically examine Rawls's theory of justice.
- How viable is a cosmopolitan theory of justice?
- Can justice apply to non-humans?

 ## Further Reading

Mill, J.S. (1972), *Utilitarianism, On Liberty, and Considerations on Representative Government*, London: Dent.
> This is the classic case for individual freedom.

Berlin, I. (1969), *Four Essays on Liberty*, Oxford: Oxford University Press.
> This is a celebrated defence of negative liberty.

Dobson, A. (1998), *Justice and the Environment*, Oxford: Oxford University Press.
> This is a wide-ranging consideration of the relationship between justice and the environment by a leading Green political theorist.

Dower, N. (1998), *World Ethics: The New Agenda*, Edinburgh: Edinburgh University Press.
> This is a useful survey of the international ethics literature.

MacCallum, G. (1967), 'Negative and Positive Freedom' in *Philosophical Review*, vol. 76.
> An influential article seeking to provide a universal definition of freedom.

Rawls, J. (1971), *A Theory of Justice*, Cambridge, MA: Harvard University Press.
> There is no substitute for reading this hugely important book.

 ## Web Links

www.freedomhouse.org/
This site attempts to measure freedom in different countries.

www.utilitarian.net/jsmill/
This is a useful site on Mill.

http://plato.stanford.edu/entries/original-position/
On Rawls.

 Visit the **Online Resource Centre** that accompanies this book to access more learning resources at **www.oxfordtextbooks.co.uk/orc/garner/**

Traditional Ideologies

Reader's Guide

After considering the general characteristics of an ideology, a range of traditional ideologies are considered in this chapter. All of these ideologies were shaped by the Enlightenment, either, in the case of liberalism, socialism, nationalism, and anarchism, adopting its key principles, or, in the case of conservatism and fascism, railing against them. Each ideology, too, cannot be understood outside the economic, social, and political environment in which it emerged. Most of the ideologies discussed have had an extraordinary impact on the development of world politics in the last two centuries, and it is fair to say that the world would have been a very different place had they not existed.

What is an Ideology?

This chapter and the next focus in detail on a range of political ideologies. Ideologies are central to this whole book because they help to shape the domestic and international political landscape. Many of the themes within them will be familiar because ideologies contain a collection of political ideas, many of which we have examined in previous chapters of this book. Liberalism, for instance, centres on the concept of liberty, whereas socialism centres on the concept of equality. In this chapter, we will examine traditional ideologies associated with the school of thought known as the **Enlightenment**. See **Box 5.1**. Liberalism, socialism, **nationalism**, and **anarchism** emerged as embodiments of the Enlightenment, whereas conservatism and fascism sought to challenge its assumptions. In the next chapter, we will move on to examine more contemporary ideologies that challenge the claims of the traditional ideologies looked at in this chapter.

The term 'ideology' was first used at the time of the French Revolution at the end of the eighteenth century by Antoine Destutt de Tracey (1754–1836). He used the term to denote a rationalistic science of ideas, which could be discovered in the same way as truths in the natural sciences. The **normative** character of ideology, however, quickly became apparent to others. For some, the word ideology has a pejorative or negative meeting. In contemporary popular usage, for instance, an ideologue is often used to denote someone with an uncompromising devotion to a set of ideas irrespective of their utility, or as simply an extremist. Marx is the best-known political thinker who defined ideology in negative terms. He used the term to mean a set of ideas that is false, deliberately designed to obscure reality in order to benefit a particular class in society. Marx's aim was to contrast ideology with the truth which his 'scientific' socialism was designed to produce.

Key Concept   Box 5.1
Enlightenment

Enlightenment—A seventeenth- and eighteenth-century intellectual and cultural movement that emphasized the application of reason to knowledge in a search for human progress. It was both a cause and effect of the decline in the authority of religion. The influence of the Enlightenment was felt in many disciplines, in arts and sciences. In politics, it is associated with the attempt to model political institutions around a set of abstract rational principles. The French Revolution is often regarded as the highlight of the Enlightenment. Its chief critic within political philosophy was Edmund Burke (1729–97) who railed against the Enlightenment in his violent attack on the French Revolution.   (Burke, 1968)

Others would regard Marxism itself as a classical example of an ideology. To so define Marxism, we need a more neutral or descriptive definition of the term. Here, an ideology might be defined as a set of ideas designed to provide a description of the existing political order, a vision of what the ideal political order ought to look like and a means, if necessary, to transform the former to the latter. An ideology therefore contains empirical, normative, and semantic elements.

Marxism is a classic case of this. Marx has often been described as the first social scientist. This is because he claimed to have discovered laws of social, political, and economic change which, he argued, enable us to predict the course of human history. Marx therefore described himself as a 'scientific socialist' to distinguish him from other socialists who put forward a normative case for socialism. However, Marx himself offers us both an **empirical** and a normative account of socialism. He seeks to tell us that socialism is desirable, it ought to happen, but he also puts forward an empirical theory which purports to determine the prospects of it happening.

A number of other features of ideologies are worth noting. First, ideologies are, more often than not, action-orientated in the sense that they seek to promote a particular social and political order for which they urge people to strive. Secondly, it is sometimes said that ideologies are less rigorous and sophisticated than 'proper' political philosophy. In reality, as Vincent (1995: 17) points out: 'ideological themes can be found on a continuum from the most banal jumbled rhetoric up to the most astute theorizing'.

Thirdly, it is often said too that the twentieth century in particular can be regarded as the age of ideologies in the sense that regimes based on particular ideological traditions—communism and fascism—wreaked havoc during this century. However, it is more appropriate to say that the twentieth century was the age of ideologies with which liberalism—which had tended to dominate in the West up to that point—profoundly disagreed. The liberal critique of fascism and communism as ideologies is a reflection of a tendency among some liberals to regard liberalism as somehow above the ideological fray. As Goodwin (2007: 35) points out: 'Liberalism appears as a necessary truth, the basis of reality, rather than as one political ideology among many'.

Fourthly, as well as containing empirical and normative elements, ideologies also seek to combine concepts that political philosophers, as we have seen, will look at individually. An attempt can be made to identify the core characteristic of a particular ideology but this is difficult, if not impossible, because all ideologies have different strands or schools, and sometimes there is considerable overlap between one ideology and another, such as when we talk about liberal versions of feminism or social democratic versions of socialism. Ideologies are, then, in the words of Festenstein and Kenny (2005: 4), 'internally pluralistic, contested, complex, and overlapping'.

One way out of this problem is to adopt the approach suggested by Freeden (1996). In a major study of the concept of political ideology, Freeden recommends identifying the morphology of an ideology. By this he means it is possible to distinguish between concepts at the core of an ideology from those which are further away from the centre and those which are at the periphery.

One final general point about political ideologies is worth making in this introductory section. It is important to recognize that ideologies reflect, as well as shape, the social and historical circumstances in which they exist. To give an illustration of this, the two main ideologies since the nineteenth century have been liberalism and socialism. It was no accident that these ideologies emerged at the time of the industrial revolution and reached their zenith in the nineteenth century. In the first place, both liberalism and socialism reflected the optimism of the time, a time when it was thought that there was nothing that human beings could not understand rationally and achieve politically and economically. Human beings could be masters of all they surveyed. This optimism derived from the dominance of so-called 'Enlightenment' thinking. Secondly, liberalism and socialism became dominant ideologies because they were associated with new social groupings created by the industrial revolution. Liberalism was largely promoted by the industrial middle class and socialism was promoted by, or in the interests of, the industrial working class.

This chapter considers those ideologies shaped by the Enlightenment whether, as in the case of liberalism and socialism, supportive of its values or, as in the case of conservatism and fascism, opposed to them. If we turn our attention to the twentieth century and beyond, and in particular to the post-1945 period, we see that the dominance of Enlightenment ideologies has begun to wane. This new ideological climate is the subject matter of chapter six.

Key points

- Traditional ideologies were shaped by the Enlightenment.
- For some, ideologies have a pejorative meaning, others adopt a more neutral term.
- Ideologies are action-orientated and seek to combine concepts.
- It is usually possible to identify the core concepts of an ideology but all ideologies have disputed meanings.
- Ideologies reflect, as well as shape, the social and historical circumstances in which they exist.

Liberalism

Liberalism is an important ideology because it has been the dominant political tradition in the West for many centuries. We have already encountered various facets of liberalism throughout this book, and many of the key Western political thinkers—Hobbes, Locke, Bentham, Mill, Rawls, and Nozick—are in the liberal tradition.

The Historical Development of Liberalism

Liberalism is a term that came into common usage in the nineteenth century where a party of that name emerged under the leadership of William Gladstone (1809–98), British Prime Minister on four separate occasions. Liberalism, and the values associated with it, however, have had a much longer history. The origins of liberalism are often traced to the rise of a capitalist political economy, and, in particular, as a defence of private property. The individualistic political philosophy of Hobbes and Locke is crucial here (Macpherson, 1962).

Liberalism is difficult to pin down, not least because of its longevity and the fact that it has gone through a variety of different formulations. The diverse character of liberalism is illustrated by the fact that it has been used to describe parties of the right, such as in Australia, and the left, such as in Canada. In some countries, it is associated with the free market whereas in others, most notably the USA, it denotes state intervention. Moreover, liberal politics has not been restricted to liberal parties. In Britain, for example, although members of the Liberal Party (now the Liberal Democrats) last held governmental office in the 1920s, much of the twentieth-century political debate in Britain has been couched in liberal terms with the Labour Party inheriting its mantle. Indeed, much of the 'social democratic' agenda promoted by the Labour Party in Britain, and many other social democratic parties in Europe, has really been liberal in character, or at least a revised version of liberalism.

The liberalism associated with the social-democratic left is a type known as 'new' or 'social' liberalism, which differs from the traditional **classical liberalism** which had its heyday in the nineteenth century. The classical tradition, drawing, in particular, on the economic theory of Adam Smith (1723–90) and the social theory of Herbert Spencer (1820–1907) emphasizes that the state's role should be limited to ensure internal and external security and to ensure that private property rights are enforced. It is partly justified on the grounds that the market is the most effective means of meeting human needs. There is also a moral dimension in that a limited state maximizes freedom and rewards those who work hardest.

Classical liberalism began to be questioned towards the end of the nineteenth century, as the extent of poverty began to be recognized and socialist ideas emerged as an alternative. From within the liberal tradition, a new emphasis on social reform began to emerge, associated with thinkers such as T.H. Green (1836–82), L.T. Hobhouse (1864–1929) and J.A. Hobson (1858–1940). This **new liberalism** saw a much more positive role for the state, in correcting the inequities of the market, but it was argued that far from reducing liberty this actually increased it by creating greater opportunities for individuals to achieve their goals. It influenced the direction of Liberal Party politics, the Liberal government elected in 1906 carrying through a range of social reforming measures including old-age pensions.

➔ See chapter twenty, page 457, for a discussion of liberal political economy.

The new liberalism came to dominant the political landscape for much of the twentieth century, although largely under the auspices of social democratic parties. In turn, however, a revised version of classical liberalism emerged to challenge it in the 1970s, under the guise of the New Right, and right-wing governments, particularly in Britain and America, were elected on programmes that were, in part, influenced by the classical liberal agenda. The academic ballast for this popular political movement was provided by thinkers such as Hayek and Nozick, whose ideas we have already touched upon in this book. Indeed, the debate between Nozick and Rawls that we encountered in chapter four is an academic version of the ideological debate between the classical and new liberal traditions.

➡ See chapter four, page 107, for Nozick's critique of Rawls's Theory of Justice.

5

Liberal Thought

One of the key questions about liberal ideology is the degree to which the two types of liberalism identified above are compatible. Bearing this in mind, we can attempt to ascertain the core meaning of the ideology. The core meaning of liberalism can be found in the concepts of liberty, tolerance, individualism, and a particular kind of equality. Liberty is *the* concept right at the centre of liberal thought, 'the primary value in the liberal creed' as Goodwin (2007: 41) puts it. For some liberal thinkers, liberty is seen as an intrinsic good; for others, such as J.S. Mill, it is a means to an end in the sense that its value is in the possibilities for self-development it produces.

The classical liberal tradition emphasizes **negative liberty**. Freedom is about removing external constraints. The new liberal tradition emphasizes **positive liberty**, whereby the state can remove obstacles to freedom. By emphasizing the collective role of the state, the new liberalism has been accused of abandoning 'true' liberalism by relegating the role of the individual. In its defence, advocates of the new liberalism argue that liberty can only be maximized through the enabling role of the state.

➡ See chapter four, page 97, for a discussion of the distinction between positive and negative liberty.

A corollary of liberty is the liberal focus on the individual. As exemplified by the **social contract** tradition of Hobbes and Locke, the individual is prior to society. The notion of rights is prominent in liberal thought precisely because of the prominence given to individuals. Individuals ought to be protected against society and the state, as seen in J.S. Mill's classic defence of individual liberty. At its extreme level, individualism denies the state's right to intervene in any aspect of the life of the individual. As we have seen, even the classical version of liberalism sees some role for the state, and therefore extreme libertarianism is best located in anarchist thought (see below).

➡ See chapter one, page 37, for discussion of the liberal social contract tradition.

The liberal focus on the individual stems from the belief that individuals are rational, and able to determine their own best interests, which they will always pursue. Thus, in the economic realm, individuals, according to the classical liberal position at least, are best left to their own devices as consumers and producers. The 'hidden hand' of the market will then ensure that economic utility is achieved.

The prominence of the individual in liberal thought involves the downgrading of the community. The community is merely an aggregate of individuals with competing interests and values. There is no room for regarding the community as a unified entity, as in the political philosophy of those such as Hegel and Rousseau. The distinction between the community and the individual is the source of the modern debate between liberals and **communitarian** thinkers. Communitarians criticize the liberal social contract tradition which envisages humans in a pre-social state. For communitarians, political principles must be derived from actual existing societies which provide identity and meaning for individuals.

→ See chapter one, page 40, for a discussion of communitarianism.

The liberal approach to equality is distinctive. Liberals regard individuals as of equal value, but they do not accept equality of outcome. Rather, the liberal position is characterized by equality of opportunity, whereby fairness is ensured because individuals, although—in theory at least—starting from the same position, are rewarded for their efforts. Of course, the free market does not allow for genuine equality of opportunity because individuals do not start out in life from the same position as some inherit advantages gained by the antecedents. It might be argued that the state intervention advocated by the new liberals actually makes equality of opportunity more of a reality. The introduction of free education and healthcare, in particular, has the effect of equalizing life chances. However, as we saw in the case of Nozick's critique of Rawls, redistributive policies can reduce the role of incentives, a central plank of the liberal emphasis on self-reliance.

Key points

- Liberalism is the dominant political tradition in the West.
- Liberalism has its classical and social reforming strands.
- The core concept of liberalism is liberty, with the classical tradition emphasizing negative liberty and the social reforming tradition emphasizing positive liberty.
- The prominence of the individual in liberal thought involves the downgrading of the community.
- Liberals advocate equality of opportunity rather than equality of outcome.

Socialism

The word socialism was first used in a working-class publication called the *Cooperative Magazine* in 1827. Socialism is an ideology, like liberalism, that is a child of the industrial revolution being associated with the emergence of an industrial working class. Socialism has been associated with working-class parties but it differs from mere trade unionism in the sense that it seeks to transform society in cooperative and egalitarian directions. Somewhat ironically, indeed, many of the advocates of socialism have in fact been middle class, and they have always faced a certain degree of hostility from working-class organizations.

Historical development

The historical development of socialism pivots around the giant figure of Karl Marx. The pre-Marxian socialists have often, following Marx himself, been described as utopian. Three thinkers—Claude-Henri Saint-Simon (1760–1825), Charles Fourier (1772–1837), and Robert Own (1771–1858)—are usually regarded as the founders of socialism. Marx regarded these thinkers as utopian in the sense that they regarded socialism as ethically desirable but had no contextual historical analysis of the possibilities of bringing about political change. Marx, by contrast, developed what he called a 'scientific' socialism which not only argued that socialism was ethically desirable but also attempted to explain the historical conditions that would bring it about.

Marx's ideas have had a huge impact on the development of socialism, and indeed world politics in general. Lenin and the Bolsheviks revised his ideas to suit Russia's circumstances, and after the Russian Revolution in 1917, the Soviet State, built on Marxist ideas, was created. This historical event resulted in the division of world socialism into two camps; on the one hand, communism, centring on the so-called 'Third International' of world communist organizations, and, on the other, **social democracy**. The roots of this division lie in debates within the German SPD prior to 1914, where there was an intellectual debate between the revisionists and the orthodox Marxists.

The revisionists, whose leading exponent was Eduard Bernstein (1850–1932), sought to revise Marxism in light of contemporary circumstances. In most central and western European countries, this revisionist Marxism, later restyled as social democracy, predominated. Marxism had more influence here than in Britain where more moderate socialist organizations had always predominated. From 1917, Marxists looked to Russia for their inspiration. Originally dominated by Lenin, his mantle was passed on, originally to a three-pronged leadership involving Trotsky, Stalin, and Bukharin, and then to Stalin alone.

➡ See chapter one, page 34, for a discussion of Marxist ideas on the state.

Means and Ends in Socialist Thought

As we have seen, all ideologies are a collection of ideas and it is often difficult to pinpoint core and peripheral ideas in their morphologies. Socialism, above all ideologies, would seem to have the largest number of competing varieties. As a result, it is tempting to use the word 'socialisms' rather than 'socialism', the former being the title of a well-known book on the subject (Wright, 1996).

In order to understand the key divisions within the socialist tradition, it is useful to distinguish between *means* and *ends*; between, that is, the methods that socialists have thought appropriate to achieve their objectives and the end goals or objectives. In terms of means, the key distinction has been between revolutionary and evolutionary socialism. In the revolutionary camp we need to make a further distinction. There are those, most notably Marx, who tended towards the assumption that a revolution would be a popular uprising. On the other hand, there are those, such as Lenin, whose preference was for a coup involving a disciplined band of revolutionaries. It was Lenin's advocacy of a disciplined party—the Bolsheviks—which created the structure that after the revolution became the Communist Party, a **political party** that dominated the Soviet Union for decades after 1917.

Evolutionary socialism has been the main alternative to revolution. It is based on the belief that with universal suffrage, socialism can be achieved through political democracy. It assumes, therefore, that the state can be responsive to working-class interests once enfranchised. This formed a central part of the division of socialist thought after the Russian Revolution.

A key thinker here was the German socialist, Eduard Bernstein. In his book, popularly known as 'Evolutionary Socialism' (1961), Bernstein argued that capitalism had not developed in the way that Marx had predicted and it was therefore time for Marxists to revise Marx's central ideas. The working class were not becoming more impoverished, and the move towards universal suffrage meant that a socialist party could win power through political democracy. Rather than being a historical inevitability, socialism, for Bernstein, would come about as a result of a growing perception of its desirability. It is questionable whether Bernstein can be described as a Marxist. His socialism is more akin to the social democratic tradition, and, indeed, Bernstein was heavily influenced by the British socialist organization, the Fabian Society.

Photo 5.1

November 1917: the distribution of newspapers on the first day of the Session of Soviets in Moscow during the Russian Revolution.

Source: Getty Images

Socialists, too, disagree about the ends of socialism. Two dimensions to this are most apparent. First, some socialists see a crucial role for the state in a socialist society, whereas others envisage a decentralized communal society. Again, the contrast between Marx and Lenin is apposite here. Marx suggests that once class conflict is eliminated, there will be no need for a state, since the capitalist state is merely a vehicle for the ruling class. At times, Marx's vision of a future communist society envisages the absence of any centralized administrative structure. This approaches an anarchist position (see below). As we saw earlier in this book, this rather optimistic scenario has been questioned. Lenin did recognize the need for a state, at least for a period of time after the communist revolution. This so-called 'dictatorship of the proletariat' was designed to defeat the enemies of the revolution, a very real threat at the time. The state, of course, remained in the Soviet Union long after this. See **Box 5.2**.

The second dimension of socialism's ends concerns the balance between public and private ownership of the means of production. Within socialist thought there is a continuum with complete public ownership at one end of the spectrum to relatively little at the other. This debate has been central to socialist debate within the West. Questions of ownership have been of fundamental importance, in particular, to debates within British social democracy. At each period of the Labour Party's existence, there have been those (the Independent Labour Party in the 1920s, the Bevanites in the 1950s, and the Bennites in the 1970s and 1980s—named, respectively, after their leading exponents Aneurin Bevan and Tony Benn) who have wanted the party to move further and faster towards greater public ownership.

Key Quote Box 5.2
Marx's Vision of Communism

Marx wrote very little about what a future communist society would look like. In the *Communist Manifesto*, however, he does say this:

When, in the course of development, class distinctions have disappeared, and all the production has been concentrated in the whole nation, the public power will lose its political character. . . . If the proletariat during its contest with the bourgeoisie is compelled, by the force of circumstances, to organize itself as a class, if, by means of a revolution, it makes itself the ruling class, and, as such, sweeps away by force the old conditions of production, then it will, along with these conditions, have swept away the conditions for the existence of class antagonisms and of classes generally, and will thereby have abolished its own supremacy as a class. (Marx and Engels, 1976: 105)

Questions to ask about this passage include:

1. Why does Marx think that classes will cease to exist under a communist regime?
2. Does this passage provide justification for the Soviet state?
3. Can the 'public power' have a non-political character?

Socialists have differed over the form that public ownership should take, with the state corporation model challenged, particularly since the 1960s, by more decentralized forms involving worker's cooperatives and even a market socialism model (Miller, 1990). The key question is, where do we draw the line? When does a particular balance between public and private ownership cease to be socialist? This debate became particularly vociferous in Britain after the 1945 Labour Government had undertaken extensive nationalization. In the 1950s, while the Bevanites wanted to go further along the public ownership route, the Gaitskellites, named after the Labour leader Hugh Gaitskill (1906–63), were prepared to settle for the mixed economy as a permanent state of affairs, with Tony Crosland's book *The Future of Socialism* (1980) providing the intellectual ballast for this position.

Key Socialist Principles

Behind these differences of means and ends, it is possible to identify a number of core socialist principles. The first of them is *a particular view of* **human nature**. Socialists tend to have an optimistic view of human nature, which, they suggest, is capable of being shaped by social, economic, and political circumstances. Liberal and conservatives tend to regard human beings as selfish, individualistic, and materialistic. Socialists, on the other hand, regard such behaviour as socially conditioned rather than innate. A socialist society would promote values of cooperation, fellowship, and compassion, thereby shaping the values of its citizenry.

The second core socialist principle is *equality*. For many, equality is the defining feature of socialism. Unlike liberals, socialists are more likely to advocate equality of outcome. This is partly because socialists see inequality as resulting not so much from differences of ability but in terms of an individual's location in a social structure. Educational attainment, in particular, is seen by socialists as a classic example of inequality at work since it is heavily influenced by social class. Equality of outcome is promoted by socialists, too, because they have a less pessimistic view of human nature. For liberals, inequality is necessary in order to provide incentives. For socialists, on the other hand, human nature can be moulded to the point where individuals would be willing to work for the good of society, irrespective of the lack of material incentives available.

The third core principle of socialism is *community and cooperation*. There is an emphasis in socialism on what humans can achieve collectively rather than individually. Therefore, there is an emphasis on the achievement of collective rather than individual goals through cooperation. Community is linked to the other two core socialist values in the sense that common ownership and equality are obvious ways in which communal values can be furthered.

Socialism, Authoritarianism, and Utopia

Many have suggested that the socialist vision is utopian. The word **utopia**, originally coined by Thomas More in the sixteenth century, is a play on two Greek words translated as good and nowhere. Utopian therefore refers to the 'good society which is nowhere', or, to put it another way, the society which is impossible of realization. This leads to the question whether socialism is similarly unrealizable.

Liberals, and especially conservatives (see below) brand utopias as unrealistic and unrealizable and suggest that socialism comes into this category. According to this argument socialists develop utopian visions of a better society in which human beings can achieve genuine **emancipation** and fulfilment as members of a community. The problem, however, is that such a society demands too much of its citizens. This might be acceptable if its effects are benign but, so the argument continues, to maintain such an egalitarian society inevitably results in an **authoritarian** state which has continually to intervene to prevent differential levels of talent and effort from eroding the socialist distribution of goods (Popper, 1962).

Such a critique is directed at the Soviet style of communism whose overbearing state was, it is argued, a direct product of socialist ideas. Whether or not this critique is justified, it is clear that the authoritarian label cannot be attached to the social democratic variety of socialism which, in any case, draws from liberalism as much as it does from Marxian varieties of socialism. Even then, as we saw in chapter four, there is a libertarian critique of redistributive versions of liberalism that claims that it illegitimately infringes liberty.

Key Points

→ See chapter four, page 107, for Nozick's libertarian critique of Rawls's Theory of Justice.

- Socialism is dominated by the work of Karl Marx, who described his socialism as scientific as opposed to the utopian variety of those socialists who preceded him.
- At the turn of the twentieth century, socialism divided into two camps, with the communists on one side and the revisionists (later to be social democrats) on the other.
- To classify different varieties of socialism, it is useful to distinguish between means and ends.
- Core socialist principles include an optimistic view of human nature, equality of outcome, and community and cooperation.
- Some argue that socialism is utopian and has authoritarian tendencies.

Conservatism

Elements of conservative thought can be found throughout history. Indeed, the Greek philosopher Plato, in urging the maintenance of the rule of the intellectual elite—the Philosopher Kings as he called them—can be regarded as the first conservative thinker. However, conservative thought received its greatest fillip as a response to the Enlightenment tradition. Whereas liberalism and socialism bought into the progressive and rationalistic values of the Enlightenment, conservatism provides a negative response to

Short Biography Box 5.3
Edmund Burke (1729–97)

Burke was born in Dublin in 1729. After studying at Trinity College in Dublin, he moved to England in 1750 where he qualified as a lawyer before settling on a career in politics. He became an MP in 1776 in a rotten borough before winning a seat in Bristol in 1775. He died in 1797, a rich man with an estate of some 600 acres in Buckinghamshire.

Burke's fame emerged from his writing and speeches on important political issues of his day. He is best known for his vitriolic best-selling attack on the French Revolution, but he also wrote and spoke on the British constitution, and the relations between Britain and India and the American colonies. There is a much discussed apparent contradiction in Burke's writings in the sense that he opposes the French Revolution but supports the American Revolution and the Indian opposition to British colonial rule.

Some put this down to an unstated fear that the French Revolution threatened the emerging capitalist class in Britain. Others argue that there was no inconsistency since Burke was applying his political principles in a logical way. Thus, he was opposed to the French Revolutionaries because they were overthrowing an established order on the grounds of abstract rational principles. On the other hand, he supported the Americans and the Indians because they were seeking to uphold long-held traditions against the encroachment of the British.

it. The classic text here is Edmund Burke's (1729–97) vitriolic attack on the French Revolution of 1789 first published in 1790 (1968). See **Box 5.3**.

Conservative political movements have not been ideologically uniform. In much of Europe, for example, they have historically been anti-liberal, reactionary, and authoritarian, whereas in Britain, conservatism has been tinged with liberalism. The nineteenth-century Conservative Party was notable for the social reforming administrations of Peel and Disraeli, and, following the creation of the post-1945 settlement by the British Labour Party, the Conservative Party largely accepted the dominance of social democratic ideas. Following the breakdown of the social democratic consensus in the 1970s, however, the Conservative Party became heavily influenced by the New Right. A similar shift to the right was noticeable in the USA with the election of President Ronald Reagan in 1980.

With its emphasis on the unconstrained free market, the New Right had more in common with classical liberalism than conservatism. Certainly, the ideological character of Thatcher's leadership was inimical to the pragmatism of conservative thought. However, the New Right also embodied a number of traditional conservative values—such as law and order, respect for authority, and the importance of traditional values—and the Thatcher Governments were prepared to use the state to enforce them. This ideological mix was described by one British academic commentator as 'the free economy and the strong state' (Gamble, 1994).

➔ See chapter one, page 34, for a discussion of the New Right theory of the state.

In the USA, the so-called 'neo-conservatism' has been more successful in challenging traditional conservatism. This has combined a brand of social authoritarianism with nationalism to create a reactionary movement which has had a large impact on the direction of US domestic and foreign policy, particularly under the presidency of George W. Bush. The major intellectual adherent of neo-conservatism in foreign policy has been the political thinker Leo Strauss (1899–1973). Strauss, with a Zionist background, argued that the USA should fight tyranny wherever it was found. Initially, this took the form of recommending a strong line against the Soviet Union, but since its collapse, the attention of neocons has turned to the threat from religious fundamentalism, seen as a challenge to conservative values. The intervention in Iraq and Afghanistan can be seen as a product of neocon ideas.

Conservative Thought

Determining the nature of conservative thought is not easy, not least because it tends to claim to be non-ideological, preferring practical principles and pragmatism over abstract reasoning. As a result, conservative thinkers have been reluctant to set out their position in a reasoned and codified fashion since to do so would be to engage in an exercise which they themselves condemn. This has been problematic, however, for taken literally, the word conservatism suggests a desire to conserve which has reactionary overtones. Conservatives, therefore, risk being accused of merely seeking to defend the status quo in order to defend existing privilege and power. This is unfortunate because conservatism can be seen as an ideology where 'certain fundamental convictions have been identified which constitute a distinct political standpoint' (Goodwin, 2007: 174).

Pride of place among these convictions is an *aversion to rationalism*. This rationalism was very much a product of the Enlightenment. It celebrated the ability of human beings to construct societies on the basis of rational principles such as—in the French Revolution—'liberty, equality, and fraternity'. There was no limit to the progress possible in human societies. For Michael Oakeshott (1901–90), a notable twentieth-century conservative, a rationalist 'stands . . . for independence of mind on all occasions, for thought free from obligation to any authority save the authority of reason' (Oakeshott, 1962: 1).

It was the rationalist temper of the French Revolution that Burke so savagely attacked. By trying to create a new society based on abstract principles, the French revolutionaries had destroyed the traditions and institutions that had evolved over the centuries. For Burke and conservatives in general, the social and political world is too complex to be susceptible of easy rational comprehension. Better then to rely on the tried and tested traditions—what Burke describes as 'prejudices'—which contain the collective wisdom of a society gained over many generations.

A number of other conservative values derive from this attack on rationalism. In the first place, the *conservative model of society is organic rather than mechanical*. In other words, society cannot be taken apart and rearranged like the parts of a machine. Rather, society is a little-understood, complex, and interdependent organism. To change one part may have an unpredictable and undesirable impact on other parts. Burke is not saying that no change is ever permissible, but it should be gradual and moderate, taking care to preserve what is valuable in the organism. There is a much-challenged assumption here that what exists does actually have value and is functional for the well-being of society. Clearly, this is not always the case and conservatives are guilty of deriving an ought—existing traditions and institutions should be preserved—from an is—the mere existence of these traditions and institutions.

The second conservative value to derive from anti-rationalism is *human imperfection*. Conservatives are sceptical about the human capacity fully to understand their social and political environment. At the very least, collective wisdom of the past and present is preferable to the abstract reasoning of a few. We should as far as possible, therefore, stick with what we know. This scepticism about human capacities follows through into the conservative *advocacy of hierarchy*. As Plato had recognized, effective self-government is a myth. Some are innately more capable of governing than others. This is the reason behind Burke's well-known justification of MPs retaining autonomy from their constituents.

Key Points

- Conservatism is a reaction to the Enlightenment tradition of political thought.
- The New Right has liberal and conservative elements.
- The underlying principles of conservatism are an aversion to rationality, an organic view of society, human imperfection, and a preference for hierarchy.

Nationalism

It is undoubtedly the case that the desire to organize political communities according to nationalistic principles has been of central importance in the past two centuries. Nationalism emerged in the nineteenth century, as the decline of monarchical power and authority eroded previous loyalties. People no longer regarded themselves as subjects and sought new ties and identities to organize their lives.

The search for national identity was initially a European phenomenon, centring on the striving for German and Italian unification, achieved in 1871 and 1861 respectively, and, after the end of the First World, national **self-determination** as set out by the US President Woodrow Wilson in the peace settlement. After the Second World War, the centre of the striving for nationalism shifted to the colonies as countries in Africa and the Middle East, in particular, sought, and largely secured, their independence. In more recent times there has been a resurgence in nationalism particularly in Eastern Europe after the collapse of the Soviet Union. Nationalism has continued to be the source of much conflict and bloodshed in countries and regions as diverse as Northern Ireland, the former Yugoslavia, Kosovo, Afghanistan, and Rwanda.

Despite the fact that nationalism is an important political concept, however, there is a question mark about its ideological character, and an even bigger question mark over its normative worth. This is based partly on the belief that it is not a universal principle as not everyone can have their nationalist objectives realized. Indeed, the achievement of one person's nationalist desires (based, say, on religion) denies it to others (based, say, on language). Nationalism also lacks political content. Its only concern is national identity. Unlike the other ideologies considered so far in this chapter, then, nationalism is not a set of interrelated ideas. It has nothing to say about the character of the political system within the nation-state, or what the role of political principles such as justice, rights and liberty might be (Goodwin, 2007: 274). Also, unlike the other ideologies we have considered so far, there is a paucity of great works advocating nationalism. It is a subject area that has largely preoccupied political scientists but not many political theorists (Hoffman and Graham, 2006: 266).

At the very least, we can say that nationalism is a confused concept. It is a simple principle in that it holds that political organization ought to be based on national identity, but the bases upon which this identity is based has varied. These have included race and language (as in Germany), religion (as in Northern Ireland and the demands for Islamic states), culture, and membership of an existing state. A profitable distinction is between civic nationalism, on the one hand, and ethnic nationalism on the other, a distinction made by the political scientist Hans Kohn (1944). **Civic nationalism** refers to loyalty to the institutions and values of a particular

Photo 5.2   Serbians Demonstrate against Declaration of Independence by Kosovo
Serbians demonstrate against the decision of the Kosovo Parliament to declare independence from Serbia. Location: Mitrovica, Serbia. Date: 18 February 2008.
Source: UN photo by Olivier Salgado

political community. **Ethnic nationalism**, by contrast, refers to loyalty to a shared inheritance based on culture, language, or religion. Whereas the former is inclusive, open to anyone who wishes to sign up to the values and institutions of a particular community, the latter is exclusive in the sense that membership is inherited and not the product of a rational choice.

Because of its inclusive character, civic nationalism would seem to be less of a threat to political order than the exclusivity inherent in ethnic nationalism. This distinction can be exaggerated, however, because even a political community based on loyalty to institutions and values has borders which have to be protected. Inclusion, while not based on religion or race, must be based on something and this has the potential for conflict. Despite its negative image, nationalism need not necessarily result in division and conflict. Liberal nationalism, for instance, while for some too romantic, sees nations as the source of internal unity and envisages cooperation between nations.

Such is the negativity associated with nationalism, however, that some traditions of political thought seek to envisage a world where national identity ceases to be an organizing principle of people's lives. Liberal internationalism, for instance, promotes **interdependence** between nations, either through the creation of supranational institutions—such as the League of Nations and now the United Nations—or through free trade between nations. For Marx and many in the socialist tradition, class, rather than the **nation**, is the chief cleavage in society. Nationalism is therefore misplaced, seen as a device to distract the working class from their exploitation. The proletariat should instead look towards unity across nations if their liberation is to be achieved, and a peaceful world created.

Key Points

- Nationalism has had an enormous impact on the development of world politics since the nineteenth century.
- Many argue that nationalism is not, properly speaking, an ideology and that it is of dubious normative worth.
- The bases on which nationalism has been justified vary.
- A profitable distinction is to be made between civic nationalism and ethnic nationalism.

Fascism

Unlike the other ideologies we have discussed in this chapter, fascism is a twentieth-century phenomenon. It is particularly associated with the relatively short-lived, and terrifying, regimes led by Mussolini (1883–1945) in Italy and Hitler (1889–1945) in Germany lasting between 1925–43 and 1933–45 respectively. Indeed, for some commentators, fascism is regarded as a distinctly interwar phenomenon (Trevor-Roper, 1947). Others disagree with this limitation (Kitchen, 1976). More attention has been

Key Concept Box 5.4
Elitism in Political Thought

The concept of **elitism** has been used in the context of a number of the ideological traditions discussed in this chapter. It is important to recognize the different ways in which the concept is being used. The classical elitists discussed in chapter one, and used to buttress the claims of fascism, were putting forward an empirical theory arguing that elites will always exist, whatever the claims of democracy. They were not claiming that such a form of rule was desirable. Both fascism and conservatism, however, are using the term in a normative sense to argue that the rule of an elite is not only inevitable but is also desirable. In National Socialism, if not Italian fascism, this elitism took on a racial connotation which is absent from conservatism. The idea of an elite norm derives from Plato who advocates the rule of an intellectual elite.

paid to the causes of the rise of fascism than its ideological character. Fascism is seen, for instance, as a product of particular political and historical circumstances, or as a product of a flawed human psychology, or of moral decay (Vincent, 1995: 145–50).

Fascism represents an extreme form of nationalism. Unlike other forms of nationalism, however, it is accompanied by a wider set of ideas. Some of these ideas are distasteful and implausible. In addition, fascism rejects abstract intellectualizing in favour of action, instinct, and emotion and as a result there are few intellectual works on which to rely, the principal exceptions being those of the Italian fascist Giovanni Gentile (1875–1944) and Hitler's *Mein Kampf* (1926/1969), the latter being of some use in explaining the character of the ideology. An added difficulty of studying fascism is that the Italian variety is different in significant respects from the German, not least in its treatment of race and its greater extremism, and there is a case, therefore, for considering Nazism as a distinct ideological phenomenon.

Despite these caveats, it would be a mistake to regard fascism as non-ideological. It is best understood in terms of its oppositional mentality. Fascism is, above all, anti-Enlightenment. It therefore opposes Enlightenment ideas such as liberalism, democracy, reason, individualism. It is also profoundly anti-Marxist. Certain elements of fascism are similar to conservatism, in particular the focus on the organic state, but fascism is also revolutionary and, in the case of Germany at least, also racist and nationalistic.

Fascism's opposition to liberalism and individualism stems from the belief that it is the community that creates individuals. Without it, they are nothing. It is therefore opposed to the liberal position that humans can be envisaged living in a pre-social state. Rather, their identity is forged through membership of a community. In fascist theory, it is the state that confers meaning upon individual lives and, as a result, individuals should be subservient to it. This provides a justification for the **totalitarian** state, one in which the individual is subsumed in the state's greater goal. In Italy, in particular, the role of corporations was, theoretically at least, to provide the means whereby society—and particularly employer and employee organizations—were to be incorporated into the state.

Accompanying the social nature of individuals is an elitist view whereby some individuals are regarded as superior to others. See **Box 5.4**. The masses are regarded as largely ignorant needing to be led by an elite, and particularly by one all-powerful leader, a Fuhrer or Duce. Italian fascists, in particular, were influenced by the elite theory of the state we encountered in chapter one. As we saw, elite\thinkers such as Pareto, Mosca, and Michels regarded elite rule as inevitable. This was largely put forward as an empirical theory with no normative overtones. What elite theory did, however, was to provide a justification for the fascist belief in the inevitability of hierarchy and the herd-like character of the masses.

In German fascism, in particular, this emphasis on inequality and hierarchy took on a racial character, with the German Aryan race regarded, as a result of the adoption of various pseudoscientific theories, as superior to other racial groups, and particularly Jews and Negroes. A belief in the German nation or *Volk* fed into a militant, aggressive, and expansionist nationalism. The goal of nationalism was therefore to establish the 'master race' across the globe, by a process of natural selection drawn from **social Darwinism**, putting into servitude, or eliminating, inferior races in the process. War and conflict was seen as inherently virtuous and character-building as well as serving the goal of racial superiority. See **Box 5.5**.

➔ See chapter one, page 33, for a discussion of the elite theory of the state.

5

 **Case Study   Box 5.5**
Neo-Nazism

There have been a large number of neo-Nazi organizations and movements in the post Second World War period, although, for obvious reasons, its adherents rarely use that term. Their goal has been to revive the ideology of National Socialism, or some variant of it. The neo-Nazi phenomenon exists in many parts of the world including the USA and many European countries, including, most notably, Austria, Russia, Belgium, Croatia, and France. It has even emerged in Germany, particularly after reunification in the 1990s, despite the extensive programme of denazification after 1945. Even Israel has not been immune as immigrants from the former Soviet Union, some of whom do not identify as Jews, have exported extreme right wing views.

There was little overt neo-Nazi activity in Europe until the 1960s. Since then, neo-Nazis have engaged in a number of common activities. Some have competed in elections; Holocaust denial has been common, or at least needs to be contextualized with the human rights abuses of the allies; Nazi regalia has been promoted; attempts have been made to gain support in student organizations; violence, against immigrants, Jews, and Muslims has been common and this has sometimes involved murder. While their activities are often shocking and newsworthy, the membership of neo-Nazi organizations remains small.

Source: Schain, Zolberg, and Hossay (eds) (2002)

Key Points

- Fascists reject abstract intellectualizing in favour of action.
- Fascism is best understood in terms of its oppositional mentality.
- Central fascist themes are the emphasis on the state's role in creating meaning for individuals, and an elitist view of humans. In Germany, the belief in the superiority of some humans took on a racial dimension.

Anarchism

Anarchism is the last of the traditional ideologies we will consider in this chapter. Anarchism has many similarities with the liberal and, particularly, socialist traditions and might have been considered in this chapter at an earlier point. It has been left until last, however, because, although it has an impeccable intellectual pedigree, it is extremely questionable whether anarchism has had any lasting impact, or is capable of having any impact, on the development of modern politics.

Anarchism dates back to the nineteenth century. Like a number of ideologies, anarchist thought has come in a number of varieties, although Goodwin (2007: 151) is probably right to say that the primary link is with the socialist tradition. Thus, anarchists such as Proudhon, (1809–65), Bakunin (1814–76), and Kropotkin (1842–1921) were all involved in practical socialist politics within the socialist International, engaging in debate, and regularly falling out, with Marx, the dominant intellectual figure within it. One of the first anarchist thinkers, Godwin (1756–1836), was an exponent of the liberal, individualist school of anarchism, but this is particularly associated with a group of twentieth-century American thinkers, and most notably Murray Rothbard (1926–95).

Despite the many differences between anarchists, they share an abhorrence of the state, which they regard as an illegitimate, even criminal, type of organization illegitimately exercising force over individuals and society, and reducing the liberty of the people. Obviously, this simple principle raises many questions. In the first place, there is the question mark over what anarchists are actually opposing. Is it just the state or is it the state, government, and any form of authority structure? Clearly, if the latter, then anarchism does rely on an optimistic view of human nature. In fact, anarchist thinkers differ here, with some holding that human nature is intrinsically good, and others holding that it is socially determined, and therefore can be shaped by the social and political environment. Whatever the exact form of the theory, anarchists all tend to argue that an anarchist society will be one in which the people will be morally correct, doing what is required of them.

Even assuming that human nature is generally good, anarchists still face problems. How are the functions of the state to be performed? For individualist anarchists such as

Rothbard, there is an assumption that the state's role could be transferred to the free market. Leaving aside the social inequality likely to be caused by market provision of education and health, it is difficult to conceive of crime and social deviancy being dealt with effectively by a private police force which lacks the authority of the state.

Similarly, how would the egalitarian ambitions of the socialist and communist anarchists be achieved without some body to enforce it? And if there is to be an authority structure of some kind to ensure a socialist distribution of resources, then what of the anarchist claim that authority structure involve the diminution of freedom? Hoffman (1975) tries to rescue anarchism. He argues that the anarchist mistake was to regard the state and the government as synonymous, whereas this is to confuse force and constraint. The state exercises force, and this is what anarchists are opposed to, but government, while inevitably requiring constraints, is not an institution exercising force. Therefore 'to link the state and government as twin enemies of freedom is to ignore the fact that stateless societies have governments, and that even in state-centric societies, the role of government is positive and empowering'. It follows then that 'without a distinction between state and government it is impossible to move beyond the state' (Hoffman and Graham, 2006: 259). This does not entirely let anarchists off the hook, however. This is because government, without a state, relies upon authority since it has no means of force to ensure its decisions are obeyed. This rather takes us back to square one; that is, how will such a society deal with those who refuse to accept the authority of the government?

Compared to the other ideologies we have considered in this chapter, anarchism would appear to have had little influence on modern politics. Strong anarchist movements existed between the 1880s and the 1930s, and anarchists briefly held power during the Spanish Civil War (Vincent, 1995: 117). Since then, there have been anarchist tendencies present in the 1960s counter-culture, the student protests and, more recently, in the environmental and anti-globalization movements. It has remained a peripheral ideology however, tainted, however unjustly, with the charge that it is a recipe for confusion and chaos.

Key Points

- Anarchism is primarily an off-shoot of socialism.
- Anarchists share an abhorrence of the state, but this principle raises many difficult questions which many argue anarchists cannot effectively answer.
- Anarchism has had relatively little influence on modern politics.

Conclusion

In this chapter we have examined a variety of traditional ideologies. Quite clearly, they have exercised an extraordinary influence on world politics, not always in the way their adherents intended. Indeed, such has been the negative impact of at least some of the ideologies discussed above that since the middle of the twentieth century, political theorists have been much more circumspect about offering the kind of overarching interpretations of the world, or 'meta narratives', that ideologies traditionally offered.

Ideologies since then have been much less ambitious and much less certain. The ideologies that have emerged in this different climate—such as **postmodernism** and environmentalism—are discussed in the next chapter. For now, we should say that it is easy to see why these new ideologies have become more important in recent years. Unlike the nineteenth century, there is now much greater scepticism about the ability of human beings to master the world. In this sense the influence of the Enlightenment has begun to wane. We are now much more cautious about universal ideologies which proclaim to understand the world and know how to put it right.

 ## Key Questions

- What is an ideology?
- Does new liberalism develop or depart from classical liberalism?
- What are the core principles of liberalism?
- Is modern social democracy socialist?
- Is socialism utopian and authoritarian?
- To what extent can conservatism be considered an ideology?
- Is nationalism an ideology?
- Did Fascism die with Hitler and Mussolini?
- Assess the claim that fascism is concerned more with political action than political ideas.
- Is anarchism naive and unrealistic?

 ## Further Reading

Bellamy, R. (2000), *Rethinking Liberalism*, London: Pinter.
   This is a collection of essays on the development of liberal thought by a noted scholar.

Freeden, M. (1996), *Ideologies and Political Theory*, Oxford: Oxford University Press.
   This is a monumental work that not only covers ideology in depth but also offers an innovative way of thinking about them.

Goodwin, B. (2007), *Using Political Ideas*, Chichester: John Wiley & Sons, 5th edn.
   This is an excellent introduction to the ideologies discussed in this chapter

O'Sullivan, N. (1976), *Conservatism*, London.
This is a well-regarded account of conservative thought.

Wright, A. (1996), *Socialisms*, London: Routledge, 2nd edn.
This reflects well the diversity of socialist thought.

 *Web Links*

www.en.wikipedia.org/wiki/Liberalism
On liberalism.

www.kirkcenter.org/burke/ebsa.html
On Edmund Burke's conservatism.

http://plato.stanford.edu/entries/nationalism/
On nationalism.

http://en.wikipedia.org/wiki/Fascism
On fascism.

www.anarchistfaq.org
On anarchism.

 Visit the **Online Resource Centre** that accompanies this book to access
more learning resources at **www.oxfordtextbooks.co.uk/orc/garner/**

6

Challenges to the Dominant Ideologies

Reader's Guide

This chapter explores a range of more contemporary ideologies which challenge the traditional ideologies encountered in chapter five. They differ from traditional ideologies in a number of ways. They are, first, less optimistic about the ability of ideologies to construct an overarching explanation of the world, not surprisingly since they emerged in the aftermath of the catastrophic impact of some traditional ideologies. They also respect difference and variety. This is a product of social and economic change which has eroded the 'Fordist' economy, brought into being a number of powerful identity groups based on gender, culture, and ethnicity, and raised question marks over the environmental sustainability of current industrial practices.

The End of History?

The so-called 'end of history' thesis was developed, most notably, by an American scholar Francis Fukuyama (1992) to denote the triumph of liberalism. Ideology, in other words, is dead, he argued, because the ideals of liberalism have spread throughout the world and now remain unchallenged. The thesis was perceived in the context of the **Cold War** where the key ideological battle was between socialism or, to be more accurate, communism and liberalism. Seen in this context, the thesis has some merit. In the 1950s, Daniel Bell (1960) had famously declared the 'end of ideology', meaning that the challenge of socialism had wilted, at least in western Europe. The collapse of communism in Eastern Europe, which occurred very soon after Fukuyama's original article appeared, merely expanded this decline. In the place of communism in eastern Europe the ideals of the market and freedom became quickly established.

What Fukuyama meant by the end of history was the dominance of one ideological narrative over another, and, as we saw in the introduction to this volume, this position underestimates the degree of political and institutional variety in the world. Another interpretation is that history cannot be understood, now, in terms of these grand ideological artefacts that seek to explain the past, present, and future, and see the human condition as one of unremitting progress (Gamble, 2000: 20–3). Given the history of the twentieth century, such scepticism is not at all surprising. The experience of Soviet-style communism appeared to show that organizing societies on the basis of ideological system-building simply does not work. The anti-Enlightenment nature of much conservative thinking seemed, then, to be increasingly relevant.

Contemporary ideologies, explored in this chapter, should be seen in the context of growing scepticism about the utility of **Enlightenment** ideologies. **Postmodernism** offers the most fundamental challenge to this modernism. The claims of any one ideology that it is able to encompass total understanding of the social and political world are rejected. Postmodernism therefore celebrates difference, accepting the subjective nature of political ideologies. For postmodernists there are, in the words of Gamble (2000: 116), 'no foundations, no objective standards, no fixed points, above all no universalism and no knowledge which is not constructed and relative'.

Much modern feminism also rejects monolithic value systems and seeks to promote the differences between men and women as politically important. The politics of difference is also explored in the context of multiculturalism, an antidote to the ethnic nationalism we discussed in the previous chapter. Another contemporary ideology, environmentalism, incorporates the growing scepticism about the human ability to master and control nature. Finally, the idea of the dominance of liberal values in the world is clearly at odds with the political and social importance of religious fundamentalism, based on a belief system very different from the largely **secular** Enlightenment ideologies looked at in the previous chapter.

➡ See chapter five, page 128, for a discussion of ethnic nationalism.

6

Key Points

- Contemporary ideologies challenge the meta-narrative character of traditional ideologies.
- Traditional ideologies are regarded as too homogeneous and certain in their orientation.

Postmodernism

For many, postmodernism is not an ideology so much as a critique of ideologies, or at least, particular types of ideology. Thus, some of the major accounts of ideologies (Vincent, 1995; Heywood, 2007; Goodwin, 2007; Hoffman and Graham, 2006) do not have separate chapters on postmodernism. Postmodernism is a label given to a wide variety of theorists in a wide variety of disciplines, not just in the social sciences but in art, architecture, and cultural studies too. It is also associated with a wide variety of academics and authors, although perhaps the two with the biggest impact on political theory have been Michel Foucault (1926–84) and Jacques Derrida (1930–2004). It is difficult to provide one all-embracing definition of postmodernism as it contains so many different emphases and nuances. At the very least, the postmodern attitude points out the necessary limitations in the project to master the nature of reality. It is therefore a direct challenge to the modernist approach.

The modernist approach, influenced by the Enlightenment, is essentially a belief in the omnipotence of reason; a confidence in the ability of reason to penetrate to the essential truth of things and to achieve progress; and a foundationalist **ontology** which argues 'that a real world exists independently of our knowledge of it' (Stoker and Marsh, 2002: 11). We saw in the previous chapter that, with the exception of conservatism, this confidence was present in post-Enlightenment ideologies, and principally liberalism and socialism. Postmodernism represents a challenge to this confidence. It suggests that the search for ultimate answers is a futile exercise as the world is too fractured, and too

➔ See chapter sixteen, page 379, for a discussion of postmodernism's contribution to international relations.

6

Key Concept Box 6.1
Ontology, Epistemology, and Foundationalism

Whereas an ontology is concerned with what there is to know about the world, epistemology asks what can we know about what exists. A key ontological question is whether there is an objectively observable 'real world' out there that is separate from our knowledge of it. Such a question is not capable of being decided by empirical information. Foundationalists argue that there is an observable real world out there, and set about trying to find out about it epistemologically. So-called 'anti-foundationalists' argue that there is not, that the world is socially constructed and that the key is to understand this process rather than scientifically to explain the world.

diverse for grand explanatory schemes or theories. Instead, difference and variety are celebrated. Moreover, an anti-foundationalist ontology is promoted whereby the world cannot be objectively observed but is socially constructed in a variety of ways. See **Box 6.1**.

For some postmodernists, the approach represents merely the description of a historical period that comes after **modernity**. Therefore, it is not a **normative** theory as much as a signpost of the way the world is heading in a more fractured and uncertain way. In politics, for instance, we can note the collapse of the homogeneous Soviet bloc in Eastern Europe and its replacement by a plurality of democratic regimes. We can also point to the decline of regimented class politics in the West, determining the nature of party systems and voting behaviour. There is now room for a greater plurality of issues, such as environmentalism and feminism, to emerge, and voting behaviour is more individualistic, electoral choice being determined by a wider array of factors. The decline in class politics is, in part, the product of the decline in manufacturing industry, and the rise of a greater variety of employment patterns, so marking the end of the **Fordist** era. See **Box 6.2**.

The postmodern age is also equated with the end of a theory of knowledge; that is, postmodernists are accused of adopting a relativistic attitude arguing that all knowledge claims, all political and moral commitments, are redundant. Clearly, such a position is antithetical to much of what we have been trying to do in the opening few chapters of this book, for a postmodernist of this ilk would reject the effort to put a rational case for democracy or freedom, or to decide between the liberty claims of liberalism against the equality claims of socialism. As such, postmodernism has been criticized for being overly destructive. As Hay (2002: 217) points out, 'by confining itself to deconstruction postmodernism never risks exposing itself to a similar critique by putting something in place of that it deconstructs'. In other words, postmodernism is criticized for its oppositional nature. In Gamble's words (116) it offers 'no guidance as to what should be done about all the modernist processes which are in full flow'.

We could respond in two ways to this charge. In the first place, we could say that the deconstruction evident in postmodernism is a valid corrective to the certainties illegitimately displayed in much political analysis. It is not the postmodernist's fault that the

Key Concept Box 6.2
Fordism

Refers to a form of large-scale mass-production that is homogeneous both in terms of the products made and also in terms of the repetitive jobs that came with it. The social structure that came with this form of mass-production consisted predominantly of unionized blue-collar workers who lived similar life styles and tended to vote en bloc for left-of-centre parties. It is named after the mass production of cars by the Ford Motor Company in the USA. We are now in a post-Fordist society where the manual working class has declined as a more varied economic structure has emerged.

world is not as modernists paint it to be. In addition, we should be careful about simplifying postmodernism. Hay (2002: 226), for instance, argues that postmodernism can be read in a more sympathetic fashion, as a position which merely questions existing beliefs in a sceptical fashion, rather than ruling them out completely. Indeed, 'postmodernism is perhaps best seen as a heightened sensitivity to the opinions and worldviews of others—a respect for others and other perspectives'.

Key Points

- Postmodernism represents a critique of particular ideologies rather than being an ideology in itself.
- The postmodern attitude points out the necessary limitations in the project of trying to master the nature of reality.
- There is a celebration of diversity and difference.
- Postmodernism has been criticized for being overly destructive without offering any guidance to action.

Feminism

Feminism starts from the assumption that women are oppressed in a variety of ways. It is also argued that political theory has, at least until recently, failed to recognize this fact, or has actively sought to justify it (Pateman, 1988). It has been common since the 1980s to divide feminism into liberal, socialist/Marxist and radical strands, although since then, as Bryson (1999: 8) points out, feminism has further fragmented into a number of different categories, some of which are mentioned below. As a result, 'feminists are profoundly and at times bitterly divided, not only over political priorities and methods, but also over goals' (Bryson, 1999: 5).

➡ See chapter sixteen, page 374, for coverage of feminism's contribution to international relations.

Liberal Feminism

Liberal feminism is often described as 'first wave' feminism in the sense that it was characteristic of feminist thought in the late nineteenth and early twentieth centuries. Its position is that women ought to have the same liberal rights as men in the public sphere, where equality is demanded in the worlds of politics and work. Two key texts of liberal feminism advocating political and legal rights for women are Mary Wollstone-craft's *A Vindication of the Rights of Women*, and J.S. Mill's *The Subjection of Women*, originally published in 1792 and 1869 respectively.

There is no doubt that substantial ground has been made in securing greater equality for women in the public arena. Women have legal and political rights in Western liberal democracies. After ferocious campaigning by the suffrage movement, women in

Photo 6.1
Six policemen successfully arrest one suffrage protester outside Buckingham Palace.
Source: Mary Evans/The Women's Library

Britain were granted the vote in 1918 and on the same terms as men in 1928. Other **liberal democracies** have followed suit.

In the workplace, too, legislative initiatives against sex discrimination, such as the British Equal Pay Act, have helped to equalize male and female pay and working conditions. Marriage laws, too, are much more enlightened, women no longer being regarded as essentially the property of men.

Without doubt, too, however, greater strides are needed in both the workplace and the political arena. Women's representation in the political arena, for instance, still lags far behind men (see Tables 6.1 and 6.2). In addition, despite equal pay legislation, women's average earnings remain less than men's, not least because women do different jobs that tend to be valued less. There is a preponderance of women in part-time and low-paid employment. Moreover, women remain the primary carers and are disadvantaged, and often deeply psychologically affected, by their enforced absence from work (Friedan, 1963). As a result of this continued inequality, some feminists argue for the introduction of measures such as **positive discrimination** designed to redress the unfair competition between men and women.

| Government office-holding 1992, 1997 and 2001 | | | | | |
Election	Governing Party	Office	Women	Men	Women as % of Total
1992	Conservative	Cabinet	2	20	9
		Junior Minister	5	62	7
1997	Labour	Cabinet	5	17	22
		Junior Minister	14	56	20
2001	Labour	Cabinet	7	16	30
		Junior Minister	23	44	34

Table 6.1   The Political Representation of Women in British Government
Source: Duncan Sutherland and Yvonne Galligan, Centre for Advancement of Women in Politics, Queen's University Belfast
www.qub.ac.uk/cawp/UKelectionhtmls/elec-shuffle.html

Liberal feminists, however, still regard the state as the 'proper and indeed the only legitimate authority for enforcing justice in general and women's rights in particular' (Jaggar, 1983: 200). This will be achieved, they argue, through the elimination of sexist attitudes in society, through education, and pressure on the state applied through interest representation and political parties.

Radical Feminism

Radical or 'second wave' feminism is a relatively recent development dating from the 1960s. There are a variety of different interpretations of radical feminism but they all share the position that the exploitation of women is more central and universal than liberal feminists think, and is not merely a product of inequality in the public realm. The crucial point is the identification of a 'patriarchal' basis to society, not just, or most importantly, in the public realm but also in family life and in relationships between men and women at all levels of society. See **Box 6.3**. Men's oppression of women, therefore, is all-pervading (Millett, 1971). Radicals argue, therefore, that 'it is not equality that women should want, but liberation (Hoffman and Graham, 2006: 329).

Some radical feminists, for instance, emphasize the sexual repression of women under **patriarchy,** that women have been effectively 'castrated' by the patriarchal culture which demands that that they be passive and submissive creatures. This was the theme of Germaine Greer's book, *The Female Eunuch,* published in 1970. Women have also suffered actual physical mutilation at the hands of a patriarchal society, not least in the

Rank	Country	Lower or Single House				Upper House or Senate			
		Elections	Seats	Women	% W	Elections	Seats	Women	% W
1	Rwanda	09 2003	80	39	48.8	09 2003	26	9	34.6
2	Sweden	09 2006	349	165	47.3	—	—	—	—
3	Finland	03 2007	200	84	42.0	—	—	—	—
4	Costa Rica	02 2006	57	22	38.6	—	—	—	—
5	Norway	09 2005	169	64	37.9	—	—	—	—
6	Denmark	02 2005	179	66	36.9	—	—	—	—
7	Netherlands	11 2006	150	55	36.7	05 2007	75	26	34.7
8	Cuba	01 2003	609	219	36.0	—	—	—	—
"	Spain	03 2004	350	126	36.0	03 2004	259	60	23.2
9	Mozambique	12 2004	250	87	34.8	—	—	—	—
10	Belgium	06 2007	150	52	34.7	06 2007	71	27	38.0
53	United Kingdom	05 2005	646	127	19.7	N/A	751	142	18.9
68	United States of America	11 2006	435	71	16.3	11 2006	100	16	16.0

Table 6.2 The Political Representation of Women in Parliaments
Source: Inter-Parliamentary Union
www.ipu.org/wmn-e/classif.htm

practice of female infanticide in China and India and female circumcision which still occurs in Africa and the Islamic world where it is estimated 80 million women are affected by it (Goodwin, 2007: 213–14).

Unlike Marxist feminists (see below), radical feminists regard patriarchy as an independent explanatory variable rooted in biology, and not therefore a product of the organization of economic classes in the capitalist system. This gender-based sphere of domination, radical feminists argue, is largely ignored by conventional political theory's focus on the state. As Pateman (1989: 3) points out, 'the public sphere', in conventional political theory 'is assumed to be capable of being understood on its own, as if it existed *sui generis*, independently of private sexual relations and domestic life'. By upholding patriarchal domination in families and **civil society**, the state therefore contributes to gender-based oppression. MacKinnon

Key Quote   Box 6.3
Kate Millett on Patriarchy

'What goes largely unexamined, often even unacknowledged . . . in our social order, is the birthright priority whereby males rule females . . . It is one which tends moreover to be sturdier than any form of segregation, and more rigorous than class stratification . . . However muted its present appearance may be, sexual dominion obtains nevertheless as perhaps the most pervasive ideology of our culture and provides its most fundamental concept of power.' (Millett, 1971: 25)

(1989: 80) puts this eloquently when she writes that: 'However autonomous of class the liberal state may appear, it is not autonomous of sex. Male power is systemic. Coercive, legitimized, and epistemic, it *is* the regime.' The feminist project, therefore, is for this form of oppression to be understood and eliminated. Only then can the state be feminized.

Race, Class, and Feminism

A number of feminist criticisms have been made of this radical strand. One is that by politicizing all aspects of our lives, feminism has **totalitarian** tendencies where 'feminists are to held accountable to their "sisters" for every aspect of their behaviour' (Bryson, 1999: 28). Another is that it, falsely, creates an image of women as helpless victims, and men as the enemy, thus undervaluing what women have achieved and reducing the possibility of utilizing men as supporters of feminism.

Perhaps the most important critique is that radical feminism has a tendency to ignore the oppression of women based on race and class. In terms of the former, it has been argued that feminism has universalized the experiences of white (usually middle class) women, thereby neglecting the specific oppression that women of colour have been subject to. There needs, therefore, to be a greater recognition of the particular experiences of black women whose life experiences cannot be merely subsumed under one all-encompassing feminist critique.

In terms of class, Marxist and social feminists put a different slant on women's exploitation (Mitchell, 1971; Barrett, 1988). The reality of capitalism is that, for both men and women, working life is equally exploitative, particularly for working-class women who, they argue, feminists often ignore. For both men and women, therefore, socialist feminists argue for a transformation of society so that working lives become more amenable and domestic lives cease to have an economic function.

Marxist feminists, in particular, are much less sanguine than the liberal strand about the possibilities of women's position improving through focusing on the state. Here, elements of the Marxist theory of the state are utilized to explain the woman's position. In one influential version of this theory, women's domestic role, where they are subservient to men, is regarded as functional for the smooth running of the capitalist economy, freeing men to work. Thus, the capitalist state has an interest in maintaining women's inferior role

(McIntosh, 1978). Crucially, here, however, the main battle lines are not the state, because the state is merely doing the bidding of the dominant class. This functionalist analysis raises some important questions, common to this type of Marxist analysis. Most notably, what propels the state to act so as to maintain the patriarchal family?

→ See chapter two, page 64, for an exploration of Marxist ideas on power and the state.

The Fragmentation of Feminism

Between liberal and radical feminism and even within the radical camp itself, there has been enormous fragmentation. Disputes have occurred, for instance, over the significance of biological differences, with some (Firestone, 1972) regarding these differences as the source of women's oppression, while others (Pateman, 1989) denying this, some seeking to recapture the importance of motherhood from a feminist viewpoint, and others seeking to emphasize the importance for women to be able to choose not to be mothers. Some feminists have violently opposed pornography (Dworkin, 1981), while other, liberal feminists, have sought to reclaim it for women (McElroy, 1995). Feminists have also differed over the character of political structures, with some wanting separatist, non-hierarchical political structures while others reject this oppositional stance and seek to build alliances with other social groups and participate in conventional political structures even though they are male dominated.

Finally, some feminists have sought to make alliances with postmodernism. Postmodernism, superficially at least, would seem to be a strange bedfellow of feminism, as the former would reject the latter's attempt to universalize a theory which explains the subordination of women. As a result, some prefer to see feminist thought as an offshoot of Enlightenment modernism.

However, postmodernism does offer something of value to feminists. In the first place, it emphasizes difference and variety which suits feminism's attempt to shift attention away from the public to the private realm. Similarly, postmodernism facilitates the differences between men and women to be celebrated, allowing women's separate roles, and values, to be regarded as equally important. It also allows an appreciation of the differences among women based on their class, race, and culture. A postmodern feminism, therefore, recognizes the difficulty of developing one approach with which to challenge a patriarchal society.

Key Points

- Feminism starts from the assumption that women are unequal to men, subject to subordination, at best, and oppression, at worst.
- Feminism is best divided into liberal, socialist, and radical strands.
- Liberal feminism seeks to achieve the same rights for women as possessed by men in the public sphere.
- Significant progress has been made in the securing of liberal rights for women, although this should not be exaggerated.

- Socialist feminists insist that more attention should be placed on working-class women whose plight is inextricably linked to the existence of the capitalist system.
- Radical feminism seeks to focus attention on patriarchal relationships in the private sphere.
- Feminist thought has undergone a great deal of fragmentation with differences evident over motherhood, pornography, political strategy, and the value of postmodernism.

Environmentalism

Concern for the natural environment is not a new phenomenon. Legislation designed to control pollution, for instance, dates back to the nineteenth century and there are probably earlier examples than this. As a distinctive issue, however, the environment did not really exist until the 1970s, and it did not become a mainstream issue for another decade. The rise of environmentalism is partly a consequence of the existence of severe objective environmental problems; the effects of air pollution, the use of pesticides in agriculture, the depletion of non-renewable resources, the extinction of many species of plants and animals, and the more recent problems of ozone depletion and climate change. A number of international gatherings—those at Stockholm in 1972 and the Earth Summit at Rio twenty years later being the most symbolic—helped to establish the state of the environment as a key issue of our time, albeit one that rarely has an impact on national elections.

Ideologically, environmental thought can be divided into two main categories. On the one hand is the reformist approach (sometimes described as light green or shallow environmentalism). On the other is the radical (dark green or deep) approach. For some political theorists, only the latter can be properly described as an ideology (Dobson, 2007). To distinguish the two, one might refer to the former as environmentalism and the latter as **ecologism**. Environmentalism can be seen, then, as a single-issue concern not necessarily inconsistent with a range of ideologies, whereas ecologism is a separate ideology with a set of distinct ideas. The differences between the two can be illustrated if we examine their major characteristics.

The Economic Realm

One major distinction between reformist and radical accounts is their approach to economic growth. Radical greens see economic growth as incompatible with environmental protection. The aversion to economic growth is partly a normative claim, that individuals will lead much more fulfilled lives in a non-materialistic society. It is primarily, however, an empirical claim, that there are natural limits to growth, and unless production and consumption levels and population size are reduced to sustainable levels, then economic and political collapse will be the result.

This empirical claim received its impetus from a report by a group of American scientists published as *The Limits to Growth* (Meadows, 1972). The report was based on a series of computer runs which factored in potential solutions to a range of environmental problems while growth in the other variables stayed the same. At each step, the authors argued, the solution did not solve the need for a cut in economic growth to forestall environmental degradation. Their conclusion was that if we failed to cut economic activity, then the point of no return would be reached not far into the current (twenty-first) century.

There have been many criticisms of the Limits to Growth report (Martell, 1994: 33–40). Not least, it has been suggested that there is no necessary trade-off between economic growth and environmental protection. This reformist challenge is based on the assertion that provided that growth is sustainable, then it is permissible from an environmental perspective. Sustainable development is therefore the centrepiece of a reformist alternative. There have been numerous definitions of **sustainable development** the best known defining it as development that 'meets the needs of the present generation without compromising the ability of future generations to meet their own needs' (World Commission on Environment and Development, 1987).

Sustainable development is notoriously vague. A more precise formulation is the principle known as **ecological modernization** (Hajer, 1997) which suggests a number of ways in which growth can be sustainable. First, growth need not necessarily occur through the use of non-renewable resources such as coal and gas. The use of renewable energy, such as wind and wave power (and even nuclear power), coupled with energy conservation, can ensure that growth remains sustainable. Secondly, the production of environmental goods—such as, for example, catalytic converters for cars or scrubs removing the pollution from power stations—can itself be a source of economic growth. Finally, it is argued that environmental damage is not cost-free economically, so that protecting the environment can be consistent with economic growth. This is the major finding of a 2006 British Government report—chaired by Sir Nicholas Stern—on climate change. Stern estimates that if temperatures rise by 5°C, up to 10 per cent of global output could be lost, and the poorest countries would lose more than 10 per cent of their output.

The Philosophical Realm

Reformists (and indeed all of the ideologies we have encountered in this chapter and the last) adopt an **anthropocentric**—or human-centred—view of the world. See **Box 6.4**. As a result, the value of non-**human nature** is extrinsic to us. We protect the environment, in other words, because it is in our interests to do so and not because we think that nature has any worthwhile interests of its own. Some radical greens, on the other hand, adopt what has been called an **ecocentric** ethic (Leopold, 1949; Fox, 1995; Eckersley, 1992). This position accords intrinsic value to both humans and to non-human parts of nature. In other words, nature has moral worth independently of human beings.

The difficulties of justifying philosophically an ecocentric ethic are considerable. For many philosophers, sentiency—or the capacity to experience pain and pleasure—is the key benchmark for moral standing. It is easy to see why damaging the interests of a human or an animal matters to her, but it is more difficult to see why damaging a tree

Key Concept Box 6.4
Anthropocentrism

Refers to a human-centred ethic where humans are regarded as having intrinsic value and non-humans have only extrinsic value. Anthropocentrism is challenged by those who want to include non-human animals as morally considerable because of their sentientcy, and also by ecocentric thinkers who regard the whole of nature as worthy of moral standing.

matters to the tree. We can clearly negatively affect a tree's interests but, following Frey (1983: 154–5), it does not seem sensible to talk about wronging the tree. Thus, polluting a river is to harm it but since the river only has extrinsic value for those sentient beings who benefit from it, it is only they who can be wronged by polluting the river.

The key question would seem to be whether establishing an ecocentric ethic is important in terms of protecting the environment. Increasingly, green thinkers argue that there are sufficient prudential grounds for protecting nature (Barry, 1999). To give

Case Study Box 6.5
Whaling and Environmental Ethics

The issue of whaling provides an interesting case study of environmental ethics in action. In 1946, the International Whaling Commission (IWC) was set up by the whaling nations (most notably Japan, Norway, and Iceland) in order to regulate whaling. The aim was to protect whale stocks so that they could continue to be hunted. The motivation behind this move, then, was clearly anthropocentric. Whales were regarded as a human resource and their value was merely extrinsic to the humans who benefited from products that derived from their capture. Such was the scale of hunting that in 1986 a moratorium on commercial whaling was introduced to try to prevent a number of whale species from becoming extinct.

Protecting the whale became an important part of the environmental movement in the 1970s. The symbol of Greenpeace activists risking their lives by sailing close to whaling ships in order to obtain documentary evidence had a significant impact on western public opinion. By the 1980s, the whaling nations were becoming outnumbered in the deliberations of the IWC and repeated attempts to restart commercial whaling since then have been resisted. The whaling nations, quite consistently with their ethical position, have argued that since whale stocks have recovered, they should be allowed to resume commercial whaling. The nations opposing this adopt a very different ethic. With the backing of public opinion, they object to whaling, not primarily because it is unsustainable, but because the practice is cruel and infringes the interests of whales. In other words, they regard whales as having intrinsic value that ought to be taken into account. As a result, the debate is unlikely to be resolved amicably because the two sides are arguing past each other.

an example, we should protect forests not because forests have intrinsic value but because it is in our interests to do so, not least because they provide crucial sinks for carbon dioxide and therefore help to control rises in the temperature of the planet. See **Box 6.5**.

The Political Realm

There is now a considerable body of green political thought (Dobson, 2007). For reformists, environmental solutions can coexist with existing political structures. By contrast, radicals argue that in order for environmental objectives to be achieved it is necessary for far-reaching social and political change. There is a division of opinion, however, on what change is necessary. In the so-called 'survivalist' literature, principally from the 1970s, there is an **authoritarian** strain. Most famous here is the work of Garrett Hardin (1968). Hardin argued that, left to their own devices, people will always despoil the environment through greed and naivety. Humans, therefore, need to be directed by a strong state, not least in reproduction habits. This authoritarian strain (seen also in the writings of Heilbroner, 1974 and Ophuls, 1973) raises question marks about the utility of democracy for environmentalism.

Most radical greens now advocate decentralized small-scale, self-sufficient anarchist-type communities linked together by loose authority structures (Schumacher, 1973; Bookchin, 1971). Despite their ability to reduce or eliminate large-scale industrial production, to enable people to be closer to nature, and to facilitate political participation and social cohesion, the environmental utility of these loose alliances has been questioned by some green thinkers (Goodin, 1992). At a time when international agreements are seen as essential for effective environmental protection, and yet difficult to achieve in the existing state system, the ability of a range of diverse range of small, self-governing communities to ensure effective coordination is, at the very least, problematic.

Finally, in the political realm, the question of **agency** has been raised. Which social class or grouping is most likely to act as the harbinger of change? A variety of candidates have been suggested, ranging from the middle class (Porritt, 1984) to the unemployed (Gorz, 1985). The issue of agency is linked to questions of justice, since those worst affected by environmental degradation are the very same people one might expect to campaign for action to deal with it. This is the rationale of the environmental justice movement which exists, in particular in the USA. Of course, justice remains separate from practical politics, and this is particularly the case for ecocentric thinkers who seek to attach moral worth to non-humans, who lack the ability to secure their own liberation.

A Distinct Ideology?

It needs to be asked, finally, how far radical environmentalism or ecologism represents a distinct ideology, separate from the other ideologies we have considered. A quick glance at the literature reveals that a number of traditional ideological positions have sought to claim environmentalism for themselves. Thus, there are works of eco-socialism (Pepper, 1993), eco-liberalism (Wissenburg, 1993), and eco-feminism (Mellor, 1982). There is even an attempt to claim the green label for fascism (Bramwell, 1989.).

On the other hand, the existence of separate Green political parties throughout the world suggests that ecologists regard their position as distinct. Clearly, the limits to growth position adds an extra dimension to political thinking. In particular, it challenges the shared optimistic vision that liberals, socialists, and Marxists have about the ability of humans to master their environment for their own infinite economic ends. Similarly distinct is the ecocentric ethic adopted by some radical greens. All traditional ideologies are incorruptibly anthropocentric in orientation, regarding the natural world as a resource for humans to exploit.

Ecology is less distinct in its political orientation. Here, it borrows from other traditions of thought—from the authoritarian implications of Hobbes' *Leviathan* to the participatory democracy of Rousseau, and the lack of hierarchy advocated by **anarchism**. In so far as these political positions are recommended for the achievement of environmental objectives there is a case for saying that they are being used in distinctive ways, but, as we have seen, there is no one favoured political position for ecologists.

Key Points

- The rise of environmentalism has been, partly at least, the product of severe environmental problems.
- Environmental thinkers can be divided into radical and reformist camps.
- In economic terms, the radicals support a limit to growth while the reformists advocate a version of sustainable development.
- In philosophic terms, the radicals hold an ecocentric ethic while the reformists hold an anthropocentric ethic.
- In political terms, radicals advocate far-reaching change while the reformist position can coexist with a variety of ideological positions.
- In its economic and political guises there is a case for saying that environmentalism is a distinct ideology, but this is less clear-cut in terms of political structures.

Multiculturalism

Multiculturalism has emerged as a direct challenge to those nationalists who desire to create distinct states based on ethnicity, and the traditional model of **citizenship**, associated above all with the work of T.H. Marshall (1950) which emphasized the need to 'promote a...common national identity among citizens' (Kymlicka, 2002: 327). By contrast, multiculturalism seeks to advocate pluralistic states based on many different religious, cultural, and ethnic identities. It has become a particularly pressing issue, in theory and practice, precisely because modern societies have become increasingly multicultural in a factual sense. The two key questions we will consider here are, first, what is the correct ideological location for multiculturalism, and, secondly, is it a positive or negative phenomenon?

Multiculturalism and Ideology

Initially, before the 1990s, multiculturalism was seen by political theorists as particularly aligned with **communitarianism**. As we saw in chapter one, communitarianism, by focusing on group rights and community cohesion and identity, is a direct challenge to the liberal focus on the autonomous individual. As Kymlicka (2002: 337) points out 'Communitarians . . . view multiculturalism as an appropriate way of protecting communities from the eroding effects of individual autonomy, and of affirming the value of community'.

➜ See chapter one, page 41, for a discussion of communitarianism.

This opposition between multiculturalism and liberalism might strike the reader as somewhat odd. After all, the liberal emphasis on the neutral state, the reluctance of liberals to countenance interfering in competing conceptions of the good (seen most notably in the later political philosophy of John Rawls), and the liberal focus on the protection of minority rights, would seem to equate liberalism with multiculturalism. This is particularly the case when one considers that liberalism emerged as a defence of religious toleration. It is not surprising, therefore, that, since the 1980s, liberals have sought to accommodate multiculturalism.

However, this accommodation presents problems for liberals. There is a potential conflict between liberal values and the upholding of minority cultural rights when the latter involves the infringing of individual rights. Thus, it would be odd for liberals to sanction illiberal practices such as forced marriages, confining women to the home, and, even worse, female circumcision (or, to be more accurate, female genital mutilation), all issues which have troubled feminists, as well as removing children from public education and apostasy (the practice of preventing individuals from rejecting a particular faith).

One way out of this dilemma for liberals is to offer limited support for multiculturalism, affirming it only when it does not involve the infringement of individual rights (Kymlicka, 2002: 340–1). Rawls (1993) essentially does this by arguing that liberals can only accept a 'reasonable pluralism', thereby not forcing it into a position where it is has to accept the moral legitimacy, say, of slavery. Kymlicka (1995) wants to go further than Rawls in a multicultural direction by arguing that the degree to which we should expect different cultures to assimilate depends upon how the minority group's position is established. Thus, refugees, and those who have chosen to emigrate, should be prepared to assimilate, whereas in the case of indigenous national minorities who have not chosen to be cultural minorities, such as the Australian aborigines and the American Indian tribes, more effort should be made to permit differentiated rights, even when they conflict with liberal principles.

While we may think that Kymlicka's principle has a great deal of validity, it is somewhat arbitrary, and it is debatable how far it remains consistent with liberal values. Others either reject multiculturalism or reject liberalism. The best example of the former is the political theorist Brian Barry (2001), who has doubts about the value of multiculturalism because it is a threat to liberal values. On the other hand, some political theorists argue that a convincing multiculturalism must go beyond the liberal objection to the infringement of individual rights, since the liberal multiculturalism of those such as Rawls and Kymlicka is heavily weighted toward liberalism. Parekh (2000), for instance, argues that we should adopt a much more pluralistic morality and be prepared to jettison liberalism when it conflicts with multiculturalism. This has the effect of offering a separate ideological status for multiculturalism, separate from liberalism and communitarianism.

Is Multiculturalism a Good Thing?

A related question is whether multiculturalism is a positive principle that we ought to adopt. This has become an issue of some political saliency, particularly in the context of 9/11, and the Islamic terrorism in Britain carried out by British citizens. Multiculturalism has been challenged primarily because of a concern for social unity, and a feeling that it is 'corrosive of long-term political unity and social stability' (Kymlicka, 2002: 366). It is for this reason that France, among European states, practises the most insistent policy of assimilation, which has caused particular controversy in the case of the wearing of religious dress. In addition, as we have indicated, the danger of moral pluralism is that it allows for the potential infringement of individual rights.

In defence of multiculturalism, it offers a solution to the inevitable cultural diversity present in modern societies. There is 'remarkably little evidence' that multiculturalism leads to social conflict. Indeed, it might be regarded as a force for social inclusion since allowing minority cultural groups to practise their differences is more likely to make them feel positive towards, and included within, the society in which they live (Kymlicka, 2002: 367). Moreover, cultural diversity brings a richness to otherwise homogeneous lives, encourages toleration of difference, and allows individuals to generate a sense of belonging. Rejecting different approaches to life, as some liberals would seem to be suggesting, also suggests an arrogance and infallibility which many argue is not justified.

Key Points

- Multiculturalism seeks to promote pluralistic states based on many different religious, cultural, and ethnic identities.
- Multiculturalism was initially aligned with communitarianism but was later adopted by liberals.
- The liberal advocacy of multiculturalism is problematic because of the need to sanction practices within minority cultures that are illiberal.

- Some liberals seek to reject multiculturalism on the grounds that it can be illiberal, others seek to qualify their support while others, writing from outside of the liberal tradition, argue that liberalism ought to be sacrificed in favour of multiculturalism.

- Multiculturalism has been attacked for its divisive nature and the potential for the infringement of liberal principles. Others defend it as one means of accommodating diversity and the very richness diversity brings.

Religious Fundamentalism

Religion is not ideological insofar as it remains a private concern among individuals and groups. It becomes ideological if it seeks to organize political principles along religious lines, and seeks political influence or power in order to achieve it. There are, of course, many instances in world history of religion playing a political role, not least the European conflicts between Catholics and Protestants in the sixteenth and seventeenth centuries.

Since then, however, many societies, influenced by the Lockean principle of religious toleration, have separated the church from the state, not least in the USA, where it is enshrined in the Constitution. In these secular regimes, religion becomes a private pursuit not impinging on the public realm, and the state remains neutral between competing faiths, providing that the practices of any one of them do not infringe the rights of any citizen, and even then there may be exceptions. Despite this, there are many contemporary examples of conflicts centring on religion, such as Northern Ireland (between Protestants and Catholics), particularly in the 1970s, Iraq (between Sunni and Shia Muslims) since the American and British invasion, and Darfur in the Sudan (between Muslims and Christians). As Goodwin (2007: 427) states 'religious differences have, for millennia, led to a waste of human life and to the undermining of the imperatives of human toleration'.

The fundamentalist religious strands, which became current in the twentieth century, are ideological precisely because they do seek to enter the political realm. To be a fundamentalist is to be convinced of the truth of the doctrine one is professing (in the case of religious fundamentalism based on an interpretation of a sacred text), and to seek to ensure that these truths are adopted by the state, even by the use of force and violence. Such is the publicity given to it that when we think of religious fundamentalism, the Islamic variety comes easily to mind. Indeed, the scholar Samuel Huntington (1996) has argued, in a controversial study, that we are now faced by a 'clash of civilisations' in which societies upholding Western values are under attack from non-Western civilizations, and particularly those dominated by Islam. So much, then, for the end of history thesis.

A number of important caveats need to made about fundamentalism in general, and religious fundamentalism in particular. First, most Muslims, Christians, and Jews are tolerant and peaceable and are content to allow for religion to remain separate from politics. In Turkey, for instance, the Islamic government has tried to combine Islam with a secular political framework. All religions—Christianity, Islam, Judaism, Hinduism, Sikhism, and even Buddhism—have their fundamentalist elements, although, by and large, they remain in a minority (Heywood, 2007: 281). Therefore, it is preferable, as one critique of Huntington has suggested, to talk about a clash between fundamentalist Muslims and fundamentalist Christians rather than a 'clash of civilisations' (Ali, 2002).

It might also be argued that fundamentalism is not limited to religion; that all ideologies have their fundamentalist elements. The obvious candidates here would be the Stalinist version of Communism and fascism in interwar Germany and Italy; but even liberalism can be said to be fundamentalist about its belief in the value of liberty, something which must be protected at all costs.

The characteristic of Islamic fundamentalism is its desire to create a theocracy (a regime based on religious principles). It is undoubtedly a potent religious force, particularly in Africa and the Middle East, receiving a fillip when the Shah of Iran was deposed by an Islamic fundamentalist regime led by Ayatollah Khomeini in 1979. Following on from the Muslim Brotherhood, formed in Egypt in 1928, a number of new militant Islamic groups have emerged, most notably Al Qaeda (literally 'the base') formed by Osama bin Laden in Afghanistan in 1988, and held responsible for the attacks on the Twin Towers in New York and the Pentagon in Washington on 11 September 2001.

In some senses Islamic fundamentalism is opposed to modernity. Thus, it is virulently anti-democrat and morally conservative, regarding modern Western values as corrupt and licentious. Nevertheless, it is 'best described . . . as a modern movement opposed to modernity' (Hoffman and Graham, 2006: 397). This is because Islamic fundamentalists (and those of the Christian variety too) have not been slow in using modern communication devices, such as the Internet, to propagate their cause and mobilize activists. It is noticeable, too, that an Islamic regime such as Iran is fully prepared to use the benefits of scientific research, as in the case of nuclear weapons' technology, to defend itself against perceived threats from the West.

As with all fundamentalist groups, the certainty of Islamic fundamentalist group's beliefs is infectious and leads to a 'capacity to generate activism and mobilize the faithful' (Heywood, 2007: 289), although it is also true that its strength derives from social and economic circumstances, often coupled with the mistakes of existing non-fundamentalist elites. Thus, rightly or wrongly, it has been claimed that the Islamic terrorist threat has been largely provoked by the response of the USA, itself influenced by its own fundamentalism, hence the label the clash of fundamentalisms.

Given that Christianity is the world's biggest religion, it would be surprising if it did not have a fundamentalist element. Christian fundamentalism is particularly associated with the Christian New Right that emerged in the USA in the 1970s. There are a range of loosely attached groupings, perhaps the best known being the Moral Majority, led by the Reverend Jerry Falwell. There has been no attempt to establish a theocracy. Instead, the Christian New Right has sought to campaign for conservative moral values—particularly against the rights given to particular social groups, such as blacks, feminists, and the gay rights movement—and against abortion.

Christian fundamentalists have sometimes resorted to violence, particularly against the staff and clients of abortion clinics, and sometimes against the intrusion of the public sector in general, such as in the Oklahoma bombing in 1995. More usually, however, Christian fundamentalists have sought to influence Republican politicians, usually through the financing of campaigns. Major progress was made by the election of Ronald Reagan in 1980 and—after the secular presidencies of George Bush Senior and Bill Clinton—George Bush Junior who is, himself, a born-again Christian.

Key points

- Religion becomes ideological if it becomes embroiled in politics.
- Religious fundamentalism can be characterized by its intention of organizing politics along religious lines.
- Not all Muslims are fundamentalists, and fundamentalism occurs in all religions and, arguably, in all ideologies.
- Religious fundamentalists, of the Muslim and Christian varieties, are anti-modernist in the sense of being morally conservative and, in the case of the former, anti-democratic too, but they are also modernist in the sense that they utilize modern communication media and campaigning strategies.

Conclusion

Whereas the ideologies we discussed in chapter five were focused on the state, the ideologies in this chapter represent a challenge to the state. This is seen first in the greater emphasis on the supranational dimension observed, in particular, in environmentalism, multiculturalism, and religious fundamentalism (Hoffman and Graham, 2006: 317–18). All have been impacted on by the phenomenon of **globalization**, a central theme of this book. The new ideologies are also a product of social and economic change, centring in particular on the decline of class as a major fault-line in world politics. This has resulted, as Goodwin (2007: 425) notes, in the 'rise of ideas and ideologies which transcend classes but focus on other group characteristics such as ethnicity, gender or religion'. Finally, environmentalism is a product of the objectively deteriorating state of the natural environment coupled with rising affluence. All of this has resulted in an ideological world which, while more dynamic and pluralistic, is less sure of itself and more open to change.

The final point to make is that the traditional ideologies considered in chapter five have responded to the challenges presented by those examined in this chapter. We have seen, for instance, how liberalism and socialism have contributed to the debate about feminism, environmentalism, and multiculturalism. Indeed, it is not clear, in the case of the latter two at least, how far they exist as distinct ideologies, rather than as particular issues to which the traditional ideologies have responded. All of this suggests that the modernist project, while not in rude health, has some life left in it.

Key Questions

- Account for the emergence of challenges to the traditional ideologies.
- What has been the impact of postmodernism on ideologies?
- Has feminism achieved its objectives?
- Does feminism have a theory of the state?
- Is there a distinct ideology of environmentalism?
- How justifiable is a non-anthropocentric ethic?
- Is multiculturalism consistent with liberalism?
- What are the strengths and weaknesses of multiculturalism?
- Under what circumstances does religion become ideological?
- Is modernism dead?

 Further Reading

Bryson, V. (2003), *Feminist Political Theory: An Introduction*, Basingstoke: Palgrave, 2nd edn.
This is an excellent introduction.

Dobson, A. (2007), *Green Political Thought*, London: Unwin Hyman, 4th edn.
This is the standard introduction to the subject.

Gray, J. (2003), *Al Qaeda and What it Means to be Modern*, London: Faber & Faber.
This is a typically incisive account of religious fundamentalism by a key thinker.

Kymlicka, W. (2002), *Contemporary Political Philosophy*, Oxford: Oxford University Press, 2nd edn, ch. 8.
This covers the multicultural debate in which he is a key participant.

Moussalli, A. (ed.) (1998), *Islamic Fundamentalism*, Reading: Ithaca Press.
This is a good collection of articles by leading experts in the field.

 Web Links

www.ipu.org/wmn-e/classif.htm
For information on women's political representation.

www.erraticimpact.com/~ecologic/
For a list of environmental links.

http://multiculturalism.aynrand.org/
A website against multiculturalism.

 Visit the **Online Resource Centre** that accompanies this book to access more learning resources at **www.oxfordtextbooks.co.uk/orc/garner/**

Part 2

Comparative Politics

by Peter Ferdinand

The next seven chapters move the focus from political theory to political institutions, from more normative to more empirical analysis. Yet this does not mean that ideas and theories, including normative ones, are less important: no study of political institutions can ignore the basic issues of political power, how it is distributed within particular states, and how it affects the distribution of resources. Democracy—how it operates and the forms that it takes, whether liberal or illiberal—will also be a recurring theme.

Normative ideas, however, are not the only type of theory to which the next chapters will introduce you. Studies of institutions are generally based upon some kind of theory that generalizes their functioning. Indeed, that is what legitimizes their study as part of the social sciences. The goal of social sciences is to go beneath the surface of empirical reality and identify underlying general trends and patterns. Knowing about particular political institutions or sets of them is only part of the objective and doing so properly is clearly essential, but locating them within a broader pattern of regularities is equally important and ultimately more satisfying. These sorts of issue provoke questions such as: why do parties exist? Is it possible to identify general patterns of their interactions? What general principles underlie electoral systems? How can we explain the behaviour of interest groups? And, more generally, how do we generalize the decisions of innumerable individuals to involve themselves in politics and to do so in particular ways? Do rational choice theories adequately explain this, or should we look elsewhere? Some of these concepts can be as essentially contested as more normative ones. What is meant by 'the state'? Or 'civil society'? Or 'political culture'? A great deal of the argument in the following chapters is structured around the different and competing understandings of these terms.

While many of these sorts of theory are easily classified as obviously 'political', this does not mean that insights from other disciplines are excluded. Politics is not a subject that seeks to explain social reality solely from within its own paradigms. It unselfconsciously borrows from other disciplines too. The next seven chapters—and also the subsequent ones on international relations—will deliberately seek to integrate insights from other disciplines. One to which we shall repeatedly return is the study of history. We shall highlight the need for a long historical perspective on the rise of the state in Europe and its spread around the world, as well as the spread of the European state system to cover the globe. Without this basis it is impossible to understand why states around the world now fairly closely resemble each other in terms of structures, or why they interact now in the ways that they do. Other disciplines also cast useful light on political phenomena. Economics plays a big role in explaining the allocation of resources within and between states. Law, too, is important for understanding the place of constitutions, the justice system, and lawyers in the structure of taking and implementing political decisions; and sociology contributes a great deal to our understanding of the relationship between classes and ethnic communities on the one hand, and the decisions taken by political authorities on the other.

Lastly let us emphasize the comparative approach. This book deliberately sets out to introduce you to politics from all regions of the world. A great many political studies concentrate on Europe and the USA. Many students become passionately interested in them. Therefore, later chapters outline the reasons why political parties emerged in the USA, and contrast the different approaches to policy making in the UK and France. Other students are more attracted to politics in the developing world or in other regions. This is an equally legitimate object of study. We discuss Islamic understandings of justice, the problems of the African state, and the debate over the merits of presidentialism in Latin America and the Philippines. What is vital is that we use consistent and compatible approaches to the analysis of institutions, whether in the developed or the developing world, so that we can identify similarities and differences in the ways in which apparently similar institutions operate in different parts of the world. There is no doubt that general institutions such as the state, political parties, or civil society look different when they are studied in Europe or the USA, as compared with other regions of the world. We want to encourage you to develop a sophisticated understanding of the similarities and the differences, their strengths and weaknesses.

Chapter seven will analyse the emergence and spread of the modern state. Chapter eight will look at constitutions, the relationship between law and politics, and federalism. Chapter nine will concentrate on legislatures. Chapter ten will turn to bureaucracies and policy making. Chapter eleven will deal with elections and political parties. Chapter twelve will look at political activity around the core institutions: civil society, interest groups, the media, and the impact of new technologies such as the Internet. Finally, chapter thirteen will discuss the significance of political culture.

Institutions and States

Reader's Guide

This is the first in a series of chapters that change the focus of analysis to domestic institutions. Political scientists spend a great deal of time analysing the behaviour of institutions and theorizing about them. All the social sciences do. This chapter will first introduce you to the concept of institutions and then different factors that structure political behaviour. Then it will present the multifaceted concept of the state. After that will come a brief historical account of the ways that the European type of state and the European state system spread around the world between the seventeenth and twentieth centuries. This will lead on to a discussion of the modern state, and some of the differences between them—strong states, weak states, and democratic states—before offering a conclusion.

Institutions

Institutions are essentially regular patterns of behaviour that provide stability and predictability to social life. Some are informal in that they have no formally laid down rules—the family, social classes, kinship groups, and such. Individuals internalize 'codes of behaviour' from them as a result of socialization, by example or out of conviction. Others are more formalized, having codified rules and organization—governments, parties, bureaucracies, legislatures, constitutions, law courts. Institutions structure the behaviour of individuals and groups. In that sense they are constraints. On the other hand, they serve as resources for the knowledgeable who navigate their way through them to achieve desired outcomes. Thus, institutions are both constraints and resources.

Students of politics tend to concentrate more upon formal institutions, which form political systems. This is especially true of those who work on Western political systems, where such institutions dominate political life. They try to identify the regular processes of change that are intrinsic to the system itself or to parts of it. Sometimes they claim to have identified regularities that can be elevated to the level of 'laws', as in the natural sciences. One example, to which we shall return in chapter eleven, concerns **Duverger's Law.** This stated that first-past-the-post electoral systems produce two-party systems. At the same time, however, political studies also focus on the environment in which these systems are situated. Any political system may be buffeted by pressures arising either in the society surrounding it, or in the international arena. This may lead to disruption or even break-down, in the form of revolutions; but in most cases, states adapt to these challenges. Political scientists attempt to identify regular patterns of adaptation as a way of generalizing more widely about the behaviour of political institutions.

➜ See chapter eleven, page 266, for a discussion of Duverger's Law.

As Steinmo put it: 'Institutions define the rules of the political game and as such they define who can play and how they play. Consequently, they ultimately can shape who wins and who loses' (Steinmo, 2001: 7555).

It is, however, important also to grasp the relationship between political institutions and the surrounding environment of other political, social, and economic forces. We will use a simplified version of structuration theory, originally formulated by Giddens, to clarify these relationships. He distinguished between 'system', 'structure', and 'structuration' (Giddens, 1979: 66). We will adapt the term 'system' to mean 'political system'. We will use the term 'structure' to mean 'political institution'. And **structuration** will refer to the complex of factors that both constrain and also provide resources for changes in the operation of institutions and the system as a whole. These can range from levels of economic development, through regional or class group activity, to the behaviour of individual political actors. In studies of politics, as in the social sciences more generally, it is rarely the case that big events or changes can be attributed to a single factor. Most political decisions are the product of the interaction of several factors. It is the relative weight of these factors that determines the specific outcome. Thus, explanation of causation is a matter of judgement.

At this point it is important to introduce another basic distinction from the categories used in studies of politics to explain political events: 'structure' versus 'agency'. Here, what is meant by 'structure' is the impact of the particular configuration of institutions. To what extent did they determine the outcome, or at least predispose a particular outcome? Sometimes this is presented in terms of 'path-determined' outcomes. The contrast is with 'agency', i.e. the effect of actions by one or more agents, whether individuals or groups of them. Since politics is a social activity, it is very rarely the case that a particular political outcome was absolutely determined by structure alone. Nor is it the case that agents have complete freedom. Their options are always constrained by structures of one kind or another.

➜ See chapter twenty for an exploration of the relationship between the state and economic institutions.

7

Key Points

- Institutions play a vital role in structuring political behaviour.
- Political, economic, and social factors all provide structuration in political life and determine particular outcomes.
- 'Structure' and 'agency' perform complementary and contrasting functions in determining outcomes.

States

Chapter one outlined the concept of the **state**, as well as some of its ambiguities. Let us recall the definition that was given there: 'the state is sovereign, its institutions are public, it is based upon being legitimate, it is in the business of domination, and it covers a particular territorial area.' To this let us add one other characteristic that will be elaborated more in chapter eight. In addition to their monopoly on the means of violence, states, especially modern states, also claim a monopoly on law-making. Pre-modern societies evolved binding rules for their members through a variety of means: edicts of rulers, clan or family traditions, religious prescriptions, and so on. They also often allowed a variety of agencies to enforce them. Modern states, however, claim the sole right to formulate laws and they insist that state courts enforce them.

At its most general the state becomes a synonym for the structure of rule and authority within a particular geographical area. It is abstract. 'In some important senses, the state is more an idea held in common by a group of people, than it is a physical organism' (Buzan, 1991: 63). We talk of the nation-state, the welfare state, and so on.

Yet there is another, more limited and more concrete use of the term. This is used to designate the apparatus of institutions and individuals who are responsible for managing public affairs. It includes executives, legislatures, courts of justice, the armed forces, central and local officials. This apparatus also collects revenue to pay for the services that it provides, whether through taxes or other forms of contributions. This use of the term is easier to grasp, but the overlap between the two levels of meaning of the term 'state' complicates the individual's relationship with the state. As Edelman wrote over forty years ago: 'The state benefits and it threatens. Now it is "us" and often it is "them". It is an abstraction, but in its name men are jailed or made rich on … defense contracts, or killed in wars' (Edelman, 1964: 1). Commentators may alternate between the two and it is important always to keep this in mind. Most of this chapter will concentrate on the more organizational features of the state, although you should not forget the broader usage of the term. We shall return to the ambiguity of the concept of the state towards the end of this chapter when we raise the issue of the meaning of the term 'democratic state'.

The rest of this chapter will focus first on the rise of the European state and then its proliferation across the world with the spread of the European state system. After that will follow a discussion of the modern state, of strong and weak states, and finally a discussion of the democratic state.

In more distant times there was a much greater variety of forms of rule in tribes and small communities around the world. The antecedents for European ideas on government are to be found in writings from classical Greece and Rome, including the idea of democracy, and they were revived during the Renaissance after centuries of oblivion. However, the modern European state emerged gradually between the seventeenth and nineteenth centuries. And then, as we shall see, it spread to other parts of the world. Although there certainly were alternative forms of rule in other parts of the world that preceded it, e.g. the imperial system of classical China, modern states in other parts of the world display key features that make them more similar to the European model than their own historical predecessors.

Key Point

- The term 'the state' is used in a great variety of ways, some concrete and some abstract. This makes detailed analysis difficult and contentious.

The Rise of the European State

→ See chapter one, page 26, for an exploration of different theoretical conceptions of the state.

The first thing to note is the growth of state capacity over the last three centuries—a key fact that has already been mentioned in chapter one and to which we will return again in chapter twenty. In chapter one we introduced you to the theoretical concept of the state. Here we will focus more upon its historical evolution. As Tilly put it, over the last 1,000 years the European state has evolved from being a wasp to being a locomotive (Tilly, 1990: 96). By this he meant that the state has evolved from a small inconvenience to the people that it ruled into becoming a powerful driver of social and economic development. As we will show in more detail in chapter fourteen, the origins of the modern state are to be found in Europe as it emerged between the seventeenth and the nineteenth centuries. Up until then, it was impossible to separate the personality of the state from the personality of the ruler. The ruler used personal appointees as officials to run the affairs of state. The ruler was also responsible for paying them and although some states did impose taxes, a great deal of the upkeep of officials came from the ruler's own property and income. A salaried bureaucracy began to emerge, and one of its most important functions was to collect and administer taxes. Gradually what emerged was a system for extracting taxes from broader sections of property owners, especially to pay for the most expensive state activity, which was warfare. Protracted wars risked bankrupting a monarch. As Tilly put it: 'War made the state and the state made war' (Tilly, 1975: 42). Time and again the need to raise funds for fighting drove further governments to devise new ways of raising money. The USA, for instance, introduced income tax in 1861 to pay for the effort of the civil war. Gradually this capacity, allied with access to a modernizing and industrializing commercial economy and a large rural population, enabled some states to dominate others (Tilly, 1990: 15). They in turn became the models with which others had to deal and, if possible, surpass.

The French Revolution transformed the powers of the state, as it introduced a level form of taxation for all its citizens and the principle of the modern mass army. This enabled the French for a while to dominate continental Europe. Britain was forced to emulate it so as to resist it. By the beginning of the nineteenth century, as Hegel recognized, the bureaucracy itself had become the state, elevating itself high above and separate from the rest of society (van Creveld, 1999: 143). This was a decisive development. First, what was expected from state officials was a primary loyalty to the state and the public good, rather than to any individual monarch or section of society. Then, secondly, they evolved rules and patterns of administration that further separated them from the rest of society. Later, Weber publicized the importance of the new bureaucratic form of public administration: impersonal, rule-based, goal-oriented activity, with promotion of officials exclusively based on merit and performance. He made it into an ideal type of social organization, which he identified, not without misgivings, as part of a process of ever-growing rationalization of social life. He emphasized the technical superiority of bureaucratic over any other form of organization. Subsequent commentators have coined the term 'Weberian' public administration to denote this type of organization.

In addition, in the eighteenth and nineteenth centuries, the economic and military might of the dominant European powers, reinforced by superior technology, enabled them to develop **empires** overseas. This spread the European type of state to other continents through colonies, albeit in a cut-down version. Administration in colonies was always more rudimentary than in the metropolitan countries, but even if it was a pale shadow of the original, it was still a recognizable copy.

➜ See chapter twenty, page 468, for an exploration of states in a globalizing world.

➜ See chapter fourteen, page 334, for a more detailed discussion of the rise of the modern state system.

7

➜ See chapter ten, page 237, for a discussion of theories of bureaucratic policy-making.

The power of the model can be seen in the response of a state such as Japan. While the imperial European powers imposed their systems on the peoples that they colonized, not all territories became colonies, although most did. Japan had cut itself off from the outside world for 300 years when, in 1854, the American Commodore Perry led a number of warships into Tokyo Bay and demanded that Japan open up to international trade. The Japanese had no ships that could challenge the Americans and they were forced to agree. This set in train a whole series of transformations of Japanese society and the state as the Japanese sought to modernize, so that they could compete with the West and make Japan 'rich and strong'. This led to the imposition at first of a more **authoritarian** system of rule with the restoration to more effective power of the Meiji emperor in 1868. The government swelled into a much larger civilian bureaucracy that could develop resources for the state. It sent representatives abroad to learn more about the political, legal, and technological strengths of the West, so that the best could be transplanted to Japan. The traditional class of independent warriors—the samurai—were forced to serve the state, either by becoming officials or officers in the new national army. In 1890 the first Japanese constitution came into force, which set limits (albeit ambiguous ones) on the powers of the Emperor. This also established a parliament and an independent judiciary. All of these reforms transformed Japan. From a backward and introverted nation it gradually transformed after 1868 into a recognizably modern state that by 1895 was able to defeat its biggest regional rival, China, and by 1904–5 was the first non-European state to win a war against a European imperial power—Russia. Japan then developed its own empire. Within a few decades Japan had exploited the new state to expand its national might in a process that had taken European nations centuries.

Turkey is another of the few examples of the few territories that did not become a Western colony but which adopted Western forms of rule so as to compete with the West. By the nineteenth century the Ottoman Empire was in decline and significantly it was the military that took the lead in looking to the West for ideas and models of reform so that Turkey could compete. It was military considerations that drove increasingly radical reforms of the state in the nineteenth and twentieth centuries. This culminated in the rise of Ataturk as president of a secular republic in 1923, who pushed through a full separation of state and religion that was modelled primarily upon principles of laicism borrowed from France (Starr, 1992: 8–15).

After independence the former colonies took over these state apparatuses and also the institutions that they had established. Whether it was the former Spanish colonies in Latin America during the nineteenth century, or the former British, French, German, and Italian colonies in the twentieth century, the newly independent states largely adopted the same basic attributes of rule, the same apparatus of institutions, even though they also in other respects usually adopted a forthrightly anti-imperialist ideology. Most importantly, they also adopted and often developed the bureaucratic machine that extracted resources from the people to pay for government. In some cases the innovation of the separation between ruler and officials that had earlier marked the rise of the modern state was now reversed. In what have been called patrimonial states, some rulers came to use the state to extract resources from the rest of society for their own benefit. This practice has been associated with African states, although it is not exclusive to that region.

As the European states grew stronger, gradually new institutions were devised to try to prevent them from becoming too despotic. Legal principles were established that would also constrain rulers, particularly through constitutions. Finer emphasized two events that were crucial in this respect: the American revolution and the French revolution.

For him:

the transcendent importance of the American Revolution is that it demonstrated for ever that quality of the Western European government we have called "law-boundedness". Here is a government which draws its powers from and can only act within a framework of fundamental law—the Constitution—which is itself interpreted by judges in the ordinary courts of the country. Could law-boundedness go further, could it receive a more striking affirmation? (Finer, 1997: 1485)

From this followed six innovations, as can be seen from **Box 7.1**.

It was the American constitution that introduced the formal principle of 'separation of powers'. To some extent this evolved from practice in Britain, which had had a constitutional monarchy since 1689, and which had been extolled by Montesquieu (1689–1755) in his work *On the Spirit of Laws* of 1748, a strong influence upon many of the framers of the American Constitution; but whereas in Britain, and in other states in continental Europe, the basis for the different houses of parliament was social class—e.g. the House of Lords and the House of Commons—now the distinction was entirely abstract and functional—the House of Representatives and the Senate. It was a more democratic form of institutionalization, which assumed that all citizens were equal and subject to the same laws.

 Box 7.1

The Governmental Innovations of the American Revolution

1. the deliberate formulation of a new frame of government by way of a popular Convention
2. a written constitution
3. a bill of rights enshrined within it
4. guaranteed protection for these rights through judicial review
5. the separation of powers along functional lines
6. the division of powers between the national and the state governments

(Finer, 01997: 1485)

At the time the combination of new institutions and principles was an experiment. No one knew whether they would all work together. However, the American Constitution has proved a model and a starting point for all subsequent writers of constitutions.

Then, only just over a decade later, another revolution further transformed the theory and practice of government: the French Revolution.

The French Revolution is the most important single event in the entire history of government. The American Revolution pales beside it. It was an earthquake. It razed and effaced all the ancient institutions of France, undermined the foundations of the other European states, and is still sending its shock-waves throughout the rest of the world. (Finer, 1997: 1517)

The governmental legacy of the French Revolution can be summarized in four main points. See **Box 7.2**.

As can be seen from this list, not all of the points can be reconciled with each other. The French Revolution celebrated the Rights of Man making all men equal, and at the same time inaugurated an era of populist dictatorship. Although the revolution had a universal appeal, France became the prototype nation-state, with nationalism as its core political ideology and it provoked a backlash among other peoples, especially in the German states, that led to the creation of nation-states throughout Europe in the nineteenth century. And although it preached universal harmony, it also devised a new form of military organization—the mass citizen army—that became the model for military organization throughout Europe. Yet in their different ways, these diverse elements became the precursors for various forms of modern government not just in Europe, but throughout the world. Both modern democracies and dictatorships, rule by law and by force, were prefigured by the French Revolution. Thus, although the French Revolution began as an attempt to create

---

 Box 7.2

The Governmental Legacy of the French Revolution

1. the Declaration of The Natural Rights of Man and the Citizen established the legal basis for the sovereignty of the democratic state, based upon the General Will.

2. nationalism—it laid down the national unity of all French citizens, and their primary obligation of loyalty to it. The Napoleonic wars spread the doctrine throughout Europe and provoked a matching response from the peoples of other nations.

3. citizen armies—in the defence of the Revolution the French state mobilized far more citizens to fight on its behalf than had ever been seen in Europe, which forced its enemies to compete.

4. neo-absolutism—the rise of the Committee of Public Safety followed by the Napoleonic dictatorship.

(Finer, 1997: 1538–66)

checks upon the absolutist monarchy, it instituted new forms of state activity that led to far greater intrusion in the lives of ordinary people than ever before. In that sense, as Finer puts it: 'all four [of these elements] are still alive, working like a leaven throughout the globe. In that sense the revolution is a Permanent Revolution. Nothing was ever like it before and nothing foreseeable will turn this Revolution back' (Finer, 1997: 1566).

Key Points

- A crucial importance in the development of the European state was the separation of state officials from personal servants of the ruler.
- Another crucial development was the separation of the state from the rest of society through institutionalization and bureaucratization.
- Warfare was a catalyst for increasing the raising of funds for the state from society and increasing the state's reach.
- The American and French Revolutions developed modern principles of government.
- This led to the invention of institutions to check the power of the state.

The Spread of the European State System

States today have two sets of roles or functions. The first consists of functions that they exercise towards their own populations. The second is those that they perform towards other states. States 'recognize' each other and by doing so confer an additional degree of legitimacy.

The rise of the European state also transformed the international system. We will briefly outline it here because it explains the spread of the European type of state across the world. We will then return to it a more detailed discussion of the state and the international system in chapter fourteen.

The modern European state system is normally taken to have resulted from the treaties that established the Peace of Westphalia in 1648 and ended the Thirty Years' War. It established the paradigm of a:

→ See chapter fourteen, page 340, for a more detailed discussion of the globalization of the modern state system.

European state . . . [that] was a sovereign, territorially delimited political unit, facing other similar units, each striving for supremacy but never achieving it owing to their rapidly adopted skill of forming combinations that would defeat such a purpose, that is, the techniques of the "balance of power" first developed by the Italian city-states in the fourteenth and fifteenth centuries. (Finer, 1997: 1306)

The Treaty of Westphalia established three principles:

1. the **sovereignty** of states and the fundamental right to **self-determination**;
2. legal equality between states;
3. non-intervention of one state in the affairs of another.

➜ See chapter fourteen, page 326, for details on the Montevideo Convention.

➜ See chapter fourteen, page 338, for more detail on Jean Bodin.

7

Today, the criteria that states use for mutual recognition were agreed under the Montevideo Convention of 1933. These principles, however, are based upon practices that were first established in the Treaty of Westphalia.

In subsequent centuries Europeans spread their patterns of interstate behaviour around the world as they built up empires, first in South America, then North America, Africa, and Asia. Western concepts of state sovereignty, originating with Bodin (see chapter fourteen), differed from traditions in other parts of the world in two respects. First, they were based upon formal legal principles. Secondly, they insisted upon the sovereignty of a state running uniformly throughout territory within prescribed boundaries. In Africa, by contrast, authority and rule were more fluid. According to Clapham:

African [states] formed islands of relatively settled government beyond which stretched deserts, forests or zones of progressively impoverished savannah which a strong ruler would seek to control but from which a weak one would retreat. Dissident or defeated groups could strike out into the borderlands to conquer or establish kingdoms of their own. (Clapham, 1996: 29)

Likewise in Southeast Asia, traditional understandings of state sovereignty focused more upon the mystical power of the ruler at the centre of the state which radiated outwards, like a force-field or like a cone of reflected light. Thus, the power was weaker the further that one went from the centre, until it ran up against a stronger force field from another state (Suwannathat–Pian, 1988: 29). In both continents states were defined by their capitals rather than by their perimeters. Therefore, traditional rulers concentrated more upon maintaining and strengthening the power at the centre and they paid less attention to what was happening on the periphery (Anderson, 1990: 21–36).

Western states imposed stronger boundaries on their territories and insisted upon undivided sovereignty right up to those borders. They drew much firmer borders, imposing them, often arbitrarily, upon peoples that they colonized. This was particularly true of South America and sub-Saharan Africa. The consequences of this for state legitimacy and viability are still with us today. When these colonies became independent, they usually took over the existing legal framework and these borders, reasserting the latter's their inviolability. After independence they then tried to build modern nation-states, attempting to forge nations out of citizens on the European model. Thus, in many parts of the world it has been the state that has created the nation, whereas in Europe it has often been the nation that has created the state.

Key Points

- The European type of state spread to lands on other continents.
- War and colonial expansion were the key elements in doing so.
- This also led to the emergence of a European-type system of states around the world.

The Modern State

Today the state has become the universal form of political organization around the world. Presently 192 states are members of the United Nations, ranging in size from China with a population of over 1.3 billion to Tuvalu with a population estimated at 12,000. In area they range from Russia with over 17 million sq. km. to Monaco with an area of 2 sq. km. This also means that a third set of functions performed by a state relate to its relations with other states. States have to manage relations with each other through diplomacy and they have to devise defence policies to protect their territory and their people against attacks from outside. Equally importantly, states recognize each other as legitimate rulers over defined areas of territory and in this way they reduce the **anarchy** that exists, at least potentially, at the global level because of the lack of a global government. This diplomatic recognition provides reassurance against attack, although it is not an infallible guarantee. On the other hand, it also means that states expect their counterparts to interact with them in familiar and predictable ways. Bureaucratic agencies in one state that deal with the outside world—and in an era of globalization this is increasingly the case—expect to find equivalent agencies in other states. This strengthening **international society** contributes to the proliferation of government agencies in individual states.

There is no doubt about the national importance of state apparatuses—given the growing share of state expenditure in individual countries' GDP, as can be seen from Table 7.1.

This charts their growth, particularly since the end of the Second World War. Figures on the size of government bureaucracies tell the same story, as seen in Table 7.2, even though there are great differences between the practices of countries over whom they count as state officials. Some states have been proportionately much bigger than these three.

How, then, do we generalize what states do? Gill has suggested that there are three basic types of internal roles performed by the modern state. The first is that of the state as partisan. In other words the state operates on the basis of, and pursues, its own interests. This is reinforced by a Weberian state bureaucracy with its own structure and procedures that resist pressures from the rest of society. This would be typical of authoritarian regimes.

The second role is that of the state as guardian. Here the state stabilizes and where necessary rebalances society in a way of which society itself is incapable. Therefore, the state is essential for social stability. This could be because of fundamental conflict in society which threatens to tear it apart. Examples of this would be **federal** or **consociational** political systems which have been designed to counter fundamental cleavages in society and to which we shall return in more detail in chapter eight. Or it could take the form of a **developmental state** already mentioned in chapter one, as in East

➡ See chapter ten, page 237, for a discussion of bureaucratic policy-making.

General government for all years	About 1870	1913	1920	1937	1960	1980	1990	1996
Australia	18.3	16.5	19.3	14.8	21.2	34.1	34.9	35.9
Austria	10.5	17	14.7	20.6	35.7	48.1	38.6	51.6
Canada			16.7	25	28.6	38.8	46	44.7
France	12.6	17	27.6	29	34.6	46.1	49.8	55
Germany	10	14.8	25	34.1	32.4	47.9	45.1	49.1
Italy	13.7	17.1	30.1	31.1	30.1	42.1	53.4	52.7
Ireland			18.8	25.5	28	48.9	41.2	42
Japan	8.8	8.3	14.8	25.4	17.5	32	31.3	35.9
New Zealand			24.6	25.3	26.9	38.1	41.3	34.7
Norway	5.9	9.3	16	11.8	29.9	43.8	54.9	49.2
Sweden	5.7	10.4	10.9	16.5	31	60.1	59.1	64.2
Switzerland	16.5	14	17	24.1	17.2	32.8	33.5	39.4
United Kingdom	9.4	12.7	26.2	30	32.2	43	39.9	43
United States	7.3	7.5	12.1	19.7	27	31.4	32.8	32.4
Average	**10.8**	**13.1**	**19.6**	**23.8**	**28**	**41.9**	**43**	**45**

Table 7.1   Growth of General Government Expenditure in Selected Countries, 1870–1996 (per cent of GDP)
Source: Tanzi, Vito, and Ludger Schuknecht (2000), *Public Spending in the Twentieth Century*, Cambridge: Cambridge University Press: 6–7

Asia, where the state directs the development of society and the economy in what it regards as a path of development that is in the **national interest**, e.g. industrialization and economic modernization.

The third type of role is the state as instrument. Here the state operates primarily as a tool in the hands of some group or groups in society at large. This could take the form of a genuine **liberal democracy**, where the people are in control of the state's actions. Alternatively it could be a state that is controlled by a particular section of society, e.g.

➜ See chapter one, page 27, for a description of the developmental state.

	1821	1985[*]
Germany	23,000[**]	855,000
UK	27,000	1,065,000
US	8,000	3,797,000

Table 7.2 Size of Government Bureaucracies, Selected Years

[*] Central government civil servants only

[**] Prussia only

Source: Finer (1997), *The History of Government from the Earliest Times,* Oxford: Oxford University Press, 3: 1624

a particular ethnic group or 'big business'; or it could even be a patrimonial state, where political actors take advantage of state power to enrich themselves and their clients. Here the state is just a tool.

In practice, any modern state performs a combination of all three roles. Most state bureaucracies operate to some extent on the basis of their own codified procedures and institutions that are intended to resist outside turbulence. Most states do develop some perspective on the desirable path of development for that society and attempt to mobilize resources to achieve it, and most states are to some extent responsive to groups outside themselves. Dictators such as President Suharto of Indonesia favour 'loyal' businessmen who do their bidding and in return enjoy special favours. Thus, what is important is the balance between these three types of roles in particular states. Are they *predominantly* partisans, guardians, or instruments?

Key Points

- The state in the West today is larger than at any time in history.

- The modern state can act predominantly either as partisan, as a guardian, or as an instrument.

Strong States and Weak States

This list of state functions, internal and external, suggests that the modern state has become more powerful than at any time in its history. There is no doubt that the twentieth century witnessed the most extreme manifestations of state power that the world has ever seen, in the form of what some analysts characterized as **totalitarian** systems, such as Hitler's Germany and Stalin's Russia. Even though state control was never as completely total as the term might imply and there still remained pockets of resistance, there was no doubt about the aspiration of their leaders for total control, or the spread of institutions to try to achieve it. Now that the archives of some of these states are open, it is possible to gain a clearer perspective on the size of such states. For example, at the time of its collapse in 1989, the German Democratic Republic had what has been described as a 'honeycomb' state, in which perhaps one sixth of the adult population were involved in one way or another in the state's 'micro-systems of power'. Over 91,000 were full-time employees of the secret police alone by the time the state collapsed, a ratio of one to every 180 people in the population and the highest for any former communist state (Fulbrook, 2005: 236, 241). Yet, however strong and all-powerful they looked, most have now collapsed.

These were extreme versions of the modern state. As the powers of the state have increased in the twentieth century, so too have been the expectations of what it can perform. Rotberg has provided a long list of the political goods or functions that a modern state might be expected to provide its citizens. Typically the most important are:

1.   human security;

2.   predictable, recognizable, systematized methods of adjudicating disputes, and regulating both the norms and the prevailing mores of a particular society or polity;

3.   freedom to participate in politics and compete for office, respect, and support for national and regional political institutions, such as legislatures and courts, tolerance of dissent and difference, and fundamental civil and human rights.

However, there are many others also expected by citizens: medical and healthcare, schools and educational institutions, roads, railways, harbours and other elements of

Photo 7.1   Fifteen Years Since Storming of Stasi Headquarters

Berlin—13 January: A security guard walks among files in the massive archives of the former Stasi, the secret police of the former East Germany. The Stasi kept detailed records on millions of East Germans in a staggering volume of documents, most of which survive in today's archive.
Source: Getty Images

physical infrastructure, communication networks, money and a banking system with a national currency, a beneficent fiscal and institutional within which citizens can pursue personal entrepreneurial goals and potentially prosper, space for the flowering of **civil society**, and methods of regulating the sharing of the environmental commons (Rotberg, 2004: 2–3). If we look at states in the developed world, we can usually find that they perform these functions to the satisfaction of their citizens, even if not perfectly. They are 'strong' or 'robust' states.

However, it is important to remember that not all states today are like that. There are many that are clearly weak. Most are to be found in the developing world. Chabal and Daloz have argued that the state in Africa is 'not just weak, but essentially vacuous, with virtually none meeting the Weberian criteria' (Chabal and Daloz, 1999: 1). Bayart amplified this by saying that in most states of sub-Saharan Africa:

> The frontiers of the state are transgressed, the informal sector is a canker on the official economy, taxes are not collected, poaching and undisciplined exploitation of mineral resources becomes endemic, weapons circulate, resettled villages split up, the people appropriate the legitimate use of force to themselves and deliver summary justice, delinquency spreads, businesses suffer from languor induced by underproductivity, delays and absences. (Bayart, 1993: 258)

Table 7.3 contains a list of the twenty 'weakest' states according to the *Foreign Policy* magazine in 2007.

The case study presents the story of Somalia which has been effectively a territory without a central state since 1991. See **Box 7.3**. This makes it the territory with the longest such experience in modern times. How did this happen? As Hobbes was quoted as saying in chapter one, this should be a region where life is 'solitary, poor, nasty, brutish and short': is this actually the case?

Thus, even though the structures of modern states are fairly similar, they vary considerably according to their capacities. This raises the question of what makes a state strong, and conversely, what makes it weak. It is possible to identify a series of factors.

Clearly, one is size. Although China enjoys the same international legal status as Monaco, in practice there is an enormous difference in their respective capacity to pursue their goals in the world.

Another factor is the strength of the economy. As the largest economy in the world, the USA possesses the capacity to finance a high level of domestic public services and respond to the preferences of its people. By contrast a poor state such as Burma is much less capable of providing a wide range of adequate services for its people.

A third factor is military might. Again, the USA as the only remaining military superpower can do far more to protect its people and territory, as well as pursue foreign policy goals, although the failures in Iraq suggest that there are more limits to this power than were previously supposed.

➜ See chapter one, page 37, for more on Hobbes and the social contract tradition.

Rank	Country
1.	Sudan
2.	Iraq
3.	Somalia
4.	Zimbabwe
5.	Chad
6.	Ivory Coast
7.	Democratic Republic of the Congo
8.	Afghanistan
9.	Guinea
10.	Central African Republic
11.	Haiti
12.	Pakistan
13.	North Korea
14.	Burma
15.	Uganda
16.	Bangladesh
17.	Nigeria
18.	Ethiopia
19.	Burundi
20.	East Timor

Table 7.3   Ranked List of the 20 Weakest States in 2007

Source: Foreign Policy Magazine (www.foreignpolicy.com/story/cms.php?story_id=3865&page + 7)

Case Study Box 7.3
Case Study: Somalia as a Failed State

Unlike many post-colonial states, especially in sub-Saharan Africa, Somalia does not suffer particularly from ethnic heterogeneity. Nor are most of its boundaries much disputed, though Somalis have also traditionally resided in what are now Ethiopia, Kenya, and Djibouti. Occupying territory as large as France, it has a population estimated in 2007 at 9.1 million, i.e. only roughly 15 per cent of the French. However, all Somalis believe they are descended from a common ancestor. The main divisions between Somalis are based upon clans and sub-clans rather than separate ethnicity. In addition, some commentators on Somalia have also stressed the strong-minded individualism of nomadic herdsmen who view authority with suspicion. The colonial and post-colonial states have all hung above the rest of society, only partially integrated into it.

In 1960 the post-independence state was formed from former British and Italian colonies. In 1969 power was seized by General Siad Barre after the assassination of the last civilian president. Barre attempted to create a modern state by suppressing traditional clan ties, but gradually the army fragmented along clan lines. Barre's regime became notoriously corrupt and its domestic support shrank to his own clan.

In 1991 he was overthrown by his former intelligence chief, Mohamed Farah Aidid, which then provoked a bloody civil war between rival militias. Initially the conflict was confined within the country, but hundreds of thousands of people died either from the ferocious fighting or subsequent starvation. In 1993 the UN, and primarily the USA, attempted to impose a peace which would mark a new role in peace-making in the post-Cold War era with Operation Restore Hope. They were initially welcomed into the capital, Mogadishu, but after a few months their unsuccessful attempts to arrest the most prominent warlord, Aidid, led to widespread civilian casualties and united Somalis against outsiders. Even the Red Cross had to be protected. Mogadishu was devastated by withering American firepower and retaliation (Peterson, 2000). The deaths and mutilation of American servicemen in the events popularized in the film *Blackhawk Down* turned American popular opinion against the intervention, and the UN later withdrew. Since then, Somalis have largely been left to their own devices.

There is no central authority. In 2003 Kenya took the lead in organizing a conference that established a Transitional Federal Government, but little progress has been made in its national legitimacy. In late 2006, forces from Ethiopia intervened to frustrate a movement for unity on the basis of Islamic courts.

Menkhaus (2007: 86–7) writes of 'a loose constellation of commercial city-states and villages separated by long stretches of pastoral statelessness'. De facto, one part of the country (Puntland) has declared autonomy, while another (Somaliland) in the north is effectively independent. The only effective administrations are at the local level, and public services (education, healthcare, welfare) have collapsed. Clans and sub-clans defend their interests using traditional customary interclan practices of recompense for injuries or damage received by their members instead of relying upon state justice, but heavily armed militias can still demand resources largely with impunity. Yet average life expectancy is estimated in the CIA's *World Factbook* at forty-eight years (though no statistics are very reliable)—higher than in many other African countries and about the same as in Nigeria. Somaliland is supposedly as safe as anywhere in the Horn of Africa. It has even established a rudimentary democratic system with elections and political parties. Therefore, insecurity is certainly a major problem in the country and there are over 450,000 Somali refugees abroad, but the extreme violence of the early 1990s has subsided. Life there is not especially short, at least by the standards of sub-Saharan Africa.

The traditional economy of trade in herds of cattle is flourishing as compared with the pre-1991 period, since the state cannot extract usurious taxes (Little, 2003). Private enterprise has found ways of providing services such as the transfer of money within and outside the country despite the lack of banks. Businessmen also buy off militiamen to provide security for their trade, so there is no state monopoly on the means of violence. Mobile phone companies prosper, while the landline service decays. The private sector has taken over the supply of public services where quick profits are possible, e.g. running ports, airports, electricity supply, but not public sanitation. Transnational corporations such as Total and GM have found ways of doing business in the country despite the lack of a stable institutional and legal system. Somalis abroad remit back home anywhere between US$500 million and 1 billion per year, which bolsters the domestic economy, especially in the cities.

Somalis have found ways of coping with the lack of a state, which they regard as 'an instrument of accumulation and domination, enriching and empowering those who control it and exploiting and harassing the rest of the population' (Menkhaus, 2007: 86–7). Yet they are disadvantaged because they cannot protect their maritime resources, having no navy, and they cannot defend their businesses against foreign discrimination. Saudi Arabia, previously the largest importer of Somali cattle, banned them because the country could no longer provide a veterinary service to prevent the spread of disease. The insecurity in urban areas has prevented any significant investment in infrastructure or industry. Moreover, in 2008, Western aid agencies warned about the danger of a renewed humanitarian catastrophe as fighting between groups escalated again and the capital Mogadishu emptied of people.

So far, we have looked primarily at external factors in estimating the strength of states, but equally important are domestic ones. First there is the issue of legitimacy. If a state lacks the consent to rule on the part of its people, then it is bound to be potentially weak, because it will need to rely more upon force to achieve acquiescence. This could be the result of dissension over its borders. Many post-colonial states have international frontiers that were imposed more or less arbitrarily, with the frequent consequence that ethnic or tribal communities straddle borders and refuse to think of themselves as citizens of at least one of the states where they are found and wish to establish their own homeland; or it could be the result of challenges to the dominant ideology of the state. Ultimately what brought down the regimes in Eastern Europe and the former Soviet Union was the lack of support for the official ideology of communism. Without that shared sense of popular legitimacy, states are brittle, however superficially strong they may look. They are vulnerable to new challenges because they lack flexibility and are slow to adapt.

A second crucial factor in the strength of states is the robustness of the state institutions themselves. To what extent can they withstand turbulence from the rest of society? Bayart, Chabal, and Daloz repeatedly emphasize the weakness of many African states as the result of the interpenetration of state, society, and the economy. Individual African politicians expect to use the state to become rich as a way of impressing others and redistributing resources to their 'clients'. 'Rich men are powerful and powerful men are rich' (Chabal and Daloz, 1999: 52). Ethnic and tribal communities expect 'their' representatives, whether democratically elected or even lowly officials in the government bureaucracy, to channel resources to them, because if they do not do so, no one will. Thus, state institutions in Africa are far less robust than in the West, because they do not stand above or apart from society in the same way. The structuration provided by the rest of the society outweighs the capacity for autonomous, rule-based behaviour on the part of the bureaucracy. The institutions are not really institutionalized, and the African state is more easily penetrated by outside forces as a result—at least for the moment. The emergence of robust African states may in part be simply a matter of time—the time that it takes for political ideas and political behaviour to adjust to the still relatively new state units. Van Creveld (1999: 306) reminds us that in the nineteenth century newly independent states in South America suffered similar fragility. Colombia had thirty civil wars, Venezuela had fifty revolutions and Bolivia sixty. According to Coronil on Venezuela at the beginning of the twentieth century:

[T]he state was so weak and precarious as a national institution that its stability and legitimacy were constantly at risk. Without a national army or an effective bureaucracy, in an indebted country that lacked a national road network or an effective system of communication, the state appeared as an unfulfilled project whose institutional form remained limited to localized sites of power with but partial dominion over the nation's territory and sway over its citizens. (Coronil, 1997: 76)

We shall see in chapter eleven that it does not look like this now. So maybe in time African states will also acquire greater robustness.

➡ See chapter eleven, page 269, for a case study on Venezuela.

To some extent this section has identified fundamental disparities between the state in the developed world and the state in the developing one today. In general, European states and the USA are strong, while those in the developing world are weaker. General theorizing about the state by Western political scientists has tended to focus on the issues associated with the strong. Recently, however, the problems of weakening states in the developed world have begun to attract more attention. Increasing globalization is beginning, but still only just beginning, to recast this debate. States in the developed world are now increasingly exercised by the erosion of their sovereignty, for example by multinational corporations and other transnational actors and forces (Marsh, Smith, and Hothi, 2006: 176). The erosion has not yet reached anything like the same level as in the developing world. Nevertheless there seems to be a spreading slow decline in the autonomy of the state in different parts of the world. To that extent the vectors of state capabilities in different parts of the world are beginning to converge again. This is an issue to which we shall return in chapter twenty.

➜ See chapter twenty, page 468, for an exploration of the impact of globalization on the study of politics.

Key Points

- There is an enormous range in the capabilities of states in different regions of the world.
- Some states are at best 'quasi' states (Jackson, 1990).
- States need legitimacy and robust institutions to be strong.
- Globalization has a growing impact on limiting state capabilities around the world.

7

A Democratic State

➜ See chapter three, page 70, for a discussion of the meaning of democracy.

Lastly, let us return to a particular widespread form of the state, which illustrates the complexity of the term, and which is at the core of much of the writing on politics. Let us come back to the democratic state, initially discussed in chapter three. The purpose of the discussion here is to demonstrate the complexity of the concept of the state in a particular form. Initially, the notion of a democratic state might seem simple. It could mean a state with elections for some or all leading positions in the state or government. But what about authoritarian states which hold elections but where the outcome can be taken for granted? We could instead specify that there have to be genuinely free and fair elections, however that might be monitored. But is that sufficient? We could say that a democratic state would also need political parties, since it is very rare to find a democracy that does without parties (although for an example, see **Box 11.3** on Uganda in chapter eleven). Does that mean that a democratic government is genuinely accountable to elected representatives? This is also normally presumed to be an essential element of a democratic state. Parties are elected to parliament in some authoritarian states, but they cannot exercise any effective check upon the government. Perhaps we should specify extra conditions that would ensure such accountability, e.g. some provision that would ensure that a government or at least individual ministers could lose office because they failed to do what 'the people' wanted. However, is democracy only about parties, parliaments, and elections? Does there need to be a

➜ See chapter eleven, page 260, for a case study on Uganda.

broad representation of major social groups in parliament? For example, should there be roughly equal representation for men and women in parliament, or other elected bodies? Are the attitudes of ordinary citizens important too in making it work? Is civil society an essential requirement for a functioning democracy? Is a democratic **political culture** also needed to make democracy work? If so, how does it emerge?

So far these questions have explored dimensions of democratic political systems but, as we argued at the beginning of this chapter, this is not the same as a democratic *state*, because the term 'state' is so much more complex. To focus upon this we need to ask wider, more abstract questions about conceptions of authority. Do views about authentic democracy vary from one country to another, or from one region of the world to another (Paley, 2002)? Bell and others have identified a different attitude towards democracy in East and Southeast Asia from that in the West, i.e. **illiberal democracy**, also mentioned in chapter one. There are still elections and political parties, but instead of liberal democracy, the state operates on the basis of more definite views about appropriate forms of social harmony. The main priority of the legal system is controlling society rather than guaranteeing rights and liberties (Bell *et al.*, 1995). The Chinese government produced a White Paper on democracy that promotes a different understanding of what it means (*White Paper on Political Democracy*, 2005). In what ways does it differ from those in liberal democracies? How far would an Islamic democracy look different from that in a Catholic society? Lastly, can only the citizens of a given state fairly judge whether their state is democratic, or can foreigners have a legitimate view?

As you can see, these are just some of the many dimensions that might contribute to the assessment of a 'democratic state'. The last point of this chapter is to encourage you to try to carry out a democratic audit of a state with which you are familiar. International IDEA, the democracy promotion institute, has set out a checklist of questions to provoke analysis by citizens about their particular countries (International IDEA, 2002a). Use this as a starting point for your own analysis. You can also get an idea of how this might work in practice from the examples given in their accompanying work (International IDEA, 2002b).

➡ See chapter twelve, page 276, for a detailed exploration of the concept of civil society.

➡ See chapter one, page 27, for a discussion of illiberal democracy.

7

Key Points

- There is a multidimensional nature to a democratic state.
- A democratic political system and a democratic state are different concepts.

Conclusion

This chapter has set the framework for the next six chapters. These will explore various dimensions of the state, whether as organization or as structures of authority. It has also illustrated the great disparity in capabilities between some states and others. The next three chapters will focus upon the most important institutions of states, while the following two will deal with broader forces that provide structure to the context of political life.

 ## Key Questions

- What is a nation-state? Does it matter whether the nation or the state came first?
- Does the state require moral authority to enjoy domestic legitimacy?
- Is state capacity simply a function of the level of economic development?
- Or is it simply a function of longevity and habituation (viz. Latin America as compared with sub-Saharan Africa)?
- How far can theories of modern stae West (see Hay *et al.*) *be applied to states in the developing world?*
- After carrying out a democratic 'audit' of a particular country, what are your conclusions?
- Was it internal dissension or external destabilization that played a bigger role in destroying the Somalian state?
- How would you try to strengthen a weak state in the developing world? Would democracy help?
- Are some states simply too weak and/or too arbitrarily constructed to justify continued international recognition? Should the international community simply let them disintegrate? What would be the consequences?
- Is the state entering a period of decline? How would you measure its effectiveness compared with earlier periods?

 ## Further Reading

Buzan, Barry (1991), *People, States and Fear*, London: Harvester International, 2nd edn, esp. ch. 2.
> A much-read study that considers both the internal and external roles of the state.

Chabal, Patrick, and Daloz, Jean-Pascal (1999), *Africa Works: Disorder as Political Instrument*, Oxford: The International Africa Institute in association with James Currey.
> This is a vivid account of the distinctive features of states in Africa.

Noah Feldman, (2008), *The Fall and Rise of the Islamic State*, Princeton, NJ: Princeton University Press.
> A sophisticated introduction to the history of the Islamic state and its contemporary evolution.

Gill, Graeme (2003), *The Nature and Development of the Modern State*, Basingstoke: Palgrave.

This is a good survey of theories of the state in the aftermath of the collapse of communism.

Hay, Colin, Michael Lister, and David Marsh (eds) (2006), *The State: Theories and Issues*, Basingstoke: Palgrave.

This is a collection of articles that discuss contemporary issues in theories of the Western state.

Leftwich, Adrian (2004), 'Theorizing the State' in Peter Burnell and Vicky Randall (eds), *Politics in the Developing World*, Oxford: Oxford University Press: 139–54.

This is an attempt to extend theories of the state to the developing world.

Van Creveld, Martin (1999), *The Rise and Decline of the State*, Cambridge: Cambridge University Press.

This is a sweeping historical survey of the rise and spread of the Western state.

 *Web Links*

www.pbs.org/ktca/liberty
Devoted to the American Revolution.

http://chnm.gmu.edu/revolution/
Devoted to the French Revolution.

www.magnacartaplus.org
Contains links to many human rights documents.

www.foreignpolicy.com/story/cms.php?story_id=3865
The most recent of regular lists of failed states.

www.china.org.cn/english/features/book/145941.htm
The Chinese 2005 White Paper on its democracy.

 Visit the **Online Resource Centre** that accompanies this book to access more learning resources at www.oxfordtextbooks.co.uk/orc/garner/

8

Law, Constitutions, and Federalism

Reader's Guide

This chapter will first discuss the importance of constitutions in determining the basic structure of the state and the fundamental rights of citizens that they establish. Then, as a reminder that the rule of law may not always be interpreted uniformly, we shall explore different ways in which states may attempt to realize justice in applying the law, focusing in particular on differences between Islamic and Western practice. Next, we shall consider the importance of constitutional courts. After that we shall turn to the institution of federalism as a way of containing the powers of the state as a way of managing diverse societies. Then we will turn to consociationalism as an alternative approach to managing such diversity. We will conclude with a brief discussion of the increasing legalization of political life.

Law and Politics

Chapter seven emphasized the power of the modern state and attempts to control it. According to Finer, one of the main Western innovations in the theory of the state was the introduction of the 'law-bounded state', although Bonnett (2004: 5) argues that it was only towards the late nineteenth century that the idea of the West being a law-governed society came to be widely accepted. In other words the decisions of the ruler(s) had to be codified and published so as to impose limits on the exercise of arbitrary power and to provide predictability in public affairs. The editor of the journal, *Foreign Affairs*, Fareed Zakaria, concurs: 'For much of modern history, what characterized governments in Europe and North America and differentiated them from those around the world, was not democracy but constitutional liberalism. The "Western model" is best symbolized not by the mass plebiscite but the impartial judge' (Zakaria, 1997: 27).

The spread of Western conceptions of law around the world is a consequence of the spread of Western ideas of the state. Previously, in traditional societies in other parts of the world, authoritative rule-making was not seen as the exclusive domain of political rulers. Binding rules on human conduct could emerge from a variety of sources, e.g. clans or tribes, and religious authorities. Although these rules may not have been specifically called 'laws', they had the same force. Because there was no single source of authority for these rules, there existed a kind of norm-creating pluralism. Moreover, traditional societies in Africa and Asia were inclined to prefer to achieve order through internalized harmony and self-regulation, rather than formal legal adjudication (Menski, 2006: 547).

Gradually, however, Western states arrogated to themselves exclusive responsibility for issuing such rules as laws, and they also codified them for the sake of consistency of application. Then, as legislatures became more common, law-making became their primary function. Gradually these practices spread around the world as Western states did. It was associated with the 'civilizing mission' that Western states set for them-selves. This monopoly on legislative activity is another essential feature of the modern state. A further refinement is that states often claim as well that the legitimacy of binding rules for society depends upon approval by the legislature. Sometimes this is described as **legal positivism**, i.e. law is what the state says it is. Other types of rule lack this legitimacy, and so lack the same degree of authority. It has become widely accepted as normal in Western states. As Twining (2000: 232) put it:

[O]ver 200 years Western legal theory has been dominated by conceptions of law that tend to be monist (one internally coherent legal system), statist (the state has a monopoly of law within its territory), and positivist (what is not created or recognised as law by the state is not law).

It is perhaps best exemplified in the principle of **secularism** in France where the civil state authorities assert their precedence over all competing sources of rule-making authority, especially religious ones. Ataturk was heavily influenced by this example in the reforms that he introduced in the 1920s which asserted Turkish state supremacy over Islamic religious authorities. There, the state's Directorate of Religious Affairs controls the mosques by employing all Muslim clerics on salaries and subjecting them to an administrative hierarchy, which supervises their pronouncements. The most striking demonstration of the state's claim to authority was the announcement in 2008 that it would seek to establish which of the Prophet's sayings or *hadith* were genuine.

The extent to which this claim to legal **monism** has become accepted can be seen in the UK in the heated opposition to the Archbishop of Canterbury's lecture in 2008 which raised the possibility of the state accepting the validity of principles of shar'iah law in regulating family life of Muslims in the UK. He did not actually propose that a system of parallel law should be established, merely that some principles of shar'iah law might be incorporated into state law. Nevertheless it was widely taken as challenging the dominant assumption of the primacy of state-approved and state-codified law. In fact, states in other parts of the world do allow greater legal pluralism. India, Pakistan, and Bangladesh, for example, do allow different religious communities

Photo 8.1   Turkey—Where East Meets West

Turkey is a country of enormous contrasts: between a culture and lifestyle resembling that of modern Western Europe and the United States, and traditions that lean more towards the Middle East and the Orient. Turkey's population is 99% Muslim, and has maintained a strong philosophy of secular democracy since the days of Ataturk. The present government is led by Prime Minister Recep Tayyip Erdogan of the pro-Islamic Justice and Ruling Party (AKP).

Source: Peter Turnley for Harper's/Corbis

the right to establish their own rules to regulate matters of faith and family rules; so legal pluralism does exist and it may spread further in the future as a result of globalization. For the moment, however, Western states still claim a monopoly on the making of law.

There is a close connection between legal and political systems. It can be said of the law, as it was for politics in chapter one, that its primary concern is the 'authoritative allocation of values in society'. Creating laws to regulate human conduct, i.e. legislation, has been one of the most basic functions performed by states since earliest times. This is 'rule by law'. For laws to be legitimate, i.e. to be accepted by citizens, states have established rules of procedure which are themselves legitimate and have to be followed. They have to be approved in legislatures, a subject to which we shall return in chapter nine. Almost all states have legislatures, although their powers and procedures may vary widely.

There is a second function performed by law. It determines what is criminal behaviour, it prescribes punishments for criminals and it provides impartial rules for binding adjudication in disputes. This is often encapsulated, especially in the West, in the concept of the **rule of law**. This goes further than rule by law. It means that everyone in a society, whether ruler, minister, or ordinary citizen is expected to obey the law. At least in theory, everyone is equal before it. For such a system to enjoy legitimacy, Fuller laid down eight preconditions for laws to be just. See **Box 8.1**. These have been widely taken as the necessary basis for the rule of law.

As enshrined in the American **constitution** and repeated widely in other constitutions since then, the legal system is a check upon the exercise of power by the executive. One essential prerequisite for it to perform that function is independence from the state, in the sense that the state accepts that judges are free to determine the merits of legal cases irrespective of the consequences for state administration. Although an impartial legal system is a check upon the freedom of manoeuvre of legislators and therefore of the majority in a democracy, the rule of law is one of the essential elements of what Western states call **good governance**, a topic to which we shall return in chapter ten. It is certainly an integral feature of **liberal democracy**. We shall return to the adjudication function of legal systems and their relationship with political systems towards the end of this chapter.

➡ See chapter ten, page 242, for a discussion of good governance.

 Box 8.1

List of Requirements for Just Laws

Laws must be: a) general in scope; b) public; c) prospective rather than retroactive; d) clear; e) consistent; f) relatively constant; g) capable of being obeyed; h) enforced as written. (Fuller, 1969: 33–94)

Constitutions

The term 'constitution' can be used in two different ways, one general and one more narrow. In the broad sense it denotes the overall structure of a state's political system. King has recently provided a broad definition. See **Box 8.2**.

This can also be expanded even wider to cover a nation's **political culture**, as when people talk about a particular decision being contrary to the nation's 'constitution', i.e. it may infringe the 'spirit' of the constitution rather than its precise terms.

The second, narrower use of the term constitution refers to a specific document that lays down the basic institutions of state and procedures for changing them, as well as the basic rights and obligations of its citizens. It also serves as the basic source of national law, so that individual laws and legal codes are expected to conform to it. It is, or should be, the core of the legal system. For most states this is a demanding requirement, which requires continual monitoring and, usually, a special constitutional court that can adjudicate whenever there seems to be a conflict. For Islamic states this is an even more onerous obligation, since it involves the harmonization of divinely inspired, avowedly universal shar'iah law with national, civil, more secular codes. For an example of an attempt to devise an Islamic constitution, see Moten (1996: Appendix B). For the more practical difficulties of a constitutional court (in this case in Egypt) trying to cope with these problems, see Lombardi (1998). This could be contrasted with the existing constitutions of Iran and Saudi Arabia.

In practice the difference between the two uses of the term constitution is not nearly as wide as it used to be. Only three states—the UK, New Zealand, and Israel—now do not have a specific constitution. The last twenty years have seen an enormous surge of constitution-writing around the world. At least eighty-one states introduced new constitutions, while a further thirty-three carried out major constitutional reform. In many cases this was a consequence of the collapse of communism and the independence of many states in the former Soviet Union and former Yugoslavia: but it also included Saudi Arabia which adopted a constitution in 1992, Algeria (1989, amended 1996), and Morocco (1996). Therefore, legitimate patterns of political behaviour become both more transparent and also more regularized. But in any case, as King (2007) reminds us, no state includes all of even the most fundamental elements of the

Key Quote   Box 8.2
King on Constitutions

'the set of the most important rules and common understandings in any given country that regulate the relations among that country's governing institutions and also the relations between that country's governing institutions and the people of that country.'

(King, 2007: 3)

political system in a single written document. For example, virtually no state establishes a particular electoral system in its constitution, yet this is a vital element in determining how power can change hands.

In addition to the details of specific constitutions, you should also bear in mind the related notion of **constitutionalism**. This can mean two things. It can encapsulate a normative outlook on the political values embodied in particular country's constitution, i.e. doing things according to its 'spirit'; or it can mean a broader normative standpoint: making the observance of constitutions the most fundamental principle of political life. At its most extreme, this could mean that constitutions, once codified, should remain inviolate. In practice no states make this an absolute principle. Constitutions do change. They are amended or even replaced. However, states generally make it very difficult by insisting upon special procedures for changing them so that such change takes place without haste and after due reflection. This notion of the special status of constitutions in general is part of constitutionalism. Respect for the primacy of the constitution remains a core element of the American political system. The same is true of continental Europe, where the memory of disastrous dictatorships accentuated the attractiveness of a robust constitutional order. The principle of rule of law does underlie a great deal of western advice on good governance to developing countries, where observance of a constitution provides greater governmental transparency and predictability for foreign investors as well as for local citizens.

Key Points

- Common usage of the term 'constitution' is ambiguous. It can mean either a legal document and/or a pattern of rule.

- Constitutions may embody aspirations for future patterns of rule, as well as regulating how that rule should be exercised now.

- Constitutionalism is a normative doctrine giving high priority to the observance of a constitution's provisions and making it effective.

Fundamental Rights

One of the basic features of constitutions is that they usually contain a list of fundamental rights of citizens. The first lists of civil rights were contained in the American Constitution and the list of the Rights of Man from the French Revolution. More recently the UN adopted in 1948 a Universal Declaration of Human Rights. A comparison of the two will show that there has been an evolution in the thinking about the range of rights to which citizens are entitled. The Rights of Man mostly concentrate upon the establishment of a legal basis for the relations between the citizen and the state, so they deal with legal due process. However, they do also focus upon more specific political rights vis-à-vis the state: freedom apart from what the law specifically forbids (Articles 4, 5) freedom of expression (Article 11), and the right both to determine the people's contributions that are made to the state and to expect an account from the state of how those resources have been used (Articles 14, 15).

However, in the twentieth century, constitutions have often gone beyond purely 'political' rights to include broader social rights. These additions usually relate to welfare provisions, but they may also specify other conditions as well. For example, many states (especially those with Catholic or Islamic societies) lay particular emphasis upon the family as the basic unit of society and assign it a privileged position. The Universal Declaration of Human Rights was an early exemplar of this trend of establishing social rights. It includes additional specific political rights that were not mentioned in the Rights of Man. It lays down that every individual has the right to freedom of thought, conscience, and religion, including the right to change them (Article 18); the right to freedom of opinion and expression, including the freedom to receive and impart information and ideas through any media and regardless of frontiers (Article 19); and the right to freedom of peaceful assembly and association (Article 20). In addition, it lays down a number of social rights as well. Everyone has the right to social security (Article 21), to work and equal pay for equal work (Article 23), to rest and leisure with reasonable limits on working hours (Article 24), to a standard of living 'adequate for the health and well-being of himself and of his family' (Article 25), to education (Article 26), and to participation in the cultural life of the community (Article 27). In theory, all states that have accepted the Universal Declaration of Human Rights have also committed themselves to observing it, whether or not its provisions are specifically incorporated into their constitutions.

At least in principle these rights are 'justiciable' within individual states, i.e. a citizen should be entitled to go to law to seek redress if s/he feels that any of these rights are being infringed by his/her government. This depends upon the willingness, and the resources, of individual citizens to pursue their own claims in the courts. More recently a further trend has emerged, especially in the USA and Catholic states, which is support for the 'right to life'. In other words citizens can take up the right of someone else, in this case the unborn, and so prevent abortions.

What is clear from this extension of the rights is that they leave a great deal of room for judicial interpretation. The various welfare and cultural rights do not lend themselves to simple yes or no adjudication. They leave open the question of amount or degree. Is a citizen of a developing country entitled to the same degree of welfare as one in Europe? What level of healthcare? Of education? It leaves open the question of the relative priorities of every sovereign government. Should the courts become involved in determining the levels of welfare spending as opposed to other claims on the budget? This is a

Photo 8.2   Young Girl Carries Water on Donkey
Young girl from an Arab nomad tribe carries water through her village on a donkey.
Source: UN photo by Stuart Price

particularly sensitive issue in democracies. Even in the case of the more 'political' rights, such as freedom of expression and association, where a yes/no adjudication by the courts is more likely, recent experience has shown that these too may increasingly have to be balanced against other public priorities. For example, the right to freedom of expression may have to be weighed against the 'right' to public security, viz. the examples of government restrictions to prevent incitement of hatred or terrorism.

Thus, although the twentieth century has seen a dramatic expansion in the range of rights to which citizens are supposedly entitled, there is still scope for individual legal systems to come up with a great variety of interpretations. All of this explains why in democracies, perhaps even more than in **authoritarian** regimes, the court system is increasingly limiting the freedom of manoeuvre of elected governments. This is true even of Britain, which did not have a Charter of Human Rights of its own, but since 1998 has subscribed to the European Convention on Human Rights as laid down in the Human Rights Act.

Increasingly, constitutions of nation-states contain not only provisions regulating the operation of specific institutions. They also contain aspirations about the direction in which their respective political systems are expected to develop. This has always been a feature of constitutions of states in Latin America, but it is increasingly prominent in Europe and also in Islamic societies. In so far as they contain provisions that are not yet realized, then they also allow greater scope for the courts to contribute to the realization of those aspirations. In that sense they allow for greater legalization of the political process. In fact they will contribute to it.

Key Points

- Over the last two centuries there has been an increasing number of universal rights.
- They have expanded from political freedoms to rights to welfare, cultural protection, and cultural respect.
- There is a potential clash between the enforcement of rights by courts and the sovereignty of parliament.

Constitutional Courts and Judicial Review

Chiefly because of the sensitivity of the issues that they are called upon to determine, all states have a constitutional court of some kind. As we shall see, this is particularly true of federal states where constitutional guarantees to subnational units are a crucial reassurance that their interests will not be repressed. Some courts may be called by that name specifically. Others may assume that role as part of a wider range of judicial functions. Even Britain, which does not have a formal constitution, entrusts the function of interpreting the legality of laws to the Appellate Committee of the House of Lords—at least until 2010, when a new Supreme Court will be established.

In most countries those who serve on these courts are either trained and experienced lawyers, or academic lawyers. France is something of an exception, however, in that its *Conseil constitutionnel* has more limited powers. It can only pass comment on a law in the short period of time between its approval in parliament and its promulgation. Once promulgated, a law in France cannot be changed, except by parliament; and it is not required that a member of the Conseil be a lawyer—sometimes they are distinguished politicians. At present, out of eleven members, two are former presidents of the republic, another two former ministers, and only two are professional lawyers.

One trend that has become more evident in recent years has been the readiness of courts in the USA and the UK to challenge government decisions through judicial review, on the grounds that fundamental rights have been infringed, or that administrators have failed to observe due process. While this has often been regarded as at the very least embarrassing or irritating for governments, the courts have justified this intrusion by the need to ensure that human rights have been duly observed, even those of condemned criminals. Although this appears to be a tendency that is spreading to other countries, France again is an exception. There the state takes the view that challenges to the constitutionality of potential human rights abuses are better raised in parliament, which has the duty of holding the government to account, than by the courts. British judges used to share this view until the 1970s, but no longer (King, 2007: 115–49).

Key Points

- States establish special courts, or legal arrangements, to safeguard constitutions.
- There is an increasing tendency to appeal for executive policy-making to be subject to standards laid down by judicial review.

Legal Adjudication of Political Problems

As these examples show, within the general trend of creeping legalization of political life, there remains considerable scope for variation in the interpretation and implementation of even universal human rights by the courts of different nations. This is not only because of the interests, or self-interest, of particular nation-states, but also because of different approaches to the ultimate objective of the justice that legal systems are expected to dispense. Approaches to the function and purpose of law also vary from one country to another. As Montada (2001) put it: the concern for justice seems an anthropological universal, but it takes many faces, because there are divergent views on what is meant by the term and how it is realized in particular legal jurisdictions. Let us outline four basic differences, and they revolve around different interpretations of the meaning of 'justice'.

The first can be summarized as a kind of legal positivism. The law of a particular country is neither more nor less than the sum of the laws which it has established.

It can be summed up by a common phrase used by French lawyers: *La loi est la loi*. This means that the wording of each individual law as approved by parliament, as well as the whole legal code, is sacrosanct. It is inappropriate for judges to seek to enquire whether any particular law is phrased inadequately. Their task is simply to enforce it.

This approach to constitutional issues is replicated in France's former colonies, but it resonates more widely too. In pre-modern China there was a school of legal thinking called the Legalists. Their main concern was to ensure that the Chinese obeyed the law. As long as they did, this would ensure order and harmony in society and prevent **anarchy**. The Legalists were not especially interested in 'justice' except in so far as an orderly society was also a just one. It was order and harmony that was just, not necessarily any particular law. They wanted to deter law-breaking, as that would be unjust. To this end, extreme punishments were 'just', however brutal for the individual law-breaker, as they would ensure justice for the rest of society. This was rule by law, but it was aimed at making people fear rulers and officials. It was law for **deterrence**.

A second approach to the social function of law was typified by communist states. Here the function of law was subordinated to some higher, non-legal goal: communism itself. Universal human rights were of lesser concern, except in the indefinite future, even if such states' constitutions specifically upheld them. Judges had to be members of the Communist party, which meant that they had to defer to the party leadership. So appeals to the courts to defend the human rights of political dissenters were bound to fail. And still in China today officials of the communist party can only be prosecuted for criminal offences after the party leadership has agreed. Thus, although in China there is increasing talk of 'rule of law' replacing 'rule by men', there is still a long way to go, at least by Western standards.

A third approach to law and society can be seen in Islamic states. In general there is no doubt about the traditional importance of justice and the law there. According to Rosen: 'Everywhere one encounters in Islamic life the idea of justice' (Rosen, 1989: 74). For Lewis, 'the traditional Islamic ideal of good government is expressed in the term "justice" ' (Lewis, 2005: 39), and according to Hallaq (2005: 193), 'if ever there was any pre-modern legal and political culture that maintained the principle of the rule of law so well, it was the culture of Islam'. However, in so far as this rule of law existed, it was more because of practice, rather than because of the explicit separation of the powers of rulers and judges as in the West: it was because both rulers and judges were supposed to defer to the revealed law of the shari'ah. In general, rulers appointed and could dismiss judges. There was no notion of ordinary people having rights vis-à-vis their rulers, unless the latter broke divine law.

On the other hand, the state did not claim the same monopoly over law-giving as western states do. Laws were mainly formulated by legal scholars, not by rulers; and there are four equally respected schools of legal scholarship to which Sunni judges could belong (the Hanafi, Maliki, Shafi'i, and Hanbali). The traditions of these schools could lead to different decisions in particular cases, especially commercial ones. People could choose their lawyers according to the type of decision they would be likely to make in a particular dispute. Moreover, there was not the same insistence upon consistency between the decisions of judges and upon binding precedents. Judges much more frankly tried to do justice according to the particular circumstances of an individual case, rather than forcing the facts to fit a set of orthodox decisions. There was no systematic codification of legal precedents. Therefore, traditionally in Islamic societies there was a tendency for political monism but legal pluralism, whereas in the West we find the obverse: a greater tendency towards political pluralism and legal monism, with legal systems expected to deliver consistent authoritative verdicts.

By contrast the fourth approach to legal justice—what we can loosely term the Western approach—places greater stress upon **procedural justice**. This means making sure that verdicts are similar and more consistent in similar sets of circumstances. It requires a greater legal bureaucracy to ensure consistency of verdicts, with one or two higher layers of appeal courts, as well as ministries of justice to administer them. It also risks delivering verdicts that are less well tailored to individual circumstances. However, it does provide greater predictability about likely outcomes to court cases. Gradually the Western approach spread more widely around the world in the nineteenth and twentieth centuries. It was part of the spread of the Western state that was described in chapter seven, and it also contributed to it, because the state took the responsibility of codifying laws and creating the judicial apparatus to achieve this. Again one of the best examples is Japan. As the Japanese state sought to respond to challenges from the West in the second half of the nineteenth century, it sent scholars to Europe to study alternative national legal systems, particularly Britain, Germany, and France, and present comparative reports on the respective merits of different legal codes. In the end Japan turned to the principles of German administrative law to provide the basis of its new code of administrative law, while it turned to Germany and France for the principles of commercial law. Turkey responded in similar ways as it sought to withstand the challenge to its own empire from Europe. From the 1870s onwards, Turkey too began to produce legal codes that grafted western legal principles and the organization of justice on to its own well-established forms of jurisprudence and courts, and these were then spread throughout its empire in the Middle East. Civil courts assumed greater authority over religious ones. Gradually the state assumed control of the legal process as it embarked on Western-style modernization.

➡ See chapter seven, page 164, for a discussion of the rise of the Western-type state.

Although the Western legal practices and norms have spread around the world, this does not mean that they have become universal and fully consistent. The decision in 2007 of President Musharraf of Pakistan to 'correct' the Supreme Court by dismissing most of the judges and replacing them with more pliant ones was a striking example of persisting differences. It resonated with earlier traditions of Islamic rulers; and in Islamic states in general, as mentioned above, there remains a shifting tension between the prescriptions and reasoning of shari'ah law and civil codes.

In addition we should also remember that other elements in the context of national legal systems may also have a significant bearing on the way law is practised. Epp, for instance, has shown how the pursuit of civil rights in a number of states with quite similar legal frameworks—the USA, India, the UK, and Canada—has varied considerably according to the legal infrastructure of individual countries. In particular, what matters is the availability of public resources to help poorer litigants pursue cases. Litigants in the USA and Canada find this much easier than in the UK or India. The consequence is that there has been a much stronger movement to pursue rights-related cases in North America, with Canada in particular undergoing what Epp describes as 'a vibrant rights revolution' since 1960. He explains this in part by the adoption in 1982 of the Charter of Rights and Freedoms, but also in part by a growing support structure for legal mobilization (advocacy organizations, government aid for litigants, lawyers, and legal scholars who changed the previous prevailing conservative mindset of the legal system) (Epp, 1998: 156, 195–6). The availability of resources for litigation has an important impact upon the pursuit of rights. What this shows is that there is a close connection between a country's legal system and the evolution of its political system. The two interact with and impact each other.

Even the simple fact of the number of lawyers that are qualified in a country will have a big impact on the place of law in a nation's public life and therefore on citizens' ability to have recourse to law. The United States has almost one million qualified lawyers, which represents about 0.3 per cent of the population. This reflects a society that is prone to litigation but the availability of lawyers no doubt also contributes to it. The UK has half that figure, Germany has a quarter, France an eighth, while Japan and India have only roughly one twenty-fifth. No doubt this also played a part in the limited pursuit of rights in India that Epp mentioned above. These figures explain the widespread perception that the Japanese are very reluctant to go to law and to the courts when they have a problem. They try to find alternative ways of resolving disputes.

This section has argued that a whole range of factors contribute to a variety of interpretations of the rule of law in the practice of legal systems in different regions of the world.

Key Points

- Orientations on appropriate functions for legal systems have traditionally varied from country to country.
- This can lead to different interpretations of even universal rights.
- There is a distinctive emphasis in Western jurisprudence on realizing procedural justice through greater consistency and bureaucratic organization.

Federalism, Consociational Democracy, and Asymmetrical Decentralization

The American Constitution was explicitly designed to restrain the power of the state. One way, as we have seen, was through the establishment of checks and balances, with the threefold division of power between executive, legislature, and judiciary. There was, however, a second way. This was through the establishment of a federal system. The territorial decentralization of power, it was hoped, would further obstruct any possible oppression. Ever since then, **federalism** has been touted as a solution to the risks of potential dictatorship. The importance of this idea can be seen in the federal constitution that was imposed upon West Germany after the Second World War. It was intended to undermine the remaining roots of Nazi dictatorship and it has justified the hopes that were placed upon it. These institutions have taken root in the German political system and have made Germany a reliable democratic partner in the heart of Europe.

In general, what is federalism? According to Robertson (1993: 184):

'Federalism' is now used to describe such a form of government, in which power is constitutionally divided between different authorities in such a way that each exercises responsibility for a particular set of functions and maintains its own institutions to discharge those functions. In a federal system each authority therefore has sovereignty within its own sphere of responsibilities, because the powers which it exercises are not delegated to it by some other authority.

What this definition emphasizes is the constitutionally backed equality between the national government and the federal units for responsibility for performing particular functions. It reassures the federal units or states that their decisions cannot be overridden by some higher authority. It is a protection against a domineering centre or worse.

To provide substance for that protection, federal systems usually establish two institutions. First, there is normally a two-chamber parliament, with the upper chamber composed of representatives from the states. The latter are given specific powers to ensure that their constitutional prerogatives cannot be legislated away without their consent. Secondly, there is usually a constitutional court to rule upon the constitutionality of legislative proposals, again aimed at reassuring the states that they cannot be coerced into submission.

Generally, however, since the American Revolution, federalism has been called upon to provide a constitutional framework for states facing two other challenges. The first is simply territorial size. Most federal states occupy a large area. As can be seen from Table 8.1, eight of the ten largest states in the world by area are federations. Of course many of them are heterogeneous in terms of population, but size is also an important issue. Here Australia is the paradigmatic example. The federation there was originally created in 1900 to allow significant devolution of power to individual states because of the difficulties of trying to run the whole country from Canberra, given the communication technologies that were available at that time. Diversity of population was not a significant factor in the decision.

In most cases, however, federalism has been proposed to provide guarantees for minority communities—usually ethnically based—that they will be able to preserve their particular way of life, their culture, their language, their religion, etc. Or, at any rate, that there will be no political challenge to them. Because of this, as can be seen from Table 8.2, federations vary considerably in size, some being very small indeed.

8

State	Federal/Unitary
Russia	F
Canada	F
USA	F
China	U
Brazil	F
Australia	F
India	F
Argentina	F
Kazakhstan	U
Sudan	F

Table 8.1 Federalism among the Ten Largest States in the World by Territory

The experience of federations is of course not always positive. There is quite a long list of those that have disintegrated, some disastrously. The collapse of the USSR has been described by President Putin as one of the greatest disasters of the twentieth century, while that of the former Yugoslavia unleashed the greatest conflict in Europe since the Second World War. See **Box 8.3**. Even where federations have survived, some have still gone through bloody civil wars, e.g. Nigeria in the 1960s, or the United States in the 1860s. The recent experience of Belgium, which in 2007 went for over 150 days without a national government, also suggests that they are not always capable of decisive national decision-making. So federations are not automatically capable by their very existence of preventing violent conflict and/or dissolution, or of providing effective government. Yet it can be argued that a prime cause of the collapse of the USSR and Yugoslavia was the lack of the legal support and the rule of law without which constitutional provisions of any kind are more vulnerable. It was not the constitutional provisions themselves. On the positive side Stepan (2004: 441) has recently declared: 'Every single long-standing democracy in a territorially based multi-lingual and multinational policy is a federal state.' And Rotimi has maintained that despite the civil war: 'federalism has long been recognized as the indispensable basis for Nigeria's identity and survival' (2004: 328).

Argentina	Germany	Pakistan
Australia	India	Russia
Austria	Iraq	St. Kitts and Nevis
Belgium	Malaysia	Sudan
Bosnia and Herzegovina	Mexico	Switzerland
Brazil	Micronesia	United Arab Emirates
Canada	Nepal	USA
Comoros	Netherlands	Venezuela
Ethiopia	Nigeria	

Table 8.2   List of Federations

Case Study   Box 8.3
The Collapse of the Former Yugoslavia

Yugoslavia was created at the end of the First World War as a state for South Slavs to prevent the return of imperial powers to treat them as colonies. However, between the wars it was bedevilled by enduring enmity between the two largest ethnic communities, the Serbs and Croats. In the Second World War it was dismembered under Axis control and hundreds of thousands were killed in fratricidal conflict.

After Liberation largely by the Communist partisans under Tito the Yugoslav state was restored, this time as a federation. Even the ruling Yugoslav Communist Party was divided into separate federal units. The six federal republics (Serbia, Croatia, Slovenia, Bosnia–Herzegovina, Macedonia, and Montenegro) had equal representation in the federal government, and after 1974 the two autonomous regions of Kosovo and Vojvodina in Serbia were granted only slightly less. Yugoslavia was by far the most genuinely federal communist state. In 1963 it created the only constitutional court in the communist world. For a long time the memory of the blood-letting during the war, a political culture that exalted the shared heroism of the partisan resistance, the pride in a Yugoslav road to socialism based upon workers' self-management, the threat of foreign intervention, as well as Tito's own robust leadership, all helped to preserve national unity. Despite occasional challenges to the leadership (in 1968 a new generation of Croat leaders tried to introduce a more liberal set of policies but were rejected by Tito), Yugoslavia stayed united and prosperous until he died in 1981.

8

Afterwards, however, the state ran into increasing difficulties. There was no cohesion in the national leadership. Tito had avoided naming a successor and he had created a federal system with a collective presidency, where the leader of each of the federal republics acted as head of state for just one year in rotation. He had emphasized the need for national decision making on the basis of 'consensus', i.e. unanimity. After he was gone, all the republic leaders put the interests of their own republic above that of the state as a whole. The national economy fragmented increasingly into republic units. Inter-republic trade actually declined. Inflation continued to increase throughout the 1980s. The national leadership agreed remedies in Belgrade and then refused to implement them when the leaders returned to their republic capitals. No one was prepared to make sacrifices for the good of the country as a whole. Popular dissatis-faction grew. All the nationalities, even the Serbs, the largest one, felt that they were the losers of the Federation. Trust disintegrated across the country.

Then in 1987 the heir apparent to the Serbian leadership, Slobodan Milošević , made a speech at an event commemorating the 600th anniversary of the defeat of the Serbs at the hands of the Ottoman Turks in Kosovo. He made an unexpected appeal for Serbs to stand up for their rights and vowed that Belgrade would back them. This provoked an emotional response across Serbia, which he then tried to turn into a movement to restore decisive national government under his leadership. Large numbers of Serbs were mobilized to march on Montenegro and then Slovenia to bring them to heel. In turn this provoked apprehension in the other republics about resurgent Serbian chauvinism. The constitutional court proved ineffective. The collapse of the communist regimes in Eastern Europe exacerbated the sense of crisis. Partly to forestall similar developments in Yugoslavia, and partly to keep Milošević at bay, the leaders of the Communist parties in Croatia and Slovenia began to call for multiparty elections.

In turn this provoked Milošević to send the federal army into Slovenia and Croatia to try to bring them to heel or, if that failed, to establish a greater Serbia which could protect all Serbs against a repeat of the genocide that they had suffered in the Second World War. With that he launched a civil war that became the biggest conflict in Europe since the Second World War and destroyed the state of Yugoslavia.

(For a discussion of various explanations for the collapse of the former Yugoslavia, see Ramet, 2005.)

➡ See chapter three, page 87, for an introduction to consociational democracy.

Yet in the 1970s the idea that federalism was the naturally most appropriate solution to the problems of division in deeply divided societies was challenged by the theory of **consociationalism**, which was initially introduced in chapter three. This was based upon the experience of a few small states with deep multiethnic and multiconfessional cleavages, largely in Europe, that had achieved intercommunal harmony and cooper-ation without a formal federal system. The first example of this to be cited was the Netherlands. The key to its success was attributed not to formal constitutional arrangements or legalism, but rather to iterated patterns of cooperation between elites in sharing power which generated and reinforced mutual trust. According to Lijphart (1977), there are four main characteristics of consociational democracies. See **Box 8.4**.

In fact, some of the other states that were later adduced as examples of the same practice ran into serious problems. Consociationalism, no more than federalism, is an automatic guarantee of social harmony. Not all of these difficulties were domestically caused. Lebanon, for instance, was destabilized by conflict between Israel and the Palestinians living in Lebanon. Cyprus was destabilized by Turkish invasion. Nevertheless since this model was usually applied to small states in general, this made them more vulnerable in the case of outside intervention. In fact most sets of consociational arrangement have proved relatively short-lived, and not just because of external intervention. Only the Netherlands has remained faithful to the model. This has suggested that the model may be more appropriate as a temporary solution to societies that have recently suffered from major division or conflict. It can help to stabilize the state through increased trust between communities, before some transition to a more permanent set of arrangements replaces it.

Nevertheless, Lijphart (1999) subsequently went on to extend his theory to other states, focusing particularly on the first point. He claimed that democracies regularly governed by coalitions that were much larger than a simple majority in parliament achieved better political and economic results because their policies were 'owned' by much broader sections of society. This ownership was then translated into a more active commitment on the part of broad sections of society to carry them out. He claimed that such more consensual methods of government are more effective in the long run in bringing substantial improvements in the living conditions for their citizens.

Box 8.4

Features of Consociationalism

- Government by grand coalition, i.e. governments included deputies from the parties representing all of the main communities, which usually required that they held far more than a bare majority of seats in parliament.
- Segmental or subcultural autonomy, i.e. each ethnic or confessional community was responsible for administering policies in specific policy areas that affected them.
- Proportional representation in the electoral system, which made simple majoritarian rule very unlikely, and proportionate representation in the distribution of posts in government bureaucracies, the distribution of public funds, and so on.
- Agreement on minority vetoes for certain types of legislation.

Whether or not these claims will be borne out by further examination of the evidence, one last development should be noted. This concerns new state practices in managing their centre–periphery relations around the world. This is a greater willingness to consider flexibility in arrangements between some states or provinces and the centre which is not offered to all those units. States no longer feel that they have to make an exclusive choice between either unitary or federal systems. They sometimes devise hybrid combinations. This can be called asymmetric decentralization or asymmetric federalism, and the general principle can be found in both federal and unitary states. A particularly striking example is Spain, which has granted much more extensive self-governing powers to some of the regions or 'autonomous communities', such as Catalonia, the Basque country, Galicia and Andalusia, than to the other thirteen, although the Catalan political scientist Colomer still calls the Spanish state 'the clearest case of failure...to build a large nation-state in Europe' (Colomer, 2007: 80). The same principle has been applied in the UK, with varying powers granted to the Scottish, Welsh, and Northern Irish assemblies. Even France, where the state has traditionally been very preoccupied with constitutional equality and the dominance of Paris, has granted greater autonomy to Corsica than to other *départements*. All of these are still formally unitary states. Federal states display the same tendency for hybridity. The Soviet Union for decades distinguished between federal republics, autonomous republics, autonomous regions, autonomous districts, all of which had different sets of powers from the more 'orthodox' provinces. Pakistan allows greater self-rule to the north-west frontier region and the federally administered tribal areas as compared with Punjab or Sindh. This means that other states that are confronted by challenges of great ethnic or religious cleavages can draw upon a much wider range of possible precedents to demonstrate flexibility. In many ways the old distinction between federal and unitary states has disappeared, as similar kinds of asymmetrical relationships are introduced into both of them.

Key Points

- Federalism has a dual role: as a check on centralized government, and as a way of managing profound social diversity.

- Federations may collapse without appropriate legal structures or widespread popular support.

- Consociationalism is an alternative approach to handling social diversity, relying on elite cooperation rather than legal formalism.

- Consociationalism may be understood more broadly as a more consensual form of rule than majoritarianism.

- There is an increasing use of asymmetric arrangements to handle diversity in both federal and unitary political systems, which erodes the differences between them.

Conclusion: Growing Legalization of Political Life

This chapter has highlighted four things. The first is the importance of constitutions as fundamental institutions that structure political systems. By establishing the basic principles for political life, they channel the political behaviour of all the inhabitants of a state in various directions and, equally importantly, prevent some other forms of political behaviour; and they help to provide greater transparency about the ways that public decisions are made.

Secondly, constitutions need a developed legal system to give life to the provisions that they contain. Without some kind of accompanying rule of law, constitutions may be flouted by government, or they may be undermined, as the example of Yugoslavia shows.

Thirdly, this still allows for different approaches by which legal systems attempt to achieve justice. Emphases vary from one state to another, and this will also mean that interpretations of universal human rights will to some extent vary from one country to another.

Fourthly, federalism as a form of government does help to prevent excessive concentration of powers in a nation's capital. It can also help to provide reassurance to some minorities that their interests will not be overridden by larger communities. It can promote harmony in heterogeneous states marked by deep cleavages. However, it is not the only structure that can achieve this. Consociationalism offers an alternative approach to the same challenge, although it has tended to succeed only in smaller states, and then over a more limited period of time. More recently, unitary states have shown greater flexibility in devising new forms of decentralization which take account of the regional differences and vary the rights that they offer to particular communities. In this way the boundaries between federal and unitary states are becoming more blurred.

Lastly, there is a trend underlying the argument of this chapter. This is the expanding role played by law in social life. The extent to which law plays a central role in the political process varies considerably from one state to another. It is certainly more pronounced in the developed world, especially the USA. However, the trend is much more widely evident. Pakistan is but one example. The attempt by President Musharraf in 2007 to curtail the independence of the Supreme Court provoked concerted resistance from lawyers as a whole, with widespread popular support.

There are two dimensions to this trend. It encompasses first a growing tendency to devise legal frameworks to regulate an increasing number of dimensions of social behaviour within individual states, and secondly an expansion of international legal activity to support globalization (Buxbaum, 2004; Lieberman, 2001). We have already mentioned the increased use of judicial review in the USA and most European states. The change in the growing salience of law and legal processes is striking in the case of a state such as China which at the beginning of its reforms in the early 1980s had only

200 lawyers and now has over 100,000. The increase in the number of trained lawyers certainly marks a change in the direction of the rule of law, even if China is still a long way from practising it in the same way that the West does. This trend does make for greater checks upon the power of the state and the executive branch of government; but it also makes politics more complicated, more difficult for non-lawyers to understand. Dahl has remarked that the American system 'is among the most opaque, confusing, and difficult to understand' among Western democracies (Dahl, 2001: 115). At roughly the same time in a survey of public opinion in the Trilateral countries (the USA, Japan, and Western Europe), King concluded:

The American people have lost confidence in their government because they have ceased to understand it . . . The American political system was probably hard for most ordinary people to understand when it was first designed in the 1780s . . . it has become even more complicated since then. (King, 2001: 91–3)

The checks on the power of the state may be greater, but is politics becoming more opaque and more esoteric, increasingly confined to a more limited political 'class'? This is an issue to which we shall return in both chapters nine and twelve.

 ## Key Questions

- Go to http://confinder.richmond.edu/country.php and find the longest and shortest constitutions in the world. What would you expect to be the consequences for the operation of the political systems of these two states? How different are they likely to be?

- What is the most absurd constitutional provision that you have come across? Does it deserve the special status?

- If accepted, what difference would the Archbishop of Canterbury's proposals on the adoption of shar'iah legal principles make to the relationship between the state and law in the UK?

- Britain has no formal constitution. What difference does that make as compared with the political arrangements and practices of any other state with which you are familiar?

- Are the French right to resist the expansion of judicial review in political life and leave constitutional challenges largely to parliament?

- Assess Dahl's arguments about the weaknesses of the American Constitution. Is there any likelihood of them being remedied?

- If federalism does indeed weaken the power of the government, does it make weaker states in the developing world too weak? What is the evidence from Nigeria, India, Brazil, and/or Pakistan?

- Do the autonomous communities of Catalonia and the Basque country in unitary Spain have greater powers for self-government than the federal Länder in Germany?

- Are federalism or consociationalism viable solutions to the internal conflict in Iraq?

- If the rule of law is a good thing, does that mean that the more laws a state has, the better?

 Further Reading

Amoretti, Ugo M. and Nancy Bermeo (eds) (2004), *Federalism and Territorial Cleavages*, Baltimore, MD: Johns Hopkins University Press.
   This is an account of the ways in which federalism can manage territorial divisions within states.

Burgess, Michael (2006), *Comparative Federalism: Theory and Practice*, London: Routledge.
   This is a recent account of the theory of federalism.

Dahl, Robert A. (2001), *How Democratic is the American Constitution?* New Haven, CT: Yale University Press.
   This is a study of weaknesses of the American Constitution, including the great difficulty of changing it.

King, Anthony (2007), *The British Constitution*, Oxford: Oxford University Press.
   This is a recent authoritative study of the British 'constitution' in the broad sense.

Lane, Jan-Erik (1996), *Constitutions and Political Theory*, Manchester: Manchester University Press.
   This is an examination of the relationship between constitutions and political theory.

Lijphart, Arend (1999), *Patterns of Democracy: Government Forms and Performance in Thirty-Six Countries*, New Haven, CT: Yale University Press.
   This states the case in favour of big coalition government, including consociationalism, as a more consensual and ultimately more effective form of rule.

 *Web Links*

http://confinder.richmond.edu/country.php
A site offering connections to all the constitutions that are online.

www.archbishopofcanterbury.org/1575
The text of the Archbishop of Canterbury's lecture.

 Visit the **Online Resource Centre** that accompanies this book to access more learning resources at **www.oxfordtextbooks.co.uk/orc/garner/**

9

Legislatures and Legislators

Reader's Guide

This chapter will first survey the functions of legislatures. It will also discuss the growing practice of measures to establish quotas to increase gender equality in legislative recruitment. Then it will consider the systemic issue of presidentialism versus parliamentarianism. It will present a classification of legislatures based upon their capability to stand up to the executive branch of government. After that comes a basic introduction to the internal structure of legislatures: the choice of single or double chambers, and the role of parliamentary committees. Then it will deal with trends in the backgrounds of members of parliament in various countries, specifically focusing upon the criticism that they constitute a 'political class'. Finally there will be a Conclusion.

Functions of Legislatures

At present there are 263 parliamentary chambers in 189 countries. This means that a little under one-third of countries have two chambers. If we bear in mind the subnational elected bodies that determine policies for more restricted areas, there are thousands of elected bodies around the world. It is no wonder that legislative studies is one of the oldest branches of political science. Within this potential diversity, there is a paradox about the main object of the studies. Gamm and Huber (2002: 313) present it clearly: 'The scholarly world of legislative studies is, overwhelmingly, a world that studies the US Congress. And the study of Congress tends to be the study of the postwar House of Representatives.' Yet this chapter will illustrate much of the diversity from around the world, not just the USA.

Legislatures are crucial institutions in any political system, but above all in democracies. A democracy would be inconceivable without a parliament. They are vital elements in the structures of power within the state and they usually, though to varying degrees, act as checks upon the freedom of manoeuvre of the state executive. Without legislatures power in the modern state would be highly concentrated and potentially oppressive. They are essential in upholding constitutions because they can publicize attempts to subvert them and they can support the courts if the executive attempts to undermine or suspend them.

There are two ways of presenting a comparative overview of legislatures, as indeed is the case for most political institutions. One way is to focus upon the functions that they perform. In that sense they or the actors who devised them are responding to a perceived need in the political system. The second way is to concentrate upon institutional arrangements that are common so as to show their similarities and differences: in this case debating chambers, standing committees, how members of staff run their offices and handle links with constituents, and so on. We shall largely concentrate on the former type of exposition—the functional—but we will examine one particular institutional issue: the differences between parliamentary and presidential political systems and their respective merits.

The functions of parliaments can be divided into three broad groupings. First, there are the representational functions, where parliaments represent either the views of citizens, or are representative of particular groups in society. Secondly, there are governmental functions: legislatures contribute to forming governments, formulating policy, ensuring the accountability of government for its actions, and enhancing government communication with citizens. Thirdly, there are procedural functions that determine the procedures under which legislatures do their work (Olson, 1994).

Representation

The original function of parliaments in Europe was to provide a forum where different classes in society could express their views to the monarch on matters of public concern.

Their role was purely consultative. There was no sense that parliaments could decide policy, let alone impose their will on monarchs. Gradually, however, they acquired greater authority as rulers saw fit to consult them when needing to raise taxes for public works, most importantly for raising armies. Thus, not only did the European state grow in response to the needs of war, as suggested in chapter seven, parliaments did so as a means of constraining the ability of monarchs to make war.

➡ See chapter seven, page 164, for a discussion of the rise of the European state system.

Inherent in parliaments, therefore, is the notion that they are representative of wider society. To be legitimate they have to 'represent' the people. However, over time different dimensions of possible representativeness have been proposed. In practice these are difficult to reconcile, not least because the composition of parliaments is also inevitably intertwined with the electoral system on which they are based, as discussed in chapter eleven. So states with different histories and different national priorities may arrive at different institutional solutions to the same problem.

➡ See chapter eleven, page 265, for a discussion of party systems.

Does representation mean that deputies should be numerically representative of particular sections of society, as were originally the Lords and Commons in the UK? Should the numbers of female representatives roughly correspond to the number of women in the population as a whole? What about ethnic minorities? One perspective on this is offered by Jacobson (1997: 207). He points out that in the US Congress, blacks and Hispanics are under-represented, though the disparity between share of population and share of representatives is not as great as in the case of women; but he condones this with a different slant on representation. 'Congress is probably quite representative of the kinds of people who achieve positions of leadership in the great majority of American institutions. What it does produce is a sample of local elites from a remarkably diverse nation.' Election to Congress is certainly an elite achievement, and so it would be both more appropriate and realistic for members of Congress to be representative of elites rather than the population as a whole. This was not, however, an explicit objective of the Founding Fathers. Rather it is a rationalization.

A more recent trend has been actively to seek to make the composition of legislators correspond more exactly to the basic structure of the population as a whole. Most obviously this has concerned the proportion of women in parliaments. Figures for parliaments in various parts of the world were shown in Table 6.2 in chapter six.

➡ See chapter six, page 143, for Table 6.2.

In that respect, communist regimes were more 'representative' than states in the West because members of their parliaments were statistically fairly representative of broad sections of society. However, in recent years there has been an active movement around the world to increase the proportion of women in national legislatures in democracies. There are now at least forty countries that have introduced quotas for female representatives in legislatures, while in a further fifty countries, political parties have adopted quotas for female candidates for election (Dahlerup, 2005: 145). At present, as Table 6.2 suggested, there is still a long way to go before such quotas will be achieved, for reasons that Matland (2005) and Dahlerup (2005) have discussed. Nevertheless it is likely to increase pressure for measures to be adopted to raise the

Photo 9.1

British Prime Minister Tony Blair faces rows of Conservative MPs during the weekly Prime Minister's Question Time in the House of Commons, London, Wednesday 12 October 2005.
Source: PA Photos

recruitment of people from other groups in society that are also regularly under-represented. In that case, at least in democracies, legislatures will undergo major transformation in the coming decades.

Or should 'representation' rather refer, as suggested in chapter three, to the role of deputies in expressing the views of their constituents? In that case, the personal character-istics of individual deputies are less important. Representation is then taken to be an expressive function. Whoever is a member of parliament expresses views on behalf of others. (S)he is understood to be a channel of communication to those in authority. This leaves open the question as to how far a representative is obliged simply to express the views of a larger community of citizens, and how far (s)he has the freedom to express personal opinions or come to individual judgements. In practice, representatives will always have some freedom to do the latter but, as we have seen in chapter three, the view that they are positively entitled to exercise their individual judgement is associated with Edmund Burke and with the practice of the House of Commons. See **Box 9.1**.

➡ See chapter three, page 72, for a discussion of representative democracy.

 Key Quote Box 9.1
Burke on the Relationship between an MP and his Constituents

'Certainly, Gentlemen, it ought to be the happiness and glory of a Representative, to live in the strictest union, the closest correspondence, and the most unreserved communi-cation with his constituents . . . But, his unbiased opinion, his mature judgement, his enlightened conscience, he ought not to sacrifice to you; to any man, or to any sett of men living . . . Your Representative owes you, not his industry only, but his judgement; and he betrays, instead of serving you, if he sacrifices it to your opinion.

Parliament is not a *Congress* of Ambassadors from different and hostile interests; which interests each must maintain, as an Agent and Advocate, against other Agents and Advocates; but Parliament is a *deliberative* Assembly of *one* Nation, with one Interest, that of the whole; where, not local Purposes, not local Prejudices ought to guide, but the general Good, resulting from the general Reason of the whole. You chose a Member indeed; but when you have chosen him, he is not Member of Bristol, but he is a Member of *Parliament*.' (Burke, 1996: 68–9, italics in original)

Some other parliamentary systems adopt a more restrictive view and enshrine the principle of recall, whereby electors can 'recall' their representatives, or rather delegates, either to be replaced or to face re-election for failure adequately to represent the views of their constituents. This is a principle instituted by the French national assembly after the revolution. It subsequently became part of the socialist tradition, so that deputies in communist and some socialist states such as China and Cuba are liable to recall if a significant number of their electors conclude that the deputy has failed to carry out the mandate. Such a provision would guard against deputies elected on a one-party ticket subsequently moving to another party without resubmitting themselves to the electorate for approval.

On the other hand, many states enshrine the principle of parliamentary immunity to protect the right of deputies to speak out without fear of prosecution or threat of libel proceedings for what they may say in parliament. This also means that occasionally, individuals will seek election as a way of preventing, or at any rate postponing, prosecution for some criminal act.

Another key question is: who are a particular deputy's electors? In general, most parliaments enshrine the principle of a direct link between an elected representative and a particular district within the country. There are a few exceptions, e.g. Israel, Peru, and the Netherlands, where voters in a single national **constituency** choose between the lists of candidates offered by different parties, so that those elected accurately represent the national preferences of the people. This ensures that members of parliament are proportionately representative, an issue to which we shall return in chapter eleven. On the other hand, critics of the Israeli system have alleged that this proportionality has exacerbated the difficulties of forming a government, since it concedes excessive power to small parties, which makes executive policy making extremely fraught. According to Amotz Asa-El (2008), a former editor of the *Jerusalem Post*:

Israel maintains the most extreme model of the proportional electoral system and the results are nothing short of disastrous. This system has been depleting Israel's political energies for decades:

➡ See chapter eleven, page 254, for a discussion of proportional representation.

it radicalised the territorial debate, debilitated the economy, obstructed long-term planning, derailed government action, distracted cabinets, diverted budgets, weakened prime ministers, destabilised governments, enabled anonymous and often incompetent people to achieve positions of great influence and responsibility and blurred the distinctions between the executive and legislative branches of government. Perhaps most crucially, it has led talented, accomplished, moral and charismatic people to abandon the political arena.

Chapter eleven will discuss the relative merits of **plurality** versus **proportional repre-sentation** systems. What is important to note here is the effect of the combination of a solely national constituency, proportional representation and a low threshold for parties to be allowed to take up seats—they only need to win 2 per cent of votes to do so in Israel, though it should be remembered that the Netherlands has the lowest threshold in the world of 0.67 per cent, and the same fragmentation and polarization does not seem to occur there. According to Asa-El, an essential element in reform will be the linking of at least some Knesset seats with specific constituencies within the country. This will increase the incentives for representatives to focus on local issues that are of concern to voters. At present its members allegedly pay scant attention to the type of local issues that are the staple of constituency politics in other countries. At least in Israel a wide range of minority views are represented in parliament. If nothing else, this does avoid the risk of neglecting the views of minorities that are not geographically concentrated in a few places so that their local representatives have to listen to them.

➜ See chapter eleven, page 253, for a discussion of plurality versus proportional representation.

For most states the connection between an individual representative and the people that (s)he represents in a territorial constituency is regarded as an essential contribution to the legitimacy of parliament. This is held to be so, even though it may lead to other distortions in the way that the people's overall views are represented. However, this raises another set of questions. Is there an optimal size for a constituency? How similar in size should they be? Further, as citizens constantly move residences, who should be responsible for redrawing constituency boundaries? Most European states assign this responsibility to public officials, but in the USA the boundaries of districts for the House of Representatives are determined by incumbents. This no doubt contributes to the fact that between 80 and 90 per cent of House races are won by incumbents.

The size of constituencies, and the redrawing of their boundaries to reflect demo-graphic changes in their population so as to ensure rough parity between different constituencies, is always a highly contentious issue. In England the maximum disparity in size between parliamentary constituencies is roughly two to one—largely because of the unique size of the Isle of Wight (Boundary Commission for England, 2007: 482–3). Otherwise it would be a great deal more even. In Wales there is only a disparity of one and a half times, but in Scotland it is three and a half times, because of a special requirement that the Orkney and the Shetland Islands form distinct constituencies.

The effect of this is to create even greater disparity within Britain as a whole. The disparity between the Isle of Wight and Na h-Eileanan an Iar is roughly five to one.

In Japan, by the end of the 1970s, urban areas had nearly four times as many eligible voters as rural areas in elections to the lower house of the parliament, the Diet. Since then the disparity has been halved by redrawing boundaries, to roughly the same level as England. But for the upper house, the House of Councillors, there is still a disparity of over five times between different prefectures (Stockwin, 1999: 128–9).

One of the most extreme manifestations of this problem is in the USA, where there is an even greater disparity between states over the number of eligible voters in senate elections. The US Constitution grants two senators to each state of the union, irrespective of size. The consequence is that now Wyoming, the state with the smallest population, has the same number of senators as California, the state with the largest population, even though California's population is 72 times larger; and even though the cumulative effect of this principle is that smaller (often more rural) states have a disproportionate impact on Senate voting, because together they can mobilize a much greater proportion of votes there than their combined populations would warrant, there is no prospect of this being changed because to do so would require a constitutional amendment, and the smaller states can muster enough votes to prevent it.

Key Points

- Members of parliament represent wider society, most often through the means of territorial districts.
- Part of their legitimacy is based upon the assumption that they are also representative of society.
- The extent and ways to which they are 'representative', however, is contentious and varies from one state to another.
- The introduction of quotas to increase recruitment of women in parliament may lead to measures to do the same for other groups under-represented there.

Governmental

Now let us turn to a number of functions performed by parliaments that can be generally termed 'governmental'. This refers to functions that are primarily concerned with forming governments, formulating policy and implementing it.

Presidentialism versus Parliamentarianism

One major function, at least in some states, is the formation of the government itself. In a parliamentary system, the head of the government is almost always decided by the parliament. Thus **parliamentarianism** denotes the principle that parliament is the final arbiter in the choice of the head of the government. The UK is one of the best-known examples. The alternative principle is **presidentialism**, which means that the head of state, whether elected or not, either determines the choice of prime minister, if there is one as in France, or is personally the head of the executive branch of government, as in the USA. In the latter case, the direct election of the president by the whole nation confers a powerful mandate. If there is a separate prime minister, the parliament can offer advice and ratify the decision, but it does not have the power to make the decision itself. In practice the implication of this distinction determines the primary direction of loyalty of members of the executive. Ministers and officials are either primarily responsible for policy to the prime minister or to the president.

In parliamentary systems the normal practice is that the prime minister is chosen because (s)he can command a majority in the parliament. Where a single party has a majority of the seats in parliament, the choice is usually easy. Where no single party has a majority, this usually involves negotiations between several parties who try to form a coalition government. If that fails, then sometimes, minority governments are formed which hold only a significant proportion of the seats in parliament, but not a majority. In that case, the government is obviously more vulnerable to defeat if the opposition can unite against it, but sometimes minority governments can survive for quite a long time by careful selection of policies.

Linz (1992) argued that parliamentarianism is more advantageous for democracy because it leads to greater stability, whereas presidentialism is more fragile. See **Box 9.2**. He based most of his case upon the experience of Latin America which has experienced a high degree of political instability over decades and where almost all regimes have been presidential. He identified one fundamental problem that caused this. Presidential democratic rule assumes a powerful executive based upon a mandate from the whole people, while at the same time legislators also lay claim to popular mandates. Therefore president and parliament are driven by their respective senses of equal public legitimacy for their views into clashes over policy, even where they agreed over the basic direction in which they would like government policy to go. It makes for a 'zero-sum' approach to policy-making, with each side striving for a winner-takes-all outcome.

By contrast, he argued, (1992a,b) parliamentary systems tend to be inherently more flexible. They encourage actors holding different political positions to negotiate

Key Debate Box 9.2
Linz and Cheibub on Presidentialism and Parliamentarianism

'Perhaps the best way to summarize the basic differences between presidential and parliamentary systems is to say that while parliamentarianism imparts flexibility to the political process, presidentialism makes it rather rigid . . . [W]hile the need for authority and predictability would seem to favour presidentialism, there are unexpected developments—ranging from the death of the incumbent to serious errors in judgement committed under the pressure of unruly circumstances—that make presidential rule less predictable and often weaker than that of a prime minister.

Presidentialism is ineluctably problematic because it operates according to the rule of "winner-take-all"—an arrangement that tends to make democratic politics a zero-sum game, with all the potential for conflict such games portend . . . [Parliamentary elections] more often give representation to a number of parties. Power-sharing and coalition-forming are fairly common . . . By contrast, the conviction that he possesses independent authority and a popular mandate is likely to imbue a president with a sense of power and mission, even if the plurality that elected him is a slender one. Given such assumptions about his standing and role, he will find the inevitable opposition to his policies far more irksome and demoralizing than would a prime minister, who knows himself to be but the spokesman for a temporary governing coalition rather than the voice of the nation or the tribune of the people.' (Linz, 1992: 122–3)

'True, presidential democracies are more unstable than parliamentary ones, but this instability is not caused by the incentives generated by presidentialism itself. Presidential democracies die not because the institutions are such that they compel actors to seek extra-constitutional solutions to their conflicts. The conflicts themselves should take some of the blame, since they are probably hard to reconcile under any institutional framework . . . One of the advantages of presidentialism is that it provides for one office with a national government.' (Cheibub, 2007: 165, 168)

compromises because they have to reconcile their own individual mandates with the potential national mandate for government. They can also keep tighter discipline among their members in parliament because they can offer the prospect of promotion to ministerial posts as an incentive to avoid challenging government policies. He found confirmation of his argument in the very successful transition to parliamentary democracy that was achieved in post-Franco Spain. This differed strikingly from the experience of many less successful transitions to democracy in Latin America.

More recently, the President of the Philippines, Gloria Macapagal-Arroyo, has accepted this view of the relative merits of presidential and parliamentary systems to propose a reform from the former to the latter. See **Box 9.3**.

On the other hand, Cheibub (2007) has argued more recently that even if presidential systems appear less stable than parliamentary ones, the reason lies not in the different forms of government themselves, but in the political contexts in which they have to operate. He has claimed that in Latin America there is a tendency for military authoritarian regimes to be replaced by democratic presidential ones, and if the transitions break down, then it is because of a more fundamental crisis of authority than because of the type of system adopted. Thus, the balance of advantages of parliamentary systems as compared with presidential ones may be less clear-cut.

In any case, in practice there are hybrid versions that synthesize these two principles. One form of this is the increasing practice of parties choosing their leader through elections that involve their wider membership rather than simply their own parliamentary

Case Study   Box 9.3
Presidentialism in the Philippines

The Philippines has had a presidential system since 1935 when it was granted greater autonomy as a colony of the USA. It gained independence in 1946. Since then it has been a democracy, with the exception of the years 1972–86, when President Marcos imposed martial law as the constitution barred him from standing for election for a third term. The system is closely modelled upon that of the USA. This means that parties remain fairly weak, with candidates for public office making more personalized appeals.

It has, however, been bedevilled by widespread corruption. In the Transparency International 2006 Corruption Perceptions Index, Philippines was ranked joint 121st, out of 163 countries. Corruption also involves elected representatives. One particular feature of Filipino politics has been the persistence of dynastic political families. Filipino **political culture** lays great stress upon family values. Individual members of these dynasties are able to pass on seats in local councils and the House of Representatives to their children or to relatives. In the Congress elected in 2001, 73 per cent of those elected to the House came from the 2nd, 3rd, or 4th generations of political families (Coronel *et al.*, 2004: 60). The personalized nature of Filipino politics makes it easier for candidates to run expensive personal campaigns, where favours could be traded between generations of political activists. Currently successful candidates for the House need to spend at least US$250,000, and $375,000 for the Senate (Rüland *et al.*, 2005: 119). Success also enables office-holders to lavish business favours upon supporters, thereby increasing the incentive to seek political office for gain.

Periodically in the 1990s proposals were aired for the introduction of a parliamentary rather than a presidential system, on the grounds that it would weaken the power of the president (an important consideration in the aftermath of Marcos' martial law), and also reduce the risk that attempts to get rid of an unpopular president would lead to impeachment and thus undermine the system as a whole (Rüland, 2003: 467–8).

In 2005 President Gloria Arroyo (herself the daughter of a former president) announced a plan to replace the presidential system with a parliamentary one. She justified this on the grounds that presidentialism favoured individuals and that a parliamentary system would strengthen the control of parties over the political system, make them more policy-oriented and reduce the scope for individuals, especially rich candidates, to escalate the costs of electoral campaigns.

While such a reform might certainly change the basic incentives for political careers, it is not so clear whether it would do anything to uproot the political culture that supports and nourishes political families. Rüland (2003) suggested several changes to electoral rules and to the legislative operations of Congress that might address the concerns of the critics. President Arroyo's plans have become bogged down in the Congress. Her plan for introducing the change by 2010 seems unlikely to be achieved, and her term of office ends in that year.

9

members. The main British parties now involve all of their membership in the selection of their leader, although (s)he has already to be an MP and the votes from different sections of the party membership may be weighted differentially. Parties in some states, for example, Canada and Germany, have their prospective candidates for leader in parliament and therefore also for becoming prime ministers, elected by conventions of all party members rather than just the representatives of those parties in parliament. As both are federal states, this allows for the possibility of a national prime-ministerial candidate being chosen who holds a post in one of the state governments rather than from the national parliament. If this happens, then the same party has to find a way of enabling that person to become a member of the national parliament. In general, these reforms have the effect of strengthening the role of party members in selecting their leader, thereby weakening the power of their parliamentary colleagues.

Another hybrid system was devised in France, and has subsequently been copied in other states, e.g. Russia. Here the president is responsible for nominating the prime minister, but the prime minister must enjoy the confidence of parliament. If the parliament passes a vote of no-confidence in the prime minister, then general elections have to be called. The original reasoning behind the introduction of this system was to make the position of the prime minister quite strong and avoid the endless wrangling between small parties that was characteristic of the Fourth Republic up until 1958. On the other hand, it can also make for rivalry between president and prime minister that can divide the government, especially when the latter has ambitions to become president later and uses the post to advance those ambitions. For many years the problem was further complicated by having different terms of office for the president and the prime minister. It was not uncommon for the president and the prime minister to come from different parties because they were elected at different times, when the relative popularity of parties had changed. This led to uneasy periods of **cohabitation**, when the rivalry between the two became much more intense and often paralysed decision making. The same effect can be observed in other states where the terms of office of directly elected heads of state and of parliaments diverge, sometimes leading to different parties controlling the two institutions, e.g. Taiwan, South Korea. The USA has often suffered from a similar problem since the Second World War. The Democrats dominated the House of Representatives between 1954 and 1994, but the Republicans controlled the presidency for more of that time, which led to frequent 'gridlock' in Washington. Even though elected presidents have constitutionally greater powers than prime ministers, and therefore ought to be able to overrule them, the fact that both can claim a mandate from the people and usually take advantage of that to appeal to public opinion to support their views means that the struggle is often quite tangled and intense. Principally for that reason, the French Constitution was amended in 2000 so that both president and prime minister now hold office for identical five-year terms. The same happened in Taiwan in 2008.

Legislation

The second function performed by parliaments today, especially in democracies, is to serve as the basic source of legislation. An alternative term for parliament is legislature, i.e. the supreme law-giver in society. It is the national legislature that determines the final shape of laws, although as we saw in chapter eight, in most states this is now qualified by the need to respect international legal conventions and in many by the practice of judicial review. To some extent, this legal function also helps to explain the relative frequency with which elected representatives have been trained as lawyers. In the USA, which reserves a very prominent role for the law in public affairs as we saw in chapter eight, roughly 40 per cent of House members were lawyers in the mid-1990s, while the equivalent figure for senators was 54 per cent (Jacobson, 1997: 207). In 2005, sixty-eight British MPs (11.7 per cent) were solicitors or barristers from the three main parties. According to the Nuffield electoral studies, this was close to the average of 12 per cent for the five parliaments elected since 1987 (Cracknell, 2005).

→ See the discussion on the growing legalization of political life in chapter eight, page 203.

In practice, however, it is the executive that is the chief initiator of legislation. According to Olson, there is a common experience around the world that 90 per cent of new legislation originates in the executive rather than in parliament, and that 90 per cent of that is adopted (Olson, 1994: 134). This is true even of the USA, where the executive cannot on its own introduce proposed new legislation into Congress: it needs to find sympathetic members of the House or Senate to do so. The picture is more complicated for members of the European Union (EU), where member states have to introduce national legislation to give force to decisions agreed in Brussels. According to a Foreign Office junior minister in 2006, roughly half of UK legislation relating to business, charities, and the voluntary sector originates in agreements between ministers in Brussels, while roughly 9 per cent of all statutory instruments originated there. Reportedly the German government estimates that around 50 per cent of all regulations governing business originates in agreements in Brussels (Miller, 2007: 12, 14). All of this means that today national legislatures primarily respond to initiatives that originate elsewhere.

→ See the discussion of legal adjudication in political life in chapter eight, page 193.

Ensuring Accountability

A third function of parliaments, especially in democracies, is holding the government to account for its actions. This is particularly important in democracies as a way of ensuring that governments honour the commitments that they made to the public when seeking election. It strengthens the incentive for credible commitments and hence increases the chances of a government being replaced at the next election for failure to keep its promises. But even in authoritarian regimes where this is unlikely, parliaments can hold executives to account. According to Olson (1994: 143–4), even under authoritarianism it is difficult for the executive always to control the legislature. He cites as examples the growing activism of the Brazilian Congress under military rule in the 1970s and 1980s, and of the Sejm under martial law in Poland in the 1980s. Another example is China. There the National People's Congress only meets for two weeks per year and thus performs more of a symbolic function as far as legislation is concerned. However, in recent years it has become an increasingly vocal critic of the policies of individual ministries, while refraining from criticizing the government, and therefore the regime, as a whole. In particular it has cast votes condemning inadequate government action to deal with issues such as corruption and crime. Thus simply having parliaments can strengthen trends toward democracy over time.

It should be noted, however, that parliaments are not the only institutions that hold the executive to account. In most states the media also perform this role, whether or not it is explicitly recognized by the state. Also, within the executive there are institutions that keep a check on what other executive agencies do—what O'Donnell (2003) called 'horizontal accountability', which he contrasted with the 'vertical accountability' performed by parliaments. Examples of such agencies are audit offices, such as the National Audit Office in the UK, which check on government spending. In practice all of these institutions contribute to the accountability of government and they often cooperate with each other.

Formation of Public Attitudes

A fourth function of legislatures is to contribute to the formation of public opinion and often to set the agenda for public debate. This is an expansion of the role of representing the views of the people to government. Here parliaments take the lead in forming public opinion as well as providing a forum. Obviously in an era of mass communications where the media play such a role in informing the public about issues of the day, the role of parliaments in this respect is more circumscribed than it was in the nineteenth century, when debates in parliament were reckoned to set the agenda for public debate. Nevertheless there are issues, for example, moral ones such as abortion or environmental ones such as GM foods, where parliamentary debates play a key role in forming public opinion, although the line between parliament forming public opinion and representing it becomes fuzzy. Debates in parliament and in parliamentary committees are regularly reported in the media. In North America the C-Span and CPAC cable networks are devoted full-time to coverage of the US Congress and Canadian parliament. Some parliaments, such as the Bundestag, the Dutch, and Scottish parliaments, have attempted to take advantage of the new communications technologies such as the Internet to stimulate public debate over current affairs. This was an attempt to develop a more reflexive approach to policy-making in society at large—the sort of **deliberative democracy** discussed in chapter three—although it seems to have had only limited success.

➜ See chapter three, page 80, for a discussion of deliberative democracy.

Another way in which parliaments can stimulate public debate in politics can be observed in Sweden. There members of parliament regularly meet with advisory commissions to formulate legislative proposals. This acts as a constraint on both the executive and the **sovereignty** of parliament, but it does help to ensure a wider range of views are involved in the legislative process, which should lead to better legislation (Olson, 1994: 135).

Key Points

- Parliaments perform a number of 'governmental' functions.
- They usually play an important role in the choice of head of government in presidential systems, and in parliamentary ones their role is decisive.
- Parliamentary and presidential systems may have different effects on the stability of democratic regimes.
- There are a number of hybrid systems that attempt to synthesize these two different forms of government.
- Cohabitation of an executive head of state and a prime minister from different parties can easily paralyse government decision-making.
- Today, parliaments mostly respond to initiatives for policy that originate from elsewhere in the political system, primarily the executive.
- Parliaments provide a means for holding governments to account for their election promises.
- Parliaments also provide a forum for national debate.

Procedural

There are also three procedural functions that legislatures perform.

Ritualizing Conflict

Parliamentary activities help to ritualize conflict. They function on the basis of debate, i.e. the expression of differing views. To that extent they legitimize diversity of views and its expression. In the Iranian parliament, for instance, though access to it is restricted to religious parties as secular ones are banned, what would otherwise be in danger of being condemned as factionalism conducted by dissident groups acquires greater respectability or legitimacy (Baktiari, 1996). Critics of democracy sometimes allege that parliaments exacerbate divisions in society by providing opportunities for dissenting opinions to be expressed. It is true that Westminster-type parliaments formalize the role of official opposition to the government. This often, it is alleged, forces the parties not in government into excessive confrontation, further exacerbated by the seating arrangements that have the government and opposition facing each other at a distance of a little over two swords' lengths. In some states such as Taiwan, national legislators exploit the media coverage of their debates to dramatize their differences so as to establish a partisan image that will help their chances of re-election, e.g. throwing lunch boxes at each other.

A response to this is that all societies have a plurality of opinions on any issue and parliament only reflects that. As far as seating arrangements are concerned, a more common arrangement is for the members of parliament to be arrayed in a semi-circle facing the speaker in a debate. Where dissension is particularly extreme, parliaments can help to resolve disputes which might otherwise take a more violent turn. In that sense they 'routinize' conflict, and even though members of parliaments sometimes use parliamentary debate to rouse public opinion in pursuit of extremist goals, it does not mean that parliaments by nature manufacture conflict. Often they can tame its excesses.

Partisanship

Although it occasionally happens that independent members are elected to parliament, in the overwhelming majority of cases legislators represent political parties as well as territorial constituencies. Even in the Chinese National People's Congress, where roughly two-thirds of deputies are members of the CCP, the remaining third have to be approved by the CCP and are expected to support the regime. Unlike the judiciary, members of parliament are expected to hold partisan ideologies that structure their overall views on political issues and priorities. This fact reinforces the role of parliaments as debating chambers out of which better legislation emerges.

Transparency

Parliaments are generally committed to openness, to publicizing issues and policies. A parliament that kept secret its deliberations would make no sense—as was the case with the Supreme Soviet in Stalin's time. It would have purely symbolic value. Although debates in parliaments in authoritarian regimes may publish only edited versions of debates rather than full transcripts, they still to some extent contribute to the publicizing of important issues. They make policy-making somewhat more open. The publication of verbatim transcripts of all their deliberations obviously does this even more. All this contributes to the more open resolution of disagreements in society and thus to its stability. However, this is a problem in societies that are most accustomed to more traditional, possibly more consensual styles of decision-making. It certainly comes as a shock to politicians who are more used only to negotiating deals behind the scenes. The greater openness can be used to embarrass politicians. It upsets and changes political culture.

Key Points

- Parliaments assume diversity of opinions and ritualize political disputes.
- They assume that legislators have partisan opinions.
- They also contribute to open policy making and dispute-resolution.

Types of Legislature

As will be obvious, legislatures vary considerably not only in their powers, but also in their relations with the surrounding political and societal structures. Mezey (1990) produced an influential typology of legislatures to try to identify the range of their possible operations. He proposed a fivefold classification based upon the principle of the capacity of a legislature to stand up to the executive.

1. Active legislatures, such as the US Congress, which is at the centre of the political system and genuinely does have the power to say no to the president as often as it feels necessary.

2. Reactive legislatures, such as the House of Commons, as well as such parliaments as those of France, Germany, India, Sweden, Japan. Here the legislature has less power to withstand the government, but it can set firm parameters within which the government has to act and it can impose sanctions on a government that infringes them.

3. Vulnerable legislatures, such as the Philippines and Italy. Here the legislature is much more pliant, in part because of local political culture that tolerates or at any rate acquiesces in legislators pursuing their own material interests. In Italy the legislature has been more vulnerable because of the difficulties of forming stable coalition governments.

4. Marginal legislatures, such as Pakistan, Peru, Nigeria, Russia under Putin. While these legislatures do perform important legislative functions, they enjoy much more tentative support from social elites. At times the executive has decided that it can do without the legislature and the latter has been unable to resist.

5. Minimal legislatures: here the examples primarily came from communist states, which met rarely and served more the purposes of symbolizing national unity and regime legitimacy than exercising any check upon the government. This is still largely true of the National People's Congress in China, and the Vietnamese National Assembly.

Key Points

- Legislatures can be classified according to the extent to which they can impose their will upon the executive.

- The factors that contribute to this capability derive both from internal factors and the broader political and social context.

Structure of Legislatures

Now let us turn to two structural features of the way that parliaments work.

Unicameral/Bicameral

As mentioned at the beginning of this chapter, roughly one-third of parliaments around the world have two chambers. Thus, one major issue in establishing a parliament concerns whether to have one (**unicameralism**) or two (**bicameralism**) chambers. In practice there is an enormous variety in the arrangements that individual nations make to order the relations between two chambers where this occurs. As of the late 1990s, out of sixty-one second chambers, only nineteen were composed exclusively of directly elected members. Fifteen were hybrids, with mixed memberships of the directly elected and the nominated, while the remaining twenty-seven contained no directly elected members (including the House of Lords). Within these three subcategories, there is still room for enormous variety in the ways in which the second chambers are constituted—for details, see Patterson and Mughan (1999: 6–7). Within this variety it is possible to identify three sorts of factor underlying them. The first is tradition. In the past two chambers allowed for the separate representation of different sections of society, usually the aristocrats in one and the ordinary people in the other. They have generally survived even in the context of a modernizing society, though Denmark took the decision to abolish its upper chamber in 1953 and Sweden did the same in 1959.

➡ See chapter eight, pages 196–200, for a discussion of federalism.

The second reason for an upper house often has to do with **federalism**. The places in it are set aside for representatives from the next lower level of government. This serves as a guarantee to them that their wishes will not be ignored by the national government. It reassures them that they do not need to contemplate leaving the union.

The third reason is the expectation that it will lead to better legislation (Tsebelis and Money, 1997). This is explained in two ways. On the one hand, there is the rationale of efficiency in terms of legislation. The need for legislation to be scrutinized in two chambers rather than one should lead to it being better fit for purpose—what Patterson and Mughan (1999: 12–16) call the principle of 'redundancy'. It allows for a second opinion on the best form of a particular law. The other reason for expecting better legislation is that the need for legislation to satisfy two chambers increases the likelihood that the final outcome will better approximate to the wishes of the population at large (which may be difficult to determine definitively given the difficulties of establishing societal preferences, as suggested by the **Arrow impossibility theorem**, as discussed in chapter eleven), especially if the two chambers have been elected or selected according to different principles or at different times. Both principles resonate with the concern expressed by Madison in *Federalist Papers 62* about the need to prevent over-hasty, too subjective legislation.

➡ See chapter eleven, page 252, for a discussion of the Arrow impossibility theorem.

According to Tsebelis and Money (1997: 4–5), the existence of one or two chambers of parliament makes little difference to the relations between the legislature and the executive, but it obviously does affect the legislative process. This largely depends on the specific powers of the two chambers and the rules that they adopt for regulating the process by which they achieve agreements. Most constitutions give greater powers to one chamber than to the other, especially where control of the government budget is concerned. This obviously determines the way in which the two houses achieve compromise in cases of disagreement. Italy is the exception that proves the rule: there the Senate and the Chamber of Deputies have coequal powers. This obviously complicates the negotiation of agreements, adding to the paralysis of Italian government, although it has been successful in preventing the return of a fascist dictatorship, as it was intended to do.

But even where one chamber is more powerful than the other, the need to find compromises still regularly affects the final version of laws. Even if one chamber lacks the power to veto proposals (as in the case of the House of Lords at present), the process of trying to achieve compromise will affect at least some legislative outcomes. The mechanism used to achieve this compromise will also affect the outcome: is it a joint committee of both houses, or does a bill have to be considered by full sessions of each chamber, and in both cases what kind of majority is needed? All this makes a difference.

Committees

In practice, legislators spend most of their time working in committees rather than in full sessions of the parliament. This is because most of the detailed consideration of proposed legislation is carried out in ad hoc committees convened to consider particular bills. In addition, most parliaments also establish permanent committees to effect regular scrutiny of the workings of individual ministries. They often interrogate ministers and senior officials, and sometimes they hold enquiries into particular issues of policy that the members think worthy of consideration or reconsideration. As some of the committee members may have long experience of parliament and government, they may be very knowledgeable about particular policy areas, in which case they can embarrass ministers or even the government as a whole. For legislators from parties not in government, this can be a very useful way of weakening the popularity of the party or parties in power, and thereby establishing their own credibility as alternatives. It is also another way of parliament fulfilling its functions of the formation of public opinion and the visibility of policy-making. However, beyond that, parliaments differ considerably in their committee arrangements. Some parliaments, such as the German and Swedish, allow these parliamentary committees to propose legislation to the house as a whole, whereas this cannot happen at Westminster. In France there are a few, large, permanent committees that divide into ad hoc committees to consider specific bills.

Key Points

- Bicameralism may offer the prospect of better legislation that corresponds more closely to the preferences of the population, but it is more time-consuming.

- The procedures for resolving disagreements between two chambers will affect the particular legislative outcomes.

- Most parliamentary work is done in committees of the legislature.

Legislators

Now let us turn to some common features of those securing election as legislators. In democracies, as has been explained above, there is a presumption that members of parliament are representative of the population at large. This is true in only the most general terms, for most people obviously do not stand for election to parliament. In general, legislators tend to be male, better educated than the average citizen, and to come from the middle class (even if they represent socialist parties).

➜ See chapter one, page 33, for a discussion of elitism.

In fact, commentators have commented on a growing tendency among Western states for the emergence of a political 'class'. The term was originally coined at the end of the nineteenth century by Gaetano Mosca, the Italian political scientist who was mentioned in chapter one. By this he meant, as Oborne (2007: 24) explains, a group that is 'self-interested, self-aware and dependent for its economic and moral status on the resources of the state'. However, according to Oborne, it did not fit the reality of that time very well, because there were significant external checks upon political figures and because the resources of the state were not so easily bent to serve them. Now, however, he argues: 'The Political Class has won its battle to control Britain . . . In an unannounced takeover of power, the public domain has been seized by the Political Class' (Oborne, 2007: 310). Nor is this argument made about Britain alone. Rizzo and Stella (2007) have made much the same claim about Italian politics, where they stigmatize 'an oligarchy of insatiable Brahmins'.

Academics as well as journalists have begun to make use of the same concept. Borchert (2003: 6), for instance, introduced the term in a study of most OECD countries and explained it as meaning the political class that 'lives off politics' and acts as a 'class for itself'. Actually, as Borchert emphasizes (2003: 16), the concept is bound to be fuzzy at the edges when applied to individual countries. It is clear that it includes legislators and elected members of lower-level public councils, as well as employees of political parties; but should it apply to judges who are publicly elected, as in the USA and Germany? Also, what about party nominees on the boards of state-owned companies in many states of Europe? Clearly, therefore, it will be difficult to achieve full comparability.

Nevertheless, this term has analytical utility and potentially much wider comparative application. As we have already seen in chapter seven, accounts of politics in African states also typically emphasize the widespread pursuit of politics for the purposes of making money (Bayart, 1993; Chabal and Daloz, 1999). So the term could be used as the basis for wider comparative studies. What Borchert and his colleagues also highlight is a more recent phenomenon specific to OECD democracies, namely the emergence of a category of political professionals who are skilled in the arts of winning elections, whether as candidates or working for candidates, and who have never had another career. In earlier periods members of parliament included a much higher proportion of people for whom politics was their second or third career, people who had had a wider experience of life, which they then brought to their legislative activity. This is no longer so common and it is now often regarded as a defect.

→ See the discussion in chapter seven, page 173, on strong states and weak states.

This trend is not uniform and it has national specifics in the way that it operates. In Japan and Ireland, for instance, a surprisingly high proportion of members of the national parliament are the children of older legislators who used to hold the same constituency. In Japan the figure had risen to 28 per cent of deputies to the Lower House of the Diet in 2003 (Usui and Colignon, 2004: 408–9), while in Ireland the figure remained fairly constant between 22 and 25 per cent between 1992 and 2002 (Gallagher *et al.*, 2003: 114). This certainly suggests class-like characteristics, but does not seem to be replicated in other countries, though there certainly are individual cases of parliamentary seats passing from father to child in other countries. The income of political professionals varies considerably from one country to another. To some extent that reflects different degrees of self-interest on the part of politicians in different countries.

If this trend towards increasing professionalization of political careers is regarded as problematic, it remains doubtful whether any specific measures can be proposed to reverse or change it. Sutherland (2004) suggested that an alternative would be random selection of individuals for service in parliaments just as juries are chosen, arguing that it is especially appropriate for British conditions. Actually, this approach resembles the one adopted in the short-lived Paris Commune of 1871, which then had a great influence on the world socialist movement. The Bolsheviks in Russia initially attempted to establish something similar in October 1917, but the rapid onset of civil war then undid it. It still has iconic significance for some socialists. Nevertheless, while it certainly might seem fairer, it is not clear that this would preserve legislative professionalism, or that it would in practice enable parliament to stand up to a much more experienced government. A succession of inexperienced members of parliament would make it easy for the executive to mislead them or conceal things from them.

Key Points

* There is an increasing trend of professionalization of political representatives
* Some have alleged that this has already led to the emergence of a 'political class'.

Conclusion

Finally, let us consider the regard in which parliaments are held by their citizenry. It might be expected that parliaments elected by the people would enjoy broad popular support, especially in democracies with free and fair elections; yet the World Values Surveys suggest differently. To some extent democratic citizens are more suspicious of their representatives. In the most recent round carried out in 1999–2002, there was an enormous range of answers to the question on the confidence that people had in their parliament, as can be seen from Table 9.1.

What this shows is a tendency for people in countries in the developing world to have greater confidence in their parliaments than citizens in the developed world. The World Values Surveys also asked questions about confidence in other institutions. Overall the average around the world for those with confidence in parliament was lower than that for national governments (50 per cent), the press and the civil service (44 per cent each), but more than political parties (30 per cent).

While this does not suggest a great challenge to the existence of parliaments, it does suggest widespread scepticism about either how parliaments or how politicians operate, or both. Arora (2003: 36) has remarked on the public image of the Indian parliament being 'at a very low ebb'—and this for a country where the World Values Survey showed a relatively high level of public confidence at 55 per cent. At the same time, we should also bear in mind Norton's comment (1998: 190) on legislatures in Western Europe. He observed that the fundamental relationship between the legislature and the executive is

Vietnam	97	Turkey	43
China	95	France	41
Tanzania	79	USA	38
Uganda	77	Germany	36
Pakistan	76	UK	36
Iran	70	Italy	34
Philippines	62	Russia	19
India	55	Macedonia	7
Sweden	51	**Average**	41
Spain	48		

Table 9.1   Confidence in Parliaments

Proportion of respondents in various countries answering 'a great deal of confidence' or 'quite a lot of confidence' to the question: 'How much confidence do you have in parliament?'

Source: Inglehart *et al.* (eds) (2004) *Human Beliefs and Values*, E075

determined by factors external to the legislature—the constitution, the political culture, the state of the economy, and so on. Therefore, when people criticize parliaments, they are often in reality complaining about something else. Mainwaring concluded something similar from a series of studies on the legislatures in the five Andean states of Bolivia, Colombia, Ecuador, Peru, and Venezuela. He and other collaborators chose this region because it has a particularly low level of public confidence in parliaments by world standards as well as those of Latin America—and this was despite the fact that all the countries in the region had experienced a widening and deepening of representation over the previous thirty years. His conclusion was that this lack of confidence was primarily the result of popular perceptions of broader deficiencies in the political system as a whole. The economies had failed to develop and so had standards of living. There were also serious problems with corruption. Thus the popular lack of confidence in legislatures reflected a deeper dissatisfaction with the failure of the political system as a whole to deliver a better quality of life to the people. While it is true that sovereign parliaments in democracies have in principle the power to change government in ways that the people want, they may not in practice be able to achieve the changes that people would want. Institutions such as the judiciary or the military, even if corrupt, may resist political pressure. Thus, assessments of legislatures are inseparable from assessments of the political system as a whole. Almost all of these Andean states can be included in the category of 'weak states' presented in chapter seven. 'Better state performance is key to promoting greater confidence in the institutions of representative democracy and greater satisfaction with democracy' (Mainwaring, 2006: 331). Policy implementation is as important as policy formulation. Chapter ten will go on to consider ways in which states formulate policies.

9

➜ See chapter seven, page 173, for a discussion of strong states and weak states.

 *Key Questions*

- How threatening for democracy is the emergence of a 'class' of 'professional' politicians in the UK? Can anything be done to prevent it?
- What should be the powers and functions of a reformed House of Lords as a second chamber?
- Does a second chamber of parliament make it more likely that laws better reflect the preferences of the whole population? Are there any circumstances in which it might not?
- Assess the arguments in favour of presidential and parliamentary systems? What evidence do the experiences of states performing democratic transitions since 1989 provide to justify one choice or the other? What difference, if any, would the replacement of presidentialism by a parliamentary system be likely to make for Filipino democracy?
- How representative should a legislature be of the citizens of a given country? In what ways?
- Assess the arguments in favour of special measures to increase gender equality among members of parliament. Should the same arguments be applied to other groups in society currently under-represented?
- How far does it matter if there is great disparity in the size of constituencies electing representatives to the same legislature? Why?
- Are citizens in democracies more critical of their representatives? Why?
- How far should parliaments seek to lead public opinion, and how far should they simply follow and represent it?
- How useful is the term 'political class' in comparing the politics of different states?

 Further Reading

Ballington, Julie and Azza Kazam (eds) (2005), *Women in Parliament: Beyond Numbers*, Stockholm: International IDEA, revised edn, www.idea.int/publications/wip2/index.cfm.#toc
  An international discussion of ways in which the number of female legislators could be increased.

Jacobson, Gary C. (1997), *The Politics of Congressional Elections*, New York: Longmans, 4th edn.
  An authoritative account of the evolution of election issues in the USA.

Lijphart, Arend (ed.) (1992), *Parliamentary Versus Presidential Government*, Oxford: Oxford University Press.
  The argument in favour of a parliamentary system.

Mehra Ajay, K. and Gert W. Kueck (eds) (2003), *The Indian Parliament: A Comparative Perspective*, Delhi: Konark Publishers.
  This presents aspects of politics and procedure in the parliament of the world's largest democracy from a European perspective.

Mosca, Gaetano (1939), *The Ruling Class*, New York: McGraw-Hill.
  This is a classic of political analysis.

Norton, Philip (ed.) (1998), *Parliaments and Governments in Western Europe,* London: Cass, 2 vols.

This is an authoritative compendium of material on various European legislatures.

Oborne, Peter (2007), *The Triumph of the Political Class,* London: Simon & Schuster.

This is a political columnist's indictment of the political class in Britain.

Sutherland, Keith (2004), *The Party's Over: Blueprint for a Very English Revolution,* Exeter: Imprint Academic.

This is a radical proposal for the random selection of members of parliament.

Tsebelis, George and Jeannette Money (1997), *Bicameralism,* Cambridge: Cambridge University Press.

This presents the issue of two chambers from an academic perspective.

 *Web Links*

www.ipu.org/parline-e/parlinesearch.asp
An International Parliamentary Union database on structure and working of parliaments around the world.

www.ipu.org/english/parlweb.htm
A link to websites of national parliaments.

www.idea.int/gender/index.cfm
The International IDEA website on democracy and gender issues.

www.official-documents.gov.uk/document/cm70/7032/7032.pdf
The most recent report of the Boundary Commission for England.

www.bcomm-scotland.gov.uk/5th_westminsterreport/index.htm
The most recent report of the Boundary Commission for Scotland.

www.bcomm-wales.gov.uk/fifth_review_e.htm
The most recent report of the Boundary Commission for Wales.

www.pippanorris.com
This includes links to many databases on British constituencies.

 Visit the **Online Resource Centre** that accompanies this book to access more learning resources at **www.oxfordtextbooks.co.uk/orc/garner/**

9

10 Bureaucracies, Policy Studies, and Governance

Reader's Guide

This chapter will first introduce the subject of the civil service and its traditional role in building up the effective power of the state. It will suggest that embedded autonomy is an appropriate way to characterize its relationship with the rest of society, using examples from economic policy-making. Then it will introduce theories of bureaucratic policy-making, taking the basic issue of relations between principals and agents as the starting point. This leads on to the more recent proliferation of agencies in government set up to implement policies devised by the political leadership but operating at arm's length from the structures of ministries. This expands the scope of study from governments to governance and, in the case of the developing world, the related subject of good governance. The domain of policy-making spreads beyond state officials or civil servants to issue networks and policy communities. Finally the Conclusion addresses the emergence of a 'network state' and what that might mean.

Civil Service

At first sight the subject of bureaucracies and policy studies is less intellectually inspiring than many other elements in an introduction to politics course. It cannot inspire in the way that the study of political ideologies can do. Nor does is it so interesting for those attracted by the whiff of political power. It deals predominantly with insiders who are subordinated to and constrained by the will of their 'political masters'. Rather than focusing upon the challenges of policy initiation and formulation, it concentrates upon the more prosaic, managerial issues of policy implementation. Yet if you remember from chapter seven the share of GDP taken by the state in modern Western societies, you will appreciate the immense significance of ensuring that all that money is well spent, i.e. allocated to the highest priority projects and managed so as to ensure successful outcomes. Misguided or mismanaged projects can waste hundreds of millions of pounds, viz. the current British government's record on big IT-related projects. Probably no other branch of political science offers the possibility of saving such large sums of money for taxpayers.

➡ See Table 7.1 in chapter seven, page 172, for figures on general government expenditure.

In chapter seven we saw how the Western-type state spread across the globe in the nineteenth and twentieth centuries. One important factor in this was that state's bureaucratic mode of operation. Weber emphasized the impact of the innovation of the large modern bureaucracy, which transformed economic organizations such as companies, but did the same for government too through the greater consistency, impartiality, and effectiveness that it brought to policy-making. See **Box 10.1**.

10

The qualitative change that it brought is associated with what came to be known as the civil service in Britain. It was the Northcote–Trevelyan Report of 1854 that laid the basis for it. This recommended the establishment of a government service divided between those responsible for routine tasks and an administrative class responsible for policy formulation. It also recommended replacement of the previous system of recruitment of officials by personal recommendation to one based upon competitive

➡ See chapter seven, page 164, for a discussion of the rise of the state system.

Key Quote   Box 10.1
Max Weber on the Efficiency of Modern Bureaucratic Organization

The decisive reason for the advance of bureaucratic organization has always been its purely *technical* superiority over any other form of organization. The fully developed bureaucratic apparatus compares with other organizations exactly as does the machine with the non-mechanical modes of production. Precision, speed, unambiguity, knowledge of the files, continuity, discretion, unity, strict subordination, reduction of friction and of material and personal costs—these are raised to the optimum point in the strictly bureaucratic administration.   (Weber, 1968: 973) examination. In principle, under the reform civil servants could move from one ministry to another without losing any of their entitlements, although in practice this did not happen so often. It served as a model for other states later setting up their own systems of administration and it eliminated corruption from the recruitment process. It survived more or less unchanged for a century.

It was also an important innovation in the development of a democratic state. Officials were supposed to be politically neutral. They were no longer serving at the whim of the monarch, except in the most formal sense. In return for abstaining from active political commitment, officials were assured of protection against malicious or capricious dismissal. They were guaranteed tenure as professionals. Whichever party was in power was entitled to the best impartial advice on policy and how to implement it. Officials could and should offer this even if it was unpalatable to their political masters. This objectivity reinforced the ability of democratically elected leaders to translate their ideas into the most appropriate and most effective policy.

The British version of the impartiality of the civil service laid particular stress upon the impartiality of officials even at the highest levels. However, there can be problems for leaders who wish to introduce radical changes in policy, especially after a change of government, when they feel that the officials through whom they have to work are still committed to the old policies because they have implemented them as effectively as they could in the past. Other states have been more ready to allow political appointees to hold senior administrative posts. The French system of administration allows for political appointees to hold posts in the office of ministers, including and especially the *chef de cabinet*, i.e. the head of a minister's office. The USA still operates a 'spoils system' (i.e. to the victor, the spoils), which allows newly elected political leaders at various levels of government to fire and hire large numbers of officials, although their ability to do so was much curtailed in the twentieth century. Currently, every incoming president has around 9,000 positions as listed in the US Government Policy and Support Positions (the 'Plum Book') to which (s)he can appoint supporters. This is a tiny proportion of the total number of federal employees which stands currently at 2.72 million, but it does represent all the most senior and politically sensitive posts. In continental Europe political leaders can also appoint supporters to top posts in state corporations, which can include public broadcasting organizations—part of what is now called *lottizzazione* ('parcelling out') in Italy. In Britain the Thatcher Government also began down this road, introducing the possibility of ministers appointing political advisers who worked in the minister's private office—though not always harmoniously, if *Yes Minister* is to be believed. During the Major government there were around 35 special advisers in Whitehall. The Blair Government doubled that to around 80 (Richards, 2008: 180).

Thus, European states developed forms of state administration that emerged from their own particular political, legal, and historical context, with the British version of the civil service operating the most stringent separation of civil servants from political roles. In general, in continental Europe they placed greater stress upon the role of law in establishing the relationship between the state and the bureaucracy, as law had played a greater role than in the UK in curbing the powers of autocratic regimes (Lynn, 2006: 58–9). It was associated with the concept of the German concept of the *Rechsstaat*, i.e. a law-based state. According to Ginsborg (2001: 217), this is most evident in the case of Italy. An official Italian government report on administrative reform in 1993 estimated that whereas in France there were 7,325 laws in force and in Germany 5,587 passed by the central government, in Italy there were 90,000 laws or regulations with legal status. Even though a later report by the Italian parliament put the figure closer to 40,000, this was still a significant excess. The effect is to place much greater constraints on the freedom of initiative of Italian civil servants and it still did not necessarily lead to a more impartial civil service. Italian officials found ways of favouring clientelistic or familial connections. Over a fifteen-year period in the 1980s and early 1990s, 60 per cent of the hirings of state officials were initially made on the basis of 'temporary' or 'precarious' contracts, which were not subject to the same strict regulations as permanent ones, but later these were converted into permanent employment (Ginsborg, 2001: 218).

There was also a greater tendency for administrative, political, and business elites to overlap. This is most evident in the case of France, where the Ecole Nationale d'Administration has trained generations of administrators, some of whom have gone on to glittering careers in the state administration, others have gone into politics with two (Giscard d'Estaing and Chirac) later becoming president, while others have become top businessmen.

The colonial powers also transferred these forms of administration to their colonies. After independence the new states took them over for their inaugural administration. The difference that this could make can be seen in the different experiences of India and Nigeria before and after independence. In India the merit system of appointment by examination was introduced in 1853, i.e. slightly earlier than in Britain itself, and the Indian Civil Service (ICS) continued to attract high-quality applicants from Britain until independence nearly a century later. It was quite small—around the 1930s the colonial state employed nearly a million people to administer a population of 353 million, but the ICS itself only employed around 1,000 and by then half of the new recruits were already Indian rather than British. This relative paucity of numbers meant that its presence was uneven around the country. Nevertheless, according to Kohli (2004: 237–40), it made long-term contributions to Indian state formation for three reasons. First, it resisted provincialism and ensured consistent all-India administration. It ensured a unity that nationalists were happy to harness later. Secondly, its competence and efficiency enabled limited, good government. Thirdly, it exemplified the idea that a modern state can put the public interest above private ones. All of this justified the praise that Weber had heaped upon modern bureaucratic administration.

10

The experience of the colonial state in Nigeria was quite different. 'In stark contrast to India, the civil service the British created in Nigeria reflected the minimal goals of British **colonialism** in that country and therefore was not very good. The numbers were relatively small; they were not well trained; and very few Nigerians were incorporated' (Kohli, 2004: 306). In fact the numbers of British officials were proportionately much greater in Nigeria than in India. In the latter there was one British official to every 353,000 in the population in the 1930s, while in Nigeria there was one to every 20,000. But the quality of the civil service in Nigeria was much lower. Recruitment continued to be on the basis of personal recommendation rather than competitive exam. Few Nigerians were recruited to the administrative service. Equally, much less emphasis was placed upon consistency of administration across the country as a whole, which meant lower resistance to division after independence (Kohli, 2004: 306–7).

Key Points

- The creation of an impartial civil service developed first the effective power of the state and then later the stability of democracy.

- European states developed different variants of the civil service and national traditions of administration.

- Colonial powers transferred these forms of government organization to their colonies, with varying long-term success.

'Embedded Autonomy' and Economic Policy-Making

The notion of a civil service closed off from the rest of society is, however, an oversimplification. Rather it would be more appropriate to borrow from developmental political economy and describe the role of the civil service with the term **embedded autonomy**. In other words civil servants are insulated from pressures from the rest of society, but not complete isolation. Their position is embedded in a set of official regulations that guarantee it, but it also grows into a habit of mind, a form of political culture. Let us see how this emerged.

It comes in particular from the successful development of East Asian states that is transforming the world economy. Nowadays there is fairly widespread agreement about the contribution that the **developmental state**, as introduced in chapter one, has made to those achievements. The success of the first of these, Japan, was subsequently attributed to the coordinating role of the Ministry of International Trade and Industry (MITI) from the 1960s (Johnson, 1982). Later accounts have challenged the leading role that Johnson attributed to MITI, arguing instead that MITI provided more of a

➜ See chapter one, page 27, for a description of the developmental state.

coordinating role for major actors in the economy, while ideas on the desirable direction of policy emerged from industry representatives (Calder, 1993). Nevertheless there is a consensus that MITI played an active role in the process.

Subsequently the lessons of the state as autonomous actor in economic policy-making were learned by other states in the region. South Korea, Taiwan, and Singapore all achieved economic breakthroughs. Evans (1995) then generalized from this some lessons about the reasons for their success. In particular he explained the prolonged economic success of South Korea in terms of the embedded autonomy that state economic decision-makers enjoyed vis-à-vis other economic actors. By this he meant that they were insulated, but not completely divorced from, pressures from various economic actors. If they had been completely divorced from the rest of society, then all of their plans would have risked unreality. They had to be aware of society's current needs and priorities. They also needed some detachment to determine what was in the public interest and follow it.

Nor is the term 'embedded autonomy' only relevant to developing economies. In their path-breaking study of economic systems in Europe and the USA, Hall and Soskice (2001) identified two distinct categories. On the one hand there is the Anglo-American 'liberal' model, which does indeed prescribe a more autonomous role for both the market and the state, as private capitalist actors determine how to interact with each other on the basis of expected comparative advantage. The contrast is with the **coordinated market economies** (CMEs) of continental Europe, particularly France and Germany. Here governments play a more active role in directing the economy through a substantial number of state-owned enterprises, in regulating competition (possibly making hostile takeovers more difficult), in managing labour relations, and in providing technical and professional education and training. In

 Case Study Box 10.2
Transport Policy in Britain and France

A study of transport policy in Britain remarked: 'Perhaps because transport is "technical", long-associated with engineering achievements and quantified design standards, it is easy to forget that as a policy it is as ideological as social welfare provision or the reform of prisons' (Glaister *et al.*, 1998: 45).

Britain and France have very similar sizes of population and levels of development, although with France being over twice the size of the UK, the demand for transport is higher. Until 1980, transport policies in the UK and France were fairly similar. Buses and trains were in the hands of the state, whether central or local. Road and railway building was commissioned and financed by the state. Both countries had national transport plans to predict and prepare for future growth in demand where the state took the leading role in realizing it. Both countries also had significant manufacturers of cars, lorries, and railway equipment. Both had one nationalized vehicle producer (British Leyland and Renault) which they wanted to see prosper. National transport policy in both countries was to a significant extent designed to support these manufacturers.

10

From 1980 the bases of the respective national transport policies began to diverge. The Thatcher Government began to introduce more market-oriented reforms into the transport sector, through privatization of first bus and then later, rail services. It concentrated on the potential savings from greater efficiencies within the supply of transport services, sacrificing industrial policies. Gradually investment priorities shifted from rail to road, partly on the grounds that this offered greater choice to consumers. One consequence of this was that the number of cars per 1,000 population in Britain rose from 78 per cent of that of France in 1980 to 90 per cent in 1990, a figure which has remained fairly constant since then.

France, on the other hand, continued to support industrial policies to sustain the manufacture of transport equipment. It also maintained a stronger commitment to public service in transport and to state planning of transport policy, buttressed by the veto power of French rail unions which the authorities were unwilling to challenge (Héritier and Knill, 2001: 283–5), until President Sarkozy. The consequence is that the French state currently spends roughly 2.3 per cent of GDP on transport whereas the British government spends about 1 per cent. This can be seen particularly clearly in the expenditure on railways where for the last twenty years the French government has spent roughly twice as much as it has on roads. This is despite the fact that France still has slightly more cars per 1,000 of the population, and 76 per cent more lorries and goods vehicles, so one might have expected the pressure from road users to be greater. By contrast in Britain expenditures on rail and road are now roughly equal after the early years of privatization when much less was spent on rail.

Over the period since 1980 the British government has extracted efficiency gains from public expenditure on transport and since privatization it has also attracted more private investment into transport infrastructure, often through public–private partnerships. This has reduced the burden on the state and freed resources for alternative uses. However, a major element of the railway privatization has been reversed with the replacement of the infrastructure company Railtrack with the not-for-dividend company Network Rail. Britain has also lost a great deal of the vehicle manufacturing plants that existed in 1980, though in compensation other foreign producers have come in to take their place. Britain has also lost most of its domestic train manufacturing capacity and now imports large amounts of equipment. New Labour's attempts at a ten-year integrated transport policy—the sort of thing that comes naturally in France—has already foundered (Glaister et al., 2006).

Meanwhile French transport planning has moved on to 'multi-modal' integration of public transport, e.g unified ticketing of passengers making a combined journey by rail and air (Abord de Chatillon, 1994). Questions remain about the optimality of state transport investments and of its scale of charges to the public (Neiertz, 1999). Nevertheless, France has retained a much greater industrial capacity to produce transport equipment. Peugeot, Citroën, and Renault are the sixth and ninth largest vehicle-manufacturing corporations in the world, and France's investment in high-speed rail networks (TGV) has started to lead to large-scale exports of rail equipment, e.g. to the USA and South Korea.

general, there is a more sceptical attitude in CMEs towards what Landier and Thesmar (2007) have characterized as 'the big, bad market'. For an example of the differences that this makes in transport policy in Britain and France, see **Box 10.2** on pp 235–6.

In both cases the state has played a key role in determining and implementing transport policy, and in both it has practised embedded autonomy, but in different ways. In Britain the central state leaders have pushed back the scope for its direct involvement with the aim of freeing up consumer choice. In France the state continues to play a stronger role in not only determining priorities but also administering transport as a public service.

The importance of bureaucracies in government policy-making in all states has generated a whole range of theories to explain how they operate.

Key Point

- The civil service needs a degree of embedded autonomy if it is to pursue the public interest, but it may realize this autonomy in different ways.

Theories of Bureaucratic Policy-Making

Theories of bureaucratic policy-making have always revolved around what are now often termed principal–agent issues. This is a set of situations found in micro-economic game theory where the actions of two or more actors need to be harmonized but their interests do not necessarily converge. A set of incentives and/or rules needs to be devised so that they do converge and activity is coordinated. In the case of a civil service this takes the form of one person (minister, 'the principal') or one group giving instructions to others ('agents') on what to do. This always involves a hierarchical relationship. Civil services (agents) are subordinated to the decisions of political leaders (principals). Of course, within the civil service, there are further nested hierarchies, with varying levels of principals having the authority to issue instructions for implementation by agents below them. Theories of bureaucratic policy-making have always sought to do two things: (a) clarify how bureaucracies actually implement decisions; (b) identify ways that will enable principals better to ensure that policy outcomes conform to the original policy objectives.

Over time, theories of bureaucratic policy-making have evolved. Allison (1971) wrote a very influential work on the Cuban missile crisis which attempted to theorize the ways that the executives in both the USA, but especially the USSR, formulated policies and interacted. He identified three competing paradigms. The first hypothesized that government as a whole, and individual ministries, operated as a single rational actor, where outcomes corresponded to the original objectives. Research quickly showed, however, that this did not seem to be the practice, at least not uniformly. It left many uncertainties about key developments during the crisis which could not be easily explained or understood on this basis.

10

The second paradigm was what Allison called 'organizational process'. This hypothe-sized that rather than government agencies designing new structures and practices to implement new policies, they adapted wherever possible existing structures and practices to the new circumstances. In other words a great deal of policy-making consists of what Allison termed 'standard operating procedures' (SOPs). Of course, outsiders trying to decipher policies from outcomes without knowing the underlying procedures would have great difficulty in identifying the SOPs—as sometimes happened to the Americans when puzzling over Soviet moves that needed an urgent response. It is often the case that outsiders will not be able to penetrate the rules of the civil service, so that they will not be able to decide whether particular policy outcomes are the result of SOPs. Determining how large a part this plays in the overall picture of policy making is bound to be problematic. However, it clearly cannot be the case that all policy-making is the product of SOPs. Hence, Allison formulated his third paradigm.

This focused instead on bureaucratic politics, i.e. the ways in which particular institutions interacted with each other that led to specific policy outcomes. This is a self-evidently reasonable thing to do, but reliably identifying this process is also as difficult for outsiders to penetrate as SOPs.

To some extent this third paradigm became an orthodoxy for analysts of bureaucratic politics, but at the same time it exacerbated frustrations about the responsiveness of bureaucratic institutions to the decisions of their political masters. It reminded analysts about the difficulty of ensuring appropriate clarity in the **principal–agent relationship**. Clear decisions by ministers (at least in theory) could become bogged down in a morass of bureaucratic politicking. Thus, it provoked a rethink at a time when economic game theory was becoming more influential in the social sciences.

As it happened, the broader context of policy making was also changing then. This too changed perspectives on policy-making and what it could be expected to achieve. Serious economic crises in the 1970s and 1980s concentrated the minds of Western governments on reducing their expenditure and getting better value for money. Neo-liberal ideas on economic reform gradually spread from the USA and displaced Keynesian approaches to policy-making. Then the collapse of communism opened the way for initiatives for government restructuring in new parts of the world. A further factor for change in Europe was the EU, both in terms of widening and deepening the union. EU expansion brought new systems of administration to former communist regimes; and EU deepening forced member states to coordinate their administration more closely, especially in the area of economic policy and the embed-ding of a single market.

What emerged was what came to be known as the **New Public Management** (NPM). This new paradigm of managerialism emphasized incentives, competition, and performance instead of the traditional values of rule-based hierarchies. 'The mantra has grown in volume: the bureaucratic paradigm is dead; long-live quasi-markets and quangos, flattened hierarchies and continuous improvement, competitive tendering and subsidiarity' (Lynn, 2006: 2). As will be obvious from this terminology, a lot of the ideas for reform came from economics and from business management.

For some critics this was fundamentally mistaken. It was based upon a confusion over the different purposes of public and private institutions. New Public Management implies that 'the public sector is not distinctive from the private sector' and that its practitioners are 'self-interested, utility maximizing administrators' like corporate executives (Olsen, 2003: 511, 522). It challenged the traditional notion of the impartial civil service and it undermined the sense, indicated in chapter seven, that the state might embody a special set of public values.

Nevertheless it has been an extremely influential approach to public sector reform. Toonen (2001: 186) has identified six features, as can be seen from **Box 10.3**.

There is a paradox about these reforms, however. The wave has spread from the more developed countries and international aid agencies now encourage developing countries to learn lessons from it. As a Moroccan Professor of Administration, Ourzik (2000: 44), said in an address to the African Training and Research Centre in Administration for Development:

➔ See the discussion of the modern state in chapter seven, page 171.

The role of the State has been shaped by a trend which is today universal, that of a State as an enabler rather than a doer, a State that regulates instead of manages. Like a genuine orchestra conductor of social and economic activities, the State is required to promote private initiative without stifling or restricting it. A State that is at once modest and ambitious, since the population still expects much of it: it must, while ensuring that overall balances are maintained, protect the environment, ensure proper land-use management, put in place new infrastructures, provide health and education services, etc.

Box 10.3

The Features of New Public Management

- A business-oriented approach to government;
- 'a quality- and performance-oriented approach to public management';
- an emphasis on improved public service delivery and functional responsiveness;
- an institutional separation of public demand functions (councils, citizens' charters), public provision (public management boards) and public service production functions (back offices, outsourcing, agencification, privatization);
- a linkage of public demand provision, and supply units by transactional devices (performance management, internal contract management, corporatization, intergovernmental covenanting and contracting, contracting out), and quality management;
- wherever possible, the retreat of bureaucratic institutions in favour of an intelligent use of markets and commercial market enterprises (deregulation, privatization, commercialization, and marketization) or virtual markets (internal competition, benchmarking, competitive tendering).

Yet the context in which these ideas were originally formulated was countries where civil services were relatively well established with traditions of impartiality and incorruptibility. In the developing world these traditions are not always so strong. True, the Indian Administrative Service retained the elite ethos of its colonial predecessor and until the 1990s maintained a firm grip upon the country and its strong public sector of the economy. Indeed, there were regular complaints about the extent of the stifling 'licence raj' of permits that they imposed upon the economy. The challenge of New Public Management (NPM) was particularly appropriate there, as the state moved towards deregulation of the economy after an economic crisis in 1991.

In Africa, however, there were many problems. On the one hand, by the early 1990s many African states were confronted with the need to reduce what had become bloated state bureaucracies. International financial institutions such as the World Bank were advocating NPM as a coherent way of doing this (Adamolekun, 2007). On the other hand, these states were also suffering from widespread official corruption. NPM did not explicitly foster an official ethic of incorruptibility. Rather, it assumed that this had already been inculcated. Nigeria can be taken as a serious, but not untypical example. As reported by Salisu (2003: 171–2), there are problems with the internal organization of the Nigerian civil service: overstaffing and poor remuneration of employees, poor assessment of labour needs, inadequate training, and lack of qualified technical support. In addition there has been considerable political interference in personnel administration, which has bred apathy, idleness and corruption. Although there have been several attempts to reorganize the structure and operation of the service so that incentives and performance are better aligned, the problem of eradicating corruption remains huge, so there is a real danger in seeking to transfer NPM here that, by treating civil servants as if they were business executives, it will undo previous efforts to inculcate an ethic of incorruptibility.

Key Points

- Theories of public administration have always revolved around principal–agent relations.
- New Public Management borrowed its basic principles from business studies and economics.
- It may undermine efforts to eradicate corruption in public administration in developing countries.

Emergence of Agencies

One key element of the NPM reforms has been the hiving off of government departments and functions to newly created separate agencies—which is encapsulated in the ugly term 'agencification'. In the UK this saw the emergence of institutions such as the Child Support Agency and the Driver and Vehicle Licensing Agency. The underlying rationale was on the one hand to simplify the tasks of government administration, and on the other more clearly to establish incentives for good performance which could lead to greater rewards for those who deliver it. In one sense it merely extended a well-established principle of public administration which is to separate 'policy' from 'implementation'. However, what was new was the proliferation of 'outside' agencies that were not directly under the control of those who made the policy. Most were hived off from existing administrative structures, though the extent to which some 'new' agencies were really separate from ministries was sometimes opaque. Implementation was to be the responsibility of a different principal, who established distinct rules and procedures for its own agents. This undermined the homogeneity of a civil service with common standards and operating procedures. The control over the performance of the agencies was often to be framed in the form of targets for desirable outcomes. Achievement of them was the standard by which the agencies would be judged. Thus the setting of targets became an expanding feature of administrative leadership.

Talbot (2004: 6) has concluded that there are really three dimensions to the idea of 'agency':

- 'structural disaggregation and/or the creation of 'task-specific' organizations;
- performance 'contracting'—some form of performance target setting, monitoring, and reporting;
- deregulation (or more properly reregulation) of controls over personnel, finance, and other management matters.'

It represented a move towards what Rhodes (1997: 87–111) has called the 'hollowing out' of the state, and what Bevir and Rhodes (2006: 74–86) have termed the 'decentring' of governance. This reflected a trend of devolving both decision-making authority to Scotland, Wales, and Northern Ireland, and also implementation authority to agencies outside Whitehall. For them it reflected a gradual change towards more autonomous steering of society by actors outside the government. This would mean greater policy-making from, if not below, at least lower down in the system. Governance meant steering society rather than guiding it, and now there would be more hands on the steering wheel.

➡ Also see chapter one, page 43, for a discussion of the 'hollowing out' thesis.

On the other hand, this was to some extent contradicted by a counter-tendency of the reforms: greater stress upon the delivery of services. One benefit of this was the focus upon the delivery of services as an activity in its own right. Trying to find ways of making consumer-friendly the delivery of services was made a higher priority. 'Delivery' became a mantra during the later years of the Blair Government. Barber (2007) was the Director of the Number 10 Delivery Unit and he has produced a very insightful insider's account of the procedures that were adopted and the lessons that could be learned for further reforms. For him better implementation is essential if the huge sums of money spent on public services are to be politically sustainable (Barber, 2007: 294). However, for the reforms to become permanent, civil servants would have to internalize them and make them the basis of their official behaviour. Blair believed this could only be achieved if the prime minister's office acquired greater power to supervise the implementation processes.

In addition, the separation of policy-making from implementation added to problems of accountability. Though an elaborate array of techniques came to be developed to clarify ways in which implementation agencies could be made accountable to the policy principals (Lynn, 2006: 139–40), accountability of policy-makers to parliament was more difficult to enforce. If particular targets were not met, was it the fault of principals who had set unrealistic ones? Was it due to lack of commitment on the part of the 'agents', i.e. the officials? Or were the targets contradictory or incompatible? If so, whose fault would it be, and who would decide? The greater the incentives for meeting targets, and also the penalties for failure to do so, the greater the danger of neglect of other work where targets were more difficult to devise, but which might still be regarded as important. It could lead to perverse effects. The effect of the whole process was to reduce the salience of politics in policy-making and make the whole policy process more technocratic. It attenuated the whole notion of ministerial responsibility.

Key Points

- The emergence of agencies charged with implementation of policies formulated elsewhere facilitated concentration upon delivery.
- In Britain the Prime Minister's Office became more directly involved in pushing through the reforms.
- There was a heavy reliance upon targets as performance indicators.
- This complicated the problems of ministerial accountability.

Governance and Good Governance

As will be clear from the above discussion, an increasing trend in political science is to blur the old distinction between state and society. Instead of focusing upon government, now there is greater stress upon governance. However, there is quite a variety of interpretations of its meaning. Pierre and Peters (2000: 1) use the term to focus on 'the capacity of government to make and implement policy—in other words, to steer society'. They emphasize, however, that sometimes the term is used to describe the structure of decision-making. From this perspective, people conceptualize it as hierarchies, or as markets, or as networks, or as communities, or as combinations of these. Sometimes it is used to concentrate on processes of steering and coordinating. And sometimes it is used rather as an analytical approach, which questions the normally accepted meaning of terms such as 'government' and 'power', as well as the distinction between state and society. These diverse uses in themselves cause confusion (Pierre and Peters, 2000: 14–27).

By contrast the UN Economic and Social Commission for Asia and the Pacific (UNESCAP) has defined governance simply as 'the process of decision-making and the process by which decisions are implemented (or not implemented)'. ('What is Good Governance?') Actually the term does not have to be used in a political context at all. For example, it is also used in the term 'corporate governance', i.e. the processes by which companies make decisions. However, when involving the state, it stretches to cover non-governmental participants in the decision-making and implementing processes. Indeed it can include circumstances when non-state actors may take the lead in formulating policies in a particular issue area, or even in their implementation. An example of the latter would be private security organizations that are hired to protect government offices or to provide protection for a country's nationals abroad, such as in Iraq. Because of their importance for the implementation process, this also gives them the freedom to make greater inputs into the policy that they are supposed to be implementing.

A related term that is now much used in international politics is **good governance**. Governments in the developing world are often encouraged to practise this, sometimes as a condition for foreign aid. Again it emphasizes the importance of non-state actors as well as government in decision-making. UNESCAP has identified eight features of this term. See **Box 10.4**.

10

Box 10.4

The Elements of Good Governance

- Participation, i.e. encouragement for the involvement of a wide range of actors in making and implementing decisions. It would contribute to, but does not actually require, democracy;
- rule of law, i.e. clear, legal frameworks that are enforced impartially. It implies respect for human rights, an independent judiciary and an incorruptible police;
- transparency, i.e. open decision-making procedures;
- responsiveness, i.e. policies that are formulated and implemented in ways that respond to social needs;
- consensus-oriented, i.e. decision-making through mediation between different interests;
- equity and inclusiveness, i.e. opportunities for all, especially the most vulnerable, to improve the conditions under which they live;

- effectiveness and efficiency, i.e. good policies to make the best use of available resources and protect the environment;
- accountability. i.e. decision-makers, both public and private, must be responsible for all their decisions to society as a whole, and there must be procedures for making sure that this happens.

UNESCAP accepts that few states meet all of these criteria, but emphasizes that without progress in most of them, real **sustainable development** is not possible.

Kayizzi-Mugerwa (2003: 17) presents the concept of good governance in more concrete terms, focusing more explicitly on institutions. According to him it includes:

1. an effective state, that enables economic growth and equitable distribution;
2. civil societies and communities that are represented in the policy-making process, with the state facilitating political and social interaction and promoting societal cohesion and stability;
3. a private sector that plays an independent and productive role in the economy.

This summary recapitulates the principle underlying the more general concept of governance, namely that it involves wider sections of society. The steering of society implicit in the term governance, and even more so in *good* governance, cannot be successfully performed without the active involvement of **civil society** and the private sector.

Key Points

- This change of focus reflected a broader perspective of focusing upon governance rather than just government.
- This blurs or ignores the distinction between state and society.
- Developing states are encouraged to introduce and practise good governance, which also downplays the state–society distinction.
- Good governance presumes wide societal involvement in the formulation and implementation of policies, as well as accountability to the people for their outcomes.

Policy Communities, 'Iron Triangles', and Issue Networks

The focus of this chapter has gradually expanded from the civil service to the totality of policy-making and steering processes. One other concept that links the two together is

Photo 10.1

A heavily-armed private security guard keeps watch in this 27 June 2004 photo as US administrator Paul Bremer tours an education facility in Hillah, Iraq.
Source: AP/PA Photos

→ See chapter two, page 63, for an exploration of elitism.

that of **policy communities**. This is an analytical concept drawn from elitist understandings of politics, which originated in the study of British politics in the 1970s (Thatcher, 2001: 7940). It was based upon the assumption that policy-making in a particular area emerged out of the interaction of officials responsible for policy in a certain area and **interest groups**. It argued that out of this regular interaction the views of officials and interest groups gradually converged. They tended to see issues and solutions to problems in congruent ways. Thus the policies that emerged were likely to enjoy greater legitimacy and have greater effectiveness because of this convergence of perspectives. Even if the officials ultimately formulated the policies, some of the ideas underlying them came from groups and individuals outside. These shared views on what policy in a particular arena should be and how it should be applied sometimes took precedence over general ideological perspectives that individuals among them might hold. An example of this would be people who in general believed in market approaches to policy-making, but wanted to rely upon state regulation to achieve more environmentally friendly results.

Another version of the same idea emerged from the study of US politics at about the same time. This was the notion of **iron triangles**. These are groups of officials, politicians, and outside experts who together formulate a set of policies towards a particular issue area. The difference from policy communities is the more explicit inclusion of politicians in them. A long-established feature of politics on Capitol Hill is the lobbying of members of Congress by business organizations, and sometimes the lobbying of some members of Congress by others. This process of lobbying helps to establish a commonality of views on policy.

A variant of this process can be found in Japan, which reflects the greater organizational power of parties. There the Liberal Democratic Party (LDP) has been in power almost continuously since 1955. Over the years it has established powerful policy committees that meet regularly with civil service counterparts to devise new policies. This has created what have been termed policy 'tribes' (*zoku*), that have made a distinctive impact upon Japanese policies because of the LDP's long hold on power. The LDP created committees for specific areas of public policy, e.g. welfare, construction, agriculture, that met regularly with representatives from the sector concerned and with ministry officials to discuss the operation of existing policies and the formulation of new ones. Traditionally they have had great opportunities to set the parameters for policy in a given area and also resist changes that were proposed from outside or above. These 'tribes' have had a great impact upon policies, often obstructing change that the prime minister would wish to introduce (Kim, 2006).

There is a problem, however, about these theories. In the urge to identify the commonality of views that emerges through close interaction, their proponents sometimes exaggerated the degree of this closeness as compared with other kinds of groupings in the **political system**, e.g. political parties, or more formalized structures of policy-making. Also, they did not necessarily allow for change taking place. The tighter the implied connections, the more difficult it was to identify spaces through which new or alternative ideas might penetrate. Clearly, policy alternatives do periodically emerge in every issue area, so there emerged instead the looser concept of **issue networks**. As Thatcher (2001: 7940) describes it:

An issue network consists of a large number of issue-skilled 'policy activists' drawn from conventional interest groups and sections of the government, together with academia and certain professions but also comprising expert individuals regardless of formal training. Participants are constantly changing, and their degree of mutual commitment and interdependence varies, although any direct material interest is often secondary to emotional or intellectual commitment.

Building upon this insight, subsequent theorizing attempted to identify typologies of networks to identify different types and to show how they interact in the overall policy process.

One of the best-known examples of such a typology was proposed by Rhodes (1997: 38). It had five elements that represented a continuum of organizational strength, running from weak (issue networks, sharing only common ideas) to strong (policy communities that share both ideas and organization):

1. issue networks, which tend to be unstable, with large numbers of members and limited vertical interdependence;

2. producer networks, most often sharing economic interests, which tend to have fluctuating membership, limited vertical interdependence and to serve the interests of producers;

3. intergovernmental networks, which tend to have limited membership, limited vertical interdependence, and extensive horizontal articulation;

4. professional networks, which are more stable, with highly restricted membership, vertical interdependence, limited horizontal articulation, and serve the interests of the profession;

5. policy or territorial communities, which are much more stable, with highly restricted membership, vertical interdependence, and limited horizontal articulation.

In general, issue networks tend to be larger, covering a wide range of interests, with fluctuating contacts between members, with regular disagreements between members, with only limited resources as a group, and with uneven powers, resources, and access. By contrast policy communities have much more limited membership, are more focused on economic or professional issues, have frequent, high-quality interaction of members, who share basic values and have access to common resources, and have a hierarchical leadership that can deliver support from members to government (Rhodes, 1997: 44).

Key Point

● Where officials and non-governmental actors are jointly involved in policy-formulation and implementation, the nature of their relations can be located somewhere on a continuum stretching from issue networks to policy communities.

Conclusion: Towards a Network State?

The focus of this chapter has widened from an initial concern with civil administration to the wider context in which policy is formulated. In previous decades civil services brought efficiencies and effectiveness to governmental policy-making, especially in Western Europe and the USA. More recently, their role has come to be more questioned by people both inside and outside government, as governments have sought to reduce their own size and increase efficiency. In Africa, issues of reforming governance became a higher priority for three, not dissimilar reasons. First, there was a recognition that weaknesses in governance were limiting the pay-offs to economic reform. Secondly, the collapse of communism deprived some African states of aid. Thirdly, Western donors could become more demanding in the conditions that they expected recipients to observe, because there were no longer any rivals in the East (Kayizzi-Mugerwa, 2003: 20).

The result has been a widening of the focus in studies devoted to policy-making. They now devote much more attention to non-governmental actors, both individuals and groups. There is a changed awareness about the primacy of the state in many areas of policy, and this in turn has weakened the emphasis upon the authority of the state to impose its will and expect compliance. How far this change can be reconciled with the persistent need to establish effective and clean administration where this does not already exist in developing countries remains to be seen.

Nevertheless, as was indicated in chapter one, there is a growing literature that envisages a hollowing out of the nation state as a response to globalization. Though some such as Weiss (1998) would contest the inevitability of such changes, we have seen in this chapter the emergence of converging approaches to administrative reform in various parts of the world that might further contribute to this process. The stress upon both governance and good governance implies a rebalancing of relationships between state and society in favour of the latter. Various commentators have looked forward to a state of the future that will look more like a network than a traditional Weberian bureaucratic hierarchy (Bobbitt, 2003). Castells (1998) visualizes the European Union as a network state of the future.

Kamarck has gone so far as to claim that we are witnessing the end of government as we have known it, at least in the USA, and the emergence of a new kind of state. She looks forward to two things: (a) 'government by network'; and (b) 'government by market'. 'Government by network' she interprets as follows:

The state makes a conscious decision to implement policy by creating a network of nongovernmental organizations through its power to contract, fund or coerce. In government by network, the state itself decides to create, activate, or empower a network for the purpose of implementing a policy. Thus the network is a self-conscious creation of a policymaker or a group of policymakers rather than a naturally occurring part of the greater society. (Kamarck, 2007: 100–1)

10

→ See chapter one, page 43, for a discussion of the 'hollowing out' thesis.

As for government by market, here she means something broader than a government or state that just relies upon markets to run the economy, though that is included in it. As she explains it: 'In...government by market, the work of government involves few, if any, public employees and no public money...the government uses state power to create a market that fulfils a public purpose' (2007: 127). Here her examples are drawn from environmental policy, where the state creates markets so as to achieve publicly desired ends, e.g. trading in carbon emissions and reducing pollution. It could also include the creation of markets in schooling, so as to put pressure on failing schools, or it could be used to stimulate the provision of welfare services without relying upon state providers.

This is an imaginative sketch of a future state that is very far removed from the Weberian-type bureaucracy; but how far can networks provide **structuration** for policies as compared with more organized institutions? Clearly, they do not have the same capacity to impose or implement policies except by persuasion. How far the traditional features of civil services such as hierarchies will survive remains to be seen, as do the ways in which they interact with the new networks that they have helped to create. Certainly, the legal basis of state administration in continental Europe will not be easily eroded.

However, it is a strong reminder of the significance of groups and organizations outside the state and civil service in determining the way that governance operates. The next few chapters will deal with the roles of some of these external political actors—parties, interest groups, and the media.

10

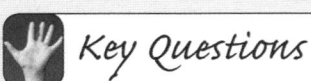 Key Questions

- Can a valid distinction be drawn between the values and motivations of public adminis-tration and business management?
- How far do the groups involved in British transport policy correspond to the different categories of issue networks and policy communities proposed by Rhodes? (See Glaister *et al.*, 2006: chs. 2, 3, 6.)
- Compare the ways in which the Thatcher and Major Governments attempted to reform transport policy with those of Presidents Chirac and Sarkozy.
- Assess the Eddington Transport Report.
- Is it unrealistic to expect civil servants to be politically impartial?
- How can civil services be made incorruptible? Will New Public Management help?
- Is good governance a Western imposition on the developing world? Did the West have it at similar levels of development? Did it matter then?
- What are the advantages and disadvantages of the 'spoils' system in the USA?

- How can agencies and officials be made accountable under the New Public Management?
- What would a network state look like? In what ways would it differ from more traditional states?

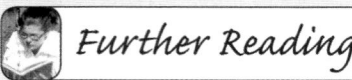

Further Reading

Barber, Michael (2007), *Instruction to Deliver,* London: Politico's.
  This is a fascinating insider's account of the Blair Government's Delivery Unit, illuminated by comparisons of the administrative load of the prime minister today with earlier periods.

The Eddington Transport Report, London: HMSO, www.dft.gov.uk/162259/187604/206711/executivesummary.
  This is a set of proposals for future UK transport policy by the former head of British Airways.

Glaister, Stephen, June Burnham, Handley Stevens, and Tony Travers (2006), *Transport Policy in Britain,* Basingstoke: Palgrave, 2nd edn.
  This is the authoritative account of the subject.

Kamarck, Elaine C. (2007), *The End of Government . . . As We Know It: Making Public Policy Work*, Boulder, CO: Lynne Rienner.
  This details the prospects for state administration transformed by new technology.

Lynn, Jr., Laurence E. (2006), *Public Management: Old and New,* London: Routledge.
  This is an account of changing approaches to public management.

Pierre, Jon, and B. Guy Peters (2000), *Governance, Politics and the State,* Basingstoke: Palgrave.
  This is a good introduction to the concept of governance and its implications.

Web Links

www.civilservant.org.uk/index.html
How to be a civil servant: a master site of information about the civil service in the UK.

www.gpoaccess.gov/plumbook
United States Government Policy and Supporting Positions. The 'spoils' list of government positions to be filled with political appointees by an incoming administration.

www.dft.gov.uk/162259/187604/206711/executivesummary
The Eddington Transport Study. A recent government study on future transport provision in the UK.

Visit the **Online Resource Centre** that accompanies this book to access more learning resources at **www.oxfordtextbooks.co.uk/orc/garner/**

Votes, Elections, Parties

Reader's Guide

Voting, elections, and parties are core institutions of democracies. They are also important in most authoritarian regimes. This chapter will first explain some of the basic issues involved in assessing the operation of voting and electoral systems. Then we will go on to look at political parties: why they emerged, how they can be classified, what functions they perform, how they interact, and finally what are the challenges facing them today.

The Voting Paradox

➔ See the discussion on the role of the state in chapter one, page 36.

➔ See the discussion on policy communities in chapter ten, page 245.

Voting is a mechanism for making collective decisions. It is also intended to be a means for ensuring that the majority preference for a candidate or a policy is reflected in the ultimate decision. It is another key ingredient in the concept of representation introduced in chapters one and ten. Determining this supposedly objective preference is extremely difficult. This is due to the mathematical problem known as the **Arrow impossibility theorem**, which asserts that when a group of people are asked to make one choice as their preference between three or more alternatives, it is impossible to conclude that one particular outcome is the one 'most preferred' unless over 50 per cent all vote for it. Let us see an example from Table 11.1 that illustrates this, where people are choosing between three alternatives (A, B, C):

None of the three alternatives wins a majority of first choices, but if we just count first choices, then C wins with ten votes out of twenty-two. If the first two choices are counted equally, then B wins, with eighteen votes out of forty-four. However, it might be fairer to give extra weight to first choices over second ones, since that would reflect more genuine strength of preference. Suppose first choices are given two points, and second choices are given one. In that case, A wins with twenty-four points out of a possible sixty-six.

We can see that all three possibilities could win, depending on the counting system used, without the actual votes changing at all. None of the options ever achieved a majority of the total votes or points available, whichever system was being used, so it would be impossible to conclude that the general preference was 'clearly' in favour of one particular option. As you can easily imagine, this problem gets worse with a greater number of alternative choices, whether they are candidates or policy options. This means that the determination of preferences depends upon the particular procedure chosen for assessing the votes. Any procedure chosen is a compromise between theory and practicality. It also explains why referenda are usually reduced to a choice between two possible alternatives. In that way, even though it might seem artificially to constrain the choices that are being voted upon, it will result in an unambiguous outcome.

No. of voters	1st choice	2nd choice	3rd choice
8	A	B	C
4	B	A	C
6	C	B	A
4	C	A	B

Table 11.1   Hypothetical Distribution of Votes

Therefore, the choice of method for assessing votes is crucial and really can alter the outcome. To give one famous example, Riker showed that when Lincoln won the presidential election in 1860 against three rivals, different methods of assessing the votes which are used in various parts of the world today could easily have led to either of two others winning equally well (Riker, 1982: 227–32). If that had happened, then the American Civil War might never have occurred and world history might have developed along quite different lines.

Key Point

- The method chosen for assessing votes plays a crucial part in determining the outcome.

Elections

Elections are methods of assessing preferences through votes. They are vital to democracy. According to Article 12 of the Universal Declaration on Democracy adopted by the Inter–Parliamentary Union in 1997: 'The key element in the exercise of democracy is the holding of free and fair elections at regular intervals enabling the people's will to be expressed' (Inter-Parliamentary Union, 1997).

For electoral systems, there are two basic alternative principles underlying them, although there are several subvariants. These are summarized in **Box 11.1**.

The first basic type is the simple **plurality**, first-past-the-post majority system. This has the advantage of simplicity. At least in theory, it allows voters to choose individual candidates rather than party representatives. It also tends to be biased in favour of producing governments with larger majorities, at the expense of more representative

 Box 11.1

Types of Electoral System

1. Majoritarian systems (first-past-the-post)

    —single member plurality systems (UK, USA, India)

    —two-round system (France)

    —alternative vote (Australia)

    —block vote (Singapore, Syria)

2. Proportional representation

    —party list (Netherlands, Israel, Brazil)

    —single transferable vote (Ireland)

3. Hybrids (Germany, Russia, Japan, Scottish Parliament, Welsh Assembly)

reflections of public opinion. This can allow governments to be more decisive. It can also facilitate a strong opposition, and broadly-based parties. It disadvantages extremist parties. On the other hand it can exclude minorities, and it can have the effect of restricting women representatives. Also in many constituencies it can lead to a large number of 'wasted' votes for a candidate who has no realistic chance of being elected, thereby discouraging those voters from voting at all (International IDEA, 2007: 36–7).

Variants of this system can include multimember constituencies where voters either have as many votes as the required number of successful candidates, in which case this can produce even stronger majorities if people vote consistently for the same party, or they have only one vote, in which case candidates can be elected with as little as 20 per cent of the vote, undermining their legitimacy. (An up-to-date list of countries practising these and all of the other alternative systems mentioned for their national legislatures can be found at www.idea.int/esd/world.cfm.)

➜ See chapter eight, page 201, for more on Lijphart and consociational democracy.

The alternative principle is **proportional representation**, where the priority is to ensure an adequate representation of the range of public opinion, irrespective of whether it strengthens or weakens the cohesion of government that results from it. This can be important for new democracies in creating a wide sense of ownership of the system. It reduces the number of 'wasted' votes, favours minorities, but also encourages parties to spread their appeal beyond their core districts. It may contribute to greater stability of policy and make coalition agreements more visible, as is argued by Lijphart. On the other hand, it is more likely to lead to coalition government and to fragmentation of the party system, with small parties able to negotiate a disproportionate say in policy-making—see the scathing condemnation of the effects of proportional representation in Israel by Asa-El in chapter nine. Holding coalition governments to account for individual decisions is more difficult under proportional representation (International IDEA, 2007: 58–9).

➜ See chapter nine, pages 210–11, for Asa-El's criticism of proportional representation.

Since first-past-the-post and proportional representation systems tend to produce different kinds of outcome, each of which have much to commend them, a more recent trend has been for countries to adopt hybrids such as the **alternative member model**, with some seats elected on the basis of a simple majority and some on the basis of proportional representation. Germany, Japan, New Zealand, and Russia, for example, have all gone down this route. This was basically what the Jenkins Commission on Electoral Reform proposed for Britain in 1997, although it was not accepted by the Blair parliament.

One alternative intermediate system is to hold two rounds of elections in constituencies where the first round does not produce an absolute majority. In the second round the candidates are reduced to the two most successful alternatives, which prevents strategic voting and ensures that there is no doubt about the preference of the majority. France does this, as do many of its former African colonies, as well as Iran and several former republics of the Soviet Union.

Altogether, of the main types of electoral system, seventy states in the world have list proportional representation, forty-seven have first-past-the-post (plus twenty-two with two-round elections), and there are twenty-one hybrids (International IDEA, 2007: 32).

Colomer has argued that electoral change around the world has tended to take place in the direction of increasingly inclusive formulas, leading to fewer risks for the parties involved. This has meant a much greater tendency for electoral reform to move from majoritarian to mixed or proportional systems, rather than the reverse. His explanation is party self-interest: when threatened by challenges from newcomers, they prefer to minimize the risk of complete extinction, which would be far greater under majoritarianism than by agreeing to a more PR-based system. This would offer greater opportunities for survival, albeit in somewhat reduced numbers of representatives elected (Colomer, 2004: 4, 58; Farrell, 2001: chs 7, 8). Dunleavy (2005) has argued that this process is now underway in Britain.

Key Points

- The two main alternative voting systems widely used are first-past-the-post and proportional representation.
- Their outcomes tend to have different virtues: stronger government versus more representative government.
- There are hybrid or intermediate alternatives that attempt to mitigate the disadvantages of theoretically purer systems.
- Voting systems have a big impact upon party systems.

Parties

One of the paradoxes about democracies is that on the one hand there is near unanimity on the indispensability of political parties. They are almost ubiquitous, even in **authoritarian** regimes. The Universal Declaration on Democracy included in Article 12 'the right to organize political parties and carry out political activities' as one of the 'essential civil and political rights' (Inter-Parliamentary Union, 1997); yet a strict public choice approach to politics would question the logic of their existence. From this perspective, individuals only rationally form groups to pursue their interests when they can be sure that the benefits that they are likely to obtain are greater than the costs of membership. This is only likely to be the case for small groups where the share of benefits that any individual member can obtain in the case of success will be larger. For big organizations such as political parties, especially at the national level, the benefits that any individual member is likely to gain are bound to be minuscule, while the costs of membership are still significant. Thus it is irrational for people to join parties. They should only form (small) **interest groups**.

Then, too, criticism is often levelled at parties because they allegedly create and exacerbate divisions in society rather than help to mitigate them. This is particularly the case where political parties exclusively represent specific ethnic communities. As we shall see from Box 11.3, this underlay the attempt in Uganda to do without parties after years of ethnically-based civil war. The same argument is repeated by the leaders of the People's Republic of China to justify the leading role of the Communist Party.

Carothers (2006: 4) expands on what he terms the 'standard lament' about political parties in various countries where he has done research:

1. Parties are corrupt, self-interested organizations dominated by power-hungry elites who only pursue their own interests or those of their rich financial backers, not those of ordinary citizens.

2. Parties do not stand for anything: there are no real differences among them. Their ideologies are symbolic at best and their platforms vague or insubstantial.

3. Parties waste too much time and energy squabbling with each other over petty issues for the sake of meaningless political advantages rather than trying to solve the country's problems in a constructive, cooperative way.

4. Parties only become active at election time when they come looking for your vote; the rest of the time you never hear from them.

5. Parties are ill-prepared for governing the country and do a bad job of it when they do manage to take power or gain places in the national legislature.

Key Points

- Parties are a vital element in modern political systems, especially democracies.
- Despite this, the rationality of party membership can be questioned.
- Parties generally suffer from low public esteem and are often associated with corruption.

Emergence of Parties

Historically, there were two phases in the development of political parties. Originally they emerged within the parliaments of the first democracies as groups of independently elected representatives who needed to find ways of cooperating in passing legislation. These were caucus parties, loose organizations of like-minded representatives. Then, later, parties became involved in the process of trying to structure the vote in popular elections. For most countries these two stages were combined, because the model of parties was imported from abroad at the same time as parliaments. For them, parties had to structure both the popular vote and also the workings of parliament, but in the case of party pioneers, such as Britain and the USA, it is possible to separate the two stages.

There is an alternative way of theorizing the emergence of parties that goes beyond the purely chronological. This concentrates on the previously unfulfilled functions that parties emerged to perform. In this approach, historical description and more abstract logic are intertwined. It seeks to explain the systemic needs that parties had to fill. This approach is most common in the USA, so let us consider how it is used to explain the emergence of parties there.

Why did parties initially emerge in Congress? This was because the task of finding a new coalition each time a proposed bill was being considered for legislation was extremely time-consuming, especially if it involved sounding out the views of each representative afresh. Forming blocs of relatively like-minded representatives simplified the negotiating process and also enlarged the influence of individual members over legislation. It was easier for groups of members to have an impact because together they were more likely to have the casting vote over a particular bill than would individual members. They could extract greater concessions in the terms of the bill, or alternatively, they could more effectively trade concessions over one bill for advantages over another—what in the USA is called 'log-rolling'. Because legislation is a repetitive process, group commitments encouraged greater confidence that commitments would be honoured than those of individuals. It was easier to hold groups of legislators to their word than it was for individuals, and thus to penalize those who broke it. Thus, relatively coherent groups of legislators provided greater predictability for other legislators or groups of them as negotiators. This crucial role of parties in structuring and facilitating the business of parliaments should always be remembered, because, as we shall see, even if today there seems greater reluctance on the part of individuals to become committed rank-and-file party members, thus provoking doubt about the future role of parties in society, their function in structuring the work of parliaments is unlikely to disappear.

The importance of this point can be seen in the very fact that they emerged in the new American Congress after Independence, when the American Founding Fathers had a distinct antipathy to any kind of party or faction, which they regarded as incompatible with real democracy. In *Federalist Paper No. 10*, Madison attacked 'factions', because they could oppress or exploit the people as a whole. He defined 'faction' as follows:

a number of citizens, whether amounting to a majority or a minority of the whole, who are united and actuated by some common impulse of passion, or of interest, adverse to the rights of other citizens, or to the permanent and aggregate interests of the community.

By the Third Congress (1793–4) like-minded legislators had begun to form groups to smooth the passage of bills. Even in the circumstances where Congress only met for one or two months per year, and therefore had a tiny legislative load compared with today, so that the problems of log-rolling were small, this predictability was still a key benefit (Aldrich, 1995: 68–96).

Later, parties began to form outside Congress as a way of mobilizing support for candidates in first presidential and then local elections. Aldrich argues that the first time that this happened was in 1828 with the emergence of the Democratic Party of supporters for General Andrew Jackson. The effectiveness of the party was first shown in the fact that he won this election, where he had lost in 1824. Moreover, he did so on the basis of a turnout that increased from 30 per cent of the electorate to over 50 per cent, so party organization motivated supporters to vote. Then, when opponents followed suit by organizing the Whig Party (though it only lasted for about twenty-five years), the combined effect of these two parties could be seen in a turnout rate of over 78 per cent in 1840. The emergence of **mass parties** both changed the course of elections and also stimulated greater interest in politics in general, at least as measured by turnout. Thus they strengthened democracy (Aldrich, 1995: 97–125).

Since then, political parties have gone through several mutations. The next was the emergence of mass parties between the second half of the nineteenth and the first half of the twentieth centuries. The effectiveness of the American parties, as well as the lessons of growing party democracy in Britain, made political parties a vital element in the extension of democracy elsewhere in Europe and later further afield. In addition, industrialization overturned traditional patterns of authority relations and drove increasing numbers of people into growing urban areas, where parties could more easily mobilize support. All the political issues associated with industrialization provided the matter for a new, more popular democracy where mass parties became the norm and where the franchise was extended to include all men and then all women. This was the era when party membership was highest. This period also entrenched a key social divide as the basis for a great deal of political activity, i.e. that between capital and labour. While not all party systems revolved around this division, many did.

To cope with this at times exponential increase in party members, and to ensure greater coordination both in their activities and also those of party elected representatives, the number of full-time party officials increased. While it brought greater professionalism to the internal workings of political parties, it also complicated the practice of democracy in internal decision-making in parties. How much weight should be given to the views of ordinary party members as opposed to those of party officials? Should they all be treated as equal? Could they be?

Since the Second World War, parties in Europe have evolved further towards what have been termed 'catch-all' parties, i.e. parties that devote less attention to ideology and more to strategies to win over the median voter, who would make the crucial difference in a general election, even though it might mean appealing to voters who would instinctively support a different party. The consequence of this change has been to strengthen the hand of the party leadership that would be needed to make these strategic decisions. An early indication of the change came in West Germany in 1959 when the Social Democratic Party renounced Marxist ideology and committed itself to a market economy and liberal pluralism.

More recently European and American parties have undergone a further mutation as they turned into **cartel parties**. As party membership has declined, this has strengthened the authority of the party machine, which in turn has become increasingly professional in its handling of all the media alternatives for putting its message across. Aldrich has particularly focused on this evolution in the case of the two American parties since the 1960s. Where previously the parties were dominated by local party machines such as that of Mayor Daley in the Democratic Party in Chicago and careers of elective office holders were made through the party machine, now parties have turned into organizations of media-savvy professionals ready to serve the needs of whichever candidates emerge to prominence. Thus the parties have become candidate-centred rather than machine-centred (Aldrich, 1995).

This historical outline of the emergence of the modern party suggests that analysis of any modern party can usefully be divided between its activities in three arenas: (a) the party-in-government (including parliament); (b) the party-in-the-electorate (i.e. its strategies for winning popular support and votes); (c) the party's internal organization (Aldrich, 1995). All parties that seek election have to establish their own synthesis of these three roles, but the political system in which they operate, the policy goals that they set themselves, and the attitudes of ordinary citizens towards them all provide **structuration** for the particular synthesis that they evolve. All of this determines their particular interpretation of intraparty democracy.

Key Points

- The first parties emerged to structure the work of legislatures.

- Later phases of development were mass parties to structure the votes of electors, catch-all parties to win more votes irrespective of ideological appeal, and cartel parties more dominated by party professionals.

- All parties seeking electoral success have to balance three sets of roles: vis-à-vis government, the electorate, and their own internal professionals.

11

Functions of Parties

Modern **political parties** are protean organizations performing an extremely wide range of functions in the pursuit of political power. Ware has provided the following definition: 'A political party is an institution that (a) seeks influence in a state, often by attempting to occupy positions in government, and (b) usually consists of more than a single interest in the society and so to some degree attempts to "aggregate interests"' (Ware, 1996: 5).

In general they perform seven functions, irrespective of whether they operate in democracies or authoritarian regimes. These are listed in **Box 11.2**.

The balance between these functions varies according to the type of state. Not all parties perform all of these functions. In democracies parties have a more prominent role in providing choice between individual political actors and between policies—indeed, in performing most of the last six functions. Authoritarian regimes place more emphasis upon the second function—though their interpretation of integration and mobilization implies more of a top-down rather than bottom-up process. However,

Box 11.2

Functions of Political Parties

- Legitimation of the political system
- Integration and mobilization of citizens
- Representation
- Structuring the popular vote
- Aggregation of diverse interests
- Recruitment of leaders for public office, thus facilitating (normally) non-violent choice between individuals
- Formulation of public policy, facilitating choice between policy options.

while it may be almost unthinkable for democracies to exist without political parties (for an exception that proves the rule, see the example of Uganda in **Box 11.3**), what is striking is the wide variety of states than contain them. Most states today, not just democracies, contain political parties. The only significant group of exceptions are many Islamic states because of the higher priority of establishing a state there according to God's will, although even Iran has political parties. Even communist regimes, which never tolerated challenges to the leading role of the Communist Party, organized regular elections at all levels of the state as a way of re-engaging the commitment of their citizens to the goals of the regime and also of demonstrating claims to popular legitimacy to the rest of the world. Authoritarian regimes too, e.g. South Korea between the 1960s and the end of the 1980s, have devoted considerable resources to holding regular elections and mobilizing support for the ruling parties, even though there was never a realistic possibility of political alternatives winning power. Thus legitimation of the political system, whatever its basic structure, remains the single most common function of political parties. The only exceptions are parties that seek to overthrow the existing political system, especially those that seek violent revolution rather than change through the ballot box.

Case Study   Box 11.3
Uganda as a No-Party State

Uganda is a rare example of a state that has attempted to practise democracy without political parties.

Since independence in 1962, Uganda has gone through civil war, genocide, and revolution. It was originally put together as a colony by Britain from a variety of former tribal kingdoms and principalities. There was no tradition of democracy, and in the less than seventy years of colonial rule, Britain only began to introduce it in the last few years. Milton Obote was elected the first president, but democratic values did not develop among the newly elected parties. Uganda effectively became a one-party state from 1964, but Obote was overthrown by Idi Amin in 1971, who declared himself president for life. Gradually the country slid into tyranny, chaos, violence, and economic collapse. In 1979 he was overthrown and Obote was reinstalled as president. This time he attempted to restore a multiparty system, but the party leaders refused to cooperate with each other and violence returned. Between 1971 and 1986 an estimated one million people died.

When the National Resistance Movement under Yoweri Museveni took over the country, he declared that the country needed a fresh political start. Political parties would be banned because they institutionalized division and antagonism in the country, as shown by the experience of 1979–86, where what was needed was unity. The new regime would try to inculcate the spirit of unity, mutual tolerance, and democracy through the dissemination of the principles that had underlain the practice of the resistance movement. This would also be better in keeping with African traditions of tribal consultation.

The constitution adopted in 1995 after nearly a decade of military and transitional rule allowed for either a multiparty political system or a democratic 'movement political system', but although political parties were not banned, the regime prevented them from organizing openly. Party representatives had to stand for election to parliament as individuals. Instead, the regime focused its efforts at democratization on local resistance councils. However, armed groups in the north still challenge the authority and the democracy of the government in Kampala.

The constitution laid down a limit of two five-year terms on any president. As Museveni's second term drew towards its close, the regime began to float the idea of a third term. This provoked unease both at home and among foreign governments that gave aid. In the end a referendum was held which approved the change to a multiparty democracy. Thus the reintroduction of open political parties was a response to both domestic and external pressure. However, in the general election called in early 2006 Museveni won a clear majority, despite opposition allegations of electoral irregularities. The Supreme Court upheld the outcome by a vote of four to three. Critics have alleged that little has changed in the way the country is ruled.

What remains to be seen is whether the era of the 'movement regime' has indeed laid the foundation for a more enduring democracy in Uganda.

Source: Mugaju and Oloka–Onyango (2000)

The ways in which parties perform these roles depend upon three things (1) the constitutional framework within which they operate, (2) the particular national system of elections, and (3) the technologies of communication available to them.

→ See chapter eight, page 196, for a discussion of federalism.

1. As we have already seen in chapter eight from the constitutional distinction between federal and non-federal regimes, the degree of central authority in a state has a key impact upon the organization of political parties. The relative powers of a party's central apparatus and local organizations to some extent reflect the relative powers of the corresponding government authorities.

2. Countries with primaries to select candidates for election to major offices have to organize their activities to a different timetable from that of other countries.

3. As television and advertising have become more powerful, parties have turned to them increasingly to get their messages across rather than relying upon more personalized direct contact with party activists, even though this has greatly inflated their costs. Now the rise of the Internet is beginning to offer new possibilities for much more personalized canvassing, with candidates contacting voters individually to respond to their particular concerns.

→ Also see chapter twelve, page 287, for a discussion of the impact of the media on politics.

Key Points

- Parties perform an extremely wide range of functions in political systems.
- These are structured by the constitutional framework of the political system, the national system of elections, and the technologies available to them for communicating with voters.

Typologies of Political Parties

Political scientists develop typologies of political parties to try to think more systematically about their activities and to make more meaningful comparisons. **Box 11.4** presents the recent typology of Gunther and Diamond which they explicitly formulated to take account of political parties in various regions of the world. It is based primarily upon the ways in which and the extent to which parties organize themselves. This means that the lower down the table we go, the more organized they are.

On the other hand we must not forget that political parties have their own ideologies. They need them to compete for power. Thus they need programmes to serve as the basis for governing. These more general programmes make them distinctively different from interest groups, which certainly wish to influence government decisions but not to take part in government themselves. It is possible, then, to construct an alternative typology that focuses more directly upon this feature.

Here is an alternative typology based upon nine general programmatic orientations in political parties around the world. It is an extension of one originally developed for Western Europe (Beyme, 1985: 29–158). It should be noted that there is still considerable variation between parties with similar general programmatic orientation in different states.

Box 11.4

Typology of Political Parties

Basic category	Variants	Sub-variants
Elite-based	Traditional local notables (esp. 19th century)	
	Clientelistic	
Electoralist	Personalistic	
	Catch-all	
	Programmatic	
Movement	Left-libertarian	
	Post-industrial extreme right	
Ethnicity-based	Exclusive ethnic	
	Congress/coalition movement	
Mass-based	Religious	Denominational
		Fundamentalist
	Nationalist	Pluralist
		Ultranationalist
	Socialist	Class/mass based
		Leninist

Source: From Gunther and Diamond (2003: 173)

1. Liberal or radical: such parties stand for equal legal and political rights, as well as free trade.

2. Conservative: such parties tend to support traditional forms of social relations, including hierarchy. They often appeal to nationalism as well. Recently,

however, some conservative parties have veered towards more radical, neo-liberal, free-market economic policies.

3. Christian democracy: this developed after the Second World War as a way of trying to find a third, Catholic-influenced, way between liberalism and socialism. While it endorsed more traditional authority relations, preferring women to stay at home and raise children, it accepted a significant role for state-provided welfare.

4. Socialism or **social democracy**: these parties advocate workers' control of the means of production. Usually they have had close connections with their trade union movement and many were affiliated to the Socialist International. They also advocate state welfare systems. However, unlike Communist parties, they accept the need to maintain market economies, even though they would prefer some form of planning too.

5. Communism: these parties were inspired by the Russian Revolution of 1917 and sought to spread the communist alternative to socialism based upon the teachings of Marx and Lenin. They were affiliated to the Communist International (Comintern) in Moscow. Such parties were also distinguished by their organizational doctrine of unconditional loyalty to the party ('democratic centralism') and strict party discipline.

6. Regional parties: these parties stand for the interests of particular regions of countries and often want, whether overtly or covertly, to establish their own states. There has been a surge of popularity for these parties in Europe over the last twenty years. Possibly the most successful has been the Lega Nord in Italy, which has occasionally participated in national coalition governments.

7. Environmental parties: these appeared more recently, initially emerging from interest groups such as Friends of the Earth. Typically, they win support from younger and middle-class voters and tend to be sceptical of free market economic policies. They advocate consensus-based decision-making and **social justice**.

8. Nationalist parties: these certainly flourished in former colonies, as the new regimes sought to establish their national values. The end of the Cold War removed some alternative poles of political organization, allowing freer rein for nationalists, for example in Eastern Europe and the former Soviet Union. Because such parties' ideology is based upon a concept of the whole nation, as opposed to the interests of a part of it, e.g. a class, they aspire to a hegemonic position in the political system, which can make cooperation difficult with other parties.

9. Islamic parties: Islamic political parties are relatively recent, because of the authoritarian nature of many Islamic regimes in the Middle East. In Iran, however, all parties represented in the Majles (parliament) are Islamic,

representing a fairly wide spread of opinions. Like nationalist parties, Islamic parties seek to speak for the whole of society rather than the interests of a part of it, and therefore they too aim for a hegemonic position in the political system.

Key Points

- Typologies facilitate more systematic comparison between party activities.

- They vary according to the primacy accorded to different basic features.

Party Systems

Any state with more than one political party also has a party system. Sartori defined these as 'the system[s] of interactions resulting from interparty competition' (Sartori, 1976: 44). These interactions are affected by (1) the nature of the political system as a whole; (2) the pattern of basic cleavages in society which underlie the differentiation between parties; (3) the channels open for competition between the parties, i.e. primarily the electoral system, though not exclusively: for example uneven availability of campaign funding to individual parties can also significantly affect electoral outcomes.

1. Clearly, the constitutional nature of the state has a fundamental impact upon the competition between parties, as parties have to operate according to its rules. Parties have to operate rather differently in liberal democratic regimes, where electoral success does lead to changes of government, from more authoritarian regimes where the rulers will not contemplate electoral overthrow and where opposition parties, if tolerated, have to be much more circumspect in their criticisms. It also matters whether a regime is presidential or parliamentarian.

2. The pattern of relations between political parties is in part determined by the fundamental cleavages in society. These are based on social history. The original version of this as it applied to politics in Europe was formulated by Lipset and Rokkan. They concluded that there were four fundamental cleavages that had structured the rise of the new mass parties in Europe either towards the end of the nineteenth century or in the first quarter of the twentieth. Since then these 'frozen' cleavages have remained the basis of West European party systems. These cleavages were: (i) centre versus periphery: this meant the competing claims of different communities within the same state for power both at the centre and in regional authorities (sometimes these were also based upon different linguistic communities, but not necessarily); (ii) state versus church: this was particularly important in Catholic states where a significant part of the challenge to the Church's temporal powers was mounted by anti-clerical liberals and radicals; (iii) land versus industry: the growth of industrialization and of industrial capitalists posed a challenge to more traditional rural elites; (iv) owner versus worker: the rise of

➜ See chapter nine, page 212, for a discussion of presidentialism versus parliamentarianism.

11

capitalism also pitted the interests of the new industrial workers against those of their employers (Lipset and Rokkan, 1967). All West European states were affected to varying degrees by these divisions, but the outcome differed in terms of actual party representation.

3. The electoral system also affects the system of political parties. A political science classic, Duverger's *Political Parties*, argued that first-past-the-post electoral systems tend to produce two-party systems—what later became known as **Duverger's Law**. By contrast, he argued, proportional representation tends to produce multiparty systems (Duverger, 1964). While these are more generalizations than uniform 'laws' (in the past, for example, Venezuela had proportional representation and also a two-party system), there is no doubt about the logic of the argument.

Given these structurating factors, most typologies of party systems focus upon the number of parties contained in them. One version gives the following fourfold classification (Ware, 1996: 159):

1. Predominant party systems, where one party occupies a dominant place in the national legislature. In developed democracies, Japan is the only example, but it has emerged in Russia because of official backing, and this situation is very common in sub-Saharan Africa, where non-ruling parties are short of resources (Doorenspleet, 2003: 205). Some authoritarian regimes, e.g. Indonesia under President Suharto, have explicitly supported the primacy of one party on the grounds that it provides opportunities for representation of different interests and groups within the constraints of a single party where unprincipled party competition would jeopardize social cohesion (Reeve, 1985).

2. Two-party systems, e.g. the USA.

3. Systems with three to five parties, e.g. France, Germany, UK.

4. Systems with more than five parties, e.g. Belgium, Denmark, Italy.

What is striking is that, once established, especially in liberal democracies, party systems tend to change very slowly—viz. Lipset and Rokkan's 'frozen' party systems of Western Europe. They can play a big part in the successful operation of a democracy, e.g. a two-party system, and they can also frustrate it, e.g. with a highly fragmented party system with many small parties, e.g. Italy since the Second World War; yet it is almost impossible to design and impose a particular system when voters' choices are genuinely free. Then, party systems just emerge and acquire a life of their own. They are not easily changed even when reformers set out to do so because of perceived and unpopular weaknesses in them. Take the case of Japan. The Liberal Democratic Party (LDP) has been in government since 1955, with the brief exception of a period in 1993–4. In the 1990s, however, the LDP became unpopular because of its association with corruption and money politics. Apart from the general need for parties for money, this corruption was attributed to the particular electoral system of multimember constituencies, where several candidates from the same party could compete with each other as well as with other parties. To try to break this, the electoral system was reformed with more first-past-the-post voting so as to try to facilitate a more genuine two-party system. It was thought that this would reduce the incentive for escalating campaign expenses and also, as Duverger's Law would predict, favour a two-party system by strengthening opposition to the LDP (Rosenbluth and Ramseyer, 1993). Yet despite the reforms, the LDP have so far upset these calculations, adapted to the new circumstances, and continued to win a majority of seats in the key lower house of the Diet (parliament). Nor has campaign spending been noticeably reduced. It is a reminder of a more general warning made by Gambetta and Warner after reviewing electoral reform in Italy: 'Several of the effects of introducing new electoral systems are seldom predictable' (Gambetta and Warner, 2004: 249).

Key Points

- Party systems are the product of sociological and institutional interactions.
- They cannot be designed in genuine democracies.
- Once formed, they are very durable and, again in democracies, difficult successfully to reform so that they realize different objectives.

Problems Facing Parties

As ever, serious problems now confront political parties, although they vary in nature from one region of the world to another. In Western Europe the traditional main parties themselves and the party systems still survive. There, the problem is one of declining party membership. In general, the mass parties that were typical of the interwar and post-war eras are a thing of the past. Although parties do not always maintain scrupulous records of members, in part because of the need to appear strong to outside observers, the trend seems clear throughout Europe, as can be seen from Table 11.2. In the case of Spain, one of the two exceptions to this general trend, it should be noted that the base year of 1980 was only five years after the death of the dictator Franco and only two years after the promulgation of a new constitution.

This means that by the end of the 1990s the average share of European populations who are party members was around 5.7 per cent, only around a third of what it had been thirty years earlier (Mair, 2005: 15). By coincidence, this figure is almost exactly the same as the share of Chinese Communist Party (CCP) members in the Chinese population by 2007—though the CCP is still, at least nominally, deliberately more selective in its membership; and yet membership of the CCP is going up, while that of parties in the West is declining.

Much thought has been devoted to the reasons for this increasing apparent reluctance for party activism in Europe. In Britain one of the objectives of the Power Inquiry held between 2004 and 2006 was to remedy this. It recommended a number of measures,

Country	Period	Change in numbers	Per cent change in original membership
France	1978–99	– 1,122,128	– 64.59
Italy	1980–98	– 2,091,887	– 51.54
UK	1980–98	– 853,156	– 50.39
Norway	1980–97	– 218,891	– 47.49
Austria	1980–99	– 446,209	– 30.21
Sweden	1980–98	– 142,533	– 28.05
Germany	1980–99	– 174,967	– 8.95
Greece	1980–98	+ 375,000	+ 166.67
Spain	1980–2000	+ 808,705	+ 250.73

Table 11.2 Trends in Changing Membership in European Parties, 1980–2000
Source: Peter Mair and Ingrid van Biezen (2001), 'Party Membership in Twenty European Democracies, 1980–2000', *Party Politics*, 7(1): 5–21

including calls for 'a responsive electoral system—which offers voters a greater choice and diversity of parties and candidates—to replace the first-past-the-post system', a minimum voting age of 16, and state funding for parties through vouchers assigned by voters at a general election (Power Inquiry, 2006). This last principle of state funding for political parties has become much more common around the world in recent years, as a way of boosting funds for the vital functions that parties perform in democracies and also as a way of trying to reduce their dependence on corporate sponsors.

Critics, however, warn of the need to ensure that this does not protect parties from new challengers and prevent newcomers from winning seats in parliament, as did happen in Venezuela (see **Box 11.5**) (International IDEA, 2003). State funding can encourage party fragmentation rather than consolidation, opening the possibility of funds for dissident factions to set themselves up as new parties, as happened in Japan in the 1990s. Other critics argue that the cause of the indifference is the sense that individuals can make no impact upon government or party decisions—a variant of the public choice argument about the 'irrationality' of membership for the party rank-and-file mentioned above. From this perspective, the only solution is to change the process of political decision-making to make it more 'relevant'. Once this had happened, people would flock back to parties.

In the USA there is an analogous problem, though it is not one of resources. In the 2004 presidential election the two parties declared combined expenditure of US$880 million,

Case Study Box 11.5
Venezuela and the Downfall of Liberal Democracy

From the time when democracy was re-established in 1958, Venezuela had
of the most stable and most liberal democracy in South America. Yet recent yea
this system pushed aside by President Chavez in favour of a more populist democ
reminder that while liberal democracy may have been presented by Fukuyama as
of history', this type of regime may be vulnerable too. How did it get into this situatio

In 1958 former dictator Pérez Jiménez was overthrown in a military coup that le
the reintroduction of democracy. In October the leaders of the three main parties sign
a pact at Punto Fijo that committed them to observing the same basic rules of the
political game for the sake of preserving democracy. Subsequently this underlay the
evolution of Venezuela into a state with effectively two parties: Acción Democrática (AD)
and Comitida de Organización Política Electoral (COPEI). The concept of 'pacted
democracy' was later cited by commentators as a model for how to establish a
successful democracy, especially in Latin America, and for many years it underpinned
US policy for promoting transitions to democracy there.

The two parties extended their reach into a wide range of other organizations: professional associations, peasant federations, state enterprises...which helped both to
strengthen their control and also to increase their membership. On the one hand the
two parties exercised very strict control over their members. On the other hand they
sought consensus between themselves wherever possible, though this did not prevent
energetic competition for power, with the presidency changing hands regularly.

This system worked well for nearly two decades, reinforced by prosperity based upon oil
wealth. From the mid-1970s, however, the economy began to stagnate and decline. Partly
this was caused by falls in the international price of oil, but partly also by corruption and
waste. Popular dissatisfaction grew and the parties did not reform. They became more
isolated from the public.

In 1998 former Lt. Colonel Hugo Chávez won a presidential election as an outsider.
He promised a 'Bolivarian' revolution, appealing to the example of the nineteenth-
century liberator from Spanish rule, Simon Bolívar, though the latter had traditionally
been seen more as a liberal and an admirer of the American Revolution. Chávez aimed
at sweeping away corruption and redistributing wealth towards the ordinary people.
He attacked the 'partocracy' (*partidocratia*) that kept all power in the hands of the two
parties and their state funding was abolished. What gradually emerged was a populist
regime that promoted social polarization rather than consensus. Chávez introduced a
new constitution that removed many of the checks upon the powers of the president.
Attempts to overthrow him through a putsch and by holding an election to recall him
from office on the grounds of misusing his position both failed. The old party system
fragmented, to be replaced by a multiparty system with numerous small parties. They

are overshadowed, however, by Chávez's dominant Fifth Republic Movement (now the United Socialist Party of Venezuela).

Aided by the additional wealth that came from increasing world oil prices, despite a more polarized society, Chávez won a second term of office in January 2007.

Sources: Coppedge (2002); McCoy and Myers (eds) (2004); Gott (2005); Corrales and Penfold (2007)

an increase of two-thirds since 2000. At least the same amount is spent every two years on elections to Congress and state legislatures. An enormous amount of this goes on media campaigning, but there is no shortage of volunteers who help on campaigns without pay. Nevertheless here too we find a trend towards declining party membership. Individuals can be motivated to join and help with the campaigns of particular candidates whom they support, but they are more fickle in their allegiance. Here too, the party professionals play a bigger role in determining party image and appeals to the electorate. This can risk the parties losing contact with the rest of society, as did happen in Venezuela.

For new democracies there is no problem in forming new political parties. As of 2004, Russia, for example, still had forty-four political parties registered with the government; yet as Hale has described, Russia's parties have failed to become dominant institutions (Hale, 2006). In Latin America, parties and party systems are still often weaker and less institutionalized, with the consequence that, as in Peru at the end of the 1990s, an elected authoritarian leader such as Fujimori can break them down

11

Photo 11.1
Supporters of Venezuelan president Hugo Chavez take part in a rally to support the constitutional amendments promoted by him, in Caracas, 30 November 2007, ahead of Sunday's referendum.
Source: AFP/Getty Images

(Levitsky and Cameron, 2003). The problem for these regimes is that political parties find it difficult to become the equivalent to the national institutions that they are in established democracies. If parties in the latter are seeing an erosion of their membership, when these parties have an established image and can adapt to changing electoral circumstances, the problem of membership is much worse in new democracies, where it is extremely difficult to grow to an effective size. For them an added complication is the lack of obvious fundamental social cleavages that can underpin a party system. With the Cold War over, socialist parties on the defensive and the emergence of post-industrial economies where social identities are more fluid, the old divisions between capital and labour no longer underpin fundamental party divides (Biezen, 2003: 37–8).

Taiwan is an exception that proves the rule. Since 1987 Taiwan has become one of the most successful new democracies. It has a stable party system, with two main parties and one or two minor ones. The two main parties—the Nationalist Party (KMT) and the Democratic Progressive Party (DPP)—do indeed confront each other over a vital basic political issue, but this is not one of the four traditional divides that Lipset and Rokkan identified. It is unique to Taiwan: the issue of independence from mainland China. The DPP would prefer formal independence, the KMT opposes it. In fact, there is disagreement within both parties over the best way to frame policies to achieve either of these goals, so there is not complete unanimity. Both parties have a wider range of policies to appeal to voters, some of which overlap and cut across the basic cleavage, preventing the antagonism from becoming irreconcilable. This is the fundamental difference between the core images of the two parties. It structures the party system. As other new democracies do not have the same fundamental cleavage, or an analogous one, then their party systems are more volatile.

Although there are many differences between the parties in the established democracies of Western Europe and the USA, and those in the newer democracies in other parts of the world, there does seem one trend of convergence. This is the enhanced importance now of party professionals in determining party 'brand' and policies to appeal to the electorate. This is the result of a combination of factors. On the one hand, this is a consequence of the reduction in rank-and-file members of previously mass parties. On the other it results from the growing importance of state funds in financing party activities. While the two main American parties do not suffer from the same problems of financial stringency, Aldrich has argued that the same change has taken place there. Since the 1960s the Democratic and Republican parties have both changed from mass parties to ones that are candidate-centred with party professionals at their service (Aldrich, 1995: 254). This convergence also makes it likely that parties in various parts of the world will seek to derive lessons from the American experience on ways of winning elections, even if the electoral systems are quite different, especially where those parties also mutate into candidate-centred organizations, as in Peru.

There is a growing divide between party professionals and the party rank-and-file. According to Mair, parties in Europe 'have reduced their presence in the wider society, and have become part of the state'. They are less concerned with playing the function of opposition and more concerned with preparing for government. 'Within politics . . . the parties are either all governing or waiting to govern' (Mair, 2005: 20).

The corollary of this is that the fundamental difference between rank-and-file party members and ordinary citizens in the internal life of parties is eroding. Some attempts to revive interest in politics may exacerbate the problem. For example, theories of **deliberative democracy** advocate new ways of consulting public opinion in policy-making by involving representative groups of ordinary citizens. One striking example came in Greece in 2006 when the PASOK party selected its candidate for mayor of one of the municipalities of Athens through consultation between a group of randomly selected citizens rather than votes from members (*First Deliberative Polling*, 2006). This privileged the decision-making role of ordinary citizens over that of both party professionals and party rank-and-file in a key area of party activity. Were this to become a more common phenomenon, it would certainly erode the boundaries separating parties from the rest of society.

→ Also see the discussion on electronic decision-making in chapter twelve, page 294.

Key Points

- Political parties are facing a range of new challenges.
- In various parts of the world the balance between rank-and-file party members and party professionals is tipping towards the latter.
- Despite the lack of esteem for them, parties remain vital for the formulation and legitimation of public policies.

Conclusion

As ever, parties and party systems are in transition, though their future shape is not clear. There seems little chance that the old mass parties will return; but parties will continue to play an important role in the way that policy choices are presented to citizens for approval. Indeed, where significant resources are at their disposal, they will have an increasing impact on the presentation of policies, managing a widening variety of media strategies. They will also continue to play important roles in structuring the work of parliaments. They will act as recruitment channels for ministerial positions, and they will certainly continue to legitimize, or be used for the purposes of legitimizing, political regimes. Although parties often suffer from a bad press, and they are sometimes accused of exacerbating social divisions rather than finding ways of reconciling them, attempts to devise alternative forms or organization such as 'movements' have failed to supplant them for long. Political parties are not a guaranteed solution to problems of political instability. They structure the formulation of public policies, but their leaders still have to make choices about priorities and they can change them. They make mistakes, antagonize people, seem self-interested; but without them a politics dominated by narrower interest groups would be even less attractive (Fiorina, 2002: 541). It remains difficult to envisage the formulation and legitimation of public policies without parties.

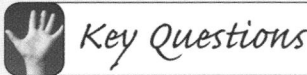

Key Questions

- What are the relative strengths and weaknesses of the various alternative means of assessing votes—e.g. simple plurality, Borda count, Condorcet count, and approval voting? (See Saari, 2001.)

- Why did New Zealand change from majoritarian voting to proportional representation in 1993? (See Nagel in Colomer, 2004.)

- Assess the pros and cons of the proposals of the 1997 Jenkins Commission on Electoral Reform in the UK. Why were they not implemented?

- How stable is the party system in any country with which you are familiar? What might upset it?

- Do you take an active part in the life of a political party? How do you justify this? How rational is it?

- Would the proposals of the Power Inquiry make any difference to your motivation?

- How appropriate is state funding of political parties? How valid are the objections?

- Are parties' programmes becoming more difficult to distinguish from each other? Are they becoming less 'ideological'?

- Are parties in other parts of the world becoming more 'American'? If so, in what ways? Does it matter?

- How well does either of the two typologies of party systems fit the political systems of countries with which you are familiar?

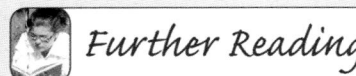

Further Reading

Aldrich, John H. (1995), *Why Parties? The Origin and Transformation of Political Parties in America*, Chicago: Chicago University Press.
   This is a theoretically informed history of the rise of parties in the USA.

Farrell, David M. (2001), Electoral Systems: A Comparative Introduction, Basingstoke: Palgrave.
   This is a very approachable introduction to the various types of electoral systems.

Gallagher, Michael, Michael Laver, and Peter Mair (2001), *Representative Government in Modern Europe: Institutions, Parties and Governments*, Boston: McGraw Hill, 3rd edn, chs 7–10.
   This is a survey of parties in various European states.

International IDEA (2007), *Electoral System Design*, Stockholm.
   This details the considerations that should underlie the choice of electoral system, especially for regimes in transition to democracy.

Katz, Richard S. and William Crotty (eds) (2006), *Handbook of Party Politics*, London: Sage.
   This is a compendium of information on many features of political parties.

Levitsky, Steven and Maxwell A. Cameron (2003), 'Democracy Without Parties? Political Parties and Regime Change in Fujimori's Peru', *Latin American Politics and Society*, 45(3): 1–33.
   This is a study of a political system whose president attempted to rule without parties—complements the case study on Uganda.

—— —— (2005), *Parliamentary Affairs* 58(3), special issue on 'The Future of Parties'.
   This is a collection of articles on the challenges to political parties.

Lewis, Paul G. (2000), *Political Parties in Post-Communist Eastern Europe*, London: Routledge.
   This presents parties in the transition states of Eastern Europe.

Mair, Peter (1997), *Party System Change*, Oxford: Oxford University Press.
   This is a theoretical discussion of how modern parties change.

Mainwaring, Scott and Timothy Scully (eds) (1995), *Building Democratic Institutions: Party Systems in Latin America*, Stanford: Stanford University Press.
   This presents party systems in Latin America.

McLean, Iain (1999), 'The Jenkins Commission and the Implications of Electoral Reform for the UK Constitution', *Government and Opposition*, 34(2) April: 143–60.
   This analyses the reasons why electoral reform was rejected after the 1997 election.

Reeve, David (1985), *Golkar of Indonesia: An Alternative to the Party System*, Singapore: Oxford University Press.
   This presents the Indonesian justification for an authoritarian ruling party as a substitute for democracy.

Mohamed Salih, M.A. (ed.) (2003), *African Political Parties*, London: Pluto.
   This is an introduction to African political parties.

Ware, Alan (1996), *Political Parties and Party Systems*, Oxford: Oxford University Press.
   This is a thorough survey of the relationship between parties and party systems.

11

 *Web Links*

www.idea.int/vt
Comprehensive source of information on voter turnout around the world.

www.psr.keele.ac.uk/parties.htm
Compendium to websites of political parties, social movements, and interest groups around the world.

www.opendemocracy.net/democracy-open_politics/article_2312.jsp
Paul Hilder, 'Open parties? A map of 21st century democracy'. Discusses alternative possible future organizational forms.

http://repositories.cdlib.org/csd/05-06
Peter Mair, 'Democracy Beyond Parties', Center for the Study of Democracy, University of California, Irvine, 2005. Discusses the changing politics of the party.

www.bepress.com/wpsr/vol3/iss3/art1/
Giovanni M. Carbone (2007), 'Political Parties and Party Systems in Africa: Themes and Research', *World Political Science Review* 3(3). A recent attempt to systematize African political parties.

 Visit the **Online Resource Centre** that accompanies this book to access more learning resources at **www.oxfordtextbooks.co.uk/orc/garner/**

Civil Society, Interest Groups, and the Media

Reader's Guide

This chapter will cover a selection of dimensions of political life outside the state and political parties. First it will look at the very popular and broad concept of 'civil society', which encompasses the activity of apparently non-political actors, certainly not 'politically' organized actors, in pursuing their goals. After that it will present interest groups and also corporatism. Next will come an introduction to 'infrapolitics', i.e. politics from below as presented by political anthropologists, particularly with regard to politics in the developing world. Then we will turn to the role of the media in political life. Finally we will consider the impact of new communications technologies on political life, and the extent to which they are transforming its practices, or may do so in the future.

Civil Society

This term was originally mentioned in the Introduction. Robertson (1993: 69) defined it as follows:

Civil society is the framework within which those without political authority live their lives—economic relationships, family and kinship structures, religious institutions and so on. It is a purely analytic concept because civil society does not exist independently of political authority, nor vice versa, and, it is generally believed, neither could long continue without the other; therefore, no very clear boundary can be drawn between the two.

A term originally formulated in the eighteenth century, **civil society** became much more widely used at the end of the 1980s when a number of regimes were overturned by tides of apparently unorganized, previously non-political forces. Some of these took place in the Far East. In 1986, the **authoritarian** President Ferdinand Marcos of the Philippines was overthrown by waves of 'people power' demonstrations in Manila supporting Corazon Aquino, the widow of one of his most famous victims, Benigno Aquino. In 1987, demonstrations in Seoul destabilized the plans for an orderly handover of power by South Korean President Chun Doo Hwan to his chosen successor, General Roh Tae Woo. This set in train a sequence of events which led to the reintroduction of democracy. In spring 1989 a demonstration in Beijing by thousands of students mourning the death of the Chinese Communist Party's former General Secretary, Hu Yaobang, turned into a massive challenge to the nation's leaders on Tiananmen Square and in many other cities of China that drew in hundreds of thousands of protestors and was only put down on 4 June with the loss of thousands of lives.

The biggest demonstration of the potential power of civil society, however, came in the autumn of that year in Eastern Europe. It was civil society that brought down the communist regimes there and hastened the end of the Soviet Union in 1991. This was despite the fact that those regimes had had decades to organize the repression of opponents and to establish very powerful secret police forces. They had brutally suppressed demonstrations in Hungary in 1956 and Czechoslovakia in 1968, which served as enduring lessons. The victory of the demonstrators in Eastern Europe was achieved with minimal casualties. It was a striking affirmation of the potential political power of civil society, if roused.

They had achieved this despite—or more likely because—other more 'regular' political groupings such as parties had been more relentlessly repressed. The Communist regimes had devoted enormous resources to identifying, dispersing, and punishing organized opposition, and yet it had all been in vain. The more amorphous civil society had overcome it—for more details, see **Box 12.1**.

After this, civil society became the focus of intense attention, as it seemed to offer the promise of an alternative, more consensual, non-coercive democratic politics. For some it acquired a normative status. It became a metaphor for the good society. See **Box 12.2**.

Photo 12.1

The 'Velvet Revolution' refers to a bloodless revolution in Czechoslovakia that saw the overthrow of the Communist government there. On 17 November 1989, a peaceful student demonstration in Prague was severely beaten back by the riot police. That event sparked a set of popular demonstrations from 19 November to late December. By 20 November the number of peaceful protestors assembled in Prague had swelled from 200,000 the day before to an estimated half a million. The Communist Party of Czechoslovakia announced on 28 November they would give up their monopoly on political power.

Source: © Hungry Eye Images

12

Would-be reformers started looking at other authoritarian regimes to try to identify analogous groupings to those in Eastern Europe in the hope that they could achieve similar results. It did not matter whether these groups were well-organized or agreed on their long-term goals. They contained the germ of freedom, if only some way could be found of incubating it. Policy-makers in Western governments and international charities had become disenchanted with giving aid to governments in the developing world which

Case Study   Box 12.1
Civil Society and the Collapse of Communism

By 1989 the communist regimes in Eastern Europe were beset by mounting difficulties. Their leaderships were ageing and the economies were stagnating. The regimes themselves had been imposed by the USSR after the Second World War and lacked popular legitimacy. Attempts by individual states to extricate themselves from Soviet tutelage had provoked brutal repression in Hungary in 1956 and Czechoslovakia in 1968. All attempts at organized political opposition were crushed.

However, the Soviet Union was descending into turmoil after four years of **perestroika**, which was failing to deliver the promised economic revival. The new Soviet leader, Gorbachev, no longer seemed to offer the same unconditional support for East European leaders in return for political loyalty as Brezhnev had done. He started pressuring them to reform their systems as he had done.

The crisis first broke out in Poland, where the regime was among those most beset by economic and political problems. There the independent trade union, Solidarity, which had been challenging the regime throughout the decade despite martial law, forced the government into round-the-table negotiations over reforms. As the price for agreeing to participate in what were expected to be rigged elections, it extracted an agreement for its own legalization. However, contrary to everyone's expectations, including its own, it won all but one of the seats that it could contest in the elections in June. This fatally undermined the legitimacy of the communist rulers and by September, Solidarity had become the dominant actor in a new government.

The ferment of expectation and resistance spread to other states. East Germans tried to flee to the West by travelling to Hungary and seeking asylum in the West German embassy. The Hungarian authorities were reluctant to suppress them, when Moscow would not commit itself unequivocally to support such action. Their indecision was noted and spread to other capitals. It further encouraged hopes of change. The aged East German leader, Honecker, was deposed, and his successors began also to make conciliatory noises. Demonstrations started taking place and, when they were not repressed, involved masses of people. By November the demonstrations had spread to Prague, and there the authorities quickly capitulated with virtually no loss of life in what came to be known as the 'Velvet Revolution'. Change was remarkably peaceful and amicable. Also in November, the new East German leadership abandoned rather feeble attempts to keep the Berlin Wall closed. With the Wall open, it was no longer possible to prevent people crossing to the West. After that, resistance in most East European regimes crumbled. The last to do so was Romania in mid-December, although it was accompanied by street fighting and the filmed execution of the former dictator Ceausescu and his wife.

The regimes collapsed remarkably easily after over forty years of repression. Through a combination of circumstances, they had become sclerotic, brittle, and weak. However, it had taken the courage and heroism of tens of thousands of demonstrators in all the states to reveal this by challenging the authorities. Although largely not organized beforehand, they quickly found ways of cooperating decisively. It was a time and movement of joyous good humour or, as one account put it, 'a carnival of revolution' (Kenney, 2002). The legend of the power of civil society was born.

12

Key Quote Box 12.2
Edwards on Civil Society

'It is a truism that civil society is what we as active citizens make it, but it is also true that "social energy", or "willed action", is the spark that ignites civil society as a force for positive social change. The determination to do something because it is the right thing to do, not because we are told to do it by governments or enticed to do it by the market, is what makes associational life a force for good, provides fuel for change in the practices of states and business, and motivates people to raise their voices in the public sphere . . . Against the background of weak democracies, strong bureaucracies, corporate power, legalism and nationalism resurgent, civil society, as both concept and reality, is essential to the prospects for a peaceful and prosperous world order in the twenty-first century . . . Warts and all, the idea of civil society remains compelling, not because it provides the tidiest of explanations but because it speaks to the best in us, and calls on the best in us to respond in kind.'   (Edwards, 2004: 111–12)

had failed to reduce poverty and in particular they were exasperated by official corruption, so they fastened on civil society and the voluntary sector as instruments to spread **good governance** and democracy. Aid money was liberally dispensed to **non-governmental organizations** (NGOs) in the developing world in the hope that they would spread their enthusiasm and experience among fellow citizens. They had the advantage of large numbers and, unlike political parties in dictatorships, they operated at the grass roots. Even existing democracies such as Japan began to pay more attention to their NGOs as potential political actors, or at any rate as institutions with legitimate political inputs to make. The 1990s was a heroic decade for civil society. It became one of the top items on the international agenda. It was this heroic aspect of civil society that many people found so inspiring. It seemed to symbolize the possibility of the downtrodden rising up and overthrowing their oppressors.

   In addition there was the economic appeal of voluntary associations for helping with welfare in developing world countries where a welfare state would be beyond their means. This was attractive for aid donors because it provided them with opportunities to ensure that their aid actually reached the grass roots, and because often they involved women, who had previously been excluded from this. It was attractive for the governments because it helped to reduce the pressure on them to provide welfare, and it was attractive for the recipients too because it provided them with opportunities to organize and stand up more for their rights. Left-inclined local authorities in developing countries occasionally experimented with ways of drawing selected groups of citizens into active participation in the compiling of budgets, for example, in Porto Alegre in Brazil (Bruce, 2004) and Kerala in India. This was blurring the distinction between civil society and elected representatives.

12

Of course, problems quickly emerged in trying to spread it around the world. On the one hand, the policy became a victim of its own success. Many NGOs in the developing world became dependent upon foreign funding for their activities. This meant that their leaders had to spend as much time if not more on devising projects that would attract foreign funding rather than ones that they themselves felt their communities needed most urgently. On the other hand, dictatorships were quickly alerted to the potential political threat from civil society and moved to hem it in. Authoritarian regimes also sought to restrict the flows of foreign aid that might be channelled their way, sometimes, like Russia, playing the nationalist card and complaining about unjustified foreign interference from organizations like the Carnegie Foundation for International Peace. Many started organizing alternative, pliant civil society organizations. This led to a plethora of new acronyms, such as GONGOs (Government Organized Non-Governmental Organizations). In Indonesia in 1990, for instance, one of President Suharto's ministers (and later successor as president), B.J. Habibie, created ICMI, an organization of Islamic intellectuals so that it could have an impact upon the authoritarian political decision-making system. They were expected to act as a think tank for new ideas on furthering Islam while promoting education. By 1994 it claimed to have 20,000 members.

On the other hand, one of the strengths of the concept for the study of comparative politics was that it could open the way to integrating regimes that lacked many of the political institutions of the developed world. It brought the study of informal social politics back in, as well as political activity at the margins of institutions. Jenkins (2005: 280–1) has explained that in India there is a long-standing tradition of political parties, especially the Congress Party, fostering associations that were part of the independence movement. This relationship has continued into the post-independence era, so a clear-cut division between the state and civil society would preclude consideration of important elements of Indian politics. The term certainly attracted a great deal of interest among students of Middle Eastern politics. Social institutions such as the salons in the Gulf states, where all sorts of subjects could be discussed including politics, or the informal 'circles' in Iranian society were known to play a significant part in political life (Eickelman, 1996: x–xi). Now there was a framework that could integrate them into broader comparisons with informal politics elsewhere in the world. Traditionally the state had played a more limited role in the lives of Muslims and non-state actors, e.g. charitable foundations, had provided a great deal of public services such as education, and water supplies. Although their role has become more limited, it is still important. So too is the role of professional organizations of doctors, engineers, teachers, and such (Ibrahim, 1995). They embody the principle of a self-organizing society separate from the state. So the concept of civil society could accommodate their activities too (Hoexter, 2002).

Not surprisingly, given the enormous interest that was generated in it, the concept of civil society remained subject to great contradictions and misunderstandings. For one thing there was disagreement over whether it was primarily an analytical term or a normative one. The concept of 'civil society' itself was subjected to quite disparate interpretations. Did it mean that all the groups shared some kind of common perspective when they pursued political goals? In particular, was it committed to an altruistic advocacy of policies that were judged to be in the public interest? Or at least were they committed to some kind of 'civility', which meant excluding from consideration groups that pursued non-civil goals? Could it include the advocacy of interest groups? Could it include clientilistic networks, mafia organizations, fundamentalist religious sects, extreme right-wing nationalist groups? Or is it a bulwark against the **anarchy** of weak or failed states? (Chabal and Daloz, 1999: 17–18.) Does some form of civil society keep Somalia together after the collapse of the state outlined in chapter seven? Or is it simply a collective noun that designates all the activities of a wide variety of groups and organizations that are not part of the state or of political society? Lastly, civil society is vulnerable to existing inequalities in society, which may privilege some groups and disadvantage or even silence others and which inhibits its normative potential.

➜ See chapter seven, page 176, for the case study on Somalia.

Beyond this, there was difficulty in translating the term into foreign languages because of extra connotations that attached to the term in English. In Chinese the most commonly used equivalent was *gongmin*, which really just indicates citizens. The same is true of *shimin*, in both Japanese and Korean, which has something of the same positive connotations that *citoyen* acquired in the French Revolution. On the other hand, right-wing critics of Japanese democracy such as Saeki (1997) stigmatize civil society as a (harmful) Western implant. Islamic societies were also suspicious about the term. Some of them were unhappy about the derivation of the term from nineteenth-century European philosophy, which they associated with an Enlightenment, i.e. secular, project. They condemned it as part of an intolerant Westernizing project. They wanted instead a term that was more compatible with Islamic traditions and goals, one that focused more upon organizations of the *ulama*, the body of Islamic scholars, so they preferred to coin their own equivalents using the Arabic word *madani*, which stressed the civility that should be found in 'civil society'—and civil society in Indonesian thus became *masyarakat madani* (Baso, 1999).

Analysts of African politics often complained that the term had been inappropriately transferred from a quite different European context.

In Africa, as in other places, 'civil society' evokes otherwise inchoate—as yet unnamed and unnameable—popular aspirations, moral concerns, sites and spaces of practice; likewise it bespeaks a scholarly effort to recalibrate worn-out methodological tools, and to find a positive politics, amid conceptual confusion. (Comaroff and Comaroff, 1999: 2–3)

Not only is there ambiguity over the meaning of the concept. There is also ambiguity over the boundaries of the phenomena that it is supposed to encompass. In simple terms it seemed to indicate the space for social activity between the state on one hand and private individuals on the other. We have already seen from chapter seven

➜ See chapter seven, page 171, for a discussion of the modern state.

12

that the boundaries of the state are also fuzzy, which then makes the boundaries of civil society equally fuzzy. As Chabal and Daloz put it (1999: 17), the fundamental problem in trying to apply the concept of civil society is that there is no clear division between the state and society. Instead there is constant interpenetration. Chandhoke (2003: 10) emphasizes that civil society is impossible without a robust legal system that can protect civil rights. On the other side, it was not always clear—or at any rate made clear—where the boundaries of 'the private' began. Did it only apply to individuals? Or did 'the private' include the family too, as has usually been the case in the West since Aristotle? (Swanson, 1992.) If it did, then it would seem to exclude the very important dimension of family-based social activity which is typical of Middle Eastern, African, and Asian societies (as well as Southern European; see Ginsborg, 2001). Hahm (2004: 454–7), for instance, has argued that the traditional Confucian view could either not accommodate the public/private distinction or made it a fluctuating one. This was because Confucian doctrine began with the development of virtue in the individual and then gradually widened its horizon to encompass the whole of society. The goal of a virtuous society was impossible without virtuous individual members of it, and individuals could not be virtuous unless they performed the necessary familial roles and rites. So distinctions between family and society were positively detrimental.

Lastly, the subsequent evolution of the civil society groups in Eastern Europe after 1989 weakened enthusiasm for it as a model for the future. In Eastern Europe itself the euphoria that surrounded the unbelievable success of groups such as the independent trade union Solidarity in Poland quickly evaporated. The hopes that such groups might form the basis for a new kind of consensual rule were quickly dashed, despite all the encouragement and approval from outside. The need to make radical changes and take drastic decisions in the face of mounting economic crises quickly revealed the difficulty for civil society organizations to maintain their cohesion. They lacked ideologies and organization forged in earlier years that would keep their members together. The crises polarized them rather than uniting them. Solidarity—the largest such organization and the one with the longest and most distinguished history of struggle against the communist authorities—quickly fragmented. Instead new political parties began to appear like mushrooms—further confirmation of their importance for democracy, however difficult the circumstances. By 1992, only three years after the collapse of the communist regime, 222 parties had been registered in Poland, although not all of them had candidates standing at elections.

All of these uncertainties have made the use of the term problematic. Yet it has now acquired such widespread usage that it is impossible to abandon it. After all their criticisms, Comaroff and Comaroff (1999: 33) conclude: 'Civil society may be deeply flawed as an analytic construct . . . But it still serves, almost alone in the age of neoliberal capital, to give shape to reformist even utopian visions' Edwards (2004). advocates positively embracing its diversity. The best that can be said is that if you use the term, you should specify clearly what you understand by it, and what you do not. But remember, as Chandhoke (2003: 33) reminds us: 'civil society is not a given; it is what its practitioners make of it.' It is as much a project to be created as a concept to be applied. Like politics more generally, it is an arena of great contestation.

Now let us turn to a subset of institutions that are often included within the notion of civil society, i.e. **interest groups**.

Key Points

- Civil society is an ambiguous term subject to a wide variety of interpretations.

- It acquired a heroic aura because of its association with the protests that brought down communist regimes in Eastern Europe.

- Subsequently it was appropriated by policy-making elites in the West as the targets for aid that they wished to distribute to grass-roots organizations in the developing world.

- There is a big disagreement over whether it can be applied in a non-European environment, and if so, how.

Interest Groups

Interest groups represent a big component of civil society. They are an essential element of democracy—it is impossible to think of a democracy without interest groups and to a limited extent they may raise or enhance the level of democratic participation in Britain (Jordan and Moloney, 2007). Interest groups also attract normative comment. For some writers they exert a baleful influence on democracy, because they may disproportionately privilege some interests at the expense of others, or of the public interest as a whole. This was the kind of attitude expressed by Madison about 'factions' that was mentioned in chapter eleven. For others they are entirely desirable because they facilitate the input of new ideas into the political process. According to this view, they are a key element in the pluralism which is an essential feature of (liberal) democracy. For rational choice theorists such as Olson, interest groups are the most rational form of political activity for ordinary citizens, because they are smaller than parties and offer a greater likelihood of return on effort. On the other hand, group interests are not just confined to democracies. All societies are prone to them, including dictatorships, even though the opportunities for expressing them may be more restricted in the latter.

➜ See the discussion on the emergence of parties in chapter eleven, page 256.

12

Interest groups have attracted an enormous amount of comment and analysis, both in general and with respect to particular political systems, and they still do. There is also a long-standing argument about the term itself. What counts as a 'group'? Does it have to be a self-consciously cohesive group, like Friends of the Earth? For groups of this kind, an alternative term is pressure group, although it is less widely used. Or could it denote a disparate group of people who share common interests but do not act in a cohesive manner, e.g. corporations or social classes? There is no definitive answer to this and analysts differ over which version to employ.

➜ See chapter one, page 30, for a discussion of pluralism.

According to Robertson (1993: 240), interest groups are 'associations formed to promote a sectional interest in the political system'. They differ from political parties in that they do not seek to present themselves as candidates for government. Instead they focus upon a narrower range of issues than a government does, although it does happen that interest groups turn into political parties, as environmental groups have done. One distinction often made is between **insider** and **outsider** interest **groups**. Insiders concentrate upon winning support through lobbying, personal contacts, etc. Outsiders rely more upon winning over public opinion through campaigning, the media, etc. While some groups may be permanently oriented towards insider or outsider roles because of their membership, the difference between the roles may also be determined by the nature of the government. For example, conservative governments are typically more inclined to treat employers' associations as insiders, giving greater attention to their views in formulating policy, while labour or socialist governments typically treat trade unions more as insiders.

Puhle (2001: 7703–4) divided interest groups into eight types (a) professional associations; (b) groups of business, commerce and industry; (c) trade unions; (d) agricultural organizations; (e) single interest groups, such as the National Rifle Association in the USA; (f) ideological interest groups, such as the British Humanist Association, or religious groups; (g) public interest groups, such as Amnesty International; (h) welfare associations, such as the Royal National Institute for the Blind.

Interest groups operate in a great many ways, but in so far as they pursue political goals, they will adapt themselves to the structure of the institutions that they wish to influence. If they want to influence the national government, then they will turn most of their attention to the capital, appealing to public opinion, lobbying ministers, officials, and members of parliament. In federal systems they will devote much attention to winning support in individual states. In more administratively dominant communities, interest groups will concentrate most of their efforts on lobbying officials, as happens in Brussels with the European Union. Schlozman (2001) suggests that the strong centralized French political system leads to weak interest groups. On the other hand, the traditions of 1789 continue to endorse a greater inclination towards direct action by interest groups, such as farmers, in France than are normal in other European states. Given the enormous range and diversity of interest group activity around the world, it is very difficult to generalize about it with overarching theories. It is the basic features of individual political systems that structure what interest groups do and how they do it.

Key Points

- There is an ambiguity in the term interest group.
- It can refer to consciously organized groups promoting interests or concerns, in which case it is an essential element in any democracy.
- Or it can refer to groups of interests in society which some actors may promote, in which case it can be found in any state.
- In either case, they are adapted to the institutional framework of a particular regime to maximize their effect.

Corporatism

One variant of interest group theory is called **corporatism**. As mentioned above, governments do not treat all interest groups equally. They will be more inclined to listen to some, i.e. 'insiders', than to others. In this model, though, the state is still responding to ideas or pressure from outside, but some states do more to formalize this relationship. They set up arrangements for regular consultation of key interest groups that represent the views of sections of society that are politically or economically strategic—what have been termed 'peak' associations, as in Britain the Confederation of British Industry and the Trades Union Congress. They do this for the sake of better policy-making, which they recognize requires regular consultation. It resonates with the tendency to focus upon governance rather than government as the most appropriate framework for national decision-making, as was outlined in chapter ten. Because this role is rather different from that of more conventional interest groups that concentrate upon expressing views to the government, Schmitter (1980) coined instead the notion of 'interest intermediation'. In other words, this more select group of organizations acts as channels for exchanging views between their members and the government, rather than necessarily promoting a set view.

→ See chapter ten, page 242, for a discussion on governance.

Schmitter also identified two distinct patterns of establishing these relationships. One, which he termed the 'societal' variant of corporatism, emerged out of pressure from below, i.e. from society or economic actors. As a consequence the choice of which of these actors the state recognizes depends partly upon these pressures from below. In the alternative variant, which he termed 'state' corporatism, it was the state that took the lead in designating its preferred partners.

Lehmbruch (2001) suggests that corporatism has been more prominent at certain periods of history and in certain groups of countries than others. The practices of corporatism were particularly important at times of Keynesian economic management in the 1960s and 1970s, when government, employers, and trade unions regularly consulted over policies that made a trade-off between levels of unemployment, wage rates, and inflation rates. Although several European countries later turned away from these methods, they remain influential in others. The Nordic countries, Germany, and France all practise variants of 'organized' or 'concerted' capitalism, as indicated in chapter ten, which still allow significant scope for negotiations between national partners as opposed to impersonal market forces in determining socio-economic policies.

→ See chapter ten, page 235, for a discussion of coordinated market economies.

Key Points

- Corporatism privileges certain national 'peak' organizations as negotiating partners for the state in determining socio-economic policies.
- There are two variants: society-led or state-led.
- It is still a common approach to governance in countries in continental Europe.

Infrapolitics and Subaltern Studies:
the State Viewed From Below

The preceding sections of this chapter have focused upon ways in which civil society responds to state actors and tries to manoeuvre them into cooperation. This is politics from below. It is important to realize that politics can be viewed through this lens, as well as through a lens focused on national governments and state leaders. Another manifestation of this comes from political anthropology. It is important to appreciate this because it is an important dimension of the study of politics, especially in the developing world, although their insights are not just confined to developing states.

One of the key concerns of political anthropologists is power and its disguises, to use the title of a book by Gledhill (1994). They focus upon the ways in which ordinary people relate to political systems: how they view rulers, defer to them and also manipulate the system for their own ends. One very influential work was Scott's 1990 book, *Domination and the Arts of Resistance*. What attracted his attention was the ways in which peasants among whom he had done fieldwork talked differently among themselves from the way that they talked to their social superiors. It alerted him to the existence of a whole world that he designated as 'infrapolitics', i.e. the subtle ways in which the powerless subvert or undermine the authority of the powerful. Most often, it depended upon ambiguity rather than direct expression of opinions. Individuals needed to avoid retribution. 'Infrapolitics is the realm of informal leadership and nonelites, of conversation and oral discourse, and of surreptitious resistance.' Because of this ambiguity, he argued, it had often been missed, or misunderstood, by outside observers. In fact, social historians such as Hobsbawm had written about such phenomena, but it was much less common among political scientists. Infrapolitics could take the form of covert resistance such as poaching, squatting on land, desertion (of slaves), evasion, and foot-dragging. It could lead to dissident subcultures of resistance: millenarian religions, folk myths of social banditry, and class heroes, e.g. Robin Hood (Scott, 1990: 200, 198).

One particular recent approach in political anthropology has been to try to see the politics and institutions of other regions of the world in their own context and in their own right, not in the shadow of Europe. Given the way in which the European state spread around the world, as outlined in chapters seven and fourteen, this is an understandable reaction. There has emerged a school of 'subaltern' studies, especially among academics in and studying South Asia. This approach too began with social history. Again the concern is with the underdogs in society and their relationship with lower-level officials, the 'subalterns'. As Gupta (2006) explained, there is relatively little ethnographic evidence of what lower level officials do in the name of the state and how this impacts upon the lives of ordinary citizens. These officials are differentially positioned in hierarchical networks of power, which means that they behave differently

12

➜ See chapter seven, page 169, for a discussion on the spread of the Western state.

➜ See chapter fourteen for a more detailed discussion on the rise and spread of the state system.

whether they are turned towards their administrative superiors or towards ordinary citizens. The consequence is, he argued, that there is no such thing as a single state. Instead there are multiple variants of the state within the same nation, with different groups having different experiences of it.

Another concern of the subaltern school is 'decentring' or 'provincializing' Europe, i.e. examining politics and society in other parts of the world in their own right and on their own terms, not as seen though a European lens (Chatterjee, 2001: 15,240). Apart from trying to give a voice to the previously underprivileged in society, it also aims at challenging those who would recommend a Western path to **modernity**. They want equality of respect with and from the West. They recommend the search for an alternative path to modernity which is not necessarily the same as in the West and is more in tune with local circumstances.

Key Points

- Political anthropology examines the connections between political attitudes and political behaviour and their cultural contexts, especially at the grassroots.

- Subaltern studies emphasize the multiplicity of ways in which the state is perceived by people because of the disparate ways in which they are treated by local officials.

- Subaltern studies also demand consideration for development strategies that are not borrowed from the West and are better adapted to local (non-Western) conditions.

The Impact of the Media

We have now moved on to considering the ways in which politics and the state is perceived by its citizens. One crucial set of actors that determines this is the media. It is difficult to exaggerate the extent to which the media structure perceptions of politics among citizens in a particular country. In addition, democracies recognize the importance of the media in upholding freedom of speech. The First Amendment to the US Constitution in 1789 established the principle of freedom of speech as an essential element of democracy. Since then this principle has increasingly figured in other states' definitions of a democracy. This also established the importance of the media in ensuring an informed democratic citizenry.

Traditionally this meant seeing the press as confronting or challenging the established authorities on behalf of ordinary people. It played a complementary role to that of opposition parties in parliament, as described in chapter nine. There developed the notion of the power of the press. It was, or at any rate could be, another of the checks on the power of the executive. This made it another branch of civil society. Journalists had the time and resources to investigate official wrongdoing that ordinary people and even politicians lacked. In fact they were sometimes granted special legal immunities.

➡ See chapter nine, page 217, for a discussion on ensuring accountability.

In the USA and some other democracies, journalists were entitled to keep sources of information confidential even if threatened with prosecution, a right that was only otherwise available to lawyers, doctors, and priests.

Sometimes, journalists have achieved dramatic changes in national politics—the *Washington Post*'s dogged investigation of the Watergate affair in 1972 ultimately led to President Nixon's resignation. Brave journalists around the world regularly put their lives at risk in the pursuit of stories. In 2006, eighty-one journalists and thirty-two media assistants were killed around the world (Reporters Without Borders, 2006).

Equally, the owners of media outlets—above all, newspaper proprietors—often see their role as one of advocates for particular political standpoints. The extent to which this can be achieved may be exaggerated—when *The Sun* claimed in 1997 that 'It Was The Sun Wot Won It' for Labour, this was only partly true. Popular exasperation with the incompetence and complacency of the outgoing Conservative government was more fundamental in creating a mood for radical change. Yet there is widespread consensus that the direction and tone of an issue like Britain's relations with the EU are heavily circumscribed by the well-known positions of major newspapers, whichever party is in power. Recent years have seen the emergence of media owners as politicians in their own right—even as prime ministers, such as Berlusconi in Italy and Thaksin Shinawatra in Thailand—instead of them seeking to act as tribunes for particular views, as previously tended to be the case.

On the other hand, all newspaper and TV companies rely on political stories to help sell their products. They have to make profits to stay in business, which means that they have to present the news in ways of which enough readers or viewers will approve. Even the BBC finds it advantageous to give governments a hard time in its reporting so as to appear impartial to its audiences, even though it is overwhelmingly paid for out of a state-determined licence fee. In China, the reporting of events has been changed by the need now for newspapers, even *The People's Daily*, to break even or make a profit. They cannot simply rely upon state subsidies. These newspapers do have to adapt their reports to some extent to fit in with the likely views of their readers. To some extent, that also leads to a preference, certainly in the West, for human interest accounts of politics rather than dry dissections of party policies, what is sometimes called 'info-tainment'—even if it leads to criticism by politicians of 'dumbing down' politics.

On the other hand, both governments and individual politicians need the media to help to sell policies and to help to win election campaigns. As the political columnist and former MP, Matthew Parris, once put it: 'Politicians run on publicity like horses run on oats' (Franklin, 2004: 5). So they also need to court the media and 'spin' policies. The ability to come up with memorable sound bites is an invaluable skill for any politician.

This means that, according to Franklin (2004: 14) politicians and the media are sometimes adversaries and sometimes accomplices. Trying to capture the complexity of that relationship is difficult, and he outlines four different theories that have been proposed to try to do so (208–28).

1. A theory of the 'powerful' media, which 'injected' messages into their audience like 'magic bullets' or battered them into acceptance; yet the methodological problems of actually identifying where and how this really happens have proved extremely challenging.

2. The 'two-step' flow of limited media influence: this suggested that the media were influential only in so far as their messages were reinforced by personal interaction of readers or viewers with local opinion-formers.

3. The theory that people 'use' the media to gratify certain needs. This approach reverses the direction of the argument by focusing upon why viewers and readers choose to respond to media messages, rather than serving as passive consumers. How can we reliably identify those 'needs', let alone the ways in which they may structure viewing and reading habits?

4. The theory that broadcasters and audiences jointly 'encode' and 'decode' political messages, but they may diverge in the ways that they do so. Journalists may 'construct' messages to convey political information, but audiences may receive and interpret them differently. In some ways this is a more realistic account of the relationship since it focuses equally on both sides. However, identifying regular social patterns in the ways that this occurs is also fraught with difficulty.

There is still no agreed consensus on the superiority of one theory over the others. It is a truism to talk about 'the power of the press', and yet it is extremely elusive and difficult to pin down. To complicate matters further, audience views of politics may be influenced by entertainment programmes as well as 'straight' news-reporting. Audiences do not neatly separate political entertainment from factual news. *Yes Minister* had an iconic status in presenting to the public the relationship between politicians and civil servants, whether or not it was always accurate. *Spitting Image* contained nuggets of satire about the Thatcher Government that audiences felt must be true at a deeper level, even if they portrayed scenes that never really happened. *The West Wing* for some people is built around the best Democratic president that the USA never had. It has spread a more positive view of American politics than numerous current affairs shows ever have. Trying to factor these elements into an analysis of the relationship between politics and the media adds further layers of complexity into an ever-fascinating subject (Street, 2001).

Now there is a further complication. New forms of communication are appearing which will upset the more traditional relations between politics and the media. This will be the subject of the next section.

Key Points

- Traditionally the media, especially the press, have been seen as an essential element of liberal democracy and a check on the power of the executive.
- Politicians and the media are by turns adversaries and accomplices.
- More recently the media have been condemned for dumbing down the coverage of politics, while politicians have been criticized for 'spinning' their activities.

- An assessment of the power of the media needs to take into account the way politics is presented in all the formats where it appears and not just in current affairs programmes.
- The way 'the power of the press' operates is extremely difficult to pin down.

The Challenge of New Technologies

In recent years new communications technologies have begun to revolutionize the role of the media in politics again. Indeed, it can be argued that they may have a bigger impact than newspapers and TV did in the past, not least because they provide additional opportunities for ordinary citizens to take advantage of the new **public space** to make an impact upon politics. They can provide civil society with new arenas for activity. There are three reasons for this. First, the Internet and mobile phones have transformed the ability of ordinary citizens to organize themselves in groups even when confronted with repression from their authorities. Secondly, they have widened the possibilities for people outside the media world to report news and make influential comment on events. In that sense they have democratized access to the media. Thirdly, they offer the future possibility of transforming decision-making institutions as well, e.g. voting and referendums. We will consider these three dimensions in turn.

Promoting Horizontal Communication

Previously, communications channels within states were mainly vertical ones. The most influential media outlets tended to congregate in national capitals. That was especially true of TV stations. Political parties and interest groups achieved results by concentrating their efforts there. The opportunities for other groups to make themselves into significant forces were constrained by the difficulties of contacting people through landline telephones and the mail. Now, however, there are much greater opportunities for would-be political actors to mobilize support using horizontal communications—mobile phones (including SMS texting) and the Internet.

In the early years of the Internet there was optimism about the possibilities that the new media offered for organizing political parties. In the USA, in particular, the enormous cost of standing for office made it very difficult for outsiders to be elected. Much was made of the success of a former wrestler, Jesse Ventura, in winning election against all expectations as Governor of Minnesota in 1998 as a third-party candidate. He made widespread use of the Internet as a cheap means to get his message across. This seemed to open the way for other outsiders to follow his example. However, the established parties quickly took note of the threat and started throwing money at their Internet strategies. They have refined the techniques of using the Internet for candidates to communicate directly with individual voters and target specific messages to their various concerns. Once again they have outflanked the challengers.

12

On the other hand the new technologies can empower groups to organize protests, as they can mobilize supporters much more quickly and unexpectedly in real time. This can still be very effective. The UK, for instance, saw mobile phones used in September 2000 to organize effective blockades of fuel storage depots by protesters who wanted to see cuts in fuel duty. The Philippines saw a much more important example at the end of 2000, with an explosion of SMS texting making a decisive contribution to the overthrow of the democratically elected President Estrada. See **Box 12.3**. Now social networking sites such as Facebook and MySpace can enable the same sort of activity.

These new possibilities for self-organization will impact both democratic and authoritarian states, although in different ways. More open systems are vulnerable to the activities

Case Study   Box 12.3
The Fall of Joseph Estrada

In 1998 Joseph Estrada was elected president of the Philippines. A former actor who had played the lead in over a hundred movies and had produced seventy, he entered politics in the late 1960s as mayor of a town in Metro Manila. Gradually his political career took off as he was elected first a senator and then, in 1992, vice-president. Coming from a poor background in a country whose politics are dominated by traditional elite families, he won the support of the poorer strata of society.

By 2000, however, his administration was in trouble. His popularity in opinion polls was sliding. He launched a costly military campaign against the Moro Islamic Liberation Front on the island of Mindanao. Then it was alleged that he had taken several million dollars in bribes from gambling and the Senate moved to impeach him. In January 2001 pro-Estrada senators blocked a key piece of evidence from being presented in court. This plunged the country into crisis (Doronila, 2001).

In Manila outraged demonstrators began to organize public demonstrations using mobile phones. In a normal week Filipinos had been exchanging 50 million text messages per day, but as the crisis deepened, this figure rose to 80 million. People intending to demonstrate passed on information about the location at very short notice to everyone they knew, who then passed it on to others. The organizers of the demonstrations quickly realized that it was this short timescale that made it extremely difficult for the authorities to respond. Hundreds of thousands of people kept gathering on or around the same street that had been the site of demonstrations of 'people power' in 1986 that had toppled President Ferdinand Marcos.

After five days of demonstrations that paralysed the capital, Estrada was forced to step down, to be replaced by Vice-President Gloria Macapagal-Arroyo. He was the first political casualty of SMS texting. Three months later he was arrested and put on trial. After proceedings lasting six years he was found guilty in 2007 and sentenced to life imprisonment. Almost immediately afterwards President Arroyo pardoned him on the grounds that he had reached the age of 70, the age at which prisoners in the Philippines are released, and in return for a commitment that he would retire from politics.

12

Photo 12.2

A sea of umbrellas used by protesters as heavy rains fall during a protest rally. Tens of thousands of Filipinos who attended the rally are opposed to President Joseph Estrada's proposal to change the constitution.
Source: © Reuters/CORBIS

of what Rheingold (2002) has termed 'smart mobs'. These are technologically sophisticated groups who use their skills to organize group protests that the authorities find difficult to prevent, even if they are aware of what is planned, because of the short warning that they are given. The fuel protesters in Britain were one example of this. It can be a kind of political blackmail. It certainly challenges the ability of the state to satisfy demands without alienating the rest of society that did not take part. The demonstrators in the Philippines were a much larger manifestation of the same phenomenon.

Obviously, authoritarian regimes place more emphasis upon controlling the freedom to organize in this way because any such protest is fundamentally more threatening. See **Box 12.4**.

China in particular has devoted enormous efforts to surveillance of the Internet. They have erected a firewall to limit the access of their own citizens to politically sensitive material abroad. They also have a large number of censors (nicknamed

Key Quote Box 12.4
Rolling Stone on the Internet and Authoritarian States

'The Internet is the censor's biggest challenge and the tyrant's worst nightmare...
Unbeknown to their governments, people in China, Iraq and Iran, among other countries, are freely communicating with people all over the world.'   (*Rolling Stone* magazine
1995 (see www.fas.org/cp/swett.html))

'Internet mamas') supervising electronic message boards and requiring that politically
or socially undesirable materials are deleted. However, technologically sophisticated
netizens use mirror servers to obtain sensitive information from abroad and outwit the
censors. The danger for these sorts of regime is that they can control the Internet in
normal times, but that the new technologies will exacerbate any serious crisis if and
when it occurs. In the absence of legitimate democratic institutions to channel protests
in a constructive direction, these technologies may increase the opportunities for
protest if and when people become very dissatisfied.

Of course, not all the groups that use the new technologies to aid organization are
benign. The Internet can be extremely useful to small extremist groups for attracting
adherents, which they would have found much more difficult to do relying upon the
older methods of personal contacts, public meetings, pamphlets, and posters. The
challenge of combating groups bent on violence or terrorism has been made more
serious for all governments, whether democratic or authoritarian.

Everyone a Blogger, Everyone a Journalist

The new media have also made it much easier for non-journalists to publish comments
and views in blogs on politics. Some have become more influential than established
commentators and are quoted by journalists, especially at times of elections. Equally,
political figures, e.g. David Cameron, whether elected or standing for election, now
increasingly publish blogs to connect with voters, though this further strengthens the
trend mentioned in chapter eleven, whereby the personal image of candidates is
enhanced at the expense of their parties.

Equally, individuals can now report breaking news as quickly as news agencies if they
happen to be in the right place at the right time. They can also publish alternative versions
of events if official government sources are perceived to be putting their own (inaccurate)
spin on what happened. Despite the controls, this has already begun to happen in China,
as the regime has been forced to reconsider and apologize for initial official explanations of
disasters or major accidents that local people thought were mistaken.

➔ See the
discussion on
problems facing
parties in chapter
eleven, page 267.

12

In both these ways, the new media have begun to change the traditional media landscape and potentially also the structure of authority in society. Gradually they are giving voices to Scott's 'infrapolitics'.

Electronic Decision-making

Evangelists for the new media have also suggested that they can be used to bring public decision-making much closer to the people than ever before. Barber (1998, 1984), for instance, has looked forward to the new technology inaugurating a new era of 'strong' democracy, i.e. a modern equivalent of the democracy of ancient Athens. However, for the moment, actual proposals have focused more upon two alternative strategies. The first is based upon local government, the other upon greater use of referendums.

The local government option has been based upon the model of town meetings in the USA, i.e. meetings of citizens in a local community to debate and decide policy. The electronic variant is to arrange for citizens to be connected through cable so that they can debate and decide online (Becker and Slaton, 2000). The expectation was that this would enable a richer form of democracy to take root locally and then gradually spread throughout the nation. It assumed that the electronic meetings would themselves propose and decide upon policy. The alternative was to organize regular electronic consultation of citizens about proposals that initially emerged either from representatives or from administrators. The model would be based more upon the referendums regularly organized in Switzerland (Budge, 1996). This latter variant is clearly a 'weaker' form of democracy than the former, though the one might lead to the other. Neither variant has yet made a great deal of progress. The same is true of research on electronic voting in Europe.

There is an important issue hanging over all such proposals. How reliable is the technology, especially for voting? A recent American report has reminded us that there are a great many potential dangers (*Asking the Right Questions About Electronic Voting*, 2005). These dangers are likely to be less great when the voting is confined to localities. Once voting is aggregated at higher levels, there is a serious danger of the integrity of the voting process being compromised. Votes could be stolen or redirected or simply dumped without the voter being aware of this. The whole process could be disrupted by viruses. Even though the existing American system of voting in many states ran into serious criticism after the shambles of the 2000 presidential election recounts, there are still good reasons for waiting until a really secure voting system can be devised. Until that happens, the more ambitious hopes for e-democracy will have to be delayed.

But although these are daunting challenges, they are not the only ones that stand in the way of politics being transformed by e-democracy. As McLean (1989) pointed out, there are other fundamental difficulties in aggregating preferences of citizens in some **direct democracy**. They relate to the difficulty of coming to a definitive view of the wishes of large numbers of people expressing preferences for a range of alternative policy proposals which they rank in quite different ways. This is another manifestation of the problem identified by the **Arrow impossibility theorem** mentioned in chapter eleven.

➔ See chapter eleven, page 252, for a discussion of the Arrow impossibility theorem.

This problem becomes even more intractable if any of the possible choices are dependent upon conditions resulting from other choices, as is almost always the case where spending priorities are involved. Thus the problems of e-democracy transforming traditional problems of democracy are not likely to be resolved in the near future.

Key Points

- New communications technologies have aroused great hopes for transforming citizen involvement in politics, by enabling outsiders and new ideas to penetrate established political systems.
- They can also enable 'smart mobs' to disrupt government and hold the public to ransom.
- Their effect is likely to be greater in states with less established, or less legitimate political institutions, especially at times of crisis.
- They also allow non-journalists to publish news stories and influential blogs.
- They may enable greater participation in local decision-making.
- Electronic voting is still subject to great risks about the integrity of the technology.

Conclusion

This chapter has concentrated on views of the state from below and attempts to influence it. It has also discussed the concept of civil society and the great impact it has had on policies of the developed world towards the developing world since the 1980s; yet, as we have seen, it also suffers from great ambiguities and contradictions, which make it another essentially contested concept. The final section focused on the impact of new communications technologies on political life. Although we are only at the beginning of the revolution in political behaviour that they herald, it is clear that they may make the concept of civil society even more unwieldy. Not only do they enable citizens within states to organize for the pursuit of political goals more easily than ever before, they also blur the boundaries between national and foreign politics even more. Neither the Internet nor mobile phones are great respecters of national frontiers. Like-minded groups can organize much more freely across them. This was already seen in the demonstrations that disrupted the 1999 WTO summit in Seattle, which brought together protest groups from around the world. Since then WTO and the annual G8 summits have tended to attract similar swarms of protesters, although not with the same degree of violence. What is clear is that these new possibilities for group self-organization are not only transforming civil society within individual states, they are also beginning to promote what can be described as **international civil society**, i.e. a global community of political activists and organizations that demand a greater say in the running of international politics. The new technologies are not merely promoting alternative views of the state from below. They are also promoting alternative views of the international order from below. Castells (1996) has written of the emergence of the 'network society'. It may also be the beginning of the 'network world'.

12

 *Key Questions*

- Go to Technorati.com and find interesting political blogs. Is there anything that makes them interesting which is different from the work of commentators in newspapers or on TV? Do they have more credibility?

- What makes a politician's blog good?

- Do TV series such as *The West Wing* and *Yes Minister* do more to shape political opinions than 'straight' political reporting? How would you measure the impact?

- Is there any point in trying to preserve public broadcasting as something distinct in an era when broadcasting possibilities are expanding almost exponentially on the Internet?

- What needs to be done to make electronic democracy work?

- How do media outlets create the sense of credibility in their coverage of politics? Do they use the same techniques for fictionalized accounts of politics as for straight political reporting?

- Is the rise of single-issue interest groups good for democracy?

- Why is there not a single model of a successful interest group that others could follow?

- Identify some of the 'weapons of the weak' with which you are familiar. How can you tell whether they are subversive of the existing order?

- How viable are alternatives to Western paths to modernization?

 Further Reading

Chadwick, Andrew (2006), *Internet Politics: States, Citizens and New Communications Technologies*, Oxford, Oxford University Press.
> This is a wide-ranging account of the impact of the new technologies on politics.

Edwards, Michael (2004), *Civil Society*, Cambridge: Polity Press.
> Here, we have committed advocacy of the potential for civil society to transform politics by the Director of the Ford Foundation's Governance and Civil Society Program.

Jordan, Grant and William A. Moloney (2007), *Democracy and Interest Groups: Enhancing Participation?*, Basingstoke: Palgrave.
> This is an enquiry into the ways in which participation in interest groups enhances democracy.

Scott, James C. (1990), *Domination and the Arts of Resistance: Hidden Transcripts*, New Haven, CT: Yale University Press.
> This is an influential examination of the ways in which ordinary people get around authoritarian rulers.

Street, John (2001), *Mass Media, Politics and Democracy*, Basingstoke: Palgrave.
> This is a very good analysis of the relationship between the media and democratic politics.

Wilson, Graham K. (1990), *Interest Groups*, Oxford: Blackwell.
> This is a well-regarded analysis of interest groups.

12

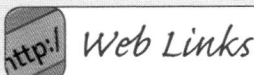

Web Links

https://fp.auburn.edu/tann/
For the TAN + N (Teledemocracy Action News + Network)

www.publicus.net
An e-democracy network

http://edc.unige.ch/
For the European E-Democracy Centre

www.social-informatics.net/evoting.htm
A still topical list of publications on e-voting up to 2006

www.socialcapitalgateway.org/eng-index.htm
Gateway to large number of sites devoted to social capital and interest group activity

 Visit the **Online Resource Centre** that accompanies this book to access more learning resources at **www.oxfordtextbooks.co.uk/orc/garner/**

12

13

Political Culture

Reader's Guide

This chapter will begin by presenting some of the ideas and objectives of the originators of the concept of political culture. Then it will look at some of the problems that emerged in analysing and applying it. It will present a case study of the difficulty of identifying the contribution of the political culture to understanding political change by looking at the failures of establishing democracy in Russia since the collapse of communism. It will then argue that despite the problems, political culture remains an important field of study in political science, because of its relation to nationalism, for instance. Finally, it will suggest an alternative approach that takes account of a place for political culture where contestation and argument are central.

Civic Culture and Political Culture

As indicated in chapter seven, all normally functioning states require legitimacy. If their rulers are not to depend upon permanent repression, they need to be accepted by their populations. This involves both an acceptance of the goals of the state and also of the ways in which their leaders emerge and rule. Earlier chapters have focused upon the ways in which the processes of selection may be made acceptable in modern states, but what also matters is the sense that the policies and the processes are deemed appropriate by and for a particular national community. In other words, it also depends upon their 'political culture'. To use one of the terms presented in chapter seven, this is one of the factors that structure the operation of political institutions and the actions of political actors.

➔ See chapter seven, page 173, for a discussion of the domestic factors affecting the strength of states.

Political culture is 'the totality of ideas and attitudes towards authority, discipline, governmental responsibilities and entitlements, and associated patterns of cultural transmission such as the education system and family life' (Robertson, 1993: 382).

One of the pioneering works that established the field of political culture was Almond and Verba's *The Civic Culture*. It took as its starting point the reasonable hypothesis that for a state to be stable, it would need a substantial congruence between the values of society and the behaviour of the government. This notion that democracy rested on a broader set of social values had after all been elaborated in Tocqueville's nineteenth-century classic text *Democracy in America*. See **Box 13.1**.

There he argued that family relations and social life in democratic America were quite different from the aristocratic societies with which he was familiar in Europe. Almond and Verba made an early use of public opinion surveys in political science to analyse the attitudes towards authority in five countries: the USA, the UK, Germany, Italy, and Mexico. The fundamental objective was not just to illustrate differing attitudes towards authority from one country to another. It also wanted to test the

13

Key Quote   Box 13.1
Alexis de Tocqueville

'It is therefore particularly mores [i.e. habits and opinions] that render the Americans of the United States . . . capable of supporting the empire of democracy, and it is again [mores] that make the various Anglo-American democracies more or less regulated and prosperous . . . I am convinced that the happiest situation and the best laws cannot maintain a constitution despite mores, whereas the latter turn even the most unfavourable positions and the worst laws to good account. The importance of mores is a common truth to which study and experience constantly lead back. It seems to me that I have it placed in my mind as a central point; I perceive it as the end of all my ideas.'
(de Tocqueville, 2000: 295)

hypothesis that popular attitudes towards politics and the state in established democracies differ from those in other political systems. For this purpose the UK and the USA were assumed to be mature democracies.

It hypothesized two things. First, there were three possible dimensions to a political culture, i.e. three collective attitudes towards politics. Schematically it identified them as 'parochial', 'subject', and 'participant'. Groups who inclined towards 'parochialism' were little interested in politics, certainly at the national level. In so far as they were interested in 'politics' at all, it was only in events and issues very close to their own locality and their direct personal interests. 'Subjects' did have a wider perspective. They were interested in national politics, but only as observers. They might cast votes in general elections but they did not feel any great ability to make a greater contribution to political life. Instead they left it to established elites to make those decisions. 'Participants', however, felt that they could and should contribute to national decision-making, not just through occasional votes. They felt they were entitled to have their views taken into account when decisions were made. This could be through membership of **interest groups**, contacts with the media, and so on.

In fact Almond and Verba assumed that all three types of political attitude are present in almost all societies. In that sense they had a model that could be applied to almost all political systems, but it was the mix of the three dimensions that determined whether a system was democratic, and if so, what kind of democracy it was. They assumed that in a mature democracy the proportion of people that adopted participant attitudes would be greatest, although they also felt that no viable democracy was possible if everyone wanted to participate. It was essential, therefore, that in a modern democracy a significant proportion of the population accepted a 'subject' status, were more deferential towards authority.

This work was part of the behavioural movement that was gathering momentum in political science around that time. It aimed at expanding the boundaries of analysis to include social forces that had an impact upon the institutions that previously had been the main focus of attention. It reflected the rethinking of the nature of modern democracy as **polyarchy** found in Dahl's *Who Governs?*, which had appeared four years earlier in 1961; and it inspired a great deal of research on political attitudes in other countries.

A companion work by Pye and Verba introduced a theme that was also widely taken up later, i.e. political culture and 'modernization'. Do political attitudes change with socio-economic development? Can political scientists deduce from this 'a better understanding of the policies and necessary investments in various socializing agents which can best produce desired changes in a nation's politics'? (Pye and Verba, 1965: 11.) They hypothesized that this would be achieved by focusing on four themes or pairs of values. See **Box 13.2**.

At the time these works on political culture offered a whole new way of conceptualizing political life, one that could apply findings from other disciplines such as psychology. They spawned a host of other works that sought to apply the same type

Box 13.2

The Four Pairs of Values of the Civic Culture

- Trust versus suspicion: to what extent do individuals in a given society trust strangers, or even people with whom they are familiar?
- Hierarchy versus equality: how far do individuals respond to traditional social hierarchies and hierarchies of power?
- Liberty versus coercion: how far do individuals and groups insist upon their freedom to act?
- Levels of loyalty and commitment: how far do individuals and groups focus their loyalty upon family or parochial grouping and how far upon the nation as a whole?

Source: Pye and Verba (1965: 22–3)

of approach to other political systems, including by people who did not share all of the original assumptions or objectives.

Sodaro has summarized and generalized these approaches by dividing the dimensions of their research into three categories, all of which offer a spectrum of alternatives:

1. attitudes towards authority: this would run from submissive at one end, through deferential and then alienated, to rebellious at the other end;

2. attitudes towards society: here there are two subdimensions. The first would run from highly consensual at one end to highly conflictual at the other, with various mixes of the two in between. The second would run from extreme individualism at one end to extreme collectivism at the other;

3. attitudes towards the state: this would run from approval for a very permissive state at one end to approval for a very interventionist state at the other (Sodaro, 2008: 300–4).

Thus the field opened up enormously, so that it is common for books on individual political systems to include parts that deal with political culture. Yet it is also one of the areas that is most challenged by sceptics. The original works by Almond, Pye, and Verba were theoretically more nuanced than many of their detractors later alleged. They did not make unqualified assertions about the explanatory power of such approaches. Yet there is no doubt about the difficulties involved in using political cultural approaches to explain political outcomes. Let us now turn to some of the objections that have been raised.

13

Key Points

- The intellectual origins of the concept of political culture lie in the attempt to identify a civic culture, i.e. a set of attitudes that make democracy work.

- This spawned enquiries that examined attitudes in individual states towards authority, society, and the state which can be combined to identify a nation's political culture.

Challenges to the Concept of Political Culture

This section will focus on five challenges to the use of the concept of political culture. The first four relate to the difficulties of operationalizing it. The fifth presents objections to the way that it was sometimes used.

1. Is there a Homogeneous National Political Culture?

The first challenge relates to the difficulty of trying to identify a single national political culture. This can be illustrated through the example of Italy. Italy has proved a fruitful object of analysis for more general theorizing about modern political culture, because it does not fit well into pictures of West European politics more generally and it was less economically developed. For example, the state in Italy enjoys much less respect from citizens than in other European states. Almond and Verba concluded that Italy had an 'alienated political culture', with relatively unrelieved social isolation and distrust (Almond and Verba, 1965: 308). The sense of deference towards public goods there is much less. In some parts of Italy, especially the south, alternative social institutions, even organized crime, may assume functions on behalf of local communities that in other countries are the preserve of the state, e.g. the maintenance of order. Even before *The Civic Culture*, the sociologist Banfield had examined this phenomenon in poor parts of Sicily. He concluded that the lack of community spirit there could be explained by what he termed **amoral familism,** i.e. people put the needs and interests of their families higher than those of the rest of society. All was for the family and the only morality was promoting the family's interests by any means. People there recognized few if any moral checks on the pursuit of those family interests. The result was a highly divided society where people were unwilling to contribute to the public good and where politics was dominated by attempts to promote families (Banfield, 1958).

More recently, however, Putnam produced another influential work on Italian political culture, *Making Democracy Work*. This focused on the north of the country, where party democracy is much stronger. After surveying the historical traditions of particular regions in the north, it concluded:

The regions characterized by civic involvement in the late twentieth century are almost precisely the same regions where cooperatives and cultural associations and mutual aid societies were most abundant in the nineteenth century, and where neighbourhood associations and religious confraternities and guilds had contributed to the flourishing communal republics of the twelfth century. (Putnam, 1993: 162)

Thus what had evolved here was a **social capital** that was translated into democratic practice. It was a striking reaffirmation of the importance of political culture in democracy.

Both works have been extremely influential, with the conclusions then being turned into hypotheses for the analysis of other states. At the same time they have both provoked great controversy—see, for example, Jackman and Miller, 2004. Nevertheless for our purposes the main point is that they both describe parts of the same country, yet come to quite different conclusions. Putnam identifies regions where there is a strong tradition of democratic involvement and public service. Banfield focuses on regions where naked self-interest determines behaviour. Even though these two works were written forty years apart, which might explain the difference, they tried to identify long-term features of their national political cultures. These two conclusions cannot be synthesized; yet *The Civic Culture* tried to identify a single national political culture. Even though it did not assume a completely homogeneous national political culture— it did examine the impact of different levels of education upon political views, for example—it did not take into account regional variations. These two works demonstrate why that is an oversimplification.

The same point could be made about Almond and Verba's analysis of politics in the UK. Again it assumed a territorially homogeneous political culture, yet only six years later the upsurge of protest and then violence in Northern Ireland, which lasted for over thirty years, showed that the claim that Britain had a single, deferential political culture was an oversimplification. So too did the subsequent rise of Scottish and Welsh **nationalism**. Yet Italy is an ethnically homogeneous nation, and the UK is fairly homogeneous.

The problem of identifying a single national political culture is even more acute in religiously divided societies or in ethnically more divided states, especially where communities speak different languages. Diversity matters, and so too does size. In the United States the Civil War ended 140 years ago, and yet it still divides political attitudes between northerners and southerners. Before 1861 the South produced most American presidents. It took 115 years for the next Southerner to be elected in his own right—Jimmy Carter in 1976 (Woodrow Wilson had moved to the North first, while Truman and Johnson moved up from being vice-president after the deaths of the incumbents). Under those circumstances, attempts to identify a common national political culture are problematic—as the authors themselves later acknowledged (Almond and Verba, 1989: 406).

2. The Problematic Link between Attitudes and Political Outcomes

A second problem in operationalizing political culture is identifying a chain of causation between the sources of political attitudes of a group of people, or even a whole society, formed largely in adolescence and youth, and national political outcomes years or even decades later. By focusing upon the sources of national values and when they are absorbed by individuals, they tended to imply that political outlooks were largely set by the time of adulthood, or at any rate soon afterwards. This greatly narrowed the scope for changing and learning in later life, e.g. in response to major events. Even if a great many decisions were made in conformity with values learnt years or decades earlier, some would still be unexpected. Every revolution, for example, represents a break with previous trends and traditions.

3. The State may Establish the Bases of Political Culture

An underlying assumption of Almond and Verba was that the legitimacy of a political system among its people at least in part depended upon a fit with pre-existing, or at any rate separately formed, social and political values. This was a plausible assumption for states with a well-defined, historical national identity such as the UK, the USA, and most of Western Europe. It assumed that political culture emerged out of a prior existing set of social values. The state had to adapt to those values; but most states in the world teach about national values as part of their school curriculum. Even Britain is planning to introduce this into its schools, and it has already begun to do so for would-be long-stay residents from abroad and those seeking naturalization (Home Office, 2007). The state tries to socialize young people into approved political values and national identity. Even though this is never likely to be the sole means by which people learn political values, nevertheless it means that the state is trying to establish in people's minds the basis of its own legitimacy. The greater its success in establishing this, the greater would be its legitimacy. National identity and national political culture are not simply accepted by a state. The state helps or tries to create or at least form it. This was a possibility that theories of political culture did not really take into account.

China can help to clarify this phenomenon. The Chinese state has over 5,000 years of recorded history, although only for the last 2,000 has the recording taken place roughly contemporaneously with the events being recorded. Not surprisingly, history plays a very important role in Chinese political culture. Mao Zedong repeatedly drew parallels between his own actions and those of previous emperors. As Jenner remarked,

Chinese governments have, for at least 2000 years, taken history much too seriously to allow the future to make its own unguided judgements about them . . . Historical myth-making has so far been remarkably effective not just in inventing a single Han Chinese ethnicity but also—and this is a far bigger triumph—in winning acceptance of it . . . The religion of the Chinese ruling classes is the Chinese state, and it is through history that the object if devotion is to be understood. (Jenner, 1992: 3–4)

This weight of officially sanctioned Chinese history has left a long shadow over Chinese political identity and Chinese political culture.

Russia is another example of the same phenomenon. Across the Eurasian landmass there are few geographical features that provide natural borders. The whole area has been subject to periodic invasion from east and west. Thus Russians identify their territory with the state that established secure borders. An enduring feature of Russian political culture is concern with state-ness (*gosudarstvennost*), i.e. the ability of the state to operate effectively and the priority of ensuring that it does. In the geographical circumstances in which Russia finds itself, a strong, effective state is regarded as a precondition for 'normal' social life, and this colours Russian attitudes towards democracy. The latter should not impede the necessary functions of the former.

The issue is even more important in states with a much shorter history, e.g. former colonies in Africa and Asia. In many cases it was the colonial regimes that determined the borders. Previously, societies were broken into smaller communities, clans, tribes, etc. Thus, as was argued in chapter seven, post-colonial states often had to determine the nation, to establish both national identity and national values. Some have been more successful at this than others. According to the most recent World Values Survey, Tanzania had the highest score of respondents (54 per cent) of any African state who regarded the existing political system as 'very good'. Another way of putting this is that Tanzania was the African political system with the greatest legitimacy. Although its founder, President Nyerere was committed to a socialist programme that proved economically unsuccessful, politically he proved more successful. He concentrated on creating a one-party state to establish national unity and he could do so because colonial rule had undermined traditional political structures and suppressed attempts at 'native rebellions'. Thus the Tanzanian African National Union could impose itself as the sole political force after independence, and it has preserved its dominance as the Revolutionary Party despite the introduction of multiparty elections in 1995 (Baregu, 1997). It has avoided exploiting tribal divisions, and it has achieved a diffuse but widespread popular support. There is widespread participation in political rallies and campaigns, but little individual political activism, despite the most intense dissatisfaction over poor economic development and corruption. Nevertheless trust in public institutions there was the highest of the twelve states surveyed by Afrobarometer in 2001. All in all it would seem that the dominant mode of political culture is that of subjects, to use the categories of Almond and Verba. Political change has been top-down but fairly flexible (Martin, 1988). It has been relatively effective in establishing political values and support for them. According to Afrobarometer, this made the country stand out by comparison with other African states (Chaligha *et al.*, 2002).

By contrast, only 8 per cent of respondents to the World Values Survey in Pakistan regarded their political system as very good—the lowest figure for any state in Asia or sub-Saharan Africa. This is not surprising, given the shocks that Pakistan has had to endure since independence in 1947. First, it was forced into a separate existence from

➔ See chapter seven, page 169 for a discussion on the spread of the Western state.

13

the rest of India at quite short notice, with over ten million Muslim refugees forced to flee there. It was divided into two parts on either side of India, with quite different attitudes towards the place of religion in public life and different historical traditions (Humayun, 1995). West Pakistan maintained control over East Pakistan, until 1971 when the East seceded with the assistance of India. Thus, the Pakistani regime was forced into casting and recasting its national identity twice within twenty-four years. And the task of maintaining popular support in a military-dominated regime was exacerbated by two wars with India in 1965 and 1971, both of which it lost. In addition significant numbers of Pakistanis reject state attempts to impose law that they regard as clashing with Islamic precepts—a major problem for a state whose Islamic identity is absolutely fundamental (Yilmaz, 2005: 126–7). Under those circumstances it is not surprising that the regime should find it difficult to establish a durable political culture, with alternating military rule and attempts at democracy, a great deal of corruption and widespread 'amoral familism' such as Banfield originally identified in Italy.

4. The Impact of Globalization

Globalization increasingly nullifies attempts to identify a national political culture. At the elite level ambitious politicians eagerly search for new ideas to win elections, manipulate the media, and mould public support. Sarkozy and Berlusconi are among the most recent examples of national leaders who have sought to use American campaign techniques to outwit their opponents and win large majorities. At the popular level, increasing migration across borders by workers means that appeals for political support can no longer rely on traditional themes and approaches, viz. the great efforts that both American parties now put into winning the Hispanic vote.

5. Political Culture is Used to Explain Why Change cannot Happen

Lastly, the argument about national political cultures is often used to justify failures in developing democracy, or even its inappropriateness. Arguments of this type usually begin by asserting that democracy is a Western concept, imply that states in other parts of the world have different cultural traditions and then use this to explain away the failures of democratization. This is the argument used in Singapore to justify the slowness of the regime there to move towards more open democracy although the standard of living has matched or even exceeded that of Europe. It was said that Asian traditions were less individualistic, more consensual than those of the West, and this made confrontational party democracy both inappropriate and less desired. 'Asians' allegedly value order and stability more highly than freedom (Emmerson, 1995).

There is certainly some truth in this claim, but the supposed incompatibility of democracy with non-Western political traditions can be exaggerated. Until the late 1980s it was regularly asserted that Confucianism was incompatible with democracy because it advocated a system of rule that rested on the authority of the head of the household and the head of the state. There was no requirement for consultation with other family members or members of society, let alone some right to joint decision-making. The authority of the head of the family and the emperor was paramount. Up until the 1980s the evidence from East Asia supported the assumption. No Confucian society did practise democracy. In a magisterial work on Asian political authority that appeared in 1985, Pye argued that, because of the paternalistic structure of authority there, 'the prospects for democracy, as understood in the West, are not good' (Pye, 1985: 339); yet only two years later, in 1987–8, two states still heavily influenced by Confucianism, Taiwan and South Korea, went democratic and have not looked back. Even though these democracies still have problems, e.g. corruption, there have been no attempts at overthrowing them. So now articles are written which argue instead that Confucianism is indeed compatible with democracy (Fukuyama, 1995). And the most recent World Values Survey in 1999–2001 showed that in the eighty countries surveyed, the average response that democracy was a 'very good' or 'fairly good' way of running a country was 91 per cent. Of the main 'Confucian' states, only one (South Korea) returned a score lower than that of the USA (which at 89 per cent was lower than the average). All the others (China, Singapore, Taiwan) ranked higher than the USA (Inglehart, 2004: E117). Of course, we should not ignore the possibility that people had different understandings of the term 'democracy'. Nevertheless it certainly does not suggest a culturally based hostility to the principle of democracy in 'Confucian' states.

Key Points

- There are a range of fundamental objections to the concept of political culture.
- It assumes homogeneous national values.
- It remains extremely difficult to operationalize.
- It is difficult plausibly to link values and political outcomes, especially at the systemic level.
- Many states educate their peoples in political values, thus making it difficult to analyse the effect of those values on policies and institutions.
- Globalization multiplies the factors affecting political values.
- Political culture is most often used to explain why systemic change does not and cannot take place.

Analysing the Significance of Political Culture: a Case Study

Let us examine a case study to show the difficulty of using arguments from political culture to claim that they cause major political outcomes. The case study will be the difficulties of making democracy work in post-Soviet Russia. See **Box 13.3**.

13

Case Study Box 13.3
Political Culture and the Collapse of Soviet Communism

It is indisputable that Russia has enjoyed less success than most states in East and Central Europe in managing the transition to democracy since 1991. Yet in autumn 1991 the Soviet Union collapsed with surprisingly little resistance and loss of life, given the size of the KGB and armed forces and the lessons of decades of Communist party indoctrination. Only three people died while challenging the authority of the plotters who attempted to depose Gorbachev in August 1991. It led to euphoria about the possibilities for a smooth and relatively painless political transition; yet by the time the World Values Survey was carried out in Russia in 2000, only 3 per cent of respondents rated the current political system as 'good' or 'very good'—the lowest figure for any country in the world (Inglehart *et al.*, 2004: E111A). Why, then, did this disillusionment take place and to what extent can Russia's political culture be blamed?

In favour of the argument is the fact that Russia had never had a full functioning democracy. Seventy-four years of communist rule had been preceded by a dozen years of limited parliamentary democracy under the last Tsar and centuries of autocracy. There was no national democratic tradition on which reformers could draw. Various foreign commentators have identified differences between Russian and West European political culture, focusing in particular upon the greater Russian predilection for various forms of collectivism—whether inspired by teachings of the Russian Orthodox Church or by communism—as opposed to individualism. In addition, the collapse of the Soviet Union took the new leaders, including President Yeltsin almost by surprise. They had no plans for a democratic transition and had to improvise as they went along. This could also be ascribed to the lingering effects of communist political culture. Few newly created political parties turned into viable national institutions—the strongest remained the Russian Communist Party which managed to retain a great deal of its Soviet assets and support. Most were only active in Moscow. The lack of a democratic political culture of give and take was exemplified by the events of 1993 when the parliament defied the president and in the end the army was authorized to intervene and shell the parliament building. President Yeltsin himself was not very preoccupied by the need to establish robust political institutions—apart from the presidency. He was suspicious of potential rivals and often went out of his way to undermine them.

On the other hand, a great many other things also went wrong in the transition. The programme of economic reforms initially led to a dramatic fall in economic output—greater than the effect of the Great Depression on the USA. Massive inflation in 1992–3 wiped out the savings of large numbers of people and then, just as the economy was beginning to recover, another financial crisis wiped out savings again in 1998. Russia was also hit by a mounting security crisis after the mid-1990s, which led to major terrorist acts in Chechnya and elsewhere, that provoked brutal military responses. This compounded the anxieties originally caused by the collapse of the Soviet Union and the independence of large swathes of territory in former republics that Russians had become used to thinking of as 'theirs'. The very survival of Russia itself seemed in doubt, and while there was significant financial help through institutions such as the World Bank and the IMF, the EU did not offer the carrot of possible EU membership to encourage persistence with economic and political reforms, as it did for the states of Eastern and Central Europe.

Under those circumstances, it is easy to understand Russia's difficulties in making a successful political transition. Clearly, political values played a part, both in terms of the persisting effects of earlier political socialization, as well as the lack of preparation for post-communism. Yet it could be argued that the combined effects of the financial crashes in undermining the regime's legitimacy and internal terrorism all played at least as big a role, if not bigger. Fish explained the failure to democratize through three variables: too much oil, too little economic liberalization, and too weak a national legislature (Fish, 2005: 247). At most, earlier political traditions might have contributed to the weakness of the legislature, but even here it was not the only factor. Russian political culture contributed both in terms of the attitudes of whole sections of society, but it would be wrong to ascribe to it overwhelming significance. The difficulty is compounded when the level of analysis is transferred to individual political leaders. President Yeltsin was clearly a product of the communist system and its system of ideological indoctrination. This showed in his difficulties in designing a post-communist regime. Yet he, more than any other political figure, brought down communism in the USSR. He was a product of communist political culture, and yet even in late middle age he moved decisively against it.

Persisting Significance of Political Culture

Despite all the problems of operationalizing the concept, it would be wrong to reject political culture entirely. There are a number of points to make in its favour. Why is it still important?

1. First, it is indisputable that there are differences between the attitudes of citizens of different states towards similar institutions and issues. As was explained in chapter seven, there are different attitudes towards the state in Western Europe and the Islamic world. While Pye's book *Asian Power and Politics* clearly underestimated the likelihood of democracy coming to Confucian states, it did also convincingly describe the importance of ritual and status in traditional politics in the region as something quite different from what is found in politics in the West.

Even the attitude towards politics in general varies considerably from one state to another. According to the World Values Survey around 2,000, only 45 per cent of

➡ See the discussion on illiberal democracy in chapter seven, page 181.

Country	Percentage	Ranking
Vietnam	80	1
Tanzania	72	2
China	71	3
Israel	70	4=
Czech Republic	70	4=
Norway	69	6
Austria	67	7=
Netherlands	67	7=
USA	66	9
Japan	64	10
Germany	61	11
India	45	34=
Turkey	40	48=
Russia	39	50=
France	37	54=
UK	37	54=
Italy	32	60
Pakistan	30	63
Venezuela	24	69=
Algeria	24	69=
Morocco	20	71
Argentina	18	72
El Salvador	15	73

Table 13.1   Percentage of Respondents in Selected Countries Agreeing that they were 'Very' or 'Somewhat' Interested in Politics

Source: Inglehart *et al*. (eds), *Human Beliefs and Values*, E023

respondents across all the countries that it surveyed agreed that they were 'very' or 'somewhat' interested in politics, but that general figure shows great variation, as can be seen from Table 13.1.

From this table it is clear that interest in politics in general varies considerably around the world, irrespective of geographical region, level of economic development, whether a state is democratic or not. This is bound to have an impact on the political culture or political cultures of individual states.

2. Secondly, governments and political actors do believe in political cultural differences and this affects policy. De Gaulle, for instance, more than once suggested, only partly in jest, that it was extremely difficult to govern an individualistic country such as France that had 246 varieties of cheese (and now there are over 350). Here are four more examples.

a) The first relates to American foreign policy making in the 1990s. During the Yugoslav civil war there was widespread brutality against civilians and many massacres. Western states debated whether to intervene, but although the UN did agree to send peacekeepers, the USA refused for a long time to get involved. There were many reasons for this—the legacy of the Vietnam experience, the feeling that European states should take the lead—but another was reportedly that President Clinton had read Kaplan's book *Balkan Ghosts* to gain background information on the region. This gave him the impression that it was a region of ancient hatreds and blood feuds, which convinced him not to risk American troops there.

b) The second concerns Huntington's *Clash of Civilizations*. This much-cited book asserted that after the end of the Cold War the major sources of international conflict would be between the major world civilizations—principally Christianity and Islam. What would provoke the clashes would be disputes over the values that others espouse, and the desire on the part of each to increase their sway in the world. The West allegedly wishes to spread democracy and the Muslim world to resist it. Even though it was not based upon any survey research, and the conclusions have been challenged by numerous commentators, including Inglehart and Norris on the basis of World Values Survey findings (Inglehart and Norris, 2003), it has attracted a great deal of attention around the world and no little support.

c) The third example comes from India. Since independence in 1947, India has prided itself upon being a secular state, with believers from all religions treated equally. This was a principle laid down by the Congress Party that ruled India until 1989. In more recent years, however, the Bharatiya Janata Party (BJP) has asserted an alternative principle of Hindutva (Hindu-ness), which would give political recognition to the dominant position in Indian society occupied by Hindus. This is based upon a quite

13

different conception of Indian political identity and would transform Indian political life (Malik and Singh, 1995).

d) The fourth example concerns the European Union. Gradually the EU has expanded from a group of six to now a group of twenty-five countries. However, possible further expansion is still on the agenda, in particular for Turkey, Serbia, Bosnia, Albania, although others such as Russia and Ukraine may also apply at some point in the future. All candidate countries are expected to comply with the so-called Copenhagen criteria laid down in 1993. See **Box 13.4**.

The first category of conditions identifies the values that would-be members should practise; yet with respect to Turkey, former French President Giscard d'Estaing has added a further set of conditions, which relate to shared European history, as he termed it 'the foundations'. These 'include the cultural contributions of ancient Greece and Rome, the religious heritage pervading European life, the creative enthusiasm of the Renaissance, the philosophy of the **Enlightenment** and the contributions of rational and scientific thought' (Giscard d'Estaing, 2004). Earlier, he had highlighted the problems of Turkey's geography, most of it lying in Asia, as well as of the size of its population and the impact on future European decision-making. He was at pains to emphasize that Turkey has its own distinguished history and culture and that its Muslim society was not a problem. However, he implied that the fact that Turkey had not shared European history presented another insuperable obstacle. Was this judgement really intended to rationalize objections based on other principles? Nevertheless, as the EU now reaches the geographical boundaries of what is generally accepted to be 'Europe', these criteria will become more important in considering possible applications from would-be members in the future, such as Ukraine and Russia. Thus, a shared history as well as a commitment to values enshrined in the Copenhagen criteria, and even some outside them, is being used, whether openly or not, to judge applications.

3. Further confirmation of the significance of a nation's political cultures can be found in the experience of trying to export or even impose democracy in other

Box 13.4

The EU's Copenhagen Criteria for New Members

A candidate country must have achieved:

- stability of institutions guaranteeing democracy, the rule of law, human rights and respect for and protection of minority rights;
- the existence of a functioning market economy as well as the capacity to cope with competitive pressure and market forces within the Union;
- the ability to take on the obligations of membership including adherence to the aims of political, economic, and monetary union.

countries. The experience of the Confucian world is that democracy can take root despite the lack of many of the preconditions that can favour it, as explained above. The success in establishing democracy in Germany and Japan after the Second World War shows that it is possible to transplant it to other countries. The more recent experience in Iraq shows that foreign models of democracy cannot simply be grafted on to indigenous social structures either. Unless occupying forces are prepared to impose their will and suppress resistance for as long as it takes to change hearts and minds, they have to take some account of local attitudes. Even if part of the explanation for the failures lies with policy errors made by the occupying forces, nevertheless the internal resistance shows that the attitudes of political actors within the country towards each other—whether individuals or groups—have also made a major contribution towards the morass in which the USA and the UK find themselves.

4. Political culture may indeed help to explain different policy outcomes. Attitudes towards the welfare state differ considerably between Europeans and Americans. Moreover, as Alesina and Glaeser recently suggested, Americans tend to have different attitudes from Europeans towards income inequality and towards income redistribution through the state. From evidence in several rounds of the World Values Survey, they ascertained that roughly 60 per cent of Americans believe that the poor are lazy, as against 26 per cent of people in the EU. On the other hand, 60 per cent of those in the EU believe that the poor are trapped in poverty, while only 29 per cent in the USA do so.

This is a marked difference and it is linked to the prominence of the welfare state issue. It was not always the case that Europeans believed in state redistribution to help the poor. How did the divergence come about? In the nineteenth century there was no welfare state on either side of the Atlantic. Alesina and Glaeser set out to try to explain how this major difference in political culture emerged. Their conclusion was that it was political traditions established by political institutions that shaped ideas about the poor. From the late nineteenth century, Europe saw the rise of labour and socialist parties that propagandized the view that the poor were trapped and deserving. The success of these parties spread the ideas of the welfare state through society, so that even their opponents accepted the validity of their claims and sought only to limit the size of the welfare state. As Esping-Andersen put it in a very influential comparative analysis of welfare systems, this amounted to a 'de-commodification' of welfare (Esping-Andersen, 1990: 35–54). Welfare came to be seen as a right, an entitlement of every citizen who needed it, however much it cost. In the USA, on the other hand, organized labour never achieved the same political success during industrialization. Partly this was because of the enduring power of the founding myth of the USA as a land of opportunity for all. Partly it was because the greater geographical size of the USA made concerted political action by workers scattered across the country much more difficult. Partly it was because many middle-class Americans saw blacks as the real poor and looked down on them for making no effort to overcome their situation. Partly it was because the eighteenth-century constitution which enshrined the property rights of recent colonizers was not subject to strong later challenge or amendment by social groups

13

with quite different attitudes and interests. Hence, welfare issues were always presented much more in terms of costs and benefits for the whole of society, with greater stress on the costs (Alesina and Glaeser, 2004).

This excellent study shows the salience and significance of political culture as an explanatory tool that can contribute to explanation of major different political outcomes. However, the difference from the Russian case study is that it does not use political culture as an exclusive explanation. Rather, it shows that it can make a substantial contribution to a full explanation for a pattern of policy outcomes. It also illustrates how that political culture was itself an amalgam of original values and more recent ones, and that it was in part created by political institutions as well as being used to legitimate new policies. This reveals a much more dynamic understanding of the way political culture can evolve and affect policy.

5. A nation's political culture is also inseparable from nationalism. It is part of its identity and without that identity nationalism would be impossible, so ways of analysing it have paralleled those applied to the study of nationalism too. We have already seen that a strong tendency in the past has been to try to identify enduring, if not permanent elements of a nation's political culture, just as one of the approaches to nationalism has emphasized its primordial nature. Here what is particularly interesting is that one of the more recent theoretical approaches to nationalism has been **ethno-symbolism**. This seeks to identify core symbols of a nation's identity that can then serve to bolster national pride. The most potent symbols have a long history. They may be subject to various interpretations by different groups over time, but this is less important. What is crucial is that they reinforce the sense of identity whenever they are appealed to, irrespective of whether one group says that they are good and another says that they are bad (Leoussi and Grosby, 2006).

Aronoff has suggested that the same process has now begun to take place in the analysis of political culture. Instead of searching for some permanent core of a nation's political culture, he suggests that a new trend there is also to focus upon common symbols of that culture (Aronoff, 2001: 11,640). Even if they give rise to radically different evaluations, whether positive or negative, they still serve to reinforce the sense of national identity. They have special significance for members of a given nation. There is an enormous possible range of these symbols in any state. They may be individuals, groups, events, achievements, even failures.

Because of the radical change of domestic policies that followed Mao Zedong's death in 1976, the People's Republic of China provides good examples of diametrically opposed official assessments of elements of Chinese political culture, which still serve to buttress the sense of national identity. Let us give two examples, first of a famous individual, and then of a symbol of national achievement. The individual is Confucius. While Mao was leading China, he wanted increasingly to radicalize popular ways of thinking and so he used Confucius as a symbol of the old, 'feudal' ways, especially during the Cultural Revolution. Big campaigns were waged against Confucius and 'Confucianists'. Since Mao's death, however, Confucius has regained official approval as a symbol of the greatness of Chinese civilization. Now the state is setting up a network of government-run Confucius Institutes abroad to spread knowledge of Chinese culture, language, and civilization around the world.

As for the symbol of national achievement, this is the Great Wall. Again, in Mao's time, the Great Wall was used as a symbol of China's 'feudal' past, the sufferings imposed upon the subservient masses by a cruel imperial system. It was used to inspire the people for socialism. Since Mao's death, however, the Great Wall has also become a symbol of China's past greatness, a reassurance that the Chinese are capable of building great monuments. It was even alleged, though wrongly, that it was the only man-made structure that can be seen from space. So it is now also presented as a symbol of the future greatness and achievements of the Chinese people (Waldron, 1993).

Most nations have symbols of historical achievements that serve or are used as sources of national pride: Greek and Roman civilizations, the French Revolution, the British Empire—these are just some of the numerous examples which have been subject to radically different interpretations but which despite, or because of, that serve to highlight particular enduring features of a nation's political culture. Chapter eleven referred to the different ways in which the memory of the liberator Simon Bolívar is used in Venezuela. Until recently he was the symbol of national heroism in standing up to Spanish colonizers, which could unite all Venezuelans. Now, however, President Chávez uses Bolívar as inspiration for standing up to the forces of globalization, especially the USA. This exacerbates the polarization in Venezuelan society between those who support Chávez and those who oppose him.

➜ See chapter eleven, page 269, for the case study on Venezuela.

Nor is this structurating role limited to historical objects or events. Values can also become symbols of national identity and pride. The British sense of 'fair play', American 'can-do' attitudes, Russians' generous 'broad nature' (as opposed to the supposed narrower, meaner West Europeans) have all served this purpose. Interviews carried out for the Commission for Racial Equality identified several such values of 'Britishness': freedoms, **rule of law**, fairness, tolerance and respect, reserve, pride, work ethic, community spirit, mutual help, stoicism, and compassion (and drunkenness), as well as the differences in perceptions of these qualities between white English, Scots, Welsh, and immigrants (Commission for Racial Equality, 2005: 25–9). Even though these different views exist, they still form core elements of a British political culture.

Symbols of failure are less often called upon to perform such functions, for obvious reasons, although 'the Dunkirk spirit' is a mixture of failure and success. But Serbia does provide one such example of failure serving as a source of national inspiration. In 1389 the young Serbian empire was destroyed by the Turks at Kosovo Polje. What followed was 500 years of Ottoman domination. This has been used to exemplify Serbian heroism in the face of overwhelming odds and refusal to surrender. It has regularly been cited by Serbs in military and political struggles down the centuries. It also came to be seen as a sacrifice that Serbs made for the sake of 'Europe', since continuing Serbian resistance to Turkish rule helped to prevent the Ottoman Empire from spreading further west, so it is used to assert Serbs' European-ness as well, even though most of the EU has sanctioned Kosova's independence.

13

Photo 13.1

Murals of South American liberator Simon Bolívar line the walls, and are ubiquitous in Venezuela. President Hugo Chavez, has renamed the country the Bolivarian Republic of Venezuela with the revolutionary spirit in mind.

Source: Aurora/Getty Images

What these examples show is that, instead of seeing political culture as some kind of national consensus on the appropriate goals and processes of politics, it should more usefully be seen as a set of narratives and symbols of national identity which different groups try to manipulate to their political advantage. Indeed, Kyogiku interestingly presented the dynamics of Japanese politics in terms of ritualized repertoires of theatrical plots with regularly appearing roles for whichever actors were involved (Kyogiku, 1987). Consensus periodically emerges, but it is never more than provisional because renewed struggles for political power break out between various groups in society; but since such groups usually want to have their interpretations accepted by society at large, they present their claims in such a way as to appeal to a wider audience and so reinforce the sense of national identity.

Key Points

- It remains indisputable that there are differences in political attitudes between citizens of different states, and that these are linked to significantly divergent policy outcomes. This includes the difficulties of transferring democracy from one state to another.

- Political actors accept this, and governments sometimes base policies upon this belief.

- Political culture is closely linked to nationalism.

Conclusion

This chapter has argued that there are many problems about operationalizing political culture, and yet that some of the insights underlying it will continue to inform political analysis in individual states and between states. It can help to clarify genuinely different attitudes towards politics between peoples in different parts of the world. For a political science that seeks to be genuinely international, this is important. It is important too because politicians and decision-makers sometimes base their policies upon their perceptions of different political values practised in various states. Because it involves notions of national identity, it is also important in that it is inseparably linked to the analysis of nationalism. Lastly, it has a broader disciplinary relevance. To return to two basic premises outlined earlier, chapter seven emphasized the crucial importance of institutions in the study of politics. Any plausible theory of political culture must allow for a two-way process of institutions constituting political values as well as being constituted by them. Chapter one emphasized the importance of power as a basic concern. The theory and analysis of political culture must leave room for contestation and arguments over power—the stuff of politics—to shape those values rather than try to demonstrate an unrealistic, supposed national consensus over values. It would be more accurate to write of the political cultures of a nation rather than a single political culture. The approach must allow scope for change and evolution. No nation's political cultures are immutable, as both society and the world outside change.

The study of political culture should indeed be consciously comparative. Every state is unique, but also not completely different. The main features of a single country's political culture can only properly be understood within a comparative context. At the very least the framework of analysis should be methodologically rigorous, capable of being applied more widely, even if a particular study does only focus on one country. In that respect, whatever the difficulties they and others later encountered in trying to operationalize the approach, the fundamental objective of the originators of the political culture approach was exactly right.

Lastly, political culture can also be linked to **constructivism** in international relations theory, which will be presented in chapter sixteen. Constructivism also focuses upon national identity. It assumes that the identity of nations determines the pattern of interactions between them; only, as you will see, this interaction is even more complicated to pin down, because it involves not only the identity of a particular state (however that is achieved) but also how it is perceived by partner states. Operationalizing a constructivist approach is even more of a challenge than doing so for the political culture of a given country.

➔ See chapter sixteen, page 372, for a discussion on constructivism.

13

Key Questions

- In 1963 Almond and Verba characterized British political culture as 'deferential civic'. Is it still? In what ways does British political behaviour differ from that of other countries with which you are familiar?

- How adequate do you think is *Life in the UK: a Guide to UK Citizenship* in laying the foundation for an understanding of 'Britishness'? Assess its contribution to understanding British political culture.

- Try to identify basic symbols associated with the political culture of one or more states with which you are familiar. How have different groups attempted to manipulate the same symbols to achieve political success?

- How much weight would you put on political cultural factors in explaining the failures of democracy in Russia?

- What are the European values of the EU? Do Russia and Turkey share (enough of) them for membership to be conceivable?

- How effective are state educational systems in instilling national political values?

- Is success in this a function of levels of development? Are states in the developing world as successful as those in the developed one?

- How far does religion structure national political culture?

- Does globalization do more to erode a nation's political culture or shape it?

- How objectively can members of a particular state analyse the political culture of their own country?

 Further Reading

Almond, Gabriel A. and Sidney Verba (1965), *The Civic Culture*, Boston, MA: Little Brown.
  This is the original classic study of the subject.

Bell, Daniel A. (2006), *Beyond Liberal Democracy: Political Thinking for an East Asian Context*, Princeton, NJ: Princeton University Press.
  This is a recent attempt to identify ways in which liberal democracy is questioned in East Asia.

Fish, M. Steven (2005), *Democracy Derailed in Russia: the Failure of Open Politics*, Cambridge: Cambridge University Press.
  This is a readable analysis of the reasons why democracy has not taken firm root in Russia since 1991.

Fukuyama, Francis (1995), 'Confucianism and Democracy', *Journal of Democracy*, 6(2) April: 20–33.
  This is an alternative view to that of Pye and Bell on the compatibility of democracy and cultural traditions in Asia.

Halman, Loek, Ruud Luijkx, and Marga van Zundert (eds) (2005), *Atlas of European Values*, Leiden: Tilburg University.
  An examination of European identity along various attitudinal dimensions, with variations by country.

Putnam, Robert (2001), *Bowling Alone: the Collapse and Revival of American Community*, New York: Simon & Schuster.
  This is a very influential study of the significance of social capital for democracy.

Pye, Lucian W. (1985), *Asian Power and Politics: the Cultural Dimensions of Authority*, Cambridge, MA: Belknap Press.
> This is a readable attempt to present Asian cultural traditions and the difficulties that they pose for democracy.

de Tocqueville, Alexis (2000) *Democracy in America*, Chicago, IL: Chicago University Press.
> This is a classic political study.

 *Web Links*

www.ethnos.co.uk/britishness.htm
Commission for Racial Equality, *Citizenship and Belonging: What is Britishness?*
An attempt to set down a set of British beliefs.

www.worldvaluessurvey.org
The website of the World Values Project at the University of Michigan.

www.europeanvalues.com
Links to various studies of European values.

 Visit the **Online Resource Centre** that accompanies this book to access more learning resources at www.oxfordtextbooks.co.uk/orc/garner/

13

Part 3

International Relations

by Stephanie Lawson

The following seven chapters introduce students to key aspects of history, theory, institutions, and themes in the study of International Relations (commonly abbreviated to IR). As the name suggests, IR has traditionally been concerned with relations between nation-states rather than politics within the state, or with the comparisons between states. The boundaries between the three broad areas of political studies, however, are often ill-defined and certainly overlap in many respects. Approaches to IR which attempt to fence off activities and developments within the state from those in the international sphere are far less plausible than they may have been in previous periods, although some would maintain that there was never a time when the concerns of the international could be neatly separated from those of the domestic, and that the distinction has always been an artificial one. At the same time, there are those today who would insist on maintaining a traditional approach, claiming that the study of IR can and must be kept separate from domestic politics in order to keep the focus squarely on the dynamics of the international system and not to cloud the issues with domestic considerations.

The trend in IR towards softening, if not erasing, the boundaries between the domestic and the international matches the trend noted in the opening part of the section on theories and institutions in this book concerning the fact that political theory is facing significant challenges due to the phenomenon of globalization and the state-transcending dynamics it has generated. Here it is noted that political theory has developed over the last few centuries on a very state-specific basis but that with issues such as 'cosmopolitan democracy' now on the agenda, political theorists can no longer remain impervious to wider developments and must now confront issues raised in both comparative and international politics. The same applies to the student of IR, now faced with a very complex world of relations not just between states but with an enormous range of non-state actors and forces. This is reflected in fields as varied as international political economy and international organizations to security studies. The challenge for IR in the present period is to integrate insights from domestic and comparative studies, including studies in political theory, into a broader conception of the 'international'. As we shall see, this has prompted some scholars to abandon the very term 'international'—and 'relations'—favouring instead terms such as 'global politics' or 'world politics'.

The chapters that follow are 'introductory' in the sense that they provide broad overviews of the principle fields of study within IR, introducing students to a range of theoretical, methodological, and empirical issues and themes rather than delving very deeply into any one of these areas. They also aim to illustrate the close link between theory, method, and practice and the fact that how people—whether private citizens, businesspeople, statesmen and women, military leaders, and so on—acquire knowledge, interpret facts and events and generally *think* about the world of IR, and thereby build up a picture of its structure and dynamics, is the basis on which they *act* in the world. This is evident when we consider matters such as sovereignty, the state, and international order in chapter fourteen. Sovereignty, for example, is not a material 'fact'. Rather, it is an idea which has a certain history and which has given rise to particular institutions and practices in the present period.

The status of other important ideas, and how they are theorized in relation to other ideas and practices, is explored further in chapters fifteen and sixteen. Here we shall see the extent to which ideas and theories contend with each other in an effort to produce a superior conception of the world of IR and therefore a better basis for acting in the world. We should also note that most of these theories, whether it is explicit or not—have a distinctive *normative* basis which make claims about how we *ought* to act in the world. This is distinct from theory which simply purports to *describe* the world. Chapter seventeen deals with the central concern of traditional IR—security (and insecurity), looking at both conventional as well as newer, alternative approaches. Chapter eighteen presents an account of the closely related areas of diplomacy and foreign policy which are key activities in the everyday world of IR but which are also based essentially on ideas about how the world works, or *ought* to work. Chapter nineteen looks at the phenomenon of international organizations which have proliferated in the contemporary world, impacting on almost every aspect of IR while chapter twenty closes the section on IR with an overview of the field of international political economy (IPE), from the modern origins of international trade and commerce to the present period of globalization and regionalization. As before, these chapters show that practice is intimately related to ideas. Chapter twenty, in particular, also provides further insight into issues of wealth and poverty, how these relate to the dynamics of contemporary IR and, once again, how we ought to act in the world in terms of whether greater justice in the distribution of resources is not merely desirable, but possible.

Sovereignty, the State, and International Order

Reader's Guide

This chapter presents an overview of International Relations (IR), starting with some basic terminological and conceptual issues and the emergence of the discipline itself. We then consider the central institution of traditional IR—the state—with special reference to their variety throughout history. We also look at empire as a form of international order, noting the extent to which this has also featured throughout time and space. Next, the rise of the modern state and state system in Europe is considered along with the theory of sovereignty and the implications for the conduct of relations between states. Sovereignty also raises ideas about the concept of anarchy which has a special place in IR thought. Finally, we consider the globalization of the European state system through imperialism and colonialism which has produced the present international state system, together with the phenomenon of weak states, quasi states, and state failure in various parts of the contemporary world.

Discipline, Definitions, and Subject Matter

Observant students may have noticed already that the naming of IR as a subject often shifts around between 'international relations', 'international politics', 'world politics', and sometimes 'global politics'. Each term has its own nuance and may be used to denote different approaches to the subject depending partly on how broadly or how narrowly one regards the scope of the subject. At the time of its emergence as a formal field of academic study in the UK in the immediate aftermath of the First World War, its practitioners were, not surprisingly, concerned primarily with the causes of war and the conditions for peace in the international sphere. The focus was therefore largely on relations between states and the maintenance of international order which the early practitioners believed ought to be studied as a specialized field in its own right, apart from political institutions within states as well as from disciplines such as law and history. In the USA, especially in the aftermath of the Second World War and in what seemed to be a dangerous climate of Cold War between the emergent superpowers, there were renewed calls to promote the specialized study of politics in the international sphere. The reflections of an American commentator on the topic in the early post-war/Cold War period provided what was to become a fairly conventional answer to the question of IR's standing and importance as a distinctive discipline, while also drawing attention to the fact that a world of sovereign states constitutes a special kind of community in which there is no centre of authority to enforce order. See **Box 14.1.**

More recently, many scholars have adopted a broader interpretation of IR as much more multifaceted than merely relations between sovereign states in an international system of states, and believe that it cannot be as neatly demarcated from other spheres of politics as some of its earlier practitioners had insisted. Domestic political and indeed social and economic concerns, it is argued, interact constantly with the international sphere and vice versa. In addition, states are not the only important actors in

Key Quote   Box 14.1
The Case for a Specialized Discipline of International Relations

'. . . The questions which arise out of relations among nations who possess their own coherence and uniqueness since they arise out of the relations in a special kind of community, namely, one made up of autonomous units without a central authority having a monopoly of power. Pulling together the scattered fragments of knowledge about them obviously serves to focus attention on them and encourage the development of more intelligent ways of handing them. Recent events have reinforced the growing conviction that the questions of international relations are too complex and dangerous to be dealt with any longer as sidelines of existing disciplines. . . .' (Dunn, 1948: 142–3) this sphere. 'World politics' or 'global politics', as some prefer to call the field, is characterized by a multiplicity of non-state actors including multinational or trans-national corporations, **non-governmental organizations** (NGOs), international or-ganized crime groups, and so on. Furthermore, 'world' or 'global' avoids having to use the word 'international', a word which has misleading connotations, as discussed below. However, if one wishes to talk about relations between states—and perhaps between non-state actors as well—in one particular part of the world, then 'world politics' or 'global politics' will not do. For example, one can talk about the international relations or international politics of the Asia-Pacific region, but not the 'world' or 'global' politics of the region.

Here we should note that the term 'global' is almost always used as an all-encompassing term referring to the entire world regardless of state boundaries. Indeed, it works to some extent to erase these boundaries. The idea of a 'global environment', for example, is often used to assert the transcendence of boundaries in the context of such issues as global warming and climate change. The idea of the global citizen, which is linked closely to ideas of **cosmopolitanism** also emphasizes the notion that we all belong to 'one world' rather than simply one country, and that humanity shares common problems, common interests, and a common fate, all of which transcend particular political communities. Cosmopolitanism also represents a different *ethical* vision of international order. Rather than limiting one's moral concerns to the bound-aries of the state, it implies a moral concern for the world and its people as a whole. See **Box 14.2**. This also raises the subject of **globalization**, which emphasizes a global interconnectedness that is conceived as transcending state boundaries and controls which many believe challenges the traditional view of international order based on independent sovereign states. Not surprisingly, globalization is a phenomenon that has been a particular focus of interest for many IR scholars in recent years, and is a topic we revisit throughout the remaining chapters.

The terms **state** and **nation** also require some scrutiny. They are often used syn-onymously or joined together to produce 'nation-state', but they refer to two quite distinct entities. Having said that, you will find that the state by itself is given several

➡ Also see chapter four, page 109, for a discussion of the cosmopolitan approach.

➡ Also see the Introduction, page 4 and chapter one, pages 43–5, for a discussion of globalization.

14

Key Quote Box 14.2
Peter Singer's One World

'We have lived with the idea of sovereign states for so long that they have come to be part of the background not only of diplomacy and public policy but also of ethics. Implicit in the term 'globalisaization' rather than the older 'internationalisaization' is the idea that we are moving beyond the era of growing ties between nations and are beginning to contemplate something beyond the existing conception of the nation-state. But this change needs to be reflected in all our levels of thought, and especially our thinking about ethics.' (Singer, 2002: 9) different dictionary meanings. For our purposes—and those of politics more generally—we need to keep in mind that 'state' refers to the notion of a distinctive political community with its own set of rules and practices and more or less separate from other such communities. For the more specific purposes of IR, 'the state' refers specifically to the modern sovereign state which possesses a 'legal personality' and which is recognized as possessing certain rights and duties. This kind of state is distinct as well from the states that generally make up a federal system, such as the individual states of which the USA is composed.

As we have seen in chapter seven, the sovereign state has been given a clear legal definition by the 1933 Montevideo Convention on the Rights and Duties of States. Of the sixteen Articles adopted, the most important are the first eleven, and of these, the first Article provides the most succinct understanding of the criteria for a modern sovereign state, namely: *a permanent population; a defined territory and a government capable of maintaining effective control over its territory and of conducting international relations with other states.*

➜ See chapter seven, page 170, for a further discussion of the Montevideo Convention.

A particularly important provision highlighting the sovereign aspect of international statehood is Article 8 which asserts the right of states not to suffer **intervention** by any other state. Article 10 emphasizes the conservation of peace as constituting the primary interest of all states. Article 11 reinforces both these messages in no uncertain terms. See **Box 14.3**. In summary, the state in IR is envisaged as a *formally constituted, sovereign political structure encompassing people, territory and institutions.* As such it interacts with similarly constituted structures in an international system of states which, ideally, is characterized by peaceful, non-coercive relations thus establishing a similarly peaceful international order conducive to the prosperity of all. One might well say, if only it were so.

We now turn to the idea of nation, a term which refers specifically to 'a people' rather than a formal, territorial entity. There is no widely agreed definition of what constitutes 'a people' beyond the fact that it denotes a species of collective identity grounded in a

14

Box 14.3

Article 11, Montevideo Convention on the Rights and Duties of States, 1933

'The contracting states definitely establish as the rule of their conduct the precise obligation not to recognize territorial acquisitions or special advantages which have been obtained by force whether this consists in the employment of arms, in threatening diplomatic representations, or in any other effective coercive measure. The territory of a state is inviolable and may not be the object of military occupation nor of other measures of force imposed by another state directly or indirectly or for any motive whatever even temporarily.'

Source: www.molossia.org/montevideo.html (accessed 17/10 /2007)

notion of shared history and culture and which may or may not lay claim to some kind of political recognition as well as a specific territory. Chapter thirteen has already discussed the problem, if not the impossibility, of identifying single national **political cultures**. We have also seen in chapter five that **nationalism** as an ideology holds that political organisaization ought to be based on 'national identity'. It therefore supports the claims of a nation to a state of its own which, since the early twentieth century, has generally been based on the apparently democratic principle of national **self-determination**. Nationalism, at least in the more extreme right-wing versions, may also seek the exclusion of 'alien' elements from an existing state to safeguard the 'authenticity' of its national character.

➡ See chapter thirteen, page 302, for a discussion of homogeneous national political culture.

However defined, 'nations' are assumed to populate sovereign states and are very often described in singular terms; that is, one state may be assumed to contain one nation. For example, the state of France is occupied by the 'French nation', Japan by the Japanese and so on. These examples indicate the commonly accepted conflation of state and people that produces the familiar term 'nation-state' which, again, reflects the principle of national self-determination. However, only a moment's critical reflection is needed to recogniseize that the matching of state and nation is seldom so neat and unproblematic. Rather, it is an ideal that has rarely, if ever, been achieved. There is virtually no state in the world encompassing a single, homogeneous nation. Many states are made up of two or more 'nations' and even these are not always distinct. The contemporary British state is comprised of recognized sub-state national entities: the Welsh, Scots, English, and Northern Irish, but these are also multilayered, especially since immigration over the centuries has brought dozens of different 'nationalities' to the British Isles thereby producing the 'multicultural' and indeed 'multinational' Britain of the contemporary period.

➡ See chapter five, page 127, for an exploration of nationalism.

A close inspection of other national entities around Europe will show similar stories. Of course, what started out as British settler colonies, which are a legacy of modern empire and of mass migration, are now among the most 'multinational' in the world today—the USA, Canada, Australia, and New Zealand in particular; but if we look to places like India and China, it is also evident that these states are made up of many different groups speaking different local languages and possessing different cultural practices. Even relatively small states can be incredibly diverse. Papua New Guinea, for example, has a population of just under six million, yet there are over 850 different languages spoken and each language group could theoretically consider itself to be 'a nation'. It is because of such diversity that states like Papua New Guinea are considered to be 'weak states', a topic we explore further below. Nonetheless, states are still widely assumed to contain singular nations and although most states are acknowledged as containing many more than one, the identity of the state will to some extent be equated with a dominant majority. Thus in the USA and Australia, for example, a dominant white English-speaking majority constitutes a mainstream.

14

This explanation of the basic distinctions between 'state' and 'nation' does not exhaust all the nuances of the terms. However, it provides some indication of how simple terms attempt to capture complex realities, and do not necessarily succeed. It also illustrates the problematic nature of the term chosen to name the peak body in international affairs, the United Nations (UN), since it is states, not nations, that constitute its membership and which are represented in its General Assembly. This brings us to the last of the key terms to be considered here, and that is the equally complex idea of the 'international'. It is not hard to pick apart the literal meanings of this word's component parts: 'inter' more or less denoting 'between and among' and 'national' referring to any given national grouping. However, it is not so much 'nations' as 'peoples' that interact formally in the 'international' sphere, but rather sovereign states as described above. But if we were to adopt the technically more correct terminology of 'interstatal' or 'interstate' relations, confusion would arise as to whether this referred to states in a federal system or sovereign states in the broader sphere.

The term 'international' was actually coined to refer to the latter sphere by the British political and legal theorist, Jeremy Bentham (1748–1832), who sought an appropriate term to describe the 'law of nations', although technically he meant law relating to independent sovereign states as they existed at the time (i.e. the established states of Europe and the USA as virtually no others were recognized as possessing 'statehood'), rather than 'nations' as described above. Bentham's use of 'nation' here exemplifies once again the difficulties in establishing clear, uncomplicated, and precise usage; but it also highlights the close association between states and nations in political as well as conceptual terms.

Key Points

- Although the distinctions between IR and other fields of politics, as well as other disciplines such as law and history, are often difficult to maintain, IR is generally differentiated as a specialized area of study if not as a separate discipline.

- The terminology of IR involves a complex of over-lapping terms such as 'nation', 'state', 'nation-state' and 'sovereign state' as well as 'international relations', 'world politics', and 'global politics', all of which have different nuances.

States and International Systems in World History

The variation in state forms and the phenomenon of empire throughout history illustrates that international systems or orders are highly variable and that the sovereign state system with which we are familiar today may very well be replaced by a different kind of system at some point in the future. Indeed, the proponents of 'globalism' believe that a transformation is presently under way in which state boundaries and controls will become increasingly meaningless. Others believe that we are entering a new era of **empire**, although there are differing views as to where its principle centre of power may lie.

To begin with states understood simply as political communities, these date more or less from the time that human groups first developed settled agricultural and/or animal husbandry practices requiring an ongoing association with a particular part of the earth's surface, and a way of organizing themselves and their resources and generally protecting themselves. As we have seen, the definition of the modern state includes a relationship between a permanent population and a certain defined territory. This part of the definition can therefore be extended back in time to cover numerous historic cases without running too much risk of anachronism, although there have also been 'stateless communities' throughout history—typically those with a nomadic lifestyle which have therefore lacked a fixed attachment to, or control over, any particular territory. The formation of states has also given rise to 'state systems' or 'international orders' which denote the ways in which political communities have systematically organized their relations with other such communities either in their immediate geographical area or further afield.

Since IR is, by and large, a discipline that developed in 'the West', it is scarcely surprising that it has looked for historical antecedents of statehood and international orders in the 'cradle of Western civilization', that is, the eastern Mediterranean region where the ancient Greek and Roman civilizations flourished. These, however, had close connections with the civilizations of northern Africa and the near east, and both Greece and Rome drew on the rich sources of knowledge and aspects of cultural practices from these regions. In turn, the communities of northern Africa and the near east were connected to other communities, and so processes of cross-cultural learning, including political knowledge, were transmitted from much further afield as well.

The 'state' of the ancient Greeks was the *polis* or 'city-state'. The largest and best known was of course the Athenian *polis*—often referred to as the archetypal model of classical democracy. The political philosophy of certain leading thinkers who gathered in Athens—many of whom, as noted in chapter three, did not actually favour democracy—has also underpinned much subsequent political theory concerning the nature and purposes of the state. Aristotle, for example, saw the state as the *natural* habitat for humans rather than as an artificial construct separating the human *from* nature. When he described 'man' as a *zōon politikon* (political animal) he did not mean that humans were naturally scheming, devious creatures. What Aristotle actually said was that since the *polis* 'belongs to the class of objects which exist by nature', it follows that the human is, 'by nature a political animal'—that is, a creature designed by *nature* to live in a *polis* (Aristotle, Iii). In IR, Athens also stands out as a historic exemplar of a state driven by the imperatives of political **realism**, especially when it fought for supremacy against the Spartans. The historian Thucydides, eyewitness to some of the events of this war and author of *The Peloponnesian War*, is similarly regarded as standing at the head of a long tradition of realist thought for his interpretation of the war and his observations on human nature. These ideas are discussed in the next chapter.

Athens for a time also headed another important form of political organization—an empire, although the best known of these in the ancient world is undoubtedly the

14

➜ See chapter three, page 72, for a discussion of the history of democracy.

Roman Empire. Developments in Rome are important to the historical growth of 'the West' especially in relation to theories of republicanism as well as the legal system of significant parts of Europe. It is also partly due to the Roman Empire that Christianity became firmly established in Europe, a development which had very significant consequences for the subsequent development of political ideas and practices.

In considering empire as a form of international system, it is important to note that, like states, empires have existed at various times throughout most of the world and have taken different forms. What they tend to share in common is the fact that they are relatively large-scale political entities made up of a number of smaller political communities (generally states) with a central controlling power, and they are also usually held together by force. While some states may also be held together by little more than force, it is more characteristic of empires; and although empires constitute a kind of international order, this is quite different from the current international state system, underpinned as it is by a theory of sovereign equality among its constituent members. In contrast, empires are characterized more explicitly by relations of domination and subordination, although as contemporary critics would be quick to point out, this can occur in the present system as well. The brief tour of historical empires sketched below also gives a better sense of the diversity of our world and the fact that not everything of historical significance happened in Europe.

The earliest known empires were situated around the river systems of the Tigris, Euphrates, and the Nile, their geographical location suggesting a certain correlation between the conditions required for successful agriculture and the establishment of settled political communities with extensive networks of relations between them. The same broad region saw the rise of the Sumerian, Egyptian, Babylonian, Assyrian, and Persian empires between about 4,000 BC and 400 BC. The methods of domination used by the controlling powers of these empires varied from direct control over smaller, subject communities to more indirect methods which allowed some autonomy to local groups provided that regular tributes were forthcoming (Stern, 2000: 57; Lawson, 2003: 24–5). Africa also produced a number of empires, both ancient and modern. Among the latter was the Mali empire which thrived between the thirteenth and seventeenth centuries and which gave rise to a significant centre for learning, as well as trade and commerce, in Timbuktu. The Ottoman Empire, with its capital in Istanbul, emerged at around the same time, but lasted until the early 1920s.

Further east, the ancient kingdoms of the Indus Valley formed a broad civilizational entity, with Hinduism and Sanskrit providing some basic cultural cohesion over much of the region. Even so, political communities within the region evinced much variety with both oligarchies and republics in evidence. The region's best-known empire was established in the north in 300 BC. Although it lasted less than a century its reputation was assured largely because one of its leading figures, Kautilya, produced a highly sophisticated text on **statecraft**, the Arthasastra, which set out the ways and means of acquiring territory, keeping it, and reaping prosperity from it. It is comparable to Machiavelli's writings on statecraft, although some see it as presenting a far harsher picture of the struggle for domination (Boesche, 2002: 253–276; Lawson, 2003: 24–25).

One of the most extensive and durable empires of all was the Chinese which lasted from the time of the Shang dynasty in the eighteenth century BC, until the early twentieth century, although there was a substantial interlude during which time it disintegrated into a number of warring states. It was during a period of chaos and violence that the ancient philosophy of Confucius, which is largely concerned with setting out the political and social arrangements conducive to good order under strong leadership and **authority**, is thought to have developed (see Lawson, 2006: 155). This is comparable to the conditions under which European theorists of **sovereignty**, which is also ultimately concerned with the same problems, were to develop their ideas.

In the early modern period, the Ottoman Turks ruled over some 14 million subjects from the Crimea to Hungary while the Moghuls pushed further towards the south and east. By the end of the sixteenth century, Islamic forces—cultural, political, and military—controlled not only the Middle East, but significant parts of Africa, Central Asia, South Asia, Southeast Asia (especially present-day Malaysia, Indonesia, and parts of the Philippines) as well as sizeable parts of Eastern Europe. There are numerous other examples

---

Pre-Modern Empires

African Empires: Ethiopian Empire (ca. 50–1974), Mali Empire (ca. 1210–1490), Songhai Empire (1468–1590), Fulani Empire (ca. 1800–1903)

Mesoamerican Empires esp. Maya Empire (ca. 300–900) Teotihuacan Empire (ca. 500–750), Aztec Empire (1325–ca. 1500)

Byzantine Empire (330–1453)

Andean Empires: Huari Empire (600–800); Inca Empire (1438–1525)

Chinese Pre-Modern Empires: including T'ang Dynasty (618–906), Sung Dynasty (906–1278)

Islamic Empires esp. Umayyid/Abbasid (661–1258), Almohad (1140–1250), Almoravid (1050–1140)

Carolingian Empire (ca. 700–810)

Bulgarian Empire (802–827, 1197–1241)

Southeast Asian Empires: Khmer Empire (877–1431), Burmese Empire (1057–1287)

Novgorod Empire (882–1054)

Medieval German Empire (962–1250)

Danish Empire (1014–1035)

Indian Empires, including Chola Empire (11th century), Empire of Mahmud of Ghazni (998–1039 AD), Mughal Empire (1526–1805)

Mongol Empire (1206–1405)

Table 14.1 A Brief Guide to Historical Empires

Source: Global Policy Forum: http://globalpolicy.org/empire//history/2005/empireslist.htm

Pre-Modern Empires Cont.
Mamluk Empire (1250–1517)
Holy Roman Empire (1254–1835)
Modern Empires
Portuguese Empire (ca. 1450–1975)
Spanish Empire (1492–1898)
Russian Empire/USSR (1552–1991)
Swedish Empire (1560–1660)
Dutch Empire (1660–1962)
British Empire (1607–ca. 1980)
French Empire (ca. 1611–ca. 1980)
Modern Chinese Empire: esp. Ch'ing Dynasty (1644–1911)
Austrian/Austro-Hungarian Empire (ca. 1700–1918) [See also Habsburg Empire]
US Empire (1776–present)
Brazilian Empire (1822–1889)
German Empire (1871–1918, 1939–1945)
Japanese Empire (1871–1945)
Italian Empire (1889–1942)
Habsburg Empire (1452–1806)
Ottoman Empire (1453–1923)

of empire throughout the world, from those of Mesoamerica to the modern Japanese Empire, showing just how common this form of international system has been (see Table 14.1).

While virtually all have left important legacies of one kind or another, those which have had the most profound impact on the structure of the present international system are the modern European empires. The largest and most powerful of these was the British Empire, although it had other rivals in Europe. France, Spain, Portugal, Holland, Denmark, Belgium, Italy, and Germany were all colonizing powers at one time or another, but none acquired the same power and influence as the British.

Given the extent to which **imperialism** and **colonialism** facilitates cultural spread, it is scarcely surprising that British—or more particularly English—culture gained significant ground around the world. This is partly manifest in the fact that English now prevails as the major international language.

Cultural spread, however, goes both ways and contemporary Britain, and significant parts of Europe, have absorbed cultural influences in turn. More generally, the history of empire, which encompasses exploration, trade, proselytization, and migration as well as other more explicitly political aspects, is also part of the history of globalization. The networks and movements of people prompted by the global reach of the modern European

Photo 14.1 Botswana

A San schoolgirl with a Setswana–English dictionary at a community school.

Source: © Giacomo Pirozzi/Panos Pictures

empires, in particular, along with technological innovations and the development of financial and economic systems that accompanied these, established much of the basis on which contemporary global **interdependence** rests.

The phenomenon of globalization has recently been linked to a new form of empire which, it is argued, is replacing the old form of state sovereignty with a different kind of sovereignty. It is said to rely neither on a territorial centre of power nor on fixed boundaries or barriers. Nor does the USA occupy a singularly privileged position, simply taking up where the old European empires left off. Rather, the new imperial order is characterized by the power of transnational corporations and forms of production owing no allegiance to territorial entities and which in fact seek to supplant their sovereignty (see Hardt and Negri, 2000: xi–xiv). Some may see this version of 'empire' as a grossly exaggerated scenario, but at the very least its proponents provide a basis for critical reflection on key aspects of the phenomenon of globalization and the growing power of deterritorialized corporations.

Some other recent commentators do regard the USA as exercising a genuine measure of imperial control, although its leaders deny any such connection. In his analysis of contemporary US **hegemony**, Niall Ferguson quotes prominent US politicians as emphatically denying that the global role of the USA today is an imperial project. George W. Bush claimed in 2000 that 'America has never been an empire . . . We may be the only great power in history that had the chance, and refused', a theme he continued when declaring a victory in Iraq in May 2003 over the forces of Saddam Hussein, insisting that while other nations had 'fought in foreign lands and remained to occupy and exploit', Americans in contrast, 'wanted nothing more than to return home' (Ferguson, 2003a). Ferguson concludes another major book on the subject of the British Empire with the observation that Americans have taken on the global role formerly played by Britain, yet without facing the fact that an empire comes with it. In short it is 'an empire in denial' (Ferguson, 2003b: 370).

Key Points

- States as political communities have existed for thousands of years and have taken a wide range of forms in terms of size and institutional features. Today, the sovereign state is the dominant form and underpins the international system although many commentators see the forces of globalization as undermining it.

- Empires as a form of international order have also existed in ancient, pre-modern, and modern periods and throughout different parts of the world. Some argue that the USA now plays an imperial role in global politics in everything but name while others see the power of transnational corporations trumping that of any state, including the USA.

The Rise of Modernity and the State System in Europe

Modernity names a complex phenomenon associated with the rise in Europe of science and technology leading to industrialization, increased military power and, with it, enormous political and social change, including diminishing religious authority. However, this did not occur in isolation from other influences. Stern (2000: 72) notes that not only were important ideas and inventions transmitted from China and Arabia, but that significant aspects of Greek and Roman learning were recovered through the work of Islamic scholars. The 'discovery' of new worlds in the Americas and the Pacific also served to acquaint Europeans with a seemingly endless array of widely varying states and societies, all of which prompted new comparisons and questions (Lawson, 2006: 60).

In the year 1500—conventionally taken to mark the beginning of the modern age—Kennedy says that it was scarcely apparent to anyone that a cluster of rather insignificant states in Western Europe 'was poised to dominate much of the rest of the earth' (Kennedy, 1989: 3). Chinese civilization at the time seemed vastly superior to any other. Technological innovation, including moveable type printing, gunpowder, paper money, and massive ironworks all contributed to an expansion of trade and industry further stimulated by an extensive programme of canal building. China also possessed an army of over a million. All this, together with an efficient hierarchical administration run by an educated Confucian bureaucracy made Chinese society 'the envy of foreign visitors' (Kennedy, 1989: 5). More generally, as we have seen, empires elsewhere were thriving and there were many other important centres of power at the beginning of the modern period.

There had been no political organization of Europe as a whole in the Renaissance or early modern periods to match the Chinese or Ottoman Empires. Rather, Medieval Europe consisted of a rather chaotic patchwork of overlapping jurisdictions and fragmented authorities, scarcely resembling a coherent state system or international order. The only institution providing any sort of unity was the Christian (Catholic) Church based in Rome, from where it imposed some religious authority on the rest of the continent. The Protestant Reformation, however, would challenge the supremacy of the established Church, triggering a massive theological and political fallout.

Key aspects of the development of European states and the state system, especially with respect to their capacity, have been covered in chapter seven. Here we should emphasize that the devastating struggle between Catholic and Protestant forces, which ended with the Peace of Westphalia in 1648, is conventionally understood to have resulted in the consolidation of certain characteristics of the modern state that are central to aspects of IR theory. These characteristics included not only the principle of religious co-existence, but also the monopoly claims by the state over such matters as declarations of war and the negotiation of peace, diplomatic representation and the authority to make treaties with foreign powers (Boucher, 1998: 224). For these reasons, Westphalia has long been regarded as the founding moment of the modern *sovereign* state. Whether or not that assessment is entirely accurate is a matter of some debate among contemporary scholars (see, for example, Clark, 2005), the finer points of which are beyond the scope of an introductory text. See **Box 14.4**.

→ See chapter seven, page 169, for a discussion of the rise and spread of the Western state.

Key Points

- 'Modernity' is a phenomenon associated with social, political, intellectual, and technological developments in Europe which brought significant changes to the political landscape, although there were influences from other parts of the world as well.

- The Peace of Westphalia is conventionally regarded as the founding moment of the doctrine of state sovereignty and therefore of the modern state.

The Emergence of Sovereignty

The principle of sovereignty has come to be regarded as effectively enclosing states within a 'hard shell', with the shell corresponding to the territorial borders. It was meant to

Case Study Box 14.4
The Peace of Westphalia

The Thirty Years War between Catholic and Protestant forces in Europe ended in 1648 with the Peace of Westphalia. This was achieved through complex diplomatic negotiations over a period of five years, ending when the Treaties of Osnabrück and Münster were signed to form a comprehensive agreement containing 128 clauses covering matters of law, religion, and ethics as well as numerous practical issues.

Some of the principles enshrined at Westphalia, such as the authority of rulers to determine the religious affiliations of their subject, were very similar to an earlier agreement, the Peace of Augsburg of 1555, so the ideas underpinning the 1648 treaty were not entirely new. However, Westphalia was infused with emergent ideas about a kind of international law which could transcend religious differences and therefore be applied universally—that is, to Catholic and Protestant states alike. The foremost thinker along these lines was the Dutch jurist Hugo Grotius (1583–1645) whose influential work, *De Iure Belli et Pacis* (*Laws of War and Peace*) confronted the problem of conflicting moralities and the need for toleration as well as setting out minimum standards for conduct. Most importantly for the development of the state system and international order, it granted co-equal juridical status to states.

Westphalia has been described as the first, and perhaps the greatest, of the modern European peace treaties, and is also considered to have established the legal foundations of modern statehood. Its principal feature in this latter respect concerns the right of rulers to conduct their affairs within their own territories free from outside interference, thus establishing the principle of autonomous political authority which underpinned the development of the doctrine of sovereignty. The articulation of principles and doctrines, however, does not mean that practice always accords with their intent. There has been little to prevent violations of both the letter and spirit of the Westphalian Peace, as the subsequent history of Europe itself shows only too clearly. The Westphalian model nonetheless provides a benchmark for both critics and supporters of the sovereign state system as well as for those who predict its eventual demise due to the irresistible state-transcending forces of globalization.

guarantee non-intervention in the internal governmental arrangements or any other domestic affairs of a state. The theory possessed an attractive simplicity. Rulers within states could follow the religious and moral principles of their choice, and could also require their subjects to conform. In addition, they could govern according to whichever form of rule they preferred. The protective shell of sovereignty thus guaranteed the complete independence of each state—or rather the ruling elements within each state—to arrange their domestic affairs as it suited them, regardless of what any external actor might think and no matter the relative standing of the state in terms of size, power, and capacity. As pointed out in the introduction to this book, the state is sovereign in the sense that it is the supreme law-making body within a particular territory with the ultimate power of life and death over individuals. The juridical sovereignty possessed by individual states remains a basic principle of international law today.

While admirable in its theoretical simplicity, the principles of state sovereignty in the international sphere have been far less straightforward in practice. This has been demonstrated in part by the fact that Europe appears to have been no less prone to warfare among its constituent states for much of the 300-year period following Westphalia. The extent to which this can be attributed to the rise of nationalism along with the modern state system is a moot point. Whatever the historical reasons for war, it is really only in the post-Second World War period that Europeans seem finally to have struck on a formula for peaceful relations. That this was achieved via a regional supra-state framework in the form of the EU, is something of an irony, because although the principle of state sovereignty was initially formulated to prevent warfare, it seems that a lasting peace has only been acquired through significant modification of its basic elements. How far the EU—and other regional experiments elsewhere in the world—will go in undermining the principle of state sovereignty remains to be seen.

Another factor to be considered here is the moral conundrum raised by the actions of states with respect to the treatment of their own citizens or any others within their borders. A strict interpretation of the theory of state sovereignty prohibits any action by actors outside the state even in cases of civil war, genocide, or other forms of human rights abuses. In the present period, however, there has been much discussion of an assumed right of **humanitarian intervention**, a nascent doctrine which seeks to trump the sovereign rights of states—or rather their rulers—to do as they please within their own borders. This accords with another recently promoted notion that the possession of sovereignty by a state confers on it the *responsibility to protect* its inhabitants.

Here we should note that the theory of state sovereignty faces two ways, possessing both external and internal dimensions. As Evans and Newnham (1998: 504) put it, the doctrine makes a double claim: 'autonomy in foreign policy and exclusive competence in internal affairs'. The latter claim depends on there being an ultimate authority within the state that is entitled to make decisions and settle disputes. Thus 'the sovereign', who may be either a person (such as a monarch) or a collective (such as a parliament representing the sovereignty of the people) is at once the highest power and the final power in the state's political system. This assumes that it cannot be subject to any other agent, domestic or foreign (Miller, 1991: 492–3). In other words, the traditional doctrine of sovereignty holds that the absoluteness and finality of sovereign power applies not only within the domestic arena but in the external realm as well.

14

As far as the external or international sphere goes, this produces, somewhat paradoxically, a condition of **anarchy**—which means, literally, 'without a ruler'. For if all states are sovereign, and therefore the final arbiters of their own destinies, there can be no higher authority placed outside and above the individual states in an international system of states. In other words, there is no ultimate authority in the international sphere that functions as a ruler (see Evans and Newnham, 1998: 504). Of course, a large, powerful state can take over lesser states by sheer force. This is what many see as the prime danger posed by the condition of anarchy in the international sphere. The disorder produced by the unfettered exercise of power is likened to a dangerous **state of nature** characterized by the absence of law and order. This is what the theory of sovereignty sets up as 'fact', and then seeks to ameliorate.

The theory of sovereignty was first worked out in relation to the sphere of domestic rather than international politics and various well-known figures contributed to its development through the centuries. Among the earliest was Jean Bodin (ca. 1530–96) who, like many others concerned with political order, lived in disordered times, experiencing civil and religious disturbances throughout much of his life. He therefore contributed to the development of sovereignty not just as a doctrine but as an 'ideology of order' (see King, 1999). However, the best-known theorist of sovereignty is undoubtedly Thomas Hobbes (1588–1679), author of *Leviathan* and generally regarded as standing in the same tradition of political realism as Thucydides and Machiavelli. He, too, lived during a period of civil war and, as mentioned in chapter one, was concerned with how an all-powerful sovereign can establish order. We consider his ideas and their contribution to IR theory in the next chapter.

➜ See the discussion on the liberal social contract tradition in chapter one, page 37.

Another important development that must be considered along with the rise of the modern European state system is the ideology of nationalism. We noted earlier the assumption implicit in the principle of self-determination that each 'nation' is entitled to a state of its own, which is highly problematic given that one could probably identify thousands of groups around the world that could make some credible claim to constituting a nation. Despite the practical difficulties, the idea that nations and states go together seems very persuasive; but like the sovereign state itself, it is a relatively recent one. Indeed, its origins lie in the same state building dynamics that emerged in post-Westphalian Europe.

At the time of Westphalia itself, the link between nation and state was practically non-existent. Sovereignty was seen as residing in the person who occupied the top position in the state's political hierarchy, such as the monarch, and he—or occasionally she—would not have regarded the masses over whom rule was exercised as constituting 'a nation'. Indeed, the people within these states remained largely undefined, acquiring some kind of common political identity only with further important developments towards the end of the eighteenth century, including the emergence of democratic ideas which required a distinct body of people—citizens—to constitute a *sovereign people*. The most likely candidate was of course 'the nation'. Although the record of democratic development in Europe remained very patchy until quite recent times, the idea of the nation caught on very rapidly, and the subsequent development of the modern state and state system brought together the three prime characteristics of the modern state—*sovereignty, territoriality, and nationality*. These characteristics also underpin an international order based on the state system.

The French Revolution of 1789 marks an important turning point in the rise of the modern European state system because it effectively converted the mass of people, hitherto known simply as 'subjects' of a monarch, into a unified body of citizens of the French state. The entity that emerged as the 'French nation', however, was far from unified. Rather, the territory covered by France, and formerly ruled by the king, was occupied by quite disparate groups speaking different languages and living by varied customs. Some legal and administrative unity existed, but this obviously did not emanate from the 'French nation' as such. It had to be imposed from above. The same applied to most other parts of Europe. In short, the emergence of democratic ideas, following closely on ideas about sovereignty, became an important vehicle for the ideology of national unification in a sovereign state (Cassels, 1996: 18–19). The power of the national idea, however, found favour not simply among democrats. It was soon to become an ideology that lent itself to all comers. Indeed, it was most warmly received by the most notorious dictators of the modern period.

Another significant development came in the wake of the Napoleonic wars. This was the **Concert of Europe**, a term designating a series of irregular conferences focused on resolving diplomatic crises between states. Beginning with the Congress of Vienna in 1815, it lasted until the mid-1850s and although the meetings were eventually discontinued, the art of diplomacy within Europe matured to a significant extent and became an important instrument of the state system. By the beginning of the nineteenth century, the modern European state system still existed more in theory than in practice, and it was still far from being regarded as a 'nation-state' system. The *national* idea, however, was a powerful driving force, becoming more and more prominent in the rhetoric of state-making movements throughout the century and which saw the emergence of new 'national' states in Greece (1830), Belgium (1831), Italy (1961), Germany (1871), and Romania, Serbia, and Montenegro (1878). By the beginning of the twentieth century, the sovereign state system with its principles of nationality was reasonably well entrenched in Europe, as well as the USA, but it scarcely existed in other parts of the world. This brings us to the subject of European colonization and decolonization, for it is largely due to these developments that the European state system became effectively globalized in the twentieth century, thus giving rise to the present international system.

Key Points

- Theories of sovereignty which came to underpin the state system developed in response to various stimuli, including both civil and inter-state war in Europe.

- In political philosophy, ideas about the 'state of nature' were associated with violence and the drive for power in a sphere of anarchy and underpinned emerging theories of state sovereignty.
- Nationalism as a form of political/cultural identity is also closely associated with the rise of the modern sovereign state and state system.

The Globalization of the Sovereign State System

As we have seen, numerous empires existed in ancient times and in many different parts of the world. The modern period did not spell the end of empires and, if anything, imperialism and colonialism not only continued with the rise of the sovereign state in Europe, but thrived under it. Furthermore, it is through the European empires that the sovereign state system was effectively transported to the rest of the world, where it has met with varying success. Early Spanish, Portuguese, and Dutch explorers and traders were followed by the British, French, Belgians, and Germans. Shipping routes and trading posts encircled the world, the latter providing a base for subsequent colonization. It was not long before almost the entire world came under the direct control of one or other of the European powers. After the Second World War, however, there was significant normative change concerning the legitimacy of colonial rule. The principle of self-determination, originally developed in relation to Europeans in the aftermath of the First World War, was now invoked as a right of colonized people and drove a decolonization movement which saw almost all former European colonies achieve independence by the end of the twentieth century.

➡ See chapter seven, page 170, for a discussion of the European concepts of borders and sovereignty on colonial territory.

Among the legacies of European colonization were more or less clear borders demarcating one colonial state from another. The imposition of such boundaries on what had often been a fluid system of occupation by native people frequently resulted in arbitrary divisions of tribes or ethnic groups between two or more different colonies, especially in Africa. The extent to which the construction of colonial and postcolonial spaces was carried out with virtually no regard for pre-existing groupings and boundaries is reflected especially in those borders which are represented by straight lines on a map. This has made the task of **nation-building**—that is, the attempt to build a coherent sense of national identity among disparate groups of people—in many of these places especially difficult.

The establishment of colonial states with their relatively clear boundaries, their administrative centres and more or less permanent, settled populations mimicked the structure of European states. When decolonization came onto the agenda, the transition from colonial state to sovereign state, in an international system of similarly structured states, seemed relative simple from a technical point of view. Sovereignty was simply transferred from the colonizing power to an indigenous elite. In the decades following

14

the end of the Second World War, most of the former colonial states from the Atlantic and Africa through to Asia and the Pacific acquired sovereign statehood on the basis of existing boundaries and with structures of governance—parliaments, electorates, a civil service, etc.—which reflected European practices. A notable exception to the territorial norm was the case of India and Pakistan where separate sovereign states were created, on the basis of religious differences, out of what had been a single overarching colonial unit. In the process of partition, at least a million people lost their lives in the violence that ensued.

In summary, virtually all former colonies became part of an international system of states based largely on the European state system, a development which effectively ensured the globalization of that system. Even those states which had not been colonized, such as Japan and Turkey as well as Thailand and Tonga, adopted the European state format. However, independent sovereign statehood has not been an outstanding success for a number of countries. While few postcolonial states have actually collapsed completely, a number have experienced major difficulties in maintaining the basic elements of effective statehood. Here is where it is useful to consider concepts such as weak states, quasi states and collapsed or failing states in some parts of the former colonial world.

→ See chapter seven, page 166, for a discussion of Japan and Turkey's adoption of the European state format.

Weak states are typically those lacking the capacity to organize and regulate their societies and to extract and deploy resources in an appropriate way (Migdal: 4). As a result, they generally cannot deliver an adequate range of political, social and economic goods to their citizens. *Quasi states* is a term that has been used in various ways, and in some usages overlaps with weak states. Robert H. Jackson uses it to describe Third World states dependent on the support of the international community and which therefore possess 'negative sovereignty' (Jackson, 1990). The idea of *failing states* applies where states, which are already weak, reach a point where factors such as corruption, incompetence, unfair distribution of resources, human rights abuses, favouritism on the basis of ethnicity, the direct involvement of the military in politics, and so on, feed into social unrest, persistent violence, economic breakdown, and political turmoil (Rotberg, 2003: 1–2). Among the states that have been described as either weak or failing states, or as quasi states, are the Congo, Sudan, Sierra Leone and Afghanistan, Columbia, Tajikistan, Haiti, Lebanon, Fiji, Solomon Islands, and Papua New Guinea while Somalia is more or less a collapsed state.

→ See chapter seven, pages 173–80, for discussion of strong and weak states.

Even though many of the problems leading to state weakness or failure may be generated from within, it is by no means fair to attribute blame to domestic actions alone. A significant range of historical and broader contemporary developments must also be considered in relation to each specific case. Colonial legacies, the activities of transnational organizations, inequitable trading regimes—all of these have contributed as well. More generally, the forces of economic globalization are often seen as especially problematic for fragile Third World states with underdeveloped capacity and little negotiating power in the international arena, all of which ensures that they remain vulnerable to failure at one level or another.

14

All these problems bring into question both the assumed benefits of the globalization of the European state system and its long-term prospects as an effective system of international order. Having said that, we can also point to the relative success of many other postcolonial states, especially in the Asian region. Also, Europe has had its share of failed states as well, the most recent being Yugoslavia which is now divided into seven sovereign entities (Slovenia, Croatia, Bosnia and Herzegovina, the Former Yugoslav Republic of Macedonia, Serbia, Montenegro, and Kosova). Furthermore, the deepening and widening of the EU, as a project in **regionalization** that at once incorporates as well as transcends sovereign states, raises questions about the future of the traditional sovereign state in its original heartland.

Key Points

- It is largely due to the global reach of the European empires and their political legacies that the European state system became the basis for the current international state system and international order.

- Formal sovereign statehood has not always delivered significant benefits, especially in the Third World where a number of weak or failing states provide little in the way of benefits to their citizens.

- The concept of a 'quasi state' is useful in highlighting the fact that some Third World states depend so much on the international community for their continuing existence that their sovereignty is essentially 'negative'.

Conclusion

This chapter has provided a broad overview of key aspects of the study of International Relations from its foundations as a discipline and its basic terminology to the substantive concepts on which it has traditionally been based, namely sovereignty, the state, and international order. It has also sketched how states and international systems, including empires, have developed over many centuries from the earliest times to the present era of globalization. Setting the rise of the contemporary international order against this world historical background helps to illustrate not only the variety of state forms and international systems in history, but also the fact that while some systems have achieved an impressive longevity, no system has ever achieved permanence. It would therefore be mistaken to assume that the present state system will necessarily remain as it is over the longer term, especially given the challenges of globalization—however the phenomenon is conceived—and the various pressures it exerts on all aspects of sovereign statehood.

14

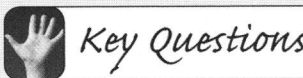

Key Questions

- What does 'International Relations' signify and how does it differ from terms such as 'world politics' or 'global politics'.

- How do empires form an international system?

- Under what circumstances did the idea of sovereign statehood arise in Europe?

- What are the distinguishing features of the modern state?

- What is the relationship between states and nations?

- What do you understand by the terms 'anarchy' and 'international order'?

- How did the European state system become globalized?

- What are the implications of weak and failing states for the state system as a whole?

- What is 'negative' sovereignty?

- What are the alternatives to the current international order?

Further Reading

Griffiths, Martin and Terry O'Callaghan (2002), *International Relations: The Key Concepts*, London: Routledge.

> This is one of a number of books which provide a good basic guide to some of the main concepts, themes, and institutions that figure prominently in the study of International Relations. It is a very useful companion to a main textbook such as the present one.

Best, Anthony, Jussi M. Hanhimaki, Kirsten E. Schulze, and Joseph A. Maiolo (2003), *An International History of the Twentieth Century*, London: Routledge.

> A wide-ranging study of international history such as this provides important additional context for the study of International Relations, giving students an appreciation of the trends that have shaped the contemporary world, including events in Europe, Asia, the Middle East, Africa, and the Americas.

Hobson, John M. (2004), *The Eastern Origins of Western Civilization*, Cambridge: Cambridge University Press.

> This book provides an interesting argument which attempts to counter the ethnocentricity apparent in mainstream accounts of the rise of 'the West' and its dominance of world affairs. It therefore provides a balance to assumptions that other regions, especially 'the East' have been passive bystanders.

Treasure, Geoffrey (2003), *The Making of Modern Europe 1648–1780*, London: Routledge.

> This study provides a deeper international history background, focusing on the growth of the state in Europe throughout the seventeenth and eighteenth centuries and major events such as the Thirty Years War and the French Revolution.

14

 **Web Links**

www.history.ac.uk/ejournal/
This free electronic journal 'aims to promote an understanding of the breadth, depth and policy relevance of international history by examining how the politics, societies, economies and traditions of countries have shaped and influenced international relations since circa 1500.'

www.history-world.org/
This is a very extensive site containing a collection of world history related essays, documents, and maps as well as music and videos including the history of the ancient world, Africa, Europe, Asia, India, the Middle East, Australia, and the Americas.

www.history.ac.uk/ihr/Focus/Empire/index.html
This contains information through various links on a range of historical empires, but with a particular focus on the British.

 Visit the **Online Resource Centre** that accompanies this book to access more learning resources at www.oxfordtextbooks.co.uk/orc/garner/

15

Traditional Theories of International Relations

Reader's Guide

Theory is a way of organizing the basic elements of our thinking about the world around us, and we can neither explain nor understand that world without some kind of theoretical framework in which the 'facts' of international politics are arranged and made sense of. Two major bodies of theory—liberalism and realism—constitute the theoretical terrain of traditional IR. Each has offered competing explanations and solutions addressing the causes of war and the conditions of peace in the international sphere. IR's theoretical development also raised some important issues of methodology involving the search for objective knowledge on the one hand, and the place of norms and standards on the other. We also look at the 'English School' of IR which focuses on the idea of international society as well as maintaining an alternative methodological pathway to that of the 'scientism'. Finally, we consider theoretical developments in the form of neoliberalism and neorealism respectively. From the start we should note that traditional theories of IR, while attempting to provide universally valid explanations of political behaviour, have been developed largely in 'the West' and therefore draw largely on European and North American experiences.

Liberalism and the Rise of IR

It is widely accepted that the main impetus for the emergence of IR as a formal academic discipline was the First World War. Although Europe had witnessed many wars in the past, the unprecedented scale of this particular conflict, which brought into our vocabulary the term 'total war'—denoting the militarization of a state's entire resources for the purpose of annihilating the enemy—prompted an urgent search for a new international order which could deliver a stable political environment providing for lasting peace and security. Under the influence of the US President, Woodrow Wilson (1856–1924), this was to be an essentially liberal order. See **Box 15.1**.

Liberal international theorists of the early twentieth century drew on a pre-existing body of philosophy in constructing their notion of international order. Ancient philosophers had emphasized the capacity of individual human reason for delineating the 'good life', although it was modern liberal thinkers who advocated concrete political action in achieving reform when the existing order was found wanting. Among the most important contributors to liberal ideas specifically in international politics are Hugo Grotius (1583–1645) and Samuel Pufendorf (1632–94), both of whom experienced the Thirty Years War discussed in chapter fourteen.

Grotius argued for the possibility of universal moral standards against which the legitimacy of actions in pursuit of self-preservation could be judged. This has featured in liberal international thought ever since. He also formulated some of the earliest ideas in the modern period about the 'sociability' of the international sphere which were highly influential in the development of later ideas about international society (Dunne, 1998: 138–9). Pufendorf, whose work was immensely influential, incorporated a basic **natural**

➡ See the case study on the Peace of Westphalia in chapter fourteen, page 336.

15

Short Biography   Box 15.1
Woodrow Wilson

Woodrow Wilson (1856–1924) served as a Democratic US president from 1913 to 1921. He brought the USA into the First World War in 1917 to help 'make the world safe for democracy', an idealist notion that has resonated in American foreign policy ever since. Wilsonian idealism was also reflected in attempts to establish a new international order at the end of the war along essentially liberal lines. A chief architect of the League of Nations, the centre piece of the new order, Wilson was unable to persuade a Republican-dominated Congress to join. But he was recognized for his efforts by the awarding of the Nobel Peace Prize in 1919. The first Chair in the emergent discipline of IR—the Woodrow Wilson Chair of International Politics at University College Wales, Aberystwyth—was established in the same year, also honouring his commitment to establishing a peaceful international order.

law of self-preservation in his work on universal jurisprudence and the law of nations. He, too, promoted the essential sociability of humans which served to counter ideas about excessive self-interestedness. (see, generally, Hochstrasser, 2000). Another major figure is Immanuel Kant (1724–1804) (ch. 4), whose seminal work, *Perpetual Peace,* was published in 1795. In order to secure lasting peace among states, he proposed a set of propositions for a law of nations founded on a federation of free states, ideas which have remained highly influential in peace theory (see Kant in Brown, Nardin, and Rengger, 2002: 432–4).

Kant further proposed that under republican forms of government, the individual concern for self-preservation, which was an entirely rational concern, would ensure that citizens effectively vetoed warmongering. This is one of the rationales behind the influential **democratic peace** thesis. Woodrow Wilson also endorsed the idea that democracies are inherently peaceful, both within themselves and in their relations with each other, and believed that if all countries were governed democratically, then warfare would be virtually eliminated. He certainly believed that if all European countries had been democracies in 1914, war would have been avoided (Lawson, 2003: 42–3).

A major theme uniting liberal thinkers from Grotius onwards, and which helps to distinguish liberal from realist thought, includes an optimistic view of the possibilities for peaceful relations. This derives from a positive view of **human nature**, at least to the extent that people can learn from their mistakes. Beyond this, liberals believe that the effect of rationally chosen, self-regarding courses of action by individuals tends to lead to better outcomes for all, or at least for the majority. Thus over time humans can *progress* towards a better state of existence as individuals as well as with respect to both life within their political communities and in the relations between communities. None of this comes about by itself. People (agents) need to make it happen. Just as human rationality *and* **agency** is required to build a satisfactory social and political order within a state, so it is required just as much, if not more, in the construction of international institutions designed specifically to overcome the negative effects of **anarchy** and to contain tendencies to war. This style of thinking was crucially import-ant in underpinning developments in the immediate aftermath of the First World War.

President Wilson led his country into war in the belief that once the forces responsible for the war were defeated, a strong international organization dedicated to preserving international peace and security could flourish. He proposed a general association of nation-states to make mutual guarantees concerning economic and political independence and territorial integrity, regardless of each state's size or capacity. This was operationalized through the 1919 Treaty of Versailles which embodied the Covenant of the League of Nations. However, the Treaty also imposed harsh reparations on Germany for loss and damage caused by the war. Described as 'one of the best examples of a peace treaty creating the pre-conditions of a future war' (Evans and Newnham, 1998: 559), many of the treaty's authors lived to regret the harshness of its provisions. We consider further aspects of the League in chapter nineteen, but for present purposes it provides a useful case study of how theory and practice are interwoven. See **Box 15.2.**

➡ See chapter nineteen, page 444, for a discus-sion of intergov-ernmental organizations.

Case Study Box 15.2
Liberal Theory and the League of Nations

It is often said that the League of Nations was a failure because it did not prevent the outbreak of the Second World War. The liberal internationalism which underpinned it was derided, at least by realists, as a form of utopianism bound to fail when faced with the realities of power politics in an anarchical international sphere; but is this to mistake cause and effect? Although some provisions allowed too much leeway in the application of sanctions, the institutional design of the League itself was workable enough, and the UN is based on many of these. As the first major attempt to set up a mechanism for collective security on such an extensive international scale it has, for all its weak points, been hailed as a considerable achievement. Other factors were far more important in undermining its chances for success. Thus, when the League, and the principles of liberal internationalism on which it was based, stand accused of failing to check the aggression of Germany, Italy, and Japan, we must remember the failure of the USA to join, the refusal to allow communist Russia to join, the aggression of France itself when it invaded a German industrial area with Belgium in an attempt to exact reparation dues, the failure of Britain to condemn this violation of League rules, all combined with the vengeful nature of the treaty's reparations provisions. A humiliated Germany was ripe for the rabidly fervent nationalism that Hitler came to espouse while the geopolitical land-scape of swathes of Eastern Europe was highly vulnerable to the aggression of a remilitarized Germany prepared for another total war. The question then is: did the League of Nations fail; or did state leaders fail the League of Nations?

Another important aspect of liberal theory pushed by Wilson and others in the wake of the First World War was the principle of **self-determination**, a term which has several nuances. First, it can refer to the right of states freely to determine their own policies and practices. Secondly, it can refer to the right of citizens to determine their own government and therefore a preferred set of policy options—a defining characteristic of **liberal democracy**. Thirdly, it can refer to the quest of a nationalist movement to secure political autonomy, which can include an act of secession to form a new sovereign state. This right to *national* self-determination further strengthens the legitimacy of the nation-state idea, discussed earlier. Historically, it should be emphasized that the principle of the self-determination of 'peoples' (understood as 'nations') originally applied within Europe only, and was not extended to include the colonized world until after 1945, except in South America.

Liberal IR theory reached a high point in the interwar years. Among the prominent liberal scholars of the time was Norman Angell, awarded the 1933 Nobel Peace Prize on the basis of his extensive writings on the futility of war. Subsequent developments, however, saw liberal ideas overshadowed as **realism** rose to prominence and its

➔ See chapter fourteen, pages 326–8, for a discussion of the nation-state.

15

proponents denounced the **idealism** implicit in liberal international theory and the perceived ineffectiveness of international institutions in the face of the realities of **power politics**. Whatever criticisms they may have attracted later, the early twentieth-century liberals have been recognized widely as the founders of IR as an academic discipline. As we shall see, liberalism was to make something of a comeback in the latter part of the twentieth century, and remains a highly influential stream of IR theory. In practical terms, it now underpins an extensive system of international law as well as the principal political institutions of contemporary **global governance** embodied in the United Nations system. It is also deeply implicated in international political economy which we discuss in chapter twenty.

Key Points

- Significant impetus for liberal international theorists of the early twentieth century, and for the establishment of IR as a distinctive academic subject, was the devastation wrought by the First World War and a determination to identify the causes of war and the conditions for peace.
- Liberal international theory is characterized by an optimism concerning the prospects of a peaceful international order established through strong international institutions underpinned by international law. It accepts that sovereign states are the key actors in international affairs but believes that their behaviour, even under conditions of anarchy, can be modified through such institutions.

The Realist Turn

The Treaty of Versailles not only failed to resolve a number of Europe's political problems, but exacerbated others. New states had been created in Eastern Europe partly in an attempt to apply the principle of national self-determination. Strategically, they were also supposed to serve as 'buffer states' between Western Europe and the emergent communist empire further east. The USSR's own brand of **internationalism** at the time was committed to the overthrow of a liberal, capitalist economic order by means of worldwide revolution. Throughout the 1920s, however, relative peace was the order of the day and even Germany had joined the League of Nations. None of this prevented the rise of Adolf Hitler, who set about building the Third Reich on an ultranationalist basis.

Developments in other parts of the world were significant too, especially the rise of Japan which had achieved extraordinary industrial growth over the previous half-century. Japan had been a member of the League of Nations and some Japanese remained committed to internationalism. But aggressive militarism and **imperialism** succeeded in a period where the effects of the Depression enhanced the influence of ultranationalists, as in Italy and Germany. The latter's invasion of Poland in 1939 led the world into its second large-scale war. Japan had already invaded China but it was not until 1940 that Japan became part of the 'Axis Alliance' with Italy and Germany and, in the following year, brought the USA into the war by attacking Pearl Harbor.

Over the period 1939–45, more than 50 million people were killed as a direct result of the Second World War—more than five times the number killed in the previous world war. Apart from the massive increase in fatalities, the death camps of Nazi Germany, in which at least six million people were murdered, highlighted the consequences of racialist nationalism gone mad. The holocaust, which refers primarily to the mass murder of Jews in this war, stands as the most notorious act of genocide in human history. Given that the discipline of IR had been founded by people dedicated to the prevention of war, and the death, destruction, and suffering it caused, this war must be seen as a devastating setback. Here is where realism enters the picture as a theory designed to explain how the world *really* is rather than how it *ought* to be.

While there is no single, concise theory that goes under the name of 'realism', virtually all realist approaches in IR take the struggle for power and security by sovereign states in the anarchic sphere of international politics as their central focus. Although it emerged as an explicit theory of IR only in the twentieth century, many of its proponents claim that they are part of a much longer tradition. The treatment of the Peloponnesian war by the historian Thucydides, mentioned in chapter fourteen, contains a dialogue commonly taken to illustrate two cardinal principles of political realism. The 'Melian Dialogue' suggests, first, that power politics is the name of the game in relations between states, and second, that issues of morality are irrelevant in the sphere of power politics. This sphere is therefore *a*moral in the sense that no moral rules can be applied, rather than *im*moral which indicates the transgression of an existing moral rule. See **Box 15.3**.

➜ See the discussion on the history of states and the international system in chapter fourteen, page 328.

 Box 15.3

The Melian Dialogue

The inhabitants of the island of Melos were neutral in the war between Athens and Sparta and would not submit to Athens. The Athenians first sent envoys with terms for a Melian surrender and Thucydides records the dialogue:

'Athenians: [We will] not go out of our way to prove at length that we have a right to rule . . . But you and we should say what we really think, and aim only at what is possible, for we both alike know that in the discussion of human affairs the question of justice only enters where the pressure of necessity is equal, and that the powerful exact what they can, and the weak grant what they must.

Melians: But must we be your enemies? Will you not receive us as friends if we are neutral and remain at peace with you?

Athenians: No, your enmity is not half so mischievous to us as your friendship; for the one is in the eyes of our subjects an argument of our power, the other of our weakness. . . .

Melians: But do you not recognize another danger? For . . . since you drive us from the plea of justice and press upon us your doctrine of expediency, we must show you what is for our interest, and, if it be for yours also, may hope to convince you: Will you not be making enemies of all who are now neutrals? . . .

Athenians: . . . you are not fighting against equals to whom you cannot yield without disgrace, but you are taking counsel whether or no you shall resist an overwhelming force. The question is not one of honour but of prudence. . . .

Melians: We know only too well how hard the struggle must be against your power, and against fortune. . . . Nevertheless we do not despair of fortune; . . . because we are righteous, and you against whom we contend are unrighteous.

Athenians: . . . of men we know, that by a law of their nature wherever they can rule they will. This law was not made by us, and we are not the first who have acted upon it; we did but inherit it, and shall bequeath it to all time, and we know that you and all mankind, if you were as strong as we are, would do as we do. . . . the path of expediency is safe, whereas justice and honour involve danger in practice . . . [and] . . . what encourages men who are invited to join in a conflict is clearly not the goodwill of those who summon them to their side, but a decided superiority in real power. . . . '   (Thucydides, V, 84–109)

Thucydides further records that the Melians refuse to surrender. The Athenians lay siege to the city and eventually force a surrender whereupon they put to death all males of military age, and enslave the women and children.

Another significant figure is Niccolò Machiavelli (1467–1527) who developed a pragmatic approach to politics, eschewing idealist imaginaries and moralizing. As mentioned in chapter fourteen, the ancient Indian text on **statecraft**, the *Arthasastra* by Kautilya, has been compared to Machiavelli's writings on the subject. A particularly important idea, often traced to Machiavelli, is *raison d'état* (**reason of state**) which is reflected in the more common contemporary phrase **national interest**. Although Machiavelli did not use the precise term 'reason of state', he urged that where the safety of the country is at stake, a ruler ought not to consider what is just or unjust, merciful or cruel, but rather what will secure 'the life of the country and maintain its liberty' (Machiavelli, Bk 3, Ch. XLI).

Perhaps the most important figure claimed for the realist tradition is Thomas Hobbes (1588–1679) (chs 1, 7). Hobbes starts by positing a **state of nature** as well as a certain human nature, both of which are assumed to be universal, that is, *constant for all times and*

15

➔ See the discussion on the history of states and the inter-national system in chapter fourteen, page 328.

all places. Hobbes' state of nature is devoid of all that is necessary for the good life. It lacks security, justice, and any sort of morality. And it lacks these elements precisely because there is no sovereign power to enforce them. The essential characteristic of this condition is anarchy. Fear and insecurity dominate people's consciousness, driving individuals to seek the means of their own preservation above all else. Since domination is the only viable means of achieving one's preservation, the inevitable result is the war of each against all. This scenario prompted Hobbes to pen his most famous line, namely, that life in the anarchic state of nature is solitary, poor, nasty, brutish, and short!

To dispel anarchy and escape this scenario into a realm of peace and security, individuals must contract together to live under a single, indisputable political authority—a sovereign power—who can enforce order and obedience to a set of laws. People retain only a fundamental right to self-preservation, since it is for this purpose that they submit to the sovereign authority in the first place. Political communities for Hobbes are therefore artificial constructs devised to alleviate the miserable, insecure conditions of the state of nature. As for relations between states, exactly the same conditions apply as for individuals in the state of nature. Since no overarching sovereign authority holds sway in the international sphere, states are condemned to exist in a realm of perpetual anarchy where survival is the name of the game—and this is achieved only through domination and the rational pursuit of pure self-interest. As for justice and morality, these simply have no place in such an environment (Lawson, 2003: 34–5).

These are some of the basic ideas on which theories of *classical* realism in IR developed from the 1930s up until about the late 1960s. Also central to this development was a critique of liberalism. Indeed, at least in its classic formulation, realism is essentially a conservative response to liberal international thought. One of the most prominent critics, E.H. Carr, is often described as a disillusioned liberal who regarded the peace settlement following the First World War as a fiasco. As he saw it, the principal defect of the liberalism in IR was an almost complete blindness to the power factor in politics which he likened to a law of nature, rather like Hobbes. One of Carr's principal arguments holds, first, that no political society, whether national or international, can exist unless people submit to certain rules of conduct. He further asserts the primacy of politics over ethics, arguing that as a matter of logic, rulers rule because of superior strength, and the ruled submit because they are weaker. **Political obligation** thus derives from the recognition that 'might is right'. In preparing the ground for a theory of realism, Carr also asserts that this theory is in fact a reaction to utopianism and cites Machiavelli as initiating a revolt against utopianism in political thought in his own time (Carr, 1948: ch. 4). See **Box 15.4**.

Carr's broader view of politics does not concede the entire ground to realism. He was also concerned to point out that when realism is attacked with its own weapons, it is just as likely to be found lacking the cold objectivity claimed by for it by its proponents as any other way of thinking (ibid.: 89). This led him to conclude that sound political thinking must be based on elements of both **utopia** and reality, for when utopianism

➔ See chapter five, page 116, for an exploration of liberalism.

15

Key Quote   Box 15.4
Machiavelli on the 'Real' versus the 'Ideal'

'... it appears to me more appropriate to follow up the real truth of a matter than the imagination of it; for many have pictured republics and principalities which in fact have never been seen and known, because how one lives is so far distant from how one ought to live that he who neglects what is done for what ought to be done sooner effects his ruin than his preservation.'   (Machiavelli quoted in Carr, 1948: 63)

'has become a hollow and intolerable sham, which serves merely as a disguise for the interests of the privileged, the realist performs an indispensable service in unmasking it.' Pure realism, on the other hand, offers 'nothing but a naked struggle for power which makes any kind of international society impossible' (ibid.: 93). As we shall see, the idea of **international society** was to become a central theme in the English School's contribution to theory.

After the Second World War, and with the onset of Cold War, IR developed rapidly in the USA and acquired a distinctive realist tone. The principle figure in post-war American theorizing was Hans Morgenthau whose ideas have been compared with those of Thucydides by contemporary authors. Richard Ned Lebow (2007: 52–70), for example, says that both Thucydides and Morgenthau see politics, in any time and any place, as subject to a basic human instinct revolving around power. Realism, like conservatism, therefore claims not to be an 'ideology'. This epithet is reserved for doctrines such as liberalism and socialism which are grounded in idealist suppositions. Realism, on the other hand, claims to provide an account of how things 'really are', thus claiming to be entirely objective.

Realism also sees politics in the domestic sphere as much the same as politics in the international sphere. The crucial difference is of course the fact that a sovereign authority resides within states and therefore makes domestic order possible. Some order is possible in the anarchic international sphere, but this is achieved only through rather fragile mechanisms. These mechanisms include, first and foremost, a **balance of power** among constituent elements of an international system. In realist theory, this balance of power has a **deterrence** effect so long as states behave in a rational manner and do not allow greed and ambition to colour their judgement. More sophisticated versions of realism allow for the possibility of a deterrence effect to also arise from certain elements of sociability in an international system. In other words, if a group of states acknowledge a 'community of interests' or are otherwise bound by some common elements of culture, conventions, personal ties, and so on, then competition for power is greatly modified and less likely to generate warfare. Some states, however, aggressively pursue what they perceive to be their own interests regardless. Thus certain states, such as Athens during the period of the Peloponnesian War, or leaders like Napoleon and Hitler in later times, cannot be deterred.

→ See chapter five, page 116, for a discussion of liberalism.

→ See chapter five, page 119, for a discussison of socialism.

15

Lebow further quotes Morgenthau's wry observation that a balance of power 'works best when needed least' (Lebow, 2007: 58). See **Box 15.5**.

Key Points

- 'Realism' as a general approach to the study of politics purports to analyze things as they *really are*, rather than as they *ought to be,* and in this way marks itself off from the idealism of liberal thought which, in the interwar years, was often derided as 'utopianism'. In developing their ideas, classical realist scholars of the mid-twentieth century claimed such thinkers as Thucydides, Machiavelli, and Hobbes as belonging to their tradition.

- Realism comes in different forms, but virtually all realist international theory takes the struggle for power and security of sovereign states in conditions of international anarchy as their central focus. These views in turn generate key ideas such as deterrence and the balance of power which help to maintain international order under such conditions.

Key Quote   Box 15.5
Hans J. Morgenthau on Power Politics

'International politics, like all politics, is a struggle for power. Whatever the ultimate aims of international politics, power is always the immediate aim. Statesmen and peoples may ultimately seek freedom, security, prosperity, or power itself. They may define their goals in terms of a religious, philosophic, economic, or social ideal. They may hope that this ideal will materialize through its own inner force, through divine intervention, or through the natural development of human affairs. But whenever they strive to realize their goal by means of international politics, they do so by striving for power'.   (Morgenthau, 1948: 13)

Some Questions of Method and Norms

We have seen in the introduction to this book that the study of politics involves different kinds of analysis and **methodology**. Among the important developments in IR following the Second World War, especially in the USA, was the impact of **behaviouralism**. As explained earlier, this is an approach to social science which rejects legal, historical, and comparative enquiry in favour of quantifiable data— aimed to produce objective, *positive* knowledge derived through the application of scientific method. Thus the closely allied term, **positivism**, signified the acquisition of a neutral, universally valid, body of knowledge about subjects such as politics and IR via the same methodology deployed in the natural sciences, including the formulation and testing of hypotheses, the collection of empirical facts, the identification of relevant variables, and the determination of cause and effect which should lead in turn to some measure of predictability in international politics. To reiterate: positivism assumes a

➡ See the Introduction, pages 16–17, for a description of behaviouralism.

15

'unity of method' for the production of knowledge in both the natural and social sciences. Because normative considerations are bracketed off as 'unscientific', positivist approaches are, by definition, largely concerned with what *is*, rather than what *ought* to be.

Normative analysis or theory, in contrast, is very much concerned with norms, values and ethics and asks questions about right and wrong, justice and injustice—of which there are many in the international sphere. Accordingly, *normative international theory* does not attempt to sell itself as 'scientific' in the sense that it is built up on the basis of neutral or 'objective' knowledge obtained through experimental procedures or statistical correlations. One cannot empirically 'test' the truth or falsity of moral claims, and issues of cause and effect are simply not of the same character as they are in fields such as physics and chemistry; but while normative theory does not develop knowledge via the testing of hypotheses and the accumulation of 'facts' through any kind of positivist methodology, it nonetheless lends itself to systematic investigation and the construction of theory based on reasoning and intuition. Thus if 'science' is simply taken to refer to the systematic accumulation of knowledge—and this is in fact its ordinary meaning (from the Latin *scientia*, knowledge)—then normative theory, when undertaken in a rigorous, organized manner, may be regarded as no less scientific than theories generated via positivist methods.

In any event, most normative theorists would argue that knowledge produced by positivist methodologies is never completely objective and that the results it produces often reflect the biases of the scientists concerned (whether these are natural or social scientists). There are many examples where bias is fairly obvious, for instance, when scientific studies commissioned by major coal or oil producers show that fossil fuels are either not to blame for global warming, or that global warming and climate change are not actually occurring at all. Even where no vested interest is obvious, it is difficult to maintain that any study in any field is entirely free of subjective biases and some go as far as to claim that all knowledge is a matter of interpretation. We consider some related issues in the next chapter.

To return briefly to the point raised above concerning the focus of positivist approaches on what *is*, rather than what *ought* to be, we should note that this suggests a close connection with some of the tenets of classical realism. As we have seen, key figures from Thucydides onwards who have been claimed for the realist tradition have been at pains to stress that one needs to accept what is 'real' in the world of politics rather than try to grasp at some unattainable 'ideal'. Politics, in this view, is about what 'is' rather than what 'ought' to be; so although realism as a theory of politics, and positivism as a methodology, are not the same thing, they seem to share certain important assumptions. Morgenthau's classical realism, however, was rather more historical and discursive than a thoroughgoing positivism could accommodate. Realism would subsequently take a more scientistic direction, as we shall see shortly.

Key points

- Positivism encompasses a belief that the same basic scientific method employed in the natural sciences can be used to produce a universally valid and normatively neutral (that is, value-free) body of knowledge about subjects such as politics and IR.

- Because realist IR is concerned with what *is*, rather than with what *ought* to be, it has certain affinities with positivism. The philosophical and historical elements of classical realism, however, are largely incompatible with positivist methodology. Even so, realism, liberalism and positivism all subscribe, in one way or another, to notions of universally valid propositions.

The English School and the Idea of International Society

While behaviouralism made its mark on social science in the USA, another group of scholars developed a very different approach to IR on the other side of the Atlantic. This group first gathered in London in 1959 and, constituting themselves as the 'British Committee' (later known as the English School), addressed themselves to fundamental questions of international theory (Dunne, 1998: xi). One member, Martin Wight, thought the entire field of IR was theoretically underdeveloped compared to the study of domestic politics. He proposed that just as political theory asks fundamental questions about the state, so international theory must ask fundamental questions about the international sphere which constituted a 'society of states'. The fact that it had not done so meant that the entire field suffered a profound intellectual poverty (Wight, 1966: 18). While individual members of the group adopted varying positions, some giving emphasis to realist perspectives while others subscribed to more liberal ideas, they shared a common interest in historical and normative approaches, thereby rejecting the scientism which had come to characterize much academic work in the USA.

As suggested in Wight's remarks, much of their theorizing revolved around the concept of international society articulated earlier by Grotius. This was understood as a society of sovereign states formed under conditions of anarchy. While English School theorists agreed that such conditions are inherently less stable than those in the domestic sphere, their emphasis was on the extent to which a stable order can nonetheless be achieved. A prominent member of the school, Hedley Bull, while accepting the basic premises of realism, proposed that state behaviour could be significantly modified through the adoption of rules and institutions. These generated an international environment and process of socialization in which norms, values and common interests came to play an important role in influencing state behaviour. See **Box 15.6**.

Despite general agreement among English School theorists on the basic principles of international society, there were diverging views on the extent to which a common core

Key Quote Box 15.6
Hedley Bull on the Society of States

'[A] society of states (or international society) exists when a group of states, conscious of certain common interests and common values, form a society in the sense that they conceive themselves to be bound by a common set of rules in their relations with one another and share in the working of common institutions'.   (Bull, 1997: 13)

of norms could be established among all states. Bull, Wight, and others were living in an era of decolonization and states very different from those of Europe were emerging around the world. Could a theory as Eurocentric as theirs apply universally? Could the norms of a society of European states really be exported to the rest of the world? These questions raised the issue of cultural difference in world politics and the fact that much theorizing in the discipline to date was characterized by an unashamed **ethnocentricity**.

With respect to the export of norms, opinion was divided. Some, including Bull, adopted **pluralism** as the basis of their approach. This recognized that different people (understood in terms of different 'cultures') invariably have different norms and values and therefore different standards of justice. If each state is a repository of those standards of justice, one must conclude that there can be no universal yardstick against which standards can be evaluated. This argument therefore tends strongly towards a notion of ethical relativism based on the idea that individual states not only have no legitimate sovereign power above them, but no moral authority above them either. The absence of a universal standard for 'right conduct' does not preclude the formation of an international society, but it does mean that such a society is fairly minimalist in that states do not need to share more substantive domestic goals, values or conceptions of justice to support a notion of international society. Rather, the latter is held together simply by agreement on the importance of international order itself, and a normative commitment to supporting the goal of peaceful *coexistence* (Dunne, 1998: 100). This position accords more or less with **communitarianism**, discussed in chapters one and four. According to this approach, morality arises within particular communities and basically holds good only for those communities. For the purposes of international relations, such moral communities are, in effect, states.

➔ See chapter one, page 41, for a discussion of communitarianism.

15

Others, however, adopted a 'solidarist' approach which recognizes the inherent plurality of values among states in the international sphere, but seeks a more robust commitment to shared norms of both domestic and international behaviour, especially when it comes to issues of serious human rights abuses. **Solidarism** therefore reflects not simply a solidarity among states making a commitment to forming a peaceful international society bound by a commitment to non-intervention, but a broader commitment to the solidarity of humankind itself. While a norm of non-intervention may be taken as a standard feature of the

➔ See chapter four, page 110, for an exploration of communitarianism and justice.

society of states in the ordinary course of events, a solidarist position allows, in principle, for this norm to be overtaken by an *extra*ordinary turn of events, such as when a population group within a state becomes a target for genocide. Solidarism therefore shares some common ground with **cosmopolitanism** which, as we saw earlier, contemplates the transcendence of state boundaries. For pluralists, however, the solidarist position and its cosmopolitan leanings moves too far away from an international society, understood as a society *of* states, towards something of a world society which de-emphasizes state boundaries and indeed the notion of a state system as such (Buzan, 2004: esp. pp. 139–60).

English School theory has experienced a significant revival in recent years. As two prominent authors have recently remarked, the importance of the English School's concern with the relationship between international order and human justice is at the heart of current debates about the relationship between state sovereignty, the strong global human rights culture, and pressures for **humanitarian intervention**, as well as the phenomenon of failing states.

Questions of clashing world-views in a multicultural international society—a concern for some of the early theorists—also seem more urgent than ever in the post-9/11 world. Furthermore, ideas of international society as articulated by earlier English School theorists are seen as highly relevant for the analysis of regional integration projects, problems of the global environment, and aspects of international political economy (Linklater and Suganami, 2006: 2).

Photo 15.1

Pakistani human rights activists hold a rally against foreign intervention in the country's politics, Saturday 15 September 2007 in Lahore, Pakistan.

Source: AP/PA Photos

Another recent study of legitimacy in IR, which involves agreement about who is entitled to participate as a prime actor in international relations as well as how actors should conduct themselves, argues that apart from underscoring the very existence of international society, questions of legitimacy have become increasingly urgent in the present period. Bodies such as the United Nations (UN) are seen as an essential repository of much legitimacy in the international sphere, especially in relation to **intervention**, humanitarian or otherwise (see Clark, 2005). In addition, important aspects of English School theorizing resonates with emergent theories of **social constructivism** which have become especially prominent in the present period and which we explore further in the next chapter.

Key Points

- The English School, while accommodating both realist and liberal perspectives, promotes the idea of a society of states underpinned by a set of common norms. Its early members also embraced historical and normative enquiry, seeking to provide IR with a basis in political philosophy which distinguished it from the positivism of much American IR.

- Two main approaches developed, one 'pluralist' which sought to accommodate varying norms, values, and standards of justice of different states within a framework of coexistence based on respect for sovereignty. 'Solidarism', in contrast, promoted a common set of norms and standards including respect for human rights and, in exceptional circumstances, a right of humanitarian intervention.

Neoliberalism and Neorealism

Further developments in the post-war period saw revisions of both liberalism and realism, resulting in the two 'neos'. Neorealism also goes by the name of 'structural' realism because of its concentrated focus on the structure of the international system itself. Neoliberalism, on the other hand, is sometimes referred to as pluralism for its much broader focus on the multiple forces at play in that system (Little, 1996: 66). The use of the term 'pluralism' here, incidentally, is not identical with the way in which it is used by English School theorists. Both usages invoke a concept of diversity, but whereas the English School usage was more concerned with the diversity of culture and values embodied within states, neoliberal 'pluralism' refers more to a plurality of actors and institutions in the international system.

Liberalism's period of renewal occurred after the Second World War when the international sphere underwent significant changes, especially with the creation of the UN organization as another attempt at creating a global institution capable of regulating the international system and of keeping a check on aggressive power politics. The UN's founders did not consider the old League such a failure that its basic institutions were rejected as a model for the new organization. Indeed, the UN incorporated many of the League's features, including a General Assembly and a Secretariat presided over by a Secretary-General, a Court of Justice, and an executive Council. In addition, specialized agencies were formed to assist in the task of building an international system with a strong economic and social framework.

The new international order after 1945 also saw substantial formal decolonization in Africa, the Middle East, Asia, and the Pacific, thus 'globalizing' the liberal idea of self-determination and, as we have seen, of the sovereign state system itself as a vehicle for self-determination. As a result, the UN's membership base was much more extensive than the old League and is therefore genuinely global in scope. All these developments were underpinned by liberal ideas and the aspiration to make the world a better place in practice, not just in theory.

In terms of intellectual development, the renewal of liberalism in the post-war period challenged what was seen as realism's simplistic approach to the nature of the international system. Like realism, liberalism accepted the anarchic character of the international sphere as well as the central role played by sovereign states. Unlike realists, liberals not only accorded international institutions (such as the UN) a crucially important role in ameliorating the negative effects of anarchy and power politics, but also came to regard the role of non-state actors as important. These include organizations ranging from transnational corporations to NGOs such as the Red Cross/Red Crescent, the International Chamber of Commerce, and so on. These bodies are said to constitute an **international civil society** which operates alongside the state system and the set of regional and international institutions based on that system.

In addition to its attention to the plurality of actors in the international system, neoliberalism also applied a finer-grained analysis to sovereign states. Whereas realists tended to regard states as unitary actors in the international sphere, neoliberals acknowledged a variety of state characteristics and modes of behaviour which were often influenced by domestic political constraints. Some of the earliest neoliberal ideas were formulated by Robert O. Keohane and Joseph S. Nye (1977) in terms of a new **interdependence** model of international relations which highlighted linkages between various actors as well as their sensitivities to the effects of actions by others in the system, both state and non-state.

This had important implications for international political economy as well, and so these liberals went beyond traditional security concerns. While it could be argued that the idea of interdependence advances very little on older ideas about alliances, interdependence is generally seen as much more complicated than the relations generated by mere security alliances, especially since the processes of industrialization and modernization, and globalization more generally, have produced many more dynamics than can be accommodated in realist theory. Thus neoliberals began to talk of **complex interdependence** to describe the principle characteristic of a modern international system with its multiple actors, agencies, and forces. Nye said a different kind of world from that depicted by realists could be imagined simply by reversing their key postulates. Thus we can see a world where states are not the only significant actors but operate alongside many others; where force is only one significant instrument among others, which include economic manipulation; and where the dominant goal is not security but welfare (Nye, 2005: 207).

As we have seen, liberalism has also been closely associated with ideas about creating positive conditions for peace. The link between theory and practice here occurs not just in the construction of international institutions but in the work of the peace movement more generally. Further intellectual support has also been developed in specialist peace studies programmes in universities and other institutions throughout the world, from the home of the Nobel Peace Prize (established in 1901) in Sweden to Japan, where peace activism, peace museums and peace studies have had a strong profile since the Second World War.

With neoliberalism providing a plausible alternative account of the international system, *neo*realism in turn restated the prime importance of power in an anarchical international sphere while modifying certain assumptions of classical realism. In refining the latter's ideas, neorealism also sought to produce a more *parsimonious* theory of IR—that is, a theory stripped down to the essentials. This was meant to enable the production of testable hypotheses in accordance with a more scientific approach. Critics would argue that this came at the expense of gross oversimplification.

The key neorealist figure in the 1970s was Kenneth Waltz whose major work, *Theory of International Politics* (1979), was highly influential in establishing the *structure* of the international state system as determining the behaviour of individual states, and not the other way around. Thus although states remained the principle actors, it was the structural attributes of the system as a whole that determined how states interacted with each other and therefore how the dynamics of the international political sphere worked. Because structure is the determinant of state behaviour, individual agents have little impact. Furthermore, this structure remains essentially anarchic regardless of how many international institutions attempt to modify its effects.

In an earlier work, Waltz (1959) had already laid out some of the groundwork for the neorealist/structural realist enterprise through his delineation of three distinct spheres or 'images' of politics: (1) individuals, (2) the state, and (3) the international system of states. In the first image, warfare among individuals is driven by negative aspects of human nature—greed, stupidity, and misdirected aggression. In the second image, conflict is mediated by the internal (domestic) organization of states. The third image takes anarchy as the essential attribute of the structure of the international system, one which makes warfare much more likely to occur because of the absence of restraints under conditions of anarchy. For Waltz, the third image provides the exclusive subject matter for IR while politics within the first or second image exert little influence on the international sphere because they do not affect its essential structure. In addition to strengthening the dividing line between the domestic and the international, this move effectively eliminated the influence of human nature on international politics. Rather, the struggle for power is determined by the structure of the system itself.

A leading contemporary realist says that the anarchic international system, in which no higher authority sits above the great powers, and in which there is no guarantee that one will not attack another, means that each state is moved by good sense to acquire sufficient power to protect itself in the event of attack: 'In essence, great powers are trapped in an iron cage where they have little choice but to compete with each other for power if they hope to survive' (Mearsheimer, 2007: 72). However, this brings other problems because the action of one state to enhance its security vis-à-vis other states in the international sphere, for example, by building up its military forces, invariably provokes other states to enhance their military capabilities in turn, thus making them more dangerous than they were before. This is, effectively, a feedback loop which results in a **security dilemma**, a concept developed much earlier in the Cold War period where the arms race was a prominent feature of power politics (see Herz, 1950). It also illustrates the key realist concept of the balance of power in so far as each state strives to adjust its capabilities to balance any change in the capabilities of other states, or at least those states that are considered relevant to the equation.

Waltz's ideas do not exhaust the range of 'neorealisms'. Other influential writers include Joseph Grieco (1988) who has elaborated on the idea of relative and absolute gains among states in terms of power and influence. Whereas liberals believe that states are content to make an absolute gain (measured against their own existing capacities rather than relative to other states), realists hold that states always seek both absolute and relative gains. Furthermore, states may well cooperate to enhance their overall position within the state system, but realists believe that states will engage in cheating behaviour if they think this will yield greater power or if continued cooperation appears likely to weaken their position.

Yet another branch of structural realism distinguishes defensive and offensive varieties and relates these to the concept of **hegemony**—a situation in which there is a dominant centre of power. Offensive realism holds that states constantly seek to enhance their power vis-à-vis others in the system which is a perfectly rational means of guaranteeing survival. A state that acquires hegemonic status enjoys the greatest measure of security precisely because of its superior power. Defensive realism, on the other hand, views hegemonic ambitions in terms of the security dilemma because the pursuit of hegemony by one state will invariably provoke a reaction in other states. Moreover, the combined power of other states may well be greater than that of the aspiring hegemon, leading ultimately to its defeat. However, realists of all varieties can see the dangers of expansionism and other ill-advised adventures abroad. Mearsheimer says that almost every realist opposed the Iraq War which has turned into a strategic disaster for the USA and its allies (2007: 86).

Ideas about absolute and relative gains, offensive realism and defensive realism are just some of the variations on the neorealist theme. Certain of these ideas may appear to critics of the neorealist project as abstract elements of an oversimplified theory of international relations, limited in its ability to ask deeper questions about the state of the political world and what the future might hold. Neorealism(s) have little to say about a range of pressing problems which go beyond the concerns of military security, from the state of global environment to imbalances in resource allocation and consumption around the world. For liberals, of course, neorealism says nothing about questions of justice either for present or future generations. There is now an emergent school of *neo*-classical realism which seeks to broaden the scope of realist theory to once again attempt a more comprehensive theorization and analysis of the mass of 'variables' which contribute to the dynamics of the international sphere (see Rose, 1998: 144–72). We may well see a realism develop along these lines in the future.

Key Points

* Important neoliberal ideas include 'complex interdependence' which recognizes multiple actors, agencies, and forces at work in the international system and more porous boundaries between domestic and international spheres. States remain significant actors, but they operate alongside many others while economic power is just as significant as force. For some, welfare is at least as important a goal as traditional security.

* Neorealism takes *structure* as the prime determinant of behaviour in the international sphere which is quite separate from the state's domestic sphere of activity and must be studied in its own terms. The 'three images' approach also eliminates human nature and individual agency as relevant factors. This narrows the scope of IR and produces a more parsimonious theory which its proponents say can generate testable hypotheses. Neorealism has now split into a variety of approaches as well as being contested by neoclassical realism.

Conclusion

This chapter has shown how, and under what circumstances, two major, competing bodies of IR theory initially developed to provide a framework for the discipline. Although much of the explicit theorizing about IR did not begin until the twentieth century, both liberalism and realism drew on existing ideas in the history of political thought to address basic problems of international order. However, each also contains different strands of thought and each has been modified over the years, so neither can be taken as a single body of theory. At the same time, both liberalism and realism assume that certain propositions are universally valid—the 'fact' of international anarchy being a prime example. These and other assumptions, as well as the positivist approaches to methodology developed in the post-war period, have been challenged by some of the more recent bodies of theory which we consider in the next chapter.

15

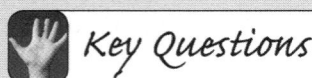 *Key Questions*

- What were the major factors behind the rise of liberal international theory in the early twentieth century and what did the early theorists hope to achieve?

- In what way does the right to national self-determination strengthen the legitimacy of the nation-state idea?

- Why did E.H. Carr describe early liberals as utopians, and was this description fair?

- What are the distinguishing features of classical realist thought?

- What is 'positivism' and in what way does it constitute an operative critique of normative theory?

- How does the idea of 'international society' contribute to our understanding of international relations?

- How could the English School accommodate both realism and liberalism and remain coherent?

- In what ways does neorealism differ from classical realism?

- What is 'pluralist' about neoliberalism and how does pluralism relate to the concept of complex interdependence?

- Is neorealism's parsimony a strength or a weakness?

 *Further Reading*

Angell, Norman (1934), *The Great Illusion*, London: W. Heinemann.

Originally published in 1910, this book provides a critique of nationalist expansionism and arms-racing in early twentieth century Europe. It is an early, influential statement of idealism which argues against the notion that national prosperity depends on a preponderance of military power. A sample of the text is available at http://net.lib.byu.edu/rdh7/wwi/1914m/illusion.html.

Aron, Raymond (2003), *Peace and War: A Theory of International Relations,* New Brunswick, NJ: Transaction Publishers.

Raymond Aron (1905–83) was a French social philosopher who wrote widely on politics (including international politics) and society. In this book he brings a range of insights to the study of IR as well as a distinctive historical approach which eschews the possibility of a 'science' of IR. It is difficult to locate his theoretical approach within any hard and fast tradition of thought—he accepts and rejects aspects of both liberalism and realism. This edition includes a new introduction which discusses the continuing relevance of Aron's thought in a post-Cold War context.

Bellamy, Alex (ed.) (2005), *International Society and its Critics,* Oxford: Oxford University Press.

This is an edited book in which leading scholars consider a range of themes and issues surrounding the notion of 'international society' and the way in which it is theorized. There is a particular focus on the English School and its relevance to the analysis of contemporary issues such as global governance, international law, and terrorism.

15

Schmidt, Brian C. (1998), *The Political Discourse of Anarchy: A Disciplinary History of International Relations,* Albany, NY: SUNY Press.

> Schmidt's book provides a detailed disciplinary history of IR from the mid-nineteenth century to the outbreak of the Second World War. It challenges conventional understandings of the presumed dichotomy between idealism and realism in the early period as well as focusing on how the concepts of sovereignty and anarchy have been used as constituent principles of the discipline. Schmidt also relates historical perspectives to current debates about IR and politics more generally.

  *Web Links*

www.irtheory.com
The International Relations (IR) Theory website is described as an online resource for students, scholars, and other professionals interested in International Relations theory.

www.geocities.com/virtualwarcollege/
Various parts of the Virtual War College site provide a general introduction to both liberalism and realism as traditions of thought in IR.

Visit the **Online Resource** Centre that accompanies this book to access more learning resources at **www.oxfordtextbooks.co.uk/orc/garner/**

15

16 Alternative Approaches to International Relations

Reader's Guide

While liberal and realist theorists of IR probe each other's ideas for faults and weaknesses, both operate within the same paradigm—an international order composed of sovereign states engaging each other under conditions of anarchy. Neither have they challenged capitalism and its implications for the global economy. Apart from Marxism, the main challenges to traditional approaches did not emerge until around the 1970s. They were subsequently given considerable impetus by the end of the Cold War which prompted many scholars to start asking new questions about the world of IR and the assumptions on which traditional theories rested. In addition to the place of Marxism in IR and some important critiques of capitalism and modernization inspired by it, this chapter considers five broad developments—Critical Theory, constructivism, feminism, postmodernism, and postcolonial theory. Aspects of these approaches have been discussed in previous chapters, especially chapter two with respect to Marxism and power, and chapter six with respect to feminism and postmodernism. Here of course the focus is once again on the implications for the study of IR.

Marxism

Although neither Karl Marx (1818–83) nor his close collaborator, Friedrich Engels (1820–95), wrote extensively on international matters, their ideas have had a very significant influence on critical approaches to the field. Over the years, however, numerous competing interpretations and diverging pathways have been generated and some theories, while influenced by Marxist thought, cannot now be classified as strictly Marxist. Here we examine several major strands of Marxist-influenced theory of direct relevance to international politics including dependency theory and world-system theory. Gramscian theory (after its founding theorist, Antonio Gramsci) and Frankfurt School theory, both also influenced by Marxism, have had a significant influence on contemporary Critical Theory in IR which we consider in a separate section. We should also note from the start that virtually all the strands discussed here are variants of 'Western Marxism' which distinguishes the legacy of Marx and Engels from the way it has been theorized in **authoritarian** communist regimes, especially in China and the former USSR. Having said that, some of the early figures in these regimes contributed to important aspects of Marxist ideas in international politics.

Chapter two introduced the theme of power in Marxist theory, explaining ideology, **hegemony,** and the way in which ruling classes maintain control and promote the legitimacy of the capitalist enterprise. The Marxian notion of ideology as 'false consciousness' is especially important in analysing the way in which the interests of any ruling class are presented as somehow natural, inevitable and desirable and therefore compatible with those of subject classes. This is 'false' in the sense that it masks the deeper 'truth' about domination and subordination, and who benefits in the process. Here we should also note the Marxist emphasis on the role of the **bourgeoisie**, generally defined as a merchant and/or propertied class wielding essential economic power and control. In their classic statement of the principles and purposes of communism, Marx and Engels describe their crucial role in the spread of capitalism around the world through the medium of **imperialism** which relates in turn to the contemporary phenomenon of **globalization**. The opening passages of the Communist Manifesto (1848) describe how the 'need of a constantly expanding market for its products chases the bourgeoisie over the entire surface of the globe', nestling, settling, and establishing connections everywhere. The first Russian communist leader, V.I. Lenin (1870–1924), developed a more elaborate critique of imperialism as the highest and final stage of capitalism and its parasitic exploitation of peripheral countries characterized by an increasing gap between rich and poor nations and also leading to wars over control of territory and resources (Lenin, 1986).

The most prominent figures working in this area in the post-Second World War period have been André Gunder Frank and Immanuel Wallerstein. Frank's dependency theory and world system analysis uses a deep historical perspective reaching back over

➜ See chapter two, page 64, for an exploration of Marxism and power.

➜ See chapter two, page 64, for a description of false consciousness.

16

several thousand years, de-centering Europe as the principal agent of historical change in the process. This distinguishes it from most versions of globalization which see Europe and the West more generally as at the centre of virtually all world-transforming dynamics, and resonates with some of the themes of chapter twelve concerning the need to both 'de-centre' and at the same time 'provincialize' Europe as well as to challenge the appropriateness of the Western path to **modernity**.

→ See the discussion on infrapolitics and subaltern studies in chapter twelve, page 286.

Frank's dependency theory is part of a larger critique of modernization and development theories applied initially to Latin America and then to the Third World in general. It explains underdevelopment in poor, peripheral countries in terms of the exploitative legacy of Western imperialism and **colonialism** rather than local cultural factors to do with 'traditionalism'. Independence has scarcely improved matters for many Third World countries because the underlying structures of exploitation remain and many postcolonial indigenous elites have simply colluded with the 'core' states (generally those of the industrialized North) in perpetuating relations of exploitation. A major focus of dependency theory is therefore on core-periphery relations and how these are embedded in the world system (Frank, 1967 and Frank and Gills, 1996).

Photo 16.1

Sweat shop 30 km south of Dhaka employing 280 garment workers including children. Factories such as these fail to comply with the most basic health and safety regulations. Most of their output is for export. 90% of the 1,600,000 garment workers in Bangladesh are employed in similar unregulated textile factories. Overtime is rarely paid. When a factory is working to a delivery deadline workers can work between 70 and 80 hours a week. Average salaries vary between 600–700 takas/month (US$12–14). There is no freedom of association, unions are forbidden, and workers can be sacked without cause.

Source: © Fernando Moleres/Panos Pictures

The world system approach of Wallerstein critiques the totality of exploitative economic and political relations from a sociological as well as historical perspective. He embraces the basic assumptions of dependency theory, but broadens critique by questioning whether the international system really is based on a nation-state model. Wallerstein's concept of *world* system is quite deliberate in not using *international*, for it depicts a capitalist world economy which transcends the nation-state model of separate political and economic units. Further, his world system 'is a *social* system, one that has boundaries, structures, member groups, rules of legitimation, and coherence' (Wallerstein, 1976: 229, emphasis added). In addition, Wallerstein provides a thought-provoking critique of how the very construction of social science forces thinking processes, especially in terms of 'development', along very restricted pathways (Wallerstein, 2001).

Key Points

- The critique of capitalism by Marx and Engels provided a basis for later critiques of traditional IR theories. Marx and Engels were also the first to observe how capitalism is implicated in the development of a global system.

- Dependency theory and world systems analysis draw on Marxist thought in critiquing theories of modernization and development, especially in relation to the Third World and the exploitative structure of the international economic and political system.

Critical Theory

Critical Theory (usually abbreviated and capitalized as CT) refers to a range of social science theorizing which is broadly concerned with critiquing traditional theories of society and politics such as liberalism, realism, and conservatism. It includes, but is not limited to, Marxist theory, although most versions of CT address the adverse impact of capitalism on social life in one way or another. The identification of problems within capitalism, and proposed remedies, however, can differ widely and many of CT's proponents have moved away from the main premises of Marxist theory and its focus on economics and class struggle while retaining a belief in the ethical notion of **emancipation** from oppressive social and material conditions.

The Italian intellectual, Antonio Gramsci (1891–1937), focused on the *naturalization* of power in the creation of hegemony by elites, arguing that ruling classes maintained power and control, even in the absence of constant coercive force, because they made prevailing inequalities seem natural, inevitable, and even right. This highlights the importance of *cultural power* in controlling 'hearts and minds'. It resonates with the Marxist conception of ideology as false consciousness, but focuses more on the consensual nature of support for hegemony. See **Box 16.1**.

Later theorists such as Robert W. Cox have found Gramsci's insights highly pertinent in explaining the *hegemony of theories and ideas* in the international sphere.

16

Short Biography   Box 16.1
Antonio Gramsci

Antonio Gramsci (1891–1937) was a political theorist and activist, at one time leading the Italian Communist Party. He was deeply opposed to fascism and was imprisoned under Mussolini's regime after the latter's rise to power. His notes and essays were published posthumously as *Prison Notebooks*. While he accepted Marx's analysis of capitalism and the idea that struggle between the ruling class and the subordinate working class was the driving force of society, Gramsci rejected the materialist basis of Marxist theory, including the notion of an 'objective reality' that could be described 'scientifically'. He argued instead that 'reality' does not exist independently of human interest, purpose or interpretation. He further proposed that 'One of the commonest totems is the belief about everything that exists, that it is "natural" that it should exist, that it could not do otherwise than exist . . .' (excerpted from 'The Modern Prince: Conceptions of the World and Practical Stances'), thus highlighting the 'naturalization' of power in the creation of hegemony by elites. In summary, Gramscian thought combines coercion and consent in a theory of hegemony to explain why the dominated (the masses) often accept domination by an elite, as well as the *values* of that elite, as part of the natural order of things. (Gramsci, 1967)

This differs from conceptions of hegemony which focus only on material (mainly economic and military) capabilities. Cox is well-known for declaring that 'theory is always *for* some one, and *for* some purpose' (Cox 1981: 128). Put another way, theories are never neutral in the selection and interpretation of the facts around us—they are reflections of subjective values and interests and therefore tend strongly to support those values and interests. It follows that facts and values do not exist independently of each other, so the idea that any theory can be 'value-free', or that knowledge can be totally objective, is insupportable.

Realism, Cox suggests, is an *ideology of the status quo*. It supports the existing international order and therefore the interests of those who prosper under it. Furthermore, by presenting it as *natural*, the existing order is perceived as inevitable and unchanging in its essentials. Any difficulties that arise within the order are seen as problems to be solved within the parameters *of* that order. The order itself does not come under challenge. Cox and other Critical Theorists insist, however, that no order is 'natural' or immune from change. All political orders, from that of the smallest community to the world at large, are humanly constructed and can in principle be reconstructed in a more just and equitable manner. CT aims to provide the intellectual framework for emancipation from unfair and unjust social, political, and economic arrangements that benefit the few at the expense of the many. To the extent that **liberalism** participates in the perpetuation of injustices and effectively justifies inequalities, especially through capitalism, it is subject to a similar critique.

16

The Frankfurt School of the 1920s and 1930s, which included figures such as Theodor Adorno, Herbert Marcuse, and Max Horkheimer, shared with Gramsci a concern for cultural and social factors, therefore placing less emphasis on economics. In recent years, Jürgen Habermas has continued the Frankfurt School's tradition of critical enquiry through a complex of ideas and arguments which analyse the problems of capitalism through new forms of social theory. Habermas's theory of communicative action holds that, under the right conditions, a consensus about 'truth' may be reached. This relies on an **epistemology** which sees knowledge about the social world emerging through a process of continuous dialogue. Because social sciences cannot proceed as the natural sciences do, they must instead see all action from the perspective of the actors involved while maintaining critiques of any and all perspectives on both empirical and normative grounds (see Smith, 1996: 27–8). To maintain that there is some neutral ground or unassailable foundation from which critique can proceed, clearly implies an eternal bedrock for ethics that is valid for all times and all places regardless of changing beliefs, values, and so on. Habermas rejects the notion of objective ethical truths that exist independently of any social world. They are made *within* a social world, but one which is wide enough to embrace everyone. This provides the basis for universally valid ethics and so Habermas's normative theory is clearly cosmopolitan in character.

Contemporary writers such as Andrew Linklater work in the CT tradition and among his projects is the extension of Habermas's emancipatory concerns to the sphere of international politics, especially with respect to how state boundaries tend to denote the limits of ethical concerns. This leads once more into the realm of **normative analysis** which, in recent years, has sought to grapple with a wide range of contemporary ethical concerns from the epistemological basis of human rights to the grounds for practical intervention in the internal affairs of sovereign states.

The most creative Critical Theories go beyond mere critique of existing theories and practices and put forward alternative visions of how the world *could* be (and *should* be). Linklater's ideas about transformative potentials for the way in which political communities are conceived and structured, for example, sets out such a vision. Although modernity has a dark side, he argues that it still carries within it the seeds of the original aims of the **Enlightenment** which are, in the final analysis, about the emancipation of people from a range of constraints, prejudices, and exploitative practices; and while modernity gave us the Westphalian state system, the 'unfinished project of modernity' envisages a post-Westphalian world in which states as political communities no longer operate in the service of inclusion and exclusion. This transformation, he suggests, seems most likely to occur in the very region which gave rise to that system in the first place and which has since produced the European Union (EU), itself a project with considerable normative potential. Habermas, too, sees very similar possibilities in the European project. See **Box 16.2**.

CT emphasizes very clearly the 'constructed' character of the social/political world, and indeed its very *reality*. It is not, however, the only body of thought in IR to have taken up the idea of the essentially constructed nature of social reality There is now a more general school of in IR which has become increasingly influential in recent years and which we consider next.

Key Quotes   Box 16.2
Linklater and Habermas on the Transformation of Political
Community

'Alternative means of organising human beings . . . seem most likely to appear in Western Europe . . . where a lasting balance between the claims of the nation and the species
may yet come to be struck. . . . Whether Europe will be the first international region which
is permanently transformed by peace rather than by war . . . is unclear. What is clear is
that it is improbable that changes in the structure of European international society will
be quickly emulated across the world as a whole. . . . Promoting the ideal of a universal
communication community in which insiders and outsiders recognize one another as
moral equals is essential where the nature of political community has become problem-
atical in the lives of its own members.'   (Linklater, 1998: 218–19)

'It is undisputed that there can be no Europe-wide democratic will-formation capable
of enacting and legitimating positively coordinated and effective redistributive policies
without an expanded basis of solidarity . . . Skeptics doubt whether this can happen,
arguing that there is no such thing as a European "people" who could constitute a
European state . . . On the other hand, peoples emerge only with the constitutions of
their states. Democracy itself is a legally mediated form of political integration. It is a form
that depends, to be sure, on a political culture shared by all citizens. But if we consider
the process by which European states of the nineteenth century gradually *created*
national consciousness and civic solidarity—the earliest modern form of collective
identity—with the help of national historiography, mass communications, and military
duty, there is no cause for defeatism. If this artificial form of "solidarity among strangers"
owes its existence to a historically influential abstraction . . . why should this learning
process not continue on, beyond national borders?'   (Habermas, 2003: 97–8)

Key Points

- CT provides an intellectual and normative framework promoting a project of emancipation from social, political and economic arrangements that benefit the few at the
  expense of the many through hegemonic control in a system of coercion and consent.

- CT emphasizes that all political, economic, and cultural orders are humanly *constructed*
  rather than dictated by nature. Once recognized, relations of domination and subordination can be challenged at their foundations rather than simply taken for granted as the
  way things are.

- Cosmopolitan elements of CT transcend nation-state barriers to produce broader, more
  inclusive notions of political community.

Constructivism

➡ See chapter
sixteen, page 372,
for a discussion of
constructivism.

It has been claimed that, unlike neorealism and neoliberalism, constructivist IR has no
direct antecedents in traditional theories of international relations, although it is

conceded that English School approaches provide useful insights for the contemporary constructivist project (Ruggie, 1998: 11). There is, however, a significant tradition of European social theory, developed in earlier periods by classical sociologists such as Emile Durkheim, Max Weber, and Karl Mannheim, from which IR constructivists have drawn. In the latter part of the twentieth century Berger and Luckman's influential work, *The Social Construction of Reality* (1966), argued that social order (embodying beliefs, norms, values, interests, rules, institutions, and so on) is an ongoing human production. As with CT, its *ontological status*—its very being or existence—is derived not from nature (i.e., biological data) but from human activity alone. To understand how social orders are produced, one's analysis must produce some theory of institutionalization incorporating a process of habitualization. This refers to social actions that come to be practised routinely and, with repetition over time, solidify into a taken-for-granted construct which we call an **institution** (59–61). If we consider the world of international relations as we know it through the lens of social constructivist theory we can see the extent to which it really is a 'world of our making'.

The premises of **social constructivism** in IR challenge the way in which both neo-realism and neoliberalism take the essential components (states) and the character of the international system (anarchic) for granted. Some constructivists are especially critical of the tendency in traditional theories to focus largely on *material* forces (e.g. guns and bombs), arguing that *ideational* forces are equally important. The latter are formed through social interaction and consist of norms, values, rules and symbols that influence how people act in the world. Furthermore, it is within the realm of ideas that *meaning* is created, including the meaning of material objects. Alexander Wendt points out, for example, that a gun in the hands of an enemy is a very different thing from the same object in the hands of an ally, adding that 'enmity is a social, not material, relation' (Wendt, 1996: 50).

Wendt's constructivism does not deny the importance of material force. Rather, it establishes the important connection between material *and* ideational forces providing a better understanding of how 'social facts' are produced. Thus fundamental institutions, such as states and their sovereign properties, are social rather then material facts constructed at an *intersubjective* level by agents (us!). **Anarchy** or **sovereignty**—or any other concept invented by humans—has no existence or meaning outside of those who think and believe in them. Thus anarchy is simply 'what states make of it' (Wendt, 1992: 391–425). The things we take for granted as the 'reality' of the world around us possess the same character—the market, the government, the EU, the UN, the stock exchange, and so on. One cannot see, feel, hear, smell, taste, or choke on any of these 'things' precisely because they are ideational, not material. When these ideational constructs begin to be treated as if they were actual 'things', this is called *reification*.

All this casts a different light on the relationship between *agents* and *structures* (people and institutions). This was discussed in chapter seven in terms of **structuration**, with many constructivists emphasizing that agents and structures are *mutually constituted*. Put another way, humans are born into an existing world—one which has

➜ See chapter seven, page 162, for a description of structuration.

both material and ideational aspects—and are shaped by that world as they grow and mature and develop their own ideational perspectives. Existing structures, which always already embody a set of norms and values, shape each emerging generation of agents. But agents can also change existing structures. After all, they were put in place by previous generations rather than set in concrete by nature and can in principle be remade or overthrown altogether provided there is a sufficient level of *norm change* among relevant actors. One constructivist, whose insights derive from a close study of post-war Japan, emphasizes the fact that institutional change is often very slow because of how deeply institutionalized certain norms can become. Thus, Peter J. Katzenstein (1996) argues that while norms are contested and contingent, they do not change constantly. He says that actors generally attribute deeper meanings to the historical battles that define collective identities than to the more transient conflicts which characterize everyday politics. Moreover, the fact that norms become entrenched through institutionalization—including authoritative legal institutions—limits the range of choice at any particular time. 'History and institutions thus give norms both importance and endurance' (3).

We should note that constructivism, like other bodies of theory, comes in different forms. Some versions, such as Wendt's, tend towards *rationalism* and do not move too far away from the dominant modes of American social science scholarship which characterize both realist and liberal approaches. For a theory to be 'rationalist' means that it subscribes to an underlying rationality which directs human behaviour towards particular ends and, further, assumes that knowledge of such matters can be obtained via empirical investigations. This is contrasted with modes of *reflectivist* scholarship, sometimes called post-positivist or interpretive, which reject the scientistic/empirical basis of rationalist approaches, thereby challenging the status of the knowledge they claim to produce (Smith, 2000: 374–402). Some versions of constructivism argue that it occupies a middle ground between rationalist approaches and reflectivist approaches (mainly postmodernist, poststructuralist, and critical), and creates new areas for both theoretical and empirical investigation (Adler, 1997: 319–63). However defined or located, constructivism has become an increasingly popular mode of IR scholarship for those seeking more complex, socially oriented accounts of the contemporary world.

Feminism and Gender Theory

Feminism in IR is no singular body of theory, but rather incorporates a range of approaches to the problem of **patriarchy** including liberal, socialist, critical, constructivist, postcolonial, and postmodern variants. Feminism therefore draws from, interacts with, contributes to and often critiques, other schools of theory. Thus 'liberal feminists', for example, will apply certain insights of liberal theory—including the essential equality of all individuals—to critique the way in which conventional liberal theory has ignored, or indeed supported, patriarchal structures of authority. Feminism is a principal strand of the broader field of gender theory which is concerned with both femininities and masculinities.

Because the study of gender issues in IR has been carried out largely by feminist scholars it has been concerned with how women have been depicted or, more often than not, written out of the script of international politics. Put another way, the sphere of the international—characterized largely by the struggle for power in an anarchical world—has often been depicted in such masculinist terms that women seem to disappear as active agents. They have been essentially passive, simply supporting men in their various roles as soldiers and statesmen. The same applies to studies of the global economy with trade and commerce depicted largely as the preserve of men. Where women became prominent in any sphere, it was always an exception to the rule.

Historically, feminist scholars began to make an impact in political studies in the 1960s and 1970s but it was not until the late 1980s that they came to question the apparent absence of women in *international* politics and economics and to highlight how traditional discourses of IR, because they were founded on masculinist assumptions, excluded women as participants. That this has been made to appear 'normal' or 'natural'—even to many women themselves—has constituted a major epistemological and ontological problem, exemplifying just why the insights provided by critical social theory are so important. Many feminists have therefore adopted critical and postpositivist approaches, for as much as any group that finds itself marginalized by a dominant mainstream, feminists have interrogated the extent to which 'knowledge' itself is often constructed to suit male interests.

As suggested above, feminism comes in various forms and even within feminist IR, there are different strands. How to characterize these is no simple matter. Here we consider two general typologies, the first setting out three broad overlapping forms reflecting certain theoretical/methodological orientations:

→ See the discussion in chapter six, page 140, on feminism.

1. *Empirical feminism* focuses on correcting the denial or misrepresentation of women as active agents in the international sphere due to such mistaken assumptions as: women are either absent from or irrelevant to international processes and activities; and/or male experiences count for both sexes.

2. *Analytical feminism* addresses gender biases more directly by highlighting the asymmetrical and socially constructed concepts of masculinity and femininity evident in IR's traditional theoretical frameworks which favour masculine interpretative practices.

3. *Normative feminism* incorporates reflection on IR theorizing and feminist concerns within a broader, explicitly normative agenda for global change. For example, normative feminism not only questions how gender hierarchies are

16

reproduced in IR theories but also how they serve to naturalize other forms of power (True, 2005: 216–29).

A different typology has been devised by two other feminist scholars which follows more closely the labels generally applied to the different IR theories and are summarized as follows:

1. *Liberal feminism* highlights the subordination of women in world politics but does not challenge the premises of traditional IR. It is similar to empirical feminism in that it investigates particular problems—say, of refugee women, gendered income inequalities, trafficking of women, rape in war, and so on— usually within a positivist framework. Liberal feminism seeks equality of women in a man's world rather than questioning the foundations of that world.

2. *Critical feminism* builds explicitly on Critical Theory, subjecting relations of domination and subordination, the play of power in world politics, and the relationship between material and ideational factors to scrutiny through a gender-sensitive lens. As a theory seeking action and not just interpretation, it promotes a project of emancipation which takes more explicit account of women's subordination.

3. *Feminist constructivism* criss-crosses the terrain of constructivist IR. Some concede much methodological ground to **positivism**, in line with the predominant mode of American constructivism. Others lean towards a postpositivist questioning of the foundations of knowledge. Common themes in feminist constructivism are attention to ideational forces and the essentially social nature of the international sphere.

4. *Feminist poststructuralism*, as with poststructuralism (or postmodernism) generally, highlights the construction of meaning through language and, in particular, the relationship between knowledge and power and the extent to which these are reflected in dichotomies or oppositions. Feminist poststructuralism critiques the way in which dichotomies such as strong/weak, rational/emotional, and public/ private, not to mention masculinity/femininity, have served to empower men at the expense of women.

5. *Postcolonial feminism* often goes hand in hand with feminist poststructuralism in exposing certain relations of domination and subordination, but focuses critique on how these relations were established through imperialism and colonialism and persist through to the present period. Postcolonial feminists, however, often critique the way in which Western feminists construct knowledge about non-Western women and also tend to treat 'women' as a universal and homogeneous category regardless of differences in culture, social class, race, and geographical location.

(Tickner and Sjoberg, 2007: 188–92.)

We next consider feminism and gender in relation to traditional IR's central concern—war—which is one of the most conspicuously gendered activities of all. Not only have great matters of state such as war been almost the sole preserve of males, but active participation has been historically confined largely to male warriors. A recent review of feminist contributions to security studies sees feminist IR as having made several key contributions. Through questioning the supposed irrelevance of women in international security and exposing the workings of gender and power in international relations, women's experiences are now taken more seriously and gender-based exclusion from decision-making roles are at least recognized. Feminist security theory has also questioned the extent to which women are actually 'secured' by the protective mantle of the state in both war *and* peace. At the same time, discourses which link women unreflectively with peace are now more likely to be balanced by recognition of the fact that women have long participated in wars, if not as warriors then at least in vital supportive roles.

The attention to gender issues forced by feminists has also helped to variegate the concept of masculinity itself (Blanchard, 2003: 1290). Others have pointed out that the 'rugged male warrior' type, often constructed as an ideal, is a stereotype which many 'real' men do not actually fit (Connell cited in Tickner, 1992: 6). More recently, Connell has argued that we need also to recognize the power relations between different kinds of masculinity 'constructed through practices that exclude and include, that intimidate, exploit, and so on. There is a gender politics within masculinity' (Connell, 2005: 37). Another scholar has investigated the male soldier's gendered construction of his own identity as masculine in relation to his ability to function as a combatant. Such constructions might explain not only the almost complete exclusion of women from warrior ranks (until recently, and then only in some armies) but also the way in which masculinity frequently depends on an 'other' constructed as feminine (and therefore opposite). It is argued further that war does not come 'naturally' to men. Rather, warriors need to be socialized and trained to make them fight effectively. Gender identity thereby 'becomes a tool with which societies induce men to fight' (Goldstein, 2001: 251–2). This tactic is also evident in the modern construction of masculinity in relation to nationalism which is linked very closely with war as well as with the manipulation of gender roles (see Mosse, 1996).

A particular aspect of war which is often highly gendered is the treatment of 'enemy' civilians. Nowhere was this illustrated more clearly than in the case of the war in Bosnia from 1992 to 1995 which saw rape used as a specific tactic of war. Men and boys were subject to another kind of treatment which brought into currency the term **ethnic cleansing**. See **Box 16.3**.

Key Points

- Feminism and gender theory provide a very different lens on the world of IR to those of traditional theories, pushing the boundaries of what is relevant to IR ever wider to incorporate more critical perspectives relevant to every aspect of the field.

16

Case Study Box 16.3
Gender and Genocide in the Bosnian War, 1992–5

With the end of the Cold War, the formerly communist Federal Republic of Yugoslavia began to disintegrate, generating bitter conflict. The province of Bosnia–Herzegovina, characterized by a multiethnic population of Catholic Croats, Orthodox Serbs, and Bosniak Muslims who had lived in relative harmony for years, became the scene of the most gruesome episodes after a referendum for independence in 1992. Some Bosnian Serbs (a minority within the province) dissented and were supported by nationalists in Serbia itself, including the arch-nationalist Serb leader, Slobodan Milošević, who backed Bosnian Serb militia.

The war that ensued saw several notorious episodes of 'ethnic cleansing' now regarded as acts of **genocide**. The most serious occurred in Srebrenica in July 1995 when an estimated 8,000 Bosniak Muslim men and boys were slaughtered by units of the Army of Republika Srpska (VRS). The subsequent trial of one Serb leader, Radislav Krstić, produced a statement in the Appeals Chamber Judgment following his case before the International Criminal Tribunal for the former Yugoslavia or ICTY, which summed up the character of the incident:

By seeking to eliminate a part of the Bosnian Muslims, the Bosnian Serb forces committed genocide. They targeted for extinction the forty thousand Bosnian Muslims living in Srebrenica, a group which was emblematic of the Bosnian Muslims in general. They stripped all the male Muslim prisoners, military and civilian, elderly and young, of their personal belongings and identification, and deliberately and methodically killed them solely on the basis of their identity. The Bosnian Serb forces were aware, when they embarked on this genocidal venture, that the harm they caused would continue to plague the Bosnian Muslims. The Appeals Chamber states unequivocally that the law condemns, in appropriate terms, the deep and lasting injury inflicted, and calls the massacre at Srebrenica by its proper name: genocide . . .   (ICTY, 2004)

Female civilians among the Bosniak Muslims and some other groups were subjected to a different kind of treatment. From an early stage, accounts emerged of women being raped as part of a systematic tactical pattern which included the phenomenon of rape camps where women were subjected to multiple rape, often with the intention of impregnating them with 'Serb' babies. This came to be seen as part of the wider pattern of genocide. In 1995, a charge of rape was brought in the ICTY, the first time ever that a sexual assault case had been prosecuted as a war crime by itself, and not as part of a larger case. The estimates of the number of women raped during the war run as high as 50,000.

The slaughter of men and boys on the one hand, and the systematic rape of women on the other, during this war, illustrate gendered aspects of warfare resulting in the most extreme forms of group violence. In recent years, rape in war (which can also be perpetrated against men as an attack on their masculinity, although it is much less common) has achieved much greater prominence as an issue in the narration of war histories generally.

16

- While sometimes regarded as simply concerned with women's issues, gender theory in IR is very much concerned with various forms of masculinity and femininity and the way in which they are deployed in both war and peace.

Postmodernism/Poststructuralism

Postmodernism names perhaps the most complex of theoretical fields in the human sciences and is manifest in a confusing array of ideas that challenge, in one way or another, the assumptions of modernity. In IR, some prefer to describe their approach as poststructuralist. This term relates to a philosophical movement known as structuralism, influential in linguistic and literary theory. *Post*structuralism emphasizes the linguistic aspects of meaning and interpretation which produce knowledges (note the plural) while rejecting the tendency to *essentialize* things—like 'masculinity' and 'femininity'—in opposition to each other as well as to present *totalized* forms of knowledge (schemes of thought which bring complex phenomena under a single overarching explanation such as 'the natural order of things'). For convenience and at the risk of oversimplification, we use the term 'postmodernism'.

→ See chapter six, page 138, for a discussion of postmodernism.

While sharing some important basic assumptions with CT and constructivism, postmodernism in IR is more radical in its epistemology, rejecting the idea that we can ever have certain grounds for knowledge. Postmodernism therefore rejects more thoroughly the essentially *modernist* assumption that we can describe the world in rational, objective terms. The best we can hope for are fleeting 'moments of clarity' which might allow us to grasp transient truths, but never final, incontestable Truths.

Postmodernism's greatest strength lies in its insights into the relationship between power and knowledge and its capacity for the critique of existing institutions, practices, and ideas. Its weakness lies in its inability to go much beyond critique and to map out a programme for positive social and political change. Some would say that, taken to its logical conclusion, postmodernism simply ends in absolute relativism, nihilism and, ultimately, incoherence. For if 'there is no truth' the very claim that this is so cannot itself be true. As a further consequence of its relativism—the notion that no 'standard' can be regarded as superior to any other, because there is no objective way of adjudicating between them—it also stands accused of creating a pernicious moral vacuum in which good and evil may be regarded simply as competing narratives.

Nonetheless, postmodern strategies provide valuable insights into the *contingent* status of knowledge and the uses to which it is put in all spheres of politics. Armed with the insight that knowledge is very often a function of power, and that such power can be used to construct **metanarratives** (understood as embodying comprehensive accounts of history, experience, and knowledge) of enormous importance, we can see how this might operate in concrete contexts. The 'war on terror', although not as 'grand' a narrative as an entire theory of history, is a good example. See **Box 16.4**.

A principle figure in the rise of postmodern thought was the French philosopher, Michel Foucault (1926–84), who pioneered a 'genealogical' form of analysis. This interrogates truth claims posing as objective knowledge about the world while concealing the machinations of power. Foucault argued that each society possesses its own 'regime of truth' that exists as a set of *discourses* and which is imposed on, and generally accepted by, society at large. Foucault further proposed that the human sciences have themselves played a leading role in this concealment, lending a mantle of authority to all kinds of knowledge claims which, in the end, can be exposed as serving power (Foucault, 1980: 13).

Case Study Box 16.4
Positioning Iraq in the Metanarrative of the War on Terror

The 'war on terror' was initiated by the attacks of 11 September 2001 ('9/11') on landmark targets in New York and Washington DC. Two warzones are currently occupied by the USA and allies—Afghanistan and Iraq—as part of the war on terror. Afghanistan was the base for the leader of the group responsible for planning and carrying out the 9/11 attacks. How did Iraq come to be part of the war on terror?

The following are well established:

1. Al Qaeda operatives, most of whom were Saudi nationals (none were Iraqi) were responsible for the 9/11 attacks in the USA in 2000. Their leader, Osama bin Laden (also a Saudi national) was based in Afghanistan which was governed by the Taliban.

2. Saddam Hussein, erstwhile president of Iraq, had no connection with Afghanistan, Al Qaeda, or the Taliban. While hostile to the USA (although previously an ally), he was a secularist and actually repressed religious fundamentalism in Iraq.

3. No weapons of mass destruction were found in Iraq.

4. The presence of terrorists in Iraq following the US-led invasion (as evidenced by a relentless campaign of suicide bombing by various factions) is due almost solely to the war on terror itself.

Despite the lack of evidence linking Iraq to the 9/11 attacks, a widespread belief developed, at least among the US public, that Iraq, along with Afghanistan, was the source of the 9/11 attacks. A *Washington Post* poll taken almost two years after the attacks, and around six months after the invasion of Iraq, found that about 70 per cent of Americans believed there was a link between 9/11 and Iraq. How did that link get there? One answer is provided in the same newspaper report which quotes Bush on establishing the link without explicitly telling falsehoods.

If the world fails to confront the threat posed by the Iraqi regime, refusing to use force, even as a last resort, free nations would assume immense and unacceptable risks. The attacks of September the 11th, 2001, showed what the enemies of America did with four airplanes. We will not wait to see what terrorists or terrorist states could do with weapons of mass destruction. (March 2003)

The battle of Iraq is one victory in a war on terror that began on September the 11, 2001 . . . The liberation of Iraq is a crucial advance in the campaign against terror. We've removed an ally of al Qaeda, and cut off a source of terrorist funding. . . . No terrorist network will gain weapons of mass destruction from the Iraqi regime, because the regime is no more . . . We have not forgotten the victims of September the 11th . . . . (May 2003, after declaring major combat in Iraq at an end; 'Hussein Link to 9/11 Lingers in Many Minds' (Milbank and Deane, 2003: A1))

This suggests that the power of the presidential office in the USA, supported by a largely conservative and uncritical media, succeeded in purveying a particular *metanarrative* about terrorism which was used to justify the war in Iraq despite the lack of evidence (either at the time or subsequently).

In contrast, support for the war in the UK has always been weaker although former Prime Minister Tony Blair used similar rhetoric on many occasions. This may be attributed to greater scepticism about the link with 9/11, a more critical press, a more critical attitude towards political leaders generally nurtured by a stronger system of government and opposition, and a less nationalistic political world view among the public at large. From a postmodern perspective, we might conclude that the power/knowledge nexus, which supports successful metanarratives, is not as strong in the UK as it is in the USA.

This resonates with Gramscian thought but differs in its refusal to illuminate an alternative path for social life, for this would simply end in another 'regime of truth' serving particular interests. Therefore, while proponents of CT have a distinct normative project in making the world a better place, it is difficult for a radical postmodernist to entertain such ambitions. Postmodernism does raise awareness of the extent to which knowledge serves power and interests and how the human sciences, which themselves exist as a set of interlocking discourses, are often deeply implicated in the production of power/knowledge. We must keep in mind, however, that power as such is not necessarily a 'bad' thing. As pointed out in chapter two, it can also be used for the 'good'.

➡ See the discussion in chapter two, page 53, on 'Is power a good thing?'

In summary, postmodern or poststructuralist analyses of international politics have interrogated various forms of the power/knowledge nexus, generally in a negative sense, as well as the grand narratives and discourses which purport to explain the nature and dynamics of the international sphere. Sovereignty, **statecraft**, anarchy, warfare, borders, identities and interests, the interpretation of history, the idea of history itself—are all subject to their critical gaze. Despite frequent complaints about the impenetrable prose characterizing much postmodern writing, postmodernism has nonetheless gained a foothold in the study of IR, highlighting the extent to which 'reality' exists not as a concrete, unalterable state of affairs 'out there', but resides ultimately in our mental structures.

16

Photo 16.2

US Marines pull down the statue of Saddam Hussein in the centre of Baghdad, 9 April 2003.

Source: Getty Images

Key Points

- Postmodernism/poststructuralism in IR shares some common ground with CT and constructivism in IR but has a much more radical epistemology derived from its rejection of modernist assumptions about knowledge.

- A common criticism is that its radical relativism deprives moral arguments in politics, or any other sphere, of any foundation and permits no adjudication between different standards.

- Despite these criticisms, postmodernism/poststructuralism in IR is valuable in showing just how tenuous truths are, including those embedded in metanarratives.

Postcolonial Theory

'Postcolonialism' is an interdisciplinary enterprise entailing a set of critical theoretical approaches to the direct and indirect effects of colonization on subject people. It is not identical with 'subaltern studies' discussed in chapter twelve, although the latter may be regarded as one specific manifestation of postcolonial theory. An important figure in the development of postcolonial thought was Edward Said (1935–2003), a professor of comparative literature whose critical work on 'Orientalism' argued that Europeans— especially the English and French but also the Germans, Russians, Spanish, Portuguese, Italians, and Swiss—had long treated the Orient as its major 'cultural contestant'. Thus Europeans defined *themselves* against, or in contrast with, the people of the Orient. But for Said, Orientalism is more than just a style of thought; it is an *activity* dedicated to the production and dissemination of knowledge *about* the Orient and thereby a means of exercising authority over it. In developing his ideas, Said drew on Gramscian ideas about hegemony as well as Foucauldian insights into the power/ knowledge nexus, which together inform his conception of Orientalism as a hegemonic discourse. Although Said's Orient consisted largely of the Middle East, his ideas have been generalized so that 'Orientalism' is used to designate almost any construction of non-European 'Others' by Europeans—or any members of 'the West' for that matter.

Within IR, postcolonialism is the medium through which traditional IR theory, along with other critical approaches, is exposed as largely Eurocentric, the implication being that it not only provides a very partial view of the wider reality of the world, but is a vital aid in controlling it. 'As a social practice, IR constitutes a space in which certain understandings of the world dominate others, specific interests are privileged over others, and practices of power and domination acquire a normalized form' (Tickner, 2003: 300).

➔ See chapter twelve, page 286, for a discussion of subaltern studies.

16

Another postcolonial critique says that traditional IR possesses a 'wilful arrogance' in its basic assumptions about the **state of nature**, anarchy, and **power politics**. The authors attack the hybrid beast, 'realism-liberalism', in particular, for its production of 'abstract, ahistorical conceptions of the state, the market, and the individual' which are in fact bound by particular cultural expressions that are essentially 'Western, white, male' (Agathangelou and Ling, 2004: 24–5); but the critique of Western IR theory extends to many Western feminist approaches as well. These stand accused of seeing the problems of women all over the world only through the eyes of a Western female self. Most versions of Marxism, Critical Theory, postmodernism, and constructivism are similarly tainted with a thorough-going Eurocentrism. Postmodernism, however, is generally regarded as anti-Eurocentric, even though it is also said to rely, along with the other critical approaches, on 'Western intellectual traditions, concepts and methods' (28).

Agathangelou and Ling go on to propose a different approach, 'worldism', which claims to be free of the taint of ethnocentric, ahistoric modes of theorizing. It embraces five 'epistemological commitments': intersubjectivity, **agency**, identity, critical syncretic engagement, and accountability (42). Their article ends on an idealist note (although the authors do not use this term); but they do quite clearly express a desire to make the world a better place, or rather to make the different worlds that people experience into better places. 'Worldism' therefore produces a pluralistic version of **idealism** in world politics based on the logic of a particular critique of existing IR theory and practice.

Another approach, this time engaging security studies in particular, is taken by Barkawi and Laffey (2006). Like the others, they take as their point of departure the 'Eurocentric' character of traditional security studies and IR more generally. They go on to argue that traditional IR's concerns with 'great power conflict' simply cannot deal with problems of the contemporary period when threats take a very different form. Al Qaeda, they point out, is neither a state nor a great power; it is a transnational network and, more import-antly, an idea around which resistance is organized globally and locally. Further, because traditional IR 'derives its core categories and assumptions about world politics from a particular understanding of European experience' this leads to 'a distorted analysis of Europe and its place in world politics'. If we are to understand security—and other—relations, we must acknowledge 'the mutual constitution of European and the non-European world and their joint role in making history' (Barkawi and Laffey, 2006: 330).

Let us now consider the tendency in postcolonial critiques of IR to invest in the very categories of world politics that they want to reject This requires casting postcolonial critiques as belonging to a broader set of takes on world politics which go by the name of 'culturalist approaches'. This is because they tend to invoke concepts of the local and the particular against a concept of the universal and the abstract. This automatically sets up a **dichotomy**. We would argue that there is a series of powerful dichotomies that go with this. One of the most pernicious is in fact the West/non-West divide. Many postcolonial critics of IR theory would agree; but what some fail to see is that their own critiques usually require that very same dichotomy, although often in an inverted form so that the non-West is romanticized while the West tends to be demonized. There is certainly plenty in this entity called 'the West' that deserves the most trenchant critiques, including the so-called war on terror in Iraq; but if we buy into the West/non-West dichotomy too uncritically, we may risk oversimplifying problems and their possible solutions (Lawson, 2006).

Conclusion

A study of IR theory shows that whenever we think about the world around us, we do so through a certain set of assumptions about the reality of that world. Different theorists obviously see the world in different ways and will interpret facts accordingly. This highlights the point that facts do not simply speak for themselves. Certainly, the different theoretical approaches reviewed in this chapter, and in the last, often make them speak in very different ways. It follows that the study of international politics cannot be taken simply as a task requiring the unproblematic accumulation and arrangements of the facts that we know (or think we know) about the world. A constructivist would be quick to point out that different theorists see the world in different ways because each has arranged and interpreted the facts about the world in a different way. Similarly, we should not necessarily regard theory as an 'abstraction' from reality but as the means by which it is actually created. We might then ask whether each theory or way of seeing the world is as good as the next, or whether some are better than others. Rushing to endorse any one theory as the 'right' one is scarcely advisable for students in an early stage of their programme. The important thing is to give each of them serious attention and to allow one's existing beliefs to be challenged.

Finally, we might ask whether, if theory 'creates' the world, then the theories reviewed here can be seen as creating it from a largely 'Western' perspective, for virtually all of them are 'Western' in origin and orientation. It can scarcely be denied that IR theories do describe (as well as criticize) an international system and set of practices created in Europe and effectively globalized via processes of colonization and decolonization. Indeed, the theories are themselves products of that very same system. As we have seen, this is something that the development of postcolonial theory within IR is beginning to challenge. However, if we examine 'Western civilization' (if there really is such a 'thing') in detail, we find that it is the result of so many historical and cultural influences, many of which travelled from East Asia and the Pacific, India, the Middle East and Africa as well as the Americas, that it is difficult to call it an entirely European project anyway. But as the discipline of IR and the way in which it is theorized continues to develop and change, and as centres of power themselves shift and change around the world, it will inevitably be enriched by insights from an ever wider academic community and set of perspectives.

16

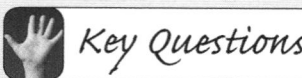 *Key Questions*

- How has Marxism impacted on theoretical development in IR?
- What are the main elements of Gramsci's notion of hegemony?
- How does the idea of 'emancipation' contribute to the critical theorization of IR?
- What is meant by 'normative theory'?
- What do constructivists mean when they speak of IR as 'social theory'?
- How do 'agents' and 'structures', and 'material' and 'ideational' factors, interact in constructivist theory?
- In what ways do the various feminist perspectives broaden the field of IR theory?
- What does a 'gender lens' expose in the construction of masculinity and femininity in IR?
- What is the relationship between power and knowledge in postmodern approaches to IR?
- Do postcolonial theories of IR really escape the West/non-West dichotomy, or do they simply reinforce it?
- Is IR theory thoroughly ethnocentric?

 Further Reading

Acharya, Amitav and Barry Buzan (eds) (2007), *Why Is There No Non-Western ITR Theory?*, Special issue of *International Relations of the Asia-Pacific,* 11(3): 287–312.

> The title of this collection of articles suggests that part of the problem with the ethnocentricity of IR theory is the lack of alternative approaches from outside 'the West'. It explores various reasons for this and speculates about future developments, using material mainly from the Asia-Pacific region.

Jarvis, D.S.L. (2000), *International Relations and the Challenge of Postmodernism: Defending the Discipline,* Columbia, SC: University of South Carolina Press.

> This book provides a readable, detailed account of the rise of postmodernism in IR, its critique of modernity, and its impact on the discipline. It makes a concerted effort to provide a 'manual' for understanding and making transparent just what the epistemological and ontological positions adopted by postmodernists are.

Jones, Branwen Gruffydd (ed.) (2006), *Decolonizing International Relations,* Lanham, MD: Rowman & Littlefield.

> The introduction argues that IR must develop greater self-awareness of its own origins, how it has been implicated in imperialism, and the problems that Eurocentrism poses for understanding the power/knowledge nexus.

Fierke, Karin M. and Knud Erik Jørgensen (eds) (2001), *Constructing International Relations: The Next Generation,* New York: M.E. Sharpe.

> The contributions to this book place the constructivist approach to IR in the wider context of social sciences around the world, thus introducing interdisciplinary perspectives and extending the analysis beyond the world of European scholarship.

16

Sylvester, Christine (2002), *Feminist International Relations: An Unfinished Journey,* Cambridge: Cambridge University Press.

> This book provides a personal and historical approach to feminism's 'journey' in IR and the difficulties encountered in giving gender relations a proper profile in the field. It touches on a range of related issues as well including, for example, elements of postcolonial theory not found in conventional scholarship.

 ## Web Links

www.marxists.org/archive/marx/

www.marxists.org/archive/gramsci/

www.marxists.org/subject/frankfurt-school/index.htm
Related sites providing useful summaries as well as archives of key works for Marx, Gramsci, and the Frankfurt School.

http://plato.stanford.edu/entries/critical-theory/
Part of the online Stanford Encyclopedia of Philosophy, it contains a wide-ranging account of critical theory with a focus on the Frankfurt School.

www.cddc.vt.edu/feminism/enin.html
A very comprehensive site covering all aspects of feminist theory.

http://plato.stanford.edu/entries/postmodernism/
Another useful entry from the Stanford Encyclopedia of Philosophy on postmodernism.

 Visit the **Online Resource Centre** that accompanies this book to access more learning resources at **www.oxfordtextbooks.co.uk/orc/garner/**

16

17

Security and Insecurity

Reader's Guide

Previous chapters have shown that IR's traditional focus has been on the security of the sovereign state, in a system of states, existing under conditions of anarchy. It follows that security has been largely concerned with the threats that states pose with respect to each other. This chapter therefore looks first at traditional concepts of security and insecurity, revisiting the Hobbesian state of nature and tracing security thinking through to the end of the Cold War. This is followed by a discussion of specific ideas about collective security as embodied in the United Nations and its Security Council, as well as the rise of security cooperation manifest in organizations such as NATO. We then consider some pressing security challenges in the post-Cold War period and the broadening of the security agenda to encompass a host of more recent concerns such as environmental security, energy security, and the diffuse concept of 'human security'. The last part provides an overview of the war on terror, raising further questions concerning how best to deal with non-conventional threats.

Security, Insecurity, and Power Politics

Traditional realist approaches to international relations have taken their cue from a number of classic texts to construct an image of the **state of nature** characterized by a permanent condition of **anarchy**. Thomas Hobbes' famous account represents the state of nature as a highly dangerous environment, lacking any effective civil structure headed by an authoritative ruler, no sense of justice or morality, and therefore no security at all for the isolated individuals who exist within it in constant fear. The most powerful individuals prevail over the weaker, although even the powerful must watch their backs constantly. Thus the anarchic state of nature offers the most *in*secure existence imaginable. The formation of states in the form of bounded political communities headed by a sovereign power, however, works to banish anarchy from within the boundaries, enabling a measure of security to prevail within states.

For realist scholars of IR, the study of life *within* the state is regarded as the proper focus for political science, whereas IR is concerned with relations between states in the sphere of international anarchy. Given the nature of anarchy, the international sphere is necessarily the locus of insecurity for sovereign states and, therefore, ultimately for the people enclosed within them. Thus, the proper concern of IR is how to maintain the survival of the sovereign state itself, for it is only when this is taken care of that people can effectively work to achieve 'the good life' within the state:

States seek to maintain their territorial integrity and the autonomy of their domestic political order. They can pursue other goals like prosperity and protecting human rights, but those aims must always take a back seat to survival, because if a state does not survive, it cannot pursue those other goals. (Mearsheimer, 2007: 74)

None of this means that the international sphere is one of perpetual chaos or warfare. Anarchy need not preclude a certain degree of order and stability. Given its underlying dynamics, peace, and security in the international sphere at any given time is tenuous. Perpetual anarchy in the international sphere thus ensures a state of perpetual underlying *in*security because even in times of apparent peace, it is always ready to unleash its destructive forces when the fragile order characterizing international relations weakens or breaks down. As we have seen, this kind of thinking crystallized in realist theory following the breakdown of international order in the lead-up to the Second World War, culminating in the turn to **power politics** in the post-war period.

The power politics approach to security as worked out by Morgenthau and his successors takes as given the notion of 'peace through strength', where 'strength' is invariably related to military capacity and underpins a robust approach to 'national security'. This is a prominent theme when foreign policy issues are raised during national election campaigns in the USA, albeit one 'that is more frequently invoked than explained or justified' (Shimko, 2005: 121). We have seen previously that the power politics approach also

17

involves considerations of both **balance of power** mechanisms and the **security dilemma** which ensures a perpetual, competitive struggle for security where, in the final analysis, states can depend only on their own resources. *Self-reliance* is therefore the watchword for security and the ultimate key to survival in the international sphere.

During the Cold War period, the use of the term 'security' by both sides came to denote much more than simply protection against invasion. On the Soviet side, 'security' and imperial expansion in Eastern and Central Europe went hand in hand, while on the other side 'any state controlling large geographical areas containing significant quantities of natural resources in a way unacceptable to the USA [presented] a threat to the "national security" of the United States' (Young and Kent, 2004: 10). The evidence since the end of the Cold War with respect to US involvement in Iraq, a country with vast oil resources, suggests that little has changed.

Another factor prominent in neorealism relates to the distribution of power in the international system and its effects on the security environment. Reflecting on the history of the state system in Europe from 1648 through to the Second World War, observers of international politics have generally agreed that the system during that period possessed a 'multipolar' character (Mearsheimer, 2007: 78–80). In other words, significant power was distributed among three or more states within the system. The Cold War period, however, was described as 'bipolar' since power was divided largely between the USA and its allies on the one hand, and the USSR and its allies on the other. The structure of **bipolarity**, together with the deterrent effect of nuclear weapons possessed by both sides, is often said to have produced the 'long peace' of the Cold War period in which major warfare was threatened but did not actually occur.

There is no agreement, however, as to whether a multipolar or bipolar system promotes greater security all round. Post-Napoleonic Europe enjoyed long periods of peace as a multipolar international system up to 1914, which rivals the Cold War period. As for the present, it is possibly too soon to tell whether the post-Cold War period of unipolarity, in which the USA appears to have achieved global **hegemony**, will prove to be more conducive to peace and security in the longer term. With the current war on terror appearing to have no end in sight, and with traditional realist theory having little to say about the nature of conflicts that are not essentially state-based and which therefore do not lend themselves to balance of power analysis, it is perhaps more fruitful to look to other approaches to the study of international politics which we consider shortly.

In the meantime, liberal approaches to security challenged the premises of **realism** in terms of traditional issues of state security, with considerable success. This is despite the apparent failures of the interwar system—that is, the League of Nations. Indeed, the strong influence of **liberal institutionalism** is evident in the extent to which the immediate post-war period saw the re-establishment of overarching international organizations designed to ameliorate the negative effects of anarchy through collective security mechanisms. Foremost among these of course is the UN which is one of the most important of the institutions set up by international treaty. See **Box 17.1**.

Key Concept Box 17.1
Treaties and Alliances

A treaty in international relations is defined simply as 'a written contract or agreement between two or more parties which is considered binding in international law' (Evans and Newnham, 1998: 542–3). A treaty may take the form of an alliance which is usually defined primarily in security terms as 'a formal agreement between two or more actors— usually states—to collaborate together on perceived mutual security issues' (Evans and Newnham: 1998: 15). The anticipated security benefits of such collaboration depend on the circumstances of each case, but generally they may include one or more of the following:

- a system of deterrence will be established or strengthened;
- a defence pact will operate in the event of a war;
- some or all of the actors will be precluded from joining other alliances (ibid.).

As instruments for securing some kind of international order, treaties and alliances have a very long history. Thucydides refers to a number of treaties between contending forces, while the histories of many other political communities around the world reveal their extensive experience in maintaining workable arrangements. Not all treaties take the form of security alliances, but historically this is probably the most common form. A treaty may be between formerly hostile parties which see a mutual advantage in establishing more peaceful relations. This does not mean that each party will cease to regard others with suspicion, nor will it guarantee future non-aggression. The non-aggression pact negotiated between Hitler and Stalin on the eve of the Second World War, for example, did not prevent Hitler from launching an invasion of Soviet territory just two years later. A treaty may also be forced on one or more of the parties at the conclusion of hostilities, to the benefit of the victorious side and/or as a punitive mechanism. The Treaty of Versailles had just such a character and, as we have seen, is often regarded as a major factor in Hitler's rise to power and support within Germany for his ultra-aggressive militarism.

The United Nations and Collective Security

As the Second World War drew to a close, delegates from fifty countries, all opponents of the Axis powers, met in San Francisco to approve a charter for a new body capable of establishing a framework for maintaining international peace and security. Work on a successor organization to the old League had been underway for some time. A meeting in London between representatives of countries committed to establishing a more secure world order was held as early as 1941. It was followed soon after by a meeting between British Prime Minister Winston Churchill and US President Franklin

17

D. Roosevelt, the outcome of which was the Atlantic Charter. This document had no legal standing but its declaratory message was a denunciation of the use of force while affirming aspirations for a new world order, when hostilities eventually ceased, which would uphold the rights of people to live in peace and freedom within the boundaries of their own states and to travel abroad in safety. A further meeting in London attended by representatives of most European governments-in-exile and the USSR pledged support. By 1943 the process of securing broad agreement on a new organization to secure world order took another step forward with a meeting in Moscow of the major powers, now including China, and another in Teheran a few months later attended by the UK, the US, the USSR, and China.

In August 1944 a proposal for a Charter was drawn up by the four major powers at the 'Dumbarton Oaks' meeting in Washington DC. By this stage, agreement had been reached on the main constituent elements of a new United Nations Organization, including a General Assembly, a Security Council, an International Court of Justice, and a Secretariat. A subsequent meeting at Yalta in the Crimea produced the all-important procedures for voting in the Security Council, and it was decided to move to a broad international conference to endorse the draft Charter. The latter was formally signed in San Francisco by representatives of fifty-one countries on 26 June 1945 with the organization coming into official existence on 24 October 1945. Its membership grew steadily as decolonization in Africa, the Middle East, South Asia, East Asia, the Pacific, and the Caribbean created newly independent states throughout the following decades, with a further increase occurring after the collapse of the Cold War and the creation of many more sovereign states in the aftermath. Membership now stands at 192.

The Charter establishes basic principles of order in support of international peace and security which every new member must sign up to. It is thus an international treaty setting out the rights and obligations of its member states in terms of the Charter's main purposes. These are contained in the Preamble to the Charter which first reaffirms 'faith in fundamental human rights, in the dignity and worth of the human person, in the equal rights of men and women and of nations large and small', and then declares its purpose as being 'to establish conditions under which justice and respect for the obligations arising from treaties and other sources of international law can be maintained' and, further, 'to promote social progress and better standards of life in larger freedom'. In pursuit of these ends, members commit themselves: to practise tolerance and live together in peace with one another as good neighbours; to unite in maintaining international peace and security; to ensure that armed force shall not be used, save in the common interest; and to employ international machinery for the promotion of the economic and social advancement of all peoples (Charter of the United Nations, Preamble, as adopted 26 June 1945). There follow nineteen chapters containing a total of 111 Articles spelling out the more detailed structure of the UN and the various powers and responsibilities of its principle organs.

17

The UN Security Council

The Security Council is set up under Chapter V of the Charter. It was originally composed of five permanent members (the UK, USA, USSR, France, and China) and six non-permanent members. There are now ten non-permanent members who serve a two-year term. The five permanent members—or 'P5'—each retain veto power over any Security Council decision. This extraordinary power reflects a belief that the new UN simply would not function without according a special place to the most prominent states, thereby rectifying a perceived weakness of the old League. More generally, the Security Council is primarily responsible for maintaining international peace and security and its functions and powers are set out accordingly. Thus the Security Council embodies the UN's aspirations to provide for 'collective security'—a term encapsulating the notion that true security cannot be obtained through the practice of 'every state for itself', but cooperatively.

The composition and functioning of the Security Council has been subject to many criticisms over the years. One is that the permanent membership, which holds such a privileged position, reflects circumstances prevailing over sixty years ago in a world where decolonization had scarcely begun. The UN's membership has almost quadrupled since then, due largely to the creation of more independent states many of which see the permanent membership as skewed unfairly in favour of the developed world. Certainly, the geographic distribution of the P5 is relatively narrow, with no representation from Africa, the Middle East, South Asia, or South America.

Photo 17.1   First Session of the United Nations Security Council

A general view of the First Session of the United Nations Security Council held on 17 January 1946 at Church House, London. NJO.

Source: UN photo by Marcel Bolomey

Reform of the permanent membership, however, seems unlikely in the near future. If reform entailed an expanded permanent membership, the veto power would be extended further making decisions on vexed issues more difficult. On the other hand, if the number of members is to stay at five who should, or would, vacate their seat to make way for a new member? One solution would be to give the European Union rather than individual European states a seat, meaning that Germany (and all other European states) would have some representation, but the UK and France are unlikely to agree. If one new member was admitted to make up the five, who would that be? Brazil, Japan, India, Nigeria, and Egypt are possible claimants, but none would be uncontroversial. If there were no permanent members at all, the dynamics of the Security Council would almost certainly change considerably and there is no guarantee that it would be for the better. Thus, reform of the Security Council will remain in the 'too hard' basket in the foreseeable future. Beyond this, some argue that the more pressing issue now is not whether the permanent membership is reformed but whether, in the light of the Iraq War, US power can be constrained (Weiss, 2003: 146–61).

In the light of the reasoning behind the both the organization as a whole and the Security Council in particular, one might ask how different theoretical approaches to IR are reflected. In the first instance, the practical imperatives driving its formation were, once again, based on the experience of warfare and the desire to minimize conflict in the international sphere. The rhetoric accompanying the various declarations was infused with idealist visions of a better world in which security for all states was the norm rather than the exception. Further, with membership open to all on equal terms, and a normative commitment to decolonization, the UN reflected a strong spirit of egalitarianism while its provisions for the social and economic advancement of all nations ensured that it would have a proactive role in areas outside mainstream security concerns.

This tendency was strengthened with the Universal Declaration of Human Rights in 1948 and an expanded humanitarian role in various areas in later years as well as provisions for the participation of NGOs. In short, the UN system may be founded squarely on the sovereign state system and its preservation, but the UN's basic principles and vision for world order extend beyond this to embrace a range of liberal ideals and a broader interpretation of the international security agenda. Thus its wide-ranging charter has seen it respond to significant non-military international security concerns such as the environment, health, food, and so on.

On the other hand, the structure of the UN's central organ—the Security Council—and the dominance of the P5 reflects a realist concern for the accommodation of power politics even within an 'idealist institution'. In addition, the broader liberal vision for collective international security expressed through the UN remains tied to a traditional state-based vision of world order focused primarily on military issues. So too do other forms of collective security, such as that embodied in the North Atlantic Treaty Organization (NATO) which we examine next.

17

The Role of NATO

The NATO alliance was instituted in 1948 in the early years of the Cold War and has played a major role in shaping world order over the last six decades. The Cold War itself had commenced almost immediately after victory was declared by the 'Grand Alliance' of forces opposed to the Axis powers. The common enemy which had held them together was gone, and jockeying for position generated mutual suspicions between the USSR and its erstwhile wartime Western allies. Economic conditions in Western Europe following the war were dire and rebuilding programs sluggish at best. This led to the 'Marshall Plan', named for US Secretary of State George Marshall who announced a large-scale plan to deliver economic aid to Europe in June 1947. European recovery was seen as vital to US interests for a number of reasons, including the restoration of its own lucrative markets as well as to strengthen Europe generally vis-à-vis the Soviet Union whose communist ideology was seen as a major threat to the 'American way'. In 1947, US president, Harry S. Truman, enunciated a doctrine which claimed a leading role for the USA in opposing the spread of communism. Together with the Marshall Plan, the broad doctrine became known as 'containment' (of communism), a term coined by US diplomat and adviser George Kennan. Although designed to play largely to his domestic audience, the Truman Doctrine had long-term international effects, legitimizing the right of the USA to intervene in civil wars abroad where communist interests were involved. Young and Kent (2002: 71) argue that the United States was to pay a substantial price in the longer term for cultivating an ideology of global dimensions which defined security in such broad terms.

It was in this general atmosphere that for NATO was established, with all its founding members committing to a basic principle of indivisible collective security. Thus, an attack on one member was to be regarded as an attack on all. Although seen essentially as a military alliance, the initial reasons for NATO's creation had as much to do with the perceived need to strengthen political will and confidence against communism as with the coordination of strategic military forces to protect Western Europe (Young and Kent, 2004: 128–9). Its initial membership consisted of ten West European states—the UK, France, Denmark, Iceland, Italy, Norway, Portugal, Belgium, the Netherlands, and Luxembourg—plus the USA and Canada. The Soviet response was to establish a rival organization incorporating its communist allies in Eastern and Central Europe, although it was seven years before the Warsaw Pact was formally instituted in 1955 as a 'Treaty of Friendship, Co-operation and Mutual Assistance'.

NATO membership expanded during the Cold War to include Greece, Turkey, West Germany, and Spain, although it suffered a setback when France withdrew from NATO's integrated military structure in 1966 following serious disagreement with the USA in important foreign policy areas. Although France remained a signatory to the 'paper treaty', it remained outside the military structure until 1993. Even then its 'long journey back' remained incomplete since it declined to participate in operations. US–France tensions aside, opinion within the USA was not always strongly supportive of a proactive role in Europe either. A significant feature of the founding of NATO is that although it symbolized the key role that the USA was playing in post-war Europe, this was a trend running counter to 'a strain of latent isolationism' deeply embedded in American politics and which was reflected in an initial reluctance to commit the USA to such a treaty (Best *et al.*, 2004: 223).

Although clearly a Cold War institution, NATO has renewed its *râison d'être* in the post-Cold War period as Europe's and the North Atlantic's prime security organiza-tion. And indeed, its membership has expanded yet again to incorporate a number of former Soviet-dominated countries—the Czech Republic, Hungary, and Poland join-ing in 1999 and Bulgaria, Estonia, Latvia, Lithuania, Romania, Slovakia, and Slovenia in 2004, bringing its current membership to twenty-six. As it welcomed the first three of its former communist members, a new 'strategic concept' was announced at a summit meeting in Washington in April 1999 and a 65 point document released, spelling out NATO's vision of its past, present, and future roles as a pre-eminent international treaty-based security organization. See **Box 17.2**. For its members, NATO is clearly seen as having a long-term future.

Box 17.2

History: Reformulating NATO's Strategic Concept

The end of the Cold War and the collapse of communism in Eastern Europe and the former USSR required a rethinking of NATO's essential mission. This resulted in the formulation of a new strategic concept which was formally announced in the following terms:

1.   At their Summit meeting in Washington in April 1999, NATO heads of state and Government approved the Alliance's new Strategic Concept.

2.   NATO has successfully ensured the freedom of its members and prevented war in Europe during the forty years of the Cold War. By combining defence with dialogue, it played an indispensable role in bringing East–West confrontation to a peaceful end. The dramatic changes in the Euro–Atlantic strategic landscape brought by the end of the Cold War were reflected in the Alliance's 1991 Strategic Concept. There have, however, been further profound political and security developments since then.

3.   The dangers of the Cold War have given way to more promising, but also challenging prospects, to new opportunities and risks. A new Europe of greater integration is emerging, and a Euro–Atlantic security structure is evolving in which NATO plays a central part. The Alliance has been at the heart of efforts to establish new patterns of cooperation and mutual understanding across the

Euro–Atlantic region and has committed itself to essential new activities in the interest of a wider stability. It has shown the depth of that commitment in its efforts to put an end to the immense human suffering created by conflict in the Balkans. The years since the end of the Cold War have also witnessed important developments in arms control, a process to which the Alliance is fully committed. The Alliance's role in these positive developments has been underpinned by the comprehensive adaptation of its approach to security and of its procedures and structures. The last ten years have also seen, however, the appearance of complex new risks to Euro–Atlantic peace and stability, including oppression, ethnic conflict, economic distress, the collapse of political order, and the proliferation of weapons of mass destruction.

4. The Alliance has an indispensable role to play in consolidating and preserving the positive changes of the recent past, and in meeting current and future security challenges. It has, therefore, a demanding agenda. It must safeguard common security interests in an environment of further, often unpredictable change. It must maintain collective defence and reinforce the transatlantic link and ensure a balance that allows the European Allies to assume greater responsibility. It must deepen its relations with its partners and prepare for the accession of new members. It must, above all, maintain the political will and the military means required by the entire range of its missions.

5. This new Strategic Concept will guide the Alliance as it pursues this agenda. It expresses NATO's enduring purpose and nature and its fundamental security tasks, identifies the central features of the new security environment, specifies the elements of the Alliance's broad approach to security, and provides guidelines for the further adaptation of its military forces.

Source: www.nato.int/docu/pr/1999/p99-065e.htm

Alternative Approaches to Security

It is now a commonplace that new security issues, and new approaches to studying security, are a feature of the post-Cold War period. This does not mean that traditional issues and approaches have withered away, as the story of NATO shows. Nor does it mean that nothing of consequence occurred before the end of the Cold War to challenge conventional approaches and alternative thinking about what constitutes security. Since at least the 1960s, the peace movement had promoted the idea that genuine security was to be obtained not simply by defeating enemies in war but by working with them to resolve conflicts. They further argued a case for rethinking security along the lines of 'positive peace', a concept which rejects peace as consisting merely in the absence of violent conflict and which focuses attention on the causes of conflict and their amelioration through cooperative social mechanisms (see Galtung, 1969: 167–91).

The peace movement itself was (and remains) multifaceted, taking on different causes and promoting different issues according to time, place and circumstance. During the Cold War period it campaigned variously against 'hot' warfare in Vietnam, Korea, and other parts of the Third World; against the advancement of nuclear technology for either military or non-military purposes; against poverty, underdevelopment, and neo-colonialism in the Third World; and for the promotion of grass-roots democracy and **social justice** in industrialized nations. There were cross-cutting links as well to other **social movements**, including the women's movement and the environmental movement, both of which were to advance their own particular conceptions of security and an alternative agenda for policy makers well before the end of the Cold War. These developments took place alongside intellectual challenges to traditional security studies coming from **postmodernism**, feminism, and critical theory more generally throughout the 1970s and 1980s.

Feminism, as part of the more general field of gender theory, has provided some interesting and challenging critiques of conventional approaches to security. Although there are very different types of feminism, as we have seen previously, a common theme is that international relations in general, and security, in particular, are not gender neutral and that a particular kind of masculinist perspective has prevailed. Beyond that, however, different feminisms have produced different and often conflicting critiques of the gender dimensions of security. One issue of particular concern to women that has received long overdue attention in recent years is that of rape in war, an issue that was highlighted during the war in Bosnia–Herzegovina as we saw in chapter sixteen. Before this, there was enormous reluctance to recognize the extent to which rape is actually used as a widespread tactic in war. Just as domestic violence against women in the home has often been concealed or downplayed, so too has violence against women in warfare.

➜ See chapter sixteen, page 378, for the case study on the Bosnian War, 1992–5.

The publicity surrounding the situation in the former Yugoslavia resonated with the increased strength of feminist voices in international politics. It also brought some long overdue attention to the same problems experienced at the end of the Second World War by German women, mainly at the hands of the victorious Red Army, and of the forced prostitution of 'comfort women' used by Japanese forces during the war in the Pacific, with instances of sexual assault in both cases running into the millions. These are clearly not the only historic cases—soldiers from many other countries have engaged in rape either en masse or individually, but almost always with impunity. It has only very recently been treated as a war crime. Indeed, the first time that sexual assault was treated separately as a war crime was in 1996 when eight Bosnian Serb military and police officers were indicted in The Hague in connection with the rape of Muslim women in the Bosnian War. This has scarcely prevented the continuation of the practice in other war zones, as reports about the plight of women refugees from the

Darfur region of western Sudan indicate (see http://web.amnesty.org/library/index/engafr 540762004), but it provides an indication that the practice of rape in war, as something that affects women in particular (although not exclusively), is no longer simply swept under the proverbial carpet, but treated as an important security issue.

Another important item on the agenda for security in the post-Cold War period has been the increasing gap between the 'haves' and the 'have nots'—with the former consisting largely of the prosperous, industrialized countries of the northern hemisphere and the latter of underdeveloped countries, most of which lie in the **global South**. We consider the issue of globalization and some of its consequences in the context of international political economy in a later chapter, but for now we need to note that the 'North–South' economic/developmental divide is often regarded as having significant security dimensions. Again, concerns about this pre-date the end of the Cold War, as the report of a UN-sponsored commission headed by former West German Chancellor and Nobel Peace Laureate, Willy Brandt, shows. Published in 1980, this influential report, entitled *North–South: A Programme for Survival*, examined in depth the range of problems arising from significant socioeconomic disparities between countries.

A feature of the report was its emphasis on the fact that both North and South had a strong mutual interest in putting an end to dependence, oppression, hunger, and general human distress. Its main recommendations related to the operation of transnational corporations, agricultural production and distribution, terms of trade, **protectionism**, energy costs, international financial institutions, foreign debt loads, levels of development assistance, population growth, and the cost of the arms race. It proposed vastly increased aid flows, arguing that the transformation of the international economy would be in the long-term interests of all counties. Further, its implementation was less an act of charity on the part of the North than a condition of mutual survival for all.

Although some developed countries saw value in acting on its recommendations, others were luke warm. Attention was focused largely on Cold War politics, especially in the USA where President Reagan evinced little interest in development oriented issues except where aid was seen as a specific counter to Soviet influence. Overall, however, aid flows did increase. Just as importantly, the commission opened up new public discourses on the relationship between global development and security by highlighting that narrow military concerns were insufficient in an era of increasing global **interdependence**. Certainly, by 1989 it was clear that the Cold War had virtually collapsed and that the time for new thinking on security in an increasingly globalized world had arrived.

In addition to the plight of millions of people in the Third World and the multifaceted security threats they faced, attention also turned more towards the environment. Again, such concerns were raised well before the end of the Cold War and the UN had held an environmental summit in 1972. However, the post-Cold War world seemed much more conducive to focusing attention on environmental issues and to expressing concerns explicitly in terms of *security*. The UN again took a lead, organizing a world summit in Rio de Janeiro in June 1992. Although wide-ranging, three

17

major concerns were given particular attention: the state of the world's forests; bio-diversity; and climate change. All three are interrelated, but it is the latter which has now become the most prominent issue (see www.un.org/geninfo/bp/enviro.html).

The summit produced the UN Convention on Climate Change which entered into force in 1994. In recognizing that the climate system is a shared resource affected by the emission of 'greenhouse gases', the Convention set up a framework for intergovernmental efforts to tackle global warming. This was followed by the Kyoto Protocol of 1997 which strengthened the Convention by committing its signatories to binding targets for the reduction of greenhouse gases (http://unfccc.int/kyoto_protocol/items/2830.php). The USA under the Bush administration and Australia under the Howard government, however, subsequently pulled out, each claiming that the emissions reduction targets would damage their respective economies and both also claiming that developing countries should not be given special treatment. Australia under a new Labor government elected in November 2007, however, changed tack leaving the USA isolated on the issue.

The consequences of global warming for security are potentially enormous. Rising sea levels—just one consequence—threaten not just the very existence of small island states and low-lying countries such as Holland, but extensive coastal regions of countries such as the USA, Australia, Bangladesh, China, and many more. Climate change will also impact on food and water security, not to mention the considerable problems that will inevitably attend mass migration from low-lying areas, impacting in turn on 'border security' with new waves of 'environmental refugees'. And while climate change sceptics have often derided the concerns voiced by environmentalists as alarmist, with some even claiming that the alarmism is part of a conspiracy against capitalism, the scientific evidence about the extent to which the earth's climate is changing as a result of greenhouse gas emission, and the devastating effects that this is likely to have, is now beyond dispute.

Other non-traditional security issues to receive more attention in the post-Cold War period include energy security, food, and water security (not just in relation to climate change), and bio-security. Energy security, in particular, is a concern that links a variety of other security concerns, both traditional non-traditional, old and new, as **Box 17.3** shows.

 Case Study Box 17.3
Securing Energy

On the eve of the First World War, Winston Churchill made a historic decision: to shift the power source of the British Navy's ships from coal to oil, intending to make the fleet faster than its German counterpart; but the switch also meant that the Royal Navy would rely not on coal from Wales but on insecure oil supplies from Persia. Energy security thus became a question of national strategy. Since then, energy security has repeatedly emerged as an significant issue. What has been the paradigm of energy security for the past three decades must be expanded to include many new factors, for energy security is lodged in wider relations among nations and how they interact.

Concerns over energy security are not limited to oil. Power blackouts on both the East and West Coasts of the USA, in Europe, and in Russia, and chronic shortages of electric power in China, India, and other developing countries, raise worries about the reliability of supply systems. Rising demand and constrained supplies of natural gas also mean that North America can no longer be self-reliant, and so the USA is joining the new global market in natural gas linking countries, continents, and prices together in an unprecedented way.

A new range of vulnerabilities also becomes more evident. Al Qaeda has threatened to attack 'hinges' of the world's economy—its critical infrastructure—of which energy is a crucial element. The world will increasingly depend on new sources from places where security systems are underdeveloped, such as the oil and natural gas fields offshore of West Africa and in the Caspian Sea.

Source: Paraphrased from Daniel Yergin (2006), 'Ensuring Energy Security', *Foreign Affairs*, 86(3) March/April: 69

Post-Cold War Conflicts

Despite significant changes in the outlook for global security at the end of the Cold War, and the notion that traditional interstate security concerns could be put aside to focus on a different range of new security issues, there was one serious interstate war of the early post-Cold War period—namely, the Gulf War of 1991. But while this episode did bring a focus back on to traditional security concerns, it also prompted visions of a new world order. This stemmed from the fact that the conflict had seen decisive action on the part of the UN Security Council when Iraq's Saddam Hussein broke the golden rule of international relations by invading another sovereign state—its neighbour Kuwait. The UN Security Council's Resolution 678 authorized member states cooperating with the official Kuwaiti government to 'use all means necessary' to oust Iraqi forces and restore international peace and security in the area. The unprecedented solidarity of the UN, and the success of multilateral action against military aggression, led President George Bush (the elder) to proclaim a new world order in which enduring peace was a real possibility. As such, it was also seen as a triumph for the UN and the ideals it embodied since, in the absence of Cold War constraints, it was now regarded as capable of achieving its original objectives as a vehicle for genuinely effective cooperative security.

While the prospects for peaceful coexistence between states were being talked up, conflict and violence within states—otherwise known as 'internal conflict'—continued unabated and was seen as a significant ongoing concern. Even where the violence and its

17

fallout is more or less contained within a state, many believe that a body such as the UN cannot simply sit by while thousands are massacred or grossly abused. In the early 1990s, there were ongoing conflicts within a number of Third World states from Africa to the Pacific, as well as in places such as Northern Ireland and Spain. In addition, the break-up of the former Soviet empire had provoked a flurry of nationalist activity. Not all of this took a violent form by any means, with the formation of the Czech Republic and Slovakia out of the former Czechoslovakia representing a model of peaceful political divorce.

The Baltic states too, eventually negotiated a peaceful path to independence and the departure of Central Asian republics from the old Soviet Union was accompanied by relatively little violence. New leaders in Moscow, however, were determined that the Russian Federation should remain intact and Chechnyan separatism, itself expressed in violent terms, has been put down ruthlessly. The Balkans also presented a particularly difficult case. While the secession of Slovenia from Yugoslavia in 1991 was managed with relatively little violence, the subsequent breakup of the Yugolsav state witnessed serious conflict between Croats, Serbs, and Muslims and saw the introduction of the term **ethnic cleansing** into our vocabulary.

In the meantime, crises in Africa produced further challenges for an international community struggling to maintain optimism about the prospects for peace and security as the Cold War receded into history only to be replaced by concerns about fragile and failing states and the associated human costs. The experience of Somalia, as discussed in chapter seven, is also widely regarded as having had a significant effect on US attitudes towards the deployment of its forces overseas. Clarke and Gosende (2003: 145) write that the 'desperate failure of Somalia intruded deeply into the sensibilities of the US Government and public' and that the experience there had a profound effect on attitudes to other crises, especially in Rwanda where the USA (along with France) forced a reduction of UN forces immediately prior to the genocide there in 1994. This event, in which some 800,000 Tutsis and moderate Hutus were massacred by extremist Hutu militia, is regarded as another monumental failure by the UN to act decisively and effectively to prevent an internal conflict from turning into a large-scale tragedy. This is a very different sentiment from that expressed at the successful conclusion of Operation Desert Storm only a few years earlier. It also shows that there have been enormous, perhaps inflated, expectations concerning what the UN can actually achieve in terms of keeping the peace in the conditions of the post-Cold War world—a world very different from that which emerged at the end of the Second World War and in which the challenges of failing states, civil wars, and large-scale humanitarian disasters were not seen as the major concerns for the world's premier international organization.

➜ See chapter seven, page 176, for the case study on Somalia.

17

From State Security to Human Security

In the meantime, a further important manifestation of new thinking was contained in another UN-sponsored publication, the *Human Development Report: 1994*

(UNDP, 1994), which was produced ahead of the World Summit for Social Development in 1995. Opening with the claim that: 'The world can never be at peace unless people have security in their daily lives' (1), and a survey of the contrast between the unprecedented prosperity achieved by some and the continuing and indeed deepening misery of so many others, the report went on to set out a case for redefining security in 'human' terms, implying a substantial shift away from security defined in terms of state or national security. The 'human' aspect here includes health security, employment security, environmental security, and security from crime as emerging issues for security around the world. Security itself was to be understood in the broadest possible terms as 'safety from the constant threats of hunger, disease, crime and repression' and 'protection from sudden and hurtful disruptions in the pattern of our daily lives—whether in our homes, in our jobs, in our communities or in our environment' (3).

As with previous UN reports, this one attracted both supporters and critics. Among the latter, a common objection was that if virtually everything came under the rubric of 'security' then the term would become meaningless. Furthermore, the broadening of the security agenda in this way meant that the important focus on *international* security may be lost or downplayed. In theoretical terms, it is not hard to see that while realists would be concerned to maintain the international/domestic distinction as a matter of practical as well as conceptual importance, liberals and others subscribing to alternative ideas about security would welcome the conceptual shift and its implications for policy. This has resulted in concerted efforts by policy-makers and others to tackle security at different levels. While not neglecting traditional state security needs, much more attention has been directed to the multiple levels at which security considerations operate. These developments, however, have been largely overshadowed by the fallout from 9/11, an event which once again brought the issue of international violence into focus, although not in a conventional manner.

Security and Insecurity After 9/11

The attacks on the World Trade Center in New York and the Pentagon in Washington by Al Qaeda operatives on 11 September 2001 (known as '9/11' following the American convention of date abbreviation), and the subsequent war on terror, has seen the US lead invasions of two separate sovereign states—Afghanistan and Iraq—and threaten others belonging to what George W. Bush famously described, in his 2002 State of the Union address, as the 'Axis of Evil'. The latter include North Korea and Iran, both of which are hostile to 'the West' and which have also been developing nuclear programmes. The war on terror more generally is not easily analysed in terms of traditional security paradigms even though the US response, in so far as it has involved military force and interstate warfare, has attempted to use traditional

17

methods. The rise of Al Qaeda and 'militant Islam' together with the responses by the USA and its allies illustrate a number of twists and variations on the theme of security. See **Box 17.4**.

Case Study   Box 17.4
The Rise of Al Qaeda and Islamic Militancy

Islamic radicalism and militancy, which is deeply intertwined with politics in the Middle East region, has been on the rise since at least the 1970s, although the essential background to these developments can be traced back much further. For present purposes it must suffice to note that both Zionist and Arab nationalist movements have been exceptionally important since the late nineteenth century although with respect to the latter, religious elements had less importance in the earlier stages partly because Arab nationalism was initially directed against the Ottoman Empire, itself a Muslim entity (see Cassels, 1996: 233).

The current Middle East geopolitical landscape has also been shaped by the outcomes of the First and Second World Wars, colonialism, and the competing claims of Palestinian and Jewish groups to territory, claims which have acquired an increasing religiosity over the years, in turn fuelling the emergence of extremist, politically driven fundamentalism in both communities. Islamic fundamentalism in the contemporary period, however, is marked not simply by opposition to the state of Israel as a Jewish entity, but to 'the West' more generally. Cassels (1996: 236) writes that pan-Islamic ideology represents an extreme form of anti-colonialism manifest in an anti-Westernism that has targeted pro-Western regimes in the Middle East.

It was in a more explicit Cold War theatre, however, that Osama bin Laden and the Al Qaeda organization emerged. Afghanistan, a country with a long history of political instability as well as strategic significance for the Soviet Union, had become a battleground for competing factions within the country over the years from the early 1970s. While the Soviets supported a Marxist government the USA, along with Pakistan, Saudi Arabia, China, the UK, and other disparate regimes, generally supported an insurrection led by the Mujahideen, whose name means 'strugglers', also related to the word *jihad* or 'holy struggle'. Initially energized by and partially united in opposition to the Soviet presence in Afghanistan, any coherence the Mujahideen possessed largely dissipated after the Soviet withdrawal in 1989.

Violent conflict between contending factions as well as with the embattled central government continued until the strongest of the resistance factions, the Taliban, gained control in 1996, imposing an uncompromising version of Islamic rule. Afghanistan thereafter became a haven for Al Qaeda, originally formed there during the struggle against the Soviets, but for a time with its main base in Sudan. In 1996, bin Laden shifted to Afghanistan from where he planned attacks on two US embassies in East Africa in

1988 and a US Navy vessel in Yemen in 2000. The most spectacular attacks, and those with the most far-reaching consequences, were obviously those of 11 September 2001 which sparked the war on terror.

Al Qaeda, known to be based in Afghanistan, was the prime suspect in the 9/11 attacks. The USA demanded that its leader, Osama bin Laden, be handed over by Afghanistan's ruling party, the Taliban, a demand supported by the UN Security Council. When the Taliban government refused to do so, the USA and allies attacked just four weeks after. NATO had already invoked Article 5 of NATO's founding charter which, as we have seen, declares that an armed attack against one member is an attack on all. Operation Enduring Freedom, as the initial intervention was called, eventually gave way to NATO's International Security Assistance Force (ISAF). A programme of political reconstruction has seen elections held, a new government put in place, and a programme of infrastructure development. However, Afghanistan barely functions as a state and insecurity at multiple levels is the order of the day. Furthermore, bin Laden remains at large and Al Qaeda now appears to be operating from remote areas in neighbouring Pakistan.

The ongoing problems in Afghanistan have been partly overshadowed by the war in Iraq, launched in March 2003 as part of the war on terror by the Bush administration and supported by the UK under the leadership of Tony Blair. This intervention, however, did not have the support of either the UN Security Council or NATO. In the Security Council, French opposition to the war was backed up by Russia and China. Support for intervention, however, was forthcoming from a 'coalition of the willing', which at one stage included almost fifty countries around the world although only Poland, Denmark, and Australia sent token military contingents. Troops from some other countries have been deployed in attempts at peace-building but operations have remained largely confined to US and UK forces. NATO and the UN have therefore played no major role in the Iraq War.

By almost any measure, the Iraq War has not gone well. Except for a short period of euphoria in May 2003 when Saddam was driven from power and Bush declared that hostilities had ended, the news has not been good. Despite elections, Iraq has teetered on the brink of civil war between Shia and Sunni factions and violent criminality has become widespread. While Al Qaeda had virtually no presence in Iraq before March 2003, the chaos there has simply opened the country up to its operatives, and indeed has become another recruiting ground for both criminal and terrorist organizations.

One major lesson from the war on terror to date is that the use of conventional military tactics against a non-conventional enemy may not only be ineffectual in defeating that enemy, but may create a score of new problems: Osama bin Laden,

17

Al Qaeda, and the Taliban have not been destroyed; a seemingly never-ending supply of suicide bombers poses a threat to civilian populations in countries around the world; and the prospects for peace and security for the people of both Afghanistan and Iraq remain bleak. Many commentators have pointed to the fact that terrorism is best dealt with by civil law enforcement agencies and the strengthening of national and international intelligence networks dedicated to the task. Although not successful on every occasion (for example, with respect to the London underground bombings of July 2005), regular policing and intelligence operations have nonetheless been successful in foiling numerous other attacks (see Peña, 2006: 289–306).

Military force is always a very blunt weapon and its consequences are often both unpredictable and uncontrollable. This is what led one of the most famous commentators on war, the Prussian military strategist Carl von Clausewitz (1780–1831), to observe that the planning and execution of war necessarily takes place in a kind of twilight where the effects of fog distort and obscure what is going on (see Clausewitz, 1993). The phrase, 'the fog of war', which is based on this observation, has become an increasingly common theme as the outcome of the war in Iraq and what the long-term future holds for the country and its inhabitants remains shrouded in uncertainty. The Chinese Taoist thinker and strategist, Sun Tzu, who lived over 2,000 ago, also advised that the best victory of all is that which is gained without fighting and pointed to various strategies for achieving this end (see Sun Tzu, 1963). These observations point to the fact that much more subtle instruments may be needed to achieve desirable security outcomes in the longer term, especially against highly unconventional threats.

Conclusion

Security and insecurity in the realm of international politics is clearly multifaceted both conceptually and in practical terms. Various institutions, practices, and policies have been developed over the years to cope with a range of security challenges. These range from those which pose a threat to international peace and security in conventional terms—that is, in terms of armed aggression by one or more states against others in the international system, to other kinds of challenges including internal conflict, environmental security, energy security, and threats from non-state actors such as terrorist organizations. These latter, non-conventional threats are among the most serious today and we may well question the appropriateness of military responses to date and ask what alternative policy approaches, attuned to the specific dynamics of the threats, are possible.

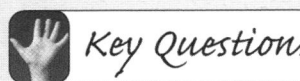
Key Questions

- How does traditional IR theory treat the concept of security and how does it relate to images of the 'state of nature'?
- How would you assess the UN's role in maintaining international peace and security since its inception?
- Does the concept of 'human security' offer a superior framework for addressing issues in the contemporary period?
- Should the nation-state remain central to how security is conceptualized in the present period with respect to both traditional and newer security issues?
- How has the peace movement challenged traditional militarist approaches to security?
- How has the agenda for international security changed in the post-Cold War period?
- In what ways does a gender perspective illuminate non-traditional security issues in IR?
- How do issues such as energy security link old and new concerns about security in IR?
- In what sense does the war on terror represent a non-traditional security threat?

Further Reading

Dalby, Simon (2002), *Environmental Security,* Minneapolis, MN: University of Minnesota Press.

This book treats the issue of environmental security from a critical theory perspective, bringing in aspects of environmental history, identities and geopolitics, and relating problems of environmental security to the expansion of modernity.

Holzgrefe, Jeff L. and Robert O. Kephane (eds) (2003), *Humanitarian Intervention: Ethical, Legal, and Political Dilemmas,* Cambridge: Cambridge University Press.

This is an edited collection bringing together experts from several disciplines to examine the dilemmas and tensions between the principle of sovereignty on the one hand and that of humanitarian intervention on the other, and the difficult position facing the UN in varying cases.

Kaldor, Mary (2006), *New and Old Wars: Organized Violence in a Global Era,* Cambridge: Polity Press, 2nd edn.

Despite the invasion of Afghanistan and Iraq, this book shows how interstate war is actually becoming an anachronism. Instead, new kinds of organized violence—'new wars'—are emerging which combine traditional aspects of war with organized crime and involve actors at various levels.

Kaplan, Lawrence S. (2004), *NATO Divided, NATO United: The Evolution of an Alliance,* Westport, CT: Praeger.

Tensions within the alliance, especially between the USA and its European partners are longstanding and despite an initial show of solidarity after 9/11, have been exacerbated by the war on terror. An interesting and insightful study encompassing the past, present, and possible futures for the Western alliance.

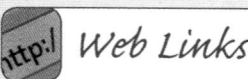

Web Links

www.un.org/reform/
Provides an overview and gives details of reports and publications on the topic of UN reform.

www.un-instraw.org/en/
www.un-instraw.org/en/index.php?option=content&task=view&id=954&Itemid=209
The main UN 'Instraw' website provides a guide to numerous sections on gender isues while the second section on gender and security sector reform provides a more specific range of resources and information.

www.envirosecurity.org
This website is hosted by the Institute for Environmental Security (IES) which is an international non-profit non-government organization established in 2002 with headquarters in The Hague.

www.terrorism-research.com/
A useful general website containing articles and information about terrorism.

www.nato.int/
www.un.org/
These are the general websites for both the UN and NATO and will lead you through an enormous number of sub-sites with important documents and other interesting material.

 Visit the **Online Resource Centre** that accompanies this book to access more learning resources at **www.oxfordtextbooks.co.uk/orc/garner/**

18

Diplomacy and Foreign Policy

Reader's Guide

Diplomacy and the conduct of foreign policy are fundamental to relations between political communities, and have been for thousands of years. In the contemporary period, diplomacy and foreign policy involve fully professionalized state bureaucracies. Alongside formal state diplomatic services are other important actors as well, from NGOs to special envoys or third party mediators tasked with special missions. In addition, there are special forms of diplomacy such as 'summit diplomacy' and 'public diplomacy', both of which have assumed increasing importance in contemporary diplomatic and foreign policy practice. Foreign policy behaviour itself is a closely related but distinctive field of study focusing on the strategies that states adopt in their relations with each other and which reflect, in turn, the pressures that governments face in either the domestic or external sphere. In this chapter we also consider the foreign and security policy of the EU which now has a role and an identity as an international actor in its own right. This further illustrates the fact that while the state remains the most important entity in the international system, it now contends with a range of other actors.

Diplomacy and Statecraft in International History

If international relations in a conventional sense refers to the pattern of interactions between states in the international system of states, then diplomacy is the principal formal mechanism through which this takes place. **Statecraft** is an allied notion denoting the skilful conduct of state affairs or, as some may put it, 'steering the ship of state', usually in the context of external relations. The practice of diplomacy has a very long history, almost certainly reaching back beyond the earliest written records. One author remarks that although we possess only hazy views of what ancient practices were really like, the beginnings of diplomacy must have occurred when the first human societies decided it was better to hear the message than to devour the messenger (see Langthorne and Hamilton, 1994: 7). To this observation we should add that it also had the advantage of being able to send the messenger back with a response, thereby establishing a basis for ongoing communications. A specific recorded reference to the utility of envoys or messengers may be found in Kautilya's ancient text, the *Arthasástra*, mentioned in chapter fourteen, and which states clearly the first principle of diplomacy: don't shoot the messenger. See **Box 18.1.**

➡ See chapter fourteen, page 328, for a discussion of the history of international state system.

Diplomacy is known to have existed in ancient China and indeed the pattern of interstate relations has been compared directly with those of early modern Europe. For a time, the existence of Chinese city-states (called *guo*) enjoyed a certain autonomy which saw alliances and diplomatic practices emerge in a multistate system well before they did so in Europe, although this effectively ended with the establishment of a universal empire in 221 BC when the scope for such practices was largely closed off (Hui, 2005: 4–5). Other studies have investigated historical patterns of diplomacy and trade between China and India, illuminating the role of Buddhism in the process (Tansen, 2003), while evidence has also been found for the practice of alliance

18

Key Quote   Box 18.1
Kautilya on an Ancient Principle of Diplomacy

'Messengers are the mouth-pieces of kings, not only of thyself, but of all; hence messengers who, in the face of weapons raised against them, have to express their mission as exactly as they are entrusted with do not, though outcasts, deserve death; where is then reason to put messengers of *Bráhman* caste to death? This is another's speech. This (*i.e.,* delivery of that speech verbatim) is the duty of messengers.'

(Chapter XVI, 'The Mission of Envoys' in Book I, 'Concerning Discipline, *Arthasástra* of Kautilya: www.mssu.edu/projectsouthasia/history/primarydocs/Arthashastra/BookI.htm)

diplomacy in the regions covered by the ancient Inca, Aztec, and Mayan empires in the Americas (see Cioffi–Revilla and Landman, 1999: 559–98). Most analyses of diplomatic history focus on developments in Europe, however, largely because it is the European state system, as well as European (and North American) scholarship on the subject, that has tended to dominate.

Formal diplomatic practices between state entities in early modern Europe are commonly regarded as having emerged in Italy where resident embassies developed by the 1450s. The Florentine political philosopher, Niccolò Machiavelli, who we encountered in earlier chapters, was among the most experienced diplomats of his time as well as one of the most famous commentators on statecraft. Machiavelli served on bodies which oversaw the conduct of Florence's war efforts and between 1500 and 1511, he acted as a government envoy on thirty-five missions, including missions to France, the Papal Court, and the German Emperor (Miller, 1991: 303). Certainly, the prime responsibility of an ambassador as a servant of the state was well understood by this time, as indicated by the oft-cited observation in Box 18.2 dating from the late fifteenth century.

The practice of maintaining embassies quickly spread to other parts of Europe where, in due course, they became part and parcel of the sovereign state system (Mattingley, 1955: 10). In seventeenth-century France the administrative machinery for managing foreign policy took on a more advanced form under the guidance of one of diplomatic history's foremost figures, Cardinal de Richelieu (1585–1642), who implemented a system in which information flowed continuously both in and out of Paris, complemented by a method of record-keeping together with a unified and controlled system of management under the authority of a single source. This was largely absent elsewhere in Europe where effective centralized government barely existed and foreign policy often depended 'on the coming and going of court favourites, the whim of a monarch and accidents of administrative chaos—to name just three possibilities' (Langhorne, 2000: 37).

Another significant development was the consolidation of the notion of *raison d'état* (**reason of state**). This expressed the idea that the state amounted to more than its ruler and the expression of his—or occasionally her—wishes (Craig and George, 1990: 5). The

Key Quote Box 18.2
The First Duty of an Ambassador

'The first duty of an ambassador is exactly the same as any other servant of a government, and that is, to do, say, advise, and think what may best serve the preservation and aggrandisement of his own state.' (Ermolao Barbaro (1454–93), Venetian noble, scholar, and ambassador at Naples and Rome (cited in Langhorne, 2000: 35))

18

term subsequently became associated with realist ideas about *machtpolitik* (**power politics**) which also implied the irrelevance of morality in the conduct of international relations and the notion that if anything is 'right', it is 'might'. In the realist paradigm, *raison d'état* requires a statecraft attuned to the inevitability of conflict rather than one seeking ends such as justice and perpetual peace. It follows that however much we might agree that these are highly desirable political goods, the *reality* is that peace and justice in the international sphere can only ever be incidental or subordinate to the main business of diplomacy, statecraft, and foreign policy, which is the preservation of the state and the advancement of its interests through whatever means it is prudent to employ. *Raison d'état* has subsequently been absorbed into the notion of **national interest** which is the more acceptable face of power politics in the contemporary period. Liberals and others concerned with the promotion of a more ethical approach to international relations, however, would not find 'national interest' cast in amoral terms acceptable. There is now much discussion of the concept of 'normative power', a quality attributed to the European Union which proponents of the concept say has been developed precisely in order to escape 'great power mentality' (Manners, 2006: 183).

In the wake of the Napoleonic wars, Europe achieved a relatively stable **balance of power** system, initially through the Congress of Vienna (1814–15) at which the great powers were represented mainly by ambassadors and their diplomatic aides. By agreeing to conduct regular meetings, the great powers established the **Concert of Europe**, an early attempt by modern states to institute a formal structure for conducting international relations. Indeed, one source says that this system was a high point in the history of diplomacy: 'They tried to avoid war, protect the status quo and, if this was impossible, to arrange for change by multilateral agreement' (Fry *et al.*, 2002: 113). Diplomacy in earlier centuries, in contrast, had consisted mainly in the representation of the individual interests of one sovereign state vis-à-vis another state, and there was no mechanism for the cooperative management of the international system more generally (ibid). Thus in the Concert system we find the first glimmerings of the kind of multilateralism that came to underpin the League of Nations and the United Nations (UN).

The Concert system declined gradually over the next half century. Later wars, such as the Crimean War of 1854–6 and the Franco–Prussian War of 1870–1, saw its virtual demise. These developments may be attributed at least partly to the rise of **nationalism** which became the principal vehicle of Europe's devastation in the next century. The years 1914–45 and 1939–45 can scarcely go down in the annals of history as bearing testimony to the capacity of European diplomacy and statecraft to ensure greater peace and stability, or as providing an exemplar of civilized behaviour to the rest of the world. Nonetheless, the basic institutions of diplomacy and statecraft in Europe remained an integral part of the sovereign state system, and were carried along with the subsequent global spread of that system.

18

Key Points

- Diplomacy and statecraft have been a feature of relations between political communities from the earliest times, appearing in various forms in different parts of the world.
- Traditional views of diplomacy and statecraft in international relations incorporate elements of realist thought such as *raison d'état* and *machtpolitik*.
- The methods of diplomacy and statecraft used today developed largely within the modern European state system which provided the initial template for the current international system.

Diplomacy in the Contemporary World

Contemporary diplomatic processes cover virtually all aspects of a state's external or foreign relations from trade to aid, negotiations about territorial borders, international treaties of all kinds, the implementation of international law, the imposition of sanctions, the mediation of hostilities, the negotiation of disputed boundaries, fishing rights in the world's oceans, framework agreements on matters concerning environmental protection and climate change, and so on. Diplomacy is not identical to foreign policy, but is rather a means (although not the only means) by which foreign policy is carried out. However, diplomacy in the contemporary period extends beyond the pursuit of any given state's own foreign policy objectives. As suggested in the above examples, it now encompasses such activities as third-party peace negotiations and the various Earth Summits which have seen extensive multilateral diplomatic activity involving a variety of actors.

We have also seen the emergence of 'track two diplomacy' which refers to informal or unofficial diplomatic efforts, sometimes undertaken by private citizens, business people, peace activists or NGOs as well as state actors. It is most commonly deployed in peace negotiations, for example, in preparing the ground for more formal talks by persuading parties in conflict to even agree to negotiate. Diplomacy, however, has not featured as a process in the war on terror to date. It seems unlikely that either the USA or the UK would consider negotiations as part of any solution while the principal figures on the other 'side' have so far been presented as incorrigible. Yet 'winning hearts and minds' among the otherwise angry and impressionable young men and women who are willing to give their lives in the cause (and take as many others with them as possible), is an objective which can only succeed through some sort of effort falling broadly under the rubric of diplomacy. We consider this again in the section on public diplomacy.

Although heads of government are now often involved directly in diplomatic activities—as we shall see shortly—the routine business of external affairs remains essentially in the hands of professional diplomatic services usually located within foreign ministries. In Britain, this is the Foreign and Commonwealth Office (FCO) while in the USA it is a function of the Department of State. Other countries may have a Department of Foreign

18

Affairs and Trade (Australia) or a Ministry of Foreign Affairs with a separate ministry for trade and related matters (e.g. Japan). Whatever they are called, such departments run diplomatic missions, usually in the form of permanent embassies around the world. Within the Commonwealth, these are called High Commissions and the head of mission is the High Commissioner rather than 'ambassador'—one of the legacies of Britain's imperial system. We should also note that many small Third World states face particular problems in maintaining embassies or high commissions, due to the high cost of premises and personnel. This makes it very difficult for them to participate on an equal footing, even though the diplomatic 'playing field' is a level one in formal legalistic terms. As in other spheres, the greater the resources, the greater the clout.

Regular diplomatic missions may be supplemented by special envoys appointed for particular purposes. Thus, Tony Blair, immediately after his resignation as prime minister, was appointed as special Middle East peace envoy representing the 'Quartet' consisting of the USA, Russia, the EU, and the UN. Other special envoys can be appointed by non-state actors such as high level religious leaders. Both the Archbishop of Canterbury and the Pope have appointed special envoys for various purposes—often in conflict situations or as special negotiators when hostages are taken. The Vatican, incidentally, has its own special status as a sovereign entity and such appointments may therefore be seen as a regular function of state.

Sometimes, special forms of diplomacy may be applied in the resolution of internal conflicts and problems. In 2000, ethnic conflict in the Solomon Islands, a former British possession in the Pacific, brought the state to the verge of collapse. With the assistance of Australia and New Zealand, a special diplomatic procedure was put in place that saw around 150 representatives from the rival factions meet 'offshore', with mediators, in Townsville, Australia. This is an example of third-party mediation which has become commonplace as conflicts within states, as well as between them, raise problems for regional and international order. Here we should also note the idea of *preventive* diplomacy which, as the term suggests, refers to diplomatic action undertaken to prevent disputes between parties from escalating into a full-scale conflict.

We noted above that there may be variations in diplomatic styles reflecting, for example, regional factors or considerations. The Association of Southeast Asia Nations (ASEAN) has promoted the 'ASEAN Way' as a distinctive style of diplomacy which, with an emphasis on consensus decision making and an almost absolute commitment to non-interference in the internal affairs of member states, is said to differ from a 'Western' style of diplomacy. Certainly, the member states of the European Union have given considerably less weight to state **sovereignty** in the interests of political and economic integration. And they have been known to openly criticize one other. To see this as reflecting a great gulf of 'cultural difference' between the two regions, however, is misleading. It belies the fact that the doctrine of state sovereignty is itself a European invention, adopted around the world for its political efficacy rather than because it was a good 'cultural fit' in any particular region. As for 'the West', this is not a coherent cultural entity in any case. The diplomatic style of the EU, for instance, has been contrasted very strongly with the hawkish approach to diplomacy and statecraft evinced by the USA in recent years, especially under the administration of George W. Bush.

Key Points

- Contemporary diplomatic practice involves different actors including professional diplomatic services, special envoys, heads of government, the UN, NGOs, and regional bodies such as the EU and ASEAN.

- Different countries or regions are said to possess certain diplomatic styles or orientations, although whether this is due to intrinsic cultural differences is a matter of debate.

- 'Track two diplomacy', undertaken by a range of non-government actors is commonly deployed in peace negotiations and is an important adjunct to formal intergovernmental modes.

Cold War Diplomacy

The study of Cold War diplomatic history is an extensive field dealing with a host of incidents, issues, and crises. These range from the expulsion of diplomats as acts of protests or for alleged spying to such major crises such as the blockade of West Berlin by the Soviets over almost a year between 1948 and 1949, and the Cuban missile crisis of 1962, triggered when the Soviets attempted to deploy nuclear warheads in Cuba. The most serious crises were, thankfully, defused by diplomatic means, thus averting major overt conflict. It is commonly believed that the Cuban missile crisis was the closest the world has ever come to 'hot' nuclear warfare, and that the crisis was resolved largely because US President Kennedy and Soviet Premier Khrushchev both recognized that the consequences would be disastrous. Strategic thinking subsequently produced a theory of **deterrence** known as 'mutually assured destruction' (MAD) which assumed that the possession of incredibly destructive weapons served as the key to preventive strategy. This remains an essential aspect of US foreign and security policy. Recent work on 'nuclear diplomacy' in the Cold War period has sought to answer the question: did the possession of nuclear weapons by both sides actually prevent a Third World War (Gaddis *et al.*, 1999)? There is no clear-cut answer to this question, but what is certain is that without systems of diplomacy operating, however clumsy they may have seemed at times, the Cold War may well have become the 'hottest' ever. Where diplomacy often did fail, however, was in relation to the Third World which bore the brunt of overt conflict conducted via conventional weaponry during the Cold War years.

Cold War diplomacy also introduced the term 'détente'—a French term for 'relaxation of tensions'—into the vocabulary of international politics. This was applied to a period between 1969 and 1979 when tensions eased due to a number of economic and geopolitical

18

circumstances including the fiasco of the Vietnam War (from the US point of view), the souring of Soviet–Chinese relations accompanied by shifting attitudes towards China in the West, the huge cost of the arms race, and the desire to attend more to domestic matters. These factors led to a number of important summit meetings and treaties which, following a Partial Test Ban Treaty in 1963, resulted in the all-important Nuclear Non-Proliferation Treaty (NPT) which opened for signature in 1968. It was subsequently extended indefinitely and currently has a total of 190 signatures, including five nuclear-weapon states—the US, France, the UK, Russia, and China. However, India and Pakistan (who both possess nuclear weapons) and Israel and North Korea (who probably possess actual nuclear weapons in the former case and possibly a covert programme in the latter) are not parties to the treaty.

The NPT was complemented by other treaties and agreements including the Stategic Arms Limitation Treaty (SALT) which had two phases—SALT I from 1969 to 1971, and SALT II from 1972 to 1979 dealing with a range of matters concerning missile deployment. The USA under Reagan, however, withdrew from the latter and adopted a more confrontational approach which saw the end of détente. Nonetheless, international treaties and conventions concerning weapons remain a crucially important part of international diplomacy and the practices and procedures put in place during the Cold War continue as vital elements of contemporary diplomacy surrounding nuclear energy and weaponry, chemical and biological weapons, and the full range of conventional weapons from weapons of mass destruction to small arms and light weapons, land mines, and so on.

Other aspects of Cold War politics and diplomacy are familiar to us through popular culture, often in the form of fiction and cinema. Although the James Bond genre has been thoroughly reinvented for the post-Cold War world, its Cold War origins are unmistakable in its central theme of spying, an activity that developed close associations with Cold War diplomacy. Real-life dramas featured throughout the Cold War as intelligence gathering by both sides deployed almost any means available. And no better on-the-ground facilities existed than embassies and their diplomatic staff. A common feature of Cold War diplomacy was the expulsion of embassy staff for alleged spying offences. The official summary of MI5 on Soviet spying under the protection of embassies is set out in **Box 18.3**.

An interesting continuity was evident in January 2006 when Moscow accused British diplomatic staff of spying in an incident reminiscent of a James Bond film

 Box 18.3

The 1971 Soviet Spy Expulsions

'During the 1960s, the Soviet Union pursued an aggressive and large-scale espionage campaign against Western countries....

By 1971, there were 550 Soviet diplomatic officials resident in the UK—more than in any other Western country, including the United States....

Between 1960 and 1971, 27 Soviet Embassy officials were asked to leave the UK for involvement in "activities incompatible with their [diplomatic] status". However, despite repeated complaints from the British Government, spying continued unabated.

The then Foreign Secretary, Sir Alec Douglas-Home, and Home Secretary Reginald Maudling sent a joint memorandum to the Prime Minister, Edward Heath. They warned that there were at least 120 Soviet intelligence officers operating in Britain . . . :

"If the cases of which we have knowledge are typical, the total damage done by these Soviet intelligence gatherers must be considerable . . . Known targets during the last few years have included the Foreign Office and Ministry of Defence; and on the commercial side, the Concorde, the Bristol "Olympus 593" aero-engine, nuclear energy projects and computer electronics."

The investigation into Soviet activities in the UK . . . came to a head on 24 September 1971 when the Government ordered 90 Soviet officials to leave the UK. It also revoked the visas of a further 15 officials who were abroad at the time . . . .

The Soviet Foreign Minister Andrei Gromyko complained bitterly of the "hooligan-like acts of the British police" and ordered 18 British diplomats to be expelled from Russia in retaliation. But the British action served its purpose. The former KGB officer Oleg Kalugin commented in his book Spymaster (1994) that "our intelligence-gathering activities in England suffered a blow from which they never recovered".'

Source: www.mi5.gov.uk/output/Page244.html

and the high-tech gadgetry designed by the ever-inventive 'M'. A BBC news report of the incident is set out in **Box 18.4**.

And it continues. Another notable episode involved the expulsion in July 2007 of four Russian diplomats from the UK following the alleged murder by radioactive isotope poisoning of former Russian agent, Alexander Litvinenko, who had later become a UK citizen. Traces of isotope were found in places visited by Russian agent, Andrei Lugovoi, who had met with Litvinenko before his death. Russia refused a request for Lugovoi's extradition to face trial for murder. When Britain's Foreign Secretary announced the expulsion of diplomats in retaliation, Moscow's immediate response was a declaration of outrage and denial, followed by the summoning of the British ambassador in Moscow to the Russian foreign office, and then the 'tit-for-tat' expulsion of four British diplomats (see www.news.bbc.co.uk/2/hi/uk_news/politics/6906481.stm, accessed 20/07/07). The murder of a British citizen allegedly by a Russian agent on British soil is obviously a serious issue, but the symbolism of diplomatic gamesmanship in cases like this sometimes seems more like set-piece theatre with a fairly predictable series of moves. The symbolism and predictability of diplomatic gamesmanship, however, may be read as part and parcel of a system of structured interactions in which countries can express deep dissatisfaction with each other while confining it to a manageable arena.

18

 **Box 18.4**

Extract from BBC News: 'UK Diplomats in Moscow Spying Row'

Monday, 23 January 2006

Russia's state security service, the FSB, has accused British diplomats of spying in Moscow. It backed claims made in a Russian TV report which showed footage of what it said was British agents retrieving data from a fake rock planted on a street. . . .

The UK Foreign Office said it was 'concerned and surprised', and denied any improper conduct. . . .The programme said four officials from the UK embassy and one Russian citizen, allegedly recruited by the British secret service, downloaded classified data from a transmitter in the rock onto palm-top computers.

Hidden camera footage appears to show individuals walking up to the rock. . . . One man is caught on camera carrying it away.

A FSB officer told Rossiya television the hi-tech stone was 'absolutely new spy technology'.

The UK embassy in Moscow has refused to comment, but the UK Foreign Office in London issued a statement.

'We are concerned and surprised at these allegations. We reject any allegation of improper conduct in our dealing with Russian NGOs . . . .'

Source: www.news.bbc.co.uk/2/hi/europe/4638136.stm accessed 18/07/07

Key Points

- The Cold War was marked by various crises in which diplomacy played a key role in preventing what may have been a Third World War featuring widespread use of nuclear weapons and the phenomenon of 'Mutually Assured Destruction'.

- Cold War diplomacy also saw the development of a system of treaties and conventions which continue to play an important role in the ongoing attempt to limit the production and distribution of a wide range of weapons.

- Although the end of the Cold War marked a sea change in world politics, continuities have been evident in certain diplomatic incidents in the contemporary period, including diplomatic dramas which illustrate the importance of symbolism in international politics and the extent to which diplomacy is at least partly a stage-managed performance.

Summit Diplomacy

It is evident from the previous sections that diplomatic practices are carried out by many different kinds of actors at different levels and in different capacities. It is increasingly the case, however, that heads of government rather than just professional diplomatic staff, will meet face-to-face over key issues. This goes by the name of 'summit diplomacy', a phrase coined by Winston Churchill in the early Cold War period to describe the top-level negotiations between key leaders at the time. But it is only in the recent past that heads of government have met more regularly to discuss or negotiate directly (Melissen, 2003: 4). Summit diplomacy itself comes in many different kinds ranging from ad hoc bilateral summits—which sometimes include a third party mediator if the issues in question involve a serious dispute—to global multilateral summits which include not only heads of government and leading UN figures but which often run parallel meetings for NGOs as well.

Among the largest and best-known multilateral summit meetings have been the Earth Summits organized by the UN. Regional or interregional summits are now also part and parcel of the regular international scene with organizations such as the Asia-Pacific Economic forum (APEC), the Organization of American States (OAS) and the Asia-Europe Meeting process (ASEM) becoming solidly institutionalized. The Commonwealth has reinvented itself as something of a diplomatic summit club in the postcolonial period with the Commonwealth Heads of Government Meeting (CHOGM) being held every two years to discuss matters of mutual interest and concern and formulate policies and initiatives at the highest level. Sometimes these are seen as little more than opportunities for international socializing at the highest level. The acronym APEC, for example, has been recast as 'A Perfect Excuse for a Chat'. But one should never underestimate the value of diplomatic socialization at any level since it invariably contributes to building **international society**.

Another very different summit of major historic importance was arranged by US President Jimmy Carter at Camp David in 1978 which led to a peace accord between Egypt and Israel which has lasted to this day. Carter, acting as a mediator, also demonstrated the efficacy of 'shuttle diplomacy' as he went back and forth between the main parties in his efforts to broker an agreement. See **Box 18.5**.

Key Points

- Summit diplomacy has become a common feature of the international political landscape since the end of the Second World War, both in ad hoc situations as well as in regularly scheduled events.

- Summit diplomacy has been used in situations as diverse as third party mediation of conflicts involving just a few individuals to large-scale multilateral negotiations over issues such as the environment.

- Summit events may be seen as helping to socialize world leaders into an 'international society' through affording opportunities for personal communication between them.

18

Case Study   Box 18.5
Arab–Israeli Relations, Summit Diplomacy, and the Camp David Accords

Camp David, a presidential retreat north of Washington DC, was the location for a summit meeting between President Anwar Sadat of Egypt and Prime Minister Menachem Begin of Israel in 1978 initiated by US President Jimmy Carter. Since the Six-Day War of 1967, Israel had occupied the Gaza Strip and the Sinai Penninsula, both former Egyptian territories. Sadat had been attempting to reclaim the Sinai since 1971 but negotiations had failed and fighting broke out again when Egypt and Syria, aided by other Arab counties, launched a joint attack on the Jewish holy day of Yom Kippur in 1973. A UN ceasefire was organized on 24 October, followed by a peacekeeping operation. Further negotiations were held with US Secretary of State, Henry Kissinger, acting as a peace broker. An interim agreement between Egypt and Israel, signed in 1975, committed both parties to renouncing further military action. Several years of inaction followed until Sadat broke the stalemate with a visit to Jerusalem in 1977. Begin reciprocated six weeks later, travelling to the Egyptian city of Ismailia. These meetings constituted the main diplomatic prelude to the Camp David Summit. Sadat believed that Gaza and the West Bank belonged to the Palestinians while the Sinai should be returned to Egypt. Begin insisted that God had given them to the Jews. After three days of direct negotiations, tensions mounted further between Sadat and Begin, leaving Carter with the impression that there was little chance of a lasting agreement. He then kept the parties separate while acting as a go-between. A single document was created and Carter worked individually with the leaders to revise it, carrying proposals and counter-proposals back and forth over a two-week period. Although these negotiations almost broke down completely on several occasions, an accord was at last reached through Carter's non-stop 'shuttle diplomacy'. The Israeli–Palestinian dispute is ongoing despite the Oslo Accords of 1993 and a further summit at Camp David in 2000 mediated by President Clinton, but there have been no hostilities between Egypt and Israel since 1978.

For the text of the 1978 Camp David Accords see: www.jimmycarterlibrary.org/documents/campdavid/accords.phtml.

Public Diplomacy

Public diplomacy, which refers primarily to the ways in which governments attempt to influence public opinion abroad, is another area that has acquired increasing importance in recent years. It utilizes the cultural power of ideas, and is implicated in the notion of 'soft power' formulated by the American liberal academic Joseph Nye. He defines this form of power in terms of the ability to achieve one's end without the use of force or even coercion, effectively by winning 'hearts and minds'. See **Box 18.6**. Interestingly, this has some resonances with Antonio Gramsci's notion of cultural power and the way in

18

Key Concept   Box 18.6
'Soft Power'

'It [soft power] is the ability to get what you want through attraction rather than coercion or payments. It arises from the attractiveness of a country's culture, political ideals, and policies. When our policies are seen as legitimate in the eyes of others, our soft power is enhanced . . . When you can get others to admire your ideals and to want what you want, you do not have to spend as much on sticks and carrots to move them in your direction. Seduction is always more effective than coercion, and many values like democracy, human rights, and individual opportunity are deeply seductive . . . But attraction can turn to repulsion if we act in an arrogant manner and destroy the real message of deeper values.'

Source: Nye, 2004a: x

which it supports **hegemony**. More generally, the role of culture in diplomacy, foreign policy, and the broader field of international relations is a highly contested field of debate with both 'culturalists' and their critics producing an abundance of literature on the issue in recent years (see Gaenslen, 1997; Lawson, 2006).

In the UK, the FCO has defined public diplomacy in terms of: 'Work aiming to inform and engage individuals and organisations overseas, in order to improve understanding of and influence for the United Kingdom in a manner consistent with governmental medium and long term goals' (www.fco.gov.uk, accessed 20/07/07). The two most prominent vehicles of public diplomacy are the British Council, which has primary responsibility for promoting British education and culture internationally through some 110 offices around the world, and the BBC World Service which is funded mainly by a grant-in-aid from the FCO, although it claims to enjoy almost complete editorial independence. Its services now include multimedia sites in Arabic, Chinese, Persian, Russian, Spanish, and Urdu (see www.bbc.co.uk/worldservice/).

The US State Department also has a dedicated Under Secretary attending to matters of public diplomacy and public affairs as well as an advisory committee on public diplomacy. The stated purpose of the Under Secretary is to provide for long-term public diplomacy by three strategic objectives:

1. offer people throughout the world a positive vision of hope and opportunity that is rooted in America's belief in freedom, justice, opportunity, and respect for all;

2. isolate and marginalize the violent extremists; confront their ideology of tyranny and hate; undermine their efforts to portray the west as in conflict with Islam by empowering mainstream voices and demonstrating respect for Muslim cultures and contributions; and

3. foster a sense of common interests and common values between Americans and people of different countries, cultures, and faiths throughout the world.

(Source: www.state.gov/r/ accessed 20/07/07.)

18

Other countries promote their own brands of public diplomacy. China, for example, has been proactive in raising its international profile over the last thirty years—all the more important for a country with a poor human rights record and which has suffered serious international image problems, especially following the Tiananmen Square massacre in 1989 when tanks confronted unarmed, peaceful pro-democracy protestors, an incident televised internationally. It is commonly believed that this was a major factor in China's failure to win a bid for the Olympic Games in 2000. The rehabilitation of China's image, however, saw a successful bid to host the 2008 games despite ongoing human rights (and other) problems which resulted in a series of protests by individuals and groups around the world when the games were actually held. More generally, China has opened over a hundred 'Confucius Institutes' around the world to teach Chinese language and culture. Meanwhile, in 2006, the government of India announced that its external affairs ministry was to create 'a new public diplomacy division to educate and influence global and domestic opinion on key policy issues and project a better image of the country commensurate with its rising international standing' (http://timesofindia. indiatimes.com/articleshow/1517855.cms, accessed 20/07/07).

Ad hoc acts of public diplomacy also abound, and include attempts by so-called 'pariah regimes' to attract favourable international attention as well as play to their domestic audiences. Examples include the release amid much fanfare by Iranian President Mahmoud Ahmadinejad of fifteen British navy personnel captured in a waterway between Iraq and Iran in March 2007. Another was the role of Hamas in gaining the release of British journalist, Alan Johnston, in July 2007 after being held for 114 days by the 'Army of Islam' in Gaza. Cuba's offer to the USA (which has no diplomatic relations with Cuba) of medical aid to the victims of Hurricane Katrina in 2005 falls into another interesting category of public diplomacy. The offer, incidentally, was declined.

Some have argued that although public diplomacy is rarely a decisive factor in the success or otherwise of particular foreign policy initiatives, it functions as an important accessory service, especially in the contemporary period in which media and telecommunications has changed so radically. It is further suggested that a new type of public diplomacy is developing in which the focus is shifting from indirectly influencing other governments, which is essentially still a state-to-state interaction, to shaping the attitudes of other societies in a more direct state-to-society interaction (Henriksen, 2006: 1). The need is especially acute for the USA in the present period where, in the Middle East in particular, it has a serious image problem. With the battle for hearts and minds so prominent in international affairs, it is clearly important for states seeking to play a prominent role on the world stage, or to attract attention and support for their various causes, to invest resources in public diplomacy for the 'soft power' it can generate.

Here we may well ask where one draws the line between public diplomacy (usually perceived as a positive thing) and propaganda (usually perceived in negative terms), or whether they are simply different sides of the same coin. Propaganda in a neutral sense simply denotes the dissemination or promotion of particular ideas and values through

18

some means of communication. In a slightly more instrumental sense, it implies an attempt to influence beliefs and behaviour rather than an objective presentation of 'the facts'; but over time it has acquired more sinister overtones and often conjures up images of deceit, distortion of facts or even 'brainwashing'. Contemporary variations on the theme of propaganda include 'spin doctoring', otherwise known as 'news management' which refers to a conscious strategy of minimizing negative images of either politicians or political events while maximizing positive images (see Jowett and O'Donnell, 2006: 2–3); and although 'spin' is most often played to a domestic audience, it clearly has an important place in the international sphere of diplomacy and statecraft as well.

Finally, let us briefly consider a variation on the idea of public diplomacy as it relates to the war on terror and the utility of soft power in winning hearts and minds. A recent article has described the war on terror as a response to a global insurgency that requires a global counter-insurgency strategy. Key to this strategy, according to the author, is winning the trust of those among the general population who support the insurgents, whether tacitly or actively, and certainly not to antagonize them. This may also require listening to and addressing their grievances. It may extend to rethinking US and UK policy in the Middle East and the larger Islamic world (Mockaitis, 2003: 21–2). There is a salutary lesson in the fact that violence is for some the 'normal' response to political grievances, which is precisely the opposite of what diplomacy is all about.

Key Points

- Public diplomacy at its most basic involves attempts by governments to influence public opinion in other countries by promoting positive images of one's country.

- Many acts of public diplomacy, from the release of hostages amid much media publicity to the every day activity of news management, involves elements of propaganda and 'spin'.

- Public diplomacy may be understood as an instrument of soft power in contrast with the methods of power politics.

Foreign Policy

Foreign policy is generally framed in terms of the strategies that states, or rather those in control of a state at any given time, adopt in their dealings with other actors in the international system or with respect to relevant issues, such as the environment, aid to developing countries, trade regimes, and so on. Whatever particular issue is at stake, the study of foreign policy invariably links the domestic and international spheres of politics. As Evans and Newnham (1998: 179) put it, foreign policy is often called a 'boundary activity' because it effectively straddles both spheres and mediates between the two.

An important factor affecting a state's foreign policy behaviour is its regional or geopolitical location. For example, although much attention is presently focused on US behaviour

18

Photo 18.1   Basra, Iraq

Propaganda leaflet distributed by British Royal Marines in Basra, appealing to Iraqi civilians for their cooperation.

Source: © Elio Colavolpe/Editing/Panos Propaganda

in relation to the Middle East, the history of US foreign policy shows how important the Americas have been for forging enduring patterns of foreign policy behaviour. It was in the context of the establishment of independent states in South America, and the attempts by European powers to maintain colonial systems there, that the USA enunciated the 'Monroe Doctrine', named for its initiator, President James Monroe. After safely concluding the purchase of Florida from Spain, Monroe announced to Congress in 1823 that the US would look to maintain an independent line on its interests in the Americas without reference to European interests. See **Box 18.7**. But this did not amount to a declaration of unqualified respect for the sovereignty of the new states emerging in the Americas. The Monroe Doctrine readily evolved into an attitude that political developments in the Americas were not just something that European powers should stay well out of, but something that the USA were entitled to intervene in unilaterally. Subsequent interference by the USA in the internal affairs of Central and South American politics—including the undermining or outright overthrow of leftist governments, whether democratically elected or not—may be seen as the logical outcome of the doctrine.

The foreign policy of the UK has followed a different trajectory in its historical development, shaped both by the dynamics of the European region as well as by its colonizing enterprises. In more recent years, it has become deeply enmeshed in 'special relationships' which have been decisive for its foreign policy. Although there are several 'special' relationships, such as the relationship with the former colonial empire through the Commonwealth as well with fellow EU members, *the* special relationship is the Anglo–American relationship. This has ebbed and flowed according to whatever issues

Key Quote   Box 18.7
The Monroe Doctrine as Announced on 2 December 1823

'...full power and instructions have been transmitted to the minister of the United States at St. Petersburg to arrange by amicable negotiation the respective rights and interests of the two nations on the northwest coast of this continent. A similar proposal has been made by His Imperial Majesty to the Government of Great Britain, which has likewise been acceded to.... In the discussions to which this interest has given rise and in the arrangements by which they may terminate the occasion has been judged proper for asserting, as a principle in which the rights and interests of the United States are involved, that the American continents, by the free and independent condition which they have assumed and maintain, are henceforth not to be considered as subjects for future colonization by any European powers....'

Source: www.yale.edu/lawweb/avalon/monroe.htm, accessed 21/07/07

18

in world politics are salient and according to the personalities involved. The term 'special relationship' actually dates from the time when Roosevelt and Churchill forged a close personal alliance during the Second World War. Another strong personal alliance developed between Margaret Thatcher and Ronald Reagan during the latter stages of the Cold War, assisted no doubt by their conservative dispositions and manifest in their mutual loathing of communism.

The spotlight was turned once again on the special relationship in recent years due to former Prime Minister Blair's unwavering support for George W. Bush in the war on terror and, especially, the invasion of Iraq which was cast by both parties as an integral part of that war even though there was no evidence linking Saddam with Al Qaeda or the events of 9/11. Blair came under much criticism at home for what seemed to be his uncritical endorsement of White House policy and support for a war that turned out to lack any firm justification. The final outcome of the Iraq War for the special relationship, and for perceptions of it in the UK, are not entirely predictable. Although it is unlikely that the relationship itself will suffer serious long-term damage, future prime ministers in the UK may well choose to make a little less of it. In an interesting study, published in 2006, comparing the impact of the Falklands War and the Iraq War, it was suggested that although the idea of the special relationship may have been weakened, there is no reason why there should be any significant move away from the relationship under any new prime minister. After all, it suggests, 'the problem with Iraq lay not in the special relationship itself' but rather with 'flawed analysis which led to flawed policy' (Freedman, 2006: 74). This issue aside, there is little evidence to suggest that the foreign policy behaviour of the US has been influenced by the UK and indeed, its avowed **unilateralism** seems to confirm this.

Key Points

- Foreign policy generally entails the strategies that governments adopt in their dealings with other actors in the international system.

- The foreign policy behaviour of states or other actors is influenced by size, capacity, geopolitical and/or historical circumstances.

- The UK's foreign policy behaviour is sometimes said to be deeply influenced by the 'special relationship' with the USA, although there is little evidence to suggest a reciprocal effect.

The EU's Common Foreign and Security Policy

The EU as a foreign policy actor represents a significant departure from the traditional sovereign state model, although it is in Europe that the model was generated in the first place. In recent years, the EU has been working to develop a Common Foreign and Security Policy (CFSP) in which is also embedded a European Security and Defence Policy (ESDP). A major factor contributing to the development of the

18

CFSP/ESDP, and indeed to the consolidation of the European movement itself, was the end of the Cold War and the perceived need for a coordinated approach to regional affairs in the wake of the collapse of Soviet hegemony in Eastern Europe. Beyond the exigencies of these particular circumstances, it has also been suggested that the challenge for the European project was more fundamental: 'From its origins, the ideal or "vocation" of Europe has been to ensure peace between former warring European nation-states and to provide the conditions for geopolitical stability built on the foundations of a commitment to liberal democracy' (Dannreuther, 2004: 1–2).

The CSFP was embedded in the 1993 Treaty on European Union (otherwise known as the Maastricht Treaty), subsequently refined in the 1999 Amsterdam Treaty and refined again in the Nice Treaty which came into effect in 2003, while the ESDP was given an operational capability in a 2001 meeting of the European Council. The CFSP's basic working profile is set out in **Box 18.8**.

These objectives clearly reflect a desire to export European political norms—especially in respect of human rights, democracy and **good governance**—to other parts of the world. As we have seen earlier, it is now said that the EU consciously projects itself as a qualitatively different kind of power in the international sphere—a 'normative power'—staking a claim 'to being a legitimate and thus a more effective international actor' (Farrell, 2005: 453). Further, while 'American unilateralism renews the legitimacy of power politics

Box 18.8

EU Common Foreign and Security Policy: Objectives and Mechanisms

The Amsterdam Treaty spells out five fundamental objectives of CFSP:

- to safeguard the common values, fundamental interests, independence and integrity of the Union in conformity with the principle of the United Nations Charter ;
- to strengthen the security of the Union in all ways;
- to preserve peace and strengthen international security, in accordance with the principles of the United Nations Charter, as well as the principle of the Helsinki Final Act and the objectives of the Paris Charter, including those on external borders;
- to promote international cooperation;
- to develop and consolidate democracy and the rule of law, and respect for human rights and fundamental freedoms.

The treaty also identifies several ways in which these objectives are to be pursued:

- defining the principles and general guidelines for the common foreign and security policy.
- deciding on common strategies.
- adopting joint actions and common positions.

Additionally, mechanisms for regular political dialogue with a whole range of third countries have been set up, usually with troika meetings at ministerial, senior officials and working group level, summits and in some cases, meetings with all Member States and the Commission at ministerial or senior officials level . . . .

Outside these regular mechanisms, the EU maintains a political presence, particularly in areas of crisis or conflict. Special Representatives have been appointed to the Great Lakes (Africa), Middle East, Stability Pact, Former Yugoslav Republic of Macedonia, Ethiopia/Eritrea and Afghanistan. These Special Representatives provide a direct link to developments in these areas and allow the EU to have an active involvement in the search for lasting solutions.'

Source: http://ec.europa.eu/external_relations/cfsp/intro/index.htm, accessed 21/07/07

on the world stage, the normative approach in the European management of international relations sustains the relevance of the very notion of global governance' (ibid.). This illustrates once again the idea of soft power versus militarism and power politics more generally in achieving foreign policy objectives.

Key Points

- The emergence of the EU as a foreign policy actor in its own right represents a significant departure from the traditional state model which Europe itself generated.

- EU foreign policy is founded on a set of ideals which attempt to project 'normative power' and which is comparable in turn to 'soft power'.

- The contrast between EU and US approaches to foreign policy undermines the notion of 'the West' constituting a coherent cultural/political entity in the international sphere.

Conclusion

→ See chapter seven, pages 173–80, for a discussion of strong and weak states.

Diplomacy implies peaceful or at least non-violent interactions between political actors and 'diplomatic solutions' are frequently contrasted with military ones. By the mid-twentieth century the traditional role of diplomacy was certainly understood as a means of maintaining an international order in the interests of peace and stability (Butterfield, 1966: 190). The sections on summit diplomacy and public diplomacy, in particular, further reinforce the image of diplomacy as a peaceful instrument of policy. But diplomacy is not always a process of negotiation between equals. States are not equal in their capacities or capabilities and stronger states are often in a superior bargaining position. Indeed, diplomacy can well be aggressive and coercive, as reflected in the phrase 'gunboat diplomacy' in which the threat of force accompanies negotiations. Clausewitz famously proposed that war is simply 'the continuation of policy by other means' and a necessary instrument of foreign policy. But he also believed that if war had no specific, desirable political purpose, it was both stupid and wrong (Howard, 1966: 197). Diplomacy can certainly be accompanied by the proverbial sabre-rattling and shade into war. However, diplomacy at its best is the very antithesis of war. It is a means by which conflicts and disagreements in the international sphere can be resolved peacefully via processes of negotiating, bargaining, and accommodation which spare all parties the prospect of death and destruction through direct violence. In the final analysis, foreign policies attuned to this end are much more likely to serve the 'national interest' than the resort to the far cruder instruments of force.

 *Key Questions*

- What distinguishes diplomacy and statecraft from other forms of political activity?
- If states are no longer considered the only relevant actors in the international sphere, do they remain the most effective when it comes to diplomatic activity?
- To what extent has diplomatic practice achieved uniformity throughout the international state system?
- Are there genuinely different styles of diplomacy according to cultural factors or is the influence of culture in this sense sometimes exaggerated?
- What role did deterrence play in 'nuclear diplomacy' during the Cold War?
- Under what circumstances is summit diplomacy likely to be effective?
- Is public diplomacy little more than propaganda on an international scale?
- Is the war on terror amenable to diplomatic solutions?
- In what ways does foreign diplomacy link the domestic and international spheres?
- What is the Monroe Doctrine and how does it illustrate the historic importance of geopolitics in US foreign policy?

 Further Reading

Berridge, G. R. (2005), *Diplomacy: Theory and Practice,* Basingstoke: Palgrave Macmillan, 3rd edn.

> This book combines theoretical and historical perspectives on various styles and modes of diplomacy, a theoretical treatise of primary characteristics of the modes of diplomacy, and includes discussion of key themes such as the art of negotiation, bilateral and multilateral diplomacy, summit diplomacy, and mediation. The author maintains a website on which he updates his work: http://grberridge.diplomacy.edu/

Kennedy, Paul (1989), *The Rise and Fall of the Great Powers: Economic Change and Military Conflict from 1500 to 2000,* London: Fontana.

> This book covers much more than diplomacy, statecraft and foreign policy but as a classic text in the general field of international history it provides much of the backdrop against which the themes of this chapter may be best understood.

18

Nathan, James (2002), *Soldiers, Statecraft, and History: Coercive Diplomacy and International Order,* Greenwood, CT: Praeger Publishers.

> This is a wide-ranging study which sets contemporary diplomatic practices against the historical backdrop of the rise of the modern state system, paying particular attention to force and coercion.

 *Web Links*

www.fco.gov.uk
Homepage of the UK Foreign and Commonwealth Office's official website.

www.state.gov/
Homepage of the US Department of State's official website.

www.ec.europa.eu/external_relations
Section of the official EU website which provides a gateway into different aspects of the EU's external affairs.

www.foreignpolicy.com
The website of the journal *Foreign Policy,* published in the USA, makes available general information and short reports on issues in current foreign policy as well as partial access to its main articles.

http://fpc.org.uk
The Foreign Policy Centre, based in the UK, describes itself as 'a leading European think tank launched under the patronage of the British Prime Minister Tony Blair to develop a vision of a fair and rule-based world order'.

http://english.hanban.edu.cn/market/HanBanE/412360.htm
Homepage of the Office of Chinese Language Council International containing information on the Confucius Institute project.

 Visit the **Online Resource Centre** that accompanies this book to access more learning resources at **www.oxfordtextbooks.co.uk/orc/garner/**

International Organizations

Reader's Guide

This chapter looks first at the nature of international organizations and the way in which they are generally understood as participants in international relations. It then reviews the rise of international organizations from a historical perspective, with special reference to developments in Europe from the nineteenth century onwards. The chapter goes on to discuss the major intergovernmental institutions that emerged in the twentieth century and which have played such an important role in shaping world order. We look briefly at the League of Nations but most attention is given to its successor, the United Nations, and its various appendages. Then there is the world of NGOs, populated with a bewildering variety of bodies. Some possess significant status in the international sphere, others have little relevance, and still others pose dangers. Finally, we consider ideas about social movements and international civil society and their relationship to the contemporary world of international organizations. In reviewing these institutions and actors we should keep in mind that liberal international theory, especially in the form of 'liberal institutionalism', as well as proponents of international society, regard robust international organizations as essential building blocks of world order.

What is an International Organization?

International organizations, from the United Nations down to voluntary organizations with constituent members in just a few countries, operate in a sphere which transcends states and the state system in one way or another. This does not mean that they are necessarily more powerful or more important than states—and certainly a realist would not regard them in this way. But like states, international organizations exist as tangible institutional products of social and political forces. Beyond that, they comprise clusters of ideas and coalitions of interest at a transnational level and generate purposeful activities in pursuit of certain desired outcomes.

They may be public or private organizations, depending on whether they are set up by state actors or by non-state actors. Most are permanent, or at least aspire to an ongoing existence, even if many fall by the wayside. They invariably possess constitutional structures, although the extent to which they possess a legal personality is often unclear. Their power varies enormously, depending on the size and the resources at their disposal. And they come in such diverse forms that it is difficult to pin them down to one clear description. The term international organization also overlaps with **international regime**. The latter concept originated as a way of understanding international cooperation. As Keohane (1993: 23) explains, highly organized and systematic cooperation characterizes much of world politics, yet there are few rules that are hierarchically enforced. Rather, they are followed voluntarily and cooperatively, becoming embedded in relations of reciprocity. An international regime, though not itself an organization as such, usually incorporates one or more international organizations whose interests centre around a particular issue or theme. A prime example is the 'international human rights regime' which revolves around a cluster of important norms and principles that give it its focus. It encompasses many organizations, including—but not limited to—the UN, and operates through processes and rules set up to promote and protect human rights at both national and international levels (see Rittberger and Zangl, 2006: 6–7).

Some definitions encompass multinational corporations and these do fit a broad conception of what constitutes an international organization. However, multinationals are often treated separately from government and non-profit actors. The *Yearbook of International Organizations 2005/2006*, which lists around 40,000 active bodies as well as several thousand inactive or near-dead entities, does not include multinationals (see www.uia.org/statistics/ organizations/types-2004.pdf, accessed 04/08/2007). We do not consider multinationals further in this chapter, but encounter them again in chapter twenty on international political economy.

Another category of international organization, which is also excluded from most standard definitions, encompasses transnational criminal organizations or TCOs. They are included here because they are becoming increasingly important actors. They have been implicated very clearly in the 'new wars' described by Kaldor (2006) as combining traditional aspects of war with organized crime and involving actors at many levels. Whereas organized crime has been very largely a concern for domestic policing agencies in earlier periods, the development of TCOs has required increased policing cooperation in the international sphere to deal with their various activities which include drugs, money laundering, people smuggling, and weapons smuggling. One author notes that the emergence of TCOs results at least partly from the same underlying changes in the international sphere that have proved conducive to the success of transnational corporations. Thus increased **interdependence** between states and the permeability of boundaries, developments in international travel and communications and the globalization of international financial networks 'have facilitated the emergence of what is, in effect, a single global market for both licit and illicit commodities' (Williams, 1997: 316). In addition to their sheer criminality, TCOs are also increasingly seen as threats to both national and international security, especially in the post-9/11 world. It has been suggested that even though they are primarily economic actors, they may facilitate the business of terror networks through the provision of money-laundering facilities, false documents, and the procurement of weapons or other material for terrorist purposes. There may also be a growing convergence between some terrorist organizations and organized crime networks (see Sanderson, 2004: 49–61; Dishman, 2005: 237–52).

For the remainder of the chapter we focus mainly on those international organizations which are more conventionally recognized as such, namely, those set up by states through multilateral agreements, sometimes called intergovernmental organizations or IGOs, and those set up by non-state or non-government actors whose primary business is not strictly commercial (or illicit)—these are the ubiquitous **non-government organizations** or NGOs. An important theme here is the interaction between different organizations in the international sphere that make a model of international relations based almost exclusively on individual sovereign states acting on their own initiative and in their own interest seem very inadequate. At the same time, those who lean heavily in the other direction by exaggerating the importance of international organizations can too easily dismiss the crucial role that states play, not simply in organizing their own affairs, but in creating the very world of international organizations that may seem to make states less important in many areas. The quote in **Box 19.1** suggests an approach which balances these views.

Key Points

- International organizations come in such a variety of forms that they are difficult to define, both with respect to their relationship with states and the state system as well as in terms of their constituent elements.

- IR scholars interested in the contribution that international organizations make to the international system as a whole tend to focus on intergovernmental organizations and non-government organizations.

19

- Although multinational corporations and terrorist and other criminal organizations operating in the international sphere do constitute international organizations of a kind, they are usually treated separately.

Key Quote Box 19.1
International Organizations

'There are two predominant views of international organizations among the general public. The first is a cynical view that emphasizes the dramatic rhetoric and seeming inability to deal with vital problems that are said to characterize international organizations and the UN in particular. According to this view, mirrored in some realist formulations, international organizations should be treated as insignificant actors on the international stage. The other view is an idealistic one. Those who hold this view envisage global solutions to the problems facing the world today, without recognition of the constraints imposed by state sovereignty. Most of the naive calls for world government are products of this view. An understanding of international organizations and global governance probably requires that neither view be accepted in its entirety, nor be wholly rejected. International organizations are neither irrelevant nor omnipotent in global politics. They play important roles in international relations, but their influence varies according to the issue area and situation confronted'. (Diehl, 2005: 3)

The Emergence of International Organizations

'History, prior to the nineteenth century, affords relatively few examples of international organizations' (Gerbet, 1981: 28). Although this is a widely accepted view, the myriad international organizations of the present era do have important precursors. We have seen in previous chapters that certain structures, systems, activities, and ideas that are generally taken as characteristic of contemporary relations between political communities did not simply emerge out of nothing in Western Europe in the modern period and then spread to the rest of the world. Just as recognizable diplomatic practices have been manifest in different times in different places, so too have recognizable international organizations. The earliest known examples appear to have been defensive leagues set up among a number of small, neighbouring states. This was the case in at least one part of China between the seventh and the fifth centuries BC where assemblies met to organize their defences, while in ancient Greece rudimentary international organizations were established to arbitrate on issues of mutual concern to a number of city-states (see, generally, Harle, 1998).

Examples of international organizations in late medieval Europe include the Hanseatic League which operated between the fourteenth and sixteenth century and in which some fifty towns joined forces for the mutual protection of their trading interests, with representatives meeting in a general assembly to decide policy by majority voting. The Swiss confederation, dating from the late 1200s, and the United Provinces of the Netherlands, which emerged in the sixteenth century, although limited territorially, effectively started out as international organizations (Gerbet, 1981: 28–9; Klabbers, 2003: 16). The Catholic Church, which held sway throughout much of Europe in earlier periods, may also be counted among the earliest international organizations, and one with considerable political as well as cultural power. It was also probably one of the first organizations to establish a near universal presence in the modern period to match its name—'catholic' meaning universal in the sense of 'all-embracing'.

The scale of international organization in earlier times was necessarily constrained by limitations on mobility and communications, as was the phenomenon of **globalization** itself. As communications and transport technologies developed, so too did the capacity to form ongoing associations which eventually gave rise to formal organizations on a much broader, more inclusive scale, and which were intended to have a more or less permanent existence. The rise of the modern state system, together with technological advances in transport and communications, therefore saw not only the enhancement of diplomatic networks and practices among states, but an accompanying growth of organizations designed to facilitate the business of international relations as such. State actors may well have looked first to their own interests, but on a very wide range of matters those interests were likely to be enhanced by cooperation with other states on a whole range of matters, especially trade. And in turn, international cooperation was best achieved through certain kinds of organizations set up for particular purposes and through which rules and procedures agreed on by member states could be operationalized.

Also discussed in the previous chapter was the **Concert of Europe** or 'Concert system' which emerged among the great powers in post-Napoleonic Europe. This was not what we would call an international organization since it lacked a constitution, a permanent secretariat, a headquarters and did not meet on a regular basis (see Gerbet, 1981: 32). It may nonetheless be seen as a precursor to other major European developments in later years. The Concert system, as we have seen, started with the 1815 Congress of Vienna which provided a benchmark for interstate cooperation on setting international boundaries and managing waterways (vital for trade) on the continent as well as establishing certain diplomatic protocols. Subsequent conferences generated as part of the Concert system established a pattern of interaction which nurtured important ideas about collective responsibility and a mutual commitment to 'concert together' against threats to the system. Most importantly, it established the idea that a state's representatives should meet not merely to sign peace treaties at the end of a war, but to meet during peaceful periods to prevent war (Archer, 1983: 7).

➜ See chapter eighteen, page 412, for a description of the Concert of Europe.

Although the Concert system virtually ceased to exist after the mid-nineteenth century, the second half of the nineteenth century did see further ad hoc conferences held on important matters of mutual interest. For example, the 1878 Congress of Berlin met to settle issues in the Balkans following the Russo–Turkish war of 1877–8 and included delegates from the major European powers and observers from several smaller European states with interests in the region as well as representatives of the Ottoman Empire. With the inclusion of the latter, the international element of such conferences was expanded beyond Europe into West Asia. Other treaties and conventions which reached beyond Europe were applied in relation to colonial territories and the USA, often with respect to the navigation of waterways to facilitate trade. The Hague Conferences of 1899 and 1907 established the principle of compulsory arbitration of disputes giving the development of international law a significant boost.

It is noteworthy also that the Congress of Vienna was the first significant international forum that took a stand on a broad humanitarian issue by condemning the slave trade as contrary to universal morality (Butler and MacCoby, 2003: 353). This was quite an unusual step for such a conference. It is no coincidence that it occurred around the time that private organizations, many with a specific philanthropic mission, started to make their presence felt on the international scene as well. The anti-slavery movement in Britain, already active domestically and a prime force behind the Congress resolution, gave rise to an early NGO when its supporters coalesced into the 'Society for the Mitigation and Gradual Abolition of Slavery Throughout the British Dominions' in 1823. Anti-Slavery International, which operates today, was originally founded in 1839 and in 1840 a World Anti-Slavery Convention was held in London (see www.antislavery.org/). Anti-Slavery International is also associated with the International Labor Organization (ILO), itself established by the Treaty of Versailles in 1919 with the status of an autonomous institution but in association with the League of Nations. It survived the demise of the League and is now a UN agency. The early anti-slavery efforts were underpinned by concerted activism on the part of British women who had formed their own local anti-slavery societies and went on to forge international links, especially across the Atlantic. In these activities we also see an emergent women's movement which spread nationally and internationally to take up various causes, including their own liberation (see, generally, Midgley, 1992).

Transport and communications technologies, so essential to both globalization and the emergence of functioning international organizations, were themselves among the most important subjects of international agreements and formal associations. For example, the year 1865 saw the foundation of the International Telegraph Union (now the International Telecommunications Union), followed in 1874 by the Universal Postal Union and in 1890 by the International Union of Railway Freight Transportation (see Klabbers, 2003: 18). The two former organizations are now UN specialized agencies, again illustrating continuities in the system of international organizations despite the massive disruption of two world wars in the twentieth century. However, improvements in transport technologies brought with it other problems, including the more rapid spread of disease, and so concerns about international public health were reflected in the 1853 International Sanitary Convention and subsequent conventions and international offices. Equally, the rapid development of industry and trade saw the introduction of an International Bureau of Weights and Measures in 1875 while on the intellectual property front the Union for the Protection of the Rights of Authors over their Literary and Artistic Property was established in 1884. Private associations at an international level began to outstrip intergovernmental ones in this period, accelerating the trend in **internationalism**. Such associations were set up in connection with every kind of activity including humanitarian, religious, ideological, scientific, and technological (Gerbet 1981: 36).

At the first World Congress of International Organizations held in Brussels in 1910, convened under the auspices of the Union of International Associations, 132 international bodies and thirteen governments were represented. A second world congress in Ghent and Brussels in 1913 saw 169 international associations and twenty-two governments represented. The last world congress of this type (the seventh), was held in 1927 after which the League of Nations assumed responsibility (www.uia.org/ta/). The overall trend to internationalism for the century before the outbreak of the First World War might have indicated that a new era of peaceful international relations was about to dawn. Other forces, including those of **nationalism**, were also at work. The death and destruction of the period 1914–18 was, for a number of key actors, the clarion call for a permanent intergovernmental organization supporting a strong framework for international law and designed above all to prevent further international conflict, a need reinforced rather than undermined by the Second World War.

Key Points

- Although forms of international organization existed before the nineteenth century, the Congress of Vienna in 1815 and subsequent conferences acted as catalysts for their rapid growth in the nineteenth century which also helped underpin a nascent body of international law.

- Private organizations also achieved a significant international presence in the nineteenth and early twentieth centuries, those with philanthropic aims contributing to the development of humanitarian principles and the idea of international morality.

- Developments in transport and communications technologies provided a boost to the growth of international organizations and themselves became the subject of international agreements and associations along with a host of other agreements.

Intergovernmental Organizations

The supremo of all IGOs is the UN—officially styled the United Nations Organization—with near universal membership of the world's states. It is self-described as a 'global association of governments facilitating cooperation in international law, security, economic development, and social equity' (www.un.org accessed 06/08/07). The early development of the UN has already been set out, as has the role of the Security

19

Council, so we focus here on other aspects of the UN's history, structure, and mission. First, it is useful to recall the key ideas behind the development of its predecessor organization, the League of Nations. These ideas were to come under attack from realists in later years for their vision of a peaceful world order founded on strong institutions of **global governance** and an explicit emphasis on the place of morality in the international sphere rather than just naked self-interest. The preface to US President Woodrow Wilson's famous Fourteen Points address to the US Congress in January 1918 stands as one of the clearest statements of the idealist vision of world order in that period. The preface was followed by a 'program of the world's peace', the fourteenth point of which proposed the formation of a general association of nations, an idea given substance by the formation of the League of Nations in the immediate aftermath of the war.

We may recall that the League of Nations, which was meant to function as a collective security organization, has sometimes been described as a failed experiment because it did not prevent the Second World War. It could also be argued, however, that the Second World War illustrated just how important it is to have a strong, functioning intergovernmental organization to provide for collective security as well as many other matters requiring international support and coordination. In any event, a number of key institutions and practices set up under its auspices survived and are enshrined in the present UN system. Certainly, the latter owes much to the previous experiment in global governance which in turn drew on the earlier experiences of the Concert system, thus demonstrating a continuity over nearly two centuries.

The UN emerged from the wartime cooperation between the major powers of the time, with many other states then joining in to create a more truly international body operating under a formal charter setting out the rights and obligations of members. The preamble to the Charter states the general principles and ideals on which the organization is based. See **Box 19.2**. The main organs of the UN are set out in the UN's official organizational chart at www.un.org/aboutun/chartlg.html.

 Box 19.2

Preamble to the Charter of the United Nations

WE THE PEOPLES OF THE UNITED NATIONS DETERMINED

- to save succeeding generations from the scourge of war, which twice in our lifetime has brought untold sorrow to mankind, and
- to reaffirm faith in fundamental human rights, in the dignity and worth of the human person, in the equal rights of men and women and of nations large and small, and
- to establish conditions under which justice and respect for the obligations arising from treaties and other sources of international law can be maintained, and
- to promote social progress and better standards of life in larger freedom,

AND FOR THESE ENDS

- to practice tolerance and live together in peace with one another as good neighbours, and
- to unite our strength to maintain international peace and security, and
- to ensure, by the acceptance of principles and the institution of methods, that armed force shall not be used, save in the common interest, and
- to employ international machinery for the promotion of the economic and social advancement of all peoples,

Source: www.un.org/aboutun/charter/index.html

The business of the first organ, the Trusteeship Council, set up for the purpose of dealing with eleven non-self-governing trust territories which had formerly been League of Nations mandate territories, was terminated in 1994 when the last trust territory, administered by the USA, chose self-government and became an independent state. The second, and most powerful, of the UN's organs is of course the Security Council discussed earlier. The third, and some may say the weakest, as well as being the largest, is the General Assembly. A common criticism is that it produces little but endless ineffective resolutions since there is no mechanism for enforcing them. This illustrates the fact that the UN General Assembly cannot be compared directly with a legislature because although its resolutions may carry normative force, and guide policy, they cannot have the same legal status as legislation produced by a parliament within a national sphere. However, it would be a mistake to dismiss the significance of the General Assembly as a debating forum. It is the one place where representatives from all states can meet on a more or less equal footing, express views and debate the full range of issues in international politics. It is, moreover, a key forum for both formal and informal diplomacy and strategic alliances on issues that come up for a vote. This does not necessarily produce desirable outcomes, let alone outcomes that satisfy everyone, but that is in the nature of any political body.

The Economic and Social Council (ECOSOC) has a mandate to initiate studies and reports and to formulate policy recommendations extending over an enormous range of economic and social issues covering living standards, full employment, international economic, social and health problems; facilitating international cultural and educational cooperation, and encouraging universal respect for human rights and fundamental freedoms. Some of the best-known UN agencies, such as the World Health Organization (WHO), the Food and Agricultural Organization (FAO), the United Nations Educational, Scientific and Cultural Organization (UNESCO), and the World Bank group all fall under its rubric. It has a major role in organizing the many major international conferences initiated by the UN and oversees the functional commissions, regional commissions, and other special bodies set out in the organizational chart. Given its scope and size ECOSOC is by far the largest of the UN's principal organs and expends more than 70 per cent of the human and financial resources of the entire UN system (see www.un.org/ecosoc/about/).

One of ECOSOC's most difficult and controversial functional commissions has been that dealing with human rights, and a brief account of developments in this area illustrates just how problematic it is to achieve coherence in regimes of global governance. The establishment of a Human Rights Commission (HRC) was mandated by the UN's Charter and reflected the abhorrence of the atrocities of the Second World War. Past wars had produced some appalling cases of cruelty and ill-treatment, but the nature of the genocidal policies of Nazi Germany was unprecedented. Beginning with the Universal Declaration of Human Rights (UDHR) which was adopted by the General Assembly in 1948, the Commission produced a raft of human rights documents and treaties over a period of almost sixty years. See **Box 19.3**. The behaviour of many governments around the world over that period, however, demonstrates clearly that the existence of the Charter, or the fact that all members of the UN must endorse the UDHR, is no guarantee that basic human rights will be respected or protected.

Another problem featuring in international debates since the Charter was first drawn up concerns what are seen as two different types of rights: civil and political rights on the one hand, and economic, social, and cultural rights on the other. The former are sometimes seen as possessing a typically 'Western' liberal character unsuited to the cultural context of non-Western countries. The most vocal proponents of this view have come from a number of Muslim and African countries and parts of East Asia, especially China. In addition, economic, social and cultural rights are often regarded as more urgent for poorer, underdeveloped countries than the right to vote. It must be noted, however, that human rights activists in such countries generally do not support these kinds of arguments.

An early division of opinion on the two different clusters of rights gave rise to the development of separate covenants for each and so in 1976 the International Covenant

Box 19.3

The Universal Declaration of Human Rights (UDHR)

The UDHR was adopted by the General Assembly of the United Nations on 10 December 1948, reflecting a moment in international history when all member states could agree, at least in principle, to a substantial list of human rights ranging from the basic right to life to a host of economic and social goods. All new members joining the UN must sign up to the UDHR.

The Preamble highlights ideals which recognize the 'inherent dignity' and 'the equal and inalienable rights of all members of the human family [as] the foundation of freedom, justice and peace in the world'; it notes the extent to which 'disregard and contempt for human rights have resulted in barbarous acts which have outraged the conscience of mankind'; and heralds 'the advent of a world in which human beings shall enjoy freedom of speech and belief and freedom from fear and want has been proclaimed as the highest aspiration of the common people.'

The Declaration itself contains thirty Articles, the first ten of which are set out below:

Article 1 All human beings are born free and equal in dignity and rights. They are endowed with reason and conscience and should act towards one another in a spirit of brotherhood.

Article 2 Everyone is entitled to all the rights and freedoms set forth in this Declaration, without distinction of any kind, such as race, colour, sex, language, religion, political or other opinion, national or social origin, property, birth or other status. Furthermore, no distinction shall be made on the basis of the political, jurisdictional or international status of the country or territory to which a person belongs, whether it be independent, trust, non-self-governing or under any other limitation of sovereignty.

Article 3 Everyone has the right to life, liberty and security of person.

Article 4 No one shall be held in slavery or servitude; slavery and the slave trade shall be prohibited in all their forms.

Article 5 No one shall be subjected to torture or to cruel, inhuman or degrading treatment or punishment.

Article 6 Everyone has the right to recognition everywhere as a person before the law.

Article 7 All are equal before the law and are entitled without any discrimination to equal protection of the law. All are entitled to equal protection against any discrimination in violation of this Declaration and against any incitement to such discrimination.

Article 8 Everyone has the right to an effective remedy by the competent national tribunals for acts violating the fundamental rights granted him by the constitution or by law.

Article 9 No one shall be subjected to arbitrary arrest, detention or exile.

Article 10 Everyone is entitled in full equality to a fair and public hearing by an independent and impartial tribunal, in the determination of his rights and obligations and of any criminal charge against him.

Source: www.un.org/Overview/rights.html, accessed13/8/07

➜ See chapter eight, page 190, for summaries of many other social and economic rights included in the UDHR.

on Civil and Political Rights (ICCPR) and the International Covenant on Economic, Social, and Cultural Rights (ICESCR), entered into force. Apart from representing two broad approaches to rights, the covenants also represent a significant attempt to advance the codification of human rights as such and to introduce an international legal framework to support their advancement. Member states are not obliged to sign up to the covenants, but those that do so agree to accept their provisions as legal obligations as well as moral obligations.

More generally, the history of human rights issues in the UN has been plagued by competing conceptions of what the UN can and cannot, or should and should not, do to advance the protection of human rights around the world. On the one hand, the UN is committed to respect for state **sovereignty** and therefore to the notion that each state is entitled to conduct its own affairs free from external interference. On the other hand, it is committed to the universality of human rights which implies that it is not only entitled, but actually enjoined, to act to promote and protect human rights wherever and whenever such action is needed. Any action—even criticism of state practices—can be construed as a violation of state sovereignty. The HRC itself was frequently caught between these imperatives and contradictions. Apart from issues of state sovereignty versus universal principles, some countries represented on the Commission at any one time were themselves countries where human rights abuses—often perpetrated by the government—were being carried out. However, countries with poor human rights records—mainly outside 'the West'—complained of being unfairly singled out for criticism. This also led to accusations of attempted interference in the internal affairs of sovereign states. By 2006, the HRC was seen as an ineffectual and largely discredited body. It was replaced by a new Human Rights Council which has new terms for membership and functions. Whether it can avoid past problems remains to be seen (see Alston, 2006).

The fifth main organ of the UN is the International Court of Justice (ICJ) located in The Hague. As with other parts of the UN system, its origins can be traced to much earlier periods and linked to the gradual development in the modern era of methods of mediation and arbitration of disputes between states. Its immediate predecessor, the Permanent Court of International Justice (PCIJ), was part of the League of Nations system and operated from 1922 until it was dissolved in 1946 to make way for the new UN court. The fifteen judges of the ICJ are elected for nine-year terms by both the UN General Assembly and the Security Council. The ICJ functions as something of a world court with the jurisdiction to decide legal disputes submitted to it by states and to give advisory opinions on legal questions at the request of UN organs or authorized agencies. Between May 1947 and August 2007, 136 cases had been entered into its General List.

A recent example was the case brought with respect to the application of the Convention on the Prevention and Punishment of the Crime of Genocide (Bosnia and Herzegovina *v.* Serbia and Montenegro) on which judgment was delivered in February 2007. The 171-page judgment dealt with a number of issues, and the case of Srebrenica in particular. This village was the scene of the single biggest massacre in Europe since the end of the Second World War when Serb forces killed approximately 8,000 Bosnian Muslim males. While the court found Serbia and Montenegro not guilty of deliberately perpetrating a genocide, it was found guilty of *failing to prevent* a genocide and therefore in breach of its obligations in international law (see www.icj-cij.org). Note that this case was separate from the trial of former Serb President Slobodan

19

Milošević which was conducted by a special tribunal, the International Criminal Tribunal for the Former Yugoslavia (ICTY) established by a UN Security Council resolution. Milošević's trial ended prematurely with his death in 2006 (although the trial had already run for four years by then) but was nonetheless seen as a landmark case because it was the first time a former head of state had been put on trial before an international criminal tribunal.

The sixth and final organ comprises the UN Secretariat and the office of the Secretary-General. The organizational map of the General Assembly alone, which currently brings together 191 member states at least annually as well as running important offices and conferences and providing services in six official languages (English, French, Arabic, Chinese, Russian, and Spanish), makes clear how extensive the demand for the services of a secretariat is (Gordenker, 2005: 16). The Secretary-General also seems to be expected to be everywhere at once, and possess an encyclopaedic knowledge not only of the UN system itself, but of all the world's troubles, both current and potential. In practice, the Secretary-General will often appoint a representative for much routine committee work. One particularly important role for the Secretary-General is to bring matters likely to affect international peace and security to the attention of the Security Council and to report regularly on operations that the UN is involved in. Although the Secretary-General has no authority beyond issuing formal warnings of trouble and delivering information, including anything gleaned from informal discussions, the importance of this function should not be underestimated.

The UN has also populated the sphere of international organizations with a plethora of agencies and special programs; the WHO, the FAO, UNICEF, and UNESCO have already been mentioned above and the UN's organizational chart lists many more. Some, like UNICEF, are well known but others such as the United Nations Population Fund (UNFPA) are unlikely to register immediately in the minds of the general public. Others have emerged in more recent years to deal with problems unheard of in earlier periods. These include the joint UN Programme on HIV/AIDS (UNAIDS). Then there are regional commissions dealing with all the major regions of the world: Africa, Europe, Latin America and the Caribbean, Asia and the Pacific, and western Asia (more commonly called the Middle East).

The UN and its agencies do not have the IGO field entirely to itself. There is also a growing number of regional organizations. The EU and ASEAN have been mentioned in previous chapters but there are many others as well, from the African Union (AU) and the Pacific Islands Forum (PIF) to numerous trading blocs such as MERCOSUR in Latin America. These reflect another significant development in the world of international organizations, and that is the trend to **regionalization** which we consider in more detail in the final chapter. For the moment, we may note that this trend, which has been gathering pace over the last few decades, is likely to have a significant impact in the future, but one which is likely to complement the role of the UN rather than compete directly with it. This points to a future in which intergovernmental organizations are likely to play an increasingly important role in world order rather than a diminishing one.

Key Points

- The League of Nations is often seen as a failure but it was nonetheless an important forerunner to the UN and a number of its institutions have been maintained as part of the latter system.

- The UN is the largest single intergovernmental organization with five functioning main organs and a plethora of programmes, agencies, commissions, funds, courts, and tribunals involved in different aspects of global governance.

- Although the UN is the principal organ of global governance it does not possess the characteristics of a 'world government' in so far as its constituent members maintain sovereign authority within their own realms and do not form a 'world state'.

Non-Governmental Organizations (NGOs)

The non-state variety of international organization sometimes goes by the acronym INGO—which simply stands for *international* non-governmental organization—but for present purposes we shall make do with the more common term NGO. Like international organizations in general, NGOs cannot be defined in a completely straightforward way. Generally speaking, however, they share the following characteristics: they are formal rather than ad hoc entities; they aspire to be self-governing according to their own constitutional set-up; they are private in the sense that they operate independently from governments; and they do not make or distribute profits. This describes both national and international bodies, so for those which operate outside of the national sphere, we need to add that they obviously have formal transnational links (see Gordenker and Weiss, 1996: 20).

There are other types of organization which fall somewhere between the government and non-government spheres and although they often claim to be NGOs, they do not really conform to the description above. Gordenker and Weiss identify three significant deviations. The first are government-organized non-government organizations or GON-GOs—entities created by governments usually as front organizations for their own purposes. These were typically produced by communist countries during the Cold War but the USA and other Western countries had some as well. Today, there is a wide variety of GONGOs many of which serve dubious causes. The excerpt from an article published in *Foreign Policy* on the subject of GONGOS, and the dangers that some of them pose, is highly instructive as to their role in the sphere of international organizations. See **Box 19.4**.

Another special type of organization is the quasi non-government organization or QUANGO which is typically funded very largely by governments but operates

➜ See chapter twelve, page 280, for a discussion of GONGOs.

Key Quote Box 19.4
Moisés Naím, 'What Is a Gongo?', *Foreign Policy,* May/June 2007

How government-sponsored groups masquerade as civil society.

'... Behind this contradictory and almost laughable tongue twister [gongo] lies an important and growing global trend that deserves more scrutiny: governments funding and controlling nongovernmental organizations (NGOs), often stealthily. Some gongos are benign, others irrelevant. But many ... are dangerous. Some act as the thuggish arm of repressive governments. Others use the practices of democracy to subtly undermine democracy at home. Abroad, the gongos of repressive regimes lobby the United Nations and other international institutions, often posing as representatives of citizen groups with lofty aims when, in fact, they are nothing but agents of the governments that fund them. Some governments embed their gongos deep in the societies of other countries and use them to advance their interests abroad.... The globalization and effectiveness of nongovernmental organizations will suffer if we don't find reliable ways of distinguishing organizations that truly represent democratic civil society from those that are tools of uncivil, undemocratic governments....'

Source: www.foreignpolicy.com/story/cms.php?story_id=3818&fpsrc=ealert070430, accessed 16/08/07

autonomously. Unlike GONGOs, the relationship to government is a transparent one and no subterfuge is intended. The third type is the donor-organized NGO or DONGO. In this case, agencies such as the United Nations Development Program (UNDP) might organize and fund NGOs to coordinate or carry out projects (Gordenker and Weiss, 1996: 20–1). A significant number of other NGOs enjoy consultative status with the UN or, more specifically, one of its councils or agencies. The UN's Economic and Social Council, for example, accords consultative status of some kind to almost 3,000 NGOs ranging from the Adventist Development Relief Agency to the World Press Freedom Committee. These are allied in turn to specific UN agencies such as UNESCO, the FAO and the WHO (see the Council's list at www.un.org/esa/coordination/ngo/pdf/INF_List.pdf).

The practice of according UN consultative status to NGOs dates back to 1946 when ECOSOC granted such status to just over forty NGOs. Growth was steady over the next forty-five years and by 1992 there were more that 700 NGOs with consultative status. As indicated above, that number has increased to almost 3,000. There are various rules and criteria governing eligibility. Among the most basic are:

1. The organization must have been in existence (officially registered with the appropriate government authorities as an NGO/non-profit) for at least two years.

2. It must have an established headquarters.

Photo 19.1   Liberian Children Wait for Polio Vaccination

The third round of the National Immunizations Days for Polio was launched in Liberia. The campaign aims to immunize 1.2 million children against the deadly disease and Liberia's Health and Social Welfare Minister Peter Coleman thanked the World Health Organization, UNICEF, and other non-governmental organizations for supporting Liberia's health sector. Location: Salamanca, Liberia. Date: 10 November 2005.

Source: UN Photo by Eric Kanalstein

3. It must possess a democratically adopted constitution, authority to speak for its members, a representative structure, appropriate mechanisms of accountability and democratic and transparent decision-making processes.

4. Its basic resources must be derived mainly from contributions of the national affiliates or other components or from individual members.

5. It must not have been established by governments or intergovernmental agreements (see www.un.org/esa/coordination/ngo/).

Many NGOs have a specific philanthropic or humanitarian purpose. Sometimes these are underpinned by religious beliefs but are just as likely to be secular. Many are aligned with broader movements such as the environmental movement, the labour movement, the ecumenical movement, the peace movement, the indigenous rights movement, and the women's movement. More will be said about the role of these broader movements below.

Examples of some of the better-known NGOs reflecting the ideals of one or other of these movements, or sometimes two or more of them, are the Worldwide Fund for Nature, Greenpeace, the World Council of Churches, the World Peace Council, the International Women's Health Coalition, Médecins Sans Frontières, and Amnesty International, to name just a few. A brief account of the Red Cross/Red Crescent Movement provides a case study of how one of the earliest NGOs operating in the international sphere has grown to be the largest humanitarian organization in the world. In addition, it was the prime mover behind the original Geneva Convention which has become the most important international convention relating to the conduct of warfare. See **Box 19.5**.

Case Study   Box 19.5
The Origins and Development of the Red Cross/Red Crescent Movement

In 1859, Henry Dunant, a travelling Swiss businessman, witnessed one of the bloodiest battles of the nineteenth century in northern Italy when Napoleon III joined with local forces to drive Austrians from the country. Dunant subsequently published a small book which depicted, among other things, the battlefield after fighting has ceased, describing not just the dead but the plight of the wounded and their desperate need for care. He went on to devise a plan for national relief societies to aid the wounded of war. In February 1863, the Société Genevoise D'utilité Publique [Geneva Society for Public Welfare] appointed a committee of five, including Dunant, to consider how the plan could be put into action.

This committee, which effectively founded the Red Cross, called for an international conference to pursue Dunant's basic objectives. Dunant put his own time and money into the project, travelling throughout much of Europe to persuade governments to send representatives. The conference was held in October 1863 with thirty-nine delegates from sixteen nations. Just under a year later, twelve nations signed an International Convention for the Amelioration of the Condition of the Wounded and Sick in Armed Forces in the Field, otherwise known as the Geneva Convention of 1864. The convention provided for guaranteed neutrality for medical personnel and officially adopted the red cross on a field of white as the identifying emblem (the red crescent was adopted in most Muslim countries). Three other conventions were later added to cover naval warfare, prisoners of war and civilians. Revisions of these conventions have been made periodically, the most extensive being in 1949 relating to the treatment of prisoners of war. The International Committee of the Red Cross remains based in Geneva and the International Federation of Red Cross and Red Crescent Societies has National Societies in 178 countries with a total membership of 115 million volunteers. The Red Cross has been associated with four Nobel Peace Prizes, with the very first Nobel Peace Prize being awarded to Henry Dunant himself in 1901.

Sources: nobelprize.org/nobel_prizes/peace/laureates/1963/red-cross-history.html; www.redcross.int/en/history/not_nobel.asp, both accessed 07/08/07

Key Points

- Intergovernmental organizations, especially the UN and its agencies, often have a close working relationship with NGOs and have established structures supporting the work of many NGOs.

- Not all NGOS are 'good' in the sense that they make a positive contribution in the international sphere. Some are merely fronts for nefarious activities by dictatorial governments and may work actively to undermine the efforts of other organizations with respect, for example, to human rights issues.

- Many NGOs are also allied with broader movements, thus contributing to a complex web of relationships between different kinds of actors, both state and non-state, in the international sphere.

Social Movements and International Civil Society

The foregoing discussion indicates that many NGOs are involved in philanthropic or humanitarian causes, some of which are embedded in broader social movements. The term social movement is generally understood to denote some kind of collective action, driven by a particular set of social concerns and emerging from society at large

19

rather than through the governmental institutions of the state. Indeed, a feature of many social movements is an oppositional posture vis-à-vis certain aspects of state or governmental activity. In this respect they are often seen as a manifestation of grass-roots democracy expressing or articulating non-mainstream issues and agendas. As we have seen, social movements often transcend the domestic sphere, an early example being the anti-slavery movement. When a movement achieves a transnational profile and popular following, it obviously achieves the status of an international or global social movement. These often reflect shifting coalitions of interests around issue-oriented activities. But what social movements and the NGOs associated with them usually represent in one way or another is a 'cause', very often in relation to what is perceived as an injustice and/or a danger: Third World poverty, environmental degradation, the oppression of indigenous communities, nuclear weapons, and so on.

These broad social movements and the world of NGOs are said to constitute a kind of **international civil society** which has an important role in the general sphere of global governance. The idea of international civil society can also be understood initially in terms of its domestic counterpart discussed in chapter twelve along with the role of NGOs and interest group politics. Civil society names a sphere of human association not mediated by the state, or at least not directly. Thus it signifies the activities of individuals as participants in groups or collectives that have a private purpose—private in the sense that they are not part of the realm of formal state or governmental activity. They include professional associations, charities, **interest groups**, businesses, and so on. Their freedom of organization and articulation of interests is widely regarded as another important manifestation of democracy, and so the repression of civil society organizations and activities is seen as characteristic of **authoritarian** systems. Many civil society groups are obviously NGOs, but some do not fall easily into the definition of the latter. Also, not all NGOs are connected to social movements. It follows that although we can often connect NGOs to social movements and in turn class these as part of civil society, we cannot simply conflate the lot into one seamless whole.

→ See chapter twelve, page 276, for discussion of domestic civil society.

Just as domestic civil society names a sphere that is autonomous of direct government control, so international civil society may be understood as standing apart from the formal, intergovernmental structures of global governance. As with social movements, international civil society may be regarded not merely as distinct from that sphere, but sometimes positioned in opposition to the realm of formal state-based or state-generated activities. It is therefore another avenue through which democratic expression can take place. Certainly, those who look for democratic transformations in the international sphere and promote a form of **cosmopolitan democracy**—a project involving the extension of democratic accountability to the global sphere as discussed in chapter three—are broadly supportive of the positive role that international civil society has to play in such a process.

→ See chapter three, page 87, for an exploration of cosmopolitan democracy.

Whether social movements and the broad sphere of international civil society, and the NGOs which are the principle vehicles of activity in these arenas, really do present a serious challenge to the traditional structures generated by state sovereignty and the state system is an open question. As we have seen, many NGOs have a close association with the UN and its programmes and agencies; so although we may distinguish NGOs from the UN as such, they have come to form an important part of the UN system as a

19

Photo 19.2
Secretary-General Ban Ki-moon (right) meets with Gerd Leipold, International Executive Director of Greenpeace. Location: United Nations, New York. Date: 19 September 2007.
Source: UN photo by Mark Garten

whole. Social movements and international civil society are therefore at least partly enmeshed in the web of relations created by international organizations including the more formal intergovernmental institutions of global governance.

Key Points

- Global social movements reflect particular sets of concerns coalescing around issues such as the environment, indigenous rights, arms control, and so on, and which engender collective action on a global scale.

- International civil society, as a sphere of action and interaction standing apart from formal intergovernmental structures and sometimes in opposition to it, constitutes the space within which both international NGOs and social movements more generally operate.

- Both social movements and international civil society are often regarded as enhancing the space and substance of democratic activity at a supranational level.

Conclusion

Realist views of how 'the international' is organized posits states and the state system as the standard units around which almost everyone and everything else revolves, and with international activity of any real consequence being generated by state actors and with state interests firmly in mind. It follows from this view that the role of virtually all other institutions and actors is subordinate, including any form of international organization.

Indeed, some realists may dismiss the whole project of global governance, composed of the efforts of both state and non-state actors, as of little relevance in the 'real world' of **power politics**. However, realist views comprise only one, admittedly influential, view of how the international system works. Liberal views, especially those described as 'liberal institutionalist', occupy a quite different general position. For liberals, it is largely through international organizations that the dangerous aspects of international **anarchy** can be ameliorated, and all states have an interest in this. Both the League of Nations and the United Nations represent a practical manifestation of liberal international theory. As for the fluid realm of NGOs, social movements, and international civil society, these may be seen as an important complement to the more formal sphere of international organization and global governance, often acting in concert with it but sometimes opposing and resisting their policies and practices. However we may regard them, international organizations have become such an integral part of the international system, and indeed of **international society**, that it is difficult to imagine a world without them.

 ## Key Questions

- What are the key characteristics of international organizations?
- How does an international regime differ from an international organization?
- How and why did international organizations emerge in the modern period?
- To what extent has there been a continuity of international organizations over the last two centuries?
- Was the League of Nations a complete failure?
- On what general principles is the UN founded?
- Is it possible for the UN to reconcile respect for state sovereignty and respect for universal human rights?
- Could the UN do more as an international organization, or is it expected to do too much as it is?
- What role do NGOs and social movements play in the international system?
- How can international civil society enhance opportunities for democratic expression?
- How can we deploy IR theory to interpret the role of international organizations in world order?

 ## Further Reading

Archibugi, Daniele, David Held, and Martin Köhler (eds) (1998), *Re-Imagining Political Community: Studies in Cosmopolitan Democracy,* Cambridge: Polity Press.
> The editors of this collection regard the interstate system as increasingly challenged by new transnational forces and organizations: multinational companies, cross-border coalitions of social interest groups, global media, and numerous (and still multiplying) international agencies. This book looks at their impact on political life within and between communities with a focus on the possibilities of democratizing the international sphere.

19

Bennett, A. Le Roy and James K. Oliver (2001), *International Organizations: Principles and Issues,* Englewood Cliffs, NJ: Prentice Hall, 7th edn.

> The authors state that they are 'normatively committed to the indispensability of global and regional, international and transnational organizations in an age when people and nation-states must adapt to a shrinking and increasingly interdependent globe and the growing demand for global governance'. The book provides a very detailed and closely argued case for this view.

Krasner, Stephen (ed.) (1983), *International Regimes,* Ithaca, NY: Cornell University Press.

> Although more than twenty-five years old, this edited collection by leading experts still provides one of the best formulations of themes and issues around which the concept of 'international regimes', which exist in the ideational realm of 'principles, norms, rules and decision-making procedures' revolves.

Ruggie, John (1998), *Constructing the World Polity: Essays on International Institutionalization,* London: Routledge.

> Ruggie has made his name as a leading constructivist and this book brings together a number of his essays written over the years, surveying the field of post-war IR theory and how constructivist theories of international organizations and institutions contribute to it.

 *Web Links*

www.libsci.sc.edu/bob/IGOs.htm#IGOS
Lists several hundred IGOs under different categories.

www.uia.org/extlinks/pub.php
Website of the Union of International Associations, self-described as the world's most comprehensive source of information on global civil society with databases and publications covering many aspects of international organizations including their history and organization and the problems and methods with which they work.

http://portal.unesco.org/shs/en/ev.php-URL_ID=4227&URL_DO=DO_TOPIC&URL_SECTION=-473.html
This is a UNESCO portal which provides a gateway to numerous IGOs.

 Visit the **Online Resource Centre** that accompanies this book to access more learning resources at **www.oxfordtextbooks.co.uk/orc/garner/**

International Political Economy

Reader's Guide

In providing an overview of the field of International Political Economy (IPE), this chapter builds on a number of themes introduced previously, including connections with IR theory. Once again, theories of IPE are discussed from an historical perspective to enable a better appreciation of how ideas, practices, and institutions develop and interact over time. And once again, it will be seen that these theories arose substantially within a European context. Significant issues include international trade, international labour, the interaction of states and markets, the nexus between wealth and power, and the problems of development and underdevelopment in the global economy, taking particular account of the North–South divide. The final section discusses the twin phenomena of globalization and regionalization and the way in which these are shaping the international economy and challenging the traditional role of the state. An underlying theme of the chapter is the link between economic and political power.

International Relations and the Study of IPE

The field of IPE has become a major focus within International Relations (IR) since the 1970s, partly in conjunction with the rise of both neoliberalism and neorealism in IR theory. A significant impetus in the development of contemporary IPE was provided by a seminal article published in 1970. Susan Strange's 'International Relations and International Economics: A Case of Mutual Neglect' pointed out that the reciprocal ignorance exhibited by the two disciplines impoverished efforts in both fields to understand the world. She argued that IR had been far too preoccupied with the political and strategic relations between governments, to the exclusion of almost everything else (Strange, 1970: 304). The field has grown enormously since then, reflecting not only increased academic awareness of the importance of the field but the substantial changes in the international sphere in that period.

The term 'political economy' suggests a merging of two aspects of social life. As a field of study, political economy lies at the intersection of political science and economics. *IPE* focuses on the interplay between political power and economic forces from the national through to the international and global level. Critical IPE has also developed strong interdisciplinary links and has incorporated insights from history, geography, demography, sociology, and anthropology. One text defines IPE as 'the study of those international problems and issues that cannot adequately be addressed by recourse to economic, political, or sociological analysis alone' with a focus on 'the elements of complex interdependence that define many of our most pressing problems today' (Balaam and Veseth, 2005: 3). Thus IPE, as with politics and IR more generally, cannot confine itself simply to the structural study of institutions or organizations but must also take account of the norms, values, and interests that they reflect. Any arrangement of the global system of production, distribution, and exchange reflects a mix of values and must therefore be understood neither as divinely ordained nor as the fortuitous outcome of mere chance, but rather 'the result of human decisions taken in the context of manmade institutions and . . . self-set rules and customs' (Strange quoted in Balaam and Veseth, 2005: 5).

Many studies in IPE take the **state** and the market to be the two main entities involved. Indeed, it is the 'parallel existence and mutual interaction' of these that create 'political economy' (Gilpin, 1987: 8). The state embodies political forces while the market, famously cast as 'the invisible hand' by the liberal philosopher Adam Smith (1723–90), is defined as 'a coordinating mechanism where sellers and buyers exchange goods and services at prices and output levels determined by supply and demand' (Cohn, 2005: 7). The relationship between states and markets is often depicted as one in permanent tension, since the efforts of state actors are primarily concerned with preserving **sovereignty** and political unity while markets thrive on openness and the absence of barriers to trade. However, their relationship is also complementary in that state action is required to protect property rights, provide infrastructure, and regulate transactions. In turn, where an economy is thriving, which it is more likely to do where trade barriers are minimal, there is often a proportional strengthening of national political and military power (7).

Students of IPE are obviously concerned mainly with the dynamics produced in the international sphere, and the interactions between states, transnational corporations, international organizations, and so on; but it needs emphasizing once again that the distinction between the domestic and the international, as with many other fields of IR, is difficult to maintain. Indeed, the rise of IPE throughout the 1970s and 1980s was due at least in part to dissatisfaction with realist theories, including the sharp division between domestic and international spheres which appeared to make little sense in an increasingly interdependent world (Crane and Amawi, 1991: 3–4).

One scholar notes that this occurred well after many foreign ministries began renaming themselves Departments of Foreign Affairs *and* Trade (Pettman, 1996: 10), indicating pragmatic recognition of their mutual importance. Those which maintain traditional names, such as the British Foreign and Commonwealth Office (FCO), nonetheless have substantial sections dealing trade issues. The FCO's Trade and Investment section today employs around 1,500 people, a reflection of the fact that one in four jobs in the UK is linked to business overseas (see www.fco.gov.uk). This illustrates that the interface between the national and international, and between politics and economy, is extremely permeable. In the EU zone, national boundaries are obviously more porous than most given the extent of European economic and political integration. This is an aspect of **regionalization,** which we consider further below.

Key Points

- IPE sits at the intersection of international politics and economics as well as incorporating other interdisciplinary insights and has developed as a major focus of study within the broader field of IR over the last four decades.

- Studies in IPE focus on states and markets. The relationship between them consists in a tangle of complex interactions ranging from the cooperative to the hostile and involving important dynamics of power and wealth.

The Age of Mercantilism

Mercantilism (from the Latin for 'merchant'), is associated specifically with political economy as both a theory and a system. It is not a theory of IR as such, but it is antagonistic to liberal thought and therefore complements **realism** in some respects. Historically, mercantilism denotes a cluster of 'ideas and policies that surrounded the doctrine of the balance of trade in European economic thinking of the seventeenth century and most of the eighteenth century' (Miller, 1991: 335). See **Box 20.1**. A basic premise of classical mercantilism is that national wealth and military power form a virtuous circle: wealth enhances military power vis-à-vis other states (and in early modern Europe this often meant superior naval power); substantial wealth is acquired through trade; trade is protected by naval power; the wealth generated by trade further enhances naval capacity; and so on.

The relentless pursuit of trade is therefore justified by its positive contribution to national strength. However, **nationalism**, not *free* trade, was the catch-cry of the mercantilist system and so national **protectionism** was the logical accompaniment to its basic principles. Thus mercantilism acquired the characteristics of a nationalist discourse which, in a post-feudal age of state-building in Europe, resonated with other ideas about national greatness. It also went hand in hand with justifications of **colonialism**. In addition, the grounds for legitimate warfare were enlarged to encompass commercial and market considerations. Overall, the legacy of early mercantilist policies was 'to concentrate physical wealth in a few European nation-states, and to create a network of global economic interdependence the remains of which can still be seen today' (Watson, 2004: 3).

Two notable sets of laws in Britain well illustrate early mercantilist principles aimed at maximizing national profits. First, the Navigation Acts dating from the mid-seventeenth century restricted the movement of goods largely to English-built ships and crews, while foreign ships were prohibited from trading in the colonies altogether. Secondly, the Corn Laws of 1815 to 1846 constituted trade barriers protecting high prices (and profits) for home-grown grain against cheaper foreign imports. Both sets of laws were embedded in a protectionist framework embracing shipping, the colonial empire, commercial activities, and the food supply. However, the cumbersome system of tariffs and prohibitions in which foreign trade had become entangled frustrated both bureaucrats and merchants as well as

 Box 20.1

The Rise of Mercantilism

Mercantilist ideas were expressed as early as 1664 in Thomas Mun's *England's Treasure by Foreign Trade*. He argued that to produce a favourable national outcome, one must observe a basic rule: 'to sell more to strangers yearly than we consume of theirs in value' (quoted in Miller, 1991: 335). These ideas were contemporaneous with an age of European imperialism when various countries vied for supplies of raw materials for emerging industries. England had significant land and naval power which it was able to project almost anywhere in the world, thereby ensuring early pre-eminence as a global power (Watson, 2004: 2). The term 'mercantilism' was rarely used until the mid- to late eighteenth century, first appearing in the work of the French *économiste,* Mirabeau. Adam Smith was largely responsible for giving the word its currency, along with the term 'political economy'.

provoking political radicals. After centuries of protectionism, Britain abruptly changed course, 'seeking to lead the world towards a peaceful order based on free commercial exchange between individuals and nations' (Howe, 1997: 1–2).

Mercantilism was clearly at odds with emergent liberal ideas in both economics and politics more generally. Conservative economic historians depicted mercantilism as *rightly* subordinating economic to political considerations of **national interest**, in line with their belief in 'the subordination of the individual to the state and to the exaltation of vigorous nationalism characteristic of mercantilism' (Viner, 1949: 4). An early nineteenth-century defender of mercantilism argued along lines similar to classical realism. Rejecting the 'cosmopolitical' world view of economic liberals which assumes peaceful relations in a politically stable environment, Friedrich List (1789–1846) argued that political economy must start from the premise that international relations are inherently conflictual, that nationalist rivalries produce the major dynamics with which political economy must grapple, and that 'true political science' must see a world characterized by free trade as 'a very unnatural one' (List, 1991: 54).

Mercantilist thinking declined following the rise of liberal thought but enjoyed a resurgence from the late nineteenth century on into the early twentieth century when nationalism was rife. Liberal ideas supporting free trade suffered a proportionate decline. This situation was not to last. Cohn (2005: 71) writes that the extreme nationalism and trade protectionism of the interwar years, and their association with the Great Depression as well as the Second World War, gave liberal economic principles in the post-war period a boost even though mainstream IR thinking took a decidedly realist turn at the same time. Since realist theorists evinced little interest in economics, specific mercantilist ideas did not figure prominently in the early post-war period of IR theorizing. However, the cycle of ideas invariably turns and 'realist IPE', as a variation on a theme of neomercantilism, was to gather support in the 1970s as the architecture of the liberal economic world appeared to be crumbling.

Key Points

- Mercantilism is a theory of international political economy based on certain balance of trade principles. Historically, it evinces nationalist, imperialist, and realist elements.

- Mercantilism opposes the ideology of the free market, favouring a strong state which not only provides security but is actively involved in the economy by promoting protectionist measures.

The Rise of Liberal Political Economy

→ See chapter five, page 116, for a discussion on liberalism.

By the late eighteenth century, liberal political economy had displaced mercantilism in prominence due largely to Adam Smith's influence. His free trade ideas were based on the division of labour, economic **interdependence** and the notion that states in an unregulated international economy would find a productive niche based on absolute advantage. This meant that each state would find the greatest benefit in producing specialized goods most efficiently and trading these with other states, who would in turn do the same. These ideas were further refined by David Ricardo (1772–1823) who expanded Smith's insights by introducing the concept of *comparative* advantage, stating that: 'The same rule which regulates the relative value of commodities in one country, does not regulate the relative value of the commodities exchanged between two or more countries' (Ricardo, 1821: 99). This suggests that even if one state has no absolute advantage in the production of any particular good, it can at least specialize in the production and export of those it can produce with a relative advantage (Cohn, 2005: 92).

Another important concept underpinning early liberal political economy was laissez-faire (literally, 'let be') meaning that the state should allow free reign to *individual initiative, competition, the pursuit of self-interest and the invisible hand of market forces*—all classic elements of liberal political economy. While the pursuit of self-interest may seem attuned only to selfish individual ends, Smith and other liberals believed that the sum of such individual actions adds to overall wealth and prosperity for the community. Liberalism thus described is a theory of the individual *in* society rather than a theory of individual, self-regarding action without reference to a wider social sphere. Because liberal theorists were opposed to mercantilist state practices, and to the abuse of state power more generally, liberal thought acquired a certain anti-statist hue from the beginning. Even so, most versions of liberalism recognize the state as essential for the organization of political life as well as for legislation to protect rights, especially property rights. In the course of explaining the principle of comparative advantage under a regime of free trade, David Ricardo very succinctly summed up classical liberal political economy ideas, and their implications for the wider world. See **Box 20.2**.

John Maynard Keynes (1883–1946) was undoubtedly the most prominent liberal thinker of the twentieth century, although he adopted a fairly pro-state position,

Key Quote Box 20.2
David Ricardo

'Under a system of perfectly free commerce, each country naturally devotes its capital and labour to such employments as are most beneficial to each. The pursuit of individual advantage is admirably connected with the universal good of the whole. By stimulating industry, by regarding ingenuity, and by using most efficaciously the peculiar powers bestowed by nature, it distributes labour most effectively and most economically: while, by increasing the general mass of production, it diffuses general benefit, and binds together, by one common tie of interest and intercourse, the universal society of nations throughout the civilized world.'   (Ricardo, 1821: 99) regarding the state as essential in producing the necessary social, political, and economic conditions for human well-being. He also believed that the sum of rational individual actions did not always add up to a rational outcome at the collective level, making it important for the state to be able to step in and make adjustments. Certainly, to treat 'the market' as the infallible source of all wisdom was a mistake. Keynes's legacy to IPE was embodied to a considerable extent in the post-war economic order supported in the US by economists such as John Kenneth Galbraith (1908–2006) who, although not often cited in IPE literature, was important in presenting a liberal case for state involvement in economy and society and maintaining a critical stance on simplistic faith in the market: 'The notion that [the market] is intrinsically and universally benign is an error of libertarians and unduly orthodox conservatives' (Galbraith, 1984: 39–42).

Key Points

- Liberalism displaced mercantilism as the leading theory of political economy with the rise of free trade ideas revolving around the division of labour, interdependence, and comparative advantage. Mercantilist ideas, however, reappear from time to time to challenge liberal orthodoxies.

- Liberal political economy promotes individual initiative, competition, the pursuit of self-interest, and the 'invisible hand' of market forces. Liberals generally believe that the sum of individual actions adds to overall wealth and prosperity although liberals such as Keynes and Galbraith were more sceptical.

Marxism and Critical IPE

The third of the classical theories of political economy is of course Marxism which, in theorizing such key matters as **class struggle**, exploitation, **imperialism**, and techno-logical change, 'contributes an essential critical approach to the operation of contem-porary political economy' (Watson, 2004: 9–10). **Class analysis** and the distribution of wealth are implicit in dependency theory and world system analysis discussed in chapter sixteen. Critical approaches to IPE in the contemporary period focus particular attention on the commodification of labour in international markets as part of the broader process of **globalization**. They are also attuned to gender and race as well as traditional class analysis. But there is still a long way to go before these issues are brought into the mainstream of discussion. As Griffin (2007: 720) argues in relation to gender, while a gendered IPE analysis is central to a proper understanding of the processes and practice of the global political economy, and while much high-quality work has been done in recent years, gender is still seen as a 'women's issue' and therefore of marginal status vis-à-vis the more important, traditional concerns.

Another study argues that international labour migration is a massive industry, one with significant race and gender dimensions as well, and rests on wage inequalities

➔ See chapter sixteen, pages 367–8, for a discussion of world system analysis and dependency theory.

between source and destination countries caused by highly uneven development with labour migration controlled by an economic logic subordinating other social and political concerns (Goss and Lindquist, 1995: 317). The other side of the coin is the search by transnational corporations for ever cheaper sources of labour. Countries providing low-cost labour are ideal bases for manufacturing industries. While supporters of the capitalist system see this as bringing benefits to the poor on the grounds that any job is better than no job, its critics see it as perpetuating and profiting massively from relations of exploitation. **Box 20.3** also highlights the very significant gender elements in international labour markets.

Case Study Box 20.3
Globalization, Labour Markets, and Gender

The global economy depends ultimately on the exploitation of labour, and in particular on the availability of cheap labour in less developed countries. Many of the labour markets are heavily gendered. For example, while Bangladeshi and Indonesian males are employed as migrant workers in construction projects in the Middle East, Singapore, and Malaysia, females from the Philippines and Indonesia are employed as domestic workers. Regulations protecting such migrants are often very weak, leaving many at the mercy of both the companies who arrange the work contracts—itself an industry—as well as the companies or individuals who employ them. Even less protected are illegal immigrant workers who are often 'trafficked' into destination countries. 'Illegals' are found throughout the world wherever there is a demand for cheap labour, from the UK and other European countries to Dubai and Kuwait, Singapore, Malaysia, and Japan. Illegal immigrant labour is a significant part of the US economy (see Kaur, 2007).

Another phenomenon observed in studies of global labour is the 'feminization of labour'. In a 'global environment of open economies, new trade regimes, and competitive export industries, global accumulation relies heavily on the work of women, both waged and unwaged, in formal sectors and in the home, in manufacturing, and in public and private services' (Moghadam, 2005: 51). Feminized labour is especially prominent in developing countries in Southeast and East Asia, parts of Latin America, the Caribbean, and North Africa where increasing numbers of women work in labour-intensive, low-wage occupations. Such jobs are commonly found in textile and garment industries as well as in electronics and pharmaceuticals.

At the same time as world trade in services has increased and global firms engage in out-sourcing, the involvement of women in various occupations and professions of the services sector has grown as well: 'Women around the world have made impressive inroads into professional services such as law, banking, accounting, computing, and architecture; in tourism-related occupations; and in the information services, including offshore airline booking, mail order, credit cards, word-processing for publishers, telephone operators, and so on' (Moghadam, 1999: 367–88).

At the other end of the spectrum is the increased trafficking of women made possible under conditions of globalization. A US Immigration support website notes that young women from relatively poorer countries are often deceived into thinking that they will be offered a good job abroad. For many, it seems to offer a way out of poverty. After arriving in the destination country, however, they soon discover that they have been brought in to work as prostitutes; and since they are thousands of miles away from home and have nowhere else to go, they are forced into this kind of work. Although the problem is more evident in the Middle East and Europe it occurs in the USA as well.

Source: www.usimmigrationsupport.org/illegal_immigration.html

Robert W. Cox is a key figure in promoting a neo-Gramscian perspective on IPE focusing on **hegemony** and the dynamics of domination and subordination, coercion, and consent. In a seminal article, Cox (1981) does not simply accept the international economic or political order as it is, but rather questions how it came into being and how it might be transformed altogether—into a more just and equitable one. The 'new political economy' promoted by Cox and others in the critical tradition also rejects the methodological **positivism** of conventional realist and liberal IPE which they see as constraining the capacity to think outside the parameters of conventional theory. A recent critical/feminist perspective also argues that IPE requires a radical rethinking of conventional theory (both realist and liberal) that questions the objectivist and rationalist **epistemology** on which they are based, and which has worked to marginalize issues concerning race, gender, and class in mainstream studies (Peterson, 2003: 21–2). Another scholar argues that the critical wing of global political economy (GPE), as he prefers to call the field, is multifaceted in its approach, incorporating gender perspectives and critiques of race and class as well as analysing a wide range of institutions including the family, the firm, the market, and the state. Above all, it scrutinizes much more thoroughly the exercise of power (Palan, 2000: 7–8).

Key Points

- Class analysis remains relevant in an international sphere where low cost labour migrates or, alternatively, manufacturing industries locate in countries providing cheap and more easily exploited labour. Protection of workers' rights in either situation is often minimal or non-existent, further minimizing costs.

- Critical IPE questions how the global political economy came into being, what interests support it (and are supported by it) and how it might be transformed. It is more sensitive to issues of class, race, and gender, incorporates a wider range of institutions into the analysis, and is attuned to issues of domination and subordination.

Photo 20.1
Demonstrators march to City Hall in California in one of several May Day marches and rallies to press for immigrant and labour rights.
Source: Getty Images

The Post-War International Economic Order

As the Second World War drew to an end, plans for a new international economic order to free up access to markets and raw materials were developed alongside those for new international political institutions. Delegates meeting at Bretton Woods, New Hampshire, in 1944 were also concerned to institute a system which stabilized exchange rates and avoided recreating the conditions which had triggered worldwide depression in the interwar years. However, contending national interests challenged pure liberal principles and the system which emerged, which Ruggie has characterized as 'embedded liberalism', reflected many compromises: 'unlike the economic nationalism of the thirties it would be multilateral in character; unlike the liberalism of the gold standard and free trade, its multilateralism would be predicated on domestic interventionism' (Ruggie, 1998: 62–84).

Institutionally, the result was the establishment of three major bodies to support the new international economic order, collectively dubbed the Bretton Woods institutions.

These were the International Monetary Fund (IMF), the International Bank for Reconstruction and Development (IBRD—later called the World Bank), and the General Agreement on Tariffs and Trade (GATT) which was signed in 1947 as an interim measure until the architecture for a more permanent institution could be worked out. It took until 1995 to establish the World Trade Organization (WTO) (see Wilkinson, 2000). In the intervening years, the GATT functioned to hold together whatever agreements could be reached on trade liberalization. See **Box 20.4**.

One of the success stories in the early post-war years was the work of the IRBD in Europe and in which the USA played a major role. Fearing communist influence in a badly damaged Europe where millions of people were struggling, US strategy was, as

Case Study Box 20.4
The WTO and the Global Trading Regime

The WTO was officially established on 1 January 1995 as an organization dedicated to liberalizing trade, providing ground rules for the conduct of international commerce, and providing a forum for negotiating trade agreements and settling disputes. It consolidated and permanently institutionalized the rules of the trading system first established in 1948 by the General Agreement on Tariffs and Trade (GATT) which had itself evolved through rounds of negotiations. The 'Uruguay Round' of 1986 was the most important of these and led finally to the creation of the WTO which has a much wider remit. While the GATT was principally concerned with trade in goods, the WTO expanded the scope to include trade in services as well and in intellectual property (inventions, creations, and designs). It is based on the principle of multilateralism, transparency, predictability, and equality of treatment. However, it has some flexibility in accommodating special national circumstances, preferential treatment and regional free trade agreements (FTAs) and is not therefore a world-wide 'free trade' organization as such. Significant rounds of negotiations have continued under the auspices of the WTO. The 'Doha Round', which commenced in 2001, aims to eliminate unfair trading practices and especially those affecting poorer countries. Negotiations stalled at a meeting in Cancun in 2003 at which agreement on agriculture, among other key issues, failed to materialize. One of the main issues is the level of agricultural subsidies maintained by rich countries at the expense of poorer countries. The EU's Common Agricultural Policy (CAP), for example, has long disadvantaged agricultural exports from the developing world. So too have the policies of most of the G8 countries, especially the USA. There is broad agreement that the process should continue but much depends on US leadership which, under the Bush administration, has been weak on such issues.

(See, generally, www.wto.org)

we have seen earlier, to contain it partly by rebuilding the economies of Western Europe via the Marshall Plan. This plan involved billions in US aid distributed in ways compatible with securing Europe as a major trading and security partner. In the meantime the IMF, which opened for business in 1948 with fairly modest credit facilities, was charged with maintaining a stable exchange rate mechanism and **balance of payments** regime although it did little in its first few years due to the focus on European reconstruction (mainly funded separately) as well as the rebuilding of Japan and aid packages to Greece and Turkey, also funded largely by the USA. In the late 1950s and 1960s the IMF's involvement in supplying credits increased, especially as decolonization progressed, and it became a major player in Third World economies. The USA continues to dominate both the IMF and the World Bank, a reflection of its early role in international financial institutions as the major supplier of funds.

Although the Bretton Woods institutions remain an important part of international economic architecture, a breakdown nonetheless occurred in the Bretton Woods exchange rate mechanism. Part of the 1944 agreement included fixing currency values according to a gold standard. In earlier periods, the British pound had served as a primary currency but after the war only the US dollar could meet international demands for liquidity. The USA agreed to convert dollars to gold at US$35.00 per ounce to facilitate the exchange rate mechanism. By the early 1970s, however, the USA was faced with rising imports and a significant trade imbalance. The huge outflows of dollars providing liquidity for the international economy which, although contributing to the USA's considerable prosperity, could not be sustained. Increased interdependence and the recovery of the European and Japanese economies, along with vastly increased financial flows, made it almost impossible to control currency values, producing adverse dynamics (see, generally, Spero and Hart, 1997: 16–21).

In 1971 the US abandoned the dollar gold standard and raised tariffs on imports. Other industrialized countries reacted by strengthening protectionism themselves. This flew in the face of GATT principles supporting free trade, thus hampering reforms. Further trouble was in store with rising inflation, commodity shortages, unaccustomed floating currencies, and then the 'oil shocks' of the mid-1970s when oil-producers quadrupled the price of oil in a year with multiple consequences for the world economy, including recession. In 1975, a meeting of seven leading industrial countries—the USA, the UK, Canada, France, Germany, Italy, and Japan (subsequently called the G7)—met to consider reform of the international monetary system, and amendments to the Articles of Agreement of the IMF were put in place in early 1976. Although this appeared to signal a return to multilateral management, the reforms did little except codify the prevailing 'nonsystem' (Spero and Hart, 1997: 23). However, the G7 (now the G8 with the inclusion of Russia), has had an ongoing existence with semi-annual meetings still being held to coordinate matters of national and international economic policy.

By the early 1980s, in the wake of both international economic developments and the fiasco of the Vietnam War, America's status as the world's leading economic and military powerhouse seemed to be declining (Keohane, 2001). The global recession hit most countries hard and the USA was no exception. Liberal economics was identified by conservative commentators as the culprit. One US-based commentator, William R. Hawkins, deployed the term 'neomercantilism' in proposing a form of economic conservatism based more squarely on national interest and dismissing the 'utopianism' of liberal economists' visions of world order based on free trade principles (Hawkins, 1984: 25–39).

Five years later, with the collapse of communism and the apparent triumph of liberal democracy, capitalism, and free market ideology, neomercantilism and realist IPE were overshadowed by strengthening discourses of neoliberal globalization in the post-Cold War world. The new world order proclaimed by liberal triumphalists such as Francis Fukuyama (1989), discussed in earlier chapters, swept all before it in a wave of optimism about the global future. Hawkins's views nonetheless provide an interesting snapshot of neomercantilist thinking on world order in the early 1980s that still resonates with realists and other conservative critics of the globalization thesis today:

Advocates of free trade, particularly libertarians, often claim that the interdependence produced by trade will usher in an era of world peace—a notion that has no foundation in either history or current events. This view was most popular just before World War I and again just after World War II. It accounts for much of the continued liberal-left support for free trade.... Technical advances in communications and transportation do seem to have brought the world closer together, but this is an illusion. The human element of competing values and ambitions has not changed. Nor has the fundamental economic assumption: at any point in time, resources are scarce relative to wants. Thus the technical advances have only provided nations with the means to carry out their rivalries on a global scale. World unity is not at hand. (Hawkins, 1984: 29–30)

Key Points

- The Bretton Woods system which emerged after the Second World War was a compromise between liberalism and nationalism. Although the 'system' is said to have collapsed by the early 1970s, the IMF, the World Bank, and the WTO underpin contemporary global economic governance.

- Following world recession in the 1970s, neomercantilism enjoyed a revival, but the end of the Cold War saw a triumphant liberalism reassert global economic openness as the basis for a prosperous new world order.

The North–South Gap

Events since the early 1970s had seen a widening North–South gap. The rising protectionism of key industrialized states influenced by neomercantilist ideas, in addition to soaring energy costs, inflation and increasing indebtedness, led to calls for a New International Economic Order (NIEO) under which meaningful reforms could be achieved in aid, foreign investment regimes, the terms of trade, financial arrangements, including loans, and a fairer overall monetary system. In the 1960s, developing countries had formed the Group of Seventy-Seven (G77) to lobby as a bloc in global forums, especially the UN and the GATT. It had limited success. Neither the oil-producing nations who formed their own Organization of Petroleum Exporting Countries (OPEC), nor the countries of the industrialized North, were prepared to contemplate significant concessions to ease the burden of poorer countries.

As discussed in chapter seventeen, the UN's Brandt Commission attempted to put underdevelopment on the reform agenda in 1980, but significant change as recommended by the Commission did not occur. In the meantime, the World Bank and IMF promoted **structural adjustment** programmes for poor, underperforming countries. These programmes, inspired by neoliberal economic orthodoxies, included the privatization of state resources, strict limitations on public spending and other austerity measures. Loans

➡ See chapter seventeen, page 399, for a description of Brandt's report.

Photo 20.2

Boys and girls sifting through garbage in search of cash-worthy items in Sao Paulo. Location: Sao Paulo, Brazil. Date: 1 January 1985.
Source: UN photo by Sidney Rezende

were made conditional on governments implementing such measures. The result in many cases was to limit access to health, education, and public utilities even further without significantly improving overall economic performance or alleviating poverty.

How does one 'theorize' the North–South gap? In terms of dependency theory, discussed in chapter sixteen, the post-war order with its mixture of liberal and mercantile/realist institutions and principles was a recipe for exploitation. World system analysis also proposes that underdevelopment and a global division of labour is actually a necessary condition for the maintenance of global capitalism. Liberal theory of course looked to other explanations for the poor performance of many Third World countries, particularly in sub-Saharan Africa where a World Bank report found that the best economic performance had occurred in the two countries that had been able to maintain parliamentary democracy—Botswana and Mauritius—and that elsewhere on the continent a 'crisis of governance' underlay a litany of political, social, and economic woes (cited in Williams and Young, 1994: 86). This report is said to have marked a watershed in World Bank thinking about the importance of **good govern-ance** in countries with poor records (ibid.). See **Box 20.5**.

→ See chapter sixteen, pages 367–9, for a discussion of dependency theory.

The North–South gap in the distribution of the world's wealth, however, is due to a complex of causes and the problems it generates cannot be resolved simply by the application of good governance principles and practices, although these are important. Third World poverty and instability often go hand-in-hand, generating humanitarian crises as well as wider security issues which impinge on developed countries. A question to be asked by any serious student of IPE is whether this is attributable in large measure to a global economic architecture favouring those who designed it?

Key Quote Box 20.5
The World Bank and Good Governance

'The Governance group of the World Bank Institute (WBI) facilitates action-oriented and participatory programs to promote good governance and curb corruption in its client countries.' (http://go.worldbank.org/8CHK6P24S0). 'We define governance as the tra-ditions and institutions by which authority in a country is exercised for the common good. This includes (i) the process by which those in authority are selected, monitored and replaced, (ii) the capacity of the government to effectively manage its resources and implement sound policies, and (iii) the respect of citizens and the state for the institutions that govern economic and social interactions among them.'

Source: http://go.worldbank.org/MKOGR258V0

→ See chapter ten, page 243, for a definition of good governance from UNESCAP.

Key Points

- The North–South gap generates serious international political, economic, and social prob-lems and although some markets thrive on the disparities, few actually defend it as just.

- Some programmes inspired by neoliberal economic thinking and formulated by the World Bank and IMF, such as structural adjustment programmes, have been criticized as compounding the problems.

Globalization and Regionalization in the Post-Cold War World

If globalization is defined in terms of 'the acceleration and intensification of mechanisms, processes, and activities . . . promoting global interdependence and perhaps, ultimately, global political and economic integration' (Griffiths and O'Callaghan, 2002: 126–7), then it is impossible to separate globalization from the study of IPE. Indeed, some analyses focus almost exclusively on the economic dimensions of the phenomenon, positing global market forces as the central dynamic: 'The world economy has internationalized its basic dynamics, it is dominated by uncontrollable market forces, and it has as its principle economic actors and major agents of change truly transnational corporations that owe allegiance to no nation-state and locate wherever on the globe market advantage dictates' (Hirst and Thompson, 1999: 1). It has other dimensions too. As Tomlinson (1999) suggests, the consequences for cultural issues under the impact of new media and communication technologies as well as the changing nature of transnational business and work practices in the global economy and so on are far-reaching. This will almost certainly influence developments in the direction of a more cosmopolitan culture, but what that culture looks like, and what it means in terms of social, political, and moral questions is by no means certain.

Previous chapters have emphasized the extent to which globalization, in that it involves deepening trends in interconnectedness which transcend state boundaries and controls, challenges the traditional view of international order based on independent sovereign states. We have also seen in chapter seven how this relates to the problems of weakening states in the developed world. Even relatively strong developed states are seen as losing their autonomy and a fair measure of regulatory capacity. What this means for the capacity of states to deliver a reasonable measure of prosperity and protection in terms of 'human security' to their citizens is a particularly vexed question in the Third World where, as we have seen, structural adjustment programmes have already had a negative impact on state capacity. Further, the 'market' is not geared to anything but producing profits and a strictly economistic approach to explaining and understanding the dynamics of globalized markets cannot address issues of justice, either within or between states. As one observer notes, globalization produces both winners and losers and its proper study requires a multiperspectival approach incorporating markets, states, and people (Woods, 1998).

➜ See chapter seven, page 173, for a discussion of strong and weak states.

Another aspect of global economic development that has attracted very significant attention over the last two decades is the enormous growth in some Asia-Pacific economies and the prospects for a 'Pacific Century'. Despite the setbacks of the financial crisis of the late 1990s, the Asia-Pacific boom is continuing apace, with the growth of China, and more recently India, attracting particular attention. What has been especially interesting about developments in the region is the extent to which many states, or rather their governments, have been proactive in creating the conditions for growth in the global economy. It has therefore hardly been a case of states versus markets but rather states promoting markets as part of a broader neo liberal developmental strategy. Writing in the mid-1990s, one commentator noted that while neo-classical (liberal) economic orthodoxy attributed the spectacular growth in the region to laissez-faire principles, detailed studies actually show that states, via direct government intervention, have played a vital role in macroeconomic planning to facilitate this growth (see Palat, 1996). Again, this suggests that strict economistic approaches are far too narrow and need to be complemented with state-centred perspectives.

Studies urging attention to the continuing importance of the state, however, have not deterred 'hyperglobalists' from making some very extravagant claims about the future of the sovereign nation-state. A leading figure among the hyperglobalists, Kenichi Ohmae, famously proposed that the nation-state was doomed to oblivion in the newly emergent borderless world which would constitute the norm for future planetary organization See **Box 20.6**.

Ohmae's remarks about the 'region-state' alert us to the second of the two phenomena to be considered in this section, and that is regionalization. Like globalization, regionalization may be regarded as a complex integrative process incorporating cultural and social

→ See chapter one, page 27, for a discussion of the concept of the developmental state.

Key Quote   Box 20.6
States, Markets, and Globalization

'During the four decades following the Great Depression, governments had little difficulty in demonstrating their capacity to tame markets, promote growth and keep social inequality within strict limits. Nowadays, markets have taken their revenge. Financial institutions decide which state policies are acceptable and which are not. In these new circumstances, governments are beholden to market forces in a way few would have predicted. Markets now define the limits of politics . . . and economists exert unprecedented influence in shaping public policy . . . Strikingly, most advanced economies have ceased to consider their home market crucial to a strong performance . . . If all this intense activity could be reduced to a single concept, it would be that of globalization. Globalization is redefining the role of the nation-state as an effective manager of the national economy . . . .'

Source: Boyer and Drache (1996: 1)

dimensions as well as political and economic ones. Again, like globalization, the primary dynamic of regionalization is usually seen to be economic. However, many regionalizing processes have an important security dimension as well. For example, the Association of Southeast Asian Nations (ASEAN), one of the longest-standing regional organizations outside Europe, was founded primarily for the purpose of securing regional peace in the **Cold War** period and has only lately been concerned with economic issues.

Although some have seen regionalization as leading to the consolidation of rival trading blocs which threaten global multilateralism, others see it as perfectly compatible with global integration (Haggard, 1997: 20). Indeed, in some parts of the world, it is regarded as a means of participating more effectively in a globalized economy by creating opportunities for economic growth via free trade and other arrangements within a regional framework. Regionalization on this account is part of the broader globalization process itself rather than a negative reaction against it.

Regionalization is proceeding apace in Africa, the Americas, North Africa and the Middle East, in the regions of the former USSR, including Central Asia, South Asia, Southeast and East Asia, and the Pacific and Caribbean. There are also organizations covering huge swathes of the globe. The Asia-Pacific Economic Cooperation (APEC) forum, for example, has grown from an initial twelve participants, to twenty-one in the late 1980s, to a current membership comprising Australia, Brunei, Canada, Chile, China, Hong Kong, Indonesia, Japan, Malaysia, Mexico, New Zealand, Papua New Guinea, Peru, Philippines, Russia, Singapore, South Korea, Taiwan, Thailand, USA, and Vietnam. Together these countries account for about 40 per cent of the world's population, 48 per cent of world trade, and almost 60 per cent of world GDP.

While regionalization is clearly occurring in most parts of the world, the extent to which it has become institutionalized varies considerably. It is most advanced, but by no means complete, in the European Union area. The EU itself has been a long time in the making—almost five decades passed from the time of the founding of the European Movement in 1943 to the Maastricht Treaty of 1992. Given that the deepening and widening processes are ongoing, the present shape and form of the project does not represent the final outcome.

Experiments in regional integration in other parts of the world are generally far less institutionalized and none approach the depth achieved by the EU where a willingness to compromise or 'pool' sovereignty to enhance integration has been key to its success. But this model has found little support outside Europe. While states in other regions may cooperate closely on a range of matters, integration is fairly superficial. National sovereignty is jealously guarded by many states, some of which were still colonies only a generation ago and cling tenaciously to an almost absolute principle of non-interference in their 'sovereign affairs', especially when it comes to matters of human rights.

None of this means that nationalism in the EU area is dead, and this includes economic nationalism. While this phenomenon has not overwhelmed the European project, it continues to operate as a persistent low level dynamic. When it interferes with Europe's liberal economic agenda, however, it can draw very pointed criticism from liberal quarters. As one recent report argued: 'Economic nationalism in the form of opposition to cross-border mergers, promotion of national champions and bailing out of domestic firms is a serious danger for economic efficiency.' It further cited public ownership as a culprit, urging that it be 'severely restricted' (Press Release on EEAG Report, 27 February 2007). This flies in the face of not merely conservative ideology, but a long tradition of **social democracy** in Europe as well.

Another important development is interregionalism—itself a phenomenon that reinforces regionalization. A notable example is the Asia-Europe Meeting (ASEM) process established in the mid-1990s. Formed primarily to enhance economic relations, it has political and cultural pillars as well. The EU members comprise 'Europe' for the purposes of the meeting process while the Asian membership now includes all the ASEAN countries plus China, Japan, and South Korea and, more recently, India, Mongolia, Pakistan, and the ASEAN Secretariat.

In summary, although regional schemes have existed for decades, a definite pattern of strengthening regionalization in the post-Cold War period is clear. It is driven primarily by economic factors but virtually all of the regional associations aspire to closer social and political ties as well. The other observable pattern is the continuing development of an overarching tripolar economic system based on the 'macroregions' of Europe, North America, and Asia—the principle powerhouses of the global economy. The formation of ASEM is generally viewed as strengthening the third leg of that system, balancing the already strong North American-European and North American-Asian legs. Seen from this perspective, globalization and regionalization are indeed complementary dynamics in the liberalization of the global economy.

We have also seen, however, that while globalization and regionalization may well be complementary in nurturing processes of economic liberalization, they may also be complementary in undermining the economic role and functions of the nation-state, the very foundation of traditional IR. Trade liberalization and financial deregulation are all about easing state-imposed restraints, if not dispensing with them altogether, even though state actors are in many cases responsible for macroeconomic policy allowing such developments. Outside the academy, dissent and critique emanates from broad **social movements** manifest in 'anti-globalization' protests—now regular occurrences at various global or regional fora. Most participants are peaceful protesters gathering under the banners of various NGOs with concerns ranging from labour rights to environmental issues, consumer protection, peace advocacy, and so on. Others are self-described anarchists whose tactics range from civil disobedience to violence, mainly against commercial property and security personnel. An early manifestation of 'global protest' was the 'Battle for Seattle' in November 1999 when around half a million demonstrators converged on a WTO ministerial meeting. More recently, the 2007 APEC meeting in Sydney saw thousands of security personnel deployed to lock down the entire city centre for several days to forestall the vigorous protests which had become a feature of the various gatherings of regional or global organizations.

While anarchists—who are by definition anti-statist—receive most of the media attention, many of the protesters are concerned with issues that have actually been the traditional preserve of the state and who see the processes of globalization and regionalization as undermining the rights and interests of ordinary people in a variety of ways. As mentioned above, these include labour rights and consumer protection as well as environmental issues. This has prompted a debate on the role of the state, and indeed the future of sovereignty in a globalizing world. See **Box 20.7**. As we have remarked elsewhere, the state will no doubt remain, but it is unlikely to be the sovereign nation-state of traditional IR theory (Lawson, 2002: 218).

Key Points

- Globalization and regionalization are complex integrative processes driven predominantly by a liberal economic logic while incorporating social and political dimensions. They generally work as complementary rather than competitive processes. Some critical IPE approaches welcome the openings provided by globalization for new social movements while remaining critical of adverse economic consequences for marginalized groups.

- Both globalization and regionalization have been seen as undermining the traditional role of the state, an unwelcome development from the perspective of neomercantilist/realist IPE as well as from traditional leftist perspectives concerned with the negative impact on state provision for social protection.

Key Quote   Box 20.7
Globalism and the Demise of the Nation-State

'The Nation-State has become an unnatural, even dysfunctional, unit for organizing human activity and managing economic endeavour in a borderless world. It represents no genuine, shared community of economic interests; it defines no meaningful flows of economic activity. In fact it overlooks the true linkages and synergies that exist among often disparate populations by combining important measures of human activity at the wrong level of analysis . . . On the global economic map the lines that matter are those defining what may be called 'region states'. The boundaries . . . are not imposed by political fiat. They are drawn by the deft but invisible hand of the global market for goods and services. They follow rather than precede, real flows of human activity, creating new but ratifying existing patterns manifest in countless individual decisions.'   (Ohmae, 1993: 78)

Conclusion

Although many students of politics and international relations tend to shy away from economics, the proper study of IR entails due attention to IPE and the relationship between states and markets and between political and economic power. We have also seen that theories of IPE developed over the last few centuries parallel those in the more general field of politics and international relations. Mercantilism and realism, together with doctrines of nationalism and sovereignty, form a theoretical cluster which, although not entirely coherent, together produce a distinctive world-view in which states are the ultimate repository of political, social, and economic life and ought to be defended as such. Many traditional social democrats as well as the more conservative proponents of communitarianism would agree.

Liberal perspectives, while acknowledging the importance of states, generally embrace a world-view which shifts the focus from discrete political and economic communities to the myriad overlapping ties between these communities. Aided by the revolution in transport, communications, and other forms of technology, these ties have produced a thoroughly interdependent world which can only benefit from a continued softening of sovereign state boundaries to provide a truly global market for goods and services. The twin phenomena of globalization and regionalization both reflect and support the liberal view of world order.

Critical IPE challenges the assumptions of both realists and liberals, urging attention to the vested interests that lie behind them and the injustices they mask. While levels of socioeconomic well-being vary considerably within countries, critical IPE sees the North–South gap in the global economy as a standing indictment of both mercantilist and liberal approaches. The challenge is to move from incremental problem-solving approaches to a stance on theory and practice which probes the deeper historical development of opportunities and constraints as well as future trajectories. Some critical approaches do not oppose all aspects of globalization and find much to be welcomed in the challenge to sovereignty. Underpinned by a normative cosmopolitanism, while also recognizing the claims of localism, critical IPE sees the emergence of global and regional social movements as vehicles for positive change as well as providing an ongoing practical critique of both liberal and realist IPE.

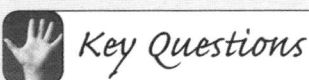 *Key Questions*

- In what sense does classical mercantilism see national wealth and military power forming a virtuous circle?
- Under what circumstances did liberalism first emerge as the dominant perspective on IPE?
- How does liberal theory justify the pursuit of economic self-interest?
- How relevant is class analysis to contemporary IPE?
- How can gender-sensitive studies contribute to IPE?
- What are the main features of critical IPE and how does it add to traditional Marxist perspectives?
- What does the North–South gap tell us about justice and injustice in the global economy?
- What is meant by the terms 'structural adjustment' and 'good governance' and how do they reflect liberal political and economic principles?
- What are some of the concerns of the 'global protest' movement?
- Do you regard globalization and/or regionalization as a genuine threat to the future of the nation-state as the foundation of world order?

 *Further Reading*

Amoore, Louise (ed.) (2005), *The Global Resistance Reader,* London: Routledge.
> This book claims to be the first comprehensive account of the exponential rise of transnational social movements in opposition to the financial, economic, and political hegemony of major international organizations such as the WTO, World Bank, and IMF with discussion of conceptual issues, substantive themes, and case studies.

Scholte, Jan Aart (2005), *Globalization: A Critical Introduction,* Basingstoke, Palgrave Macmillan, 2nd edn.
> Globalization for Scholte consists largely in deterritorialization, giving increasing significance to transborder global relations between people and organizations as communication and production are increasingly freed from geographic constraints. Thus the main focus is on the rise of supraterritoriality which is abundantly illustrated throughout the book.

Breslin, Shaun, Christopher W. Hughes, Nicola Philips, and Ben Rosamund (eds) (2002), *New Regionalisms in the Global Political Economy: Theories and Cases,* London: Routledge.
> A comprehensive set of contributions by leading authors on regionalism and the issues it raises in terms of sovereignty, autonomy, identity, environmental concerns, and financial crises, set in a broad comparative perspective.

Ravenhill, John (ed.) (2008), *Global Political Economy,* Oxford: Oxford University Press, 2nd edn.
> This is a detailed introduction to the subject matter of IPE with fourteen chapters by expert contributors covering theoretical approaches, global trade, finance and production, the implications of globalization for the state, and issues concerning the environment, the global South, and regionalism.

 *Web Links*

www.iisd.org/
International Institute for Sustainable Development: contains wide-ranging information on the developing world.

www.oecd.org/
Organization for Economic Cooperation and Development (OECD): is an invaluable source of statistical data.

www.ilo.org/
International Labour Organization (ILO): also provides statistical data but more general information on international agreements and issues.

http://europa.eu/index_en.htm
This is the (English language) gateway to the European Union website which contains an enormous amount of information. Note that all the regional organizations mentioned above have websites which are easily found with a search engine.

Visit the **Online Resource Centre** that accompanies this book to access more learning resources at **www.oxfordtextbooks.co.uk/orc/garner/**

Conclusion

by Peter Ferdinand

Reader's Guide

This chapter brings together the threads of the various arguments that have run throughout the book. It argues first that the study of political philosophy, political institutions, and international relations are closely interlinked. Secondly, it argues that the study of politics cannot be divorced from the study of other social sciences—economics, philosophy, law, sociology, psychology, and also history. In fact globalization has made those connections more important. Thirdly, it suggests that the study of politics should be seen as a genuinely international and comparative enterprise, which does not automatically assume the pre-eminence of the sovereign state, nor a privileged position for Europe or the USA. Having said that, we must acknowledge that more works have been written on political systems there than in other parts of the world, and scholars located in the West have tended to dominate academic publishing.

The Study of Politics in Context

This book has been divided into three equal parts—political philosophy, political institutions, and international relations—largely for convenience. Yet the ideas and institutions that they present are closely interlinked. Certainly, international relations are part of the same intellectual universe as the study of political theories, institutions, and comparative politics. The study of normative political philosophy, for example, cannot be kept apart from the empirical study of political institutions and the latter clearly operate at both domestic and international levels. Political systems are dependent for their stability upon their legitimacy, the reasons why members of that society believe them to be appropriate and acceptable—therefore they have recourse to ideas in order to legitimize them. Where sufficient members of a society believe the political system to be illegitimate, political rulers will need to employ a significant degree of coercion to remain in power.

Of course, most states explicitly set out to educate and/or socialize their people into supporting them, which is yet another argument in favour of seeing the normative and empirical dimensions of politics as connected. Nevertheless, what people think democracy is and how they assess it, for example, is inseparable from the way in which they make it operate. The discussion of the concepts of 'power' and 'justice', which were presented largely in the context of domestic political systems, is equally valid for the international arena. There is obviously a connection between national political systems and the international one. The international system as it has developed on Westphalian principles assumes equality and equal sovereignty between nation states. The Montevideo criteria for determining recognition of one state by another, as discussed in chapters seven and fourteen, include the capacity of national governments to control all of their territory. For many states, especially in the developing world, stability depends at least as much on a benign international environment as upon domestic circumstances.

➜ See page 170, in chapter seven for a discussion of the Montevideo Convention.

➜ See page 326, in chapter fourteen for a further discussion of the Montevideo Convention.

This book is also based upon another fundamental assumption, namely that the study of politics is eclectic, overlapping with other disciplines in terms of subject matter, theories and methods. These overlaps occur mainly in the social sciences, but they include history and philosophy as well. In the latter case, political philosophy has traditionally been preoccupied with identifying the polity that will enable human beings to live the good life, and in this quest moral and political philosophy become largely inseparable. Similarly, one of the recurring themes of this volume has been the impact of history upon the spread of both European-type states and the Westphalian state system around the world.

In the social sciences, economics is a discipline with a high degree of formal abstraction, yet there is an increasing recognition that institutions play a key role in determining many economic outcomes—exemplified by the New Institutionalist school. The study of political economy—domestic and international—is based on methods from politics and economics. In addition, economic abstractions form the basis of rational choice theories of politics, such as the economic theory of democracy examined in chapter three. Here it is assumed that political parties and voters have the utility-maximizing characteristics of actors—businesses and consumers—in the economic sphere. Parties will therefore be preoccupied with winning political power and voters will be concerned with exercising electoral choice in a way that will further their interests.

➜ See chapter three, pages 77–8, for a discussion of the economic theory of democracy.

The overlap between sociology and politics is equally apparent. For example, social stratification clearly plays a big part in the emergence of politicians and in voting patterns. The study of power, examined in chapter two, employs concepts and models of society developed by political sociologists. Chapter eight emphasized the overlap between law and politics in determining the rules that decide who gets what, when, and how in society. Psychology too overlaps with the study of politics. For example, chapter eleven illustrated ways in which it can contribute to our understanding of voting behaviour, and many themes in political philosophy are dependent on assumptions made about human nature. In addition, policy studies often involve methods of analysis and data derived from a great variety of disciplines, not just social science ones. Studies of environmental policy-making, for instance, often involve approaches drawn from natural sciences too—indeed policy analysis often benefits from scientific or technological understanding. It is evident, then, that a sophisticated understanding of political processes, whether national or international, will often require insights derived from other disciplines. This should not be taken to imply, however, that politics is simply a hybrid discipline, made up of concepts and modes of analysis borrowed from other disciplines. It clearly has its own specific preoccupations—most notably, **political obligation**, political ideologies, political institutions, and political behaviour at both the domestic and international levels, focusing on recurring regularities in political thinking and action. For some, echoing Aristotle, it is even seen as the master human science.

The Impact of Globalization

The distinctions between domestic and international politics and between the domestic politics of individual nation states, as this book has shown, have been further eroded by trends in globalization. Here are some examples.

1.   Economic crises in individual states are more difficult to prevent from spreading to others. The most recent example is the 'subprime' mortgage crisis in the USA which has caused one British as well as a few German banks to require state intervention, and hundreds of billions of dollars of losses in banks worldwide. All of this has a serious effect not only on international financial markets, but also on the economic policies of governments around the world.

2.   There have been increasing flows of people across national borders in search of work or refuge. In Britain, for instance, the 2001 Census showed that 7.53 per cent of the population had been born abroad, as compared with 5.75 per cent in the 1991 census. Migrant workers and their families play a significant role not only in the political life of their new countries, but also often as diasporas of the countries from which they came. This is especially well-documented for politics in the USA and is an increasingly frequent phenomenon within the EU, but it can be found elsewhere around the world too.

3.   Concern for the environment has also become pre-eminently a global issue, as states increasingly accept the need jointly to move towards policies of sustainable development, which will constrain the domestic policy choices of individual states.

➡ See chapter twenty, pages 468–71, for a discussion of regionalism.

4.   There has been an increase in regional organizations where states agree to pool elements of their sovereignty in exchange for the promise of coordinated policies and action. For centuries states have done this in the form of military alliances. In more recent decades, however, this has spread to organizations with economic and non-military political objectives. The best example of this is the EU, which has the closest ties between its members of all regional organizations, but there has been a proliferation of them elsewhere, for example, ASEAN, Mercosur, NAFTA, and so on.

5.   Since the 1970s there have been two waves of democratization spreading around the world. According to Freedom House, 40 per cent of states in the world (i.e. sixty-six) were electoral democracies in 1987 and in 2007 this proportion had risen to 63 per cent (i.e. 121). The collapse of one authoritarian regime sometimes encourages opponents in other ones, as happened in Eastern Europe and then the former Soviet Union between 1989 and 1991—hence the 'wave'-like phenomenon. And then political actors within states look elsewhere for ideas on political organization, for example, constitutional provisions, electoral arrangements, ways of running electoral campaigns, the reorganization of civil services, and so on. Equally, democratic states also sometimes seek to promote the spread of democracy through various forms of external assistance, ranging from training in the techniques of political professionalism to outright intervention.

6.   Ideas for the reform of policies in specific areas spread through international **epistemic communities** of professionals who share common orientations towards the most effective ways of delivering the policy objectives, irrespective of the particular state in which they live. Ideas of reforms to welfare policies, for example, spread from the USA to Western Europe. Ideas on educational policies have spread around the EU as individual states are confronted with the evidence from league tables of achievements of their pupils in mastering basic skills. Equally important has been the role of the Intergovernmental Panel on Climate Change, a group of climate scientists from around the world who have played a significant role in getting the issue of global warming on to the political agenda.

7. The proliferation and globalization of media institutions and sources of information, accelerated by the rise of the Internet and other forms of electronic communication as outlined in chapter twelve, have facilitated the emergence of the beginnings of a global civil society, that is, transnational organizations of political activists. Whether it is organizations such as Greenpeace, Médecins sans Frontières, Amnesty International, Oxfam, Caritas, the Red Crescent, the World Wide Fund for Nature or events such as Live Aid concerts, they all raise concerns above the level of the nation state.

➡ See chapter twelve, page 287, for a discussion on the impact of the media.

Globalization presents enormous challenges to the academic study of politics. Above all, it has made the study of international politics that much more important. Political philosophers, too, will have to reorient their focus from the nation-state, the character of which, since the sixteenth century, they have helped to shape. Globalization has, at the very least, increased the pressures on the state, complicating the activities of national governments.

Another trend challenges governments from the opposite direction, from below, in the form of decentralization. Sub-units of nation-states demand greater autonomy or independence. The declaration of independence by Kosova from Serbia is the most recent example. It was preceded by the disintegration of the former Soviet Union and the former Yugoslavia which gave rise to many new sovereign states, or which in some cases restored sovereignty to earlier independent countries. Elsewhere in the world we have seen a successful bid for independence in East Timor, while there are continuing demands for independence for the Basque country, Scotland, Northern Cyprus, and the Kurds and secessionist movements in Tibet, the Philippines, and Thailand, to name just a few. At the same time the state is being eroded at another level through the spread of neoliberal market ideas which advocate a clearer separation of the state from market operations, exemplified by the increasing trend towards establishing the independence of central banks from government intervention, which makes state control of the national economic less direct. Rapley (2006) also emphasized the role of criminal gangs in carving out and controlling 'statelets' of neighbourhoods that coexist in delicate, 'often symbiotic' relationships with nation-states. Examples include the favelas in Brazil, or the ganglands of Kingston, Jamaica. Often these gangs are linked with broader networks of transnational crime, challenging the traditional state from both outside and inside.

➡ See chapter one, page 43, for a description of the 'hollowing out' thesis.

All of this has contributed to the 'hollowing out' of the state evoked in chapters one and ten, with forces both above and below national governments sucking the vitality out of the state, the institution that has dominated both the practice and the study of politics around the world. Some commentators, such as Scholte (2005), have even gone so far as to identify 'globalization' with the deterritorialization of social, economic, and technical processes, which flow around the globe without significant obstacle. Others counter this by pointing to a different form of state activity at the international level, namely transnationalism. Slaughter (1997), for instance, has pointed to the rise of new

➡ See chapter ten, page 241, for more on the 'hollowing out' of the state.

networks of nodes of cooperation between branches of national governments. She points to the increasing webs of relations that link the courts and ministries of justice of individual states. This leads them to cooperate in new approaches to solving problems and sometimes to convergence. Certainly judges in one jurisdiction are often more aware now of the thinking of judges in others on similar issues—and this applies not just to the EU, which has the greatest integration of a supranational court with national ones. According to Slaughter (1997: 184), '[t]he state is not disappearing; it is disaggregating into its separate, functional distinct parts'.

New Medievalism

The end of the Cold War certainly transformed international relations and our understanding of it. One approach to the changing international order—the most optimistic—was the 'End of History' thesis of Fukuyama (1992). This proclaimed the victory of the West not merely in material terms, but also in ideological terms. The liberal democratic and capitalist model of politics and economics had prevailed over communist authoritarianism, and the future convergence of the rest of the world to the Western model seemed assured, even if it was likely to take some time. Although Eastern Europe has indeed mostly evolved in that direction, while most of Southeast Asia and East Asia have at least embraced the capitalist part of the model, convergence around the core values and practices of liberal democracy and capitalism has not occurred in other important parts of the world, especially in the Middle East. Furthermore, the failure of Anglo-American intervention to ignite that kind of support in Iraq has provoked a great deal of justified scepticism about the ability of these core Western countries to export their preferred model of politics and economics.

An alternative scenario has been promoted in the form of a 'new medievalism', mentioned in chapter one, which denotes a coming era characterized by multiple and overlapping international authority and loyalties. This scenario has at least two variants. One variant stresses the lack of established order, even anarchy, resulting from the weakening of the nation-state as an institution, as outlined in chapters one and seven. At its most extreme, the 'new medievalism' emphasizes the erosion of traditional sources of stability and the lack of any adequate alternative to replace it. Above all, this is attributed to the 'hollowing out' of state capacity. As emphasized in chapters seven and fourteen, the nation-state has generally been much weaker in the developing world for decades, but the phenomenon is now growing in the developed world as well. From this perspective, order in the global international system, for long predicated on the pre-eminence of nation-states, is now under threat and as yet no alternative structure of order has emerged to replace it. In other words, the world is moving towards greater anarchy, as was supposedly the case in the Middle Ages. The alternative variant accepts

→ See chapter one, page 44, for a description of 'new Medievalism'.

→ See chapter seven, page 173, discussion of the problems of weakening states.

→ See chapter seven, page 173, for a discussion of weak states in the developing world.

→ See chapter fourteen, page 341, for a further discussion of weak states.

the erosion of traditional poles of authority but instead argues that the Middle Ages were not as anarchic or 'dark' as is sometimes presented. There were sources of order and authority which restrained tendencies to anarchy. Advocates of this point of view generally rely on European parallels and emphasize the importance of universal authorities such as the Catholic Church and the Holy Roman Empire. There was no international system as we conceive of it in today's terms, but it was not chaotic. Conflict between various centres of power would erupt, spread, and then die down—it was not endemic. According to the more positive view of the Middle Ages, it was a time of international pluralism, with conflict restrained or moderated by overarching, mainly religious, ideologies. Admittedly this is another version of the world seen through European lenses, for it takes no account of what was happening in other parts of the world at the same time. It thus universalizes the European experience without taking account of the many imperial systems, stretching from Africa through to China and the Americas, as surveyed in chapter fourteen.

➔ See chapter fourteen, page 328, for a discussion of states and empires in world history.

Those who take this more positive view of the Middle Ages suggest that there are alternative poles of authority that prevent chaos today. Friedrichs (2001) for example argues that the post-international world is held together by the organizational claims of the surviving nation-state system and the transnational market economy, bolstered by international organizations such as the UN, the IMF, and the WTO. He suggests that this is analogous to the medieval system which was held together by the competing universalistic claims of Empire and Church.

Whether one believes that the world is becoming more anarchic, or whether it retains the capacity for self-stabilization, the permeability of national boundaries and of the power of national governments by outside forces seems indisputable. This makes the connection between the study of domestic and international politics, and the need for political philosophers to theorize these developments, even stronger.

Decentring the West? The Rise of the South?

Whether or not the new system is stable or more anarchic, one political trend does seem to be emerging across the globe. This is the rise of new centres of power. This is so even though the USA continues unchallenged as the sole superpower, with an economy that will remain the most powerful in the world for the next two decades, with conventional and nuclear military resources that dwarf all others, and with a significant claim to soft power too, despite the travails of Iraq. The EU is now emerging as a more powerful and cohesive economic and political power on the world stage. It sometimes seeks to offer a different approach to international politics, one based more upon diplomacy and upon establishing standards for law-based international behaviour. Despite its failings, it has achieved the most basic objective

➔ See chapter eighteen, pages 427–8, for a discussion of the different diplomatic styles of the USA and EU.

of banishing interstate war from the European continent, at least since 1945 and with good prospects of that continuing into the future. Given the experience of the three major Franco-German wars between 1870 and 1945, this is a great achievement. Furthermore, the gradual integration that has taken place has led to much greater prosperity. All this has made the EU a standard against which regional integration projects in other parts of the world are measured, although we must be careful not to assume it is a model that other regional projects can, and must, follow.

From this perspective the 'West' appears as powerful now as at any time since the end of the Second World War. A Western model of modernity could seem as influential and attractive as ever. And yet other actors in the world are gaining in confidence. Three states or groups of states exemplify the change. First, there is the rise of powerful states in Asia. Japan has been an economic giant for some decades, but now China, and more recently India, have come into focus as both economic and military contenders for great power status. China is sometimes presented in the USA as the country most likely to challenge American ascendancy in the coming decades. Whether or not this turns out to be the case, there is no doubting the significance of the change compared to the twentieth century and indeed the second half of the nineteenth, when China was so preoccupied with internal disorder and its consequences that it was unable to play a leading role in world affairs. Now the 'rise' of China has become a standard topic of discussion and debate, including inside China itself. Similarly, India's economic take-off since the early 1990s adds to the challenge to the West.

The second big change is the increasing self-confidence of the Islamic world. Throughout the nineteenth and twentieth centuries, the Islamic world declined significantly vis-à-vis the West. The dissolution of its most powerful grouping—the Ottoman Empire—led both to military occupation by Western countries and, equally importantly, a sense of inferiority in the face of Western modernity, as exemplified by the Ataturk secularist revolution of the 1920s mentioned in chapter seven. Even the use of the oil 'card' by Saudi Arabia and others in the 1970s did not essentially change this. Now things are different. Younger generations of Muslims, it seems, feel more self-assured, less deferential towards the West. The same is true of various Islamic governments. Having said that, we must remain very careful not to draw a simplistic dividing line between the 'Islamic world' and 'the West'. There are many overlapping interests and alliances between these two rather generalized entities. After all, Turkey is a member of NATO—a largely 'Western' alliance, as well as a candidate for EU membership. Many Islamic countries are allies of the USA in the war on terror.

➔ See chapter seven, page 166, for a description of Turkey's radical reforms.

The third big change is the resurgence of Russia. In one sense this does not represent such a big break with recent history. After all, the Soviet Union was the rival superpower from the end of the Second World War until the Union's collapse in 1991. Russia's reappearance as a global player should not, then, be so surprising. What is significant about Russia's resurgence is the Putin regime's much greater disdain for supposed Western superiority, even as it continues sometimes to proclaim itself as of the West; and this is spite of the fact that the West lavished considerable resources, both financial and advice, on Russia to try to smooth its transition from a communist regime to, hopefully, democracy and a market economy.

All these new actors demand greater respect. This is symptomatic of a wider change of attitude in other parts of the world towards the 'West'. It is no longer the object of the same deference as during most of the nineteenth and twentieth centuries. While its levels of economic development and technological prowess remain undisputed, it is no longer seen to embody the only path to 'modernity', a path that nations in other parts of the world are obliged to follow if they are going to achieve the same levels of development. Indeed there is an increasing body of people who argue that the Western style and level of development is out of keeping with the new priority of an ethic of environmentally friendly, sustainable development. They advocate a search for alternative solutions. It is an attitude that resonates with those who argue that the centre of gravity of world development, especially economically, is moving gradually away from the West to other regions or groups of countries. Equally, the developing world's refusal, despite enormous pressure from the USA, to agree to binding commitments on reducing carbon emissions at least until they are given the resources to cope with the consequences, reveals a much more confident persona. This behaviour is predicated on the developing world's insistence that developed countries have been largely responsible for climate change and therefore should take action to deal with it.

This inclination resonates with the emergence of two other schools of political analysis. The first is the 'subaltern studies' school described in chapter twelve. This rejects the idea of automatically assigning superiority and paying greater attention to the 'winners' of development. These 'winners' include both elites within individual states and also, internationally, the developed world. Instead, from this perspective, analysts should pay more attention to the 'subalterns', i.e. the underdogs. The latter point is encapsulated in the title of an article by the American academic and black activist, Cornel West (1991), 'Decentring Europe', as well as a book by the Indian anthropologist, Dipak Chakrabarty (2000), *Provincializing Europe*, that is, treating Europe 'merely' as the equal of other regions of the world.

➡ See chapter twelve, page 286, for a discussion of subaltern studies.

To some extent this approach echoes postmodernism, as briefly outlined in chapter six and further discussed in chapter sixteen. The orientation underlying it is the rejection of 'god-like' scientific authorities. Rather, it encourages and advocates pluralism. It has been criticized, with some justice, for taking this too far, for excessive relativism. Postmodernists are more noted for seeking to undermine the claims to objectivity of particular academic authorities than for establishing the validity of alternative claims. Yet the basic principle underlying this book is compatible with their outlook. We do not believe that Western political systems should automatically enjoy greater esteem than those in other parts of the world. Politics in other parts of the world is equally deserving of study.

➡ See chapter six, page 138, for a discussion of postmodernism.

➡ See chapter sixteen page 379, for a further discussion of postmodernism.

It is certainly true that, as was repeatedly emphasized in the second section of the book, Western ideas, explored in Part 1, and institutions have spread around the world and in many ways set the standard for what could be regarded as 'modern' political systems. It is a historical fact that democracy, for example, spread from Europe and the USA to other parts of the world in the twentieth century. 'Political science' is often seen as primarily a western academic discipline; and although critics continue to argue that 'Western' political institutions such as political parties are inappropriate for non-Western societies with different traditions, it is striking that viable alternative forms of political activism and political organization have proved remarkably limited. In the 1960s and 1970s, for instance, leaders of Third World states such as Sukarno in Indonesia and Nyerere in Tanzania advocated forms of political organization and decision-making that were more in keeping with the traditions of village societies; yet these alternative forms have not prospered. To some extent this was the result of other dimensions of modernization. Increasing urbanization, for example, undermined the appeal of traditional rural forms of decision-making.

It is worth reiterating, however, that there is no obvious logical reason why forms of political organization found in the West should acquire automatic pre-eminence. Nor is it obvious that political institutions in the West are all in rude health. One of the arguments underlying chapter eleven was that political parties in the West suffer from great problems, not least the lack of esteem in which they are held by their potential supporters. Concepts underlying such forms are not always easily translated from western, especially Anglophone, contexts to other parts of the world. Chapter twelve, for example, showed how the concept of 'civil society' was based upon assumptions derived from Western experience which were not easily translated into Islamic or Asiatic societies. Yet we all tend to assess political institutions in other countries through lenses that were fashioned in our own societies. The state, political parties, interest groups, federalism—these are just some of the key terms of political discourse which look and behave differently from one political system to another. Just because we think we know what they mean in systems with which we are familiar, this does not mean that they are identical elsewhere.

→ See chapter eleven, page 267, for a discussion of the problems facing parties.

→ See chapter twelve, page 276, for a discussion of civil society.

The Study of Politics in a Globalizing World

If it is indeed the case that other regions of the world are becoming more significant in world affairs, one other consequence also follows for the study of politics. It will become even more important to know about them and incorporate them into the analysis of how politics operates around the world. Moreover, political philosophers as well as IR scholars will have to engage more than they have done with the ideas underlying non-Western political practice. As this Conclusion has indicated, two key themes emphasized in this book have been, first, the declining importance of the sovereign state, and secondly, the growing significance of non-Western parts of the world. Both present enormous challenges for the political analyst. The impact of globalization reinforces the importance of the study of international politics and the need for political philosophers to reorient their traditional focus on the state. Likewise, the growing significance of the non-Western world will have to be taken into account by students of comparative politics and international relations. Political philosophers too will have to engage more than they have done with the ideas underlying non-Western political practice. This does not mean that the state has, or is likely to, become a peripheral concern of the political analyst. Nor does it mean that politics in Europe or the USA will become unimportant. Describing and analysing politics in the West and their impact on world affairs will remain absorbing. The evolution of these political systems and the ideas underlying them will still attract wide interest and offer alternative possible reforms for each other when the systems or individual institutions run into difficulties. What happens on both sides of the Atlantic will also have a major impact upon world affairs for decades to come. Nevertheless the previous dominance of the state and Western theory and practice has been eroded. It is uncertain where these developments will lead, and because of this the study of politics at the beginning of the twenty-first century will continue to be exciting and invigorating.

Glossary

Agency   In social science literature denotes the fact of something happening or existing because of an actor's action. The contrast is with a state of affairs that is chiefly determined by impersonal factors (historical, economic, etc.) over which human actors have little control. Hence the frequent use of the combined term structure-agency to pose the question whether background factors or human action were the primary causes.

Alternative member model   A hybrid voting system that combines strengths of both **majoritarianism** and **proportional representation**: votes are cast both for individual candidates within a constituency and for a general list of candidates from separate parties.

Amoral familism   The exaltation of family interests above all other moral considerations, originally coined by the sociologist Banfield to describe social relations in Sicily.

Anarchy   In its simplest sense anarchy denotes an absence of political rule or sovereign authority. In traditional International Relations theory, states are said to exist in an anarchic international sphere because there is no sovereign authority standing above individual states.

Anthropocentric   An ethic which prioritizes the interests of humans over all other forms of life.

Arrow's impossibility theorem   A mathematical theorem formulated by the economist Kenneth Arrow which shows the impossibility of determining the 'optimal' ranking of preferences by members of a society when no alternative choice receives an absolute majority.

Authoritarian   Refers to rule which is unaccountable and restrictive of personal liberty.

Authority   A situation whereby an individual or group is regarded as having the right to exercise power, and is thereby acting legitimately.

Balance of payments   Refers to a country's international economic transactions over a certain period showing the sum of all ingoing and outgoing sums between individuals, businesses, and government agencies in that country in relation to those in the rest of the world.

Balance of power   A system of relations between states where the goal is to maintain an equilibrium of power, thus preventing the dominance of any one state.

Behaviouralism   An approach that stresses the importation of the scientific method in the study of social phenomena. Objective measurement of the social world is the goal, values to be completely jettisoned from social enquiry.

Bicameralism   The principle of having two separate chambers of a national parliament.

Bipolarity   In international politics generally describes a distribution of power in which two states possess a preponderance of economic, military, and political power and influence either internationally or in a particular region. Bipolarity during the Cold War referred to the power and influence of the USA vis-à-vis that of the USSR.

Bourgeoisie   Term appearing frequently in Marxist analysis and referring to a merchant and/or propertied class possessing essential economic power and control.

Cartel parties   A type of party that has evolved from the **mass party** with more limited membership and dominated by professional politicians.

Citizenship   The granting of social and political rights to enable individuals to participate in state decision-making.

Civic culture   A variety of **political culture,** where citizens predominantly feel capable of taking an active part in politics.

Civic nationalism   Refers to loyalty to the institutions and values of a particular political community; sometimes presented as a more moderate form of nationalism.

Civil society   Consists of institutions, such as interest groups, which stand in an intermediary position between the individual and the state. See also **International civil society**.

Class analysis   Associated with traditional Marxism which places socio-economic class (e.g. proletariat, peasantry, bourgeoisie, aristocracy) at the centre of virtually all political analysis.

Classical liberalism   Emphasizes that the state's role should be limited to ensure internal and external security and to ensure that private property rights are enforced.

Cohabitation   Occurs when a country's president comes from one party and the prime minister from a different one.

Cold War   A description of the states system existing between the end of the Second World War in 1945 and the collapse of Soviet communism by the early 1990s. On the one side was the United States, the dominant power in the West; on the other was the Soviet Union, the dominant power in the East.

Colonialism   A mode of domination involving the subjugation of one population group and their territory to another, usually through settling the territory with sufficient people from the colonizing group to impose direct or indirect rule over the native population and to maintain control over resources and external relations. It is a common manifestation of **imperialism** but is not identical with it.

Communitarianism   A strand of thought which argues that individuals gain their rights and duties within particular communities. It is often contrasted with **cosmopolitanism.**

Concert of Europe   Term used to designate a largely informal agreement among the major powers of nineteenth-century Europe to act together—or 'concert' together—on matters of mutual concern. It emerged following the Congress of Vienna (1814–15) and was manifest principally in irregular diplomatic meetings and conferences aimed at the peaceful resolution of differences.

Consociational democracy   A means whereby the elites of different parts of a heterogeneous community can share power and integrate society.

Constituency   An electoral district.

Constitution   The complex of relations between a state's governing institutions and the people, including the understandings that are involved. Most of these relations are usually codified in a single document.

Constitutionalism   The principle that assigns a special significance to constitutions and rule of law in national life.

Constructivism   Sometimes called *social* constructivism, it refers to the notion that the 'reality' of the world around us is constructed intersubjectively through social interaction which gives meaning to material objects and practices; thus 'reality' is not simply an objective truth detached from a social base.

Coordinated market economies   Where firms depend more heavily on non-market relationships to coordinate their activities than in liberal Anglo-American economies; more typically found in continental Europe.

Corporatism   Traditionally, corporatism referred to the top-down model where the state, as in the fascist model, incorporates economic interests in order to control them and civil society in general. Modern societal or neo-corporatism, on the other hand, reflects a genuine attempt by governments to incorporate economic interests, trade union and business interests, into the decision-making process.

Cosmopolitan democracy   A system of popular control of supranational institutions and processes.

Cosmopolitanism   A position which holds that humans ought to be regarded as a single moral community to which universal principles apply irrespective of national boundaries.

Cultural pluralism   The descriptive fact of the existence of different norms of behaviour determined by culture. Can be regarded as normatively desirable or undesirable.

Deliberative democracy   A model of democracy emphasizing the role of discussion and debate as a means of reaching rational, legitimate, and altruistic decisions.

Democracy   Refers to a political system in which there is self-government.

Democratic elitism   An attempt, most associated with Joseph Schumpeter, to reconcile elitism with democracy. According to this model, voters have the opportunity to choose between competing teams of leaders.

Democratic peace   A thesis which holds that countries that are governed democratically do not go to war against each other.

Deontological   An ethical theory which holds that certain end states (as in the case of a natural right) are to be upheld because they are right in themselves, irrespective of the consequences which accrue from them in particular circumstances.

Deterrence   Both a theory and a strategy in IR based on the notion that the possession of powerful weapons will deter aggression by other countries. During the Cold War, *nuclear deterrence* was a widely supported strategy.

Developmental state   A state, such as Japan, which prioritizes economic resources for rapid development and which uses carrots and sticks to induce private economic institutions to comply.

Dichotomy   A division into two mutually exclusive or contradictory entities or groups such as 'the West' and the 'non-West'.

Direct democracy   Refers to a system whereby the people rule directly and not through representatives.

Duverger's Law   The conclusion by the French political scientist Maurice Duverger that first-past-the-post electoral systems lead to two-party systems.

Ecocentric   An ethic which removes humans from the centre of the moral universe and accords intrinsic value to non-human parts of nature.

Ecological modernization   A version of sustainable development which seeks to show how liberal capitalist societies can be reformed in an environmentally sustainable way.

Ecologism   An ideology that stresses the interdependence of all forms of life, and which is often used to denote the moral dethroning of humans.

Elitism   In a normative sense refers to the rule of the most able. From an empirical perspective it refers to the existence of a ruling group beyond popular control in all societies of any complexity.

Elitist theory of democracy   See **Democratic elitism**.

Emancipation   A common theme in Critical Theory which denotes a normative aspiration to liberate people from unfair economic, social and political conditions.

Embedded autonomy   The insulation of state economic policy-makers in **developmental states** from short-term political pressures.

Empire   Shares a common etymology with **imperialism** and denotes a system in which one country or centre of power dominates and controls other, weaker countries either directly or indirectly using either force, the threat of force, or some other means of coercion.

Empirical analysis   refers to the measurement of factual information, of what is rather than what ought to be.

Enlightenment   A seventeenth- and eighteenth-century intellectual and cultural movement that emphasized the application of reason to knowledge in a search for human progress.

Epistemic communities   Groups of specialists in various countries who share a common approach to a policy area that transcends national differences.

Epistemology   Refers to the task of establishing what can be known about what exists.

Ethnic cleansing   A term which emerged during the breakup of the former Yugoslavia and which referred to attempts to physically rid (i.e. 'cleanse') a particular area of people from a certain ethnic group by either driving them out or murdering them.

Ethnic nationalism   Refers to loyalty to a shared inheritance based on culture, language, or religion.

Ethnocentricity   The tendency to see and interpret the world primarily from the perspective of one's own cultural, ethnic, or national group. It often entails elements of hierarchy in that one tends to regard one's own culture as superior, or at least preferable, to others.

Ethnosymbolism   The manipulation of mainly cultural symbols to strengthen national identity.

Federalism   The principle that within a state different territorial units have the authority to make certain policies without interference from the centre.

Fordism   Refers to a form of large-scale mass-production that is homogeneous both in terms of the products made and also in terms of the repetitive jobs that came with it.

General will   A concept, associated with Rousseau, which holds that the state ought to promote an altruistic morality rather than the selfish interests of individuals.

Global governance   This term extends the concept of **governance** as defined below, and refers loosely to the 'architecture' constituted by various authoritative political, social, and economic structures and actors that interconnect and interact in the absence of actual 'government' in the global sphere.

Global justice   The application of principles of justice at a global rather than a national level.

Global South   This term corresponds more or less to what was commonly referred to as the 'Third World'. It designates poorer, underdeveloped countries most of which lie geographically south of the equator. Correspondingly, it requires a 'North' which is sometimes used as an alternate designation for 'the West'.

Globalization   A term used to describe the process of increasing economic, political, social, and cultural interdependence which has, for good or ill, reduced the autonomy of sovereign states.

Good governance   A set of principles formulated by international financial institutions to make the government of developing states fair, effective, and free from corruption.

Governance   A term often preferred now to government since it reflects the broader nature of modern government which includes not just the traditional institutions of government but also the other inputs into decisions that steer society such as sub-national and supranational institutions, the workings of the market, and the role of interest groups.

Harm principle   A position, associated with John Stuart Mill, that actions are to be allowed unless the effect of them is to harm others.

Hegemony   Generally embodies the concept of political, social, and economic domination. In IR it may refer to the general dominance of a particular country over others. It was developed as an important concept in Critical Theory by Antonio Gramsci and is used to theorize relations of domination and subordination in both domestic and international spheres.

Human nature   Refers to innate and immutable human characteristics. Hobbes, for instance, regards the competitive and self-serving nature of humans as necessitating an all-powerful state. Other strands of thought either regard human nature in a more positive light or, as with Marx, suggest that human character depends upon the social and economic structure of society.

Humanitarian intervention   This term implies direct intervention by one country, or a group of countries, in the internal affairs of another country, on the grounds that such intervention is justified by humanitarian concerns relating, for example, to genocide. See also **Intervention**.

Idealism   This term has invited numerous interpretations in philosophy, politics, and International Relations. For the purposes of IR, it is usually taken to refer to a particular school of liberal thought which emerged in the wake of the First World War and which envisaged opportunities for significant positive change in world affairs and which aimed in particular at eliminating warfare. It remains an appropriate designation for any

school of thought in IR which promotes visions of a better world order in which peace and justice are the order of the day.

Illiberal democracy   Describes states where competitive elections are held but in which there is relatively little protection of rights and liberties, and state control over the means of communication ensures that governing parties are rarely defeated at the polls.

Imperialism   Literally, 'to command', and denoting the exercise of power by one group over another. It is sometimes used synonymously with **colonialism** but is broader in its application because it does not necessarily involve actual physical occupation of the territory in question or direct rule over the subjugated people.

Insider groups   Interest groups enjoying a privileged relationship with government.

Institutions   Regular patterns of behaviour that provide stability and regularity in social life; sometimes these patterns are given organizational form with specific rules of behaviour and of membership.

Interdependence/complex interdependence   While interdependence in IR refers to the notion developed mainly in liberal theory that states in fact are interconnected through a web of relations, primarily in the economic field, which makes warfare less likely (and less desirable as a foreign policy strategy), *complex* interdependence simply introduces more variables as relevant to the equation, therefore deepening the complexity of interdependence and strengthening the case for seeing the world as far more pluralistic than, say, neorealist theories allow.

Interest groups   Political actors who seek collectively to press specific interests upon governments (sometimes also called pressure groups).

Intergenerational justice   Principles of justice relating to non-contemporaries; i.e. between those living now and those still to be born.

International civil society   Refers broadly to the realm of non-state actors, including interest groups and voluntary associations, in the international sphere.

International regime   An idea developed by Stephen Krasner which encapsulates the way in which groups of actors in certain issue areas converge around a set of principles, norms, rules, and procedures. An example is the international human rights regime.

International society   A concept associated with the English School of International Relations indicating that the condition of anarchy in the international sphere does not preclude the development of a society of states characterized by peaceful working relations.

Internationalism   Refers to both a belief in the benefits of international political and economic cooperation and a movement that advocates practical action in support of these objectives.

Intervention   In International Relations, usually refers to direct intervention by one or more states in the internal affairs of another, by either military or non-military means. *Humanitarian* intervention refers to any intervention which is claimed to have a primarily humanitarian purpose, such as intervening to prevent genocide.

Intragenerational justice   Principles of justice relating to contemporaries, that is those who are living at the same time.

Iron triangles   Groups of politicians, officials, and outside experts who regularly formulate government policy in particular issue areas to the exclusion of wider social groups.

Issue networks   Looser groups of officials and outsiders who regularly share ideas in particular policy areas.

Legal positivism   A form of legal theory that asserts that law is simply what the state says it is.

Liberal democracy   Describes states—such as the USA, the United Kingdom, and India—which are characterized by free and fair elections involving universal suffrage, together with a liberal political framework consisting of a relatively high degree of personal liberty and the protection of individual rights.

Liberal institutionalism   Closely associated with liberal internationalism, this concept focuses more attention on the ability of international institutions to ameliorate the negative effects of anarchy in the international system.

Machtpolitik   See **Power politics**.

Mass parties   Political parties typically in the first half of the twentieth century that attracted millions of grass-roots members.

Meritocratic theory of justice   Advocates distributing resources to those who display some merit, such as innate ability, and therefore deserve to be rewarded.

Metanarrative   This concept, sometimes called a 'grand narrative', refers to a total philosophy or historical explanation of the social and political world presented as an ultimate truth.

Methodology   Refers primarily to the particular way(s) in which knowledge is produced. Methodologies vary considerably depending on the type of research being carried out to produce knowledge in different fields—historical, anthropological, linguistic, biological, medical, etc. Different methodologies invariably incorporate their own assumptions and rationales about the nature of knowledge, although these are not always stated explicitly.

Modernity   Modernity is a temporal and cultural phenomenon linked not only to the rise of industrialization in Europe and North America but also to profound changes in social and political thought which are closely associated with the intellectual movement known as the Enlightenment.

Monism   The view that there are no fundamental divisions in phenomena.

Nation   A named community, often referred to as 'a people', usually occupying a homeland and sharing one or more cultural elements, such as a common history, language, religion, customs, etc. Nations may or may not have a state of their own.

Nation-building   A process in which a state is created and then an attempt is made to mould sometimes quite diverse groups into a coherent, functional 'nation'.

National interest   A concept closely associated with *raison d'état* and power politics. It suggests that the interests of the state (or at least of one's own state) is paramount over any other consideration in the international sphere. Although regarded as a foundational concept in realist approaches it is as easily used to justify idealist approaches as well indicating that what is actually in the national interest may be highly contested.

Nationalism   In politics and International Relations, nationalism refers to doctrine or ideology which holds that 'the nation' is more or less entitled to political autonomy, usually in a state of its own.

Natural law   Law conceived as both universal and eternal, applying to all people in all places and at all times, because it derives either from 'nature' or God as distinct from local laws arising within specific communities.

Natural rights Rights which humans are said to possess irrespective of the particular legal and political system under which they live.

Negative liberty Holds that liberty can be increased by removing external obstacles, provided by physical incarceration or law, to it.

Neo-medievalism A system of governance resembling Europe in the Middle Ages where authority belongs to an overlapping array of local, national, and supranational institutions.

New liberalism A version of liberalism that advocates a more positive role for the state than classical liberalism. Argues that the state, in correcting the inequities of the market, can increase liberty by creating greater opportunities for individuals to achieve their goals.

New Public Management An approach to the reform of government bureaucracies in the 1990s that sought to introduce methods of business administration.

Night-watchman state A model in which the state concentrates on ensuring external and internal security, playing little role in civil society and the economy where the economic market is allowed to operate relatively unhindered.

Non-governmental organizations (NGOs) A term applying to almost any organization that operates independently from government, whether at the local, national, or international level.

Normative analysis Refers to analysis which asks ought rather than is type questions, therefore forming the basis of political philosophy. It does not seek to ask, therefore, whether democracy, or freedom, or a pluralist state exists, but whether these outcomes are desirable ones.

Ontology Relates to what exists. It asks what is there to know? Is there, for instance, a political world out there capable of being observed or is the reality, to at least some degree, created by the meanings or ideas we impose upon it?

Organized capitalism See **Coordinated market economies**.

Original position A device used by John Rawls to denote a position where individuals meet to decide the rules of justice governing the society in which they are to live.

Outsider groups Interest groups that enjoy no special relationship with the government and thus seek to press their case from the outside.

Parliamentarianism The principle that governments are formed by prime ministers, rather than heads of state, who are primarily responsible to parliament.

Paternalism The practice, often associated with conservatism, of restricting the liberty of individuals in order to benefit them.

Patriarchy Refers to male domination and corresponding female oppression.

Perestroika The policy of attempted restructuring of the Soviet political system under President Gorbachev in the late 1980s.

Pluralism Originated as a normative argument against monism or sameness. In political theory it is most associated with a theory of the state which holds that political power is diffuse, all organized groups having some influence on state outputs. In IR it is associated with one of two main approaches adopted by the 'English School' as well as with neoliberal theory which highlights the multiplicity, or plurality, of forces at work in the international system.

Plurality A simple majority in voting (sometimes also known as first-past-the-post), as distinct from an absolute majority (i.e. 50 per cent plus one).

Policy communities Groups of officials and experts in particular policy areas who regularly consult each other.

Political culture The aggregate attitudes of members of a society towards the institutions of rule and how they should operate.

Political obligation A central preoccupation of political theorists asking why, if at all, individuals ought to obey the state. There have been a variety of different answers to this question ranging from the divine right of kings to rule to the modern claim that democracy is the basis for authority.

Political party A group of political activists who aspire to form or be part of the government on the basis of a programme of policies.

Political system The totality of institutions within a state and all the connections between them.

Polyarchy A term coined by Robert Dahl. It refers to a society where government outcomes are a product of the competition between groups. The rule of minorities, not majorities, is postulated as the normal condition of pluralist democracies.

Positive discrimination   Refers to the practice of discriminating in favour of those disadvantaged groups who, it is argued, would remain disadvantaged unless affirmative action was taken in their favour.

Positive liberty   A theory which holds that liberty can be increased either by state action or by removing internal obstacles such as immorality or irrationality.

Positivism   An approach which believes it is possible to generate empirical statements without any evaluative connotations. At an extreme level, the so-called logical positivists argue that only empirical statements, together with those that are true by definition, are meaningful, thereby ruling out the value of normative statements.

Postmodernism   A multi-faceted theoretical approach which challenges the certainties and dualisms of modernism. It therefore promotes pluralism and difference.

Power   The ability to make others do something that they would not have chosen to do.

Power politics (*machtpolitik*)   A view of politics associated with realism and which generally takes morality and justice to be irrelevant to the conduct of international relations, a view predicated in turn on the notion that 'might is right'.

Presidentialism   The principle that the president of a republic is the head of the government.

Principal–agent relations   Identifies the differentiation of roles between the giver of instructions, usually in government administration, and the implementer.

Procedural justice   The distribution of goods according to a set of rules, irrespective of the outcome.

Proportional representation   A family of voting systems that make their highest priority a close approximation between the votes given to all the parties putting up candidates and the number of seats into which this is translated in parliament.

Protectionism   An economic strategy, usually associated with a national policy of trade restriction in the form of tariffs and quotas, which attempts to protect domestic industries, businesses, and jobs from competition from abroad.

Public space   The arena (real or virtual) in which any member of society is free to express views on any issue of interest to the public. Sometimes associated with the German philosopher Habermas, who stressed its key importance for democracy and the difficulty of maintaining it under capitalism.

Realism   Denotes a complex array of theories and ideas in the human sciences, especially philosophy, sociology, politics, and International Relations. In the latter, it names a general approach to theory which takes power politics, national interest, and similar concepts as foundational to action in the international sphere, and opposes idealism in liberal and critical theories.

Reason of state (*raison d'état*)   See **National interest**.

Rechtsstaat   Literally, a law-based state, as distinct from a state where the ruler or executive is free to adopt policies and change them as they see fit.

Regionalization   A process in which a number of states in a given geographical area come together for mutually beneficial purposes, often forming a regional association. Some, like the EU, are highly institutionalized and have myriad economic, social, and political interconnections, while others may have minimal rules and less ambitious purposes.

Representative democracy   Refers to a system whereby the people choose others to represent their interests, rather than making decisions themselves.

Rule of law   The principle that everyone in a state, the executive included, is subject to the same impersonal laws.

Secularism   In political terms, it refers to the removal of religion from a privileged position in the state.

Security dilemma   A concept in International Relations, developed principally in realist thought, in which the condition of anarchy is seen to prompt states to engage in self-regarding behaviour in order to survive. The dilemma arises when efforts by one state to enhance its own security (such as acquiring superior weaponry) provokes insecurity in another state, which may then respond by building up its own military capacity.

Self-determination   A doctrine that emerged in the early twentieth century in relation to the right of 'peoples' (nations) to determine their own political future, thus embodying elements of both democracy and nationalism.

Social capital   The aggregate set of attitudes and networks that enable members of a society willingly to cooperate in pursuit of joint projects.

Social contract   A device used by a number of political thinkers, most recently John Rawls, to justify a particular form of state. It is conceived as a voluntary agreement that individuals make in a state of nature, which is a society before government is set up.

Social constructivism   See **Constructivism**.

Social Darwinism   The application of Darwin's theory of natural selection to social life. It was used by the social theorist Herbert Spencer to justify a laissez-faire approach to social policy to ensure that only the fittest survive.

Social democracy   An approach which, after the Russian Revolution in 1917, became associated with liberal democracies that engaged in redistributive policies and the creation of a welfare state.

Social justice   The principle that goods ought to be distributed according to a principle based on need, merit, or pure equality.

Social movement   Refers to largely informal broad-based movements composed of groups and individuals coalescing around key issue areas on a voluntary and often spontaneous basis. Examples include the environmental movement, women's movement, peace movement, and anti-globalization movement.

Solidarism   A term applied to a branch of thought in English School International Relations theory which seeks to promote greater protection of human rights internationally, even where this overrides, at least in principle, the rights of states to non-intervention in domestic politics.

Sovereignty   Refers to self-government either at the level of the individual or at the level of the state. To say a state is sovereign is to claim that it has a monopoly of force over the people and institutions in a given territorial area.

State   A two-level concept: a) the government executive of a country, sometimes also known as a nation-state; b) the whole structure of political authority in a country.

Statecraft   The skilful conduct of state affairs, usually in the context of external relations.

State of nature   A concept with a long history in political and social thought which posits a hypothetical vision of how people lived before the institution of civil government and society. There are various competing versions of the state of nature, some portraying it as dangerous while others see it in a more positive light.

Structural adjustment   Used in application to economic policies imposed on countries—usually poor and under-developed—by the World Bank and the International Monetary Fund as a condition for obtaining loans, so as to reduce fiscal deficits. Specific policies have included privatization, cuts in government expenditure on public services, devaluation, tariff cuts, and so on.

Structuration   A concept derived from the sociologist Anthony Giddens, which here designates all the factors that both constrain and also provide resources for the functioning of a political system.

Sustainable development   A term that seeks to denote the compatibility between environmental protection and economic growth.

Totalitarian   Refers to an extreme version of authoritarian rule, in which the state controls all aspects of society and the economy.

Unicameralism   The principle of having a single chamber of a national parliament.

Unilateralism   Refers to the tendency of a state to pursue its preferred foreign policy strategies regardless of whether there is support from international bodies (such as the UN or NATO) or indeed regardless of any international law.

Utilitarianism   A consequentialist ethical theory which argues that the behaviour of individuals and governments should be judged according to the degree to which their actions maximize pleasure or happiness.

Utopia   Refers to an ideal state of affairs which does not exist but which can be aimed for. The search for utopias is seen by some as a worthwhile exercise to expand the limits of human imagination, and by others as a recipe for illiberal, authoritarian, and even totalitarian societies.

References

Introduction

Arneson, R. (2000), 'The Priority of the Right Over the Good Rides Again' in P. Kelly (ed.), *Impartiality, Neutrality and Justice. Re-reading Brian Barry's Justice as Impartiality*, Edinburgh: Edinburgh University Press: 60–86.

Ayer, A.J. (1971), *Language, Truth and Logic*, Harmondsworth: Penguin, 2nd edn.

Bell, D. (1960), *The End of Ideology*, Glencoe, IL: Free Press.

Berlin, I. (1969), *Four Essays on Liberty*, Oxford: Oxford University Press.

Bevir, R. and R.A.W. Rhodes (2002), 'Interpretive Theory' in D. Marsh and G. Stoker, *Theory and Methods in Political Science*, Basingstoke: Palgrave: 131–52.

Crick, B. (1962), *In Defence of Politics*, London: Weidenfeld & Nicolson.

Dahl, R. (1991), *Modern Political Analysis*, Englewood Cliffs, NJ: Prentice-Hall, 5th edn.

Dworkin, R. (1987), *Taking Rights Seriously*, London: Duckworth.

Fukuyama, F. (1992), *The End of History and the Last Man*, Harmondsworth: Penguin.

Gallie, W. (1955/6), 'Essentially Contested Concepts' in *Proceedings of the Aristotelian Society*, Vol. 56.

Gamble, A. (2000), *Politics and Fate*, Cambridge: Polity Press.

Garner, R. (2005), *The Political Theory of Animal Rights*, Manchester: Manchester University Press.

Gerth, H. and C. Wright Mills (1946), *From Max Weber: Essays in Sociology*, London: Routledge and Kegan Paul.

Goodwin, B. (2007), *Using Political Ideas*, Chichester: John Wiley & Sons, 5th edn.

Hay, C. (2002), *Political Analysis*, Basingstoke: Palgrave.

Held, D. and A. Leftwich (1984), 'A Discipline of Politics?' in A. Leftwich (ed.), *What is Politics? The Activity and its Study*, Oxford: Blackwell.

Heywood, A. (2004), *Political Theory: An Introduction*, Basingstoke: Palgrave Macmillan, 3rd edn.

Hoffman, J. (1995), *Beyond the State*, Cambridge: Polity Press.

Laslett, P. (1956), 'Introduction', *Philosophy, Politics and Society*, series one, Oxford: Blackwell.

Lasswell, H. (1936), *Politics: Who Gets What, When, How?*, New York: McGraw-Hill.

Leftwich, A. (ed.) (1984), *What is Politics? The Activity and its Study*, Oxford: Blackwell.

Marx, K. and F. Engels (1848/1976), *The Communist Manifesto*, Harmondsworth: Penguin.

Nagel, T. (1987), 'Moral Conflict and Political Legitimacy', *Philosophy and Public Affairs*, 16(3): 215–40.

Rawls, J. (1971) *A Theory of Justice*, Cambridge, MA: Harvard University Press.

Stoker, G. (2006), *Why Politics Matter*, Basingstoke: Palgrave.

Stoker, G. and D. Marsh (2002), 'Introduction' in D. Marsh and G. Stoker, *Theory and Methods in Political Science*, Basingstoke: Palgrave: 1–16.

Thomas, G. (1993), *An Introduction to Ethics*, London: Duckworth.

Waldron, J. (1989), 'Legislation and Moral Neutrality' in R. Goodin and A. Reeve (eds), *Liberal Neutrality*, London: Routledge: 61–83.

Wolff, J. (1996), *An Introduction to Political Philosophy*, Oxford: Oxford University Press.

Part 1

Dahl, R. (1991), *Modern Political Analysis*, Englewood Cliffs, NJ: Prentice-Hall, 5th edn.

Horton, J. (1984), 'Political Philosophy and Politics' in A. Leftwich (ed.), *What is Politics? The Activity and its Study*, Oxford: Blackwell: 106–23.

Chapter 1

Arblaster, A. (1984), *The Rise and Decline of Western Liberalism*, Oxford: Basil Blackwell.

Avineri, S. and A. de-Shalt (eds) (1992), *Communitarianism and Individualism*, Oxford: Oxford University Press.

Bentham, J. (1948), *An Introduction to the Principles of Morals and Legislation*, New York: Hafner Press.

Blom-Hansen, J. (2000), 'Still Corporatism in Scandinavia?', *Scandinavian Political Studies*, 23(2): 157–78.

Brandt, R. (1992), *Morality, Utilitarianism, and Rights*, Cambridge: Cambridge University Press.

Britten, S. (1977), *The Economic Consequences of Democracy*, London: Temple Smith.

Burnham, J. (1941), *The Managerial Revolution*, New York: Day.

Carruthers, P. (1992), *The Animals Issue*. Cambridge: Cambridge University Press.

Cunningham, F. (2002), *Theories of Democracy*, London: Routledge.

Dahl, R. (1958), 'A Critique of the Ruling Elite Model', *American Political Science Review*, 52.

Dahl, R. (1963), *Who Governs?*, New Haven, CT: Yale University Press.

Dahl, R. (1971), *Polyarchy*, New Haven, CT: Yale University Press.

Dearlove, J. and Saunders, P. (2000), *Introduction to British Politics*, Cambridge: Polity Press, 3rd edn.

Dunleavy, P. and B. O'Leary (1987), *Theories of the State*, Basingstoke: Macmillan.

Dworkin, R. (1978), *Taking Rights Seriously*, London: Duckworth.

Dye, T. (2000), *The Irony of Democracy*, Harcourt Brace.

Gallie, W. (1955/6), 'Essentially Contested Concepts' in *Proceedings of the Aristotelian Society*, Vol. 56.

Hague, R. and M. Harrop (2007), *Comparative Government and Politics*, Basingstoke: Palgrave, 7th edn.

Heater, D. (1999), *What is Citizenship?*, Cambridge: Polity Press.

Hegel, G.W.F. (1942), *Philosophy of Right*, Oxford: Oxford University Press.

Held, D. (1989), *Political Theory and the Modern State*, Cambridge: Polity Press.

Hobbes, T. (1651/1992), *Leviathan*. Cambridge: Cambridge University Press.

Hoffman, J. and P. Graham (2006), *Introduction to Political Theory*, Harlow: Pearson.

Jessop, B. (1990), *State Theory*, Cambridge: Polity Press.

Johnson, C. (1995), *Japan: Who Governs? The Rise of the Developmental State*, New York: Norton.

Jones, P. (1994), *Rights*, Basingstoke: Macmillan.

Kymlicka, W. (2002), *Contemporary Political Philosophy*, Oxford: Oxford University Press, 2nd edn.

Lijphart, A. and M. Crepaz (1991), 'Corporatism and Consensus in Eighteen Countries: Conceptual and Empirical Linkages', *British Journal of Political Science*, 21: 235–46.

Locke, J. (1690/1988), *Two Treatises of Government*. Cambridge: Cambridge University Press.

MacIntyre, A. (1985), *After Virtue: A Study in Moral Theory*, London: Duckworth, 2nd edn.

Macpherson, C.B. (1962), *The Political Theory of Possessive Individualism*, Oxford: Oxford University Press.

Marquand, D. (1988), *The Unprincipled Society*, London: Jonathan Cape.

Mills, C. Wright (1956), *The Power Elite*, New York: Oxford University Press.

Mulhall, S. and A. Swift (1996), *Liberals and Communitarians*, Oxford: Blackwell.

Niskanen, W. (1971), *Bureaucracy and Representative Government*, Chicago, IL: Aldine.

Ohmae, K. (1995), *The End of the Nation State*, London: Harper Collins.

Plamenatz, J. (1963), *Man and Society*, Vol. 2, London: Longman.

Plant, R. (1991), *Modern Political Thought*, Oxford: Basil Blackwell.

Rawls, J. (1993), *Political Liberalism*, New York: Columbia University Press.

Robertson, R. (1992), *Globalization: Social Theory and Global Culture*, London: Sage.

Slaughter, A. (2003), *A New World Order*, Princeton, NJ: Princeton University Press.

Smith, N. (1990), *The Politics of Agricultural Support in Britain*, Aldershot: Dartmouth.

Talos, E. and B. Kittel (2002), 'Austria in the 1990s: The Routine of Social Partnership in Question' in S. Berger and H. Compston (eds), *Policy Concertation and Social Partnership in Western Europe*, New York: Berghahn Books.

Tilly, C. (1975), 'Reflections on the History of European State-Making' in C. Tilly (ed.), *The Formation of National States in Western Europe*, Princeton, NJ: Princeton University Press.

Walzer, M. (1990), 'The Communitarian Critique of Liberalism', *Political Theory*, 18(1): 6–23.

Chapter 2

Bachrach, P. and M. Baratz (1963), 'Decisions and Non-Decisions', *American Political Science Review*, 57: 632–42.

Bachrach, P. and M. Baratz (1970), *Power and Poverty: Theory and Practice*, New York: Oxford University Press.

Barry, N. (2000), *An Introduction to Modern Political Theory*, Basingstoke: Macmillan, 4th edn.

Blowers, A. (1984), *Something in the Air: Corporate Power and the Environment*, London: Harper & Row.

Crenson, M. (1971), *The Un-Politics of Air Pollution*, Baltimore, MD: Johns Hopkins University Press.

Dahl, R. (1963), *Who Governs?*, New Haven, CT: Yale University Press.

Dearlove, J. and Saunders, P. (2000), *Introduction to British Politics*, Cambridge: Polity Press, 3rd edn.

Foucault, M. (1977), *Discipline and Punishment*, Harmondsworth: Penguin.

Gerth, H. and C. Wright Mills (1946), *From Max Weber: Essays in Sociology*, London: Routledge & Kegan Paul.

Goodwin, B. (2007), *Using Political Ideas*, Chichester: John Wiley & Sons, 5th edn.

Gramsci, A. (1971), *Selections From Prison Notebooks*, London: Lawrence & Wishart.

Hay, C. (1997), 'Divided by a Common Language: Political Theory and the Concept of Power', *Politics*, 17(1): 45–52.

Hay, C. (1999), 'Marxism and the State' in A. Gamble, D. Marsh, and T. Tant (eds), *Marxism and Social Science*, London: Macmillan.

Hay, C. (2002), *Political Analysis*, Basingstoke: Palgrave.

Hewitt, C. (1974), 'Policy-Making in Postwar Britain: a National-Level Test of Elitist and Pluralist Hypotheses', *British Journal of Political Science*: 187–216.

Heywood, A. (2004), *Political Theory: An Introduction*, Basingstoke: Palgrave Macmillan.

Hoffman, J. and P. Graham (2006), *Introduction to Political Theory*, Harlow: Pearson.

Lindblom, C. (1977), *Politics and Markets*, New York: Basic Books.

Lukes, S. (2005), *Power: A Radical View*, Basingstoke: Palgrave Macmillan, 2nd edn.

Marcuse, H. (1964), *One-Dimensional Man: Studies in the Ideology of Advanced Industrial Society*, Boston, MA: Beacon.

McLellan, D. (1980), *The Thought of Karl Marx*, Basingstoke: Macmillan.

Miliband, R. (1978), *The State in Capitalist Society*, New York: Basic Books.

Mills, C. Wright (1956), *The Power Elite*, New York: Oxford University Press.

Polsby, N. (1980), *Community Power and Political Theory*, New Haven, CT: Yale University Press, 2nd edn.

Poulantzas, N. (1973), *Political Power and Social Classes*, London: New Left Books.

Poulantzas, N. (1976), 'The Capitalist State: a Reply to Miliband and Laclau', *New Left Review*, 95: 63–83.

Russell, B. (1938), *Power: A New Social Analysis*, London: Allen & Unwin.

Scott, J. (1990), *Domination and the Arts of Resistance*, New Haven, CT: Yale University Press.

Scruton, R. (2001), *The Meaning of Conservatism*, Basingstoke: Palgrave Macmillan, 3rd edn.

Westergaard, J. and H. Resler (1975), *Class in a Capitalist Society*, London: Heinemann.

Chapter 3

Arblaster, A. (2002), *Democracy*, Milton Keynes: Open University Press.

Bachrach, P. (1967), *The Theory of Democratic Elitism*, London: London University Press.

Barry, B. (1970), *Sociologists, Economics and Democracy*, Basingstoke: Collier Macmillan.

Bessette, J. (1994), *The Mild Voice of Reason: Deliberative Democracy and American National Government,* Chicago, IL: Chicago University Press.

Cunningham, F. (2002), *Theories of Democracy*, London: Routledge.

Downs, A. (1957), *An Economic Theory of Democracy,* New York: Harper & Row.

Dryzek, J. (2000), *Deliberative Democracy and Beyond*, Oxford: Oxford University Press.

Duncan, G. and S. Lukes (1964), 'The New Democracy' in S. Lukes (ed.), *Essays in Social Theory*, London: Macmillan.

Dunleavy, P. and H. Ward (1981), 'Exogenous Voter Preferences and Parties with State Power: Some Internal Problems of Economic Theories of Party Competition', *British Journal of Political Science*, 11: 351–80.

Hague, R. and M. Harrop (2007), *Comparative Government and Politics*, Basingstoke: Palgrave, 7th edn.

Held, D. (2006), *Models of Democracy*, Cambridge: Polity Press, 3rd edn.

Hoffman, J. and P. Graham (2006), *Introduction to Political Theory*, Harlow: Pearson.

Kornhauser, W. (1960), *The Politics of Mass Society*, Glencoe, IL: Free Press.

Levitsky, Steven and Way Lucan (2002), 'Assessing the Quality of Democracy', *Journal of Democracy*, 13(2), April: 51–65.

Lively, J. (1975), *Democracy*, Oxford: Blackwell.

Macpherson, C.B. (1966), *The Real World of Democracy*, Oxford: Oxford University Press.

Macpherson, C.B. (1977), *The Life and Times of Liberal Democracy*, Oxford: Oxford University Press.

Mauzy, D. and R. Milne (2002), *Singapore Politics: Under the People's Action Party*, London: Routledge.

Miliband R. (1972), *Parliamentary Socialism*, London: Merlin.

Pateman, C. (1970), *Participation and Democratic Theory*, Cambridge: Cambridge University Press.

Robertson, D. (1976), *A Theory of Party Competition*, London: Wiley.

Rousseau, J. (1913), *The Social Contract and Discourses*, London: Dent.

Schumpeter, J. (1961), *Capitalism, Socialism and Democracy*, New York: Harper & Row.

Stoker, G. (2006), *Why Politics Matter*, Basingstoke: Palgrave.

Stokes, D. (1963), 'Spatial Models of Party Competition', *American Political Science Review*, 57: 19–28.

Talmon, J. (1952), *The Origins of Totalitarian Democracy*. London: Secker & Warburg.

Wolff, R.P. (1970), *In Defence of Anarchism*, New York: Harper & Row.

Worthington, R. (2002), *Governance in Singapore*, London: Routledge/Curzon.

Wright, A. (1979), *G.D.H. Cole and Socialist Democracy*, Oxford: Clarendon Press.

Zakaria, F. (2003), *The Future of Freedom: Illiberal Democracy at Home and Abroad*, London: Norton.

Chapter 4

Barry, B. (1999), 'Sustainability and Intergenerational Justice' in A. Dobson, *Fairness and Futurity: Essays on Sustainability and Justice*, Oxford: Oxford University Press.

Barry, N. (2000), *An Introduction to Modern Political Thought*, Basingstoke: Macmillan, 4th edn.

Beitz, C. (1979), *Political Theory and International Relations*, Princeton, NJ: Princeton University Press.

Benn, S. (1971), 'Privacy, Freedom and Respect for Persons' in J. Pennock and J. Chapman (eds), *Nomos XIII Privacy*, New York: Atherton.

Berlin, I. (1969), *Four Essays on Liberty*, Oxford: Oxford University Press.

Bramwell, A. (1989), *Ecology in the Twentieth Century*, New Haven, CT: Yale Unversity Press.

Cohen, G. (1979), 'Capitalism, Freedom and the Proletariat' in A. Ryan (ed.), *The Idea of Freedom*, Oxford: Oxford University Press.

Daniels, N. (1975), *Reading Rawls*, New York: Basic Books.

Devlin, P. (1965), *The Enforcement of Morals*, Oxford: Oxford University Press.

Dworkin, R. (1978), *Taking Rights Seriously*, London: Duckworth.

Fox, W. (1984), 'Deep Ecology: A New Philosophy of our Times', *The Ecologist*, 14(5): 199–200.

Garner, R. (2005), *The Political Theory of Animal Rights*, Manchester: Manchester University Press.

Gray, T. (1991), *Freedom*, Atlantic Highlands NJ: Humanities Press International Inc.

Hart, H. (1967), 'Are There any Natural Rights' in A. Quinton (ed.), *Political Philosophy*, Oxford: Oxford University Press.

Kukathas, C. and P Pettit (1990), *Rawls: A Theory of Justice and its Critics*, Oxford: Polity Press.

Linklater, A. (2008), 'Globalization and the Transformation of Political Community' in J Baylis, S. Smith, and P. Owens (eds), *The Globalization of World Politics*, Oxford: Oxford University Press.

Mill, J.S. (1972), *Utilitarianism, On Liberty, and Considerations on Representative Government*, London: Dent.

Miller, D. (1976), *Social Justice*, Oxford: Clarendon Press.

Nozick, R. (1974), *Anarchy, State and Utopia*, Oxford: Blackwell.

Pogge, T. (1989), *Realizing Rawls*, Ithaca, NY: Cornell University Press.

Rawls, J. (1971), *A Theory of Justice*, Cambridge, MA: Harvard University Press.

Rawls, J. (1999), *The Law of Peoples*, Cambridge, MA: Harvard University Press.

Singer, P. (2002), *One World: The Ethics of Globalization*, Melbourne: Text Publishing.

Taylor, P. (1986), *Respect for Nature*, Princeton, NJ: Princeton University Press.

Walzer, M. (1985), *Spheres of Justice*, New York: Basic Books.

Walzer, M. (1994), *Thick and Thin: Moral Arguments at Home and Abroad*, Notre Dame, IN: University of Notre Dame Press.

Wolff, J. (1996), *An Introduction to Political Philosophy*, Oxford: Oxford University Press.

Wolff, R. (1977), *Understanding Rawls*, Princetonm, NJ: Princeton University Press.

Chapter 5

Bernstein, E. (1961), *Evolutionary Socialism*, New York: Schocken Books.

Burke, E. [1790] (1968), *Reflections on the Revolution in France*, Harmondsworth: Penguin.

Crosland, C.A.R. (1980), *The Future of Socialism*, London: Jonathan Cape.

Festenstein, M. and M. Kenny (2005), *Political Ideologies*, Oxford: Oxford University Press.

Freeden, M. (1996), *Ideologies and Political Theory*, Oxford: Oxford University Press.

Gamble, A. (1994), *The Free Economy and the Strong State*, London: Macmillan, 2nd edn.

Goodwin, B. (2007), *Using Political Ideas*, Chichester: John Wiley & Sons, 5th edn.

Hitler, A. (1926/1969), *Mein Kampf*, London: Hutchinson.

Hoffman, J. (1995), *Beyond the State*, Cambridge: Polity Press.

Hoffman, J. and P. Graham (2006), *Introduction to Political Theory*, Harlow, Pearson.

Kitchen, M. (1976), *Fascism*, Basingstoke: Macmillan.

Kohn, H. (1944), *The Idea of Nationalism*, London: Macmillan

Macpherson, C.B. (1962), *The Political Theory of Possessive Individualism*, Oxford: Oxford University Press.

Marx, K. and F. Engels (1976), *The Communist Manifesto*, Harmondsworth: Penguin.

Miller, D. (1990), *Market, State and Community: Theoretical Foundations to Market Socialism*, Oxford: Clarendon Press.

Oakeshott, M. (1962), *Rationalism in Politics and Other Essays*, New York: Routledge, Chapman & Hall.

Popper, K. (1962), *The Open Society and its Enemies Vol. II, Hegel and Marx*, London: Routledge & Kegan Paul.

Schain M., A. Zolberg, and P. Hossay (eds) (2002), *Shadows Over Europe: The Development and Impact of the Extreme Right in Western Europe*, Basingstoke: Palgrave Macmillan.

Trevor Roper, H. (1947), *The Last Days of Hitler*, London: Macmillan.

Vincent, A. (1995), *Modern Political Ideologies*, Oxford: Blackwell, 2nd edn.

Wright, A. (1996), *Socialisms*, London: Routledge.

Chapter 6

Ali, T. (2002), *The Clash of Fundamentalisms*, London: Verso.

Barrett, M. (1988), *Women's Oppression Today*, London: Verso.

Barry, B. (2001), *Culture and Equality: An Egalitarian Critique of Multiculturalism*, Cambridge: Polity Press.

Barry, J. (1999), *Rethinking Green Politics*, London: Sage.

Bell, D. (1960), *The End of Ideology*, Glencoe, IL: Free Press.

Bookchin, M. (1971), *Post Scarcity Anarchism*, Berkeley, CA: Ramparts.

Bramwell, A. (1989), *Ecology in the Twentieth Century*, New Haven, CT: Yale University Press.

Bryson, V. (1999), *Feminist Debates*, Basingstoke: Macmillan.

Dobson, A. (2007), *Green Political Thought*, London: Unwin Hyman, 4th edn.

Dworkin, A. (1981), *Pornography: Men Possessing Women*, London: Women's Press.

Eckersley, R. (1992), *Environmentalism and Political Theory*, London: UCL Press.

Firestone, S. (1972), *The Dialetic of Sex*, London: Paladin.

Fox, W. (1995), *Toward a Transpersonal Ecology: Developing New Foundations for Environmentalism*, Totnes: Resurgence.

Frey, R.K. (1983), *Rights, Killing and Suffering*, Oxford: Clarendon Press.

Friedan, B. (1963), *The Feminine Mystique*, Harmondsworth: Penguin.

Fukuyama, F. (1992), *The End of History and the Last Man*, Harmondsworth: Penguin.

Gamble, A. (2000), *Politics and Fate*, Cambridge: Polity Press.

Goodin, R. (1992), *Green Political Theory*, Cambridge: Polity Press.

Goodwin, B. (2007), *Using Political Ideas*, Chichester: John Wiley & Sons, 5th edn.

Gorz, A. (1985), *Paths to Paradise*, London: Pluto.

Greer, G. (1970), *The Female Eunuch*, New York: McGraw-Hill.

Hajer, M. (1997), *The Politics of Environmental Discourse*, Oxford: Clarendon Press.

Hardin, G. (1968), 'The Tragedy of the Commons', *Science*, 162: 1243–8.

Hay, C. (2002), *Political Analysis*, Basingstoke: Palgrave.

Heilbroner, R. (1974), *An Inquiry into the Human Prospect*, New York: Norton.

Heywood, A. (2007), *Political Ideologies*, Basingstoke: Palgrave.

Hoffman, J. and P. Graham (2006), *Introduction to Political Theory*, Harlow: Pearson.

Huntington, S. (1996), *The Clash of Civilizations*, New York: Simon & Schuster.

Jaggar, A. (1983), *Feminist Politics and Human Nature*, Lanham, MD: Rowman & Littlefield.

Kymlicka, W. (1995), *Multicultural Citizenship: A Liberal Theory of Minority Rights*, Oxford: Oxford University Press.

Kymlicka, W. (2002), *Contemporary Political Philosophy*, Oxford: Oxford University Press, 2nd edn.

Leopold, A. (1949), *A Sand County Almanac*, Oxford: Oxford University Press.

MacKinnon, C. (1989), *Towards a Feminist Theory of the State*, London: Harvard University Press.

Marshall, T.H. (1950), *Citizenship and Social Class, and other Essays*, Cambridge: Cambridge University Press.

Martell, L. (1994), *Ecology and Society*, Cambridge: Polity Press.

McElroy, W. (1995), *A Woman's Right to Pornography*, New York: St. Martin's Press.

McIntosh, M. (1978), 'The State and the Oppression of Women' in A. Kuhn and A. Wolpe (eds), *Feminism and Materialism*, London: Routledge & Kegan Paul.

Meadows, D. *et. al.* (1972), *The Limits to Growth*, New York: Universe.

Mill, J.S. (1970), *The Subjection of Women*, Cambridge, MA: MIT Press.

Millett, K. (1971), *Sexual Politics*, New York: Granada Publishing.

Mitchell, J. (1971), *Woman's Estate*, Harmondsworth: Penguin.

Ophuls, W. (1973), 'Leviathan or Oblivion' in H. Daly (ed.), *Toward a Steady State Economy*, San Francisco, CA: Freeman: 215–30.

Parekh, B. (2000), *Rethinking Multiculturalism: Cultural Diversity and Political Theory*, Cambridge, MA: Harvard University Press.

Pateman, C. (1988), *The Sexual Contract*, Oxford: Polity Press.

Pateman, C. (1989), *The Disorder of Women*, Oxford: Polity Press.

Pepper, D. (1993), *Eco-Socialism: From Deep Ecology to Social Justice*, London: Routledge.

Porritt, J. (1984), *Seeing Green*, Oxford: Basil Blackwell.

Rawls, J. (1993), *Political Liberalism*, New York: Columbia University Press.

Schumacher, E. (1973), *Small is Beautiful: Economics as if People Mattered*, London: Blond and Briggs.

Stoker, G. and Marsh, D. (2002), 'Introduction' in D. Marsh and G. Stoker: *Theory and Methods in Political Science*, Basingstoke: Palgrave: 1–16.

Vincent, A. (1995), *Modern Political Ideologies*, Oxford: Blackwell, 2nd edn.

Wissenburg, M. (1993), 'The Idea of Nature and the Nature of Distributive Justice' in A. Dobson and P. Lucardie (eds), *The Politics of Nature: Explorations in Green Political Thought*, London: Routledge: 3–20.

Woolstonecraft, M. (1792/1978), *Vindication of the Rights of Women*, Harmondsworth: Penguin.

World Commission on Environment and Development (1987), *Our Common Future*, Oxford: Oxford University Press.

Chapter 7

Anderson, Bendict O'G (1990), *Language and Power: Exploring Political Cultures in Indonesia*, Ithaca, NY: Cornell University Press.

Bayart, Jean-François (1993), *The State in Africa: the Politics of the Belly*, London: Longman.

Bell, Daniel A., David Brown, Kanishka Jayasuriya, and David Martin Jones (1995), *Towards Illiberal Democracy in Pacific Asia*, Basingstoke: Macmillan.

Buzan, Barry (1991), *People, States and Fear*, London: Harvester Wheatsheaf, 2nd edn.

Chabal, Patrick, and Jean-Pascal Daloz (1999), *Africa Works: Disorder as Political Instrument,* Oxford: The International Africa Institute in association with James Currey.

Clapham, Christopher (1996), *Africa and the International System: the Politics of State Survival*, Cambridge: Cambridge University Press.

Coronil, Fernando (1997), *The Magical State: Nature, Money, and Modernity in Venezuela*, Chicago, IL: Chicago University Press.

Edelman, Murray (1964), *The Symbolic Uses of Politics*, Urbana, IL: University of Illinois Press.

Finer, S.E. (1997), *The History of Government from the Earliest Times*, vol. 3, *Empires, Monarchies and the Modern State*, Oxford: Oxford University Press.

Fulbrook, Mary (2005), *The People's State: East German Society from Hitler to Honecker*, New Haven, CT and London: Yale University Press.

Giddens, Anthony (1979), *Central Problems in Social Theory: Action, Structure and Contradiction in Social Analysis*, Basingstoke: Macmillan.

Gill, Graeme (2003), *The Nature and Development of the Modern State*, Basingstoke: Palgrave.

International IDEA (2002a), *Handbook on Democracy Assessment*, The Hague: Kluwer.

International IDEA (2002b), *The State of Democracy*, The Hague: Kluwer.

Jackson, Robert H. (1990), *Quasi-States: Sovereignty, International Relations and the Third World*, Cambridge: Cambridge University Press.

Little, Peter D. (2003), *Somalia: Economy Without State*, Oxford: The International African Institute in association with James Currey.

Marsh, David, Nicola J. Smith, and Nicola Hothi (2006), 'Globalization and the State' in Colin Hay, Michael Lister, and David Marsh (eds), *The State: Theories and Issues*, Basingstoke: Palgrave: 172–89.

Menkhaus, Ken (2007), 'Governance without Government in Somalia', *International Security* 31(3): 74–106.

Paley, Julia (2002), 'Toward an Anthropology of Democracy', *Annual Review of Anthropology*, 31: 469–96.

Peterson, Scott (2000), *Me Against My Brother: At War in Somalia, Sudan, and Rwanda*, New York and London: Routledge.

Rotberg, Robert I. (ed.) (2004), *When States Fail: Causes and Consequences*, Princeton, NJ: Princeton University Press.

Starr, June (1992), *Law as Metaphor: From Islamic Courts to the Palace of Justice*, Albany, NY: State University of New York Press.

Steinmo, S. (2001), 'Institutionalism' in Neil J. Smelser and Paul Baltes (eds), *International Encyclopedia of the Social and Behavioral Sciences*, Amsterdam: Elsevier, vol.11: 7554–8.

Suwannathat-Pian, Kobkua (1988), *Thai-Malay Relations*, Oxford: Oxford University Press.

Tanzi, Vito and Ludger Schuknecht (2000), *Public Spending in the Twentieth Century*, Cambridge: Cambridge University Press: 6–7.

Tilly, Charles (1975), *The Formation of National States in Europe*, Princeton, NJ: Princeton University Press.

Tilly, Charles (1990), *Coercion, Capital and European States, AD 990–1990*, Oxford: Blackwell.

van Creveld, Martin (1999), *The Rise and Decline of the State*, Cambridge: Cambridge University Press.

Weber, Max (1968), *Economy and Society: an Outline of Interpretive Sociology*, edited by Guenther Roth and Claus Wittich, New York: Bedminster Press, vol. 3.

White Paper on Political Democracy (2005), www.china.org.cn/english/features/book/145941.htm.

Chapter 8

Bonnett, Alastair (2004), *The Idea of the West: Culture, Politics and History*, Basingstoke: Palgrave.

Buxbaum, R.M. (2004), 'Law, Diffusion of' in Neil J. Smelser and Paul B. Baltes (eds), *International Encyclopedia of the Social and Behavioral Sciences*, Amsterdam: Elsevier: 1–7.

Colomer, Josep M. (2007), *Great Empires, Small Nations*, London: Routledge.

Dahl, Robert A. (2001), *How Democratic is the American Constitution?*, New Haven, CT: Yale University Press.

Epp, Charles B. (1998), *The Rights Revolution: Lawyers, Activists, and Supreme Courts in Comparative Perspective*, Chicago, IL: Chicago University Press.

Fuller, Lon L. (1969), *The Morality of Law*, New Haven, CT: Yale University Press, rev. edn.

Hallaq, Wael B. (2005), *The Origins and Evolution of Islamic Law*, Cambridge: Cambridge University Press.

King, Anthony (2001), 'Distrust of Government: Explaining American Exceptionalism' in Susan J. Pharr and Robert D. Putnam (eds), *Disaffected Democracies: What's Troubling the Trilateral Countries?*, Princeton, NJ: Princeton University Press: 74–98.

King, Anthony (2007), *The British Constitution*, Oxford: Oxford University Press.

Lewis, Bernard (2005), 'Freedom and Justice in the Modern Middle East', *Foreign Affairs*, 84(3): 36–51.

Lieberman, J.K. (2001), 'Legalization' in Neil J. Smelser and Paul B. Baltes (eds), *International Encyclopedia of the Social and Behavioral Sciences*, Amsterdam: Elsevier: 8693–7.

Lijphart, Arend (1977), *Democracy in Plural Societies: A Comparative Explanation*, New Haven, CT: Yale University Press.

Lijphart, Arend (1999), *Patterns of Democracy: Government Forms and Performance in Thirty-Six Countries*, New Haven, CT: Yale University Press.

Lombardi, Clark Benner (1998), 'Islamic Law as a Source of Constitutional Law in Egypt: The Constitutionalization of the Sharia in a Modern Arab State', *Columbia Journal of Transnational Law*, 37(1): 81–123.

Menski, Werner (2006), *Comparative Law in a Global Context: the Legal Systems of Asia and Africa*, Cambridge: Cambridge University Press.

Montada, L. (2001), 'Justice and its Many Faces: Cultural Concerns' in Neil J. Smelser and Paul B. Baltes (eds), *International Encyclopedia of the Social and Behavioral Sciences*, Amsterdam: Elsevier: 8037–42.

Moten, Abdul Rashid (1996), *Political Science: An Islamic Perspective*, Basingstoke: Macmillan.

Ramet, Sabrina P. (2005), *Thinking About Yugoslavia: Scholarly Debates about the Yugoslav Breakup and the Wars in Bosnia and Kosovo*, Cambridge: Cambridge University Press.

Robertson, David (1993), *The Penguin Dictionary of Politics*, Harmondsworth: Penguin.

Rosen, Lawrence (1989), *The Anthropology of Justice: Law as Culture in Islamic Society*, Cambridge: Cambridge University Press.

Stepan, Alfred (2004), 'Federalism and Democracy: Beyond the US Model' in Ugo Amoretti and Nancy Bermeo (eds), *Federalism and Territorial Cleavages*, Baltimore, MD: Johns Hopkins University Press: 441–56.

Twining, William (2000), *Globalisation and Legal Theory*, London: Butterworth.

Watt, W. Montgomery (1968), *Islamic Political Thought*, Edinburgh: Edinburgh University Press.

Yilmaz, Ihsan (2005), *Muslim Laws, Politics and Society in Modern Nation States: Dynamic Legal Pluralisms in England Turkey and Pakistan*, Aldershot: Ashgate.

Zakaria, Fareed (1997), 'The Rise of Illiberal Democracy', *Foreign Affairs*, 76(6), Nov.–Dec.: 22–43.

Chapter 9

Arora, Balveer (2003), 'The Indian Parliament and Democracy' in Ajay K. Mehra and Gert W. Kueck (eds), *The Indian Parliament: A Comparative Perspective*, Delhi: Konarck Publishers: 14–37.

Asa-El, Amotz (2008), 'Israel's Electoral Complex', *Azure*, Winter, No. 31, www.azure.org.il/magazine/magazine.asp?id=410.

Baktiari, Bahman (1996), *Parliamentary Politics in Iran: the Institutionalization of Factional Politics*, Gainesville, FL: Florida University Press.

Bayart, Jean-François (1993), *The State in Africa: the Politics of the Belly*, London: Longman.

Borchert, Jens, and Jürgen Zeiss (2003), *The Political Class in Advanced Democracies*, Oxford: Oxford University Press.

Boundary Commission for England (2007), *Fifth Periodical Report*, London: HMSO, cm7032, vol. 1.

Burke, Edmund (1996), *The Writings and Speeches of Edmund Burke* (edited by W.M. Elofson with John A. Woods), Oxford: Clarendon Press, vol. 3.

Chabal, Patrick, and Jean-Pascal Daloz (1999), *Africa Works: Disorder as Political Instrument*, Oxford: The International African Institute in association with James Currey.

Cheibub, Jose Antonio (2007), *Presidentialism, Parliamentarianism and Democracy*, Cambridge: Cambridge University Press.

Coronel, Sheila S., Yvonne T. Chua, Luz and Cruz Rimban, and B. Booma (2004), *The Rulemakers: How the Wealthy and Well-Born Dominate Congress*, Quezon City: Philippine Center for Investigative Journalism.

Cracknell, Richard (2005), 'Social Background of MPs', www.parliament.uk/commons/lib/research/notes/snsg-01528.pdf.

Dahlerup, Drude (2005), 'Increasing Women's Political Representation: New Trends in Gender Quotas' in Julie Ballington and Azza Karam (eds), *Women in Parliament: Beyond Numbers*, Stockholm: International IDEA, rev. edn: 141–53.

Gallagher, Michael, Michael March, and Paul Mitchell (eds) (2003), *How Ireland Voted*, Basingstoke: Palgrave.

Gamm, Gerald, and John Huber (2002), 'Legislatures as Political Institutions: Beyond the Contemporary Congress' in Ira Katznelson and Helen V. Milner (eds), *Political Science: State of the Discipline*, New York: Norton for the American Political Science Association: 313–41.

Inglehart, Ronald, Miguel Basáñez, Jaime Díez-Madrano, Loek Halman, and Ruud Luijkx (eds) (2004), *Human Beliefs and Values*, Mexico: Siglo XXI Editores.

Jacobson, Gary C. (1997), *The Politics of Congressional Elections*, New York: Longman, 4th edn.

Linz, Juan J. (1992), 'The Perils of Presidentialism' in Arend Lijphart (ed.), *Parliamentary Versus Presidential Government*, Oxford: Oxford University Press: 118–27.

Mainwaring, Scott (2006), 'State Deficiencies, Party Competition, and Confidence in Democratic Representation in the Andes' in Scott Mainwaring, Ana María Bejarano, and Eduardo Pizarro Leongómez (eds), *The Crisis of Democratic Representation in the Andes*, Stanford, CA: Stanford University Press: 295–345.

Matland, Richard E. (2005), 'Enhancing Women's Political Participation: Legislative Recruitment and Electoral Systems' in Julie Ballington and Azza Kazam (eds), *Women in Parliament: Beyond Numbers*, Stockholm: International IDEA, revised edn: 93–111.

Mezey, Michael (1990), 'Classifying Legislatures' in Philip Norton (ed.), *Legislatures*, Oxford: Oxford University Press: 149–76.

Miller, Vaughne (2007), 'EU Legislation', www.parliament.uk/commons/lib/research/notes/snia-02888.pdf.

Norton, Philip (ed.) (1998), *Parliaments and Governments in Western Europe*, London: Cass, vol. 1.

Oborne, Peter (2007), *The Triumph of the Political Class*, London: Simon & Schuster.

Rizzo, Sergio and Gian Antonio Stella (2007), *La casta: così i politici italiani sono diventati intoccabili*, Milan: Rizzoli.

O'Donnell, Guillermo (2003), 'Horizontal Accountability: the Legal Institutionalization of Mistrust' in Scott Mainwaring and Christopher Welna (eds), *Democratic Accountability in Latin America*, Oxford: Oxford University Press: 34–54.

Olson, David M. (1994), *Democratic Legislative Institutions: A Comparative View*, New York: M.E. Sharpe.

Patterson, Samuel C. and Anthony Mughan (eds) (1999), *Senates: Bicameralism in the Contemporary World*, Columbus, OH: Ohio State University Press.

Rüland, Jürgen (2003), 'Constitutional Debates in the Philippines: From Presidentialism to Parliamentarianism?', *Asian Survey*, 43(3): 461–84.

Rüland, Jürgen, Clemens Jürgenmeyer, Michael H. Nelson, and Patrick Ziegenhain (2005), *Parliaments and Political Change in Asia*, Singapore: ISEAS.

Stockwin, J.A.A. (1999), *Governing Japan*, Oxford: Blackwell, 3rd edn.

Sutherland, Keith (2004), *The Party's Over: Blueprint for a Very English Revolution*, Exeter: Imprint Academic.

Tsebelis, George and Jeannette Money (1997), *Bicameralism*, Cambridge: Cambridge University Press.

Usui, Chikako and Richard A. Colignon (2004), 'Continuity and Change in Paths to High Political Office: Ex-Bureaucrats and Hereditary Politicians', *Asian Business and Management*, 3(4): 395–416.

Chapter 10

Abord de Chatillon, Renaud (1994), *La politique des transports en France*, Paris: Eds Eska.

Adamolekun, Ladipo (2007), 'Africa: Rehabilitating Civil Service Institutions—Main Issues and Implementation Progress' in Jos C.N. Raadschelders, Teho A.J. Toonen, and Frits M. Van der Meer (eds), *The Civil Service in the 21st Century: Comparative Perspectives*, Basingstoke: Palgrave: 82–99.

Allison, Graham T. (1971), *Essence of Decision: Explaining the Cuban Missile Crisis*, Boston, MA: Little Brown.

Barber, Michael (2007), *Instruction to Deliver: Tony Blair, Public Services and the Challenge of Achieving Targets*, London: Politico's.

Bevir, Mark, and Rhodes, R.A.W. (2006), *Governance Stories*, London: Routledge.

Calder, Kent E. (1993), *Strategic Capitalism: Private Business and Public Purpose in Japanese Industrial Finance*, Princeton, NJ: Princeton University Press.

Bobbitt, Philip (2003), *The Shield of Achilles: War, Peace and the Course of History*, London: Penguin.

Castells, Manuel (1998), *The End of Millennium*, *The Information Age: Economy, Society and Culture*, Oxford: Blackwell, vol.3.

Eddington Transport Report, The, December (2006), www.dft. gov.uk/162259/187604/206711/executivesummary.

Evans, Peter B. (1995), *Embedded Autonomy: States and Industrial Transformation*, Princeton, NJ: Princeton University Press.

Ginsborg, Paul (2001), *Italy and Its Discontents*, London: Allen Lane, The Penguin Press.

Glaister, Stephen, Jane Burnham, Handley Stevens, and Tony Travers (1998), *Transport Policy in Britain*, Basingstoke: Macmillan.

Glaister, Stephen, Jane Burnham, Handley Stevens, and Tony Travers (2006), *Transport Policy in Britain*, Basingstoke: Palgrave, 2nd edn.

Hall, Peter A. and David Soskice (eds) (2001), *Varieties of Capitalism: the Institutional Foundations of Comparative Advantage*, Oxford: Oxford University Press.

Héritier, Adrienne and Christoph Knill (2001), 'Differential Responses to European Policies: A Comparison' in Adrienne

Héritier, Dieter Kerwer, Christoph Knill, Dirk Lehmkuhl, Michael Teutsch, and Anne-Cécile Douillet, *Differential Europe: The European Union Impact on National Policy-Making*, Lanham, MD: Rowman & Littlefield: 257–94.

Johnson, Chalmers A. (1982), *MITI and the Japanese Miracle*, Stanford, CA: Stanford University Press.

Kamarck, Elaine C. (2007), *The End of Government . . . As We Know It: Making Public Policy Work*, Boulder, CO: Lynne Rienner.

Kayizzi-Mugerwa, Steve (2003), 'Introduction' in Steve Kayizzi-Mugerwa (ed.), *Reforming Africa's Institutions: Ownership, Incentives, and Capabilities*, Tokyo, NY, Paris: UNUP and UNU WIDER.

Kim, Wangsik (2006), 'Government Executive and Policy Reform in Japan', *International Review of Public Administration*, 10(2): 21–35.

Kohli, Atul (2004), *State-Directed Development: Political Power and Industrialization in the Global Periphery*, Cambridge: Cambridge University Press.

Landier, Augustin and Thesmar, David (2007), *Le grand méchant marché*, Paris: Flammarion.

Lynn, Laurence E. (2006), *Public Management: Old and New*, Abingdon: Routledge.

Neiertz, Nicolas (1999), *La coordination des transports en France: de 1918 a nos jours*, Paris: CHEEF.

Olsen, Johan P. (2003), 'Towards a European Administrative Space?', *Journal of European Public Policy*, 10(4): 506–31.

Ourzik, Abdelouahad (2000), 'Public Service in Africa: New Challenges', in *African Public Service: New Challenges, Professionalism and Ethics*, New York: United Nations, 43–9.

Pierre, Jon and Guy B. Peters (2000), *Governance, Politics and the State*, Basingstoke: Macmillan.

Rhodes, R.A.W. (1997), *Understanding Governance: Policy Networks, Governance, Reflexivity and Accountability*, Buckingham: Open University Press.

Richards, David (2008), *New Labour and the Civil Service: Reconstituting the Whitehall Model*, Basingstoke: Palgrave.

Salisu, Mohammed (2003), 'Incentive Structure, Civil Service Efficiency and the Hidden Economy in Nigeria' in Steve Kayizzi-Mugerwa (ed.), *Reforming Africa's Institutions: Ownership, Incentives, and Capabilities*, Tokyo, New York, Paris: UNUP and UNU/WIDER.

Talbot, Colin (2004), 'The Agency Idea: Sometimes Old, Sometimes New, Sometimes Borrowed, Sometimes Untrue' in Christopher Pollitt and Colin Talbot (eds), *Unbundled Government: A Critical Analysis of the Global Trend to Agencies, Quangos and Contractualisation*, Abingdon: Routledge: 3–21.

Thatcher, M. (2001), 'Issue Networks: Iron Triangles, Subgovernments, and Policy Communities' in Neil J. Smelser and Paul B. Baltes (eds), *International Encyclopedia of the Social and Behavioral Sciences*, Amsterdam: Elsevier: 7940–2.

Toonen, Theo A.J. (2001), 'The Comparative Dimension of Administrative Reform: Creating Open Villages and Redesigning the Politics of Administration' in B.Guy Peters and Jon

Pierre (eds), *Politicians, Bureaucrats and Administrative Reform*, Abingdon: Routledge: 183–201.

UN Economic and Social Commission for Asia and the Pacific, 'What is Good Governance?', www.unescap.org/pdd/prs/ProjectActivities/Ongoing/gg/governance.asp.

Weber, Max (1968), *Economy and Society: an Outline of Interpretive Sociology*, New York: Bedminster Press, vol. 3.

Weiss, Linda (1998), *The Myth of the Powerless State: Governing the Economy in a Global Era*, Cambridge: Polity Press.

Chapter 11

Aldrich, John H. (1995), *Why Parties? The Origin and Transformation of Political Parties in America*, Chicago, IL: Chicago University Press.

Beyme, Klaus von (1985), *Political Parties in Western Democracies*, Aldershot: Gower.

Biezen, Ingrid van (2003), *Political Parties in New Democracies: Party Organization in Southern and East-Central Europe*, Basingstoke: Palgrave.

Carothers, Thomas (2006), *Confronting the Weakest Link: Aiding Political Parties in New Democracies*, Washington, DC: Carnegie Endowment.

Colomer, Josep M. (ed.) (2004), 'The Strategy and History of Electoral System Choice' in Josep M. Colomer (ed.), *Handbook of Electoral System Choice*, Basingstoke: Palgrave: 1–73.

Coppedge, Michael (2002), 'Venezuela: Popular Sovereignty Versus Liberal Democracy' in Jorge I. Dominguez and Michael Shifter (eds), *Constructing Democratic Governance*, Baltimore: Johns Hopkins University Press, 2nd edn: 165–92.

Corrales, Javier and Michael Penfold (2007), 'Venezuela: Crowding Out the Opposition', *Journal of Democracy* 18(2), April: 99–113.

Doorenspleet, Renske (2003), 'Political Parties, Party Systems and Democracy in Sub-Saharan Africa' in M.A. Mohamed Salih (ed.), *African Political Parties*, London: Pluto: 169–87.

Dunleavy, Patrick (2005), 'Facing Up to Multi-Party Politics: How Partisan Dealignment and PR Voting Have Fundamentally Changed Britain's Party System', *Parliamentary Affairs*, 58(3): 503–32.

Duverger, Maurice (1964), *Political Parties*, London: Methuen, 3rd edn.

Farrell, David M. (2001), *Electoral Systems: a Comparative Introduction*, Basingstoke: Palgrave.

Fiorina, Morris P. (2002), 'Parties, Participation, and Representation in America: Old Theories Face New Realities' in Ira N. Katznelson and Helen V. Milner (eds), *Political Science: State of the Discipline*, New York: Norton, for the American Political Science Association.

First Deliberative Polling® for Candidate Selection in Marousi, Greece (2006), http://cdd.stanford.edu/polls/greece/2006/marousi-summary.pdf.

Gambetta, Diego and Steven Warner (2004), 'Italy: Lofty Ambitions and Unintended Consequences' in Josep M. Colomer (ed.), *Handbook of Electoral System Choice*, Basingstoke: Palgrave: 237–52.

Gott, Richard (2005), *Hugo Chavez and the Bolivarian Revolution*, London: Verso.

Gunther, Richard and Diamond, Larry (2003), 'Species of Political Parties: A New Typology', *Party Politics*, 9(2): 167–99.

Hale, Henry E. (2006), *Why Not Parties in Russia? Democracy, Federalism, and the State*, Cambridge: Cambridge University Press.

International IDEA (2003), *Funding of Political Parties and Election Campaigns*, Stockholm.

International IDEA (2007), *Electoral System Design*, Stockholm.

Inter-Parliamentary Union (1997), *Universal Declaration on Democracy*, www.ipu.org/cnl-e/161-dem.htm.

Levitsky, Steven and Maxwell A. Cameron (2003), 'Democracy Without Parties? Political Parties and Regime Change in Fujimori's Peru', *Latin American Politics and Society*, 45(3): 1–33.

Lipset, Seymour Martin and Stein Rokkan (eds) (1967), *Party Systems and Voter Alignments: Cross National Perspectives*, New York: Free Press.

McCoy, Jennifer L. and David L. Myers (eds) (2004), *The Unravelling of Representative Democracy in Venezuela*, Baltimore, MD: Johns Hopkins University Press.

Mair, Peter (2005), 'Democracy Beyond Parties', *Center for the Study of Democracy*, University of California, Irvine, http://repositories.cdlib.org/csd/05–06.

Mair, Peter and Ingrid van Biezen (2001), 'Party Membership in Twenty European Democracies, 1980–2000', *Party Politics*, 7(1): 5–21.

Mugaju, Justus, and J. Oloka-Onyango (eds) (2000), *No-Party Democracy in Uganda: Myths and Realities*, Kampala: Fountain Publishers.

Power Inquiry (2006), *Power to the People*, www.makeitanissue.org.uk/2007/01/power_commission_archive.php#more.

Reeve, David (1985), *Golkar of Indonesia: An Alternative to the Party System*, Singapore: Oxford University Press.

Riker, William H. (1982), *Liberalism Against Populism: A Confrontation Between the Theory of Democracy and the Theory of Social Choice*, San Francisco, CA: Freeman.

Rosenbluth, Frances and Mark Ramseyer (1993), *Japan's Political Marketplace*, Cambridge, MA: Harvard University Press.

Saari, Donald G. (2001), *Chaotic Elections! A Mathematician Looks at Voting*, Providence, RI: American Mathematical Society.

Sartori, Giovanni (1976), *Parties and Party Systems: A Framework for Analysis*, Cambridge: Cambridge University Press.

Ware, Alan (1996), *Political Parties and Party Systems*, Oxford: Oxford University Press.

Chapter 12

Asking the Right Questions About Electronic Voting (2005), http://books.nap.edu/openbook.php?record_id=11449&page.

Barber, Benjamin (1984), *Strong Democracy: Participatory Politics for a New Age*, Berkeley, CA: University of California Press.

Barber, Benjamin (1998), 'Three Scenarios for the Future of Technology and Strong Democracy', *Political Science Quarterly*, 113: 573–89.

Baso, Ahmad (1999), *Civil Society versus Masyarakat Madani: Arkeologi Pemikiran 'Civil Society' dalam Islam Indonesia*, Bandung: Pustaka Hidayah.

Becker, Ted, and Christa Daryl Slaton (2000), *The Future of Teledemocracy*, Westport, CT: Praeger.

Bruce, Iain (ed.) (2004), *The Porto Alegre Alternative: Direct Democracy in Action*, London: Pluto Press.

Budge, Ian (1996), *The New Challenge of Direct Democracy*, Cambridge: Polity Press.

Castells, Manuel (1996), *The Rise of the Network Society*, Oxford: Blackwell.

Chabal, Patrick and Jean-Pascal Daloz (1999), *Africa Works: Disorder as Political Instrument*, Oxford: The International Africa Institute in association with James Currey.

Chandhoke, Neera (2003), *The Conceits of Civil Society*, New Delhi: Oxford University Press.

Chatterjee, P. (2001), 'Subaltern History' in Neil J. Smelser and Paul B. Baltes (eds), *International Encyclopedia of the Social and Behavioral Sciences*, Amsterdam: Elsevier: 15237–41.

Comaroff, John L., and Jean Comaroff (eds) (1999), *Civil Society and the Political Imagination in Africa: Critical Perspectives*, Chicago, IL: Chicago University Press.

Doronila, Amando (2001), *The Fall of Joseph Estrada: the Inside Story*, Pasig City: Anvil Publishing and Philippine Daily Inquirer.

Edwards, Michael (2004), *Civil Society*, Cambridge: Polity Press.

Eickelman, Dale F. (1996), 'Foreword' in Augustus Richard Norton (ed.), *Civil Society in the Middle East*, Leiden: J.Brill, vol. 2: ix–xiv.

Franklin, Bob (2004), *Packaging Politics: Political Communications in Britain's Media Democracy*, London: Hodder Headline.

Ginsborg, Paul (2001), *Italy and its Discontents 1980–2001*, London: Allen Lane, The Penguin Press.

Gledhill, John (1994), *Power and Its Disguises: Anthropological Perspectives on Politics*, London: Pluto.

Gupta, Akhil (2006), 'Blurred Boundaries: The Discourse of Corruption, the Culture of Politics and the Imagined State' in Aradhana Sharma and Akhil Gupta (eds), *The Anthropology of the State: a Reader*, Oxford: Blackwell: 211–42.

Hahm, Chaihark (2004), 'Disputing Civil Society in a Confucian Context', *Korea Observer* 35(3), Autumn: 433–62.

Hoexter, Miriam (2002), 'The Waqf and the Public Sphere' in Miriam Hoexter, Shmuel N. Eisenstadt, and Nehemia Levtzion (eds), *The Public Sphere in Muslim Societies*, Albany, NY: State Univ. of New York Press: 1, 19–38.

Ibrahim, Saad Eddin (1995), 'Civil Society and Prospects of Democratization in the Arab World' in Augustus Richard Norton (ed.), *Civil Society in the Middle East*, Leiden: E.J. Brill, vol. 1: 27–54.

Jenkins, Rob (2005), 'Civil Society: Active or Passive?—India' in Peter Burnell and Vicky Randall (eds), *Politics in the Developing World*, Oxford: Oxford University Press: 275–85.

Jordan, Grant and Maloney, William A. (2007), *Democracy and Interest Groups: Enhancing Participation?*, Basingstoke: Palgrave.

Kenney, Padraic (2002), *A Carnival of Revolution: Central Europe, 1989*, Princeton, NJ: Princeton University Press.

Lehmbruch, Gerhard (2001), 'Corporatism' in Neil J. Smelser and Paul R. Baltes (eds), *International Encyclopedia of the Social and Behavioral Sciences*, Amsterdam: Elsevier: 2813–6.

McLean, Iain (1989), *Democracy and New Technology*, Cambridge: Polity Press.

Migdal, Joel S. (2001), *State in Society: Studying How States and Societies Transform and Constitute One Another*, Cambridge: Cambridge University Press.

Puhle, H.-J. (2001), 'History of Interest Groups' in Neil J. Smelser and Paul B. Baltes (eds), *International Encyclopedia of the Social and Behavioral Sciences*, Amsterdam: Elsevier: 7703–8.

Reporters Without Borders (2006), 'Press Freedom Round-up 2006', www.rsf.org/article.php3?id_article=20286.

Rheingold, Howard (2002), *Smart Mobs: the Next Social Revolution*, Cambridge, MA: Perseus.

Robertson, David (1993), *The Penguin Dictionary of Politics*, Harmondsworth: Penguin.

Saeki, Keishi (1997), *Gendai minshushugino byōri*, Tokyo: NHK Books.

Schlozman, K.L. (2001), 'Interest Groups' in Neil J. Smelser and Paul B. Baltes (eds), *International Encyclopedia of the Social and Behavioral Sciences*, Amsterdam: Elsevier: 7700–3.

Schmitter, Philippe (1980), 'Modes of Interest Intermediation and Models of Societal Change in Western Europe' in Philippe Schmitter and Gerhard Lehmbruch (eds), *Trends Towards Corporatist Intermediation*, Beverly Hills, CA: Sage: 63–94.

Swanson, Judith A. (1992), *The Public and the Private in Aristotle's Political Philosophy*, Ithaca, NY: Cornell University Press.

Chapter 13

Alesina, Alberto and Edward L. Glaeser (2004), *Fighting Poverty in the US and Europe: a World of Difference*, Oxford: Oxford University Press.

Almond, Gabriel A. and Sidney Verba (1965), *The Civic Culture*, Boston, MA: Little Brown.

Almond, Gabriel A. and Verba, Sidney (eds) (1989), *The Civic Culture Revisited*, Newbury Park, CA: Sage.

Aronoff, M.J. (2001), 'Political Culture' in Neil J. Smelser and Paul H. Baltes (eds), *International Encyclopedia of the Social and Behavioral Sciences*, Amsterdam: Elsevier: 11,640–4.

Banfield, Edward C. (1958), *The Moral Basis of a Backward Society*, Glencoe, IL: Chicago University Press.

Baregu, Mwesiga (1997), 'Political Culture and the Party-State in Tanzania' in Research for Democracy in Tanzania Project, *Political Culture and Popular Participation in Tanzania*, Dar es Salaam: Dept. of Political Science and Public Administration, University of Dar es Salaam.

Chaligha, Amon, Robert Mattes, Michael Bratton, and Yul Derek Davids (2002), 'Uncritical Citizens or Patient Trustees? Tanzanians' Views of Economic and Political Reform', *Afrobarometer Working Paper No. 18*.

Commission for Racial Equality (2005), *Citizenship and Belonging: What is Britishness?*, London, www.cre.gov.uk/downloads/what_is_britishness.pdf.

Dahl, Robert (1961), *Who Governs? Democracy and Power in an American City*, New Haven, CT: Yale University Press.

Emmerson, Donald, K. (1995), 'Singapore and the "Asian Values" Debate', *Journal of Democracy*, 6(4): 95–105.

Esping-Andersen, Gøsta (1990), *The Three Worlds of Welfare Capitalism*, Cambridge: Polity Press.

Fish, M. Steven (2005), *Democracy Derailed in Russia: the Failure of Open Politics*, Cambridge: Cambridge University Press.

Fukuyama, Francis (1995), 'Confucianism and Democracy', *Journal of Democracy*, 6(2), April: 20–33.

Giscard d'Estaing, Valéry (2004), 'A better European bridge to Turkey', *Financial Times*, 24 Nov.

Home Office (2007), *Life in the UK: a Journey to Citizenship 2007*, London: HMSO.

Humayun, Syed (1995), 'Pakistan: One State, two Nations: an Analysis of Political Anatomy of United Pakistan' in Verinder Grover and Ranjana Arora (eds), *Political System in Pakistan*, New Delhi: Deep and Deep, vol. 3: 593–613.

Huntington, Samuel (1996), *The Clash of Civilizations and the Remaking of World Order*, New York: Simon & Schuster.

Inglehart, Ronald and Pippa Norris (2003), 'The True Clash of Civilizations', *Foreign Policy*, March–April: 67–74.

Inglehart, Ronald, Michael Basañez, Jaime Diéz-Medrano, Loek Halman, and Ruud Luijkx (2004), *Human Beliefs and Values*, Mexico: Siglo XXI Editores.

Jackman, Robert W., and Ross A. Miller (2004), *Before Norms: Institutions and Civic Culture*, Ann Arbor, MI: University of Michigan Press.

Jenner, W.J.F. (1992), *The Tyranny of History: the Roots of China's Crisis*, Harmondsworth: Allen Lane.

Kaplan, Robert D. (2005), *Balkan Ghosts: A Journey Through History*, New York: Picador.

Kyogoku, Jin-ichi (1987), *The Political Dynamics of Japan*, Tokyo: Tokyo University Press.

Leoussi, Athena and Stephen Grosby (eds) (2006), *Nationalism and Ethnosymbolism: History, Culture and Ethnicity in the Formation of Nations*, Edinburgh: Edinburgh University Press.

Robertson, David (1993), *The Penguin Dictionary of Politics*, Harmondsworth: Penguin.

Malik, Yogendra K., and V.B. Singh (1995), *Hindu Nationalists in India: the Rise of the Bharatiya Janata Party*, New Delhi: Vistaar Publications.

Martin, Denis C. (1988), *Tanzania: l'Invention d'une Culture Politique,* Paris: Presses de la Fondation Nationale de Science Politique et Karthala.

Putnam, Robert (1993), *Making Democracy Work: Civic Traditions in Modern Italy*, Princeton, NJ: Princeton University Press.

Pye, Lucian W. (1985), *Asian Power and Politics: the Cultural Dimensions of Authority*, Cambridge, MA: Belknap Press.

Pye, Lucian W. and Verba, Sidney (eds) (1965), *Political Culture and Political Development*, Princeton, NJ: Princeton University Press.

Sodaro, Michael (2008), *Comparative Politics: a Global Introduction*, Boston, MA: McGraw Hill, 3rd edn.

de Tocqueville, Alexis (2000), *Democracy in America*, Chicago, IL: Chicago University Press.

Waldron, Arthur (1993), 'Representing China: the Great Wall and Cultural Nationalism in the Twentieth Century' in Harumi Befu (ed.), *Cultural Nationalism in East Asia: Representation and Identity*, Berkeley, CA: Research Papers and Policy Studies, Institute of East Asia Studies: 36–60.

Yilmaz, Ihsan (2005), *Muslim Laws, Politics and Society in Modern Nation States: Dynamic Legal Pluralisms in England Turkey and Pakistan*, Aldershot: Ashgate.

Chapter 14

Aristotle (1981), *The Politics*, trans. T.A. Sinclair, rev. T. J. Saunders, London: Penguin.

Boesche, Roger (2002), 'Moderate Machiavelli? Contrasting The Prince with the Arthasastra of Kautilya', *Critical Horizons*, 3(2): 253–76.

Boucher, David (1998), *Political Theories of International Relations: From Thucydides to the Present*, Oxford: Oxford University Press.

Cassels, Alan (1996), *Ideology and International Relations in the Modern World*, London: Routledge.

Clarke, Ian (2005), *Legitimacy and International Society*, Oxford: Oxford University Press.

Dunn, Frederick S. (1948), 'The Scope of International Relations', *World Politics*, 1(1): 142–6.

Evans, Graham and Jeffrey Newnham (1998), *The Penguin Dictionary of International Relations*, London: Penguin.

Ferguson, Niall (2003a), 'Hegemony or Empire', *Foreign Affairs*, 82(5), Sept./Oct.: 154

Ferguson, Niall (2003b), *Empire: How Britain Made the Modern World*, London: Allen Lane.

Hall, John (ed.) (1986), *States in History*, Oxford: Basil Blackwell.

Hardt, Michael and Negri Antonio (2000), *Empire*, Cambridge, MA: Harvard University Press.

Jackson, Robert H. (1990), *Quasi-States: Sovereignty, International Relations, and the Third World*, Cambridge: Cambridge University Press.

Kennedy, Paul (1989), *The Rise and Fall of the Great Powers: Economic Change and Military Conflict from 1500 to 2000*, London: Fontana.

King, Preston (1999), *The Ideology of Order: A Comparative Analysis of Jean Bodin and Thomas Hobbes*, London: Frank Cass.

Lawson, Stephanie (2002), *The New Agenda for International Relations: From Polarization to Globalization in World Politics?*, Cambridge: Polity Press.

Lawson, Stephanie (2003), *International Relations*, Cambridge: Polity Press.

Lawson, Stephanie (2006), *Culture and Context in World Politics*, London: Palgrave Macmillan.

Migdal, Joel S. (1988), *Strong Societies and Weak States: State–Society Relations and State Capabilities in the Third World*, Princeton, NJ: Princeton University Press.

Miller, David (ed.) (1991), *The Blackwell Encyclopaedia of Political Thought*, Oxford: Blackwell Publishers.

Montevideo Convention on the Rights and Duties of States (1933), at www.molossia.org/montevideo.html (accessed 17/10/2007).

Rotberg, Robert I. (ed.) (2003), 'Failed States, Collapsed State, Weak States: Causes and Indicators' in Robert I. Rotberg (ed.), *State Failure and State Weakness in a Time of Terror*, Cambridge, MA and Washington DC: World Peace Foundation and Brookings Institution Press.

Singer, Peter (2002), *One World: The Ethics of Globalisation*, Melbourne: ext Publishing.

Stern, Geoffrey (2000), *The Structure of International Society*, London: Pinter.

Chapter 15

Brown, Chris, Terry Nardin, and Nicholas Rengger (eds) (2002), *International Relations in Political Thought: Texts from the Ancient Greeks to the First World War*, Cambridge: Cambridge University Press.

Bull, Hedley (1997), *The Anarchical Society: A Study of Order in World Politics*, Basingstoke: Macmillan, 2nd edn.

Buzan, Barry (2004), *From International Society to World Society: English School Theory and the Social Structure of Globalisation*, Cambridge: Cambridge University Press.

Carr, Edward Hallett ([1939] 1948), *The Twenty Years' Crisis 1919–1939: An Introduction to the Study of International Relations*, London: Macmillan.

Clark, Ian (2005), *Legitimacy in International Society*, Oxford: Oxford University Press.

Dunne, Tim (1998), *Inventing English Society: A History of the English School*, Basingstoke: Macmillan.

Evans, Graham and Jeffrey Newnham (1998), *The Penguin Dictionary of International Relations*, London: Penguin.

Grieco, Joseph M. (1988), 'Anarchy and the Limits of Cooperation: A Realist Critique of the Newest Liberal Institutionalism', *International Organization*, 42(3): 485–507.

Herz, John M. (1950), 'Idealist Internationalism and the Security Dilemma', *World Politics*, 3(2): 157–80.

Hochstrasser, T.J. (2000), *Natural Law Theories in the Early Enlightenment*, Cambridge: Cambridge University Press.

Kaplan, Morton A. (2005), *System and Process in International Politics*, Colchester: ECPR Press.

Keohane, Robert O., and Joseph S. Nye (1977), *Power and Interdependence : World Politics in Transition*, Boston, MA: Little, Brown.

Lawson, Stephanie (2003), *International Relations*, Cambridge: Polity Press.

Lebow, Richard Ned (2007), 'Classical Realism' in Tim Dunne, Milja Kurki, and Steve Smith (eds), *International Relations Theories: Discipline and Diversity*, Oxford: Oxford University Press: 52–70.

Linklater, Andrew and Hidemi Suganami (2006), *The English School of International Relations: A Reassessment*, Cambridge: Cambridge University Press.

Little, Richard (1996), 'The Growing Relevance of Pluralism?' in Steve Smith, Ken Booth and Marysia Zalewski (eds), *International Theory: Positivism and Beyond*, Cambridge: Cambridge University Press.

Machiavelli, Niccolò, (2005), *The Prince*, trans. George Bull, London: Penguin.

Mearsheimer, John J. (2007), 'Structural Realism' in Tim Dunne, Milja Kurki, and Steve Smith (eds), *Theories of International Relations: Discipline and Diversity*, Oxford: Oxford University Press.

Morgenthau, Hans J. (1948), *Politics Among Nations: The Struggle for Power and Peace*, New York: Alfred A. Knopf.

Nye, Joseph S. Jr (2005), *Understanding International Conflicts: An Introduction to Theory and History*, New York: Pearson Longman, 5th edn.

Rose, Gideon (1998), 'Neoclassical Realism and Theories of Foreign Policy', *World Politics*, 51(1): 144–72.

Smith, Steve, Ken Booth and Marysia Zalewski (eds) (1996), *International Theory: Positivism and Beyond*, Cambridge: Cambridge University Press.

Thucydides (1972), *History of the Peloponnesian War*, London: Penguin.

Waltz, Kenneth (1959), *Man, State and War*, New York: Colombia University Press.

Waltz, Kenneth (1979), *Theory of International Politics*, London: Addison Wesley.

Wight, Martin (1966), 'Why is There no International Theory' in Martin Wight and Herbert Butterfield (eds), *Diplomatic Investigations: Essays in the Theory of International Politics*, London: Allen & Unwin.

Wight, Martin and Herbert Butterfield (eds) (1966), *Diplomatic Investigations: Essays in the Theory of International Politics*, London: Allen & Unwin.

Zimmern, Alfred (1997), *Prospects of Democracy and Other Essays*, London: Ayer Publishing.

Chapter 16

Adler, Emmanuel (1997), 'Seizing the Middle Ground: Constructivism in World Politics', *European Journal of International Relations*, 3(3): 319–63.

Agathangelou, Anna and Lily Ling (2004), 'The House of IR: From Family Power Politics to the *Poisies* of Worldism', *International Studies Review*, 6(1): 21–49.

Barkawi, Tarak and Mark Laffey (2006), 'The Postcolonial Moment in Security Studies', *Review of International Studies*, 32 (2): 329–52.

Berger, Peter L. and Thomas Luckman (1966), *The Social Construction of Reality: A Treatise in the Sociology of Knowledge,* New York: Anchor Books.

Blanchard, Eric M. (2003), 'Gender, International Relations, and the Development of Feminist Security Theory', *Signs: Journal of Women in Culture and Society*, 28: 1289–312.

Connell, R.W. (2005), *Masculinities*, Cambridge: Polity Press, 2nd edn.

Cox, Robert (1981), 'Social Forces, States and World Orders: Beyond International Relations Theory', *Millennium Journal of International Studies*, 10(2): 126–55.

Dunne, Tim (1998), *Inventing International Society: A History of the English School*, London: Macmillan.

Dunne, Tim; Milja Kurki, and Steve Smith (eds) (2007), *Theories of International Relations: Discipline and Diversity*, Oxford: Oxford University Press.

Enloe, Cynthia (1993), 'Bananas, Beaches and Bases' in Linda S. Kauffman (ed.), *American Feminist Thought at Century's End: A Reader*, Cambridge, MA: Blackwell Publishing: 441–64.

Foucault, Michel (1980), *Power/Knowledge: Selected Interviews and Other Writings*, ed. and transl. Colin Gordon, Brighton: Harvester Press.

Frank, Andre Gunder (1967), *Capitalism and Underdevelopment in Latin America: Historical Studies of Chile and Brazil*, New York: Monthly Review Press.

Frank, Andre Gunder and Barry K. Gills (eds) (1996), *The World System: Five Hundred Years or Five Thousand?*, London: Routledge.

Goldstein Joshua S. (2001), *War and Gender: How Gender Shapes the War System and ViceVersa*, Cambridge: Cambridge University Press.

Gramsci, Antonio (1967), *The Modern Prince, and other Writings*, New York: International Publishers.

Habermas, Jürgen (2003), 'Toward a Cosmopolitan Europe', *Journal of Democracy*, 14(4): 86–100.

International Criminal Tribunal for Former Yugoslavia (ICTY), *Appeals Chamber Judgement in the Case of the Prosecutor v. Radislav Krstić*, ICTY, 19 April 2004, www.un.org/icty/krstic/Appeal/judgement/krs-aj040419e.pdf accessed 13/11/07.

Katzenstein Peter J. (1996), *Cultural Norms and National Security: Police and Military in Postwar Japan*, Ithaca, NY: Cornell University Press.

Lapid, Yosef and Friedrich Kratochwil (eds) (1996), *The Return of Culture and Identity in IR Theory*, Boulder, CO: Lynne Rienner.

Lawson, Stephanie (2006), *Culture and Context in World Politics*, Basingstoke, Palgrave Macmillan.

Lenin, V. I. (1986), *Imperialism: The Highest Stage of Capitalism*, Moscow: Progress Publishers.

Linklater, Andrew (1998), *The Transformation of Political Community: Ethical Foundations of the Post-Westphalian Era*, Cambridge: Polity Press.

Dana Milbank and Claudia Deane (2003), 'Hussein Link to 9/11 Lingers in Many Minds', *Washington Post*, 6 September: A1.

Mosse, George L. (1996), *The Image of Man: The Creation of Modern Masculinity*, New York: Oxford University Press.

Onuf, Nicholas (1989), *World of Our Making: Rules and Rule in Social Theory and International Relations*, Columbia, SC: University of South Carolina Press.

Ruggie, John Gerard (1998), *Constructing the World Polity: Essays on International Institutionalization*, London: Routledge.

Smith, Steve (1996), Positivism and Beyond' in Steve Smith, Ken Booth, and Marysia Zalewski (eds), *International Theory: Positivism and Beyond*, Cambridge: Cambridge University Press: 11–44.

Smith, Steve, (2000) 'The Discipline of International Relations; Still an American Social Science?', *British Journal of Politics and International Relations*, 2(3): 374–402.

Tickner, Arlene (2003), 'Seeing IR Differently: Notes from the Third World', *Millennium*, 32(2): 295–324.

Tickner, J. Ann (1992), *Gender in International Relations: Feminist Perspectives on Achieving Global Security*, New York: Columbia University Press.

Tickner, J. Ann and Laura Sjoberg (2007), 'Feminism' in Dunne, Kurki, and Smith (eds), *Theories of International Relations: Discipline and Diversity*, OXford: OXford University Press: 185–202.

True, Jacqueline (2005), 'Feminism' in Scott Burchill *et al.*, *Theories of International Relations*, Basingstoke: Palgrave Macmillan, 3rd edn: 213–34.

Wallerstein Immanuel (1976), *The Modern World-System: Capitalist Agriculture and the Origins of the European World-Economy in the Sixteenth Century*, New York: Academic Press.

Wallerstein Immanuel (2001), *Unthinking Social Science: The Limits of Nineteenth-Century Paradigms*, Philadelphia: Temple University Press, 2nd edn.

Wendt, Alexander (1992), 'Anarchy is What States Make of it: The Social Construction of Power Politics', *International Organization*, 46(2): 391–425.

Wendt, Alexander (1996), 'Identity and Structural Change in International Politics' in Yosef Lapid and Friedrich Kratochwil (eds), *The Return of Culture and Identity in IR Theory*, Boulder, CO: Lynne Rienner: 47–64.

Chapter 17

Best, Anthony, Jussi M. Hanhimaki, Kirsten E. Schulze, and Joseph A. Maiolo (2004), *An International History of the Twentieth Century*, London: Routledge.

Boutros-Ghali, Boutros (1992), *An Agenda for Peace* (Report of the Secretary-General pursuant to the statement adopted by the Summit Meeting of the Security Council on 31 January) New York: United Nations.

Cassels, Alan (1996), *Ideology and International Relations in the Modern World*, London: Routledge.

Clarke, Walter S. and Robert Gosende (2003), 'Somalia: Can a Collapsed State Reconstitute Itself?'' in Robert I. Rotberg (ed.), *State Failure and State Weakness in a Time of Terror*, Cambridge and Washington: World Peace Foundation and Brookings Institution Press: 129–58.

Clausewitz, Carl von (1993), *On War*, rev. edn, transl. Michael Howard and Peter Paret, New York: Alfred A. Knopf.

Dunne, Tim, Milja Kurki and Steve Smith (eds) (2007), *Theories of International Relations: Discipline and Diversity*, Oxford: Oxford University Press.

Evans, Graham and Jeffrey Newnham (1998), *The Penguin Dictionary of International Relations*, London: Penguin.

Feldman, Linda (2003), 'The Impact of Bush Linking 9/11 and Iraq', *Christian Science Monitor*, online edn, 14 March at www.csmonitor.com/2003/0314/p02s01-woiq.html (accessed 9/6/07).

Galtung, Johan (1969), 'Violence, Peace, and Peace Research', *Journal of Peace Research*, 6(3): 167–91.

Independent Commission on International Development Issues (1980), *North–South, A Programme for Survival : Report of the Independent Commission on International Development Issues*, Boston, MA: MIT Press.

Lawson, Stephanie (ed.) (1995), *The New Agenda for International Security: Cooperating For Peace and Beyond*, St Leonards: Allen & Unwin.

Mearsheimer, John J. (2007), 'Structural Realism' in Tim Dunne, Milja Kurki, and Steve Smith (eds), *Theories of International Relations: Discipline and Diversity*, Oxford: Oxford University Press.

Mearsheimer, John J. and Stephen S. Walt (2002), *Can Saddam Be Contained? History Says Yes*, Cambridge, MA: Harvard University, Belfer Center for Science and International Affairs International Security Program Occasional Paper, November.

Kent, John and John W. Young (2003), *International Relations Since 1945: A Global History*, Oxford: Oxford University Press.

Peña, Charles V. (2006), 'A Smaller Military to Fight the War on Terror, *Orbis*, 50(2): 289–306.

Rotberg, Robert I. (ed.) (2003), *State Failure and State Weakness in a Time of Terror*, Cambridge and Washington: World Peace Foundation and Brookings Institution Press.

Shimko, Keither L. (2005), *International Relations: Themes and Perspectives*, Boston, MA: Houghton Mifflin.

Sun Tzu (1963), *The Art of War*, transl. Samuel B. Griffith, Oxford: Clarendon Press.

United Nations (1945), Preamble to the Charter, as adopted 26 June at www.un.org/aboutun/charter/.

United Nations Development Program (1994), *Human Development Report: 1994*, New York: United Nations.

Weiss, Thomas G. (2003), 'The Illusion of UN Security Council Reform', *Washington Quarterly*, 26(4): 147–61.

Yergin, Daniel (2006), 'Ensuring Energy Security', *Foreign Affairs*, 86(3), March/April: 69–82.

Young, John W. and John Kent (2004), *International Relations Since 1945: A Global History*, Oxford: Oxford University Press.

Chapter 18

Butterfield, Herbert and Martin Wight (eds) (1966), *Diplomatic Investigation: Essays in the Theory of International Politics*, London: George Allen & Unwin.

Butterfield, Herbert (1966), 'The New Diplomacy and Historical Diplomacy' in Herbert Butterfield and Martin Wight (eds), *Diplomatic Investigation: Essays in the Theory of International Politics*, London: George Allen & Unwin: 181–92.

Cioffi-Revilla, Claudio and Todd Landman (1999), 'Evolution of Maya Polities in the Ancient Mesoamerican System', *International Studies Quarterly*, 43(4): 559–98.

Craig, Gordon A. and Alexander L. George (1990), *Force and Statecraft: Diplomatic Problems of Our Times*, New York: Oxford University Press, 2nd edn.

Dannreuther, Roland (ed.) (2004), *European Union Foreign and Security Policy: Towards a Neighbourhood Strategy*, London: Routledge.

Dannreuther, Roland (2004), 'Introduction: Setting the Framework' in Roland Dannreuther (ed.), *European Union Foreign and Security Policy: Towards a Neighbourhood Strategy*, London: Routledge, 1–11.

Evans, Graham and Jeffrey Newnham (1988), *Penguin Dictionary of International Relations*, London: Penguin.

Farrell, Mary (2005), 'EU External Relations: Exporting the EU Model of Governance', *European Foreign Affairs Review*, 10(4): 451–62.

Freedman, Lawrence (2006), 'The Special Relationship: Then and Now', *Foreign Affairs*, 85(3), May/June: 61–74.

Gaddis, John Lewis, Philip H. Gordon, Ernest R. May, and Jonathan Rosenberg (eds), *Cold War Statesmen Confront the Bomb: Nuclear Diplomacy Since 1945*, New York: Oxford University Press, 1999.

Gaenslen, Fritz (1997), 'Advancing Cultural Explanations' in Valerie M. Hudson (ed.), *Culture and Foreign Policy*, Boulder, Co: Lynne Reinner: 265–79.

Henriksen, Alan K. (2006), *What Can Public Diplomacy Achieve* (Discussion Papers in Diplomacy), The Hague: Institute of International Relations. www.clingendael.nl/publications/2006/20060900_cdsp_ paper_dip_b.pdf (accessed 20/07/07).

Howard, Michael (1966), 'War as an Instrument of Policy' in Herbert Butterfield and Martin Wight (eds), *Diplomatic Investigation: Essays in the Theory of International Politics*, London: George Allen & Unwin: 193–205.

Hudson, Valerie M. (ed.) (1997), *Culture and Foreign Policy*, Boulder, CO: Lynne Reinner.

Hui, Victoria Tin-bor (2005), *War and State Formation in Ancient China and Early Modern Europe*, Cambridge: Cambridge University Press.

Jowett, Garth S. and Victoria O'Donnell (2006), *Propaganda and Persuasion*, Thousand Oaks, CA: Sage.

Kautilya (nd), *Arthasástra*, www.mssu.edu/projectsouthasia/history/primarydocs/Arthashastra/BookI.htm.

Langhorne, Richard (2000), 'Full Circle: New Principals and Old Consequences in the Modern Diplomatic System', *Diplomacy and Statecraft*, 11(1): 33–46.

Lawson, Stephanie (2006), *Culture and Context in World Politics*, Basingstoke: Palgrave Macmillan.

Manners, Ian (2006), 'Normative Power Europe Reconsidered: Beyond the Crossroads, *Journal of European Public Policy*, 13(2): 182–99.

Mattingley, Garrett (1955), *Renaissance Diplomacy*, Boston, MA: Houghton Mifflin.

Melissen, Jan (2003), *Summit Diplomacy Coming of Age* (Discussion Papers in Diplomacy), The Hague, Netherlands Institute of International Relations, www.nbiz.nl/publications/2003/20030500_cli_paper_dip_issue86.pdf accessed 15/0707.

Miller, David (ed.) (1991), *The Blackwell Encyclopaedia of Political Thought*, Oxford: Blackwell Publishers.

Mockaitis, Thomas R. (2003), 'Winning Hearts and Minds in the "War on Terrorism"', *Small Wars and Insurgencies,* 14(1): 21–38.

Nye, Joseph S. Jr (2004), *Soft Power: The Means to Success in World Politics*, New York: Public Affairs.

Tansen, San (2003), *Buddhism, Diplomacy and Trade: The Realignment of Sino-Indian Relations 600–1400*, Honolulu: University of Hawaii Press.

Web:

ec.europa.eu/external_relations/cfsp/intro/index.htm

www.jimmycarterlibrary.org/documents/campdavid /accords.phtml

www.mi5.gov.uk/output/Page244.html

www.mssu.edu/projectsouthasia/history/primarydocs/Artha-shastra/BookI.htm

www.yale.edu/lawweb/avalon/monroe.htm

Chapter 19

Abi-Saab, Georges (ed.) (1981), *The Concept of International Organization*, Paris: UNESCO.

Alston, Philip (2006), 'Reconceiving The UN Human Rights Regime: Challenges Confronting the New UN Human Rights Council', *Melbourne Journal of International Law*, 7(1), at bar.austlii.edu.au/au/journals/MelbJIL/2006/.

Archer, Clive (1983), *International Organizations*, London: Allen & Unwin.

Butler, Geoffrey G. and Simon MacCoby (2003), *Development of International Law*, Union, NJ: Lawbook Exchange.

Diehl, Paul F. (ed.) (2005), *The Politics of Global Governance: International Organizations in an Interdependent World*, Boulder, CO: Lynne Rienner, 3rd edn.

Diehl, Paul F. (2005), 'Introduction' in *The Politics of Global Governance: International Organizations in an Interdependent World*, Boulder, CO: Lynne Rienner: 3–8.

Dishman, Chris (2005), 'The Leaderless Nexus: When Crime and Terror Converge', *Studies in Conflict and Terrorism*, 28(3): 237–52.

Gerbet, Pierre (1981), 'Rise and Development of International Organizations' in Georges Abi-Saab (ed.), *The Concept of International Organization*, Paris: UNESCO: 27–49.

Gordenker, Leon (2005), *The UN Secretary-General and Secretariat*, London: Routledge.

Gordenker, Leon and Thomas G. Weiss (1996), 'Pluralizing Global Governance: Analytical Approaches and Dimensions' in Thomas G. Weiss and Leon Gordenker (eds), *NGOs, the UN and Global Governance*, Boulder, CO: Lynne Rienner.

Haas, Ernst B. (1990), *When Knowledge is Power: Three Models of Change in International Organizations*, Berkeley, CA: University of California Press.

Harle, Vilho (1998), *Ideas of Social Order in the Ancient World*, Westport, CT, Greenwood Press.

Kaldor, Mary (2006), *New and Old Wars: Organized Violence in a Global Era*, Cambridge: Polity Press, 2nd edn.

Keohane, Robert O. (1993), 'The Analysis of International Regimes: Towards a European-American Research Programme' in Volker Rittberger and Peter Mayer (eds), *International Regime Theory*, Oxford: Oxford University Press.

Klabbers, Jan (2003), *An Introduction to International Institutional Law*, Cambridge: Cambridge University Press.

Midgley, Claire (1992), *Women Against Slavery: The British Campaigns, 1780–1870*, London: Routledge.

Naím, Moisés (2007), 'What Is a Gongo?', *Foreign Policy*, May/June www.foreignpolicy.com/story/cms.php?story_id=3818&fpsrc=ealert070430.

Sanderson, Thomas M. (2004), 'Transnational Terror and Organized Crime: Blurring the Lines', *SAIS Review*, 24(1): 49–61.

Rittberger, Volker and Bernhard Zangl (2006), *International Organization: Polity, Politics and Policies*, Basingstoke: Palgrave.

Rittberger, Volker and Peter Mayer (eds) (1993), *International Regime Theory*, Oxford: Oxford University Press.

Union of International Associations (2006), *Yearbook of International Organizations 2005/2006*, 12th edn at www.uia.org/statistics/organizations/types-2004.pdf.

Weiss, Thomas G. and Leon Gordenker (eds), *NGOs, the UN and Global Governance*, Boulder, CO: Lynne Rienner.

Williams, Phil (1997), 'Transnational Criminal Organizations and International Security' in John Arquilla and David Ronfeldt (eds), *In Athena's Camp: Preparing for Conflict in the Information Age*, Santa Monica, CA: Rand Corporation: 315–37.

Web:

nobelprize.org/nobel_prizes/peace/laureates/1963/red-cross-history.html

www.antislavery.org/

www.icj-cij.org

www.redcross.int/en/history/not_nobel.asp

www.un.org

Chapter 20

David N. Balaam and Michael Veseth (2005), *Introduction to International Political Economy*, Upper Saddle River, NJ: Pearson Education, 3rd edn.

Boyer, Robert and Daniel Drache (1996), *States Against Markets: The Limits of Globalization*, London: Routledge.

Cohn, Theodore H. (2005), *Global Political Economy: Theory and Practice*, New York: Pearson Longman, 3rd edn.

Cox, Robert W. (1981), 'Social Forces, States and World Orders: Beyond International Relations Theory', *Millennium: Journal of International Studies*, 10: 126–55.

Crane, George T. and Abla Amawi (eds) (1991), *The Theoretical Evolution of International Political Economy: A Reader*, Oxford: Oxford University Press.

Crane, George T. and Abla Amawi (eds), (1991), 'Introduction: Theories of International Political Economy' in *The Theoretical Evolution of International Political Economy: A Reader*, Oxford: Oxford University Press: 3–33.

European Economic Advisory Group (EEAG) (2007), *Report on the European Economy*, Press release at www.cesifo-group.de/portal/page/portal/ifoHome/B-politik/70eeagreport/40PUBLEEAG 2007/_PUBLEEAG2007?item_link=eeag2007-press-englisch. htm, accessed 21/11/07.

Flynn, Dennis O. and Arturo Giráldez (1995), 'Born with a "Silver Spoon": The Origin of World Trade in 1571', *Journal of World History*, 6: 201–21.

Galbraith, J.K. (1984), 'Comment', *National Review*, 36(6): 39–42.

Gilpin, Robert with Jean M. Gilpin (1987), *The Political Economy of International Relations*, Princeton, NJ: Princeton University Press.

Goss, Joss and Bruce Lindquist (1995), 'Conceptualizing International Labor Migration: A Structuration Perspective', *International Migration Review*, 29(2): 317–51.

Griffin, Penny (2007), 'Refashioning IPE: What and How Gender Analysis Teaches International (Global), Political Economy', *Review of International Political Economy*, 14(4): 719–36.

Griffiths, Martin and Terry O'Callaghan (2002), *International Relations: The Key Concepts*, London: Routledge.

Haggard, Stephan (1997), 'The Political Economy of Regionalism in Asia and the Americas' in Edward D. Mansfield and Helen V. Milner (eds), *The Political Economy of Regionalism*, New York: Columbia University Press: 20–49.

Hawkins, William R. (1984), 'Neomercantilism: Is There a Case for Tariffs?, *National Review*, 36(6): 25–39.

Hirst, Paul and Graeme Thompson (1999), *Globalization in Question*, Cambridge: Polity Press, 2nd edn.

Howe, Anthony (1997), *Free Trade and Liberal England 1846–1946*, Oxford: Oxford University Press.

Kaur, Amarjit (2007), 'International Labour Migration in Southeast Asia: Governance of Migration and Women Domestic Workers', *Intersections: Gender, History and Culture in the Asian Context*, Issue 15, May.

Keohane, Robert O. (2001), *After Hegemony: Cooperation and Discord in the World Political Economy*, Princeton, NJ: Princeton University Press.

Lawson, Stephanie (2002), 'After the Fall: International Theory and the State' in Stephanie Lawson (ed.), *The New Agenda for International Relations*, Cambridge: Polity Press.

Lawson, Stephanie (ed.) (2002), *The New Agenda for International Relations*, Cambridge: Polity Press.

List, Frederich (1991), 'Political and Cosmopolitical Economy' in George T. Crane and Abla Amawi (eds), 'Introduction: Theories of International Political Economy' in *The Theoretical Evolution of International Political Economy: A Reader*, Oxford: Oxford University Press: 48–54.

Lawler, Kevin and Hamid Seddighi (2001), *International Economics: Theories, Themes and Debates*, Harlow: Pearson Education.

Magnusson, Lars (1994), *Mercantilism: The Shaping of an Economic Language*, London: Routledge.

Miller, David (ed.) (1991), *The Blackwell Encyclopaedia of Political Thought*, Oxford: Blackwell Publishers.

Moghadan, Valentine M. (2005), *Globalizing Women: Transnational Feminist Networks*, Baltimore, MD: Johns Hopkins University Press.

Moghadan, Valentine M. (1999), 'Gender and Globalization: Female Labor and Women's Mobilization', *Journal of World-Systems Research*, 5(2): 367–88.

O'Brien, Robert, Anne Marie Goetz, Jan Aart Scholte, and Marc Williams (2000), *Contesting Global Governance: Multilateral Economic Institutions and Global Social Movements*, Cambridge, Cambridge University Press.

Ohmae, Kenichi (1993), 'The Rise of the Region-State', *Foreign Affairs*, 72(2): 78–87.

Palan, Ronen (2000), 'New Trends in Global Political Economy' in Ronen Palan (ed.), *Global Political Economy: Contemporary Theories*, London: Routledge: 7–18.

Palat, Ravi Arvind (1996), 'Pacific Century: Myth or Reality', *Theory and Society*, 25(3): 303–47.

Peterson, V. Spike (2003), *A Critical Rewriting of Global Political Economy: Integrating Reproductive, Productive and Virtual Economies*, London: Routledge.

Pettman, Ralph (1996), *Understanding International Political Economy: With Readings for the Fatigued*, Boulder, Co: Lynne Rienner.

Ricardo, David (1821), *On the Principles of Political Economy and Taxation*, London: John Murray, 3rd edn.

Ronen Palan (ed.) (2000), *Global Political Economy: Contemporary Theories*, London: Routledge.

Ruggie, John Gerard (1998), *Constructing the World Polity: Essays on International Institutionalization*, London: Routledge.

Spero, Joan E. and Jeffrey A. Hart (1997), *The Politics of International Economic Relations*, New York: St Martin's Press, 5th edn.

Strange, Susan (1970), 'International Relations and International Economics: A Case of Mutual Neglect', *International Affairs*, 46(2): 304–15.

Tomlinson, John (1999), *Globalization and Culture*, Chicago, IL: Chicago University Press.

Viner, Jacob (1949), 'Power Versus Plenty as Objectives of Foreign Policy in the Seventeenth and Eighteenth Centuries', *World Politics*, 1(2): 1–29.

Watson, Alison M.S. (2004), *An Introduction to International Political Economy*, London: Continuum.

Wilkinson, Rorden (2000), *Multilateralism and the World Trade Organisation: The Architecture and Extension of International Trade Regulation*, London: Routledge.

Williams, David and Tom Young (1994), 'Governance, the World, Bank and Liberal Theory', *Political Studies*, 42(1): 84–100.

Woods, Ngaire (1998), 'Editorial Introduction: Globalization: Definitions, Debates and Implications', *Oxford Development Studies*, 26(1): 5–13.

Web:

www.fco.gov.uk

www.brettonwoods.org/institutions.html

Conclusion

Chakrabarty, Dipak (2000), *Provincializing Europe*, Princeton, NJ: Princeton University Press.

Friedrichs, Jörg (2001), 'The Meaning of New Medievalism', *European Journal of International Relations*, 7(4): 475–502.

Fukuyama, Francis (1992), *The End of History and the Last Man*, London: Penguin.

Rapley, John (2006), 'The New Middle Ages', Foreign Affairs, 85(3): 95–103.

Scholte, Jan Art (2005), *Globalization: a Critical Introduction*, Basingstoke: Palgrave, 2nd edn.

Slaughter, Anne-Marie, (1997), 'The Real New World Order', *Foreign Affairs*, 76(5), Sept.–Oct.: 183–97.

West, Cornel (1991), 'Decentring Europe: A Memorial Lecture for James Snead', *Critical Quarterly*, 33(1): 1–19.

Index

D